Yanks and Limeys

Yanks and Limeys

Alliance Warfare in the Second World War

NIALL BARR

JONATHAN CAPE
LONDON

1 3 5 7 9 10 8 6 4 2

Jonathan Cape, an imprint of Vintage Publishing,
20 Vauxhall Bridge Road,
London SW1V 2SA

Jonathan Cape is part of the Penguin Random House group of companies whose addresses can
be found at global.penguinrandomhouse.com.

Penguin
Random House
UK

First published by Jonathan Cape in 2015

www.vintage-books.co.uk

A CIP catalogue record for this book is available from the British Library

ISBN 9780224079228

Typeset in Dante MT Std by Palimpsest Book Production Ltd, Falkirk, Stirlingshire

Printed and bound in Great Britain by Clays Ltd, St Ives plc

Penguin Random House is committed to a sustainable future for our business,
our readers and our planet.
This book is made from Forest Stewardship Council® certified paper.

MIX
Paper from
responsible sources
FSC
www.fsc.org   FSC® C018179

Contents

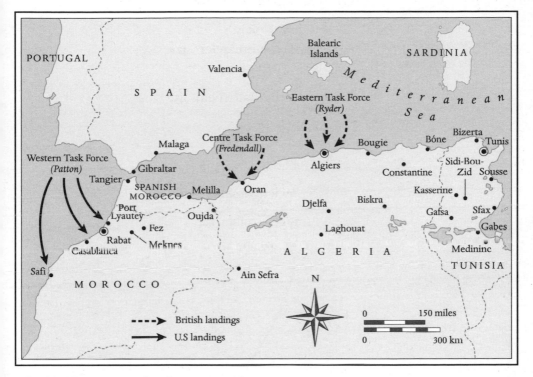

Allied landings in North Africa, November 1942

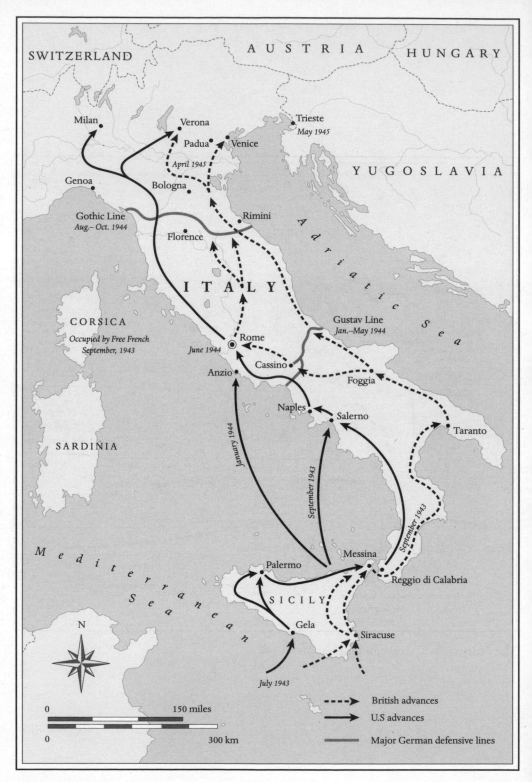

Italy, 1943–45

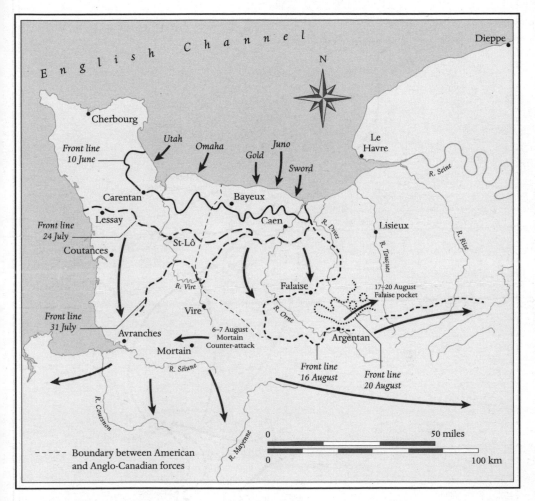

The Normandy Campaign June–August 1944

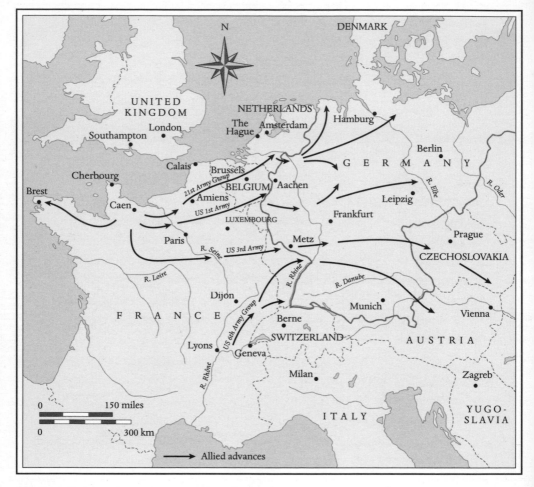

The North-West Europe Campaign, 1944–45

Yanks and Limeys

Introduction

One of the great pleasures of working at the Joint Services Command and Staff College in Shrivenham is that almost every day I walk past some outstanding work of art portraying Britain's military past. There is a sculptor's macquette of an equestrian figure that holds particular resonance for me, and although it is placed in the forum of the building, where hundreds of students and staff congregate, few recognise the figure or are aware of its significance. The mounted figure is Field Marshal Sir John Dill, and the full-size bronze statue cannot be seen on the Mall or in Whitehall in London, but in Arlington National Cemetery, Washington DC. Dill is indeed virtually unknown in Britain today, yet he played a crucial part in cementing the military relationship between Britain and America in the Second World War.[1] It was this almost daily reminder of the Anglo-American alliance that ultimately led to the creation of this book.

It might be questioned why another book on the Anglo-American alliance in the Second World War is necessary. Celebrated at the time, and commented upon endlessly since, the experience of the wartime alliance between the two countries has become almost the foundation myth of what has often been called 'the special relationship', one that has waxed and waned over the succeeding decades. There is little doubt that the shared crisis of that war brought Britain and America 'closer than ever before, or ever again'.[2] The sheer depth, scale and scope of the alliance between Britain and the United States during the Second World War is hard to comprehend even now. General George Marshall, the Chief of Staff of the US Army, rightly called it 'the most complete unification of military effort ever achieved by two Allied nations'.[3]

Once the United States became committed to the war in Europe, the two allies cooperated in an unprecedented way. While the personal relationship between Prime Minister Winston Churchill and President Franklin D. Roosevelt was vital in smoothing over many issues and arguments, the level of military cooperation achieved was equally crucial. An internal British staff history noted that 'The complete integration of Anglo-American Planning and Intelligence during World War II, like many other aspects of the direction of the War, was something which had not been attempted previously in history as between Allies.'[4] The formation of the Combined Chiefs of Staff, in which strategic objectives could be discussed and arguments resolved, represented a new departure in the management of vast military forces stationed all over the globe. From November 1942, British and American forces were deployed together on operations in North Africa, and subsequently saw service in Sicily, Italy, France and Germany. General George Marshall and General Sir Alan Brooke, as the chiefs of the American and British armies respectively, oversaw the raising, training and deployment of two enormous armies in multiple theatres of war. The strategic position of the British Isles led to the influx of over one million GIs during 1943–4 as part of the preparation for Operation Overlord, the invasion of occupied Europe. This involved a level of contact between British people and American soldiers, sailors and airmen that could not have been envisaged before the war.[5]

This is not to deny that the well-known strategic disagreements between the allies were serious or, on occasion, threatened the cohesion of the alliance; what was remarkable was that such diverging views were aired jointly within an organisation that enabled the alliance to continue.[6] The fact that it held together and reached a successful conclusion in 1945 was proof of its overall effectiveness. Nonetheless, there were numerous frictions and frequent instances of members of both armies becoming frustrated by the inefficiency of having to work with a partner rather than acting simply as an independent national army.

Not surprisingly, commentators and historians have attempted to understand the nature of this alliance ever since. There are many fine works that explain and discuss the political and personal relationship between Winston Churchill and Franklin Roosevelt,[7] and scholars have also worked to assess the diplomatic, economic and social factors involved in the collaboration. But at root, this was primarily a military alliance, which saw the resources of the British and American navies, armies and air forces fused into one. This book thus aims to trace the relationship between the British and American armies throughout the conflict. In so doing, it explores how the relationship developed over time from rather inauspicious beginnings. It also takes account of the breadth and depth of an association that began far from the battle fronts and well outside the purview of any of the later famous commanders. This can only be achieved by examining the high-level strategic decisions, as well as the operational choices of the commanders in the field and the way in which ordinary soldiers worked and fought alongside one another. Above all else, I have attempted to provide as balanced an account as possible, which I hope does not succumb to the partisanship of believing that the right answers to the problems faced by either army lay on just one side of the Atlantic.

Within this broad remit, the book concerns itself solely with the European theatre; the relationship of the two armies in the Far East was very different and beyond the scope of this work. It does not attempt to explore the relationship between the two navies or air forces. At no point can the book be considered an exhaustive history of the alliance or of the campaigns fought by either army. It is, rather, about two armies as they fought in the largest war in history, and an attempt to explain how they cooperated, learned from, and also, at times, ignored one another. Tracing the path followed by the two armies also helps to assess whether they were able to fight effectively alongside one another. One of the most vexed questions of any military alliance is whether the hard-won lessons of one army can be learnt by its partner. Examining how two armies cooperated is always difficult, since their main focus is, understandably, the enemy, rather than their relationship with their ally. This means that the true nature of the cooperation often leaves only fragmentary traces in the historical record. Armies, which by their nature represent an expression of national will and power, have often found co-operation with allies difficult. The history of alliance warfare has often been a doleful tale of rivalry, distrust, recrimination and defeat.

There remains a cloud of nostalgia and a haze of myths concerning the relationship between the United States and Great Britain during the Second World War that can obscure the reality of the partnership and make it difficult for us to properly understand the value and effectiveness of the military cooperation that led to ultimate victory. Given the attention lavished upon it, the Anglo-American alliance can often be mistaken for an isolated case rather than as simply part of a long history of alliance warfare. And just as the colossal figures of Roosevelt and Churchill can obscure as much as they reveal about the reality of the political relationship between the US and Britain, so too can the iconic personas of Eisenhower, Patton and Montgomery hinder our view of the collective endeavours of the two armies during the war. This book seeks to show how the relations between these generals evolved over the course of the war, but also to show that their relations did not necessarily impact on much of the essential cooperation that went on, almost unnoticed, at the time.

It is, of course, impossible to encompass all of the many and varied facets of this relationship, from the strategic to the tactical, in a single volume. One of the methods used is to emphasise the efforts of a multitude of individuals – famous and otherwise – who worked together to defeat Hitler's Germany. Thus the book offers a series of snapshots of events, people and personalities operating at many different levels that were key to the functioning and development of the military relationship. Characters such as Raymond Lee, the US attaché in London in 1940, Bonner Fellers, the US attaché in Cairo in 1941–2, and Charles Bolte, one of the early US observers in Britain, can give a different and much less well-known picture of what the cooperation and competition

between these two armies was really like. Their tales are woven
into a wider narrative that tries to make some sense of the course
of the war while also illustrating how the imperatives of the
conflict changed the relationship between the armed forces of
Britain and America.

It would be quite impossible to ignore the great contributions
of certain individuals, but this book does seek to go further –
deeper into the past, and across the breadth and depth of the
experience of the armies – to appreciate the relationship as a
whole. Understanding the shared history – however sparse – of
the two armies *before* the Second World War helps to explain the
starting point for the relationship *during* the war. The Second
World War did not mark the start of the relationship. Long before
that conflict, Britain and the United States of America had developed an unusual and complicated association, which had its origins
in the first attempts at English colonisation on the continent of
North America.[8] While it would be absurd to suggest that the
experiences of the eighteenth and nineteenth centuries directly
shaped the way the two armies adapted to one another in the
Second World War, it would be equally mistaken to reject this
intermittently shared history as irrelevant. While the British Army
looked back to the Civil War of the 1640s and the Restoration of
1660 for its origins, the United States Army was born in battle
fighting against the British redcoats. The subsequent century and
a half saw many fresh pressures and influences that shaped them
both.

There was thus a complex family legacy that existed between
the two armies, in which British and American soldiers had
alternatively cooperated with and fought against one another,
emulated and ignored each other in almost equal measures.
There remained faint but significant echoes of those days, which
influenced the two armies and sometimes shaped the perceptions and actions of the men who were called upon to fight
Hitler's Germany. Perhaps most curiously of all, many of the
attitudes and opinions expressed by British regulars and American
provincials about their respective allies and enemies in the

eighteenth century had reverberations that could still be heard, however faintly, during the twentieth century. If we are to understand the two armies in the Second World War, we must start long before that conflict began.

I

Family Legacy

In February 1755, two British ships made landfall off the Hampton Roads, Virginia. On board were the first regular British troops to arrive in the American colonies for over fifty years. These British soldiers, numbering more than 1,000 men, formed the core of the command of General Edward Braddock, newly created commander-in-chief of the British colonies in North America. Braddock had been sent to check the expansion of the French, who had begun to encroach on British possessions. The French strategy was only now becoming clear to the American colonists: they planned to stake their claim to the enormous hinterland beyond the British colonies on the American seaboard. By building a chain of forts, the French hoped to link their possessions in Canada with their settlements in Louisiana. If they were successful, British America might eventually be confined to the coast.

Two years earlier, in late 1753, Lieutenant Governor Dinwiddie of Virginia had sent a young surveyor, Major George Washington, to remonstrate with the French in the critical area of the Ohio valley. After a series of exchanges, the French had made it clear that the land was now theirs, and London had charged the colonies to drive them out 'by force of arms'.[1] In April 1754, Washington, now promoted to the rank of lieutenant colonel in the Virginia Volunteers, had led 159 men from Alexandria to deal with the French at the Ohio forks. He soon had his first taste of battle when he ambushed a small detachment of French soldiers near Great Meadows in the backwoods of Pennsylvania. In the ensuing skirmish, the French leader, Ensign Jumonville, was killed, and the surviving French claimed that they had in fact been on a diplomatic mission attempting to contact Washington. Washington prepared a small fort, Fort Necessity, at Great Meadows to await the French reaction.

On 3 July, the French and their Indian allies attacked. After a day of fighting, with the Virginians hemmed in around Fort Necessity, and having suffered 30 dead and 70 wounded, Washington sued for terms. The next morning, he and his men were allowed to march out of the fort, but he had been forced to sign terms that amounted to a confession that his killing of Jumonville had been an assassination rather than an act of war.[2] Far from dealing with the French threat to the Ohio valley, Washington's expedition had actually increased the French influence with the Indian tribes in the area. The Fourth of July would remain Washington's least favourite date in the calendar. These minor incidents in the backwoods of Pennsylvania precipitated outright war between Britain and France, which soon became a global conflict, with both powers competing for influence and territory in Europe, America and India. With the failure of the American colonies to deal with their security difficulties themselves, it was entirely logical that the British government decided to send regular troops to North America.

When General Braddock arrived with his troops in February 1755, he was received enthusiastically by the colonial authorities. Here was a clear sign that the British government was taking colonial problems seriously. Braddock had an enormous task before him. He proposed a four-pronged assault on the ring of French forts that hemmed in British North America. He himself would take the two regiments of British regulars and march on Fort Duquesne at the Ohio Forks; meanwhile, further freshly raised colonial regiments would attack Niagara and Crown Point on the borders of French Canada, while a New England force would conquer Acadia in Newfoundland. However, Braddock's timetable was soon derailed. The colonial authorities could not – or would not – supply him with sufficient men and materiel for his long march. It was not until 10 May that he felt able to begin his campaign, with his regulars now augmented with nine companies of the newly raised Virginia Regiment. Braddock complained of the Virginia Regiment that 'their slothful and languid disposition renders them very unfit for military service'.[3] The new recruits were indeed unimpressive, but for good reason. The colonial military system, such as it was, relied for defence upon the militia, which was supposed to include virtually all able-bodied men. However, many militia men refused to leave their home districts, which meant that for offensive operations, colonies would raise provincial regiments of volunteers who enlisted for one campaign only.[4] The ranks of these regiments tended to be filled with impoverished, recent immigrants or men who had yet to make a success in the new land. Given the lack of training and the temporary nature of provincial service, there was no equivalent of a 'standing' army in which continuity, experience and training could develop professional soldiers. Braddock's sharp manner also alienated friendly Indians, who claimed that he 'looked upon us as dogs, and would never hear anything that we said to him'.[5] George Washington, on the other hand, impressed Braddock, and although he could not secure a regular commission for the ambitious young man, he did take him along as his aide-de-camp and adviser on the expedition.

The advance of the expedition towards Fort Duquesne was painfully slow: 300 axemen had to cut a road through the virgin forest to enable the supply wagons and guns to traverse the steep ridges and valleys of the Allegheny mountains. Eventually, on 9 July 1755, after much toil, Braddock knew that one more march would put him within sight of his goal. When the army crossed the Monongahela River for the second time, the regimental standards were unfurled and the bands played in a deliberate attempt to overawe any watching French. Thomas Walker, a British soldier, claimed that 'A finer sight could not have been beheld, the shining barrels of the muskets, the excellent order of the men, the cleanliness of their appearance, the joy depicted on every face at being so near Fort Duquesne, the highest object of their wishes. The music re-echoed through the mountains.'[6] Washington later claimed that it was the finest military sight that he ever saw. Braddock and his officers had been apprehensive of a French attack, but they had now marched so close to the fort that they imagined there would be little if any resistance.

Yet soon after the crossing, Braddock's advance guard was unexpectedly attacked by a mixed force of 108 French regulars, 146 Canadians and 600 Indians, led by Captain Daniel-Hyacinthe-Marie Lienard de Beaujeu, who emulated his Indian allies by going into battle stripped to the waist with only a silver gorget around his throat to show his rank.[7] While the Indians fired from the cover of the dense woodland, the British wheeled into line, shoulder to shoulder, to deliver the controlled volleys of musketry that their drill sergeants had taught them were the key to victory on the battlefield. Unable to see their enemy, the British troops fired volley after volley into the trees with little effect, although one of their first rounds did kill Beaujeu. Indeed, it appears that many of the French troops melted away soon after the action began; it was the Indians, using their traditional tactics of rushing forward and firing from the cover of the trees, who continued the fight.

Eventually, with their ranks thinned by the sharp sniping of the invisible Indians, the remaining British troops broke and ran back just as Braddock appeared bringing up the main body of the British battalions. Very soon the entire force was clumped together in a confused mass, firing in all directions. Braddock shouted and swore at his men to re-form the line as the sniping continued. Terrified by the war whoops of their invisible enemies, the regulars even fired upon the Virginian volunteers. When some of the Virginians sought cover behind the trees to fight 'Indian style', Braddock forced them back into line.

After three hours of this unequal fight, Braddock, who had four horses shot under him, ordered a retreat. Soon after, he was shot off his horse and the British troops began to run. Washington said that 'when we endeavoured to rally them, it was with as much success as if we had attempted to stop the wild bears of the mountains'.[8] All was confusion, and the baggage and wounded were left to the Indians as the panic-stricken British and Virginians fled the field. One historian later explained that 'British officers have declared that no pen could describe the scene . . . Regulars and provincials splashed in panic and dire confusion through the ford they had crossed in such pomp but three hours before. Arms and accoutrements were flung away in the terror with which men fled from these ghastly shambles.'[9] The wounded Braddock, in severe pain, was dragged away by his aide-de-camp against his will. The retreat continued even though there was no pursuit, and on 13 July, Braddock died from his wounds. His final words were: 'Who would have thought it? We shall better know how to deal with them another time'; but it was not given to him to learn from the disaster that had overcome him and his men.[10]

The shocking reality of Braddock's defeat brought serious consequences for the American colonies. Britain had attempted but failed to protect them. Their frontiers were now open to continued French expansion and the depredations of Indian war parties. Angry colonists sought to apportion blame for the disaster, and the British officers, attempting to exonerate themselves, blamed their own men. Robert Orme, one of Braddock's aides-de-camp, later stated that 'when the General found it impossible to persuade them to advance, and no enemy appeared in view; and nevertheless a vast number of officers were killed, by exposing themselves before the men; he endeavoured to retreat them in good order, but the panic was so great that he could not succeed'.[11] It might seem unfair to blame the ordinary soldiers for the disaster, but there was an unpleasant grain of truth in Orme's assessment. The red-coated soldiers who looked so fine to the colonists' untutored eyes were not the hardened veterans of the British Army who had won an unassailable battlefield reputation fighting against the French armies of Louis XIV and Marshal de Saxe. The War Office, desperately short of troops as it invariably was, had scraped together two understrength battalions for Braddock's expedition. These had hastily recruited some new soldiers in Essex and Ireland before they sailed for America, but even then had to make up their numbers by recruiting more men when they arrived in Virginia. The core of old soldiers had worked hard to drill and train the new recruits before the expedition began, but the fact was that very few of the 'British' soldiers who fought with Braddock had ever seen service before. It was not so very surprising that in their first action against an alien opponent whom they could not see, most of the men panicked and eventually ran away. Unfortunately, the colonists, who had believed British infantry to be invincible, now took a very different attitude towards the redcoats. The Americans blamed the British for the disaster, while the British blamed the colonists for their unsteadiness under fire. Almost everyone blamed Braddock. Washington commented: 'It is impossible to relate the different accounts that was given of our late unhappy engagement; but all tended greatly to the disadvantage of the poor deceased General, who is censured on all hands.'[12]

British soldier Charles Lee, who had marched with Braddock and later rose to high rank during the War of Independence, wrote that he hoped 'there will come a day when justice will be done to this man's memory, who has left few behind him that are his Equals, in courage, honesty and zeal for the Publick'.[13] Washington, who knew Braddock as well as any American, was also forgiving towards his fallen general: 'He was brave even to a fault and in regular service would have done honor to his profession. He was generous and disinterested – but plain and blunt in his manner, even to rudeness.'[14] Braddock had promised Washington his support in gaining a regular commission in the British Army, but Washington's hopes faded with the death of his patron.

However, these supportive voices were drowned out by the colonists' howls of protest at the disaster. Benjamin Franklin's assessment of Braddock seems to have established the dominant American view not only of this one unfortunate commander, but of British officers in general. Franklin admitted that Braddock was 'a brave man, and might probably have made a good figure in some European war. But he had too much self-confidence; too high an opinion of the validity of regular troops; too mean a one of both Americans and Indians.'[15] Franklin's view of Braddock's disastrous defeat established a pattern of American military thought that became remarkably enduring; Braddock and his disastrous expedition were long remembered in the United States, although soon forgotten in Britain.* The history of the two countries, let alone

* The Braddock Road is still named from its original starting point just outside Alexandria, Virginia. Braddock was buried in the middle of the road that bore his name and Washington had the whole army march over his grave to erase any trace of it from plundering Indians. His remains were found and reburied a few yards away. American public subscription also paid for a fine memorial to this unfortunate general, which was erected in 1913.

the history of their armies, was remembered very differently on either side of the Atlantic.

James Fenimore Cooper, in his classic novel *The Last of the Mohicans*, read by generations of American schoolchildren, illustrates how the events of 1755 were remembered in America.* Cooper stated that the colonists:

> had recently seen a chosen army from that country, which, reverencing as a mother, they had blindly believed invincible – an army led by a chief who had been selected from a crowd of trained warriors, for his rare military endowments, disgracefully routed by a handful of French and Indians, and only saved from annihilation by the coolness and spirit of a Virginian boy, whose riper fame has since diffused itself, with the steady influence of moral truth, to the uttermost confines of Christendom.[16]

He went on to claim of this Virginian boy that:

> Washington . . . saved the remnants of the British army, on this occasion, by his decision and courage. The reputation earned by Washington in this battle was the principal cause of his being selected to command the American armies at a later day. It is a circumstance worthy of observation, that while all America rang with his well-merited reputation, his name does not occur in any European account of the battle; at least the author has searched for it without success. In this manner does the mother country absorb even the fame, under that system of rule.[17]

Cooper protested too much and accorded Washington far greater importance in the retreat than he would ever have claimed himself. Yet the image of Braddock and his expedition that became fixed in the American mind was one of a brave but arrogant man, stubborn and unwilling to listen to American counsels, whose inflexibility brought a disaster that fell hardest upon the American colonists and

---

* The depiction of Indian attacks in the 1995 film *Last of the Mohicans* owes more to the received memory of Braddock's defeat than to the historical events at Fort William Henry in 1757.

their families. At the same time, it was believed that the clear courage
and resourcefulness of the Virginians, as personified by George
Washington, was deliberately ignored by the British. From Braddock's
time on, the soldiers of the American provincial regiments and
militias began to lose their respect for British military prowess
and developed a new interpretation of these events. Far from the
British officers being able to teach the colonists the art of war, it
was believed that only Americans knew how to fight on their continent, since the nature of the terrain, environment and enemy meant
that there were distinctive forms of combat unique to the American
continent. This led to another strand of American military thought:
that the American military did not need to learn from the British
but could and would learn its own lessons in its own way from its
own experience. This theme of old world arrogance and fresh new
world military thinking became an important strand that threaded
its way through the relations between the British and American
armies in the Second World War.

Ironically enough, the reaction to Braddock's disaster by the
British commander-in-chief, Prince Augustus Frederick, Duke of
Cumberland, belied the image of the British Army that was already
being created and fixed in American minds. Cumberland was a
tough and brutal soldier whose battlefield skills had waned but
who still possessed a great ability to organise and reform the army.
He understood that the tactics and drill suitable for European
battlefields had 'proved a broken reed' in America, and that change
and innovation were necessary.[18] Cumberland took up the suggestion of a Swiss soldier of fortune, Jacques Prevost, who offered to
raise a regiment of four battalions in America, with many of its
original officers coming from Germany and Switzerland. Amongst
these first officers was Henri Bouquet, a Swiss officer in Dutch
service, who became the colonel of the first battalion of this new
regiment and later won renown in the French and Indian wars that
followed.

With remarkable speed, Prevost's plan was enacted. On Christmas
Day 1755, Lord Loudon, Braddock's successor to the post of
commander-in-chief of the army in North America, became
colonel-in-chief of the new 62nd Royal American Regiment of

Foot.*[19] The first soldiers of the regiment were Swiss and German mercenaries, augmented by recruits from the American colonies. This ad hoc recruitment of a polyglot regiment was just one example of a familiar situation for the British Army of drawing soldiers from many different nationalities yet still building an effective fighting force.

Far from blindly persisting with the rigid drills made famous by Frederick the Great's Prussian infantry, the British Army in North America embraced the need for light infantry 'capable of contending with the Red Indian in his native forest by combining the qualities of the scout with the discipline of the trained soldier'.[20] The dramatic example of the Royal Americans – who cut the skirts off their coats, chopped their tricorne hats into 'jockey caps' more suitable for the forest and took to wearing Indian leggings – was soon followed by the 80th Regiment, known as Gage's Light Infantry, and the famous Rangers raised by Robert Rogers. Many other lessons were learned by the British Army, which, far from being arrogant and inflexible, proved itself capable of rapid adaptation and flexibility.

Although the British met with further disasters and crises as the war with the French expanded in North America, one of the expeditions that proved just how much they had learnt and absorbed from their American experience was the renewed attempt to seize Fort Duquesne in the summer of 1758. Brigadier John Forbes was given command of 6,000 men, the vast majority colonial volunteers, to take the fort. Four companies of the Royal Americans under Bouquet accompanied the column to act as scouts. Bouquet even acquired 16 longer-ranged rifles for his sharpshooters and devised new drills for forest fighting. The most famous of these new orders was 'tree all', which meant that the men should break ranks and each find a tree to hide behind and snipe at the enemy. Far from such forms of fighting being exclusively or distinctively American, Bouquet's men demonstrated that the British had adopted and become masters of 'Indian fighting' while maintaining the discipline and order essential to a regular army.

* The regiment was soon renumbered the 60th Royal American Regiment.

This time there was no mistake. Forbes and Bouquet, his second in command, decided to build fortified depots every 40 miles along their route, so that in the final advance they could muster the maximum number of men without the encumbrance of a large supply train. George Washington advised that the expedition should follow Braddock's original road, which seems to have been based on his desire to stimulate Virginian trade, but Forbes disagreed and insisted on cutting a fresh road on a shorter route from Pennsylvania. The advance was agonisingly slow, but steady. There was a major reverse when an advance party was ambushed in scenes reminiscent of Braddock's defeat, but this only delayed the final outcome. Forbes had also established much friendlier relations with the Indians, and when the French called their allies to fight again in the autumn, most of them refused and simply returned home. On the night of 24 November 1758, the small French garrison blew up their own fort and retired towards Canada. Forbes, now seriously ill, entered the ruins the next day and renamed the rebuilt stockade Fort Pitt in honour of the British First Minister, who had masterminded the campaign in America.

With Fort Duquesne captured, alongside another success at Fort Frontenac nearby, the French position in America had been shaken, and in 1759, the miraculous 'year of victories', it was entirely broken. The brief but bloody battle on the plains of Abraham outside Quebec in 1759, which saw generals Wolfe and Montcalm both mortally wounded, also led to the end of French power in Canada. When the Treaty of Paris was signed on 10 February 1763, the French surrendered all of Canada to the British, in formal recognition of the victories won by British arms. The treaty also saw the formal expulsion of French influence from India. After the grievous start with Braddock's expedition, British power and influence had expanded in an entirely unprecedented and unexpected way. When Forbes marched away from Fort Pitt, he left behind a detachment of Virginian provincials to 'fix this noble fine country, to all her perpetuity, under the dominion of Great Britain'.[21] In a great war for empire, Britain had achieved an outstanding success, but few people in 1763, least of all the colonists of British North America, could have predicted that this very victory would precipitate the crisis that led to the American Revolution.

The Seven Years War had cost the British treasury enormous sums of money, and once peace was declared, there was a real need to tighten expenditure and replenish the coffers. The British garrisons on the frontier, often composed of Royal Americans, were reduced to absurd levels now that there was no threat from the French. The Indians, used to receiving gifts and aid from both sides during the war, now found that all such bounty ceased. More significantly, the British government decided that the American colonies should help to pay for defence afforded them by the 10,000 regular troops now garrisoned in North America. It was this thinking that led to the passing of the Stamp Act.

As far as Parliament was concerned, the great victory that Britain had won had ensured the success of her empire and extended her dominion across vast swathes of territory worldwide. And dominion meant control. The American colonies, who had signally failed to provide for their own defence and seemed unable to organise effective military establishments, would have to be encouraged to accept greater direction and control from London to ensure that the French would never be able to return in strength to the North American continent. Yet the colonies' growing sense of their own abilities and powers of decision, fostered by the success of the provincial regiments during the war, made them ever more unwilling to accept such control. The dispute between Parliament and the colonies that began as a justifiable claim of 'No taxation without representation' soon became infused with much more powerful ideas of liberty and independence.

As the crisis developed, New England stood out as the most vociferous and unruly opponent of the British government's measures. Eventually the government decided to use military force to coerce New England and thus demonstrate to all the colonies that any dissension would be met with brutal military repression. The reality, however, was that by giving the colonists the same treatment as rebels, the British ensured that their fear of a colonial revolt became reality. As the rhetoric and protests of both sides became more heated, Boston was garrisoned with troops. In response, the New England militia began to ready itself for combat from 1774 onwards by holding regular training sessions and organising the best volunteers as 'minutemen', who would be ready to take up their arms at a moment's notice, a tried and tested technique for countering the rapid threats of Indian warfare.[22] While the militia as a military institution had decayed in most of the colonies, New England was an exception: its militia had been called out frequently to deal with the threat of Indians on the frontier, defend against French incursions or mount expeditions against the French in Canada. When the British marched on Concord, they encountered a 'hornets' nest' of minutemen at Lexington that they would not have met in any other American colony in 1775.

With this initial foray to seize a reported arms dump, the conflict was finally precipitated into open war. Major General Thomas Gage, the British governor of Massachusetts and commander-in-chief of the army in North America, had become doubtful about Parliament's policy of repression when he returned to the colonies in 1774. Gage, after all, had long experience of warfare in America. He had led the vanguard of Braddock's army in 1755 and become familiar with the strength and resolution of the colonists during the French and Indian wars. He soon realised that his 4,000-strong garrison at Boston was inadequate to hold down an entire province of angry colonists, and was more likely to trigger further resistance. Nonetheless, Gage was ordered by Lord Dartmouth, Secretary of State for the Colonies, to make a show of force in the countryside around Boston, and he duly obeyed. The British column of 900 regulars, composed of grenadiers and light infantry, were being observed right from the start of their march, and by the time they reached Lexington Green, there were groups of minutemen waiting for them. The 'shot heard around the world' was almost certainly fired by a colonist, but as the British column retreated back to Boston, sniped at on all sides, they encountered all the problems that have beset regular forces when dealing with a 'war amongst the people'.

The events at Lexington and Concord have, of course, gone down in American legend. The apparent military lesson espoused at the time, and frequently since, was that free citizens, fired with liberty, needed only weapons to defeat regular soldiers who were held to the colours by brutal discipline alone. As Kathleen Burk has argued, the popular conception of the American Revolution remains powerful even today: 'The Revolution is the American Foundation Myth, a tale of unity and valour, of right versus wrong, of the simple God-fearing American fighting for his home and his liberty against the arrogant freedom-destroying Briton.'[23] Burk has observed that the reality was much more complex, as was the subsequent war and the nature of the military problems it represented. Perhaps the war was not entirely 'unwinnable' for the British Army, but a regular army ordered to hold down a rebellious population that has become fired by a competing ideology has always faced acute difficulties. As General Sir William Howe, another unsuccessful British commander-in-chief in North America, later explained to Parliament: 'If I had laid waste the country . . . would it not have had the effect of alienating the minds of the Americans from His Majesty's government, rather than terrifying them into obedience?'[24] British policy towards the American rebels tended to vacillate between conciliation and coercion and thus achieved neither.

The siege of Boston developed almost organically from the raising of the New England militia and the failure of the British to break out from the stranglehold. The Continental Congress, consisting of delegates from all 13 colonies, appointed George Washington as the commander-in-chief of American forces, the newly formed Continental Army. Not only had Washington worn his uniform as a colonel of militia to all the debates on the formation of the Continental Army, but he had a sound military reputation. Washington did, however, have rivals for the post. One of the most serious contenders was Major Horatio Gates, who later became commander-in-chief of the Northern Division, since he was a regular officer who had served with distinction in the 60th Royal Americans. The war caused agonies of loyalty within the Royal Americans, as it did throughout American society, which merely emphasised the fact that it was not just a conflict between competing forms of government but also a bitter civil war. Some soldiers of the 60th could not bring themselves to fight against the people they had pledged to protect, while others, including Gates, joined the rebellion against the British.

Washington's later stature and eventual success as commander-in-chief of the Continental Army has often overshadowed the debate in Congress about the nature of the resistance to the British. Charles Lee, who had also served with Braddock, argued eloquently for a distinctively 'American' form of resistance through the use of militia, provincials and irregular guerrilla combat – adapting the Indian style of warfare. On the other hand, Washington was adamant that under his command the Continental Army had to be developed into a regular force that could meet the British Army in open battle on its own terms.

The battle that has gone down in history as Bunker Hill (even though most of the fighting took place on the neighbouring but less memorable Brede's Hill) revealed the enormity of the problem facing the British Army in the conflict and the importance of its meaning to the people of America. The British Grenadiers who stormed Brede's Hill displayed all the virtues of British regular troops: steadiness under fire, a willingness to close with the enemy and a determination to win. They took the American positions and forced the defenders to flee. However, they suffered heavily in the process. Bunker Hill was a British military victory, but more importantly it was a profound American political success. The British could win any number of such victories without being able to subdue the American will to resist. Thomas Gage seems to have understood the nature of the American resistance he had faced. He wrote in his official report:

> These people shew a spirit and conduct against us, they never shewed against the French, and every body has judged them from their former appearance, and behaviour, when joined with the kings forces in the last war; which has led many into great mistakes.
>
> They are now spirited up by a rage and entousiasm [*sic*], as great as ever people were possessed of, and you must proceed in earnest or give the business up.[25]

As Clausewitz later observed, a people fired with passion could ignore the 'verdict of battle' and continue the struggle even in the face of military disaster. This was an entirely different kind of conflict, one with which the British Army was ill-equipped to deal.

However, Washington and his officers also faced a fundamental problem. The *rage militaire* that had grown up around the armed militia during the siege of Boston began to dissipate when the British evacuated the city. After the initial wave of enthusiasm, willingness to serve in the army began to wane. American patriots were fighting for liberty, but the soldiers of the Continental Army had to surrender that liberty in order to fight for the common good. And as the wealthier middle-class members of the militia could not, or would not, leave their farms or businesses, the Continentals had to be recruited from younger, poorer men with less of a stake in society. These men then needed to be subjected to military discipline rather than simple patriotic fervour in order to keep them in the ranks and ensure that their behaviour did not injure the wider cause. The Continental Army never became the exact copy of the British Army that Washington had aspired to join, but, through force of circumstance, it did become an 'American approximation of them',[26] much to the chagrin of the more radical believers in the concept of American liberty.

Almost all American veterans agreed that the encampment of the Continental Army during the winter of 1777–8 at Valley Forge was fundamental in shaping it into an effective fighting force capable of standing up to the British Army in a straight fight.[27] This period was a winter of discontent for many of the American soldiers. In a repeat of Braddock's experience, neither the Congress nor the ramshackle and venal quartermaster's department was able to procure and deliver sufficient supplies to keep the soldiers clothed and fed properly and, not surprisingly, desertion was rife. Despite these hardships, Washington took the breathing space in operations as an opportunity to train his men. He initially relied upon his own personal library of British military manuals to develop training and drill for his recruits, but he also sought advice from the number of European officers who had been attracted to the Continental

Army. The most important of these was undoubtedly Baron
Friedrich Wilhelm von Steuben. He was a soldier of fortune, and
thus in some respects very similar to Henri Bouquet, but although
he was rumoured to have been a general in Frederick the Great's
army, the truth was much more prosaic. Steuben had affected the
noble titles 'Baron' and 'von' to give himself greater credibility in
America, but in fact he had served as a junior captain in the Prussian
army for just two years before being cashiered in 1763, when
Frederick had purged the officer corps of its non-noble members.*
Nonetheless, he was seized upon by Washington as an officer who
understood the secrets of the famed Prussian drill. While the British
had learnt from Braddock's defeat that close-order tactics on their
own were not enough in America, Washington knew that without
them victory would never come.

Von Steuben could speak German and French but not English,
and his first day as drill master resulted in complete confusion and
frustration since he found it difficult to remember the English
translations of his German orders, which had been helpfully written
out for him by his aide, a future Secretary of the US Treasury,
Alexander Hamilton. But eventually, with Hamilton's assistance,
von Steuben's careful training of these raw American soldiers paid
dividends. Von Steuben was impressed by the capacity for rapid
learning displayed by his adoptive countrymen, and came to realise
that teaching these independent-minded men was not a simple
matter of rote learning. He commented that 'The genius of this
nation is not in the least to be compared with that of the Prussians,
Austrians or French. You say to your soldier, "Do this, and he doeth
it"; but I am obliged to say, "This is the reason why you ought to
do that", and then he does it.'[28] Each night, von Steuben wrote a
chapter of what became his 'Blue Book', which was inevitably
based upon Prussian rather than British principles. His text,
published in 1779 as Steuben's Regulations for the Order and Discipline
of the Troops of the United States, remained the official military
manual of the United States army for the next 33 years. Doctrine
remained an important aspect of American military thinking and

---

* Clausewitz's father suffered a similar fate.

was a blend of ideas drawn from both American experience and European military thought. However, although Washington had wished initially to emulate his British opponents, the American Army would remain far more receptive to French and German military ideas than to British ones.

When the Continental Army was established, its first and principal enemy was the British Army. Yet just as the British Army consistently underestimated the resolve and determination of its American opponents, so the Continentals often misunderstood the redcoats. The image that became fixed in the American imagination was of a brutalised automaton controlled by fierce discipline and capable of wanton acts of cruelty. There are few stories concerning the British Army's treatment of Americans during the Revolutionary War that sum up the American view of the redcoat as effectively as that of Andrew Jackson. He grew up in North Carolina, where the war, precipitated by British military policy, developed into a bitter guerrilla struggle between loyalists and rebels. Jackson volunteered for the Continental Army at the tender age of 14; almost as soon as he had enlisted, he was captured by British dragoons operating in support of a group of American loyalists. He was ordered by a British dragoon officer to clean his boots, but, with creditable confidence, refused and instead demanded to be treated as a prisoner of war. The officer flew into a rage and cut at him with his sword. Jackson parried the blow with his hand and suffered a serious wound. His brother Robert, who was wounded in the head in a similar incident, later died from his injuries. Understandably, Jackson blamed the British for his loss: 'Thus early in life did Jackson become a soldier of the Republic and an unalterable enemy of Britain.'[29] Jackson's experience, sadly, was often repeated throughout the south, and the image of the red-coated soldier as a brutal oppressor became fixed in the American imagination.

For obvious reasons the Revolutionary War absorbed all the energies and attention of the Continental Army, since the outcome of the fighting meant survival or destruction as an independent nation. But for the British government and the British Army, rivalry and competition with the French in Europe and across the globe remained vital issues even as the war against the colonies continued. Indeed, in the aftermath of the disastrous defeat at Saratoga in 1777, the French entry into the war made the global situation much more serious for Britain and in some respects turned the struggle for the colonies into a sideshow. The French became the main target and opponent of the war. French assistance and, in particular, naval power proved decisive to the outcome at Yorktown in 1781, when, after a brief siege, the British general Cornwallis had to admit defeat. His troops may or may not have marched out of their battered defences to the tune of the popular song 'The World Turned Upside Down', but the French officers certainly invited Cornwallis and his officers to a lavish dinner while snubbing the Americans. Washington and his officers may have won, but they were not considered gentlemen. The news of Yorktown brought the King and Parliament to their senses and peace negotiations were begun.

The British Army emerged from the War of Independence with its reputation shattered. It is not too much to say that the army languished in the doldrums for almost twenty years, with the occasional minor development. Meanwhile the new Army of the United States was learning some pretty hard lessons in a series of campaigns against Indian tribes on the old 'north-west frontier'. When Arthur St Clair led an expedition of poorly trained regulars and militia into the wilderness in 1791, the force dissolved under Indian attack in scenes reminiscent of Braddock's disaster. This suggested that the supposedly distinctive American characteristics of 'Indian' fighting could be unlearned as rapidly as they had been learned.[30] The demands of policing and conflict on the frontier would absorb much of the US Army's energies for most of the nineteenth century.

Relations with the British in Canada remained tense. Not surprisingly, in the aftermath of the Revolutionary War, the idea of learning from one another or cooperation between the British and American armies was unthinkable. In its early years of existence, the United States' main enemies, both potential and actual, remained the indigenous Indians and the British. Meanwhile, British energies and attention were fully absorbed in the struggle against Revolutionary and then Napoleonic France. Britain's dominance, indeed supremacy, at sea was confirmed after the Battle of Trafalgar in 1805. Meanwhile, after a series of unfortunate expeditions, the British Army began to restore its reputation under a young general, Arthur Wellesley, later the Duke of Wellington. From his first major action at the Battle of Vimiero, fought in the blistering heat of a Portuguese summer, Wellesley's combination of the light infantry tactics first learnt at the hands of American Indians and the two-deep line first used in the War of Independence proved its worth against the French tactics of light skirmishers and heavy columns that had brought defeat to all their other European opponents.

However, the demands of prosecuting the long and deadly struggle against France meant that the British government became increasingly ruthless in its relations with neutral states. The second 'war of independence', or War of 1812, arose out of American frustration at British maritime policies that consistently violated their shipping rights and unilaterally closed American trade with valuable partners. The main bone of contention became two Orders in Council of November 1807, which in effect imposed colonial regulation on American trade: no foreign ship could sail or trade without British licence. This was a reaction to Napoleon's continental system, which aimed to exclude British trade from the continent, but it bore hardest upon the American republic. While the British considered these measures perfectly justified since they were doing the lion's share of work defending the world's liberty against the great French 'ogre', the Americans understandably saw things rather differently.

The pressure placed upon American commerce was only enhanced by the bitter divisions in American politics between the Federalists, who were broadly sympathetic to the British, and the Republicans, who were determined upon war as a means of ensuring that republican principles were maintained. The president at the time, Thomas Jefferson – a Francophile from the days of the Revolution, and inveterately anti-British – and his successor, James Madison, saw British policies as a direct attack upon American independence. Eventually, American room for manoeuvre disappeared: the republic either had to fight to maintain its sovereignty as an independent state or, in effect, surrender those rights to Britain. Not surprisingly, Madison and Congress decided upon war. Ironically, American patience became exhausted at precisely the time that a new British administration was moving to repeal the Orders in Council. The British government repealed the legislation on 16 June 1812 and Congress declared war on the 18th. Although the war was primarily caused by these maritime issues, many Americans also saw it as an opportunity to deal with the problem of Canada. In August 1812, Jefferson argued that 'The acquisition of Canada this year, as far as the neighbourhood of Quebec, will be a mere matter of marching, and will give us experience for the attack of Halifax . . . and the final expulsion of England from the American continent.'[31]

However, the war took a very different course from how either protagonist had imagined it. In fact, the American invasion of Canada, which began on 12 July 1812, soon went badly wrong. Much of the problem lay in the neglect of the American regular army in the years leading up to hostilities. The Republican principles that Jefferson and Madison espoused suggested that a regular army was incompatible with true liberty. Jefferson favoured the militia – the people in arms – but neither he nor Madison went as far as abolishing the regular army. This meant that the regular United States army in 1812 had a strength of under 7,000 men and was mainly officered by old veterans of the Revolutionary War and by political appointees. The burden of America's defence would have to fall on volunteers and militia.[32]

With British forces strained by the demands of war with France, the overstretched Royal Navy squadrons in American waters were initially humbled by the small but powerful American navy before fresh squadrons tipped the naval war decisively in the British favour. Meanwhile, the very small regular forces, supported by Canadian militia, that made up the garrisons of British Canada were able to delay and defeat the ill-organised and virtually unsupplied American attempts to seize Canada. In 1813, American efforts met with greater success when a raid was able to capture the town of York (present day Toronto), which was then the capital of Canada; when they withdrew, the American forces torched the parliament buildings and the governor's house. Although the fighting continued in Canada, its effects were inconclusive, with each side making offensive moves that were then defeated by the other. The balance of forces shifted in the British favour when, with Napoleon's abdication in May 1814, they were able to release ships and troops from Europe for service in America.

The American government decided upon a pre-emptive invasion of Canada to seize key ground before the anticipated flood of British reinforcements could turn the war against them. The campaign that followed was bloody and abortive, but it was crucial for the survival and reputation of the US Army. Brigadier Winfield Scott had intensively prepared his brigade by drilling them for 10 hours a day: 'the echoes from Valley Forge, 35 years earlier could be heard at Buffalo in 1814'.[33] With a certain irony, Scott used a verbatim translation of the French 1791 regulations as his manual, even though these were considered obsolete in Europe, which had seen enormous changes in military tactics since the Revolutionary Wars. His men were clothed in short grey jackets due to a shortage of blue cloth, and this made them resemble militia rather than regulars in appearance. At the short but sharp Battle of Chippawa on 5 July 1814, the British commander, Major General Phineas Riall, seemingly mistook Scott's brigade for 'mere' Buffalo militia, but on witnessing their steady advance under fire is reputed to have said, 'Why, these are regulars!' Riall's words, suitably embellished to 'Those are regulars, by God!', became a matter of pride for the US Army and were used on countless recruiting posters. It is also said that the cadets of the United States Military Academy at West Point wear grey dress uniforms in remembrance of the American regulars at Chippawa.[34] The performance of Scott's brigade in the battle became legendary and enabled the US regular army to rescue its pride after an otherwise undistinguished performance during the war. The battle might have been more of a skirmish, with 2,100 British and 3,500 American troops engaged, and it might be the case that the only recorded source for Riall's words comes from Winfield Scott himself, but whatever the truth, the memory of Chippawa became a powerful one for the United States army.[35] Henry Adams later commented that:

The battle of Chippawa was the only occasion during the war when
equal bodies of regular troops met face to face, in extended lines
on an open plain in broad daylight, without advantage of position;
and never again after that combat was an army of American regulars beaten by British troops. Small as the affair was, and unimpor-
tant in military results, it gave the United States army a character
and pride it had never before possessed.[36]

Perhaps most significantly, by trumpeting the success at Chippawa,
the American Army was still measuring itself against the British
Army. After a larger and bloodily indecisive battle at Lundy's Lane,
the Americans were eventually forced to withdraw from Canada,
but the campaign simply cemented Scott's reputation and the prestige of the regular US Army. After these events, no American
government could deny the need for a regular army, however
distasteful its existence might be to its founding principles.

British reinforcements from Europe did soon make their mark on
the war in America but never materialised in the numbers that the
Americans had feared. The Duke of Wellington refused the opportunity to take command of the army in America and 'give Jonathan
one good thrashing',*[37] and only a small fraction of the Peninsular
Army was ever sent across the Atlantic. Nonetheless, the element
that was sent had a disproportionate effect upon the war. Major
General Robert Ross took a new expedition, composed of Peninsular
War veterans, to mount diversionary raids on the coast to distract
American attention from Canada. George Gleig took part in Ross's
expedition as a young subaltern and afterwards wrote a lively
account of the campaign.†[38] He admitted that 'the hostilities carried
on in the Chesapeake resembled the expeditions of the ancient
Danes against Great Britain, rather than a modern war between
civilized nations', but that, in the main, the British soldiers, unlike
the Vikings, did respect private property.[39]

In August 1814, Ross saw a chance to march on Washington itself,
which appeared practically unguarded. The British were able to sail

---

* 'Jonathan' was an early term for an American, later replaced by 'Uncle Sam'.
† He later took Holy Orders and became Wellington's personal chaplain.

up the Chesapeake and land close to the American capital without any opposition. As Ross's 4,000-strong force marched towards Washington, Madison and the War Department struggled to organise 6,000 militia men, leavened by only 350 regulars and a handful of sailors. The Americans decided to make a stand at the village of Bladensburg, four miles from the capital. Here was an echo of the minutemen of Lexington Green, as the citizen soldiery of Maryland, Virginia and Pennsylvannia were called from their homes to defend their new national capital. Yet there was a terrible irony in the fighting that took place at Bladensburg. Gleig had served under Wellington during the Battle of the Pyrenees against Napoleon's Army of Spain, and he and his men had been schooled in the light infantry system developed by Sir John Moore that had originated with Henri Bouquet and the Royal Americans. Now those same tactics, enhanced by their experience of European warfare, were used against the Americans. Gleig's criticism of the American defence of their capital was scathing:

> In America, every man is a shot from his very boyhood, and every man serves in the militia; but to bring an army of raw militia-men, however excellent they might be as shots, into a fair field against regular troops, could end in nothing but defeat. When two lines oppose each other, very little depends upon the accuracy with which individuals take aim. It is then that the habit of acting in concert, the confidence which each man feels in his companions, and the rapidity and good order in which different movements can be executed, are alone of real service . . . they displayed great want of military knowledge in the disposition of both their infantry and artillery . . . The troops were drawn up in three straight lines, like so many regiments upon a gala parade . . . In maintaining them-selves, likewise, when attacked, they exhibited neither skill nor resolution . . . Of the personal courage of the Americans, there can be no doubt; they are, individually taken, as brave a nation as any in the world. But they are not soldiers; they have not the experience nor the habits of soldiers. It was the height of folly, therefore, to bring them into a situation where nothing except that experience and those habits will avail.[40]

Gleig's criticisms concerning the habits and experience of American soldiery would linger long, however unfairly, in British military minds. Bladensburg simply confirmed the British conviction that the inexperienced citizen soldiers of the militia could not stand against well-drilled regulars. Although the American regulars, artillery and some of the militia fought well at Bladensburg, the vast majority of the raw militia and volunteers were thrown into confusion and did not stand the test of battle. The British veterans, although outnumbered two to one, were able to rout the American force in a matter of three hours.

Ross rode into Washington with a flag of truce, with the intention of negotiating a ransom so that the town would not be destroyed. However, he was fired upon from a house and his horse was killed, and after this the British troops were sent in to destroy all the government buildings in an act of revenge: 'In this general devastation were included the Senate-house, the President's palace, an extensive dock-yard and arsenal, barracks for two or three thousand men' as well as the Library of Congress.[41] Some British officers even sat down to enjoy President Madison's dinner, which had been prepared for him, before proceeding to torch his palace. The British soldiers did however spare private property from the destruction. Gleig wrote that:

> You can conceive nothing finer than the sight which met them as they drew near to the town. The sky was brilliantly illumined by the different conflagrations; and a dark red light was thrown upon the road, sufficient to permit each man to view distinctly his comrade's face. Except the burning of St Sebastian's, I do not recollect to have witnessed, at any period of my life, a scene more striking or more sublime.[42]

San Sebastian was the last fortress town that had fallen to Wellington's army in Spain. During its plundering, accidental fires began that destroyed the town. Washington actually suffered less damage than many Spanish towns, but it proved that war could have very painful consequences.*

* The pillaging of Ciudad Rodrigo, Badajoz and San Sebastian were notorious blots on the character of the British Army. The inhabitants of San Sebastian believed – probably

While the British had humiliated Madison and the American republic, as well as causing much destruction, they could not conquer. Ross's force left Washington and marched on Baltimore, but made no headway against its much stronger defences. Ultimately, the British burning of Washington reflected little credit upon the British Army and came to be seen in America and Europe, if not in Britain, for what it was: wanton destruction designed to punish an opponent.

Gleig and his fellow officers remained unrepentant. In musing on any future conflict between Britain and America, he arrived at an idea of chilling prescience, arguing that:

> in absolute monarchies, where war is more properly the pastime of kings, than the desire of subjects, non-combatants ought to be dealt with as humanely as possible. Not so, however, in States governed by popular assemblies. By compelling the constituents to experience the real hardships and miseries of warfare, you will soon compel the representatives to a vote of peace; and surely that line of conduct is, upon the whole, most humane, which puts the speediest period to the cruelties of war.[43]

Gleig had understood something of the new character of America in realising that it was governed by 'popular assemblies', but his view of how to fight against such a system prefigured the destruction wrought on the South during America's greatest conflict, the Civil War. Sadly, his prediction that inflicting the misery of war upon entire populations would bring a swift end to any conflict was mistaken, as the American Civil War and both world wars were to prove.

By the winter of 1814, both sides began to realise that the war was wholly unproductive and unlikely to end in any decisive result. The Treaty of Ghent was signed on 24 December 1814, and although both sides claimed victory, the result was inconclusive to say the least. Perhaps the principal point was that the United States had, through fighting this second 'war of independence', ensured its

---

wrongly – that the British had deliberately destroyed their town in order to reduce Spanish competition for trade after the war.

sovereignty and settled some of the worst arguments between the
Federalists and Republicans. The British came to realise that waging
war against the United States would be more costly and require
greater effort and preparation than any potential benefit was likely
to yield. Yet although most British and American observers recognised the essentially unproductive and inconclusive nature of the
war, Canada had defended her independence. American visions of
an entirely united North America had been frustrated and the
continued existence of loyalist Canada had been guaranteed in part
by the British Army but more importantly by the Canadian militia.
Ironically enough, given the importance of Chippawa to the US
Army, the experience of the war provided powerful stimulus in
Canada for the 'militia myth', the idea that Canada was defended
against the depredations of the Americans primarily by its sturdy
loyalist militia.[44]

It was perhaps typical of a war that had started at the very
moment the main *casus belli* had been removed that the last battle
was fought after the peace had already been signed. It took over
two weeks for the news to reach America, and in that time, the
Battle of New Orleans had been fought and won by the Americans.
At New Orleans, Andrew Jackson, commanding a motley force of
volunteers and militia, had his revenge on the British when they
bungled an attack on some improvised defences. The battle elevated
Jackson to the same status of military hero as Scott had achieved
after Chippawa.

The Battle of New Orleans was an unhappy disaster for the
British forces involved, but there was a tragic sequel for Sir John
Lambert's brigade. His men fought and won the last action of the
American war when they took Fort Bowyer near Mobile, and were
soon embarked on ships for home. They reached Portsmouth in
May 1815, only to be re-embarked almost immediately. Napoleon
had returned to France and a new European war was looming.
The brigade set out from Ghent early on the morning of 16 June,
and by dint of forced marching covered 51 miles in little more than
two days and nights, with only two halts.[45] They reached Wellington's
allied army posted along the ridge south of Mont-Saint-Jean at
11 a.m. on the morning of 18 June. The battle that followed dwarfed

any of the engagements in America, which seemed mere skirmishes compared to the carnage that took place at Waterloo. After an extended rest during the morning and early afternoon, the 27th Inniskillings, one of Lambert's battalions, was ordered forward to defend the critical crossroads above La Haye Sainte farm. For the next four hours, they had to hold their position against French cavalry charges, artillery fire and musketry. By the end of that long afternoon they had suffered 450 casualties amongst their 750 officers and men, and had taken heavier losses than any other British battalion present at Waterloo.[46]

The battles of New Orleans and Waterloo were thus inextricably linked by the experience of Lambert's brigade. The British, by virtue of their dominance of the sea, were able to switch troops from one continent to another seemingly at will. Yet for the soldiers of the British Army, such flexibility and mobility also posed significant challenges. British Army units could never prepare for service in a specific theatre of war because they might be sent to any number of locations. Lambert and his men had been expected to participate in a difficult campaign against the Americans in Louisiana and then, in a matter of months, switch to fighting the French in Belgium in one of the most intense battles of the Napoleonic Wars, without faltering. No other army of the time could make such demands upon its soldiers. The dilemma of preparing troops for potentially very different conflicts would remain with the British Army throughout the nineteenth century and into the twentieth. Colonel G. F. R. Henderson, the great British military historian of the American Civil War, commented in 1900:

> It is as useless to anticipate in what quarter of the globe our troops may be next employed as to guess at the tactics, the armament or even the colour . . . of our next enemy. Each new expedition demands special equipment, special methods of supply and special tactical devices, and sometimes special armament.[47]

With the eventual end of the Napoleonic Wars, Europe entered a long period of peace. Yet the British Army throughout the nineteenth century had to wrestle with important conflicting demands. It had to stand ready to deal with threatened invasions from the continent, while also meeting imperial commitments. It also mounted offensive campaigns to expand that empire, which grew at the rate of 100,000 square miles per year between 1815 and 1865.[48] The problems that beset the British Army in the Crimea in 1854–5 were in part due to the fact that the army at home had ossified under the long shadow of the Duke of Wellington. This process was personified by the personal tragedy of Lord Raglan, who as a young man had been Wellington's dashing aide-de-camp and military secretary in Spain, but presided over an ill-prepared and appallingly supplied British Army in the Crimea as a sick and increasingly embittered old man. Yet the more significant problem was that the army had fought campaigns in places as far distant as Afghanistan, Baluchistan and New Zealand but had not been organised or prepared to mount an expedition against a European opponent.[49]

Winfield Scott's influence on the US Army came in some respects to resemble Wellington's upon the British Army. Scott became the US Army's 'unofficial drillmaster and authority on tactics, molding American military practice to European theory'.[50] Both armies were heavily influenced by the work of Baron Antoine Jomini, whose *Summary of the Art of War*, which codified and explained Napoleon's system, formed the foundation for military education in both countries. Scott had worked hard to ensure that the US Army was ready for its next great test, which came with the Mexican War of 1845–6, and his influence continued until the outbreak of the Civil War, by which time his tactical ideas, if not his strategic concepts, were badly outmoded. Throughout this period, the American Army still viewed the British Army as one of its principal potential enemies. The US Corps of Engineers spent decades constructing forts and other coastal defences along the eastern seaboard of the United States to ensure that the British depredations of 1814 would not happen again. As the American engineers fortified their coastline, so the British developed the forts and citadels that protected Canada.[51]

However, the majority of the tiny United States Army spent most of the succeeding decades absorbed in the task of policing the ever-moving frontier between the United States and the indigenous Indians. Whatever the theories of war taught at West Point might have been, for most soldiers the reality was the tough practical life of a soldier in a small, isolated garrison. As one Civil War general later put it: 'During my army service, I learned all about commanding fifty United States dragoons and forgot every-thing else.'[52]

In many respects, the experience of soldiering in the British Army during the nineteenth century was similar; with the notable exceptions of the Crimea and the Indian Mutiny, most military tasks amounted to acting as a military constabulary in the growing reaches of the British Empire. Yet while the British fought numerous serious campaigns in the years after the Indian Mutiny, none approached the scale or intensity of the American Civil War, which ripped America apart and produced a cataclysm costing 620,000 lives. It began with a great wave of enthusiasm in 1861, but became a grim war of exhaustion and attrition which only ended when the Southern states had been ravaged and comprehensively beaten on the battlefield.* It is hard to argue against Shelby Foote's eloquent belief that any true knowledge of the United States 'has to be based on an understanding of the Civil War . . . It defined us . . . if you're going to understand the American character in the twentieth century you have to learn about this enormous catastrophe of the nineteenth century. It was the crossroads of our being, and it was a hell of a crossroads: the suffering, the enormous tragedy of the whole thing.'[53] The losses suffered at Antietam, where 22,000 Americans were killed or wounded, remains the single bloodiest day in American military history. However, while Americans saw this as a unique experience, it was, in fact, America's first introduc-tion to the kind of mass casualties that had become common in Europe during the Revolutionary and Napoleonic Wars.[54] While many aspects of the war looked back to the Napoleonic legacy, there were also facets that were harbingers of the future: the North and South both deployed mass armies of volunteers and utilised the fruits of the Industrial Revolution in the telegraph, railroad and improved weaponry. The battles of the Civil War were bloody

* The Northern states were usually referred to as the Union, while the Southern states were known as the Confederacy.

affairs but seemed indecisive next to the Napoleonic examples that the American generals had all studied at West Point.

The war put great strain on America's relationship with Britain. Britain's neutrality (even as her factories and shipyards produced weapons and warships for both sides) infuriated the North, but it was the *Trent* incident that brought the two countries closer to war than at any other time since 1812. The *Trent*, a British mail ship, was stopped by the USS *San Jacinto* on 8 November 1861 and the two Southern agents on board were seized, in complete contravention of international law, and taken to Boston. Ironically, it was British behaviour similar to this that had precipitated the 1812 war; this time, after serious diplomatic exchanges, war was averted. William Gladstone's speech in October 1862 urging the North to 'drink the cup' and accept the secession of the South also put severe strain on relations. Northern resentment over Britain's position of neutrality was so strong that it was not until the turn of the century that the grievance had properly faded.

By 1865, the North had emerged victorious and now possessed first-class military forces. Some hotheads amongst the Union even advocated turning the Great Army of the Republic northwards to seize Canada. Although this threat never entirely emerged, the last invasion of Canada from America did take place in 1866, when an 'army' of Irish Fenians crossed the border. After a series of skirmishes, the Fenians were defeated by Canadian militia and British regulars. The British government had found its defence expenditure on Canada an increasing burden and was never really willing to spend sufficiently to create a credible defence force. When the Confederation of the Canadas united to become the Dominion of Canada on 1 July 1867, it marked an opportunity for Britain to divest itself of these responsibilities. In 1869, Gladstone, now Prime Minister, announced Britain's intention to remove all British forces from Canada, and the last British regulars left in November 1871.[55] British troops would never campaign again in North America, breaking a continuity of experience dating back to Braddock's expedition. The defence of Canada in the future would have to be borne by the new Canadian government, which continued to rely upon the traditional solution of the militia.

While most Americans saw their Civil War as distinctively American, it was of intense interest to the officers of European armies, who sent over numerous observers to learn what they could of the modern conditions of war.[56] Although it was studied intensively, however, the American experience was often seen as unworthy of emulation: what, after all, could the professional officers and well-drilled conscripts of Europe learn from the actions of hastily raised and unmilitary volunteer forces? The Prussian field marshal Helmuth von Moltke, mastermind of the Prussian victories of 1870–1, may not have actually said that the armies of the Civil War were like 'two armed mobs chasing each other around the countryside', but the phrase did sum up many European attitudes.

British interest in the American war was soon overtaken by events on the continent, and in particular the dramatic emergence of German military power as demonstrated in the Franco-Prussian War. Attention turned to von Moltke's mastery of mobilisation and rapid movement through his use of what became known as the Great General Staff. The combats of even a few years ago now seemed outdated in the era of the French Chassepot rifle and the Millatreusse, an early machine gun. While the American Army had assiduously studied and copied French military thinking, doctrine and dress before and during the Civil War, after 1871 they – along with almost every other military, including the British Army – switched their allegiance to the Prussian model.

The Civil War nonetheless cast a very long shadow in America. American politics was bedevilled by memories of the war until the turn of the century, and its legacy to the US Army lasted much longer. There was an outpouring of documents and books on its causes and course. During the war, the United States had emerged as a first-rate military power, and American officers could now refer to home-grown examples of large-scale warfare rather than European ones. Through the voluminous tomes of *Battles and Leaders of the Civil War*,[57] amongst other books, future generations of officers learnt of American battles that matched European ones in their scale and intensity. Memories of the Civil War were still very much alive during the First World War and important even during the Second World War. It is perhaps strangely instructive

to realise that the seventy-fifth anniversary of the Battle of
Gettysburg, which saw the last reunion of Union and Confederate
veterans, took place in 1938.* The future commanders of the US
Army in the Second World War all absorbed the history of the
Civil War with enthusiasm, but in this they were simply representative of their generation, which looked back with pride to that
seminal moment in American military history.

Although the Civil War was a crucial experience for the American
republic, it did not mean that America had somehow become
enamoured with large standing armies. The Civil War was seen as
a national emergency, and after that crisis had passed, the regular
army was allowed to decline into a small frontier force again.
Nonetheless, the 'Indian wars' took on a new intensity after 1865,
as greater numbers of white settlers headed west and took land
from the indigenous Indians. Over the next 25 years, the US Army
played a central role in 'winning the west', with countless skirmishes, raids, battles and campaigns against the plains Indians who
fought against the encroachment of the United States.[58]

It was Colonel G. F. R. Henderson who revived British interest
in the American Civil War. Henderson's work and lectures at the
British Staff College became the mainstay of military history for
the British Army and influenced the generation of officers who
would command in the First World War. His most influential work
was undoubtedly *Stonewall Jackson*, in which he analysed Thomas
Jackson as a military commander in minute and telling detail,
emphasising speed, manoeuvre and the use of cavalry as mounted
riflemen who could raid far into an enemy's rear. It was significant
that Henderson, and the other writers who followed him, concentrated upon the period of Confederate victories and the early war
of manoeuvre and mobility, which was more closely akin to
Napoleon's methods. Henderson realised the importance of Grant
and Sherman, though other writers tended to underplay the direct
attritional strategy that Grant had been forced to adopt during the
last years of the war to wear down and ultimately overwhelm
the Confederacy.[59]

* The events of the First World War are already further in the past as I write this than
Gettysburg was when the Second World War broke out in Europe.

While Henderson was a skilled and intelligent military historian with an unrivalled feel for his subject, most British officers imbibed his knowledge in a bastardised form. Year after year, British officers had to pass the Staff College entrance examination, which asked questions concerning Jackson's Valley campaign of 1862 in excruciating detail. This bled the subject of most of its real significance and forced officers to view the campaign and indeed the entire war from a very narrow military technical perspective. Thus the British Army of the late nineteenth century certainly continued to benefit from American experience, but at one remove: these were lessons learned in the classroom rather than on the battlefield. These examples later dovetailed neatly with the practical experience of the British Army in South Africa, where wide, sweeping movements by cavalry and mounted infantry in the style of Jackson and Sheridan had helped to achieve decisive successes over the Boers after the initial disasters of 'Black Week' in 1899. There was thus at least an indirect link running from Jeb Stuart and Sheridan's cavalry of the Civil War through to the British cavalry and mounted infantry of the Boer War.

However, the British and American armies had actually grown apart over the course of the century. They were no longer likely enemies but nor were they potential allies. Although both had engaged in what might be termed colonial policing, they did not look to one another for information, advice or inspiration. When Elihu Root, the US Secretary of War, reformed the army in the wake of the Spanish–American War of 1898 and the subsequent Philippine Insurrection, he examined German rather than British organisation. Root was perhaps the first, but certainly not the last, US Secretary of War who hoped to utilise American business principles to reshape defence; he argued that 'it does seem a pity that the Government of the United States should be the only great industrial establishment that cannot profit by the lessons which the world of industry and of commerce has learned to such good effect', and the precise shape that these reforms took was distinctively American.[60] Nonetheless, the establishment of the post of Chief of Staff as the senior military adviser to the President through the Secretary of War, a General Staff to work under him, and a

War College to train and educate senior officers all stemmed from the German example.

Similarly, the British reforms that followed the Boer War were designed to solve particular British problems but were also inspired by the predominance of German military thinking at the time. Richard Haldane, as Secretary of State for War, introduced a series of reforms that reshaped the British Army and focused its attention on the 100,000-strong British Expeditionary Force, which would be ready for deployment in Europe or anywhere around the Empire. Haldane established a General Staff, although the British version never had the power or prestige of the Great German General Staff; his reforms included the abolition of the post of commander-in-chief and its replacement with Chief of the Imperial General Staff, who would act as the senior military adviser to the Prime Minister and cabinet. The establishment of the Territorial Army brought a final break with the shared military tradition on both sides of the Atlantic, in which forces were organised into regulars, volunteers and militia. These reforms were not due to experiences in America but were a summation of colonial experience and the distillation of European influence.

The British Expeditionary Force of 1914 has often been acclaimed as the best-trained and equipped army that Britain ever sent to war. Its excellence was a result of the shock administered to the army by the Boers but was also the fruit of a hundred years of tough campaigning in the Empire. Yet there were also echoes of the British experience in America. The Boer War had finally broken down all distinctions between the line infantry and the light infantry, which meant that every infantry soldier in the new British Expeditionary Force was trained and drilled in a system that had originated with Sir John Moore and looked back to the raising of the 60th Royal Americans in 1755. The Cavalry Division of the BEF maintained its belief in the close-order charge but every trooper carried a carbine that enabled him to act as a mounted infantryman in the role that had been pioneered during the American Civil War. The British Army of 1914 had been partially shaped, however indirectly, by its contact with America.

Sir John French, who was appointed the commander of the

British Expeditionary Force in 1914, had never attended Staff College and thus had never heard one of Henderson's lectures or read his work. French had emerged from the Boer War as a military hero for his decisive victory in 1899 at Elandslaagte, where he had utilised cavalry and mounted infantry to outmanoeuvre the Boers, culminating in a close-order cavalry charge.[61] However, when the British Expeditionary Force went to war in 1914, it encountered radically different conditions of warfare, which produced a traumatic shock very similar to that of the unfortunate General Braddock but on an altogether different scale. French later wrote that:

> No previous experience, no conclusion I had been able to draw from campaigns in which I had taken part, or from a close study of the new conditions in which the war of today is waged, has led me to anticipate a war of positions. All my thoughts, all my prospective plans, all my possible alternatives of actions, were concentrated upon a war of movement and manoeuvre.[62]

The new war overturned British assumptions and set at a discount much of the hard-won experience and knowledge gained over the previous century. It ushered in a new era of industrialised mass warfare, which engulfed the whole of Europe, and ultimately the world.

2

The Great War

Dwight David Eisenhower's wedding day was 1 July 1916. The United States was still at peace but the army had been placed on a war footing due to the crisis in Mexico. Eisenhower was a young army lieutenant who had managed to secure a 20-day furlough from his unit in order to marry his sweetheart, Mamie Geneva Doud. The wedding took place at noon in the music room of the Doud family home in Denver, Colorado. Mamie looked beautiful in her wedding dress fashioned in the latest style, something that her father's wealth as a successful businessman made possible. Dwight and Mamie would remember the day with warmth and nostalgia throughout their lives. Although Congress had just passed the National Defence Act, which allowed for the creation of a national reserve for the regular army, and 'preparedness parades' were taking place in towns and cities across the country, for almost all Americans 1 July 1916 was filled with the normal happenings of an ordinary day in peacetime.

Yet that same day had a very different meaning in Britain. France, Russia and the British Empire had been fighting a global war with the Central Powers of Germany and Austria-Hungary for nearly two years. The British Expeditionary Force, which had gone to France in August 1914 with 100,000 men, had swelled to over one million, and 1 July 1916 saw the opening of what became known as the Battle of the Somme. At 7.30 a.m., along a 20-mile front, 60,000 British soldiers went 'over the top' in an attack that aimed to break through the German defences north of the River Somme. There had been a seven-day preliminary bombardment,

which had seen 1,500,000 shells fired at the German defences.[1]
The British were confident that such an unprecedented bombardment would have left few soldiers alive in the German front-line
trenches. But as the soldiers of 13 British divisions climbed out
of their trenches, they were met with a storm of artillery and
machine-gun fire. Within two hours, 21,000 men had been killed
and 37,000 wounded. It was the worst single day in the British
Army's long history.

The events of 1 July 1916 were made even more painful for the
British Army, and the British people, because of the nature of the
army that went over the top that morning. Many of the units
involved were formed from the mass of volunteers who had flocked
to the colours in 1914 and 1915 as part of Kitchener's 'New Armies'.
These volunteers had joined up, and were allowed to serve, in 'Pals'
battalions of men drawn from the same community, units that
drew upon strong local identities to create a unique spirit. These
men were not regular soldiers but very much 'civilians in uniform',
in many respects the direct descendants of the militia and the
volunteer regiments of the nineteenth century. They were imbued
with enthusiasm, pride and strong local identity, but their training
had been decidedly sketchy and their military experience and knowledge was no more than skin deep. They were a British mirror of
the American volunteer regiments that had marched to war in 1861.
Just like the first soldiers of the American Civil War, the Pals
battalions were filled with confident young men and a strong
fighting spirit. However, when they met concentrated German
artillery and machine-gun fire on the morning of 1 July, the principle
of 'those who join together can serve together' proved to have a
tragic cost.

Brigadier Hubert Rees, the commander of the 94th Brigade,
which mounted a 'diversionary attack' on the northern sector of
the Somme front, later wrote that:

The result of the HE shells, shrapnel, machine-gun and rifle fire
was such that hardly any of our men reached the German front
trench. The lines which advanced in such admirable order, melted
away under fire; yet not a man wavered, broke the ranks or

attempted to go back. I have never seen, indeed could never have imagined such a magnificent display of gallantry, discipline and determination.[2]

Rees's brigade was composed of four Pals battalions from Sheffield, Barnsley and Accrington. The men from Accrington, who went over the top in the officially named 11th Battalion, the East Lancashire Regiment, but who were known as the Accrington Pals, suffered one of the most grievous losses of any infantry battalion that day: 585 killed, wounded or missing out of the 720 men who went over the top.*[3] The battalion had been effectively destroyed in less than two hours. The impact of these losses on the small northern mill town was devastating. The local paper soon became filled with the photographs and short biographies of men who had been killed or remained missing. Percy Holmes, whose brother served in the battalion, remembered that 'when the news came through to Accrington that the Pals had been wiped out. I don't think there was a street in Accrington and district that didn't have their blinds drawn, and the bell at Christ Church tolled all the day'.[4]

Similar stories were repeated in communities across Britain in the weeks after the first day of the Somme. These events mirrored scenes that had taken place across America after battles like Antietam and Gettysburg half a century earlier. Yet the first of July 1916 only marked the opening of a battle that ground on until November 1916, at the cost of over 419,000 British casualties. The historian A. J. P. Taylor once remarked that British 'idealism died on the Somme', and there is little doubting the profound influence that this battle had upon the British psyche.[5] The Somme can be regarded as the first British exposure to the mass casualties of industrialised warfare, and that shock had reverberations that deeply influenced the generation that fought in the Second World War.

The sharp contrast between the happy ceremony at the Douds' home in Denver and the tragedy that engulfed the British Fourth Army on the same day dramatically illustrates a fracture of experience in the histories of Britain and America during the second

---

* 235 killed and 350 wounded, most within half an hour of the start of the attack.

decade of the twentieth century. The Battle of the Somme meant very little, if anything, to the American people, for understandable reasons: it was not part of their experience or history. Yet for the British people, and even for families who did not lose a relative in the Great War (although they were in a distinct minority), the memory and losses of the Somme, and the war in general, became an important, sometimes dominating, part of life. The rituals of remembrance that developed in the wake of the war demonstrate its impact on the country. These were both widespread public demonstrations of the acknowledgement of loss and private outpourings of intense grief.[6] America fought in the Great War, and suffered heavy casualties in doing so, but her participation was mercifully relatively brief. The war did not affect every town, village and homestead and thus did not mark the same watershed. America began and ended the war with her belief in herself and her ideals unshaken. The same could not be said in Britain.

This gulf of experience – and understanding – had a profound influence upon the attitudes and thinking of the key decision-makers when the two countries became allies in 1941. The Great War had been a fundamental and formative experience for the vast majority of the senior British officers of the Second World War, but this was not the case for the majority of senior US officers, the exception being those who had made it to France. It is also impor-tant to remember that most of the officers and men of the two armies in the Second World War were too young to have fought in the First World War. That had been the war of their fathers and uncles, and many had learnt little of their experience, since most veterans were tight-lipped with their families about their memories. It was thus generally through the more senior officers that the experience of the Great War remained a direct memory and central to the relationship between the armies in the Second World War, even though that experience highlighted the contrast and differences between the two armies.

The Great War was a formative experience for men like Alan Brooke, Harold Alexander, Bernard Montgomery, George Patton and George Marshall precisely because they were relatively junior officers at the time. The higher-level complexities and tensions of coalition warfare did not intrude greatly upon their horizons as they learnt their trade as soldiers. Nonetheless, the organisation and structure for coalition war that the British, French, Belgians, Russians, Italians and later Americans fitfully constructed during the course of the Great War had a significant impact upon the nature and organisation of the alliance of the Second World War.

It has to be said that relations between the British and French governments, as well as their military commanders, were often far from cordial during the Great War. Although a new under-standing had developed between Britain and France from 1904 onwards, the two countries had a long history of enmity and competition and, with the doleful exception of the Crimean War, very little experience of working together. The intense pressure produced from prosecuting the Great War exposed major fissures in the alliance, particularly as Britain and France could be considered 'equal' senior partners but with very different strengths, weaknesses and national interests. In a war in which almost any operation resulted in heavy casualties, and where the military balance on the Western Front was measured bluntly in terms of manpower and the corresponding length of trenches held, the great anxiety of all the Allied commanders was the suspicion that they were being asked to bear the heaviest burden of the fighting. The relationship between Britain and France generated a great deal of friction and resultant heat before they hit upon, seemingly almost by accident, a winning formula of cooperation, which did not last beyond the Armistice.

The military relationship did not start well. Field Marshal Sir John French, the commander of the British Expeditionary Force, was sent to France with explicit instructions from Field Marshal Lord Horatio Kitchener, the British Secretary of State for War, 'to co-operate with the French, but to avoid heavy losses'. [7] While doing so he was to coordinate with French planning but not to come under French command. Kitchener's instructions were 'neces-sarily vague and even contradictory', and contained within them 'lay the germs of controversies that would bedevil the British Command throughout the war'. [8] This ambiguous situation was exacerbated by the fact that Kitchener's instructions were kept secret from the French, who for the first nine months of the war laboured under the misapprehension that the BEF was actually under their command.[9] Unfortunately, Sir John French took an instant dislike to his French counterparts, and the early months of the war were riven by misunderstandings and bitter recriminations between the Allied commanders.

Although the size and scale of the fighting on the Western Front seemed to demand some form of centralised command, neither the British nor the French were willing to compromise sufficiently to make this a reality. General Fox Conner, head of the American Expeditionary Force's (AEF) Operations Division in 1917–18, later commented perceptively that:

> there is no necessity of entering an extensive speculation as to why the Allies did not formally agree upon the principle of an Allied Commander-in-Chief until more than three and a half years after the outbreak of war. Neither in 1914 nor at any other time would the French have anything to do with a High Commander who was not a Frenchman. Not until 1918 would the British, on the Western Front, *openly* consent to be under a High Commander who was a Frenchman. No amount of academic discussion as to the right or wrong of either the British or the French attitude can alter these simple, if somewhat brutal, facts.
>
> But the absence of a common Commander-in-Chief did not mean a complete failure of the several General headquarters to work together to a common end.[10]

Under these circumstances, the best that could be arranged was 'cooperation', however loosely defined, between the British and French commanders on the Western Front. In fact, the British, French and Russians made a number of attempts to coordinate their offensives during 1915 and 1916, but these often foundered due to the practicalities of organising vast armies across hundreds of miles.

When General Sir Douglas Haig became commander of the BEF in December 1915, Kitchener issued him with a set of instructions

very similar to those he had given Sir John French. Haig's relationship with his French counterparts was generally better than Sir
John's – not least because Haig could speak to his opposite numbers
in their language without the aid of a translator[11] – but there
remained numerous tensions. Since the French held the dominant
military position within the alliance for most of the war, Haig was
placed in the delicate position of steering a course between
conducting a campaign in France that met the British government's
objectives while ensuring that he did not lose his independence
to the French.[12] He realised that one of his primary tasks was
'putting the British case' to the French while working with them
to get 'decisive results in their plan of operations'.[13]

The Allied aspiration to achieve decisive results certainly foundered during 1916 with the murderous battles of Verdun and the
Somme, but 1917 saw an entirely changed situation, in which
the British and French had to accommodate a new and unexpected
ally. President Woodrow Wilson had worked hard to keep the United
States out of the European war, but when the Germans renewed
their gambit of unrestricted submarine warfare in a desperate bid
to strangle the vital British sea lines of communications with North
America, Wilson's room for manoeuvre evaporated. Faced with
continued violation of American neutrality by German submarines,
Wilson had little choice but to declare war. Ironically enough, the
United States entered the war for the very same reason that had
precipitated the War of 1812 against the British: the protection of
the rights of neutral shipping. When Wilson addressed Congress
on 17 April 1917, he declared that 'the world must be made safe for
democracy'. From the outset, he made it clear that the United States
was fighting to protect its own interests, but even though he insisted
on 'co-belligerent' status rather than becoming 'allied' with Britain,
France and Russia, it was difficult to escape the fact that the United
States had crossed an important Rubicon. In the eighteenth century,
Britain and France had fought for control of North America. In the
nineteenth century, the United States had conquered a continent
and, through the Civil War, itself. In the twentieth century, it had
now intervened to settle European affairs.

★   ★   ★

The entry of the United States into the war was greeted with jubilation in London and Paris. The arrival of General John Pershing in France on 13 June 1917, followed by the first few elements of what became the 1st Infantry Division of the AEF on 26 June, caused a wave of enthusiasm throughout France. When the 16th US Infantry Regiment marched through Paris on Independence Day, 4 July 1917, Pershing and his staff made a point of visiting the Marquis de Lafayette's tomb, where he was reported to have said, 'Lafayette, we are here'.* Lafayette's French Expeditionary Force had helped to turn the tide of the war against the British in 1781, and now the French earnestly hoped that Pershing's US Army would repay that debt in France's hour of need.

It is easy to forget just how dramatic and symbolic the arrival of an American army in France was in 1917. Its presence physically overturned Jefferson's injunction to the young republic that it must avoid all 'entangling alliances' with the old powers of Europe. It was the US Army's first experience of cooperating with allied forces since the War of Independence, and the attitudes, assessments and behaviour of the Allies throughout 1917–18 were long remembered and later helped to shape the relationship between the British and American armies of the Second World War.

The need for American support in 1917 was acute. After rousing itself to one last great effort in the Nivelle offensive of April 1917, the French army had suffered widespread mutinies in the depressing aftermath of yet another failed attack, and the burden of the war on the Western Front now had to be carried by the British. Pétain, the new commander of the French, undertook a defensive policy, with only a few strictly limited attacks upon the German positions. He planned to husband the strength of the French army and rebuild its morale after the mutinies until the Americans could make their presence felt on the battle fronts.

It was popularly expected that the United States would quickly send a large expeditionary force to France and support it with limitless resources. These hopes were very soon dashed as the true

---

* The phrase was actually uttered during a speech by Colonel Charles E. Stanton, one of Pershing's aides, but it was always reported – and remembered – as being said by Pershing himself.

state of American unpreparedness dawned on Allied leaders.
Pershing's vision of a great American field army seemed to disap-
pear when faced with the reality of enormous practical difficulties.
The United States had entered the war to protect its shipping rights
as a neutral, not to become embroiled in a bloody conflict.
Consequently, no real preparation had been made prior to the
outbreak of war to organise or equip an expeditionary force. Indeed,
President Wilson was only persuaded of the need for such a force
as late as March 1917. American industry was completely unprepared
to churn out the vast scale of equipment and supplies necessary to
sustain a large American army in France. The AEF lacked almost
everything, from artillery, tanks, mortars, aircraft and transport to
steel helmets. In the event, virtually all these shortfalls had to be
made up by the Allies: American soldiers in France were equipped
with an unhappy mixture of British and French equipment, and
only 100 American guns reached the army before the Armistice.
All of the large, complicated but essential systems of supply and
maintenance would have to be developed from scratch.

Perhaps worst of all, Pershing's army lacked the fully developed
military brain and nervous system of experienced commanders
and staff officers. John Charteris, Haig's Chief of Intelligence,
commented that 'it will be a very difficult job for them to get a
serviceable Staff going even in a year's time. They have very few
trained staff officers, and those who are trained have nothing like
the knowledge that our Staff College officers had in 1914.'[14] Indeed,
on the outbreak of war, the War Department staff consisted of six
regular officers, with no plans or procedure for mobilisation. The
army's ranks contained just 133,000 men, with no functioning organisation larger than a regiment, and there were only 600,000 rifles
and 600 obsolete artillery pieces in its armouries. On 18 May 1917,
President Wilson signed the Selective Service Act, which made the
entire manpower of the United States available for service in
the armed forces, but even though 10 million men were available
for mobilisation, there were no plans, structure or organisation
with which to accomplish the task, and the army was entirely
unprepared to cope with the massive expansion needed for training
and organisation. While Pershing and the first American troops

had arrived in France soon after the American declaration of war, they were not followed by the expected flood of American manpower. The German policy of unrestricted submarine warfare was causing heavy losses to shipping in the Atlantic, which made it difficult to find space for American soldiers on board ship in addition to the enormous quantities of supplies needed to keep the Allied war effort going.

These hard facts caused grave disappointment to the Allies, whose armies and populations were growing increasingly war-weary. It rendered the common French refrain of 'Wait for the Americans' a mere slogan. It would take years for the United States to build, train and equip a functioning army from the raw, unshaped material of 1917. Charteris noted in July 1917: 'It cannot possibly develop into anything big within six months, probably not for a year. Ours took two years, and the Americans have the Atlantic to cross instead of the Channel.'[15] Even at the beginning of 1918 it looked likely that American deployment might not be complete until 1920 – by which time the Allies would be broken and exhausted.

However, what American troops lacked in training, logistic support and equipment, they made up for in enthusiasm. American 'square' divisions were composed of 28,000 men, double the number of their British, French or German equivalents. They were unwieldy formations that were difficult to manoeuvre – a problem magnified by their small and inexperienced staff. With the exception of the regular units and the marines, all of the AEF's manpower was essentially composed of untrained civilians in uniform. When Charteris saw some American troops on the march, he made a link to the British experience of the war, calling the Americans 'very fine-looking fellows, but strangely stern and silent, and almost sad-featured. All the same, these Americans look very formidable troops. They are, of course, the first-fruits of the nation, and naturally their physique is far better than any in our units, or in the French units now. They are every bit as good as the first Kitchener divisions were.'[16]

The soldiers of the AEF were indeed similar to the British volunteers of 1914 and 1915: full of enthusiasm but entirely untried and untested in war.

The British and French both came to the conclusion that the most efficient and rapid way of involving the Americans in the war would be to 'amalgamate' American troops into existing French and British divisions for training and later combat. This would mean that American infantry companies or battalions could serve within the supporting infrastructure that the Allies had already developed. This would rectify what were seen as the glaring American deficiencies in trained and experienced commanders and staff, communications, artillery and supporting arms, while bolstering existing British and French formations, which possessed all of these important attributes but were running short of infantry.

While amalgamation appeared to be a neat and tidy solution for the British and French, it was highly unpalatable for the American government: in essence, American soldiers would be used to absorb British and French losses without any corresponding political advantage. Wilson was determined that an independent American Army should be formed, and he had given the commander of the AEF, General Pershing, plenipotentiary powers to ensure that he could carry out American policy. Pershing was adamantly opposed to the idea of amalgamation. He held fast to one overriding concept: he planned to train and prepare a great American field army, which, while the exhausted British and French held the line, would deliver the final crushing blow to the German armies on the Western Front. He realised that if amalgamation was allowed, the great American Army he planned to form would be broken up into a thousand fragments, which would sustain the British and French armies but leave the United States with no independent military force. Marshal Joffre, seemingly alone amongst French opinion, understood why Pershing consistently opposed these schemes: 'No great nation, having a proper consciousness of its own dignity – and America perhaps less than any other – would allow its citizens to be incorporated like poor relations in the ranks of some other army and fight under a foreign flag.'[17]

There was more than a little irony in the fact that Douglas Haig, who vigorously defended his position as commander of the independent British Expeditionary Force, and consistently maintained that he was responsible only to his own government, became an enthusiastic supporter of the scheme to amalgamate American troops into the depleted ranks of British divisions. Fox Conner later related that:

> It was not until summer [1918] that the British stopped their efforts to utilize our troops virtually as replacements. The French never stopped . . . This 'amalgamation' idea which was never quieted until the last American soldier left the Rhine was only military in so far as the French, in the bottom of their hearts, consider no American quite sane enough for either command or staff duty. But the amalgamation plans were largely political. In spite of the warnings of Tardieu and Joffre, the French politicians thought that they could fill their depleted ranks, release their older classes, and postpone incorporating their younger classes through one form or another of 'amalgamation'.[18]

Eventually, due to the paucity of training facilities, Pershing was forced to allow the temporary integration of American units into Allied formations for training and to gain limited combat experience, but on the understanding that they would serve in major operations only under American command. Ultimately, nine US Divisions served with the British while 25 US divisions (constituting the vast majority of the AEF combat troops) served at one time or another with the French, many of them for considerable periods.[19] This was an extraordinary military experiment that ensured a far greater degree of contact between the three armies than was usual. The French and British had fought alongside each other for three years but rarely intermingled. Perhaps not surprisingly, French military methods, training and equipment eventually had a greater influence upon the AEF than did those of the British.

Pershing was right to be concerned about the amalgamation schemes. They meant that he had, in essence, given up control of his army. He also held strong opinions about the nature of his new allies. He believed that the British and French armies had been cowed by the fighting on the Western Front into accepting an attritional form of trench warfare that did not seek a decisive outcome. He was convinced that the only way to win the war was through 'open warfare': 'it was my opinion that victory could not be won by the costly process of attrition, but it must be won by driving the enemy out into the open and engaging him in a war of movement'.[20] American doctrine, and Pershing's tactical instructions, emphasised the fact that the infantry alone, using their rifles, along with American marksmanship and dash, would be able to win the victory.[21] Pershing's views certainly influenced the AEF: one respondent to a post-war survey on relations with the French replied that the French were good instructors but laid 'undue stress upon trench warfare . . . The French looked upon the rifle as a good foundation to which to attach a bayonet – and little more. The Americans knew that it had vastly greater importance as a projectile weapon, and refused to neglect training toward that end.'[22]

Pershing never seems to have realised or accepted that the doctrine of battle he rigidly espoused was not alien to the British or the French. In fact, it was virtually identical to the doctrine of the British Army in 1914. The infantry of the BEF in 1914 had, after all, been perhaps the epitome of a small, skilled and experienced force that emphasised marksmanship and rapid rifle fire above everything else. Yet the vast majority of these highly trained and experienced regular soldiers had been killed or wounded by 1917. Indeed, most French and British commanders during the war had seen the conditions of trench warfare as an aberration, and constantly sought a decisive breakthrough, after which they could return to the familiar conditions of open warfare. Very few of the Allied offensives had been launched with anything other than such a breakthrough in mind, but all had foundered on the reality of the conditions on the Western Front, where powerful artillery, defence in depth and machine guns could destroy any unsupported infantry assault.

Pershing's suspicion concerning British and French training went further. He feared that American units that trained with the British and French would become tainted by their mistaken doctrine of trench fighting and would thus be less able to conduct the open warfare that he believed would lead to victory. Pershing's views were, in many respects, a reflection of his nostalgia for the old

American regular army and its limited campaigns in Cuba, the Philippines and Mexico, where individual marksmanship was important. His hard line on doctrine was also a military version of the attitudes of American particularism, which sought to differentiate the conditions of the American continent and its people from the 'old world' of Europe. However, Pershing's insistence on drilling his men in open warfare techniques meant that American troops, when they started to reach the front in numbers during the summer of 1918, were often sketchily and inappropriately trained. The British and French efforts to train American troops also showed quite starkly the limits to which armies can transmit experience and knowledge to one another. While the British and French had shared techniques – such as the creeping barrage – their employment of such methods and conduct of battles remained very different. Similarly, the AEF, even though it was largely trained and equipped by the British and French, held to its own, distinctively American approach to battle.

American surveys of this amalgamation experience were prepared soon after the Armistice and provide a fascinating snapshot of American relations with Allied officers and troops. On 10 December 1918, Pershing instructed the commanders of all US corps, divisions and brigades that had served with the British or French armies to compile confidential reports on the relations they had experienced with these foreign armies. The replies betrayed many of the problems that are bound to beset such surveys: the American commanders were far more likely to provide an unvarnished account of their allies than of themselves. Relations between American and British officers were difficult at first. The Americans blamed this on the fact that 'the Britisher never addressed any other officer, English or Allied, with whom he was not already acquainted, and if conversation with one such became imperative, did not disclose his identity'.[23] It took time for this reserve to be broken down and such stand-offishness was compounded by what the US 27th Division considered a 'superiority complex' exhibited by the average English officer, who, particularly in the junior grades, was rather overbearing. It was noted by the US 60th Infantry Brigade that 'Tommy considered himself a superior soldier to the American and took no pains to conceal it . . . In fact he took every opportunity to impress upon the mind of the American soldier that such was the case. Our soldiers resented any such attitude and denied that it was based upon fact.'[24]

The 35th Division explained that, even though it only served with the British for three weeks, which was perhaps 'too short a period to dissolve the barrier of British reticence', its officers and men 'did not get along very well with the British. They did not like the British non-coms, or the British soldiers, or the British officers . . . There were occasional fights between our men and theirs. This did not aid in cementing the entente.'[25]

The commanders invariably replied that their relations with the British were 'excellent' or 'most cordial', while one infantry brigade replied that relations with the British were good but 'with Scotch, Very Good'. The American II Corps, whose troops spent the longest time in British and Australian company, assessed that in terms of relative efficiency the 'British were old and experienced; Americans young and dashing'. Only the 80th Division stated that the 'British were of the best; Americans 90% as efficient'. Many of the responses commented on the slow and deliberate nature of the British conduct of operations. It 'seemed to some impetuous Americans as lacking intensity of purpose', but over time the Americans 'learned to exercise a like deliberation and so achieve equal objectives at smaller cost'.[26] The American belief that the British Army was slow and methodical thus probably originated during the First World War, although it was to become a common refrain in the Second.

The soldiers of II Corps were attached to the Australian Corps and it was reported that the 'American held mingled feelings of respect and disapproval' towards the Australians. It was conceded that the Australian soldier 'combined caution with aggressiveness, and so managed to restrict casualties, but some of his other characteristics were not so pleasing'. While British discipline was considered 'excellent' by the Americans – although many Americans suspected that it was 'a manifestation of meek submission rather than the proud attribute of the trained soldier' – Australian troops were found to be almost 'devoid of discipline'. The 27th Division Commander reported systematic looting of the bodies of American

dead by Australian soldiers who constituted the following echelon
in the assault on the Hindenburg Line, and observed that their
officers were prone to refer to such practices 'in a light hearted
manner'. AEF opinion was certainly that the American soldier
possessed superior initiative to that of the Englishman – and equal
to that of the Australian. One American commander commented
that 'his men were twice as intelligent as the British'.[26]

British social customs also caused misunderstanding. The
Americans 'were at first amused at the constant English effort to put
the war out of mind. This was manifested by their fidelity to the
afternoon tea hour, entertainments behind the lines, etc.' They
soon found, however, that these simple diversions could and did
produce moments of forgetfulness that were lifesaving from the
standpoint of maintaining morale, and well worthy of adoption.
But American troops who had to share British rations universally
condemned them. It was considered that British rations 'were
terrible from the American soldier's standpoint, no matter where
encountered. Especially disliked was the substitution of tea for
coffee, and the lack of good red meat in the diet. The Britisher's
jam and cheese, on which he appeared to thrive, were anathema
to the American.'[28]

Whatever the faults of the British or his rations, however, it was
agreed that:

> the Englishman knew how to handle himself in battle, and to reach
> his objective with a minimum of casualties. He acted with delib-
> eration, rather than dash, but this was an indication of sound good
> sense rather than lack of courage, of which he possessed full
> measure. He did not equal the American in initiative or intelligence.
> His rations were unappetizing and unsustaining . . . [but] he main-
> tained extremely attractive canteens.
>
> The American officer found his British cousin, English and
> Imperial, cordial and friendly, easy to get along with, and always,
> except perhaps in the case of some of the lower grades, of good
> morale. The Englishman's social customs were frigidly peculiar, but
> he was willing to admit this, and to make honest and successful
> effort to reshape them. He was invariably brave, often exposing

himself unnecessarily . . . He was not unduly sensitive to honest criticism, indeed not so much as the American, but ready to acknowledge shortcomings when they actually existed.[29]

American views of the French army were also generally positive, but again there were exceptions. It was found that the vast majority of respondents to the survey considered relations to be cordial or good, and few language difficulties arose as long as there were some officers or men who could speak both languages to hand. In their absence, however, serious problems could emerge. French accommodation for the troops was often 'so far short of American standards, that there was much grumbling throughout the AEF as to the type of habitation furnished. American soldiers, unlike the French, were not used to sharing stables and lofts in common with barnyard fowl and domestic animals of assorted varieties, and frequently, weather permitting, preferred to bivouac in the open.'[30]

American troops and officers also all commented on the unsanitary conditions left by French troops when taking over trench positions from them. They also commented upon the exhaustion of the French army and their willingness 'to leave the German undisturbed in his front-line trenches if he would play a similar game'. While Anglo-American relations appear to have begun rather frostily and become progressively better, the reverse seems to have been the case between the French and the Americans. After the Armistice, there was an increasing anti-American feeling amongst the French and an increasing anti-French feeling amongst the Americans, who accused the French people of profiteering, ingratitude and inhospitality.[31]

While the growing AEF engaged in training behind the lines, the British and French armies on the Western Front were facing a very grim strategic situation. By late 1917, Russia was convulsed by its second, Bolshevik, revolution, and on 24 October, the combined Austro-German offensive against the Italians opened in what became known as the Battle of Caporetto. With the collapse of the Russian war effort, and the disintegration of the Italian front, the British and French finally accepted the need for a body that could coordinate the activities of the Allies more efficiently. This resulted in the formation of the Supreme War Council on 7 November 1917, with both military and political representatives from each of the major allies 'to watch over the general conduct of the war'.[32] Even though the Allied governments continued to quarrel over every issue, including where the Council should meet, the Supreme War Council provided an important precedent and a working model of cooperation for Anglo-French relations in the Second World War.

However, while the Council did very important and effective work on a whole range of issues, most notably the efficient allocation and coordination of shipping and industrial resources, it was unable to break the logjam over the question of coordination on the Western Front.[33] Haig, in particular, resisted any attempt to subordinate his army to an overall commander who would, inevitably, be French. The British and French governments also used the Council meetings as a means to pressure the Americans. Since most of the shipping used to transport American soldiers across the Atlantic would be British, it was argued that the first six American divisions should be sent to work with the British Army.[34] Not surprisingly, this was an unattractive bargain for Pershing, who held to his position of building up an independent national army, but it meant that the British were less than forthcoming with shipping to assist the Americans. This unseemly haggling over 'ships for souls' proved extremely damaging to the relationship between the two armies in the longer term.[35] It was almost certainly at the root of the American attitude that the British were inveterate intriguers who always had an undisclosed ulterior motive.

Nonetheless, it is also clear that Pershing did not fully understand the strategic pressures faced by the British and French in the winter of 1917–18. Germany had won the war in the east, and this enabled the Germans to transfer large numbers of troops to the Western Front. By March 1918, they had an overall superiority of manpower there – a situation that hadn't occurred since 1914. The French army was still in the process of recovery from its mutinies and the British were exhausted from the gruelling and bloody Passchendaele offensive. Meanwhile, Pershing's fledgling forces had yet to make any significant impact on the military situation. General Erich Ludendorff, the Quartermaster General and de facto dictator of Imperial Germany, decided to gamble everything on a series of offensives to overwhelm the British and French before the Americans could permanently tip the scales against Germany.

When Ludendorff's great offensive, code-named Michael, was launched on 21 March 1918, the British were not surprised by the direction or scale of the assault, but they were shocked by its ferocity and success. The combined tactics of a hurricane bombardment and the infiltration of specially trained 'stormtroop' infantry overwhelmed the defences of the British Fifth Army north of the Somme. By 23 March, it was clear that the Germans, for the first time in the war, had breached the Western Front. Many British troops fought stubbornly, but by 30 March, Gough's Fifth Army had been virtually destroyed. Its ranks now numbered just 9,500 men – less than a division. It was during this first offensive that Ludendorff and the German army came closest to success. The Germans inflicted roughly 350,000 casualties on the Allies, including 90,000 prisoners, and took 1,000 guns while advancing over 40 miles into Allied positions.

Nevertheless, the Allied powers of resilience were far beyond Ludendorff's expectations. He had expected that the surprise, speed and ferocity of the German attack mounted on the junction between the two allies would effectively force them apart and allow the Germans to defeat each in detail. This situation very nearly arose when Pétain suffered a critical loss of nerve. Charteris noted in his diary on 25 March 1918:

The situation is very serious both in the battle and behind it . . . Pétain met D. H. last night at Dury, and told him that if the German attack were pressed on on our right, he had ordered the local French commander [General Fayolle] to withdraw south west and cover Paris. That would leave a clean gap between our army and the French, and the Germans would get right through[36] . . . Pétain must have lost his judgement. The whole basic principle of the Allied strategy since 1914 has been for the French and British Armies to keep united. The one thing the Germans must most desire is to separate them.[37]

In fairness to Pétain, he had been shocked and disconcerted by the break-up of the British Fifth Army, which was now threatening to unhinge his line, but if he had acted on his instincts, it would have heralded defeat for the Allies. This was the supreme crisis of the war, because the informal arrangement between Haig and Pétain to share reserves had broken down just when a coordinated response was most needed. Haig – not without self-interest – now pushed for the concept of a commander-in-chief to direct both armies on the Western Front and send reserves to where they were needed, even though this was a proposal he had been stubbornly fighting against for the past two years. Charteris wrote that 'D. H. has telegraphed home asking that a Generalissimo for the whole Western front be appointed at once as the only possible means of having Pétain overruled . . . D. H. has also appealed direct to Clemenceau and Foch to try and get one or other of them to take action.'[38] Haig had belatedly realised that the only solution was to accept the need for an overall commander, who would almost certainly be French but who would realise the need to send reserves to the threatened sector around the Somme.

On 26 March, there were three separate conferences in the *mairie* of the small town of Doullens to the north of the threatened sector. Haig first met with his army commanders to reshuffle the divisions of the BEF in order to cover the gaping hole opposite the remnants of the Fifth Army. He then spoke with Lord Milner, the Secretary of State for War, and General Sir Henry Wilson, the Chief of the Imperial General Staff, to explain the crisis and develop possible solutions. At the next and most important meeting, Haig, Milner and Wilson met with General Ferdinand Foch, Prime Minister Clemenceau and President Poincaré. Foch dramatically stressed that the union between the French and British armies must be maintained, and that the city of Amiens, with its vital rail and road hub, must be held at all costs: if it fell to the Germans, the breach between the French and British would probably be irreparable. Clemenceau suggested that Foch coordinate the deployment of the French and British forces in the Amiens area, with those specific tasks of covering Amiens and preserving the link between the two armies. It was Haig who saw the flaw in such a plan – since Foch would be subordinate to both Haig and Pétain, he would have no control over what reserves were sent to the Amiens sector – and urged that Foch be given command of all British and French troops in France and Flanders. Charteris observed that 'the whole and sole object is to override Pétain and get the French to send reinforcements to prevent the British and French Armies being separated'.[39] It was finally agreed, after debate, that Foch would become the generalissimo for the whole of the Western Front. The Allies had finally adopted a policy of coordination, albeit imperfect, which had a great influence on the conduct of the war, and provided an important model for the Allies of the Second World War.

With the German threat to Amiens still looming, Pershing visited Foch at his new headquarters. During the tense meeting, in which Foch explained the grim situation, Pershing bent from his unyielding position on amalgamation: 'At this moment there are no other questions but of fighting. I have come to tell you that the American people will be proud to take part in the greatest battle of history.' Although he had made a fine gesture, his offer had little practical effect. The most dangerous German offensive was stemmed by combined French and British effort, with little practical assistance from the Americans.[40]

Indeed, it was highly significant that neither the British nor the French had seen fit to invite American representatives to the conference at Doullens. This meant that one of the most important decisions of the war was taken without reference to their new-world allies. It was only at the Beauvais Conference, on 3 April 1918, when discussions were held to define more accurately the powers of General Foch, that the Americans were invited.[41] Even then, the draft of the resolution detailing Foch's powers omitted mention of the American army. When Pershing noticed this and brought it to the attention of the Conference, Pétain rudely replied: 'There is no American Army as such, as its units are either in training or are amalgamated with the British and French.'[42] Pétain's remarks accurately caught the British and French attitude towards the American commander and his army, yet ironically, they also revealed why Pershing had been right to insist upon the development of an independent American army: without it, he would have had no say whatsoever in the strategy and conduct of the war on the Western Front. The Beauvais Conference saw the AEF finally placed under Foch's, and therefore Allied, command.

The crisis of spring 1918 had finally brought about an Allied Supreme Commander, albeit one armed only with a piece of paper and the force of his personality, but it also had other important effects. The recognition that only American manpower could save the Allies on the Western Front, however it was deployed or commanded, broke the logjam over shipping for the AEF. By June 1918, 250,000 American soldiers were crossing the Atlantic every month.[43] Pershing also ordered the 1st US Infantry Division into action, perhaps before it was fully ready, at Cantigny on 27 April 1918. This minor battle saw an attack by one American regiment, which then had to hold the ground it had gained against fierce German counter-attacks over the next three days. Cantigny was a minor engagement in the context of the Western Front but it made a highly important symbolic point: the Americans were now actively engaged in the war. However small, this first American attack began to demonstrate what an American Army might achieve at just the moment when Pershing was under renewed pressure to amalgamate American units into British and French formations.[44]

Indeed, Haig became very frustrated with Pershing during the meeting of the Supreme War Council at Abbeville on 1–2 May 1918. He vented to his diary: 'I thought Pershing was very obstinate, and stupid . . . He hankers after a "great self-contained American Army" but seeing that he has neither Commanders of Divisions, of Corps, nor of Armies, nor Staffs for same, it is ridiculous to think such an Army could function unaided in less than two years time.'[45] Haig's frustration reveals the pressure he was under as the British commander but also the patronising attitude that Pershing and his staff officers often had to deal with in their dealings with the British and French. Such attitudes simply made them work harder to prove themselves.

Meanwhile, Ludendorff had mounted further offensives in an increasingly desperate attempt to win the war. Planned without any guiding strategic concept other than ultimate victory, each successive German attack during the spring of 1918 was impressive in its sound and fury, but all were denied any strategic result. Georgette, the offensive mounted from 9 to 21 April against the British Third Army in Flanders, made little progress, apart from the abandonment by the British of the dubious gains of Passchendaele. Bluecher, the attack launched against the French on the Chemin des Dames on 27 May, again shocked the Allies with its scale and ferocity. Within three days the Germans forced three river lines, advanced 40 miles and took 65,000 prisoners. However, the US 2nd and 3rd Divisions won their spurs in combat at Belleau Wood for their part in blunting the German drive. Gneisenau, fought around Metz, was less successful, and the limited French counter-attack of 12 June showed that Allied powers of resistance remained undiminished.

Left without any strategy other than continuing on the offensive, Ludendorff mounted one last attack, which he gave the unfortunate name of Friedensturm, or Peace Offensive, thus raising the German people's hopes of victory. These hopes were to be cruelly shattered. Both the French and British had learnt to absorb the initial blow of the German offensives by leaving the front areas largely devoid of troops. The Friedensturm, around the city of Rheims, was halted on its first day, 16 July, by the French defence. Two days later, the Germans were vigorously counter-attacked by Mangin's Sixth Army with supporting American divisions in the first major Allied offensive since March.

This counter-attack on 18 July was an event of the greatest importance even though its impetus petered out two days later. For the German High Command, the French counter-attack meant the final failure of Ludendorff's offensive strategy. German strength was at an end and the British and French armies had managed to survive the greatest onslaught of the war. While both had taken terrific batterings, they were still in the field and capable of offensive action. Their governments had not fallen apart in diplomatic wrangling, nor had they sued separately for peace. Furthermore, what Ludendorff had feared and Allied leaders had hoped for had finally come to pass: the American Expeditionary Force was now over one million strong and beginning to make its presence felt on the battlefield. This contribution to Allied military strength was vital, because while Britain and France could only hope to manage the rate of decline in the strength of their armies, the Americans were now beginning to draw on their seemingly limitless manpower. Ludendorff's last throw of the dice had failed. Yet while the balance of the war had irrevocably shifted, this change was almost invisible to the protagonists. Until the Allies could actually impose their will on the German army, thus proving the extent of the German defeat, the situation remained in the balance. While the Germans had lost the war by July 1918, the Allies had still to win it.

One very small battle in the British sector provided a harbinger of the future on the Western Front; the Battle of Hamel was much more significant than its size would have suggested. The attack on the village of Le Hamel on 4 July 1918 by the Australian Corps of the British Fourth Army, with two companies of American infantry attached, was considered, even at the time, a model operation. This minor assault aimed to take advantage of German weakness and combined surprise, artillery, tanks, aircraft and infantry into an effective all-arms attack that overwhelmed the German defence. The planning and execution was a world – and a military genera-tion – away from Pershing's ideas of the primacy of the rifle and the infantry soldier.

General Monash, the commander of the Australian Corps, had deliberately planned to use 60 tanks to compensate for his declining strength in manpower. The plan had been to add one American infantry company to each of the six Australian infantry battalions to bring these depleted units back up to full strength. However, when Pershing heard of the plan, he insisted on cancelling American support. Pershing's veto over the use of American troops in the operation caused resentment amongst the American companies themselves, eager as they were to see combat.* After some frantic

---

* There is more than a little irony here. Pershing was well known to the British and French for what they saw as his stubborn refusal to use his troops in combat before he believed they were ready. This form of veto is today called a 'red card' in military

last-minute telephone calls, most of the American companies were removed – much against their will – from the order of battle, but it was too late to turn back the two that had already moved up to the starting line.[46] The all-arms assault achieved complete surprise over the German defenders. Within twenty minutes the Australian and American infantry had reached their objectives, suffering only light casualties – in Western Front terms at least. Hamel proved that the combined use of all-arms could indeed compensate for the lack of infantry. The British Army had moved increasingly towards a mechanised form of methodical warfare that emphasised firepower at the expense of manpower.

For the two American infantry companies that took part in the attack at Le Hamel, 4 July 1918 became a red-letter day. Not only was it Independence Day, but it marked the start of a successful cooperation between the Americans and the Australians in the British Fourth Army that would last until the Australians were pulled out of the line on 5 October 1918. However, such small-scale use of American forces also confirmed Pershing's fears that the American Army might be broken up and used by the British and French in a manner that would dilute any American political influence. Le Hamel was, after all, known at the time and remembered ever after as an Australian victory.

This minor attack in July was followed on 8 August 1918 by a combined-arms assault by an entire British Army in what became known as the Battle of Amiens. The Fourth Army, with the Australian and Canadian Corps to the van, utilised the techniques of Le Hamel but on a much vaster scale and with much more impressive results. This time, Pershing allowed greater American participation, and even the British were surprised by the scale of the success, which saw the leading troops advance nearly nine miles. It was not for nothing that Ludendorff called the Battle of Amiens the 'Black Day' for the German army.

---

circles, deriving from a football analogy. In the recent campaign in Afghanistan, contingents of the multinational forces frequently had their involvement in forthcoming operations vetoed by their national capital. It is now the Americans who are scornful of such vetoes, to the extent that their soldiers labelled ISAF (International Stabilization Aghanistan Force) 'I Saw Americans Fight'.

Just as German resistance was beginning to stiffen in the face of the Fourth Army's advance, Pershing explained to Haig on 12 August 1918 that he planned to withdraw the five American divisions that had been training with the British as soon as possible. He wanted to add them to the growing American Army that was now cooperating on the French part of the front. Pershing was marking the end of the devil's bargain of 'ships for souls' that had been struck under very different circumstances. Haig, understandably, was outraged by the request. He argued that the American divisions were not yet fully trained or ready but that once they were, they would be best cooperating with the British who had trained them. When Pershing insisted, Haig was forced to relent, but he fumed in his diary: 'What will history say regarding this action of the Americans leaving the British zone of operations when the decisive battle of the war is at its height and the decision is still in doubt!'[47] Relations between Haig and Pershing in the closing months of the war were far from happy.

However, Pershing had good reason to withdraw his forces. On 24 June, Foch had agreed to his long-held plan for an American assault on the Saint-Mihiel salient. The AEF staff had considered this sector for over a year and now the time seemed right to enact the operation. Pershing was gathering his forces from the British sector to build the First American Army, which became active on 10 August 1918.[48] Large numbers of staff officers at the new First Army and at AEF GHQ were plunged into a frenzy of preparation, writing a series of plans only to have them modified or scrapped. The chief inspiration behind the Saint-Mihiel plans was the chief of the Operations Section at AEF GHQ, General Fox Conner, among whose assistants was the newly promoted Colonel George Marshall. Marshall had witnessed first-hand the birth pangs and eventual growth of the AEF from a tiny unformed embryo into a fully fledged army. He went on to become the 'organiser of victory' as the US Army's Chief of Staff in the Second World War, but he had learnt his trade during the Great War.

During the summer of 1916, Marshall supervised the rather unmilitary summer training of civilian volunteers in their camp at Monterey, California.[49] However, in the spring of 1917, in a stroke of luck and as recognition of his abilities, he managed to land a place on the staff of the 1st US Infantry Division, who were scheduled to be sent out to France. Marshall arrived in France in June 1917 and thus had first-hand experience of the construction of the AEF from the ground up. In his staff job as Chief of Operations, he was only too well aware of the enormous deficiencies and the lack of equipment, training and experience in the nascent division. The 1st US Division first saw combat in November 1917, serving with the French in the front lines, and went into the line as a division in December 1917. There was a great deal of pressure on these first representatives of the American Army in France, and none was harder upon them than Pershing himself. On one occasion when he had finished a tour of inspection that did not meet his exacting standards, he gave General Sibert and his staff a severe dressing-down. It was Marshall who had the temerity to stand up to him and explain the difficulties that the division was operating under. From that time, he was marked by Pershing as a forthright officer who could be trusted.

Marshall had been in the thick of the planning for the attack on Cantigny, and his talents were recognised by promotion to the Operations Section of AEF GHQ. In American eyes, he had become a 'superlative staff officer',[50] but it is worth noting that the British and French would not have recognised either Marshall or Conner as experienced staff officers. After the initial draft plan was submitted on 9 August 1918, Marshall wrote another three draft plans in as many weeks. To British and French eyes this would simply have seemed like inexperience. Their army staffs had to produce workable plans much more rapidly for a front that was now moving at a rate of no less than a mile a day. However, their staff officers had up to four years' experience of war and a whole raft of standard procedures and doctrine to draw upon, whereas Marshall was starting almost from scratch. The very fact that Marshall drafted the plans for the whole operation, as well as the detailed artillery plan and parts of the deception plan, demonstrated that there were insufficient trained and experienced staff officers in the corps and division HQs to deal with these issues.

As Conner, Marshall and Grant worked frantically to prepare

the plans, Pershing had a stormy interview with Foch over the coming operation. Foch believed that with the Germans now in full retreat, the Saint-Mihiel salient no longer offered the opportunities that had attracted American attention in the first place. He argued that Pershing should abandon the plans and take part in a combined Franco-American drive in the Meuse-Argonne sector, which now promised greater results. He taunted Pershing: 'Do you want a part in the coming battle?' to which Pershing replied, 'Only with an American Army.'[51] Saint-Mihiel might have lost its military value but Pershing was determined to mount an operation that could be seen as the first attack of an independent American Army. Eventually a compromise was worked out: the Saint-Mihiel operation would go ahead, but as soon as the salient had been reduced, the Americans were to move to an entirely new sector near the Meuse river and the Argonne forest and prepare for an attack in combination with the French Fourth Army. Like many compromises, this proved to be the worst of both worlds. With the Saint-Mihiel attack planned for 12 September and the opening of the Meuse-Argonne offensive on the 26th, Conner and his team had to plan both battles at the same time and work out how an entire army could be shifted from one sector to another within a matter of days.

As far as Foch and Haig were concerned, the American attack at Saint-Mihiel was now an almost irrelevant sideshow, but for Pershing it was the first chance to prove what the American Army could do. It was certainly not a small operation: 550,000 American and 110,000 French troops would take part. Even though almost all of the equipment, artillery, aircraft and tanks was borrowed from the British and French, this was a fully fledged American Army going into combat, 18 months after Wilson's declaration of war.[52] At 0100 hours on 12 September 1918, the brief preliminary bombardment of the German trenches began, and at 0500 hours the Doughboys and *poilus* clambered out of their trenches into the attack. Much of the wire in front of the German trenches remained uncut – an oversight that had led to tragedy on the Somme in 1916 – but this time German resistance and, crucially, artillery fire was light. American engineers and pioneers blew and cut holes in the wire and, astonishingly, used chicken wire to form rough bridges over the low German wire. The American infantry managed to breach the defences and take their objectives, capturing 450 guns and 16,000 prisoners and suffering the relatively light loss of 7,000 casualties. However, part of the reason for this surprising success was that the Germans were already in the process of withdrawing from the salient.

The ease of the assault came as a disappointment to Lieutenant Colonel George S. Patton. Patton had accompanied Pershing during his 1916 expedition to hunt down the Mexican rebel leader Pancho Villa, and gained fame for shooting one of Villa's subordinates in a gunfight at San Miguelito.[53] Due to Pershing's patronage, he went to France as commander of the AEF's advance headquarters troops. He also served as one of Pershing's aides on many of his visits to Allied dignitaries, where he met almost all of the senior British and French commanders. Haig, on meeting the young captain, noted in his diary that 'The ADC is a fire-eater! [who] longs for the fray.'[54] Patton did indeed thirst to see combat, and with Pershing's support he became the first American officer to be assigned to the new US Tank Corps. He organised the first AEF Light Tank School at the AEF's headquarters near Langres, learned all he could about these new vehicles from the French and trained the first American tank crew. By April 1918, his work was recognised by promotion to lieutenant colonel and the command of the first US tank battalion. He first saw combat, along with his men, on the morning of 12 September 1918, but was frustrated by the relative lack of opposition.

Saint-Mihiel had proved that the new American Army could at least mount successful operations on the Western Front, but it did not quite justify Pershing's elation and sense of vindication. He was effusive when discussing the results of the operation with Dennis Nolan, the AEF Chief of Intelligence, arguing that it was the liberty found in America, combined with the opportunities of the new world, that meant that the US 'had developed a type of manhood superior in initiative to that existing abroad, which given approximately equal training and discipline, developed a superior soldier to that existing abroad'.[55] Such attitudes would have been met with cold disbelief by both the British and French.

That Pershing's triumph was rather premature was cruelly emphasised in the next phase of operations, which saw the American Army pulled out of the front line and transferred 40 miles further north to the Meuse-Argonne sector. The Meuse-Argonne offensive was a very different proposition to the Saint-Mihiel attack. The Germans' defences were very strong, and this time they were fighting to maintain one of their key communication centres behind the front. When the attack began, on 26 September, German resistance was much heavier than it had been at Saint-Mihiel. Patton was seriously wounded while attempting to bring his tanks forward that morning, and he would not command troops in combat again until the Second World War. After initial success on the first few days of the attack, the American advance stalled in the face of increased German resistance and heavy casualties. Marshall was ordered to gather in yet more divisions to regain momentum.

With most of the American strength now concentrated under Pershing's hand, only the II American Corps, composed of the 27th New York and the 30th Tennessee divisions, were left in the British sector. They took part in an important series of attacks with the British Fourth Army that became known as 'the breaking of the Hindenburg Line'. The Hindenburg Line was a formidable series of defences constructed by the Germans in 1916 and 1917, and was generally considered to be impregnable. However, the Fourth Army was able to approach through a tough series of battles, and by 28 September was ready to assault the main position. The two American divisions were used to shore up Major General Sir John Monash's Australian Corps, which had provided a crucial cutting edge in many of the Fourth Army's attacks since 8 August 1918. The Australians relied on volunteers to refill their ranks, and the corps was becoming seriously short of manpower after its involvement in intense fighting since the beginning of August. It was suggested and agreed that the II American Corps could come under Monash's command for the assault. General G. W. Read, the American commander, even allowed Monash to amalgamate the staff of the two corps so that his inexperienced staff officers could learn by working alongside Australian officers in the headquarters.[56]

The two American divisions were committed first to an attack to reach the Hindenburg Line and then in the assault on the main defences on 29 September. Monash's plan for the assault was highly ambitious against such formidable defences, and the American troops encountered severe difficulties in the thick fog and confusion of battle. Unfortunately, the 27th American Division had decided to forgo the protection of a creeping barrage for the first 1,000 yards of its advance. The tanks that were brought up to support the division encountered strong anti-tank defences and many of them were knocked out. The division made little progress and suffered very heavy casualties in its attempt to breach the main defences. Further south, the 30th American Division had the support of a creeping barrage and managed to press on into the German defences. However, due to confusion caused by early-morning fog, which obscured vision, and inexperience, which meant that the American troops had not properly 'mopped up' German positions as they advanced through them, when the 5th Australian Division passed through the American positions, it suffered heavy casualties. Although the Americans and Australians were on the main axis of attack, the Fourth Army actually encountered unexpected success further south, where the men of the 46th (North Midland) Division managed to capture a bridge intact and swim the canal.

General Sir Henry Rawlinson blamed the inexperienced American troops for the relatively disappointing results of the attack on the main axis, writing in his diary: 'The Americans appear to be in a state of hopeless confusion and will not I fear be able to function as a Corps . . . I fear casualties have been heavy but it is their own fault.'[57] Rawlinson's assessment of the American performance was unfair. It is generally agreed that their objectives were too ambitious even for experienced troops and that the problems they encountered could not have been foreseen. Prejudice concerning uneven American combat performance was to cast a long shadow over British attitudes to the American Army.

For Haig and the BEF, the breaching of the Hindenburg Line was seen as the beginning of the end. The Germans had been thrown off their final prepared defensive line, which they had believed was impregnable. By 4 October, they had been forced to accept the inevitable: they would have to sue for an armistice. Pershing's army had thus not achieved quite the objective he desired: it would not fight the final deciding battle of the war in open warfare but amongst the shattered trees of the Argonne forest. As German resistance began to weaken, scattered American forces raced to reach Sedan, but the Armistice came too soon for them to enter the city in triumph.

The very last day of the Great War also revealed a signal difference in British and American attitudes towards the lives of ordinary soldiers. While Douglas Haig and the British High Command had accepted the loss of hundreds of thousands of men during the great battles of the war, they had no desire to see such loss on the final day. Similarly, when Arthur Currie of the Canadian Corps ordered a controversial attack and the occupation of the town of Mons on 11 November, resulting in the death of one Canadian soldier, he had to face a court case brought against him in Canada that dragged on into the 1930s. Yet the American First army launched a full-scale attack just seven hours before the Armistice was to come into effect. This meant that the Americans were fighting and suffering heavy casualties until the last moment of the Great War.[58]

Ultimately, the American effort in the Great War had been impressive: 2,084,000 American soldiers landed in France and 1,390,000 saw front-line service. By November 1918, there were more American troops in France than there were British, and they were occupying a larger portion of the front. But American divisions had been in the line of battle for only 200 days, from 25 April to 11 November 1918, and their casualties had been comparatively light, with 50,300 American soldiers killed in action compared with the British loss of more than 900,000 men over the course of four long, hard years. The fact was that while the British and French breathed a sigh of relief that the nightmare of war was finally over, the Armistice had come too soon for Pershing to really show what his great American Army could do.

The news of the Armistice was also greeted with dismay by Eisenhower. In common with all of his contemporaries, he had been desperate to be sent to France so that he could lead troops in action, but his repeated requests for overseas service were denied.

Much to his frustration, the closest he got to combat was at the tank training centre of Camp Colt, established near the Civil War battlefield of Gettysburg, Pennsylvania. Although Eisenhower proved himself to be a capable leader who displayed attention to detail and sound organisational ability, and was already showing talent as a trainer of troops, it was difficult to properly prepare the men of the fledgling US Tank Corps for armoured warfare without any tanks. Eventually, in June 1918, one unarmed Renault light tank was delivered to Camp Colt for training purposes. It was the first tank ever to reach America, demonstrating how woefully ill-equipped the US Army remained after over a year at war. Eisenhower was rapidly promoted from captain to temporary lieutenant colonel in October 1918. Yet just one month later, his hopes for overseas service were finally dashed with the news of the Armistice on 11 November. The great army that America was still hurriedly building was even more rapidly demobilised. Eisenhower dropped back to become a captain again; he would not reach his former rank for another eighteen years.

With the seemingly sudden end of the war, Pershing, frustratingly single-minded and stubborn though the British and French considered him to be, had been proven correct in holding to his vision. If the American army of the Great War had suffered complete amalgamation with the British and French, its officers and men, like Marshall and Patton, would never have gained the vital experience – however brief – of the higher command of formations in modern war. Its officers and soldiers might have had more combat experience of infantry fighting but would have remained innocent of the complexities of the use of combined arms, the handling and conduct of larger formations such as divisions and corps in battle, and the importance of a modern supply system. In short, the US Army would never have gained the experience or knowledge necessary to build the great armies of the Second World War.

It was not surprising that, ultimately, each of the Allies believed that their efforts had won the war. The French, who had shouldered the burden of the fighting and its terrifying losses from the very first day, were convinced that their involvement had eventually brought victory. The British were equally certain that their naval and military might had contributed the most to the outcome. Meanwhile the Americans were in no doubt that the great American Army had achieved the vision that Pershing had set for it in overwhelming the Germans in the last battles of the war.

All of these views contained a germ of truth in them but missed the essential, wider perspective. Sir Frederick Maurice, the former British Director of Military Operations, wrote:

> Germany could not have been beaten in the field, as she was beaten, without the intimate co-operation of all the Allied armies on the Western Front directed by a great leader, nor without the co-ordination for a common purpose of all the resources of the Allies, naval, military, industrial and economic. If victory is to be attributed to any one cause, then that cause is not to be found in the wisdom of any one statesman, the valour of any one army, the prowess of any one navy, or the skill of any one general.[59]

Yet this wider appreciation of how the Allies had finally defeated Imperial Germany never became part of the received memory of the Great War. Instead, each of the participants concentrated upon their own perceived successes and, in the case of Britain and France, upon the heavy, almost unbearable cost of victory. Within ten years, the war came to be seen as a pyrrhic victory bought at too great a cost, and the Allies, who had won due to the power of their collaboration, had become largely estranged from one another. While the British and French maintained a strained relationship during the twenties and thirties, the United States abandoned the complexities of 'entangling alliances' for its more traditional policy of isolationism.

During the crisis of spring 1918, Charteris had confided to his diary that:

> The news that the Americans are lending their men to fill the gaps in our ranks is good, and makes the final issue perfectly safe. It is sad for us to have come to this pass owing solely to the dilatoriness of the Government. It is humiliating to us as a nation, but perhaps

out of that there may come great good both to us and the world. For it may bind Britain and America closer together in the post-war years. If we ever fall seriously apart, the world will have to face another conflict which will make this one seem trivial.[60]

One of the many tragedies of the Great War and its aftermath was that Britain and America did move apart, and there was almost no meaningful contact between the officers and men of the British and American armies for over twenty years. One of the consequences was that when the next conflict emerged, a conflict that did indeed make the Great War seem almost trivial, the two armies were strangers to one another just as they had been in 1917.

3

Tanks in Washington

General George Marshall was sworn in as the Chief of Staff of the United States army on the morning of 1 September 1939. Marshall had reached the pinnacle of any soldier's career in peacetime: he was now head of the army and chief adviser to the President on military matters.[1] However, the army that he presided over was small and shrunken, and had been starved of funds even before the Great Depression hit America. Restricted in size by an Act of Congress in 1920, when Marshall took command the army and the army air corps had fewer than 200,000 men in their ranks and possessed very little modern equipment of any kind. In terms of size, if not in potential, the US Army ranked seventeenth in the world, behind Finland, Poland and Romania.[2] Most of its officers had grown old serving in the same rank for decades.

The fact was that the US government had little use for a large regular army. The United States had retreated into isolationism after the Great War. With the failure of President Wilson to persuade Congress to sign up to the League of Nations Covenant in 1919, the country had returned to its Jeffersonian ideal of rejecting all entangling alliances. America remained neutral throughout the twenties and thirties; Congress had sought, through a series of Neutrality Acts, to ensure that it would not become ensnared in another European war. The army was still wedded to the concept of 'hemispheric defence', which meant that its forces would be used to defend the Americas but would go no further. The brutal truth, which Marshall understood but few of his fellow citizens realised, was that the army was incapable of defending even the continental United States against a determined adversary.

Such worries would have mattered little in a time of peace but Marshall reached the head of his profession in wartime. News of the German invasion of Poland arrived in Washington just a few hours before he was sworn in, and two days later, Britain and France declared war on Hitler's Germany. Even though the United States was not directly involved, Marshall knew that the army would have to prepare for war, not peace. He began his term as Chief of Staff with all the constraints that had bedevilled his predecessors and brought stagnation for nearly twenty years, but he would also have to face the challenge of guiding the US Army through its greatest expansion in history.

Poland put up a brave defence, but its armed forces were overwhelmed by the rapid German attack and later by Stalin's Red Army, which invaded from the east. The country was subdued in just four weeks. After this short, sharp campaign, which demonstrated German prowess with modern weaponry, the war, with the exception of the campaign at sea, sank into a lull that was quickly dubbed by journalists 'the phoney war'. Marshall faced great difficulties in persuading the President and Congress that the army needed to be enlarged and provided with modern weaponry. He initially found President Franklin D. Roosevelt a difficult master and seemingly unsympathetic to the army's plight. Roosevelt had been a junior under-secretary to the navy in the First World War and was much more interested and informed on naval matters. It was significant that when he began his extraordinary personal correspondence in September 1939 with Winston Churchill, then First Sea Lord at the Admiralty, he signed it 'Former Naval Person'. Marshall once complained, 'At least Mr President, stop speaking of the Army as "they" and the navy as "us".'[3] For the President, and indeed for Congress, the US Navy remained the first line of defence.

While large sections of American public opinion viewed the conflict in Europe with dismay, there was an equal determination that the United States should take no part in another European squabble. It was understood that the US Navy might need to be reinforced, but there was a belief that a larger army would only strengthen the hand of those who might seek to intervene in the war. The memory of Wilson's 'preparedness parades' of 1916 now had unfortunate repercussions; any expansion of the army was viewed by many Congressmen as a sign of the government starting down a path that would lead inexorably to involvement in another European war. There were also echoes of the American suspicion of regular armies, and their trust in the minutemen, who could defend their homes without the need for such a thing. In such a situation, it was almost impossible for Marshall to argue publicly for an expanded force, and Congress actually decided to cut the army's budget by 10 per cent in April 1940, just as the German invasion of Norway and Denmark began.[4]

Marshall spent much of his time on the issues of industrial mobilisation, because he understood that these were matters of the first importance. He knew that years of preparation would be necessary before an expanded US army could be ready for service. He had learnt the lesson from his experiences in the Great War that there was simply no point in inducting large numbers of American civilians into the army if there were not the weapons, clothing and supplies to equip them when they joined. It is also not surprising that the first important contacts that concerned the British and American armies during the Second World War occurred in industrial production, or that such contacts began as purely business relationships. The Second World War was just as much a war of machines and industrial production as it was a war of armies, fleets and air forces, and without mass industrial mobilisation none of the major protagonists could have continued for long. The Americans and British had also shared one vice during the interwar years: they had allowed their armies to shrink below the danger level, and when the time came for expansion, both had to scrabble to develop the industrial capacity that would be needed to arm and equip them.

Although President Roosevelt was attempting to move American policy towards his aim of all assistance to the Allies 'short of war', there were numerous obstacles in his path.[5] Large sections of American public opinion viewed with suspicion any attempt to supply the Allies. Many people believed that British purchase of munitions in America during the Great War had implicated the United States in the conflict and eventually brought about its involvement. Just as importantly, the British, along with all the other Allies, had defaulted on their enormous war loans when the US government called in those debts in the crisis of the Great Depression. The US Neutrality Acts, modified by Congress as late as 1938, were specifically designed to prevent warring countries buying war materiel from the United States. Similarly, the Johnson Act of 1934 forbade the extending of credit or loans to any foreign power wishing to purchase supplies in the United States of America. Roosevelt's room for manoeuvre in assisting Britain and France against the dictators was therefore slight, but he had long experience, through his New Deal measures to help America through the Great Depression, in finding ways through the complexity of the country's governing system. Thus he was able to persuade Congress to pass revisions to the Neutrality Act on 4 November 1939 that repealed the arms embargo. It was then possible for Britain and France to place orders in the United States for a limited range of supplies, but strictly on a 'cash and carry' basis. All orders had to be paid for in full and in dollars, and transported in British and French ships.[6]

Meanwhile, the British government had been exploring every means of maximising the country's war effort. While Britain had begun to mobilise from 1936 onwards, it was clear that Germany had stolen a march on the Western allies and was considerably more prepared for war. British rearmament had progressed slowly and had concentrated upon building up the strength of the Royal Navy and Royal Air Force. If the American Army had been a victim of isolationism, the British Army had almost been too busy: there had been numerous campaigns and expeditions throughout the Empire during the interwar years. But despite this activity, the army had been very much the Cinderella of the three services, receiving far less funding from the Defence Estimates until 1938, when it was really too late to prepare it adequately for war.[7] As British factories attempted to build up their facilities and production, the Ministry of Supply began to look elsewhere to develop the extra capacity for war production that would be needed, but none of the dominions or colonies had substantial munitions industries.

During the Great War, the British Isles had acted as 'the arsenal of the Empire', whereby raw materials from all over the Empire and beyond were utilised in British factories to produce the mountains of munitions and materiel required for the war effort. This policy had remained unchanged during the interwar years, but now, with the threat of air attacks and a lack of immediate capacity in British factories, the government decided to develop the dominions' ability to produce munitions for the common war effort. In September 1939, a British Purchasing Commission was established in Canada, designed to place 'educational' contracts to stimulate Canadian capacity to produce war materiel.[8] A British Purchasing Commission was also established in New York, under the leadership of the Rt Hon. Arthur B. Purvis, to coordinate the myriad contracts that were soon agreed with American industry to supply Britain's war needs. The first orders, which neatly circumvented the Neutrality Acts, were for Valentine tank transmissions and suspension parts. By the spring of 1940, the Allies had set up a Combined Industrial Production Mission to buy war materiel in America.[9] While these moves fitted Roosevelt's policy of helping the Allies and stimulating American industry without raising the ire of Congress, Marshall viewed many of the developments with dismay. He was concentrated upon the needs of the US Army and its planned expansion, and he feared that British and French orders would take up all the spare capacity of American industrial production.

Events began to move with astonishing speed in Europe from April 1940. The German invasion of Norway wrong-footed the Allies and brought yet more success to Hitler's forces. The Allied response became an embarrassing catalogue of failures and incompetence that seemed to point to Neville Chamberlain's incapacity as a war leader. After a heated debate in the House of Commons, Chamberlain was forced to resign, which gave Winston Churchill the political opportunity he had sought for most of his life. He became Prime Minister on the day the Germans launched their long-expected assault on France and the Low Countries. The astonishingly rapid German advance through France gave a vivid demonstration of the impact of modern armoured forces acting in combination with airpower. After just ten days of fighting,

German panzers had breached the French defences on the River Meuse and driven straight for the Channel coast, cutting off the British and French armies in the Low Countries.

Under the pressure of these disastrous conditions, the military alliance between Britain and France began to pull apart. The Allies had seemingly learnt the lesson of the Great War by agreeing to place the BEF under French supreme command, but this also tied the British force to the French plans for defence. Yet the French scheme to advance into Belgium in the event of a German attack, and evidence of French unpreparedness and poor morale, dismayed Alan Brooke, commander of II Corps, and his fellow corps commander General Sir John Dill, to the extent that they were labelled pessimists by General Pownall, Lord Gort's Chief Of Staff.[10]

When the Germans broke through the French defences at Sedan, after traversing the Ardennes in just two days, the military situation of the Allies deteriorated rapidly. As the German advance turned into a seemingly unstoppable torrent, relations between the British and French High Command broke down. With the situation worsening by the hour, Lord Gort could get no orders from his French superior, General Billotte, the French commander of the northern armies. General Ironside, then Chief of the Imperial General Staff (CIGS), who was visiting Gort, went to see Billotte at Lens, where he was having a conference with his generals. Ironside later related that he 'found Billotte in a state of complete incompetence. He had no plan whatever and was doing nothing.' When all that Billotte could say was that he had no plan, Ironside insisted that he must make a plan immediately and issue orders. Ironside even 'took him by his jacket and shook him to emphasize my advice, for I could not give him an order'.[11] Such a stormy interview was sadly closer to Sir John French's poor relations with French commanders in 1914 than it was to the determination displayed by Haig and Foch at Doullens in 1918. Faced with paralysis in the French High Command, Gort had to make up his own mind and issue his own orders to begin the retreat of the BEF to the coast, in the hope that some of the force might be evacuated back to Britain in what was to become known as Operation Dynamo.

It was in these disastrous conditions that Alan Brooke, Bernard

Montgomery and Harold Alexander cemented their reputations as professional soldiers. During the next 14 days of dismay, uncertainty and retreat, Brooke showed his true mettle. Brian Horrocks, then commander of the 2nd Middlesex machine-gun battalion, claimed that Brooke was 'the man who really saved the BEF . . . I felt vaguely at the time that this alert, seemingly iron man without a nerve in his body, whom I met from time to time at 3rd Division headquarters and who gave out his orders in short clipped sentences, was a great soldier . . . We regarded him as a highly efficient military machine.'[12] General Adam, commander of the III British Corps, described Brooke's handling of his corps as 'perfect'.[13] Horrocks himself earned Montgomery's approval for his coolness under fire and professional performance at Dunkirk, although he personally always remembered the retreat to Dunkirk with the twin feelings of 'shame and exhaustion'. Montgomery too came in for his share of praise, with his handling of his 3rd Division confirming Brooke's already high estimation of this awkward general.[14]

Soon the British Expeditionary Force was fighting for its existence in the Dunkirk perimeter. Harold Alexander had commanded the 1st Division competently during the retreat, but it was during the chaos of Dunkirk that he first gained fame as commander of the BEF's rearguard.[15] Showing his characteristic coolness under fire, he was not only the last British general officer, but one of the last British soldiers to leave the port. Before dawn on 3 June, Alexander and Captain Tennant, the senior naval officer at Dunkirk, made a final tour of the beaches and port before leaving on the last ship for Dover.[16] Over the course of the extraordinary improvisation of Operation Dynamo, the soldiers of the British Expeditionary Force were rescued from the east mole of Dunkirk harbour and the beaches of La Panne in unexpected numbers between 28 May and 3 June: 338,000 British and French troops were evacuated in what Churchill rightly described as a 'miracle of deliverance'.

The BEF might have been saved, but the French position was now disastrous. By 12 June 1940, Colonel Michael Scanlon, the US Assistant Military Attaché for Air in London, was reporting to

Washington that 'Should France capitulate Great Britain must resist invasion for which energetic action [is] being taken. Number of German warships, transports, aircraft and troops including parachute being mobilised Norway indicates preparation for probable invasion of Irish Free State or Britain. Situation most critical.'[17]

With Europe ablaze and the situation changing so rapidly, Marshall needed an experienced and high-ranking officer to act as his eyes and ears in London so that he could gain reliable first-hand intelligence. The man he selected for the job was Brigadier General Raymond E. Lee, who had already served as the United States military attaché in London from 1935 to 1939. Born in 1886 in St Louis, Missouri, he gained a degree in civil engineering from the University of Missouri but then decided to become a professional soldier. He had served with distinction during the Great War as the commander of the 15th Field Artillery Regiment, and was later Head of the Field Artillery in Washington. A military attaché is, in many respects, a legalised spy whose job is to gain access to people and information, assess and evaluate such material and report back to his government. Lee was already familiar with the workings and personalities of the people at the British War Office, and, possessed of a sharp and perceptive mind, he could be trusted to gain a clear and accurate picture of events and developments to send back to Marshall and Roosevelt in Washington.[18]

Lee was an exceptional individual with many of the gifts required to be a successful military attaché. It was said of him that he had been 'given looks, style, courage, sturdiness, sympathy, humour, the capacity for indignation, and a balancing sense of fairness'.[19] He was a cultured man with a love of the arts and the well-cut suits he purchased from Savile Row. These attributes served him well, as they ensured that he was as comfortable in military circles as he was at an English house party, and thus able to mingle effortlessly with Britain's governing elite. He was also a convinced Anglophile; on the day that Britain and France declared war, he had sent a telegram to his old friend Hastings Ismay that read: 'Let the British move up; God bless your arms.'[20] However, he always maintained a balanced sense of judgement and understood that his first responsibility was to act in the interests of the United States.

It may also have been the case that Roosevelt and Marshall wanted someone who could counterbalance the views of Senator Joseph Kennedy, the United States ambassador in London, who, as a prominent Irish-American, was an important and wealthy Democratic sponsor for the forthcoming presidential election in November. Kennedy, however, was a confirmed isolationist and an Anglophobe; his wish to see the British humbled became father to his belief that Britain was finished.

After Lee's briefings and interviews in Washington in preparation for his return to London, he wrote in his diary: 'The President has for two years been hugely alarmed by a possible victory of the Nazis but has been unable to interest either the people or the politicians. Now there is a sudden interest in this war – the United States is profoundly aware of the consequences of an Allied defeat.'[21] Lee reached London on 21 June, the day before the French signed an armistice with the Germans. He now had an extremely important and delicate task: to assess whether the British could successfully resist German air attack and a likely invasion, or whether they would collapse in exactly the same way as Poland, Norway, Denmark, Holland, Belgium and France had done. Many Americans had already decided that the British were likely to succumb to a rapid German assault. On his flight over to London, Lee noticed that all the other passengers spoke only of Britain and France's defeat.[22]

Nonetheless, Lee worked quickly to re-establish old contacts and gain interviews with high-ranking British officers in order to form his own assessment of the situation. Just four days after his arrival, he was signalling to Washington that he had had a series of 'interesting interviews' at the War Office. His first was with General Sir John Dill, who would later go on to play a critical part in relations between the British and American armies. Dill had hoped to become Chief of the Imperial General Staff before the war, but Leslie Hore Belisha, the controversial Secretary of State for War, chose instead to appoint Major General Lord Gort, who subsequently took the BEF to France. Even then, Dill was passed over for the post of CIGS, which went to General Sir Edmund Ironside; Dill was instead given command of I Corps in France. These appointments had caused him 'deep disappointment, although he took pains to conceal it'.[23] However, Dill missed the German attack in France; in April he returned to the War Office to take up the new post of Vice Chief of the Imperial General Staff. On 27 May, he replaced General Ironside as CIGS, and thus finally reached the position he had desired for so long. However, it was by now a poisoned chalice. Britain's military position was at its bleakest since 1805, or even 1066. Worse still, Dill, the consummate professional and gentleman, soon found it virtually impossible to work with the irrepressible Prime Minister and Minister for War, Winston Churchill. Dill told Lee that there had been 'little fight in the French', with the exception of 'certain units', which he saw as the main reason for the collapse in France. He also argued that the 'British Army fought successfully' and had held a 'huge front line . . . against infiltration'. He went on to admit frankly that they were 'now greatly handicapped [by a] shortage [of] materials, with their first requirements being destroyers and the second more planes'.[24]

Lee also interviewed Major General Sir Hastings Ismay, known as 'Pug' to his friends, who was now Chief of Staff to the Minister of Defence and Deputy Secretary to the War Cabinet. Ismay and Lee had become friends during Lee's former tour as military attaché, and in 1940 they stayed in adjoining flats at the Savoy Hotel. Although Ismay never held a military command during the Second World War, and had served in Somaliland throughout the Great War, thus missing the action that many of his contemporaries had experienced, he was one of the most important and influential British soldiers of his generation. An officer of the Indian rather than the British Army, in the twenties he had spent five years as Assistant Secretary to the Committee of Imperial Defence under Sir Maurice Hankey, who had been the power behind the throne during Lloyd George's premiership in the Great War and had continued as the administrative linchpin in British government ever since. Together with a range of other postings in India and at the War Office, these years prepared him as Hankey's eventual successor. In 1936, Ismay became Deputy Secretary to Hankey at the Committee of Imperial Defence, and in due course, Secretary, following Hankey's retirement in 1938.

Ismay was thus at the heart of British defence thinking and the Whitehall machine well before the outbreak of war. When Churchill became Prime Minister in May 1940, Ismay became his principal staff officer, and the military secretariat ('a first-class administrative machine'),[25] which he had already developed, became integral to the British conduct of the war. He worked in closer proximity to Churchill than anyone else, and personally handled much of his military correspondence. He sat on the Chiefs of Staff Committees as Churchill's personal representative, but he was also in direct touch with the commanders in the field, since when any of them came to London, it was to Ismay that they gave their first briefing. He was right 'in the middle of the web' of Britain's war effort.[26] Not surprisingly, Ismay's closeness to the Prime Minister meant that not every soldier trusted him; it was only over time that most came to recognise his unshakeable character.

Ismay became of vital importance not only to Britain's war effort but to the emerging relationship with the United States. In speaking to him, Lee was also gaining access to Churchill's thoughts, and Lee's record of the conversation gives hints of Churchill's grandiloquent phrases. Ismay told Lee that the 'situation [was] now so serious [that the] whole structure [of] Western civilization depends upon [the] British Navy and 5,000 air pilots'. Another of Churchill's main concerns after the fall of France was the position of the French fleet. He was desperately worried that the powerful French navy might be taken by the Germans to overwhelm the Royal Navy. Ismay also claimed that Britain was 'better garrisoned' than 'ever in history' and that the army required no additional troops to defend the British Isles, but that supplies from America in the form of destroyers, planes, automatic anti-aircraft weapons, field guns, anti-tank guns and rifles were now wanted immediately.[27]

British requirements for supplies and equipment from American factories had indeed shifted from a slow and cautious approach aimed at circumventing the Neutrality Acts while preserving Britain's finances, to an immediate and desperate need. The Royal Air Force needed more planes, the Royal Navy needed more ships, and the British Army needed supplies of every kind. While the RAF was preparing to deal with a massive air attack and the Royal

Navy was stretched beyond its limits in a greatly expanded naval war, the army had lost virtually everything. While 338,000 British and French troops had been successfully evacuated from Dunkirk, almost all of their tanks, trucks, guns, rifles, ammunition and supplies had been left behind. No complete count of the losses could ever be made, but they included 180,000 rifles, 10,700 Bren guns, 509 two-pounder anti-tank guns, 509 cruiser tanks, and 180 infantry tanks.[28] Even such figures do not really convey the truly shocking losses of all kinds of supplies, from artillery pieces to telephones and binoculars, amounting to the equivalent of ten divisions' worth of equipment. The British Army had been saved but had effectively been disarmed. The BEF had managed somehow to transport 13 tanks across the Channel, but they left 691 behind in France. The army had just 340 tanks and armoured cars left to defend the shores of Britain from the threat of imminent invasion.[29]

It was in these circumstances that Roosevelt's extraordinary correspondence with Churchill, along with the numerous reports from Lee and other American observers in London, moved the President to action. Roosevelt had first taken the unprecedented step of writing to Churchill when he rejoined the British cabinet as First Lord of the Admiralty on 11 September 1939. Roosevelt's relations with Neville Chamberlain were frosty to say the least, and the President sought another channel of communication with an important member of the cabinet. Although Roosevelt and Churchill had met briefly in 1918, neither had sought each other's advice or company over the intervening years, and Churchill seems to have forgotten all about this early meeting, much to Roosevelt's chagrin.[30] Roosevelt began the correspondence with the excuse that 'It is because you and I occupied similar positions in the World War that I want you to know how glad I am that you are back again in the Admiralty.'[31] Churchill sought Chamberlain's permission to continue the correspondence, but restricted his replies to naval matters while he remained First Lord of Admiralty. In fact, the amount of correspondence between the two men was initially small and brief, but when Churchill became Prime Minister, he wrote to Roosevelt that he was 'sure you would not wish me to discontinue our intimate, private correspondence' even though 'the scene has darkened swiftly'.[32] Even in this first letter to Roosevelt as Prime Minister, Churchill made a direct plea to Roosevelt, for 'forty or fifty of your older destroyers', along with a long list of other materiel.[33] The now established correspondence became of enormous value to both men, as it gave them a means of contacting each other directly without the necessity of moving through the often tortuous method of diplomatic communication. Their secret correspondence and the close personal relationship that developed between the two leaders was at the heart of all cooperation between Britain and America during the war.

Faced with contradictory military and diplomatic advice on the chances of Britain's survival, Roosevelt decided to send an unofficial personal representative to view the situation first hand and report back. The man chosen – at the behest of Frank Knox, the Secretary of the Navy, and Henry Stimson, the Secretary of War – was William S. Donovan. He had distinguished himself in the Great War fighting in the battles of the Marne and Saint-Mihiel, and had been awarded the Congressional Medal of Honor for his bravery in the Argonne. Donovan's Republican political views were unusual for a Catholic of Irish descent, but his support for Roosevelt, combined with his unimpeachable military record, meant that the President had even considered him as a potential candidate for Defence Secretary. Given the vague yet important nature of his visit, Donovan was able to arrive quietly in Britain, but was soon granted unprecedented access by the British establishment. He was received by the King, Churchill and the cabinet; he toured factories, met with the US military attachés, and was also shown British radar, coastal defences and the work of the Secret Intelligence Service. Indeed, his observations of British methods of intelligence-gathering became the inspiration behind his establishment of the Office of Strategic Services, the forerunner of the CIA. On his return to the United States, Donovan confirmed Lee's view that Britain would survive the oncoming assault, and urged the immediate transfer of the destroyers.[34]

Roosevelt had great difficulty in meeting the British request for destroyers, since it required 'the specific authorization of the

Congress',[35] but in answer to Churchill's direct plea for assistance, and worried that a disarmed British Army might succumb to a German assault, he ordered the War Department to organise the immediate dispatch of 'surplus' war materiel. These weapons had been stored in America since 1919 and included 500,000 Enfield rifles, 50,000 old Lewis, Vickers and Browning machine guns and 130 million rounds of small-arms ammunition. They also included (ironically enough) 820 French 75 mm field guns, which had been manufactured in Britain but shipped to America, and one million rounds of artillery ammunition as well as bulk powder for 155 mm guns.[36] While the British rather ungratefully described these weapons as being 'of ancient pattern',[37] the presidential order met with spirited protest from the War Department. The transfers would denude the US's already severely limited stock of munitions, and while these old weapons would never have gone to arm American front-line units, they could have been used for training purposes. But it was the field guns that caused real argument. Major Walter Bedell Smith, then Assistant Secretary of the General Staff and later a key member of the Anglo-American armies as Eisenhower's Chief of Staff, displayed, not for the first or last time, his dyspeptic temper by collaring Brigadier General Edwin M. Watson, military aide to the President, and bluntly declaring that the transfer of these guns was 'dangerous to the national defense', since they remained part of the mobilisation stocks of the army. Smith went on to threaten that 'if we were required to mobilize after having released guns necessary . . . and were found to be short in artillery materiel that everyone who was a party to the deal might hope to be found hanging from a lamp-post'.[38]

Such arguments represented a fundamental disagreement between Roosevelt and Marshall and his planners. Even in June 1940, Roosevelt was convinced that his armed forces should not confine their plans to the worst possible scenario, which included the demise of Britain. His belief was that Britain would probably survive (a view no doubt bolstered by Lee's reports), particularly if given aid by America, and that the military planners should work on this basis. The Joint Planning Committee, meanwhile, found it difficult to believe that Britain would 'continue to be an active combatant'.[39] Such views reinforced Marshall's opinion that, with such straitened circumstances, the US Army needed to concentrate all its energies upon hemispheric defence, rather than extending its meagre resources yet further.

Arguments delayed the deal for three weeks, but eventually Roosevelt repeated his direct order and the transfers were made. The fact was that this assistance to Britain was easier to accomplish than the destroyers Churchill had placed at the top of his list, and so the sale of surplus War Department stock was the first immediate aid given by the United States in the aftermath of Dunkirk. It was possible to sidestep the Neutrality Acts by selling the equipment to private companies as war surplus and then immediately selling it on to the British in a process that was managed by the soon-to-be-defunct Anglo-French Purchasing Board.[40] But it was the 'bases for destroyers' deal announced by Roosevelt in September 1940, in which 99-year leases on British bases in Bermuda, the Caribbean and Newfoundland were given in exchange for 50 obsolete destroyers, that gained the most publicity. The British valued both deals more as a precious statement of intent than the low military value of the destroyers and equipment that actually crossed the Atlantic.

The actual impact of these weapons was much less dramatic than might have been hoped by either Roosevelt or Churchill. In an early demonstration of the difficulties that can be caused by seemingly minor differences in military equipment, the rifles were of the wrong calibre. The Enfield rifles supplied by the Americans were, as their name suggested, of British design and manufacture, but they had been produced to the American standard rifle calibre of 0.300 inches, while the Enfield rifles used by the British Army were manufactured to the British standard calibre of 0.303 inches. This difference meant that British ammunition could not be fired from the American rifles or vice versa, and therefore to give these rifles to regular British Army units would have caused enormous complications and confusion in ammunition supply. Problems of supply based on the fact that the two armies had different designs and standards for weapons and equipment of all kinds would prove intractable in the years ahead. In the event, the rifles were given to the newly raised Local Defence Volunteers, soon to be known as the Home Guard, who were naturally delighted to receive weapons of any sort, as they had been drilling with ancient pikes and broom handles in many cases. However, they struggled to remove the thick packing grease that had preserved the rifles in storage since 1918. It required the efforts of 250 female volunteers in Cambridge for two weeks just to clean 8,000 of the rifles.[41] After all the effort and argument required in getting these guns to the British, they were never fired in anger.

As these heated arguments over destroyers, rifles and guns took place in Washington, so the British took steps to deal with the French fleet. With its armies defeated and Paris occupied by the victorious German forces, the French government had little choice but to seek terms. The Franco-German armistice of 22 June 1940 saw the occupation of northern France by the Germans and the creation of a new Vichy French regime. The terms of the armistice were harsh but did leave the new French government in possession of all of the French colonies and the second largest fleet of warships in Europe. Desperately concerned that these ships might soon fall into the hands of the Germans and thus tip the naval balance decisively against the Royal Navy, the British cabinet decided to act to ensure that the French ships could not be used against them.

Their actions led to the Anglo-French alliance collapsing in acrimony, bitterness and bloodshed. While the French fleet in Alexandria came to a reasonable understanding with the British, a tragedy unfolded at the harbour of Mers-el-Kebir just outside Oran, in French North Africa. On 3 July 1940, a British naval task force under Vice Admiral Sir James Somerville offered the French Admiral Gensoul four hard choices: join the Allies, sail to a British port where the ships would be held for the duration of the war, sail to a French port in West Africa where they could be demilitarised, or scuttle them. A tense stand-off ended with the British firing on the French ships whose crewmen had, only weeks before, been their friends and allies; 1,297 French sailors were killed in the ensuing bombardment.[42] This act not only demonstrated the desperate strategic situation facing Britain but also emphasised British resolve to continue the war at all costs.

In London, General Lee heard the news on 4 July, which, as he noted, was 'still a holiday for Americans. I slept late. My explanation to the club valet was accepted, although from his dazed expression I am not at all certain that he ever knew that the United States had won its independence.'[43] Lee also witnessed Churchill's speech to the House of Commons that day on the attack. He wrote that although Churchill was 'a most ordinary and undistinguished little rotund figure', he was 'the greatest political orator alive . . . Cheers from every corner of the chamber greeted his every point . . . and when he had finished, the decorum of the Parliament vanished. All were on their feet, shouting, cheering and waving order papers and handkerchiefs like mad.' While Lee applauded the action as a 'dashing old fashioned, Nelsonian cutting-out expedition', which 'shows that the British are not going to sit quietly and watch Hitler's plans mature', it brought an end to an alliance that had begun with the Entente Cordiale in 1904.[44] And the attack at Mers-el-Kebir was just the start of hostilities between Britain and France; British forces would spend the next two years fighting an undeclared war against Vichy French forces in Dakar, Syria, Madagascar and Tunisia. Mers-el-Kebir stands as a terrible warning of what can happen when an alliance between two states collapses.

One week later, Lee wrote in his diary that he dined with 'Pug and Kathleen Ismay . . . Pug is all optimism now, when two weeks ago he was anxious, strained and wishing that Hitler might be going east.'[45] Hitler had granted the British an unasked-for breathing space, and the worst of the chaos and confusion in the aftermath of Dunkirk and the French defeat had subsided. But it could only be a hiatus. As Britain readied itself for the expected onslaught, Lee began to send assessments of the situation to Washington that gave a realistic but hopeful outlook. On 25 July he stated that:

[The] Nature and intensity [of] German efforts cannot be determined but consensus of opinion [in] this office today is this country [is] not likely to be subdued unless considerable enemy mechanized forces can be landed which will require [that] Germany [gains] command of the air. This might be attained in time by sheer attrition or sooner by continuous bombardment and/or lavish use of gas (hitherto unemployed) on British airdromes . . . Food supplies plentiful, morale of whole population extremely high. Principal strategic weak point Ireland. Principal immediate deficiency in air phase is not sufficient pilots, in land phase not enough tanks and antitank weapons.[46]

As long as the RAF did not lose the coming fight for air superiority over Britain, it was highly unlikely that any invasion attempt could succeed, given the power of the Royal Navy and the relative weakness of the Kriegsmarine. While Lee was definitely expressing a minority opinion in stating in his next signal 'No question ultimate success',[47] and one with which his ambassador vehemently disagreed, his judgements were based on military realities and a close understanding of British strengths and weaknesses. There seems little doubt that Lee's assessments gave Roosevelt sufficient confidence to continue his policy of support, since there was more than an outside chance that Britain would survive.

While Lee was establishing himself in London, and sending back his reports to Roosevelt and Marshall, the British in their turn were beginning to send a stream of representatives to the United States. Unfortunately, the pressure of events and the desperate need for weapons of every kind meant that they sent a series of representatives rather than one high-level mission that could coordinate the demands of all the services.[48] One of these 'uncorrelated expedients' was an obscure military mission sent to deal with the single issue of tanks, which represented the first tangible cooperation between the British and American armies in the Second World War.[49]

It was only on the outbreak of war in 1939 that the British government fully woke up to its long-standing neglect of the importance of the tank in modern warfare. The financial stringency brought on by the Great Depression had stunted Britain's capacity in the design and production of armoured vehicles. The British and French governments both soon realised that the Germans had a decisive advantage in their capacity to produce tanks. Not only were German factories now tooled up to produce large numbers, but the German acquisition of the considerable Czechoslovakian armaments industry, most notably the famous Skoda armaments factory, meant that they were able to manufacture far more armoured fighting vehicles than existing Allied capacity would allow.

The French were the first to see the potential of having their tanks manufactured in America, in an environment safe from attack and with seemingly unlimited natural resources. It was after these initial French approaches had met with success that the British Ministry of Supply rather belatedly decided to organise a tank mission to discover if British tanks could also be produced in American factories. Negotiations had begun for the production of French Hotchkiss, Somua and Char B1 Bis tanks in American plants,[50] but before these plans had begun to bear fruit, the Germans attacked in the west.

Strangely enough, the head of the mission was not a soldier, but a British businessman. Mr Michael Dewar arrived in New York in July 1940 on what might have appeared to be a relatively innocuous business trip. Dewar was a noted British industrialist and the chairman of British Timken Limited, a major manufacturer of bearings, whose parent company was based in the United States. However, his trip was not connected with his own business interests but because he had offered his services to the British Ministry of Supply, which organised the whole of Britain's industrial war effort. Dewar had first gained experience in armaments manufacture through his apprenticeship at Vickers. During the Great War he joined the Royal Engineers but was soon transferred to the Ministry of Munitions and later became the Director of the National Projectile Factories and Assistant Controller of Shell Manufacture. As a member of a Ministry of Labour delegation in 1925, he had later studied employment and industrial conditions in both Canada and the United States.[51] He was thus an ideal candidate to lead a mission to persuade the US government and US Army Ordnance Department to allow the manufacture of British-designed tanks in American factories.

There was an important precedent for Anglo-American cooperation on tank production. The so-called 'Liberty Tank' programme of the Great War had been a joint British and American project to produce sufficient modern tanks for both armies for the envisaged spring offensive of 1919. Components manufactured in Britain and America were to be assembled in a purpose-built factory in France. Of course, the end of the war brought the nascent programme to an end. In spite of this precedent, the common ground between Britain and America was much less fertile for Anglo-American industrial cooperation in 1940 than it had been in 1918.

It was thus in the very different circumstances of July 1940 that Dewar arrived in America. The mission was initially composed of a very small team, but Dewar was soon joined by Brigadier Douglas Pratt, who had also been involved in the army's modernisation as the Assistant Director of Mechanisation in 1938–9, and who, even in the plain clothes he had to wear so as not to arouse the suspicions of any American isolationists, looked every inch a British Army officer. Pratt's main claim to fame was that he had commanded the 1st Army Tank Brigade, composed of heavily armoured infantry tanks, which had counter-attacked at Arras on 21 May 1940 and given Rommel's 7th Panzer Division a severe shock.[52] He could thus speak with authority on the use of tanks and give views on their design based on combat experience.[53]

Within 48 hours of arrival, Dewar realised that New York, the unofficial economic capital of the United States, was not the right place to conduct his business. He and Pratt moved to Washington DC, where the president of the Cincinnati Milling Machine Company – a business connection of Dewar's – gave Dewar the use of his suite at the Carlton Hotel. It was there that the mission first set up its office.[54] These humble beginnings marked the birth of what became known as the British Army Staff in America, which played an important, even vital, but frequently overlooked part in the Anglo-American war effort.

July 1940 was not an auspicious time for a new British mission to begin negotiations in America. The French army had signed large numbers of contracts with American companies for trucks that now seemed unlikely to be honoured. Even when the British Purchasing Commission took over these contracts, American firms had learnt their lesson and now expected significant down-payments in dollars before they would accept any new orders. More importantly, few people in the American capital believed it would be long before Britain shared the fate of France.

The main organisation with which Dewar had to negotiate was the National Defence Advisory Commission. Roosevelt had deferred existing plans for economic mobilisation in 1939, but the events of April and May 1940 made it imperative that the United States begin that transformation. The President established the Office for Emergency Management on 25 May 1940, which demonstrated his intent to begin American rearmament in earnest, and reactivated the National Defence Advisory Commission, which had operated during the Great War. The existing legislation made it relatively easy to resurrect this body and enabled the President to keep control of the process of mobilisation. Out of the seven advisers on the Commission, Dewar first had to persuade William S. Knudsen – who, as the president of General Motors Corporation, was now responsible for industrial production – on the merits of the British case for tank production.[35]

However, at his first meeting with Mr Knudsen and his assistant, Mr Biggars, Dewar was 'plainly informed that purely British designs of war material would not be permitted to be manufactured in the United States'. Knudsen went on to say that the general opinion in America was that Britain had only 'one chance in three of survival against Germany, and the Military Authorities do not want to have, in production, supplies of material of any kind which, in the event of a British collapse, are useless to the United States'. Roosevelt's administration was attempting to develop American capacity to produce war equipment for the now rapidly expanding US armed forces, and it therefore simply did not make sense for American factories to build British designs. The Defence Advisory Commission insisted that the mission would only be allowed to purchase American tanks; they could place contracts with American firms for the still evolving US designs as long as they were paid for in advance in US dollars. This had the advantage for the US Ordnance Board of 'priming the pump' of the US tank industry; then, if Britain fell, the orders and the tanks could be appropriated for the US Army.

Dewar was also told that the Americans were more than satisfied with the main mechanical components of their own tank designs. The radial air-cooled engine, transmission, track and suspension had all been proven and were in production. These tried and tested components were what made the American tanks such reliable and easily maintained vehicles. Nor was the US Ordnance Department impressed with the British designs that they saw. When, after great difficulty, the British managed to deliver an Infantry Tank Mark II, known as the Matilda, to the Aberdeen Proving Ground in Maryland in September 1940, American assessments were far from favoura-ble.* Although this was the same type of tank that had given Rommel such a shock, the Americans considered it to be cramped, difficult to maintain and lacking in engine power for its size and weight. They were much more impressed with its crew, who, as members of the 7th Royal Tank Regiment, had fought at Arras,[56] but still seem to have resisted attempts to persuade them of the merits of the British layout and design. Charles Bonesteel, a young engineer officer, later remembered that, while visiting Aberdeen Proving Ground, he met 'a poor young British tank officer who'd been through the war until the British retreat and evacuation from Dunkirk. He was drinking himself to death out of frustration, and crying inwardly at our total lack of willingness to accept the lessons already bought with British blood.'[57] American unwillingness to accept British design features and British reluctance to order the current American designs developed into an impasse.

The fact was that just as the Americans had little faith in the continued existence of the United Kingdom, the Ministry of Supply had little faith in the American ability to design modern battle-worthy tanks. The United States army had only limited experience with tanks and heavy armoured equipment before 1940. Apart from a brief introduction to the use of armour in 1918 and the produc-tion of the Liberty Tank in 1919–20, they had invested little in tank development during the interwar period. Only prototype models rather than large production runs had been purchased, and while Walter Christie, an American tank designer, had produced many

---

* This Matilda tank, named 'Grampus', still sits outside at Aberdeen Proving Ground, although it is now in a rather sorry state.

influential blueprints, none had been taken up for volume production. Ironically enough, although the British had enthusiastically adopted Christie's suspension system, the US Ordnance Board had rejected it as insufficiently reliable. The United States army had invested in proving the mechanical components that would be necessary for tanks, but it had no modern designs ready to pull off the shelf when it became clear that there was a pressing need for such weapons.

Marshall himself became involved in this impasse. He later remembered that:

> Our tanks were easily the most mobile, the most perfectly controlled of all the tanks. But they were deficient, very decidedly, in their fighting qualities, in the arrangement of the tanks so they could be fought with efficiency. So we had the British disapproving our model, and ourselves being very contemptuous of theirs. When the issue was the British had it right on the fighting part and we had it right on the mobility of the tank, and not until I got a prominent, informed Britisher in my office and told him, 'Now just what, confidentially between you and me . . . is wrong about the tank affair' – and he told me what they saw and I looked into it and found out about our side of it and that we were both wrong. Then it was comparatively easy to get the matter adjusted – doing it all behind the scenes . . . Well that was the case in so many things.[38]

The prominent informed Britisher mentioned by Marshall was almost certainly Brigadier Pratt, who had the knowledge, experience and confidence to argue the British case and give the Chief of Staff the information he wanted. Marshall employed this behind-the-scenes approach on numerous occasions to achieve his objectives and often used a personal interview with a British officer to get to the heart of the matter and sort out the controversy.

Marshall also knew that this impasse was wasting time when time was of the essence. He knew that he would need thousands of tanks in the coming years to equip the US Army, and he wanted to ensure that they were the best available. The National Munitions Program of 30 June 1940, which marked the real start of American

rearmament in response to the collapse of France, had called for
the production of 1,741 tanks within just 18 months, yet at the time
this Act was signed in Congress, the Rock Island Arsenal in Illinois
was still in the process of hand-building the three pilot models of
the new M2A1 medium tank.[59] It has to be said that this initial
American attempt to design a modern medium tank was unin-
spiring. It had the virtue of proven mechanical components, but it
was lightly armoured and armed with the same 37 mm gun as was
fitted to the light tanks. Pratt knew from his experience in France
that tanks required larger armament and thicker armour. The M2
would not have stood the test of battle.

Nonetheless, it was on the basis of the M2 that the US Army
placed its first orders with the Chrysler Corporation, who began
planning the construction of a great 'tank arsenal'. Two months
later, on 28 August 1940, the US General Staff, influenced by reports
of German tanks from Europe, and quite possibly with some indirect input from Dewar and Pratt, cancelled the M2 order and
replaced it with the improved M3, which was designed in just 60
days. The haste was obvious in the layout of the tank. The M3 hull
was essentially a stretched and expanded version of the M2, with
a 75 mm gun mounted in a sponson. The turret, equipped with a
37 mm gun, was then constructed on top. Douglas Pratt first saw
a wooden mock-up of the new tank at Aberdeen Proving Ground
in October 1940 and complained that it was 'as high as the tower
of babel', but he also admitted that he would 'rather fight in it
than any other tank'.[60] The M3 may have been a rushed compromise, but the British mission saw its potential. The main British
influence upon the design clearly came from Pratt, who, with
Marshall's blessing, had crucially argued for heavier armour of
50 mm rather than the proposed 30 mm, and made a number of
detailed suggestions for the fighting compartment. With these
modifications, the British chiefs approved the procurement of the
tank.[61]

Given their desperate need for tanks of almost any design, the
mission worked quickly to place contracts with American firms.
While the Ministry of Supply recommended that the initial contracts
should not exceed 1,500,[62] Dewar had been given a relatively free

hand in negotiation. He recognised the need to ensure the volume production of tanks, and in fact placed orders for 2,085. The first contract, for 500 tanks, was signed with the Pullman Standard Car Manufacturing Company on 18 September 1940, and the last, for 400, with the Lima Locomotive Works on 27 November 1940.[63] The sums of money involved in these contracts were truly staggering. The total cost of material and charges was in excess of $132,000,000, and the British government was committed to advancing over $16,570,000 in capital assistance to help the American firms finance the enormous expansion of buildings, plant and machinery necessary to fulfil the contracts.[64] Placing such large contracts – with hefty payments in advance – was a huge leap of faith. Dewar had signed contracts for an American medium tank that was still in the process of design, with factories that had no experience of tank production; millions of pounds of sterling could have been wasted on a programme that did not come to fruition or ultimately produced an unsatisfactory tank. Such sums were far beyond what had been envisaged by the Ministry of Supply just a year before. In November 1939, it had been estimated that the purchase of tanks and transport might require an expenditure of £1,100,000. One year later, the tank mission had committed the British government to fifteen times that level of expenditure.[65] This was priming the pump of American industrial capacity on a grand scale. The mission had engaged in what can only be described as panic-buying, but this eventually resulted in the British Army having sufficient battle-worthy tanks for the campaigns of 1942 onwards.

With the orders placed, the efforts of the mission shifted to persuading the Americans to develop their tank design in accordance with British requirements.[66] The members of the mission never seemed to have questioned their assumption that, having paid for the tanks, they could and should influence the design. Given that the United States was still a neutral power, the plans for the new tank would normally have been regarded as a military secret of the first importance. The willingness of the US Army Ordnance Board and the Defence Advisory Commission not only to share the design but to accept some suggestions from the British revealed a level of trust and cooperation that came to be taken for granted by both the British and the Americans during the Second World War. In fact, clearly with Marshall's blessing, Pratt soon developed 'extremely close personal contact' with the US Tank Design Department, and Dewar with the National Defence Advisory Commission and the procurement arm of the War Department.[67] Yet perhaps the main reason why the American authorities were willing to allow British influence was that the design itself was still in a state of flux when the mission arrived in the US. Ultimately, Pratt and Dewar persuaded the American designers to make a number of improvements.[68] L. H. Carr, a British tank designer, joined the mission in August 1940 and designed a turret that would be manufactured for the British-ordered M3s. This turret had a lower profile and enabled the radio to be fitted according to British practice. The British Tank Mission had thus influenced the fundamental design and developed a British version of an American tank.[69]

Within just a few months in 1940, the tank mission had not only secured production for thousands of tanks for the British Army, but had also developed a close working relationship on tank design. By March 1941, even though not a single M3 had rolled off the production line, Dewar could write to Geoffrey Burton in the Ministry of Supply: 'I am so thankful that we pushed ahead with the Tank programme here without delay, as if we had meandered on as they did with the Gun Programme until it was too late, and we had no more money, we should have been in a hopeless position.'[70] By that time, it was apparent that the tank programme would almost certainly be successful, and the real risk – that of not placing orders at all – was clear.

While the tank mission started the process of military-industrial cooperation between the British and American armies, Roosevelt carefully ratcheted up the involvement of the United States in British military affairs through highly secret staff talks in London. It was in August 1940, with the fierce fight for air superiority already going on in Britain's skies, that the first tentative staff meetings between British and American representatives took place. These meetings had had a long gestation period and originated in the ideas of Lord Lothian, the British ambassador to the United States, and his energetic advocacy of the British position in Washington. On 17 June 1940, as the Anglo-French alliance was nearing its end, Lothian had asked Roosevelt whether 'the time had come for further secret staff talks as to how the British and American navies, and if necessary air forces should deal with the various situations which might arise in the near future . . . The President thought that this would be a good thing and that it ought to take place at once.'[71] American and British naval cooperation had begun as early as 1936, with attempts to find a joint solution to diplomatic and naval problems in the Pacific.[72] In some respects, Lothian's suggestion was merely a continuation of this previous practice, and he hoped that such staff talks would 'help to bring home to the United States the gravity of the position it stands in itself and the truth that the sooner it throws itself into the business of defending Great Britain the more likely it is to avoid disaster to itself'.[73]

Although the talks had originated in Lothian's loose – and rather unfortunate – concept of a 'Maginot Line of the sea', the prospective representatives were soon widened to include an 'officer qualified to discuss air matters' and later even 'a suitable Army representative to attend the conversations as an observer' but not a full participant.[74] It is highly significant that while both Roosevelt and Lothian believed that their respective navies and air forces had important issues to discuss and might find useful ways of co-operation, it did not occur to either man that the two armies could do the same. Indeed, it was later considered 'significant that any Army officer had been sent at all, for it was the first time that any Army officer had been given the authority, and the opportunity, to discuss future plans with the British'.[75]

Yet as the time for the meetings approached, even Raymond Lee, who had to organise the arrival of the American contingent, was confused as to their real purpose. The British, he noted, had spent 24 hours in a departmental committee discussing security, and it had been decided to hold the talks in the strictest secrecy, with the minimum number of officials, clerks and stenographers.[76] The meetings were to be referred to as the 'Anglo-American Standardisation of Arms Committee' to provide a suitable cover for what were much broader staff conversations, although this was later changed to the vaguely disparaging 'Buffalo Bill'.[77] But while the British may have hoped that the talks might even presage an American entry into the war, Lee believed that they 'completely overrate the significance of these two men. If the US Government really intended coming to some understanding they would send officers of a different calibre to these, who are fair but no heavy-weights.'[78] Roosevelt was acting in typical fashion: not informing anyone of his real intentions and simply dropping a stone into the water to see what the ripples revealed. Joseph Kennedy, in particular, became resentful of the President's personal intervention in what he regarded as his sphere as US ambassador.

The British, meanwhile, were extremely anxious to impress the Americans and very worried about how they should deal with the awkward subject of the war. The fact was that the British strategic position was little short of disastrous, and the British Chiefs of Staff were concerned that:

> there is a danger that discussion of the grave and complex problems with which we are grappling and to which we have now become accustomed at home, in the Middle East, in Africa and in the Far East, may cause the American representatives to take an unduly pessimistic view of the future and thereby prejudice American support. Alternatively, it might lead them to a fuller realisation of the situation and so encourage them to take an increasing part in the struggle.[79]

Equally, the chiefs believed that there was a real risk of estranging American official opinion if the Americans felt they 'were not being open with them'. Lee had warned the chiefs that there were still people in the administration who had been shocked about the true situation when America entered the war in 1917 and were determined that this should not happen again. It was finally agreed that the 'conversations should be conducted on the basis of complete frankness', a policy Churchill heartily endorsed.[80]

The American delegation, which consisted of Admiral Ghormley, Assistant to the Chief of Naval Operations, Brigadier General

Strong, Deputy Chief of the General Staff, and General Delos C. Emmons, Commanding General, General Headquarters Air Force, arrived in London on 15 August, just in time to witness the first German air raid over the city. Their first series of briefings took place in the American embassy, including an introduction by Kennedy in which he attacked Churchill's handling of the war and the British in general for their 'bungling' over the political, military and economic situation.[81] They were then brought to the offices of the War Cabinet in Richmond Terrace, at the heart of Whitehall, for the first official meeting with the British.[82] These same rooms had been witness to the secret Anglo-French staff talks of February 1939, but it was hoped that the current meetings might have a happier outcome.[83] The delegates were certainly high-ranking and influential officers and the visit was viewed by the Americans as an important preliminary move by the President, but the British were immediately disappointed when they learnt that the delegates had not been given any powers to act as a joint military mission, nor were they authorised to make any commitments on behalf of their services.[84] They had arrived in Britain simply as observers; their orders were to look and learn. The British did not understand the American approach to such talks, but the fact was that Roosevelt could not afford to give official attribution to these meetings. Just as Marshall had worked behind the scenes to resolve the tank impasse, so Roosevelt used this unofficial delegation to learn more about the situation in Britain. This might have provided an early lesson in the complex world of American politics, but the British were, perhaps understandably, simply confused by the arrival of yet more observers without any power to negotiate.

The first briefing by the British Chiefs of Staff was on the overall course of the war. This told the sorry story of the Norwegian fiasco and the fall of France while firmly placing the blame for the disaster on the French:

From the first moment when it became apparent that the main German thrust had broken through the French line and that the enemy had established a deep bridgehead across the river, we were faced with a growing attitude of defeatism on the part of the French.

There seemed to be little fight in their commanders or in many of their units, and their assurances of counter-attack seldom materialised. Their resistance was, indeed, only maintained as long as it was by the most strenuous efforts of our own air forces.[85]

There is little question that the British attempted to place their own efforts in the best possible light at the expense of the now absent French, and Lee described the account as 'long and naive'.[86] After an hour of tentative and circular discussion in which little had been accomplished, the observers were taken to meet Anthony Eden, who brightened the mood considerably, much to Lee's relief.[87]

The delegation spent the next ten days on an extensive tour of military installations, but the British did not treat them as just another group of tourists. On their very first afternoon, the party was taken to the House of Commons to witness Winston Churchill in action. Churchill's speech to the House that day included his paean of praise to the young pilots of the RAF, in which he uttered the famous phrase: 'Never in the field of human conflict was so much owed by so many to so few.' Two days later, Kennedy, Lee and the observers were invited to a dinner at 10 Downing Street with the War Cabinet.[88] The British were making full use of their secret weapon in the form of Churchill's formidable powers of oratory and personality to influence the American observers. Churchill's relationship with Roosevelt may have been the linchpin of the Anglo-American alliance, but some of the first Americans he attempted to charm in person were Ghormley, Strong and Emmons.

The series of visits that the British had scheduled included Fighter Command Headquarters, Coastal Command, an armoured division on Salisbury Plain, the navy at Plymouth, and a trip to the embattled port of Dover, again in the company of Churchill.[89] It was not until the end of August that there were further meetings to discuss British strategy and further potential avenues of American aid and cooperation. At the third meeting, on 31 August 1940, Air Chief Marshal Sir Cyril Newall, the Chief of the Air Staff, outlined Britain's plans for the conduct of the war. His statement to the American observers was based on the Chiefs of Staff's assessment of future

strategy, and he provided a remarkably clear and candid outline of
British thinking on how the war should be prosecuted. [90] He declared
that 'our main object was the defeat of Germany', which was a
bold statement given that Britain was currently preparing to resist
a German invasion, but he argued that in two aspects, economic
pressure and the war in the air, Britain was already engaged 'in a
relentless offensive'. This might have been official policy, but in
practice it remained mere wishful thinking. The security of the
United Kingdom was 'absolutely vital', but the chiefs maintained
that 'we are confident of our ability to withstand any attacks on
this country', and their whole policy was based on this assumption. [91]
The most immediate overseas threat lay in the Middle East; an attack
on Egypt was regarded as imminent, and the Italians did indeed
launch an ineffectual assault in September 1940.

Newall then looked ahead to British policy for the defeat of
Germany: 'The foundation of our strategy is to wear her down by
ever-increasing force of economic pressure. This, we believe, we
shall succeed in doing.' Another essential element of British strategy
was 'to pursue a continuous and relentless air offensive against both
Germany and Italy and to develop the scale of our attack as quickly
as our resources will permit'. He admitted that economic pressure
alone was unlikely to be decisive and that Britain would have to
build up her offensive power. He also revealed that the British
believed that the elimination of Italy would relieve the pressure on
the Middle East and assist the blockade against Germany. In his
summary, he outlined the key planks of Britain's military strategy:

1.   To ensure the security of the United Kingdom and our Imperial
     possessions and interests.
2.   To maintain command of sea communications in the oceans,
     in Home waters and the Eastern Mediterranean, and to regain
     command throughout the Mediterranean.
3.   To intensify economic pressure.
4.   To intensify our air offensive against both Germany and Italy.
5.   To build up our resources to an extent which will enable us
     to undertake major offensive operations on land as opportu-
     nity offers. [92]

Newall had provided the observers with a very clear blueprint
of British strategy for the war and one that remained remarkably
consistent throughout the conflict. This emphasised air and naval
power, which, through bombing and blockade, would slowly
weaken Germany. It was, in many respects, simply a modern version
of the British 'peripheral' strategy of the Napoleonic wars, which
sought to wear down an opponent without necessarily challenging
him directly on the continent of Europe. It was not surprising that
Rear Admiral Ghormley sought to clarify whether the Chiefs of
Staff believed that the war could only be finally decided on land.
Newall replied that 'in the long run it was inevitable that the Army
should deliver the coup de grace. We hoped, however, for a serious
weakening in the morale and fighting efficiency of the German
machine, if not a complete breakdown, which would make the
task of the Army much more easy.' [93] Even the fact that Newall
used the phrase 'coup de grace' was significant, as it suggested that
Germany would have to be virtually defeated before a British army
would ever land again on the continent. Britain was simply too
weak in 1940, and indeed for much of the rest of the war, to
contemplate mounting an invasion unless the German armed forces
had been worn down by other means. British strategy in the Second
World War was always based on a gradual attritional approach,
which would take time and patience to work. However, the concept
of a slow strangling of the German economy such as had occurred
in the Great War seemed a pipe dream in the context of 1940, when
the Germans occupied much of Eastern Europe and were engaged
in building U-boat bases on the Atlantic coast of a defeated France.
Nonetheless, Newall's brief contained the foundations of much of
British strategic thought for the rest of the war. Many of the later
misunderstandings, confusions and disagreements that flared up
between the British and Americans were inherent and obvious in
his survey long before the Americans even contemplated active
participation in the European war.

Ghormley also asked whether the British Chiefs of Staff were
relying on receiving the continued economic and industrial support
of the United States, and, indeed, whether they counted upon
America's eventual active cooperation for their future plans. Newall

replied that 'we were certainly relying on the continued economic and industrial co-operation of the United States in ever-increasing volume', and that 'the economic and industrial co-operation of the United States were fundamental to our whole strategy'. However, he neatly sidestepped the issue of active cooperation, claiming that this was a matter for 'high policy'. Nonetheless, the fact remained that without the active involvement of the United States, Britain's future prospects were bleak indeed.

It cannot be said that the Buffalo Bill meetings achieved any concrete results for either party. After these rather inconclusive talks, the American observers eventually left for Washington in mid-September, by which time Lee was heartily sick of their presence in London. He confided to his diary that 'They had seen all and are now cumbering the ground.'[94] While Admiral Ghormley remained in Britain as a 'special observer', Emmons and Strong returned to Washington, where they were interviewed by Marshall. Both men returned with favourable impressions of the British, although these were almost certainly based more on their experiences touring Britain and its defences than on their discussions with the British Chiefs of Staff. They had new respect for the determination and calm response of the British to the Luftwaffe raids, and had gained a real appreciation of British methods of defence against air attack.[95] However, Marshall quickly pulled them up short as they waxed lyrical about British stoicism under assault and told them not to jump to conclusions from the 'specialized situation at that time'. He reminded them of Pershing's difficulties in dealing with the British and his troubles with their confirmed 'beliefs' during the Great War, and cautioned them that the Germans 'had always been six months ahead of the Allies' in this one. Emmons and Strong's written report was thus more cautious in its approach and findings. Perhaps the most significant result of the visit was that the American planning staff now agreed that it was likely that Britain would survive but that they should continue to plan for the 'worst possible situation', which included a successful German invasion of Britain and the destruction of the Royal Navy.[96] Marshall also recommended that the Air Corps should send further observers to Britain and the Middle East to study British methods in greater detail, and Brigadier General James E. Chaney was later sent to Britain as result.[97] Clearly, the direct impact of the observers' visit was limited in the War Department.

However, the observers also gave a series of interviews with reporters that highlighted the defiant mood in Britain. Brigadier General Strong was reported in *The Times* as saying: 'Britain is determined to win if it is humanly possible. If she cannot win, she is going down with every man fighting and her flag flying. The British are confident that in the long run they will win the war and the present indications are that they not only can but will do it.'[98] Lee was pleased with such reports, as undoubtedly were the British, but it was a small result for such an intensive visit by high-ranking American officers.

When British Army planners considered the information they had received from Strong and Lee, it appeared that there was still little room for meaningful cooperation between the two armies, although the US Army was far from ready to mount any overseas operation. The British estimated that, at the very earliest, it would take 'several months' to put any American expeditionary force into the field, with the possible exception of the US Marine Corps Striking Force of 2,000 men on each coast. Not, of course, that the US War Department was even considering this possibility; it remained wholly committed to the concept of hemispheric defence. It was understood by the British planners that US Army policy was 'at present directed towards training and equipping a force of 1,200,000 men by the earliest possible date, rather than a smaller force at an earlier date', although it was estimated that by midsummer 1941, the US might be able to field six divisions. They also pointed out that during 1918, American troops in France had still been equipped with British and French materiel, and that as vast as the momentum of the American arms production was, it would take 'a correspondingly long time to get under way'. This meant that the two American armoured divisions were unlikely to be fully equipped before the early summer of 1941, and that further progress would be dependent on the growth of the industrial programme. Their summary noted that:

(a) The US could not at present put an Expeditionary Force into the field.

(b) In 3 months *given sufficient notice* a small force of 3 divisions could be made available.

(c) In 6 months this might be doubled.

(d) In 12 months a considerable force of 9 Regular, 4 or 5 National Guard, 2 Armoured and 1 or 2 Cavalry.

(e) The present US policy is to create a large Army of 1,200,000 men as soon as possible (target date is July 1942 but it is not likely to be realized) and not a smaller force in a shorter time. This policy would have to be reversed to make (b) and possibly (c) a practical proposition.

(f) Entry of US in to the war would increase the figure of (d) and possibly of (c).[99]

The British planners' assessment that the US Army would not be ready for combat operations overseas before the summer of 1942 proved remarkably prescient, although it gave little comfort. However, they then ruminated on the issue of what might be asked of the Americans if they did produce some troops at an earlier stage. It was agreed that the relief of the British division garrisoning Iceland would be a great advantage and easily accomplished. It was also recognised that while the military value would be limited, there might be considerable political advantage in the dispatch of 'a token force' of one brigade group to Britain. Such a force would 'be a tangible sign of American participation, but would also give USA a very direct and personal interest in the defeat of any attempt at invasion'. However, it was recognised that the 'disadvantages of having considerable American contingents in UK should not be overlooked: these are largely administrative – pay and accommodation: there may also be local trouble particularly if there are no active operations. There will also be the question of command to be settled.'[100] The planners of 1940 seem to have considered an American contingent on the same scale as the Canadian forces that had arrived in the UK during 1940; they cannot have imagined in their wildest dreams that the American presence in the UK would swell to millions of men just a few years later.

★　　★　　★

Lee, perceptive as ever, had already sensed the turn of events in the air battle over Britain. On 15 September, he gave his strongest prediction to Washington that Britain would survive the German air assault:

> What is very puzzling about the past month performances is the dissipation and misuse of German air power. Conclusion is that he is badly informed as to extent of damages inflicted and temper British people. If invasion requires preliminary neutralization RAF and Navy, and crippling of industries and public determination Hitler is further from success than he was a month ago.[101]

In fact, Lee had predicted two months earlier that 15 September would mark the 'edge of the blitzkrieg season. I believe Hitler will attack this island with everything he has at any moment from now on. I also believe that if he is not successful by the fifteenth of September, he will never be.'[102] Lee had divined with clarity the date that later came to be seen as the turning of the tide in the Battle of Britain. And although the British could not know it at the time, the threat of invasion had effectively evaporated by 17 September, when Hitler first ordered the indefinite postponement of Operation Sealion.

By the end of September 1940, with no sign of a German invasion, and the Italian advance into Egypt having stalled, it was becoming clear that Britain had surmounted the immediate and 'supreme crisis'.[103] Yet although the German invasion would now never come, Hitler still hoped to coerce Britain through a destructive bombing campaign. The Germans switched to the night bombing of factories and cities in an effort to cripple Britain's industry and demoralise her population.

As the German raids intensified, Lee provided Roosevelt and Marshall with detailed assessments of bomb damage on a daily basis. If the Second World War was a conflict of industrial production and home-front mobilisation as well as armies, navies and air forces, it was equally a war fought in the realms of propaganda and public opinion. London became a magnet for American reporters attempting to convey the dramatic events of the Blitz to

their readers and listeners back home. In fact, Lee became annoyed
with much of the lurid nature of American reporting about the
Blitz, which suggested that the entire city of London was little
more than a heap of smoking ruins. On one occasion, at the height
of the bombing, he called a meeting with the American correspondents in London. They noticed that there was a pile of diction-
aries on his desk; he went on to say that 'he was disturbed by the
frequency with which the word "devastated" was used to describe
the condition of London' in American press reports. He then 'read
the definition of "devastated" to the reporters and invited them to
come to the window to see whether the scene matched the definition. "London is not devastated, gentlemen," he said, "and if you
want one soldier's opinion, it will not be devastated."'[104]

Edward R. Murrow, an American radio broadcaster working for
CBS, brought his impressions of Britain's struggle and the sounds
of the Blitz into millions of American homes.[105] He had, after a
battle with the Ministry of Information, been given remarkably
free rein to report upon events as he saw them. Murrow, who
opened his reports with his famous phrase, 'This . . . is London',
gave many of them from the rooftops of the city, where he
witnessed and recorded the atmosphere of London under aerial
bombardment. Perhaps more than anyone else, Murrow brought
the reality of the war to the American people. Britain's continued
resistance, combined with favourable reporting by American correspondents, began to make a real impact on American public
opinion.[106] On 25 June 1940, Gallup, the polling organisation, had
found that 64 per cent of Americans believed it was more important
to stay out of the war than to help Britain. By 20 October, that
figure was even, and by 19 November, polls were showing that
60 per cent believed that it was now more important to help Britain
than to stay out of the war.[107] Roosevelt's re-election as president
for an unprecedented third term, combined with this gradual shift
in public opinion, gave him the foundation to continue his policy
of all aid to Britain 'short of war'. By December 1940, Britain had
shown her ability to weather the immediate storm, but Churchill
and his government now faced an impending financial crisis that
threatened to wreck her chances of continuing the war.

4

Special Observers

By December 1940, Churchill and his cabinet colleagues had to confront the very unpalatable fact that the country was facing bankruptcy. The weakness of Britain's economic position seemed completely at odds with the image of the British Empire. Every British schoolchild knew that one third of the world's surface was 'pink' and under Britain's control. Military textbooks such as Cole's *Imperial Military Geography* assessed in detail the vast range of resources from the dominions, from foodstuffs to iron and coal, that the British could call upon during wartime.[1] Even when Britain faced Hitler's Germany supposedly alone in the summer of 1940, the country was relying on the resources and support of an enormous, if desperately overstretched, empire.

At least some of these assumptions were based on reality. During the Second World War, Britain managed to produce 60 per cent of its war requirements from its own resources. However, while the Empire could provide the British Isles with a whole range of raw materials, it could not provide all of the ships, planes, tanks and guns that Britain needed. Over the course of the war, 40 per cent of Britain's war requirements came from the United States and Canada.[2] The large orders, including those of the tank mission, placed in the United States since June 1940 were vital for Britain's war effort, but they had also drained the British exchequer of dollars to pay for them.

The problem was that Britain had to buy its wartime needs from America on a strictly commercial basis. There could be no return to the practice of borrowing the money required;[3] Roosevelt's policy of 'cash and carry' meant that all British orders had to be paid for in gold, securities or dollars – not sterling. During the first months of the war, the British had attempted to control the problem of dollar reserves by placing strict controls on purchasing in the United States and by mounting a limited foreign export drive to bring in currency. Both these policies simply served to confuse and anger the Americans. However, after the emergency of the summer of 1940, Britain needed to turn all of her industry over to war production and to buy as many supplies from America as she could. Her dollar reserves then reduced at an alarming rate, and on 7 December 1940, Churchill wrote to Roosevelt that 'The moment approaches when we shall no longer be able to pay cash for shipping and other supplies. While we will do our utmost . . . I believe that you will agree it would be wrong in principle and mutually disadvantageous if . . . Great Britain were to be divested of all saleable assets . . . such a course would not be in the moral or economic interests of either of our countries.'[4] Britain had already sold numerous investments and securities but had reached the end of her easily realisable assets. Churchill knew that the orders placed in America for December 1940 and January–February 1941 amounted to $1,000 million, yet the country's remaining gold reserves and dollar balance totalled just $574 million.[5]

The issue came to a head over the last $42 million of Britain's gold reserves, held at Cape Town in South Africa. Sir Frederick Phillips, the senior British Treasury representative in Washington, had suggested that the Americans might be able to acquire the gold in South Africa, but he did so without informing the British cabinet. There was outrage in London when they were informed that Roosevelt intended to send the USS *Louisville* to Cape Town to pick up the gold. Churchill drafted a letter to Roosevelt protesting that this act would 'wear the aspect of a sheriff collecting the last assets of a helpless debtor. It was not fitting that any nation should put itself wholly in the hands of another.'[6] The South African gold represented a large proportion of Britain's reserves, which now stood at less than half a billion dollars, while the United States held 22 billion dollars in gold.[7] While the British government considered the American action high-handed and grasping, to many Americans the safe arrival of $42 million in gold would seem to give the lie to British claims that they were bankrupt. Although Churchill eventually sent a more conciliatory message, his original, angry letter was perhaps closer to the truth. Britain's war effort – even after just one year of conflict – had placed an intolerable burden upon her finances and her future was now in the hands of the United States of America. Without American aid and assistance above and beyond the commercial basis of 'cash and carry', Britain would not be able to continue the war.

Roosevelt, secure in his third term as president, soon began to prepare American public opinion for his solution to Britain's inability to pay in cash for the products it needed. At the end of December 1940, in one of his famous fireside chats, Roosevelt used a homely analogy to explain to the American people why Britain would need long-term aid from the United States. He explained that if your neighbour's house was on fire, you would not argue about the cost of your hose that he wanted to borrow; you would simply lend him the hose and get it back after the fire was out.[8] Roosevelt's fire hose was what became known as Lend-Lease. America, he told the American people, was to become the 'arsenal of Democracy'. He asked Congress for legislation to implement Lend-Lease in his State of the Nation address on 6 January 1941. This provoked an intense national debate over just how far the United States should help Britain and all the other countries clamouring to buy munitions. Although the bill eventually passed through both houses of Congress, its passage could not be taken for granted, and it left the British in a very uncertain situation. The core of the bill would enable the United States government to 'sell, transfer, exchange, lend, lease or otherwise dispose of war materials for the government of any country whose defense the President deems vital to the defense of the United States'.[9] The obvious benefit 'in kind' that the United States expected to receive was the use of those weapons against Germany. However, the debate in Congress and across the country became very heated indeed. The British government and its purchasers in America spent the next three months in a period of uncertainty, unsure of how orders already placed were going to be paid for. For the British, such delays were intolerable, since Britain's war production plans for the next two years were now inextricably bound up with the supply of American equipment.

On 9 January 1941, Harry Hopkins arrived in London to act as Roosevelt's personal representative.[10] The visit had originated in a desire by the President to 'sit down together' with Churchill in person, but the pressure of vital work had made this impossible and eventually Hopkins persuaded the President to let him go on his behalf.[11] Hopkins had been one of Roosevelt's New Deal 'fixers' for many years and, even though seriously ill, stayed in the White House as the President's erstwhile national security adviser from May 1940 until January 1944.[12] In January 1941, as he told broadcaster Ed Murrow, he was 'to be a catalytic agent between two prima donnas'.[13] Hopkins had initially been sceptical about Churchill and his dominance of the British war effort, but Churchill was completely frank with him and a personal friendship between the two men quickly developed. Even after their first meeting, it is clear that Hopkins warmed to the Prime Minister, and Churchill is said to have felt sure that he had established 'a definite heart-to-heart contact with the President'.[14] Hopkins was able to give Churchill some of the details of the financial solution to Britain's problems: Britain would have to pay as much gold and dollars as she had left, but in return the United States would manufacture and supply what she needed and then lease it to her, with payment delayed until after the war. With Lend-Lease, Britain was allowed to run up an astronomical debt but avoided bankruptcy in the short term and was no longer entirely helpless. It would, however, leave the British economy in a very uncertain position when or if the war ended.

Churchill took Hopkins on a punishing round of meetings, tours and visits, and his legendary capacity for working long into the night exhausted the American. However, this whirlwind schedule clearly had the effect that Churchill desired. In one of his many letters to Roosevelt during the trip, Hopkins wrote that 'This island needs our help now, Mr President, with everything we can give them.'[15] At a dinner given by the Lord Provost of Glasgow, Hopkins was called on to say some words after Churchill's speech, which had made flattering references to the 'Democracy of the great American

Republic'. Hopkins, caught uncharacteristically unprepared, quoted the Book of Ruth: 'Whither thou goest, I will go; and where thou lodgest, I will lodge, thy people shall be my people, and thy God my God. Even to the end.' It is said that Churchill wept at the words, and one of the company reported that Hopkins' words 'seemed like a rope thrown to a drowning man'.[16] Hopkins' short speech was censored, but word of it reached many ears and it had a powerful effect in Britain, even though it had given a much greater assurance of support than he had meant to imply.[17] On the very day that Hopkins went to Chequers to say goodbye to the Churchill family, news was received that the Lend-Lease Bill had passed the House of Representatives by 260 votes to 165.

By throwing the rope of Lend-Lease, Roosevelt ensured that Britain did not drown, but it also meant that she became completely bound and tied to the United States of America. All of Churchill's subsequent actions, and indeed the subsequent relations between the two powers, have to be understood within this broader framework. None of the complicated and tense negotiations surrounding the Lend-Lease Bill could be considered direct influences upon the relationship between the two armies in the Second World War, but it would be equally wrong to imagine that Britain's financial predicament and her reliance upon American aid had no effect on her military and their operations. However, the passage of the Lend-Lease Bill was only one of three interrelated events in the winter of 1941, and it was in this febrile period of uncertainty that Britain's need to influence American opinion first impacted directly upon her sailors, soldiers and airmen.

As the United States Congress debated the provisions of the Lend-Lease Bill, American and British military staff representatives met in Washington on 29 January to discuss closer cooperation in the event that the United States should join the war.[18] This was the start of the formal American–British Conversations, known as ABC-1, which continued until 27 March. With his position secured by re-election, Roosevelt could take the next step towards collaboration with the British, yet the very fact that such staff conversations were taking place remained highly sensitive for the US government. The

United States was still a neutral power, and yet she was now indulging in future war planning with a belligerent state. Although Roosevelt was the true instigator of these meetings, he did not officially call for them, nor would he sign the eventual report that was prepared.[19] Indeed, Marshall warned the British representatives when he welcomed them to Washington that any public knowledge of the fact that the conversations were taking place could have a disastrous effect upon the Lend-Lease Bill.[20] Just like the Buffalo Bill meetings the previous summer, these talks took place in the strictest secrecy.

The purpose of the meetings was to 'determine the best methods by which the US and British Commonwealth could defeat Germany should the United States be compelled to resort to war', and to coordinate their military efforts and plans more closely.[21] In so doing, the meetings discussed the general principles that would guide the military collaboration of the two states but were not to imply any political commitment. This was an unofficial yet significant statement of quasi-alliance between the two countries, which also began the process of airing strategic views setting the tone and pattern for the eventual formation of the Combined Chiefs of Staff.[22]

Perhaps the most important result of the discussions lay in the agreement of the 'Broad Strategic Objective', which was declared as 'the defeat of Germany and her Allies'. It was agreed that if Japan did enter the war, the strategy in the Far East would be defensive. Annex III of the report laid out the 'Joint Basic War Plan Number One . . . for war against the Axis Powers', which later became known as Rainbow 5. These general offensive policies were clearly based upon the set of priorities outlined in the Buffalo Bill talks the previous summer. In the absence of any fully developed American plan for the defeat of Germany, there was a continued reliance upon the British peripheral approach of economic pressure, aerial bombardment, raiding and the need for an eventual land offensive against Germany. For the higher direction of this war, the report recommended 'the provision of the necessary machinery along the lines of a Supreme War Council for the co-ordination of the political and military direction of the War'.[23] This recommendation was clearly based upon the Great War experience of both the British and Americans in working with the French.

Although the talks were wide-ranging, the most concrete progress was achieved in the maritime sphere, where the division of the globe into areas of defined responsibility was more straightforward. Clear protocols were established for naval cooperation and communication, but there remained little concrete detail or progress on land forces. This was not surprising: both the US and the UK were maritime powers who had to use the sea to project air and land power overseas. The military forces the two powers could provide for any possible land operations were meagre. In the United Kingdom, British forces numbered 28 divisions, including one in Iceland; four independent brigade groups; one armoured division and four forming; and one army tank brigade and two forming. This was sufficient to defend the United Kingdom but little else. It was noted that a maximum of four US infantry divisions and two armoured divisions would be trained and equipped by 1 September 1941. Not surprisingly, the army fell back upon the plans discussed at the Buffalo Bill meetings. It was agreed that when the US entered the war, it would relieve the British forces in Iceland, provide troops to defend the naval and air bases for US use in the UK, and send one reinforced regiment (known as a brigade group) for service in the United Kingdom.

The central result of the conversations was that the Chiefs of Staff of the US and British armed forces 'agreed to collaborate continuously in the planning and executing of operations'.[24] One of the main recommendations of the report was that official military missions should be established in both Washington and London to further and deepen the transfer of information and cooperation between the two nascent allies. These organisations would then be able to work on the details of the agreed policies and plans and ensure that 'the change over from peace to war may be effected rapidly and smoothly when the time comes'.[25] These staff conversations were highly significant, even given the vagueness of many of their provisions, since they represented the first tangible acknowledgement that Britain and America might well fight as allies during the war.

Yet while the military representatives were debating future plans and policies in Washington, Churchill and his military advisers in

London had to wrestle with the immediate needs of an ongoing war. Even though Britain was enduring almost nightly bombing during the Blitz, the focus of their strategic attention shifted from the defence of Great Britain to the situation in the Mediterranean and its surrounding countries. British control of Egypt was seen as the linchpin of the defence of the entire Middle East, and second in importance only to the defence of the United Kingdom. Italian ambitions in the Mediterranean had caused the British much concern before the war, but the reality of Italian military power proved much less daunting than Mussolini's grandiloquent boasts. The Italian Tenth Army, under Marshal Graziani, had launched an advance into Egypt from Libya in September 1940, but this ground to a halt after only 60 miles. British plans then concentrated upon ejecting the Italians and thus securing Egypt.

Mussolini, increasingly desperate for a diplomatic and military triumph, decided, without reference to his military chiefs, to declare war on Greece on 28 October 1940. Far from being an easy victory, the Italian invasion across the Albanian mountains turned into a bloody fiasco. The Greeks were able to contain the advance and then throw back the ill-organised and supplied Italian armies into Albania. Churchill saw this successful Greek resistance as an opportunity to buttress the British position in the Mediterranean and a possible means of building a pro-British coalition of Balkan states that could resist Axis diplomatic and military pressure. On 2 November 1940, he informed Anthony Eden, who in his capacity as Secretary of State for War was touring the Middle East, that the 'Greek situation must now dominate all others and aid to Greece must be studied, lest the whole Turkish position be lost through proof that England never kept her guarantees'.[26] Churchill also saw it as essential to demonstrate to America that Britain meant to fight and would support anyone who resisted German aggression. German predominance threatened to completely change the balance of power in the Balkans, and if Britain stood aside and allowed Greece to be overwhelmed, the arguments of the America First movement and other isolationists would only be strengthened. While the political motivation for support to Greece appeared obvious, the issue drove a major wedge between Churchill and his military advisers. Sir John Dill knew that any campaign in Greece would stretch the meagre British forces in the Mediterranean beyond breaking point, with scarcely enough aircraft available to cover even the operations in Egypt. Dill's caution and arguments in favour of husbanding British strength were rewarded by Churchill calling him the 'dead hand of inanition' to his face. However, even Eden, usually one of Churchill's strongest supporters, considered his ideas 'strategic folly': he believed that the security of Egypt was more important than Greece.[27]

Nonetheless, at Churchill's insistence, three Blenheim and two Gladiator squadrons were dispatched to Greece in November 1940 and hurriedly repainted with Greek markings. Eden knew that Wavell, the Commander in Chief Middle East, was planning an operation to attack the Italians in Egypt, and Churchill believed that such a victory would 'probably turn the scale' and enable him to move troops to support the Greeks. But Wavell kept Churchill in the dark about the date, leaving the Prime Minister waiting in a frenzy of impatience. On 4 December 1940, at a meeting with Eden and Dill, Churchill asked again for news of Wavell's forthcoming operation, and was indignant when neither Eden nor Dill could give him an exact date. Eden wrote in his diary that Churchill became 'critical of army and generals. "High time army did something" etc. I made it plain that I did not believe in fussing Wavell with questions. I knew his plan, he knew our view, he had best be left to get on with it.'[28] This kind of passive, compliant patience was simply not in Winston Churchill's character. While Eden did not become overly anxious about the meeting, Dill later went to see his friend General Sir John Kennedy and told him:

> I cannot tell you how angry the Prime Minister has made me. What he said about the Army tonight I can never forgive. He complained he could get nothing done by the Army. Then he said he wished he had Papagos to run it.* He asked me to wait and have a drink with him after the meeting, but I refused and left Anthony there by himself.[29]

---

* Since Papagos was the head of the Greek army, this calculated insult stung Dill to his core.

This was only one of many, many arguments and outbursts between Churchill and his military advisers during the war.

The tide of the war in the Mediterranean appeared to be flowing in the British favour during November and December 1940. The Royal Navy struck a major blow at the Italian fleet at Taranto on 11 November, and just four days after Churchill's tirade against the army, Wavell's Western Desert Force mounted an astonishingly successful attack against the Italians in Egypt. Within three days, the Italian army had been routed and pursued back into Libya. These successes seemed to offer hope that the series of German successes in northern Europe might be counterbalanced by the maintenance and even the strengthening of the British position in the Mediterranean.

Perhaps not surprisingly, Roosevelt again became interested in assessing Britain's fortunes in the area. After the success of his previous mission to London, he decided to send William Donovan to observe and report on the British strategic situation. While Donovan had been able to slip into London unobserved in July 1940, his departure from Baltimore now caused a flare of media attention, with reporters announcing his arrival in London.[30] William Stephenson, the head of British Security Coordination in America, accompanied Donovan to London and noted that 'he can play a great role, perhaps a vital one, but it may not be consistent with orthodox diplomacy nor confined in its channels'.[31] The British were by now well aware that Donovan represented a direct route to Roosevelt. He spent five days in London being briefed on all manner of subjects before leaving on his tour of the Mediterranean. His guide was Lieutenant Colonel Vivian Dykes, known as 'the best man in the Cabinet Secretariat', and an individual who came to play a central part in Anglo-American cooperation.[32] As Dykes noted in a signal to Andrew Cunningham, commander-in-chief of the Mediterranean fleet at Alexandria, it was believed that:

> Donovan exercises controlling influence over Knox, strong influence over Stimson, friendly advisory influence over President . . . Being a Republican, a Catholic, and of Irish descent, he has following of the strongest opposition to the Administration . . . There is no

doubt that we can achieve infinitely more through Donovan than through any other individual.[33]

While the British believed that they might favourably influence Roosevelt by wooing Donovan, it is also clear that Donovan exerted influence upon the British. Donovan and Dykes flew to Egypt, then embarked on a whirlwind tour of the Balkan countries, including Yugoslavia, Greece and Turkey. Churchill had asked Donovan to tour these countries both to gain intelligence and to influence their decision-making process, and Donovan went on to play a part in British strategy over Greece. The Greek premier, President Metaxas, had refused all overt British offers of help, fearing that such support might be enough to precipitate German intervention but would not be sufficient to defend Greece against invasion. However, when Metaxas died on 29 January 1941, his successor, Alexander Koryzis, decided to ask for help. On 5 February 1941, the Western Desert Force set the seal on perhaps the greatest military victory achieved by the British Army in the Second World War. At the Battle of Beda Fomm, the Italian Tenth Army was trapped and destroyed. Since the British offensive had begun, 110,000 Italians had been taken prisoner, and the road to Tripoli was wide open. Churchill and Eden, now Foreign Secretary, believed the desert battle had been won and that they could now send troops to Greece to counter the German infiltration of the Balkans.

After his tour of the Balkans in January, Donovan returned to Cairo to meet with Wavell and Air Marshal Longmore on 8 February 1941, the very day that Koryzis asked for a decision on the size and composition of the forces that Britain was prepared to send to Greece. Donovan, with his first-hand experience of the Balkans, gave the two British commanders his impression of the situation:

> He put over very well his idea of looking at the Mediterranean not as an east–west corridor, but as a no man's land between two opposing fronts. The north–south conception seemed to strike Wavell very forcibly, and he was clearly impressed by Donovan's insistence on the need for keeping a foothold in the Balkans.[34]

Donovan also forcibly expressed the importance of keeping American public opinion on side, since although the Lend-Lease Bill had passed the House of Representatives, it had yet to be heard in the Senate. Wavell was aware of the risks but now believed the political reasons to be inseparable from the military ones. He concluded that 'I think we are more likely to be playing the enemy's game by remaining inactive than by taking action in the Balkans. Provided that conversations with the Greeks show that there is a good chance of establishing a front against the Germans with our assistance, I think we should take it.' General Marshall-Cornwall, the commander of British Troops Egypt, was horrified when he learned of Wavell's change of heart and blurted out to his chief that it was a gamble that could only lead to military disaster. Wavell replied, 'Possibly, but strategy is only the hand-maid of policy, and here political considerations must come first. The policy of our government is to build up a Balkan Front.'[35]

That day, 10 February 1941, was, as far as such matters can ever be dated, the moment of decision for British support to Greece. When the Defence Committee met that night, Churchill decided against allowing an advance on Tripoli, and for military assistance to Greece. As Eden put it: 'If another country to which we had given such a pledge were to fall to the Axis powers without a real effort to prevent it, the effect, especially in the United States must be deplorable.' This was the real crux of the issue. Churchill and Eden were only too well aware that the Lend-Lease Bill was making its way through Congress at this moment. The House Foreign Affairs Committee had sat and heard evidence since January before voting 17 to 8 in favour of the bill. The legislation then went to the House of Representatives on 3 February 1941, and was passed by 260 votes to 165 on 8 February. However, there remained the final hurdle of the US Senate, which was due to begin debating the bill the following week, on 17 February. As far as the British were concerned, the issue remained in the balance. The British decisions over Greece were thus taken in an atmosphere where the political repercussions in America were potentially more important than the military realities facing any British force sent to the Balkans. The meeting was a stormy one, in which Dill continued to resist the Prime Minister's view. Dill spoke to Kennedy that evening after the meeting:

> I gave it as my view that all the troops in the Middle East are fully employed and that none are available for Greece. The Prime Minister lost his temper with me. I could see the blood coming up his great neck and his eyes began to flash. He said: 'What you need out there is a Court Martial and a firing squad. Wavell has 300,000 men, etc. etc.' I should have said Whom do you want to shoot exactly? but I did not think of it till afterwards.[36]

Nonetheless, Churchill ordered Dill and Eden to leave the next day for Egypt, Turkey and Greece to investigate all of the military and political details. British civil–military relations had become just as dysfunctional as they had been in the Great War, but this time the premier, in the form of Churchill's dominating personality, held the whip hand.

On 11 February, Churchill's telegram reached Wavell in Cairo. It informed him that 'Destruction of Greece will eclipse victories you have gained in Libya, and may affect decisively Turkish attitude, especially if we have shown ourselves callous of fate of allies. You must now therefore conform your plans to larger interests at stake.' Four divisions were to be made ready for Greece, and no advance on Tripoli was allowed. That same day, Dill and Eden left Britain for Greece. Dill had a long talk with Kennedy before he left. Kennedy felt that:

> the British Government was now trying to force an unsound policy down Wavell's throat, and down the throats of the Greeks and the Turks. He believed that we would be playing into the hands of the Germans and that any force sent to Greece was certain to be annihilated or driven out again. He felt that although it had been argued that British prestige would suffer in America if we did not go to the rescue of Greece, it would suffer still more in the end when we failed.[37]

Sadly, Kennedy's predictions proved correct.

On 22 February, Eden, Dill and Wavell reached an agreement

with the Greek government for the dispatch of a British expeditionary force (although most of the men were actually from Australia and New Zealand). Churchill and Eden had achieved their policy goal, as, to some extent, had Roosevelt. On his return to the United States, Donovan, at Roosevelt's request, gave 'an unofficial report to the American people' in a nationwide radio broadcast in which he argued powerfully for greater support of Britain. However, the policy of support to Greece that Churchill had espoused and Donovan had enthusiastically supported was soon to crash in ruins.

On 7 March 1941, the War Cabinet met to confirm the decision to send the 58,000-strong Lustre Force to Greece. That same night, Harry Hopkins telephoned Churchill to let him know that the Lend-Lease Bill had passed in the Senate by 60 votes to 31. Roosevelt signed two directives within hours of the passage of the Bill, the first of which stated that the defence of Great Britain was vital to the defence of the United States.[38] Britain was allocated $4,376 million for the next six months to 'continue resisting aggression'. The second directive is much less well known. This declared that Greece was also essential to American security and ordered the immediate transfer of fifty 75 mm guns and 150,000 shells, as well as other military equipment.[39] None of these supplies reached Greece before the Germans intervened.

The German reaction to overt British support for Greece and a pro-British coup in Yugoslavia was swift and violent. Hitler also responded to the British victories in North Africa by dispatching a German 'blocking force' under the command of a young Lieutenant General Erwin Rommel. He went on the offensive in Libya, meeting with only weak resistance, and the port of Tobruk was soon under siege. Meanwhile, the German forces committed to Yugoslavia and Greece made shockingly rapid progress. Lustre Force was bundled unceremoniously out of Greece, and by 27 April Athens had fallen and Koryzis had committed suicide. This catalogue of disasters gave the lie to any presumed British expertise in strategy. It was also remembered by the Americans when the British continued to push for a Mediterranean strategy later in the war.

Donovan had been employed on a highly influential but nonetheless transitory visit; the permanent 'eyes and ears' of the US

Army in the region was the American military attaché in Cairo, Major Bonner L. Fellers, who became the main conduit for information on the British war in the Mediterranean. While the US Army had little strategic interest in the Mediterranean theatre, it was realised that the British experience of fighting in the region – most notably in the deserts of Egypt and Libya – might offer up valuable information on modern warfare. The German army had demonstrated very dramatically the power of modern, fast-moving mechanised formations during the campaigns in Poland and France, and the US Army was only too well aware of the need to gain reliable information about the reality of modern armoured warfare to ensure that US troops would be ready if or when they were committed to battle against the German Wehrmacht. However, there were few military partners, with the exception of the British, to whom the United States could turn to learn about these new forms of warfare. In the early period of the war, the Americans gleaned as much as possible from French sources, but this was impossible after the defeat of France in 1940. The Soviet Red Army, even once it became an ally of the United States in late 1941, kept its combat experience and military technology strictly to itself, and the Western Allies remained remarkably ill-informed on the Red Army throughout the war.

From 1940 onwards, Fellers headed up a team of American liaison officers and observers who were attached to the British Western Desert Force and its later incarnation as the British Eighth Army. Not surprisingly, the British authorities in London and Cairo were alive to the importance of impressing Fellers and gave him unprecedented access to personnel and information that allowed him and his team to gain extensive knowledge of British methods and derive many lessons from the desert fighting as it developed. But having provided Washington with glowing reports concerning Operation Compass and the British victories against the Italians, Fellers' cables during the spring and summer of 1941 accurately chronicled the subsequent series of disasters that brought the British position in the Middle East to the edge of a precipice. Far from being able to establish a Balkan front against Hitler, as Churchill and Eden had wished, intervention in Greece merely brought an overwhelming

German reaction. The British soon had to evacuate their troops from Greece and Crete, and the Royal Navy was punished severely by intense Luftwaffe attacks as it struggled to evacuate the troops back to Egypt. Meanwhile, having stripped their forces in North Africa to support the Greek adventure, the British were unprepared when Rommel mounted an unexpectedly early and ferocious offensive that took him to the gates of Tobruk in Libya. With the near-simultaneous boiling-up of trouble in both Iraq and Syria, for a time it seemed as if the entire British position in the Middle East might be lost.

Perhaps not surprisingly, Fellers' initial enthusiasm began to wane. However, he was still clearly being influenced by the British opinions that were being voiced to him, even while relaying the seriousness of the situation. He argued that in this desperate situation, 'Loss of Egypt might mean loss of war. Recommend War Department take all possible steps quickly to alleviate existing shortages in material and aircraft.'[40] Fellers drew much from the disastrous British experience in Greece and gave a particularly prescient warning about the necessity of airpower to support and protect naval units at sea, after the Royal Navy's harrowing experience under Luftwaffe attack during the battle and evacuation of Crete.

He also showed admiration for the courage of the British soldiers he met, if not for their organisation and methods of war:

> No race possess more fortitude and fearless determination than the British. During forty days of trying desert combat I never heard a word of complaint from Officer or soldier. They will never surrender. Somehow they know they will muddle through. The British fight best against great odds. Inadequate equipment is no discouragement. They are masters at improvisation. Yet in their willingness to improvise lies a weakness for in modern war improvisation is effective only against an inadequate enemy. The British Army is not quite in phase with the tempo of high centralization and coordination demanded by the machine age.[41]

Fellers had identified a key cultural difference that would continue to cloud the relationship between the two armies. As many

American officers were later to find, the British could indeed 'muddle through' with shortages and inadequate equipment. But while British officers saw this as a positive, even an essential virtue, the Americans took a very different view. Standard doctrine, methods and practice were essential to ensure that the rapidly expanding American Army could fight as one in the coming battles, and improvisation suggested an incoherent and dangerous jumble of differing approaches that could lead to chaos amongst the large and geographically dispersed American units.

Fellers reserved his most trenchant criticisms for the British command system in the theatre. In assessing the run of defeats that Britain had suffered, he commented that:

> There should be one Middle East Commander personally respon-
> sible for the success or failure of all operation. He should have
> under his control all means available – sea, land and air – for
> accomplishment of his mission . . . With Crete, Britain suffered her
> fourth tragic major defeat and because of divided responsibility
> inherent within her command system she has not the slightest idea
> who is responsible. The truth is that no one is responsible. It is a
> convenient system which protects all commanders, dilutes respon-
> sibilities, glosses over failure, provides iron clad alibis, but it won't
> win wars.[42]

In ascribing the string of defeats to the British command system, Fellers seems not to have been aware of the intense political pressure under which British commanders operated. Churchill had short-circuited many of the checks and balances of the British civil–military relationship, and Roosevelt's indirect encouragement through the agency of Donovan's tour had only added to the considerable demands. This level of political interference was alien to American commanders, who operated in a system with much more clearly defined boundaries between political direction and military execution. The British High Command in the Middle East and Mediterranean operated as a committee system, with three co-equal commanders-in-chief, one for each of the three services. In 1941, these posts were filled by General Sir Archibald Wavell as

Commander-in-Chief Middle East, Admiral Sir Andrew Cunningham as Commander-in-Chief Mediterranean Fleet, and Air Vice Marshal Sir Arthur Longmore as Air Commander-in-Chief Middle East. The theory behind the system was that each service chief could discuss his strategic needs and requirements with his equals and all three could decide upon the strategic priorities – and their attendant resources – together. There is little doubt that in the straitened circumstances of 1941, this system broke down, particularly over the issue of air cover for Greece and Crete. Fellers' suggested solution of one supreme commander who held ultimate responsibility for the entire theatre – air, land and sea – was a concept that found much favour in the American Army. Marshall, based on his experience in the Great War, was already a convinced advocate of the concept of supreme theatre command, but Fellers' cables from Egypt may well have provided the US Army's Chief of Staff with the final corroboration he needed that the British committee system was unworkable and needed to be avoided at all costs.

The British forces in Greece and North Africa had also lost yet more equipment, and were now facing a severe deficiency. This included 200 tanks, elevating the importance of the tank mission in Washington yet further. Fellers cabled the War Department in April that 'British sorely need cruiser tanks, air and motor transport',[43] and Wavell wrote to Dill at the end of May 1941 pleading for more tanks. He explained that his present strength amounted to 230 cruiser tanks and 237 infantry tanks and that even by the beginning of September his tank strength would amount to only the 7th Armoured Division, with one of its brigades being equipped with the American M3 light tank, whose 'value at present is unknown and only one regiment of which likely to be fit to take the field. American tanks are air cooled and behaviour in hot climate uncertain.' The reinforcements allotted to Wavell were insufficient to meet his needs after the serious losses of the previous months, and he warned that if Egypt were to be held, it was imperative that further reinforcements of tanks were sent forthwith.[44]

Dill's reply was not encouraging: he regretted that it was impossible to meet Wavell's demands. In a note to Churchill, he explained that Wavell's requirements could not be fulfilled even if every cruiser tank in the UK was dispatched to the Middle East. He also pointed out that 'Since the beginning of the war we have been unable to complete the equipment of a single armoured formation in this country.' The allotment of any more tanks to the Middle East would retard the development of the armoured formations in Britain, and with the continued threat of invasion it was impossible to send more tanks to Egypt. Britain's dearth of tanks and lack of production simply meant that no 'large scale offensive armoured operations' were possible 'in the near future'.[45]

In such a serious situation, the tank mission to the United States became crucial. With Britain unable to meet her needs out of her own production, the importance of the American M3 light and medium tanks to fill the gap was placed in sharp relief. Much of the mission's work in 1941 remained preparatory in managing the British contracts that had already been placed and then working out the details of how the Lend-Lease system of allocations would actually function. However, there was a new focus on getting the first viable American product, the M3 light tank, into the hands of British troops in Egypt.[46]

Meanwhile, Britain and America were taking the first tentative steps towards a functioning alliance by exchanging military missions. Since the duties of such missions were similar to those 'which the United States might send to an allied country in time of war', the American mission in London was known as the Special Observer Group (SPOB), in an attempt to conceal the real importance of the commitment.[47] This small group comprised 16 officers, one warrant officer and 11 enlisted men, who had all been personally selected by Marshall,[48] and on 19 May 1941, the SPOB opened its temporary headquarters in the American embassy building in Grosvenor Square. Major General James E. Chaney was selected to head the group, as he had already visited Britain during October and November 1940 and reported upon British air defence methods. It contained a predominance of US Army Air Force officers, as it was believed that the primary American forces based in Britain would be the USAAF bombardment groups mentioned in ABC-1.[49] There was little to suggest that this small collection of officers and men, wearing civilian clothes to disguise their purpose, would become the core of the United States army forces in Britain.[50]

Charles Bolte, who served with the SPOB, later explained that it was an 'undercover group that went over with a purpose and a method that was not clearly defined by Washington or certainly understood by the ambassador and the military attaché at the embassy'; nor was it understood, as he also admitted, by the British.[51] In fact, the main purpose of the SPOB was to ensure 'that the machinery would be ready so that the change-over from peace to war would be effected rapidly and smoothly if the United States decided to come into the conflict': essentially to plan and coordinate the details concerning transportation, reception, location and accommodation of US Army personnel that might be sent to Britain.[52] The group was to assist in the allocation of US equipment under the terms of Lend-Lease, but in reality most of this work was done by the US authorities working in conjunction with the British Joint Staff Mission. Chaney was also to advise Marshall on the employment of US forces in Britain. However, the misunderstanding surrounding its role limited the effectiveness of the Special Observer Group. The fact that it was forbidden to enter into any form of political commitments or negotiations meant that its duties were fixed to the preparation of plans stemming from ABC-1: it could not alter or modify those plans in the light of developments. These difficulties made it much harder to achieve the concrete progress desired by both militaries.

Most of the SPOB's work lay in observing, reporting and making detailed plans for the agreements laid out in ABC-1. These included developing American plans to occupy Iceland, selecting the location of potential US naval and air bases, and calculating the number of ground troops required to defend them. They were also expected to find a site for the Token Force, the single brigade to be dispatched to Britain, and formulate the initial plans for a US bomber force in Britain. In addition, in a duplication of Lee's work as military attaché, they were to observe and report on British organisation and methods. However, since the provisions of ABC-1 would only become active if or when the United States entered the war, there was an atmosphere of unreality and a lack of urgency to most of the group's activities.

This situation seems not to have been helped by Chaney's style of command. John Dahlquist, Assistant Chief of Staff, commented on 31 July 1941 that 'I am not very happy in my job. I seem to have little confidence in General Chaney. He seems to be so involved in insignificant details at times and so tied to the plan under which we are working.'[53] It also has to be said that many of the officers in the group did not have any confidence in the plans that had been agreed at ABC-1 when they saw the reality on the ground. Perhaps the most obvious example of such problems was that of the Token Force, which had originated in the minds of British planners back in 1940. It was suggested to the Americans that a suitable location for the force would be in Kent, near Dungeness, where there was spare accommodation.[54] Such a location would, of course, also have ensured that the American force would be quickly involved in the defence against any German invasion. During a flight over Dungeness, Charles Bolte commented that the British defences were 'pretty pathetic', and another of the group, George Griner, had 'practically paled' when he saw the defences and said that he 'wanted to pack up and go home'.[55] General McNarney, the Chief of Staff, said that evening after the reconnaissance that he felt 'like a murderer' at the thought of committing American troops to those positions. This was perhaps the first, although certainly not the last, time that a decision taken at the highest level of Anglo-American decision-making would prove to have controversial effects amongst those actually responsible for enacting them. On this occasion, the results of the reconnaissance proved decisive. Although further work was carried out on possible accommodation, the concept of the Token Force was quietly shelved during the autumn of 1941.

Work that did eventually bear fruit concerned the identification and construction of bases in Northern Ireland and Scotland. These were to be naval and air bases, which, since they would be used primarily by US forces, would be defended by the US Army. Plans for such installations began soon after the arrival of the special observers, and on 12 June 1941 contracts were signed for the construction of a naval base for destroyers on anti-submarine patrol at Londonderry, while bases for Catalina flying boats were to be built at Lough Erne in Northern Ireland and at Rosneath in Scotland. However, although these bases were 'ostensibly being built by the British for the British', they were in fact 'being built by American contractors with American money for American use', in clear contravention of America's position as a neutral power.[56]

While the members of the American Special Observer Group represented the first serious expansion of US liaison and planning in Britain, the British Army already had three military missions operating in the United States by July 1941. The tank mission, which had been joined by the Pakenham-Walsh mission, had been rechristened No. 200 Mission and had been joined in April 1941 by No. 29 Military Mission (Intelligence), headed by Lieutenant General Sir Colville Wemyss, who had gone to establish contact with the American intelligence organisations. In June, Lieutenant Colonel Vogel was sent as a representative of the Director of Military Operations to discuss the operational aspects of the Lend-Lease agreement, and in early July, No. 208 Mission (DQMG North America) arrived to act as the Quartermaster General's representative to supervise the storage and internal movement of the now large quantities of British military stores in America.

Problems arose due to the increasing number and overlapping nature of the missions, so at the end of July 1941 they were amalgamated into one organisation, the British Army Staff, commanded by Wemyss. Even at its inception, the British Army Staff comprised 65 officers and 230 military and civilian personnel, which was considerably larger than its American counterpart in London. Just like the American observers, the British Army Staff dressed in plain clothes and appeared to be part of the embassy, but while the Americans worked in a cloud of uncertainty, the British were already clear on their role and purpose. Much of their task lay in ensuring that British needs were highlighted in the allocation of Lend-Lease supplies. Once these supplies had been allocated, there remained the enormous task of checking and dispatching the growing quantities of munitions and supplies produced in America for British Army use.[57]

While the American observers were specifically prohibited from entering into any political commitments, the members of the British missions sought to influence American decision-making. Initially, however, they found it just as difficult as the American observers to gain up-to-date knowledge of unfolding events. Lieutenant General A. T. Cornwall-Jones pleaded in a letter to London on 24 April 1941 that it was essential that the members of the mission in Washington were 'kept in the picture out here', since 'unless they can speak with knowledge and assurance', their authority and position would rapidly deteriorate.[58] Cornwall-Jones was arguing that the mission had to act as the truly personal representative of the British Chiefs of Staff because:

> The President acts alone (or at least only with Hopkins and one or two others). He takes decisions without prior consultation with his Chiefs of Staff, and based entirely on the appreciations and knowledge that comes to him through all sorts of regular and irregular channels. If he can be led to understand that he has an authoritative British source in Washington at his elbow, who will always tell him the truth and give him considered military opinion, he is more likely to act along lines most commensurate with our views.[59]

Cornwall-Jones' aspiration to gain access to the President's ear was precisely what most American isolationists feared. In fact, it took time for the British missions to be placed fully 'in the picture', and for much of 1941 they gained only limited traction in the corridors of American power.

Back in London, one important element of the ABC-1 plan was activated well ahead of schedule, providing the American observers with plenty of work. This was the American occupation of Iceland. The British, anxious to deny these Danish possessions to the Germans, had occupied the Faroe Islands on 11 April and Iceland on 9 May 1940. Iceland was highly important as a potential naval and air base that could extend air patrols across the vital North Atlantic convoy routes. It also provided a staging point on the transatlantic air route and had potential as a trans-shipment point for personnel and supplies from American to British vessels.[60] Although ABC-1 had stated that American troops would relieve the British only when the US entered the war, Britain's need for troops at home and in the Middle East, combined with a desire for a tangible symbol of American support, led Churchill to request an accelerated relief of the British garrison in Iceland. This request dovetailed with Roosevelt's extension of the security zone of the United States to 25 degrees west longitude, which brought Greenland and the Azores within the western hemisphere in April 1941.

On 4 June 1941, Roosevelt ordered the US Army to prepare a plan for the immediate relief of British troops in Iceland, but the President soon found that the army was both unwilling and unable to comply with the directive. Not only would Congressional approval be required to send army units to Iceland, but the removal of regular troops and equipment to form an expeditionary force would disrupt the entire training programme of the 1.5 million raw recruits now in the US Army.[61] Much to his chagrin, Marshall had to advise that the task should be undertaken by the US Marines. The next day, Roosevelt turned to Admiral Harold R. Stark, Chief of Naval Operations, to get a Marine brigade ready to sail in five days. Since the Marines were all volunteers, there were no political restrictions on their deployment, but the mission caused similar disruption to their training programme.

On 11 June, members of the Special Observer Group reached Iceland, where they conducted a thorough inspection of its accommodation, and were warned by the British about the lack of facilities. The observers saw the need for much more accommodation while also noting that British medical and dental provision for soldiers fell far below American standards.[62] The question of command proved a thorny issue – as it did on numerous occasions throughout the war. The British believed that the Marines should be under their command, but Admiral Stark argued that US troops, who remained theoretically neutral, could not be placed under the command of a belligerent. Eventually the Marines' commander, Brigadier General John Marston, received orders to coordinate 'with the defense operations of the British by the method of mutual cooperation'.[63]

On 22 June 1941, the day the 1st Marine Brigade left Charleston harbour, Operation Barbarossa began. This was the German invasion of the Soviet Union, which changed the entire strategic calculus of the war. It removed the immediate threat of invasion from the United Kingdom but brought fresh anxieties for British and American planners. While the size and power of the Russian Red Army had become legendary, possessing as it did more than 22,000 front-line aircraft, over 20,000 tanks, and well over three million men in uniform, in the summer of 1941 much of this strength appeared to count for little. The Red Army had effectively been beheaded in the course of Stalin's savage purges, and his tight control of its deployment left it critically vulnerable to the German attack. The German army made rapid inroads against the Red Army and captured unprecedented tracts of territory and vast numbers of prisoners over the first few weeks of the campaign. Starved of hard information by the Soviet authorities, both British and American representatives in Moscow began to fear that the Red Army, like the Polish and French armies, might collapse under the weight of the blows directed at it. Yet given the mutual hostility and suspicion that existed between Britain and the Soviet Union, there could be no emulation of the growing cooperation that existed between Britain and America.

The great land battles of the war were fought on the Russian steppe without direct assistance from either the British or American armies. Eventually the war in the east came to represent the same grim attritional killing match as the Western Front had in the Great War. The events of the Eastern Front, however dimly aware of their reality the British and American armies might have been, remained of vital importance to the Anglo-American alliance throughout the rest of the war. The fact is that for much of the Second World War, the British and American armies were too unprepared and simply too small to have stood the test of battle against the full force of the German army. It was well understood at the time, if not perhaps fully admitted afterwards, that the vast majority of the German Wehrmacht was engaged on the Eastern Front.

Meanwhile, the Marines continued their journey northwards, escorted by a powerful task force, which included a battleship, two cruisers and ten destroyers. In fact, the Icelandic government was highly reluctant to 'invite' US forces to their island, and it was only after much political wrangling and considerable delay that an agreement was reached on 1 July 1941.[64] The 4,374 men of the First Provisional Marine Corps Brigade began landing at Reykjavik on 7 July 1941, while the 33rd Pursuit Squadron of the US Army Air Force flew from the USS *Wasp* to the air station at Reykjavik under British air escort. It was only after numerous changes of plan and considerable effort that the lead elements of the US 5th Infantry Division under Major General Bonesteel landed on the island on 15 September 1941 to reinforce the Marines. While the commitment of the Marines and the 5th Infantry Division marked the largest deployment of US troops outside America since 1919, the contrast with the titanic struggle on the Eastern Front could not have been greater. The United States army was still far from ready for war.

On their arrival, the Marines found that the British 'could not have been more cordial, generous, and helpful',[65] going so far as to provide rations for the first ten days of the Americans' stay on the island and even vacating some of their permanent camps to make room for the Marines.[66] In the event, the directive of mutual cooperation 'worked to the entire satisfaction of the British commander and the Brigade. The British complied with our requests and we complied with theirs. It was as simple as that. A British commander less sympathetic than General Curtis might have upset the applecart but under that talented officer no incident of conflict occurred.'[67]

Much to the disappointment of the British, the American takeover on Iceland was only gradual, and the replacement of British troops continued slowly throughout the autumn and winter of 1941. Even on 30 May 1942, there were still 11,757 British troops on the island, and it was not until 29 September that the British numbers dropped to 774.[68] The occupation of Iceland was a major and difficult first task for the US Marines and army. The dearth of facilities, combined with the harsh weather, and the need to guard 2,500 miles of isolated and vulnerable shoreline, led to the troops of the 5th Infantry Division being widely dispersed in some 90 separate camps. Roosevelt's motivation for the occupation of Iceland was clearly inspired by the growing involvement of the US Navy in the campaign against the U-boats in the Atlantic, but this relatively minor event marked the first overt cooperation between the two armies during the war.

During the summer of 1941, both armies began to give more serious thought to their potential strategy in the event of an alliance between Britain and the United States. The US War Department undertook a long-range review of what forces would be required to defeat Germany in the event of war. What became known as the Victory Program originated in the uncertainty caused by the Lend-Lease system of allocation between the British and American armies. American industrial capacity and production had been pulled in many different directions since 1940 due to the competing demands of the US services, the British and now the Soviets. While the British often had been able to present the Americans with a clear statement of requirement, and American needs had often been overruled in favour of British demands, the US Army still did not have a clear estimate of the ultimate size of the force it would require, making it hard for it to argue its case in the heated debates over Lend-Lease allocations.[69] The President thus directed the army and navy to study their production requirements should they be asked to enter the war.[70] The Victory Program was an attempt to plan exactly what forces the United States would require to achieve its own objectives, estimating the final size and shape of the US Army and thus the overall requirements for equipment and munitions. This programme would therefore set the scale of the campaigns that the US Army would be able to conduct.[71]

It was remarkable, then, that the bulk of such an important task was given into the hands of a major in the War Plans Department. Marshall had, however, recognised Albert C. Wedemeyer as an unusual and intelligent officer of promise, and it was Wedemeyer who provided the animating force behind the difficult calculations required to develop the Victory Program. Wedemeyer was a Midwesterner who had engaged in much study and reflection during the 17 long years he had spent as a lieutenant. He also had an influential sponsor in the form of his father-in-law, General Stanley D. Embick. Both men believed that the United States had been dragged into the Great War by British and French scheming, and both looked favourably on the views of the America First organisation. Wedemeyer felt little sympathy towards the British and tended to suspect that they were attempting to embroil the United States into the war for their own ends. He had attended the Command and General Staff School at Leavenworth, but, alone amongst his peers in the US Army, he had also studied at the German Kriegsakademie from 1936 to 1938. Wedemeyer's strategic education had thus been conducted by the very army he was now planning to defeat. Perhaps not surprisingly, he felt little enmity towards the Germans, and the great German military theorists whom he had studied at the Kriegsakademie clearly influenced his thinking.

Clausewitz's theories in particular – notably the importance of seeking decisive battle and destroying the enemy at the crucial point – were a clear factor in Wedemeyer's strategic thinking, and they found their way into the American Victory Program. The basic concept of the programme was to resist all Axis penetration of the western hemisphere while maintaining the flow of military aid to the United Kingdom and other countries. Major military commitments were to be avoided in the Far East, since the principal theatre was to be Europe. While Wedemeyer and the army planners accepted the need for indirect approaches such as blockade, propaganda and the use of airpower to wear down and apply pressure on Germany while the United States built up its military strength, the whole programme was predicated on the need for a powerful army, which would take the war to the European continent.[72] The final objective was the 'total defeat of Germany'; Wedemeyer, in an important appendix, made it clear that the United States army could only achieve this through combat:

> We must prepare to fight Germany by actually coming to grips with and defeating her ground forces and definitely breaking her will to combat . . . Air and sea forces will make important contributions, but effective and adequate ground forces must be available to close with and destroy the enemy inside his citadel.[73]

The mission outlined was startlingly simple: engage the German Wehrmacht and defeat it in open battle. The quickest way to end the war was by means of a power drive into Germany that would finish only in the ruins of Berlin. This was a very clear statement of intent, in which the echo of Clausewitz could be heard distinctly. Such a policy would require an enormous army that could match the German army in the field. Since he estimated that the Axis would field 400 divisions by July 1943, Wedemeyer's basic calculations suggested that, in order to provide the traditional ratio of two-to-one superiority in attack, the Allies would require 800 divisions. As the British and others could provide at most 100 divisions, the United States would have to build 700 divisions in an army of 22 million men. Thankfully, it was realised that such calculations led to impossible figures, and it was also recognised that numbers alone could not win the war. The United States would have to compensate for its lack of divisions with air and naval power while achieving local superiority rather than overall superiority in numbers.[74] Nonetheless, the Victory Program envisaged the complete mobilisation of America's vast resources for war. America would outbuild Germany gun for gun, tank for tank, plane for plane. A total of 8,795,658 men would have to be drafted and trained to fight, organised into 215 divisions. Of these, two million would serve in the USAAF, and a total of five million men would need to be transported overseas, requiring the use of at least 2,500 ships.[75]

It is not surprising that many of the army planners and industrialists in Washington, along with the US Navy, were aghast at the implications of such a plan, and the astonishingly ambitious targets of the Victory Program did not survive long. The United States only ever deployed 90, rather than 200, divisions, and the Allied forces generally had little or no advantage in overall numbers during the hard-fought campaigns of 1942–5. Despite this, the Victory Program was essential in providing a clear statement of requirement and a strategy for the United States to follow in the event of war.

The British also reviewed their strategy in the summer of 1941, and the document that was produced showed the divergence of opinion between the two potential allies. Put simply, the security of the United Kingdom and the defence of the Middle East remained the cornerstones of British strategy, but there was no clear vision of how to achieve victory in the war. Britain simply could not afford to mobilise forces on the level of the Victory Program or even provide the numbers of divisions she had fielded in the Great War. British manpower forecasts estimated that, out of a total male population of 16.57 million, a maximum of 2.73 million could be spared for the army by January 1943.[76] By the autumn of 1943, this army might be built up into a force of 59½ divisions. Given that the German army could field at least 250 divisions, it was clear that Britain simply could not build a force to match the Germans. While it was true that Britain had long experience in using local superiority to achieve limited success against a stronger opponent, British planners noted that:

> In the old days, sea power gave us flexibility and we were often able to employ inferior numbers against outlying inferior forces. With the advent of air power, mechanisation and improvements in land communications . . . the advantage has passed to Germany.
>
> Nowhere on the Continent, even if it were possible for us to land, could we subsequently prevent the existing German Army and Air Force concentrating quickly in a strength we could not resist.[77]

These facts were depressing indeed. They meant, simply, that there was no prospect of a British army, even with full American help, being able to land on the continent, 'to close with and destroy the enemy inside his citadel'.[78] Even Churchill had to agree that the army would not play the main role in the defeat of Germany. This meant, of course, that the planners had to consider alternative approaches that might offer some chance, however remote, of actually winning the war. The British had to plan to use blockade, propaganda and bombing almost as ends in themselves to weaken the German war machine. Indeed, the Chiefs of Staff admitted that 'It is in bombing, on a scale undreamt of in the last war, that we find the new weapon on which we must principally depend for the destruction of German economic life and morale.'[79]

Any return to the continent for the army could only be after these methods had worn down German resistance almost to the point of collapse. Britain would not raise another vast army on the scale of the Great War. Instead, it hoped to utilise subversion and propaganda to create armies of 'local patriots' in countries across Europe who would rise in revolt against the Germans. It was believed that, with proper preparation, these methods could 'produce the anarchy of Ireland in 1920 or Palestine in 1936 throughout the chosen theatres of operations'.[80] In essence, the hope was that Europe would liberate itself. The British forces involved would be modern armoured divisions that would hand captured areas over to the patriot forces and continue the drive into Germany.

The British plans seem not to have dwelt on the fact that the British Army itself had successfully quelled similar revolts, nor were the planners overly concerned with what the possible cost to civilian populations across Europe might be. This emphasis upon 'patriot armies' represented a search for another force to replace the manpower and fighting capacity that had been lost when the French army collapsed in 1940. It is clear that, while the Victory Program may have been overoptimistic in terms of its size and scope, Wedemeyer had at least grasped the need to mount a major land campaign to defeat Germany. The British, in their failure to confront this necessity, had produced a plan that was highly unlikely to ever actually work. As Churchill had long realised, the primary and immediate focus for British strategy lay not in the defeat of Germany but in the necessity to persuade the United States to enter the war. The Chiefs of Staff understood that the direct involvement of the United States 'would not only make victory certain, but might also make it swift'.[81]

When Churchill sailed to Placentia Bay to meet with President Roosevelt in August 1941, many of the British representatives expected the Prime Minister to somehow extract an immediate declaration of war from the President. That expectation was, however, based more on British need than a realistic sense of Roosevelt's policies. This face-to-face meeting enabled a real and personal friendship to develop between the two leaders, which became of incalculable benefit to the strength of the Anglo-American alliance during the war. Much business was also conducted on board the warships HMS *Prince of Wales* and USS *Augusta*, resulting in the highly publicised Atlantic Charter. This document, which seemed to offer much at the time, was a 'classic statement of American liberalism' in declaring basic freedoms as shared goals between the two countries.[82] However, while the leaders and their military chiefs discussed much of importance, Roosevelt was determined not to discuss the United States' entry into the war.

The British might have been sorely disappointed that the meeting of the two leaders had not resulted in immediate US entry into the war, but the possibility that Britain and America might well be wartime allies was clearly becoming increasingly likely. And although both countries had taken important ideas from the experience of the Great War, there remained deep suspicions and unhelpful assumptions on both sides. Perhaps the predominant reason for these was the simple fact that neither army really knew the other. Lieutenant General Frederick E. Morgan later explained that it was:

> hard now to realize the depth of the ignorance that existed among British soldiers concerning the United States Army and all its works, and vice versa, before 1939. There can hardly have been a single case of a United States Army officer, other than official attachés, paying more than a formal courtesy visit to any of our military units or establishments in Europe. A certain amount of polo was played but that seems to have been the extent of the liaison that existed between the two forces.[83]

Contact between the two armies had been very limited indeed during the interwar years, and with the exception of the relatively small military missions, little had changed during the first two years of this war. As late as July 1941, Lieutenant General Wemyss, the head of the British Army Staff in Washington, wrote to London with the plea that British officers should be attached to the American Army during their forthcoming manoeuvres:

> I believe that our knowledge of the US Army and its ways is probably more meagre than in the case of European Armies. This is the result of lack of opportunities for direct contacts and the

interchange of officers which elsewhere has been so helpful. We may shortly have the Americans as our Allies, when it will be to our mutual advantage to have officers with practical experience of their Army.[84]

Wemyss realised that it was 'only through attachments of British Officers to American units that we can hope to transmit to them our ideas and tactical doctrine' or that fuller knowledge of American methods could be learned by the British. It seems astonishing that almost no attempt had been made by the British Army to study and understand the American Army. And while the American Special Observer Group had made attempts to learn from British practice, many of their recommendations had fallen on unreceptive ground in America.

Charles Bonesteel, who had been sent as an observer for the Engineer Board of the US Army in December 1940, became very impressed by the British innovation of 'battle schools'. This form of training was highly controversial, as it exposed trainees to live firing and explosions in an attempt to 'innoculate' them to the sights and sounds of battle. Bonesteel wrote a series of reports on these schools and advocated the American adoption of similar methods, but received no response. When he returned to the United States, he managed to interest Brigadier Clarence Huebner in the idea, who then organised another team of observers to report on the British methods. However, Bonesteel was disappointed with their final response, which was that 'there was nothing to be learned, nothing applicable to American training methods, and this delayed our initial basic training involving obstacles, live fire and that stuff for, I think, about a year. God knows how many casualties that we might have avoided.'[85]

One British idea that Bonesteel did manage to interest the US Army in was the Bailey bridge. Designed by Donald Bailey, this was a prefabricated truss bridge with easily transportable components, which required no special tools to construct. Bonesteel was able to work with Frank Besson, a junior officer on the US Engineer Board, to develop specifications for the bridge components so that they could be produced in the United States and Canada.[86] The

Bailey bridge became a standard Allied design and one of the most widely used bridges by British and American engineer units during the war. Bonesteel believed that part of the problem stopping the American take-up of British ideas lay in 'pride of authorship', or what might be termed the 'not invented here' syndrome, but it also lay in a generally poor American opinion of the British Army. Bonesteel thought that the British had learnt important lessons and paid for them in blood, but the withdrawals and defeats they had suffered meant that the attitude of many American officers could be summed up as: 'What the hell have the British got to give us? They just foul it up.'[87]

Perceptions of American impatience with British lessons and hard-won combat experience have to be tempered with the enormity of the challenge facing the US in training this new 'Grand Army of the Republic'. In common with all the armies and soldiers of the Second World War, the US Army was filled with civilians in uniform. In this sense it approximated the eighteenth-century conception of a militia rather than that of professional regular soldiers. These citizen soldiers had to be trained from scratch in an army that was expanding exponentially from a very small and straitened base of experienced officers and regular soldiers. This, as much as any reservations about British methods, explains why Lieutenant General Lesley McNair, of the US Army General Headquarters, and later Head of Army Ground Forces, adopted standardised methods of training that could not be changed easily without throwing the whole developing machine out of gear.

McNair established a four-part training programme that began with 13 weeks of individual and small-unit training. This was followed by a series of tests, with the third phase utilised to correct any major errors or problems that had been identified. The final phase consisted of higher-level formation training for the new divisions, corps and armies that had been created.[88] Across all the training establishments in 1941, the phrase 'Time is Short' was pinned up to instil a wartime spirit of urgency into this peacetime 'emergency' army.

This enormous training programme culminated in the GHQ

manoeuvres in Louisiana and Carolina during the autumn of 1941. These were vast exercises that tested all of the newly formed army corps and armies in wide, sweeping mock-battles. They took place over 30,000 square miles and involved more than 400,000 soldiers, organised into Lieutenant General Ben Lear's Second Army, with two corps and eight divisions, which fought against Lieutenant General Walter Krueger's Third Army of two corps and ten divisions. Over 1,000 aircraft flew in support of the two armies.[89] Although the US Army was, as yet, 'playing at war', the fact that 61 soldiers died during the exercises demonstrates how serious these games really were.[90]

When a Louisiana senator complained about the disruption caused by the exercise, Marshall explained that 'I want the mistake down in Louisiana, not over in Europe, and the only way to do this thing is to try it out, and if it doesn't work, find out what we need to make it work.'[91] While the doctrine for the infantry and artillery was seen as sound, tank doctrine was radically altered as a result of the tests. Some, particularly the tank destroyer doctrine, remained controversial. Marshall also used this time as a means of testing the men he had identified as the true potential commanders of the new army. Dwight Eisenhower performed well as Krueger's Chief of Staff, while George Patton blazed a trail as a talented commander of armour. Men such as Omar Bradley, Leonard T. 'Gee' Gerow and Terry Allen also rose to prominence at least in part due to their performance on the manoeuvres. Over 740,000 men had taken part, and the manoeuvres had served their purpose in weeding out unfit officers, testing untried doctrine, revealing flaws in training, and giving real experience in the movement and supply of large formations.[92]

As the American Army continued its largest ever peacetime exercises before officially entering the war, the British Army in Egypt began one of its most intense and hardest-fought battles of the desert war. Operation Crusader, designed to defeat Rommel's army and relieve the besieged port of Tobruk, opened on 18 November 1941 with a re-equipped force renamed the British Eighth Army. This battle was of particular interest to Fellers and his team of observers because the American M3 light tank was going to be used in action for the first time. A small team of American ordnance officers and men, led by Captain Joseph Colby, who had actually designed the M3 medium tank, had arrived in Egypt in July 'to see the light tank in operation under actual fighting conditions'.[93] It had been decided to equip the 4th Armoured Brigade of the British Eighth Army with the M3 light tanks, and the American detachment established an operating and maintenance school at Tel El Kebir to train the British crews in its use. They were welcomed 'with open arms' and were able to deal with many of the minor problems and snags that afflict most weapons in their first use.[94] By September 1941, Colby could report, through Fellers, that the 'light tank M3 has operated 1500 miles under severe desert conditions without mechanical failure . . . radial aircooled engines, controlled differential, rubber jointed track, general design make American tanks far superior to any on Western Desert from standpoint of reliability and convenience for battle'.[95]

However, while sufficient tanks had arrived to equip the 4th Armoured Brigade for the forthcoming offensive, some of the working difficulties of the Lend-Lease system were revealed in the fact that, as late as 15 October, there were only 260 rounds per gun for 166 American tanks. The British had to plead with the Americans to rush a further 50,000 rounds to the theatre to ensure that the brigade would not run out of ammunition during the coming battle.[96] The following day, 16 October, was a red-letter day in Egypt, since it saw the arrival of the first two American M3 medium tanks at Suez.[97]

On 10 November 1941, Fellers' assessment of the British Eighth Army was that its training was still inadequate, its supply problems had not been solved and its air-to-ground communication remained poor. In spite of these problems, he predicted that the British, mainly due to their 'unquestioned courage and superior air and tank strength will win a decisive much needed victory'.[98] Three days later, Fellers and his team left for the desert to observe the British offensive.[99] Once again his reports began optimistically; in one of his early dispatches he was able to state that 'In savage tank battle November 19th and 20th 164 American M3 tanks of 4th

Armoured Brigade stopped main German tank attack' and that the 'British have achieved complete Brilliant victories'.[100] However, as the fighting progressed and Rommel put all of his forces into the battle, Fellers' reports became more pessimistic and critical of the British performance.

The battles that swirled in the desert around Tobruk were fierce, and with American observers and technicians working and living in British units, it was perhaps inevitable that some of them would become casualties of the fighting. On 23 November, Major Michael Buckley was taken prisoner, and two days later Staff Sergeant Delmer E. Park became one of the first American soldiers to die in the Second World War when he was fatally wounded by gunfire from a German armoured car.[101] Sergeant Floyd E. Coleman, while working with the 8th Hussars, was wounded in the arm by a strafing run from a German aircraft at some point during the battle.[102] Coleman's wound was relatively minor, but under ordinary circumstances he would have been entitled to the Purple Heart medal. Yet since the United States was still neutral and the Middle East observers and technicians were on a sensitive and secret mission, none of these men could receive official American recognition for their service or sacrifice.

It was during this fierce fighting that the British tank crews of 4th Armoured Brigade came to appreciate the qualities of their new American tanks. While the M3 light tank was no better armoured than the equivalent British tank and its 37 mm gun was perhaps marginally inferior to the British two-pounder gun, the crews soon realised that the tank was much more reliable and easy to maintain than its British counterparts. Fellers was able to report that 'Personnel of 4th Armoured Brigade are enthusiastic in their praise of American tanks and developed confidence in their vehicles never before known in British Army. This Action has conclusively demonstrated to all concerned that American Light tank . . . is the most mobile best armoured and by far most reliable vehicle in Western Desert.'[103]

This was high praise indeed for the American tank, and was in marked contrast to the reception accorded to the new British Crusader tank, which also saw its debut in the eponymous battle.

It was almost as if all of the industrial difficulties that had bedevilled British tank production since Dunkirk came home to roost in the Crusader. The tank had been rushed into production and suffered from overheating, problems with maintenance and weak tracks. However, both the British and American tanks were seriously under-gunned compared to their German counterparts. Fellers reported that the M3 light tank was out-ranged by German 50 mm and 75 mm guns, which meant that German tanks could engage it from positions beyond the effective range of the 37 mm gun. This placed the British crews at a significant disadvantage. He also reported on the German use of the 88 mm anti-aircraft gun to cover the flanks of every German armoured formation. It was only during the Crusader battles that the British began to understand that Germans combined their panzer formations with a concealed anti-tank-gun screen. The damage such tactics could inflict on British armoured formations provided a salutary lesson for the American observers. Fellers recommended that the American Army invest in armour-piercing guns of not less than 75 mm but preferably 90 mm calibre. Sadly, these calls appear to have fallen on deaf ears in the army's ordnance department. While development of the new Sherman tank was ongoing, there was no equivalent research into more powerful armament.[104]

The American involvement in Operation Crusader was highly significant and the observers drew important information and lessons on a myriad of subjects from what they saw. What is less clear is the actual impact of this information on the US Army. It would appear that some of the most important and salient points of Fellers' reports were lost in the white noise of an army that was too busy training, preparing and organising to take full notice of the lessons learned by another army in an alien and unfamiliar theatre of war.

Fellers saved his most startling conclusion until the Crusader battle had been fought and won. Tobruk was finally relieved, and with the British now following up Rommel's retreating army, he revealed that he had lost faith in Britain's ability to win the war. By the time he wrote his review of Operation Crusader, the United States was no longer a neutral observer of the conflict. The Japanese

surprise attack on Pearl Harbor on 7 December 1941 had, in one
shocking act, brought America into the war as an active participant.
Despite this, Fellers' recommendation was that the United States
army should have as little to do with the British Army as was
possible. He argued that it was:

> absolutely essential that the United States Army have its own separate
> theatre of operation, separate line of communication, separate base.
> My personal admiration for the bravery and fortitude of the British
> is without limit. However, British methods are lax, their attitude
> casual, their follow up lack[ing], their sense of coordination faulty;
> they cannot fully attune their army doctrine with the tempo of
> mechanical warfare. 15 months intimate association, of which consid-
> erable time was spent observing actual combat, compels me to report
> that I am positive our forces can never work in the same theatre
> effectively and in close harmony with the British.[105]

This was a devastating critique from the one American officer who
had watched the British Army at close quarters.

While Fellers emphasised the distance between the two armies and
recommended that the US Army should remain resolutely aloof
from the British, John Dahlquist recorded the isolation and frustration felt by the members of the American Special Observer Group
in London. This sense of being cut off came not so much from
the British as from the lack of information and orders that
reached the group from Washington. The observers had the distinct
feeling that they had been forgotten, and existed in a backwater,
far from the decision-makers in Washington. When news of Pearl
Harbor came through over the radio, Dahlquist felt 'It was so
incomprehensible that at first I could not believe it.'[106] Over the
next few days, the group were filled with consternation at the
gloomy news from the Pacific, but received little news: 'Still nothing
but fragmentary reports of what happened. Indications are that
there is too much hysteria at home. We are doing very little in the
office and seem to be entirely cut off from the War Department.
The pessimism which has flooded some people . . . is astounding

to me.' When Charles Bolte, the Chief of Staff, became angry over the fact that some of the US offices in London were closed on a Saturday afternoon now that the United States was at war, Dahlquist could only respond that there was practically 'nothing to do', war or no war.[107]

Churchill and his military advisers had rushed to Washington in the wake of the Japanese attack to meet with Roosevelt and the American Chiefs of Staff. At the Washington conference, the British and Americans made a series of critically important decisions that would shape the response of both countries for the rest of the war. However, no news of these events reached the observers in London. It was not until early January 1942 that the mood of despondency and frustration felt by the special observers was swept away. The US and British Chiefs of Staff had come to a series of agreements concerning the conduct of the war, and the long-delayed action became urgent and immediate. On 6 January, Dahlquist recorded that:

> The balloon went up today. War Department cable came in about 10 o'clock telling us that 16,000 troops would arrive in North Ireland in two weeks. Bolte had just called a staff conference to warn us that we should not let down because of lack of objectives. I am now both Plans and G-1. The situation has changed completely overnight.[108]

The American observers themselves underwent a radical change: they were no longer members of a neutral military mission but the advance element for a United States theatre of operations. Uniforms blossomed in Grosvenor Square as the newly designated Headquarters, European Theater of Operations (ETO) sprang into action, and the War Department began preparations to send not hundreds but tens of thousands of troops to Northern Ireland.[109] The experience of the American observers in London was almost an analogy for the United States as a whole. The country had spent 1941 as a special observer of a far-distant war, while preparing her forces for the likely eventuality of active participation. With the Japanese attack on Pearl Harbor, the United States was no longer an observer but had been dragged into the war that had torn Europe apart. For better or for worse, the British and Americans would now have to work alongside one another.

5

Combining the Chiefs

By the winter of 1941, Sir John Dill was mentally and physically exhausted. He had been worn down by the unremitting crises of 1940–1 and the constant criticism of Winston Churchill. Unable to conceal his contempt, Churchill had taunted him with the nickname 'Dilly Dally'. While dealing with the Prime Minister and Britain's stricken strategic situation, Dill had also had to cope with the paralysis and subsequent death of his first wife. It seemed that he had reached the end of both his tether and his military career. When Churchill decided to rid himself of his unsatisfactory CIGS and replace him with General Alan Brooke, who had made such a success of preparing the army's defences in Britain, Dill was consigned to suffer true military oblivion: he was to go to India as Governor of Bombay.[1]

Brooke took up his new post on 1 December 1941, and immediately made an impression. John Kennedy knew that Brooke could be 'tough and impatient' but also found that 'it was a delight to work with him. He was quick and decided; his freshness made a new impact; he infected the War Office and the Chiefs of Staff with his own vitality; the change of tempo was immediate and immense.'[2] But just six days after Brooke had begun to drive the War Office forward, the Japanese attack on Pearl Harbor completely altered the strategic and military situation. Churchill was determined to go to Washington not only to thrash out the details of the alliance with the United States as soon as possible but also to ensure that 'American help to this country does not dry up'.[3]

Even though many members of the American administration had wanted to delay the arrival of the British until after the New

Year, Churchill and his entourage sailed across the Atlantic immediately, braving stormy seas aboard the battleship HMS *Duke of
York* to reach the Hampton Roads on 22 December. The Prime
Minister was rapidly installed in the White House, and the personal
friendship between the two leaders continued to grow, feeding
suspicion amongst American military leaders that the British were
gaining unfettered access to, and thus undue influence with, the
President. This highly unusual situation also resulted in Dill's rescue
from oblivion. Only he had the knowledge and experience to carry
the day with the Americans at such short notice, and so Brooke
remained in London acting as the sole military adviser to Clement
Attlee, the Deputy Prime Minister, whilst Dill went to Washington
in his place. This meant that Dill, not Brooke, would be present
as the British Army's representative at the Arcadia conference, held
during December 1941 and January 1942. Brooke then argued forcefully with Churchill to retain Dill as his representative in Washington
after the talks had finished. This eventually resulted in his transformation from a burnt-out and discredited CIGS into a vital prop
of the Anglo-American alliance in Washington.

A large number of subjects were discussed during the meetings,
which were held on twelve occasions between 24 December 1941
and 14 January 1942, though no real agreement or decisions were
reached. The very first item concerned the defence of the British
Isles, which was followed by the possible dispatch of US heavy
bombers to Britain and then the long-foreseen relief of British
troops in Northern Ireland and Iceland.[4] From the very beginning,
all participants accepted the principle, if not the spirit, of dealing
with Germany first before tackling Japan. Since gaining a reaffirma-
tion of the 'Germany first' policy had been one of Churchill's main
reasons for rushing to Washington, he was broadly pleased with
the result of the discussions. However, at the same time as
confirming this policy, Arcadia also included protracted discussions
on the need for reinforcements in the Far East due to the rapidly
deteriorating situation. Longer-term plans were also discussed for
the occupation of French North Africa in an operation code-named
Gymnast, which by the end of the conference had become
Super-Gymnast. It was agreed that neither Britain nor America

had the forces to conduct the operation independently, but that jointly sufficient troops could be scraped together. Although planning documents did mention a return to the European continent, it was acknowledged that this was only likely in 1943.

Much of the debate and discussion at Arcadia dealt with broad issues rather than details. One of the major reasons for this was that neither ally wished to commit itself too early to a particular course of action. The other major reason lay in the state of indescribable chaos existing in Washington so soon after Pearl Harbor,[5] which caught the British by surprise. They had long understood the necessity for efficient machinery in order to coordinate the demands of managing a global empire. All these organs of state had, by late 1941, been hammered together by Churchill, who kept tight personal control over them and was also served by a supremely efficient secretariat, which acted to bind together British decision-making. In Washington, Ian Jacob, Military Assistant Secretary to the War Cabinet and a key member of Churchill's entourage, found that, to his eyes, 'the American machine of Government seems hopelessly disorganized'.[6] It soon transpired that the Americans had no such thing as a joint secretariat that took and maintained agreed minutes for each meeting. Instead, Admiral Stark and General Marshall each gave his own 'idea of what had happened'.[7] The time-honoured suspicion and rivalry between the US Navy and army meant that, as Jacob identified, they had no established way of sharing information. At one point during the meetings, it was reported that the Joint Planning Committee had agreed a particular paper. Admiral Stark asked: 'Do you mean a paper agreed by the Army, the Navy, and the British?'[8] This comment revealed the enormous gulf between the two American services, which would have to cooperate in order to win the war. Given this state of affairs, the British soon realised that their own ideas concerning the orderly management of government machinery would not necessarily work in cooperation with the Americans. Instead, they found that it was much more efficient to deal direct with the key decision-makers.

Marshall was only too well aware of the state of disorganisation in the War Department, and realised that many of the administrative

structures had barely changed since Pershing's day. He had hoped
to delay the arrival of the British until the New Year to enable
him to conduct a root-and-branch reorganisation of his department
before having to sort out major strategy with America's new allies.
It was for these reasons, amongst others, that he called Eisenhower
to the War Department five days after Pearl Harbor to serve as the
Assistant Director of the War Plans Division. This was a grave
disappointment for Eisenhower, who had been trying to get a
posting to command troops for well over a year. In his correspondence with his long-time friend George Patton, Eisenhower had
revealed his deep desire to lead troops and leave staff posts
behind. What he could not know was that Marshall had identified
him as an officer of high promise who could be relied upon to get
results. His long and weary apprenticeship as a staff officer under
General Douglas MacArthur in the thirties, and as Chief of Staff
of the Third Army in 1940–1, had prepared him not for the leadership of troops in the field but for command at an altogether higher
level.

Eisenhower was thus thrust into the chaos of the War Department,
and indeed the Arcadian discussions, straight from the concerns of
managing an army staff. Along with his new colleagues at the War
Plans Division, he was faced with a truly daunting situation: a
desperate and worsening position in the Far East, and the first
serious discussions with America's new, strange and rather awkward
British allies. Eisenhower noted in his diary on 5 January that 'The
conversations with the British grow wearisome. They're difficult
to talk to, apparently afraid someone is trying to tell them what to
do and how to do it. Their practice of war is dilatory.'[9] Eisenhower's
comments demonstrate that not all of the faults lay on the American
side during the discussions.

Nonetheless, perhaps the most important and significant aspect
of the Arcadia conference was the act of the British and American
Chiefs of Staff actually meeting together around the table. This
represented a physical acceptance of the concept of the Combined
Chiefs of Staff: that British and American strategy in the war would
be decided through face-to-face meetings between the respective
military heads of each service, who, in dialogue with the Prime

Minister and President, would then hammer out the priorities, resources and purpose of Allied strategy. This, in and of itself, was of enormous importance, since it ensured that the British and Americans would decide upon an agreed policy for the war based on open discussion and debate. The wonder was not that Allied strategy was fiercely debated and threw up all kinds of arguments and disagreements over the subsequent months and years, but that the debates and discussions took place at all.

Christmas Day 1941 saw Roosevelt and Churchill take part in the White House celebrations of the season, but it was also the day on which George Marshall raised an issue he saw as fundamental to Allied cooperation: unity of command. Marshall expressed his views forcibly, stating that in each Allied theatre there must be one man in command of the air, ground and maritime forces. He went on:

> We cannot manage by cooperation. Human frailties are such that there would be emphatic unwillingness to place portions of troops under another service. If we make a plan for unified command now, it will solve nine-tenths of our troubles . . . I favour one man being in control, but operating under a controlled directive from here. We had to come to this in the First World War, but it was not until 1918 that it was accomplished and much valuable time, blood, and treasure had been needlessly sacrificed. If we could decide on a unified command now, it would be a great advance over what was accomplished during the World War.[10]

Marshall was making a heartfelt plea based on his experience of the Great War and his conviction that the British committee system of command by a triumvirate of service chiefs in each theatre was unworkable and positively dangerous. While Jacob considered this to be merely a 'parrot cry' of Marshall's and not a serious proposition, Vivian Dykes believed that it was 'a fine bold conception – but who is the *man*?'[11] No one present at the time could possibly have realised that the man who would make the principle of Allied supreme command a reality was in fact participating in the conference: Brigadier General Dwight D. Eisenhower.

The one area where it was possible at the time to consider a single supreme commander was South East Asia, which became known as the ABDA Command (American-British-Dutch-Australian). Marshall had attempted to sweeten the pill of unified command by proposing the appointment of a British officer, General Sir Archibald Wavell, for the role. He gave Eisenhower the task of producing the draft directive from the Combined Chiefs of Staff to this new supreme commander. Eisenhower later commented that memories of the episode could still make him shudder:

> We spent days in the effort; we sweated blood to be fair in defining under what conditions a man could appeal to his own government, and what were the exact limitations on the authority of the Supreme Commander, etc. And the result was just as worthless as the paper it was written on. The only thing of value that possibly came out of it was the realization, by all those who worked on it, of its worthlessness.[12]

All the wrangling was of no help in shoring up the Allied position in the Far East: the ABDA area fell to the Japanese almost immediately after the conference and before Wavell had had a chance to organise his meagre forces. Yet the effort in thrashing out a common directive did serve a very valuable purpose. Firstly, Marshall's insistence on the principle of unity of command was accepted, however grudgingly, by the British. Secondly, the Allied staffs had had an object lesson in the futility of drafting a directive that covered all eventualities and circumstances: when Eisenhower became an Allied Supreme Commander later that year, his directive from the Combined Chiefs allowed him much more latitude and freedom than that written for Wavell.

Perhaps the most important issues discussed at Arcadia were the arrangements for how collaboration between the Allies should be continued after the conference. It was realised that there could only be one Combined Chiefs of Staff organisation, and the Americans were determined that it should operate in Washington. There was considerable doubt during the conference over the shape and purpose of any permanent organisation for cooperation. After all,

Washington operated not on smoothly oiled government machinery but through a web of personal relationships. Many people involved advocated an inner council of Dill, Marshall and Admiral Ernest King, the head of the US Navy, to actually decide on strategy, with an official Combined Chiefs of Staff meeting once a month 'for purely formal purposes'.[13] In the event, the Combined Chiefs of Staff Committee became a living organisation where the complex and intractable issues of Allied strategy were thrashed out face-to-face in weekly meetings. This meant that the friendship and mutual regard that had already developed between Dill and Marshall by the end of the Arcadia conference promoted rather than eroded the importance of the formal meetings.[14]

In many respects, the friendship between Dill and Marshall was highly unusual, yet in others perhaps perfectly understandable. Both men were the archetype of their service: Dill with a distinguished military career stretching back to the Boer War, Marshall with an equal reputation in the American Army. But whereas Dill's military assistant from December 1942 until 1944, Reginald Bourne, remembered his superior fondly 'It is difficult to convey to those who never met him the aura of integrity which wrapped Dill like a mantle; few Generals have inspired such deep affection'[15] Marshall's demeanour, particularly to subordinates, might be characterised as piercing and glacial. Marshall was not on first-name terms with anyone; even Roosevelt only called him 'George' once, and quickly learnt his error. These two men, who had both experienced the real loneliness of command as head of their service in difficult times, came to understand and trust one another implicitly. Their friendship, founded on mutual regard, trust and common purpose, came to smooth over many of the roughest patches of Allied argument during the war.

However, no individual relationship could have made something as complicated as the Combined Chiefs of Staff a reality. Just as important was the development of a well-oiled administration to ensure that communication between the allies, and between different departments, remained open. Central to this was the appointment of two very different but complementary military secretaries. Just as it was decided that Dill was to remain in

Washington as Churchill's personal representative, so it was decided that Vivian Dykes would not return to London to take up the post of Director of Plans in the War Office but rather would remain as the British military secretary for the Combined Chiefs of Staff. Dykes was a thoroughly efficient military secretary with wide experience and expertise based on his close working relationship with General Sir Hastings Ismay, and became an essential part of the attempt to persuade the Americans to adopt British methods of working. During Arcadia, he confided to his diary: 'They have apparently realised that their efforts at keeping minutes in parallel with ours make them look too amateurish as they now accept ours as agreed after vetting the drafts. This is a big advance.'[16]

Dykes' counterpart and eventual superior on the secretariat was an equally impressive American officer: Walter Bedell Smith. He had first attracted Marshall's attention at the Infantry School, Fort Benning, in 1930–1. In October 1939, he was appointed as Assistant Secretary to the General Staff, where he quickly became one of Marshall's key staff officers. Marshall needed men who had the confidence to deal with complex problems and make decisions themselves without waiting for his approval. Officers newly appointed to the General Staff would often find themselves in his office being asked for an assessment of an issue and suggestions as to how to resolve the matter, a test that many otherwise admirable officers failed under Marshall's steely stare, but Bedell Smith thrived in this environment.[17] When, on 4 July 1941, Bedell Smith took over as Secretary to the General Staff, he essentially became the chief of staff to the Chief of Staff. He revelled in his reputation as 'the toughest son-of-a bitch in the War Department', but he had also become a supremely effective staff officer and an indispensable assistant to Marshall.[18] Just as the friendship between Marshall and Dill became a powerful support to the Combined Chiefs of Staff, so too did the growing respect and friendship between Walter Bedell Smith and Vivian Dykes. As the respective heads of the US and British secretariats for the Combined Chiefs, Smith and Dykes worked together to sort out the agendas and agree the minutes of the meetings. Slowly but surely they ironed out many of the earlier problems of process, thus ensuring that the meetings of the

Combined Chiefs of Staff could focus on the real issues of Allied strategy.

Brooke, who had not been a party to the discussions in Washington, was shocked to learn of the new arrangements when Churchill returned to London in January 1942. The new CIGS was appalled that the British had surrendered their right to host (and thereby manage) the deliberations of the Combined Chiefs of Staff. He spluttered that they had 'sold our birthright for a plate of porridge'.[19] Brooke was convinced that the meetings should have been held in London, where the wide experience and knowledge of the British regarding global organisation and decision-making could have been utilised to best effect. While in one sense he may have been right, he was swimming against the tide. Although in the winter of 1941 the United States was still scrabbling to mobilise its industrial and military strength, and reeling from the blows in the Far East, it would soon become a military and industrial giant of far greater strength and power than the United Kingdom. The Anglo-American alliance would not be a British show with a walk-on part for the latecomers. Brooke's unwillingness to accept that the power of the United States made the location of the combined organisation inevitable was to become a theme of his tenure as CIGS and ensured that his relations with Marshall were never quite as cordial as those of his predecessor.

Although the Combined Chiefs of Staff was established to organise and manage the demands of a truly global conflict, the disastrous course of the war in the Far East became a major preoccupation of the Allies during the first few months of 1942. When, on 16 February, Major General 'Gee' Gerow handed over charge of the War Plans Division to Eisenhower, he joked: 'Well, I got Pearl Harbor on the book; lost the Philippine Islands, Singapore, Sumatra, and all the NEI [North East Indies] north of the barrier. Let's see what you can do.'[20] The Allied situation looked as bleak as it ever would do. For the British, the disasters in the Far East had been capped by the fall of Singapore on 15 February. The loss of this vital naval base and fortress destroyed Britain's military position and prestige in the Far East, and was one of the largest nails in the coffin of the Empire.

With such disasters making the headlines in early 1942, it is not surprising that the augmentation of American support in the Middle East continued unremarked. Yet such support was not only a demonstration of American assistance in a vital strategic area, but also a means of ensuring that the growing stream of Lend-Lease equipment was put to good use. In November 1941, the increasing number of American servicemen in Egypt had been reorganised into a technical mission to supervise Lend-Lease support under the command of Brigadier General Russell L. Maxwell.[21] One of the members of this mission, whose work ensured that Lend-Lease weapons and ammunition functioned properly, was George B. Jarrett. He was a lowly US Army ordnance officer, but his experience demonstrated just how closely the British and Americans could work when there was a spirit of friendliness and cooperation. Jarrett was what the British would term a 'boffin', and by his own admission was 'teched in the head'.[22] He had been fascinated with weapons and ammunition since he was a boy, and during the twenties he had even made trips over to France to collect all kinds of materiel from the First World War battlefields. By 1930, he had collected so many weapons and assortments that he was able to open a museum on the steel pier at Atlantic City. Nine years later, his collection included 12 field pieces, a tank, eight aircraft and a collection of military uniforms from around the world. Jarrett was an obsessive collector. However, he also possessed an unrivalled knowledge of weapons and ordnance, and, in particular, of the munitions that had been used by the US Army. In November 1939, he was recruited to the Ordnance School at Aberdeen Proving Ground, where he could put his specialist interest to use. In February 1942, after serving two years as the head of the Ammunition Section at Aberdeen, Jarrett was sent to Egypt to work as an ammunition advisor in Maxwell's new mission in Cairo, where he was one of only 22 US Army personnel in the Middle East, a figure that would grow to over 13,000 by the end of the year.

Real problems were by now emerging in the British use of American equipment, most notably the M3 medium tanks that had been so hurriedly ordered by Dewar's mission in 1940 and which began arriving in volume during the spring of 1942. British Army ordnance officers were unfamiliar with American tanks, and the ammunition for use in the M3 was different to the British equivalents. Jarrett's main task became testing the American ammunition and then training the British how to use it effectively. He worked closely with the artillery office at GHQ Middle East, which included Lieutenant Colonel Neville, Major Northy RAOC, and Lieutenant Colonel Berkeley-Miller RAC.

The British had realised that their tanks and anti-tank guns were becoming progressively outmatched by German armour throughout the course of 1941. The standard British tank and anti-tank gun, the two-pounder, was now decisively out-ranged by the better armed and more heavily armoured German tanks. Not surprisingly, the M3 medium tank with its heavy armour and 75 mm gun received an 'enthusiastic welcome' in the Middle East. Unfortunately, much of the ammunition was of poor quality. Jarrett found that the supplies of US 75 mm high explosive ammunition and fuses that had been ordered by Dewar's mission were surplus stocks of First World War vintage, and were not suitable for tank use. Fired from a tank gun on a flat trajectory, the fuse would not activate, and the shell would simply bounce across the desert without exploding. It was in this situation that Jarrett's in-depth knowledge born from his passion for ammunition made a real difference. He realised that original French 'creep' fuses would fit the shells and produce the desired effect. A special mission was sent to Syria to source fuses from the large quantities of ammunition that had fallen into Allied hands after the campaign against the Vichy French forces there. Over 90,000 French fuses, most of them dating from 1915, were discovered and sent to Egypt, where they could be fitted to the tank shells. Luckily this local expedient worked, since it was not until October 1942 that the new round and fuse, obtained on Lend-Lease, became available.

A similar problem emerged with the armour-piercing ammunition for the tank. Once again, the US Ordnance Department was still designing and testing the anti-tank shot for the 75 mm gun when the British Tank Mission desperately needed to source ammunition. Instead of waiting for the more effective round, the mission placed orders for a 75 mm monobloc solid anti-tank round, which was produced in America, Canada and the UK to meet the demand. Perhaps not surprisingly, this ammunition was of poor quality and ineffective against German tanks. After test-firing a shot at a British Valentine tank with successful results, the tests were repeated, at Jarrett's insistence, against a captured German tank. He 'was heart-sick as the projectiles began bouncing off the hull'.[23] A few of the new American rounds were ordered by Jarrett for testing, but it was clear that bulk quantities would not arrive in time for the coming battle. Major Northy, an Australian serving in the RAOC Ammunition Section, came up with an unorthodox but brilliant idea. Using captured German 7.5 cm ammunition designed for the Panzer IV, he realised that by pulling the German round out of its cartridge case, grinding down its rotating band, and then fitting it into the American cartridge case, a much better anti-tank round could be improvised. Seventeen thousand rounds of this composite ammunition were produced and used successfully during the Gazala battles in May and June 1942. It is not too much to say that without these expedients, the debut of the M3 medium tank would have been very disappointing. Instead, Bonner Fellers was able to provide early information on its good performance.

The American M3 medium tank – named the Grant by the British – fitted with the British turret, proved to be an extremely important weapon for the British armoured regiments: it was the first tank that could outmatch the German opposition. Even though the positioning of the 75 mm gun was awkward, it could fire an extremely effective high-explosive shell (once modified by Jarrett), which finally gave British crews the opportunity to deal with German anti-tank guns. The Grant was admired for its reliability, hitting power and strong armour, and it came to be known during the campaign as the 'ELH', or 'Egypt's Last Hope'. In a campaign in which Royal Armoured Corps crews had been trained to accept that their weapon was the decisive element on the battlefield, the Grant stood out as the most powerful tank available to the British. The advent of the M3 medium tank on the battlefield was an achievement of which the American Ordnance Department, American industry, the British Tank Mission and George Jarrett could be justly proud. All had played their part in ensuring its success.

Jarrett was subsequently ordered by General Maxwell to establish the US Ordnance Training School, as part of the Royal Armoured Corps School at Abbassia. This opened with 16 students on 4 May 1942 with the aim of training British tank crew and fitters, who could then pass on specialised instructions on the repair and maintenance of US tanks. Jarrett later explained:

> Bill [Captain Summerbell, his deputy] and I always got along well with all the British officers, largely because we had a job to do in the interests of the Allied war effort, and made an effort to. There have been countless incidents where jealousies and differences of opinion have made harmonious working difficult between the British and American officers in Middle East and later on in SHAEF [the Supreme Headquarters Allied Expeditionary Force]. Bill and I were determined to make the grade and deliver some finely trained men to the 8th Army.[24]

Within two weeks, Jarrett had taught a combined group of British and Americans, who then went round the British armoured brigades to carry on the instruction in their units. Jarrett eventually returned to Aberdeen Proving Ground in December 1942, with a glowing report from Colonel E. S. Gruver, his commanding officer: 'this officer has been an outstanding example of unselfish and energetic assistance to our Allies in the Middle East'.[25]

Jarrett's brief collaboration with the British Army was crucial in ensuring that the Lend-Lease system actually gave the British battle-winning tanks. It was perhaps easier for a technical specialist to work cordially with other like-minded individuals, but his experience demonstrates that British and American soldiers could indeed work together very effectively towards a common goal. However, examples such as Jarrett's of 'unselfish and energetic assistance' have tended to be obscured by the fierce strategic disagreements that began between the leaders of the British and American armies in the spring of 1942.

It was not surprising that there were severe disagreements in the realm of strategy. Marshall and Brooke were not simply looking after their own personal interests and careers; they were responsible for vital aspects of national interest. Their decisions affected millions of citizen soldiers, and both men were only too conscious of the heavy burden of responsibility that lay on their shoulders. It was essential that they held to their convictions and argued to the last extremity for what they believed to be the correct course of action, because these were issues that could decide the lives of thousands of men.

In the aftermath of Arcadia, and his reorganisation of the War Department, what Marshall needed most of all was a coherent strategy for the conduct of the war. While Gymnast, the invasion of French North Africa, had been considered at the Arcadia conference, the Combined Chiefs of Staff had agreed to drop the operation in March 1942, due to the worsening situation in Libya.[26] Marshall thus needed a single target that would focus all the efforts in training and production of the US Army.[27] In fact, Eisenhower had already expressed the fundamental idea. At the height of his frustration in dealing with the numerous crises at the War Department, he had written:

> We've got to go to Europe and fight, and we've got to quit wasting resources all over the world, and still worse, wasting time. If we're to keep Russia in, save the Middle East, India, and Burma, we've got to begin slugging with air at West Europe, to be followed by a land attack as soon as possible.[28]

Eisenhower had, in a few brief words, encapsulated what became the American Army's strategy for victory. Marshall was equally convinced that the best way to win the war was an attack upon Germany at the earliest opportunity. Any other operation would simply waste time and resources that could be better spent on the main effort. These basic concepts remained at the heart of Marshall's thinking for the next two years, until the invasion of Europe finally took place.

In February 1942, Eisenhower had written a study of the South-West Pacific that had emphasised the need for a definite plan of operations in Europe. While he recognised that defence in the

Pacific remained important, he saw that 'an attack through Western Europe' as soon as possible would provide the United States with the shortest route to victory. The British Isles had already become an established base for US troops and provided the perfect platform to build up forces for such an invasion, as well as offering the shortest shipping routes across the Atlantic to move the vast quantities of men and materiel that would be required.[29] This was a coherent and logical military strategy, which had, after all, been outlined in Wedemeyer's Victory Program. However, Marshall and his planners also understood the insistent demands of the US Navy for greater resources for the Pacific, as well as growing public clamour for action against the enemy that had brought the United States into the war.[30] If 'Germany First' was to become a reality, it also had to happen fast.

By 27 March, Eisenhower and the War Department planners had prepared an outline plan for 'Operations in Western Europe', which became known as the Marshall Memorandum. There were three main parts to the plan. The first was the proposal to concentrate the majority of American combat troops in the United Kingdom. This would require the shipping of vast quantities of men and materiel to Britain in an operation code-named Bolero. The second phase of the plan, code-named Roundup, involved a cross-Channel attack in the spring of 1943 with as much force as could be mustered: a total of 48 American and British divisions supported by 5,800 aircraft. However, the American planners were also concerned to make Europe an 'active sector' as soon as possible, and proposed an operation, code-named Sledgehammer, which would be mounted in the autumn of 1942 and would see five divisions making an emergency landing in France. This was to cover the twin eventualities of a Russian collapse and, conversely, an unexpected weakening of the German position.[31] The memorandum was just the sort of plan Marshall had been looking for, and he was quickly able to win the support of Stimson, the Secretary of State for War, and Roosevelt. Indeed, Roosevelt directed Marshall and Hopkins to go to London and secure the support of the British for the plan as soon as possible.[32]

This meant that Marshall paid his first trip to the British Isles,

in the company of Harry Hopkins and Wedemeyer, in early April
1942. While he did tour a number of airbases and make time to
visit the recently arrived army units in Northern Ireland, his primary
purpose was to secure British agreement for his aggressive strategy
against Germany. However, even before he had arrived in London,
the British Combined Staff planners had calculated that a return
to the continent in September 1942 was not a practical proposition.
They noted that by 15 September 1942, 'there would be only 2½
armoured and 13 other divisions available, instead of the 10 armoured
and 18 other divisions estimated to be required', which led them to
the conclusion that 'it is not possible during 1942 to put the ground
forces considered necessary on the Continent'.[33] Their estimates did
reveal that 'An invasion of the Continent early in 1943 is a possibility,
provided that Russia is still actively fighting and containing the
majority of the German forces, and provided that an early decision
is made to concentrate the maximum effort upon this operation
and to accept such reductions in the scope of operations in other
theatres as may be required.'[34] Ultimately, these obvious caveats
would cause the greatest arguments and disagreements in Allied
strategy during the war. While Marshall continued to insist that
the alliance should 'concentrate the maximum effort' on the cross-
Channel attack, the British constantly sought to increase 'the scope
of operations in other theatres', namely the Mediterranean.

Marshall expounded his strategy to the British chiefs on 9 April
1942. The virtues of speed and decision were inherent in the
plan. Indeed, the War Department's ability to identify the centre
of gravity of their opponents, even in the midst of the chaos
and uncertainty of spring 1942, was a major achievement in itself.
The centrepiece of Marshall's vision was Roundup: the invasion
of France in April 1943. The United States would provide the
lion's share of the resources for this invasion in the form of one
million men in 30 divisions supported by 3,250 aircraft.[35] Certainly
none of the British were in disagreement with Bolero, the first
element of Marshall's plan. The shipping of vast American
resources in men and materiel to the United Kingdom could only
ensure Britain's survival. The Token Force of the ABC conversations would become a mighty American Army based in Britain

for the projected invasion. The British understood that such a concentration would 'fit all eventualities', including a cross-Channel attack or the dispatch of American forces elsewhere, while also ensuring the defence of the United Kingdom in the event of a Russian collapse.[36] Equally, the British Chiefs of Staff had few concrete objections to the idea of a return to the European continent in 1943.

The devil, as with most strategic visions, lay in the detail. The real difficulty in Marshall's memorandum lay in the provision of shipping and landing craft. These issues were to dog Allied decision-making for the next two years. The American planners admitted that they could only transport 40 per cent of the American troops required, which meant that the majority would have to be carried in British ships. Meanwhile, the current lack of landing craft could only be made good through a vastly expanded building programme, which as yet had not been agreed.[37] However, the real sticking point was Sledgehammer, the proposed landing in France in the autumn of 1942. Brooke wrote in his diary that Marshall 'gave us a long talk on his views concerning the desirability of starting western front next September and that the USA forces would take part. However, the total force which they could transport by then only consisted of 2½ divisions! No very great contribution. Furthermore they had not begun to realise what all the implications of their proposed plan were!'[38]

It is clear that neither the British planners nor Brooke believed Sledgehammer to be a feasible operation of war even before Marshall arrived in London, yet no one disabused the head of the American Army of his illusions. This led Wedemeyer to accuse the British chiefs not of a personal 'will to deceive' but of 'elastic scruples' when the issues concerned matters of British national interest.[39] Wedemeyer painted a traditional picture of a perfidious Albion being served by wily military advisers who used 'the British power of diplomatic finesse' to subvert and undermine Marshall's ideas while seeming to support them, but the truth was perhaps rather more prosaic.[40] The scale and scope of Marshall's proposals seem to have taken the British chiefs by surprise. Geoffrey Bourne, a British officer working in the Joint Staff Mission in Washington who accompanied Marshall on his trip, commented that the British planners were tending to view the war 'in several distinct and separate sections' rather than as a whole.[41] It seemed to him that the British planners had not 'formulated any definite ideas upon United strategy as opposed to purely British strategy'.[42] He felt that they:

> had never contemplated anything on the scale of the Marshall Plan. They had to temporise and say that they were examining it . . . This probably explains the ready acceptance of the Marshall Plan by the British Chiefs of Staff, but it seems curious that the suggestion and the broad outline of this Continental plan should have come from US and not from British sources.[43]

It would appear that the British chiefs and planners had some difficulty in properly visualising the magnitude of the operation Marshall was proposing. The planners had been considering Roundup, phase two of Marshall's plan, as an attack by five brigades from a total assaulting force of ten divisions. It would appear that the British had been fighting under the severe constraints of limited resources for so long that they had lost the ability to think big.

These circumstances meant that the British chiefs were highly unlikely to develop their full reservations concerning the plan during the initial meetings. The eventual fate of Bolero, Roundup and Sledgehammer was as much to do with the working through of all the implications as it was to do with any British duplicity. It took time for the British to understand the full implications of the plan, even if they did not quite understand that all three elements of the memorandum had to be accepted if Marshall was to have any chance of seeing his strategy through to fruition.

In fact, time was just as important as location to Marshall and the War Department planners. While the British chiefs could afford to wait, Marshall could not. Indeed, all previous British strategy had been predicated on the basis of using the lengthy process of air bombardment, naval blockade and time to weaken the Germans before beginning to consider a ground invasion. While the British may have considered the American plan a mere sketch, which showed no appreciation of the real consequences, and Brooke certainly considered that Marshall possessed more than a little strategic naivety, they did not fully understand the political and inter-service rivalries that shaped Marshall's thinking. Marshall knew he had to win through the Washington political process before anything else could happen. He needed ground combat in Europe in 1942 to justify the concentration of the US Army in the United Kingdom – both of which would lead to the eventual full invasion in 1943. The absence of such activity would only serve to intensify the demands of the US Navy, General MacArthur and the American public for greater action in the Pacific. Equally important was the fear, widespread amongst the War Department planners, that Russian resistance might well collapse in 1942 if the Allies did not provide direct assistance by distracting the Germans. It is clear that the British did not fully understand this imperative in the spring of 1942, but this did not mean that they were guilty of Machiavellian duplicity.

In the week-long discussions, the British emphasised the importance of holding the Middle East, India, Burma and the Indian Ocean. The Americans understandably saw this as an expression of Britain's imperial interest that ignored the main imperative of keeping the Russians in the war. However, on 14 April 1942, the British chiefs agreed in principle, although expressing more than a few reservations, to Marshall's proposal that the main offensive effort would take place in 1943, and also that planning would begin for an emergency landing in September 1942 should it prove necessary. The detailed planning for both Roundup and Sledgehammer was to be done in London, a decision that ultimately gave the British ownership of the details and problems involved in both operations. In the case of Sledgehammer, this would eventually amount to a form of veto.[44]

Marshall had managed to wring agreement, if only in principle, from the British, indicating sound progress. Dill however, in a letter to Brooke, mentioned that while Marshall had been 'most successful in selling his plan to you . . . he has not yet sold it to Admiral King or the US Naval Staff'.[45] Dill realised that King and the navy were 'still concentrating almost entirely on the Pacific war'; he had read one navy document that mentioned 'the US Army's Bolero plan', which hardly inspired confidence that Marshall's strategy had their complete support.[46] In fact, the US Navy's preoccupation with rebuilding its naval strength in the Pacific overrode any other considerations. Dill knew that the army and navy staff found it difficult to reconcile these deep internal divisions, and since 'they do not like to wash their dirty linen in our presence, they naturally do not relish trying to put down United strategy in black and white'.[47] Marshall and his staff officers had to fight another campaign during May 1942 to prevent further resources being drained away to the Pacific. Although Marshall was able to wring further confirmation from the President of the priority accorded to Bolero, the fact was that its status was never fully secure in the near-constant duelling between the army and navy. Ultimately, the United States war effort approximated an army war in Europe and a navy war in the Pacific.

A further demonstration of the US Army's commitment to the European theatre occurred in May 1942, when a high-profile display of American Lend-Lease equipment was staged at Horse Guards Parade in London. This included the first Sherman tank to reach Britain, and when Churchill visited the display on 12 May 1942, he happily clambered into it.[48] Although the significance of the name 'Michael' given to the tank seems to have eluded the Prime Minister and the admiring throng, this was in fact a sincere American gesture in honour of Michael Dewar and the British Tank Mission. The advent of the Sherman tank represented the culmination of the close Anglo-American cooperation over tank design and production.

As part of maintaining the momentum behind his memorandum, and to 'effectuate closer cooperation between the US and British Planning agencies', Marshall sent Eisenhower, Generals Henry H. Arnold, head of the US Army Air Force, Brehon B. Somervell, head of the Army Services of Supply, and Mark Clark, Chief of Staff Army Ground Forces, on a visit to London in May 1942 to observe and assist in the planning for Bolero and Roundup.[49] Long discussions were held with General Chaney and the American and British planners in London on the range of issues thrown up by the implications of the movement of vast numbers of men and supplies across the Atlantic. After a full conference with General Chaney and his staff, Eisenhower visited a British Army exercise in Kent. While attending a lecture concerning the exercise, Eisenhower, a heavy smoker at the best of times, lit up a cigarette. Almost immediately, the British Army commander broke off from his exposition and, sniffing the air, demanded to know who was smoking. Eisenhower, rather taken aback, replied that he was. The British officer said curtly, 'I don't permit smoking in my office', making it quite clear that his American visitor should put out his cigarette forthwith, and Eisenhower did so. Thus it was that Major General Dwight D. Eisenhower and Lieutenant General Bernard Law Montgomery first met. It was not a particularly auspicious start to a relationship that has come to dominate a significant part of the received memory of the Anglo-American alliance,[50] although Eisenhower nonetheless recorded his impression that Montgomery was 'a decisive type who appears to be extremely energetic and professionally able'.[51]

Eisenhower's first meeting with Admiral Mountbatten was more cordial. As Head of Combined Operations, Mountbatten was responsible for the use of commandos and the development of amphibious assault tactics. The two men quickly discovered a mutual regard for each other. Brooke, on the other hand, fenced determinedly with Eisenhower during a Chiefs of Staff meeting over the issue of a single commander for the assault echelon in any amphibious landing.[52] Even though it was clear that the British Chiefs of Staff were beginning to raise all kinds of doubts and questions concerning Sledgehammer and Roundup, this seemed to be in order to settle the myriad problems and questions that were bound to arise. Soon after Eisenhower's return to Washington, Marshall informed him that he was considering sending him to London to replace Chaney and give some impetus to Bolero, Sledgehammer and Roundup. As Eisenhower prepared to leave for Britain, Churchill and his chiefs were making plans to return to Washington to revisit Marshall's memorandum.

Dill wrote to Brooke on 15 June 1942 to give him insight into the deliberations of the President. The letter was a classic example of how Dill now acted as a trusted interlocutor between American and British decision-makers. This meant that, on occasions, he was able to keep Churchill and the British Chiefs of Staff as well informed about the President's intentions as Marshall, King and Arnold – and sometimes better. Dill mentioned that Roosevelt was clearly worried about the course of the battle in Libya, the need to keep the Russians in the war and the problem of finding an active theatre of war for the growing American forces. His crucial nugget of information was that Roosevelt seemed to be less convinced by the idea of a 1942 cross-Channel attack due to the obvious problems involved. Meanwhile, he reported, Marshall remained adamantly in favour of such an attack because he believed that, unless the plans were pushed forward now, the Allies might lose the chance of mounting a larger invasion the following year. Equally, Roosevelt was still considering the possibility of:

Casablanca. President believes he might carry out purely American offensive (some six divisions) this year, aiming at control of North Africa and ultimate capture of Tripoli. He believes French would do little more than offer token resistance and considers Americans would be less unwelcome than British. Further he considers (perhaps 'hopes' is better word) that Bolero and Casablanca need not necessarily be mutually exclusive.[53]

Gymnast had been a favourite of the Prime Minister for a long time, but it seemed to hold equal appeal for the President. It is clear that, in June 1942, Roosevelt already saw the potential for a purely American assault that would satisfy the key requirement of employing substantial American forces in combat, in their own theatre.

Roosevelt was indeed concerned about the fighting in Libya. The War Department was receiving increasingly pessimistic reports from the US military attaché in Cairo, Colonel Bonner Fellers. Rommel had attacked the British Gazala Line on 26 May, and the tide of battle appeared to be going increasingly against the British. Fellers had long been negotiating for greater access to British information. He argued that:

My reports to Washington are and have been based upon personal observations, observations of assistants, information gathered from British sources. Often information is gained on a basis of friendship rather than because of my official position . . . I hold it is imperative that our War Department be provided with an absolutely official picture of the situation in this theatre.[54]

He complained that it was often difficult to gain access to all the military information he desired, as the British feared that his reports might diverge from the details provided by Dill, and that such sensitive information might not be safeguarded in Washington.[55] The difficulty faced by the British was the lack of coordination between Maxwell's technical mission in Egypt and Bonner Fellers' independent role as military attaché. However, they realised that Fellers reported directly to Marshall, and it was thus agreed in March 1942 that he was entitled to seek 'most secret information on any subject connected with the war effort',[56] though the directive did limit the types of information he could receive and aimed to ensure that he checked with Middle East Headquarters about any sensitive material. The fact that it began by stating that 'He is the representative of the United States War Department and his task is to keep the Chief of Staff of the US Army informed regarding the British situation in the Middle East' overshadowed the restrictions,[57] however, and officers in most headquarters were only too happy to provide him with detailed information, working under the impression that they would be helping to put the British case in Washington.

Fellers achieved even greater access to British sources in mid-May 1942. General Auchinleck, Commander-in-Chief Middle East, had finally allowed him to sit in on some commander-in-chief conferences, the Joint Intelligence Committee, the Joint Planning Staff, and training conferences.[58] This meant that he was able to provide an even higher level of detail to Washington once the critical Battle of Gazala opened on 26 May 1942, when Rommel swept around the desert flank of the 8th Army's defences and into their rear. Fellers moved up to the front to ensure that he could give accurate reports, and he was able to recount every British move and give the map-grid location of every British headquarters during the battle. Ironically, Dill was complaining to London at the same time that the information he received about the fighting was very thin and did not give him sufficient information for frank discussions with Marshall. He later complained that the President was 'getting his hot news from American Observers and I have no idea how accurate it is'.[59]

Unfortunately, Fellers' unfettered access, and indeed the very zeal with which he accomplished his job as military attaché, proved disastrous to British fortunes in the desert. Quite unknown to anyone in Washington, London or Cairo, every message he sent was being intercepted and decoded by Italian intelligence. Within hours, a translated copy of each of his cables to Washington was winging its way to Rommel's headquarters. The Italian intelligence service (known as SIM) had achieved a 'magnificent coup'.[60] In August 1941, a clerk working in the American embassy in Rome had been persuaded by SIM to take a photocopy of the American military attaché code, known as the Black Code, and replace the original before anyone noticed. This meant that all messages sent in this code could be intercepted and read at exactly the same time as their intended recipients in Washington were doing the same.[61] Although the Italians and Germans were able to read messages from every US military attaché, the most important were those from Bonner Fellers because of their frankness and detail and their bearing on the campaign in the desert. Not surprisingly, his reports became known as 'the Good Source' by German and Italian intelligence, while Rommel jokingly called him 'my bonnie fellow'. Hans Otto Behrendt, Rommel's intelligence officer, later confirmed that the vast majority of the Panzerarmee's information concerning British strength, losses and locations came from 'the Good Source'.[62]

When Churchill arrived back in America, Roosevelt took him to his house at Hyde Park in upstate New York. Both Brooke and Marshall fretted on 19 June 1942 as to just what the two political leaders might be cooking up as they drove around the grounds of Roosevelt's home. Well primed by Dill, Churchill was expounding on the advantages of Gymnast as an alternative to the risky proposition of a cross-Channel attack later that year. This was precisely what neither Brooke nor Marshall would have wished to hear, and the discussions between the two leaders began to pull apart the shaky consensus of the Allies and reshape it in an unexpected direction. One of the underlying motivations behind Churchill's revival of Gymnast was anxiety over the situation in Libya. It appeared that the Eighth Army had fought hard against Rommel's Panzerarmee in a swirling, confusing fight on the Gazala Line, but that it had now lost that particular round of desert combat.

Two days later, Churchill and Roosevelt were in the Oval Office of the White House when the President was handed a pink slip of paper: Tobruk had fallen. The Libyan fortress that had held out against Rommel during 1941 and become a powerful symbol of the British will to resist Nazi Germany had been taken. Rommel's road to Egypt was open. Churchill, not wishing to accept the news from an American source, asked Ismay to get confirmation from London, but before he could do so, another message arrived reinforcing the news. Churchill later admitted that it was 'one of the heaviest blows I can recall during the war. Not only were its military effects grievous, but it had affected the reputation of the British armies . . . I did not attempt to hide from the President the shock I had received. It was a bitter moment. Defeat is one thing; disgrace is another.'[63]

The fall of Tobruk was indeed a serious blow for Churchill. Coming after a litany of disaster from Norway to Singapore, this final defeat called into question Britain's military prowess, her value as an ally and Churchill's capacity as her war leader. In this moment of crisis, the relationship between the Allied leaders could easily have fallen apart in recrimination: many military alliances have fractured under the stress of bad news. Yet Roosevelt responded with sympathy and generosity, simply asking, 'What can we do to help?'[64] Years later, Churchill remembered this painful episode in the Oval Office as a defining moment in the Anglo-American alliance that brought the two leaders together.

Churchill's immediate response was to ask for Sherman tanks to help stem the tide, and Marshall worked hard over the next day to develop plans to send the entire US 2nd Armored Division under the command of George Patton to Egypt. The British were understandably reluctant to see American combat forces in a theatre they considered their own responsibility, and in the event it was decided to send 300 Sherman tanks and 100 self-propelled 105 mm guns – the equipment of a US armoured division – to reinforce the British. This act of generosity meant taking tanks out of the hands of American troops who had just received them, but nonetheless Marshall did not hesitate to give the order.[65]

Fellers had, by this time, lost all faith in the British. He reported in great detail on the British catastrophe, and provided a searing judgement on the Eighth Army:

> With numerically superior forces, with tanks, planes, artillery, means of transport, and reserves of every kind, the British army has twice failed to defeat the Axis forces in Libya. Under the present command and with the measures taken in a hit or miss fashion the granting of 'lend-lease' alone cannot ensure a victory. The Eighth Army has failed to maintain the morale of its troops; its tactical conceptions were always wrong, it neglected completely cooperation between the various arms; its reactions to the lightning changes of the battlefield were always slow.[66]

This was indeed a damning analysis. There is no question that many of the Eighth Army's tactical methods were lamentable, and it appeared to Fellers that they were not only wasting the largesse of Lend-Lease but were incapable of organising for victory. The terrible irony was that it was his own thorough reports that had given Rommel the vital information he needed to defeat the British. In detailing the alarming losses suffered at Gazala, Fellers handed Rommel his last intelligence coup. Out of 1,142 tanks in service at the start of the battle, 1,009 had been knocked out by 16 June. This vital information was greeted with dismay in Washington and delight at Rommel's headquarters. Fellers' report ended with the grim conclusion:

> 1.   The army has been defeated primarily because of the incompetency of its leaders; 2. If Rommel intends to take the Delta, now is the time; 3. The British must make haste to offer at least

Disaster at the Monongahela.

After a confused ambush in the backwoods of Pennsylvania, Major General Braddock falls mortally wounded from his horse while a dismayed Washington looks on. This engagement, on 9 July 1755, marked the start of what would become known as the French and Indian Wars.

Two worlds on one day.

Dwight D. Eisenhower and Mamie Dowd on their wedding day,
1 July 1916.

A support company of the Tyneside Irish Brigade moving forward on the first day of
the battle of the Somme, 1 July 1916. The British Army suffered its worst loss of life
on one day in just a few short hours.

Tommies and Doughboys.

British and American soldiers discuss baseball at Pas, France, 18 May 1918.
Relations between British and American soldiers in the Great War were
generally good, although Americans did not like British rations.

American soldiers of the 77th Division undergoing trench training with British
instructors from the 39th Division in France, 22 May 1918. Pershing feared that
such instruction would train the 'dash' out of his riflemen.

A meeting of minds.

General George Marshall and General Sir John Dill on board HMS *Prince of Wales* Placentia Bay, August 1941. The friendship which developed between these two men was of fundamental importance for the Anglo-American alliance.

Roosevelt, Churchill and their assembled chiefs attend Church Service on board HMS *Prince of Wales* August, 1941. The Atlantic Conference resulted in the announcement of the Atlantic Charter but not, as Churchill had hoped, a US declaration of war.

Lend-Lease.

US instructors educate British crews on the finer points of the new M3 Grant tank in Egypt, spring 1942. Although an interim design, the Grant tank provided British tank crews with the chance to fight their German opponents on equal terms.

The first Sherman tank in Britain arrives for a display of war equipment at Horse Guards Parade, April 1942. The British Army named the US M4 Medium Tank the 'Sherman', after the American Civil War General. The American Ordnance Department, in turn, named this M4 'Michael' in honour of Michael Dewar, head of the British Tank Mission.

One of the first American M3 light tanks to arrive in Egypt, 19 July 1941. These tanks were a powerful symbol and indeed some of the first fruits of Lend-Lease.

Over there.

Private Milburn Henke, one of the first US soldiers to arrive in Britain, steps onto the quay at Belfast Northern Ireland January 1942.

GIs enjoying a pint at a NAAFI in Britain. American views on British beer were not always polite and encounters in British pubs between American and British soldiers were not always calculated to improve relations.

Tunisia.

Lance-Sergeant Brown and Sergeant Randall greet each other during the link-up between the British Eighth Army and US II Corps in Tunisia, 7 April 1943. The campaign had proved to be one of the most difficult and divisive fought by the Allies.

A Churchill tank of the North Irish Horse with stretcher bearers of the East Surrey Regiment during the final, successful attack on Longstop Hill, 23 April 1943. It had been a different matter for the tired Allied soldiers in the previous December.

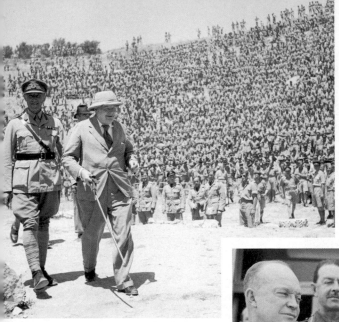

Winston Churchill and Lieutenant General Kenneth Anderson leave the Roman amphitheatre at Carthage on 1 June 1943. Anderson's awkward relations with both British subordinates and American allies meant that he never held another operational command during the war.

High Command.

Eisenhower, Alexander, Churchill and Ismay in Tunis on Christmas Day 1943. Churchill was in the process of engineering what became Operation Shingle.

'We came, we saw and we were conquered.'

The Combined Chiefs of Staff at Casablanca, January 1943: (left to right) King, Marshall, Dykes, Wedemeyer, Ismay, Mountbatten, Pound, Brooke, Portal and Dill.

a respectable resistance to the forces of the Axis; 4. To hold
the Middle East the British must be supplied immediately, in
order of importance, with a large number of bombers, tanks,
artillery.[67]

Not surprisingly, Rommel chose to follow Fellers' advice and
pursue the defeated Eighth Army into Egypt. However, the British
secret service had finally identified the nature and source of the
leak through their own decrypts of German Enigma transmissions.
All German military radio traffic was encrypted through the use
of the highly sophisticated Enigma electro-mechanical device.
While the Germans believed that the enigma codes were unbreak-
able, British code-breakers working at Bletchley Park had been able
to crack the Enigma traffic in 1940. Intelligence gained from the
Enigma decrypts was known as 'Ultra' and remained vital and
highly secret throughout the war. Without Britain's success in
decrypting Enigma, the American diplomatic code might have
continued to provide a rich source of intelligence for the Axis. The
British were horrified by the implications of the leak. If Fellers had
become aware of the 'Ultra' secret, one of Britain's most powerful
intelligence weapons could have been neutralised overnight.
However, by 29 June 1942, Fellers' reports were no longer being
read by German and Italian intelligence, and soon afterwards he
was complaining to Washington that he could not gain access to
important British information. But the damage had most assuredly
already been done. The entire episode emphasised the danger as
well as the benefits of close cooperation between allies. Yet in
one of the strange ironies of history, while Rommel accepted
Fellers' assessment of the situation, Marshall did not. The Chief
of Staff of the United States army kept faith with his allies even
in the face of such alarming reports from Cairo.

While Fellers clearly believed the situation was virtually hope-
less, the Eighth Army, now under the direct command of General
Auchinleck, turned to fight Rommel's seemingly unstoppable
army at El Alamein. It was a moment of supreme crisis for the
British in Egypt, and for Churchill, who had by now returned to
London. While Auchinleck and the Eighth Army faced the

onslaught of Rommel's army, Churchill faced a vote of no confidence in the House of Commons. Dill, keen to counter the pessimistic views of Marshall's staff concerning the 'probable outcome of the present battle', asked London for information concerning Auchinleck's intentions. London replied that they would not divulge 'Auchinleck's plan for fighting battle. Although situation is critical, Auchinleck's reports of morale of 8th Army do not justify extreme pessimism evinced by Americans in Egypt'.[68] Most War Department staff in Washington clearly believed that the British would fail yet again, and that the collapse of the entire British position in Egypt was now only a matter of time.

Churchill, meanwhile, went on an immediate offensive against his opponents in the House of Commons and won the motion by the convincing margin of 425 votes to 25. Nonetheless, this vote in the Commons demonstrated that Churchill's room for manoeuvre on Allied strategy was limited. The Prime Minister could not sanction a risky operation like Sledgehammer, which would primarily use British troops, without the possibility of severe political consequences. Nonetheless, he had surmounted the immediate political challenge, and by 4 July 1942 it was clear that after three days of intense fighting, Auchinleck and the Eighth Army had managed to hold Rommel at the very gates of Egypt. Yet while this marked at least a temporary easing of the tide of Allied defeat – and in retrospect the high-water mark of the Axis in the desert – the storm over Allied strategy was only just beginning.

6

Cats and Bulldogs

On 22 July 1942, Eisenhower confided to his aide, Harry Butcher, that he feared the day might well go down in history as 'one of the blackest days of the war' for the Allies.[1] There were many reasons why Eisenhower might have considered this day as particularly depressing. He might have had in mind the disastrous outcome of Operation Splendour, the Eighth Army's second attempt to destroy Rommel's Panzerarmee Afrika at El Alamein in Egypt, which failed amidst confusion and heavy casualties.*[2] He might also have been referring to the imminent encirclement of the Soviet forces at Rostov-on-Don and the seemingly unstoppable advance of the German summer offensive, which had now reached the gates of the Caucasus.[3] Had Eisenhower still been in charge of the Operations Division, his reference might well have been connected with the almost unrelieved gloom emanating from the battle fronts, but he was actually referring to the fact that, after days of heated argument and debate, the British Chiefs of Staff had finally and conclusively refused to agree to Operation Sledgehammer. This threw all of the Allied plans against Germany into flux and called into question the feasibility of Operation Roundup as well. As far as Eisenhower was concerned, after months of long and wearing staff work on Marshall's conception of a major cross-Channel attack in 1943, he was 'right back to December fifteenth': square one.

After his initial visit to London in the spring of 1942, Eisenhower had returned to the British capital on 24 June, but this time he arrived not as a staff officer or as an aide, but as a commander.

---

* In fact, news of the failure did not reach London and Washington until the next day.

Marshall had appointed him Commanding General European Theater of Operations (ETO), replacing General Chaney, who had held this new post for just 12 days. Although he arrived without fanfare, Eisenhower lost no time in stamping his authority over the American officers at Grosvenor Square. On 25 June, he held a conference with the heads of the staff sections in which he told them that their primary responsibility was to get an American army ready for a full-scale invasion of France. He explained that they must all 'push incessantly toward the attainment of the objective, which is to have an army in the field, ready to attack by spring, 1943' and that he expected 'an atmosphere of the utmost earnestness coupled with determined enthusiasm and optimism' to characterise the entire staff and every command in England.[4] A few days later, Dahlquist noted in his diary that 'Eisenhower indicated in no uncertain terms that he planned to run the theater' and that there would be none of the confusion and vacillation that had developed under Chaney.[5]

However, although Eisenhower had crossed the Atlantic to drive forwards Marshall's plans for an early cross-Channel attack, those proposals were meeting increased resistance from the British. Marshall and his advisers in the Operations Division (OPD) were becoming concerned about the possibility of a Soviet collapse under the renewed hammer blows of the German summer offensive. Rather than wait passively, they were willing to take any risk in order to forestall that possibility and provide at least limited Allied assistance. An emergency landing on the French coast in the autumn of 1942 might well end in disaster but it would distract at least some German attention: it was perhaps the only action the Allies could take to support the Soviets directly. OPD saw the operation as 'a sacrifice for the common good'.[6] Given that such an assault would have to be conducted with mainly British forces, the British chiefs became increasingly sceptical about Sledgehammer. The truth was that they had never really considered it a practical act of war and had no intention of sacrificing four British divisions. The British Army had suffered so many disasters during the war that the concept of deliberately courting another was out of the question.

Yet as the British became more forthright in their opposition to Sledgehammer, Marshall was faced with an intractable dilemma. If Britain would not support a cross-Channel attack in 1942, where was the growing strength of the US Army to be applied? US planners considered Gymnast, an invasion of French North Africa, to have almost no military value, and suspected that British enthusiasm for it disguised an attempt to subvert American strength for their own imperial objectives.

By the first week in July, both the British cabinet and the Chiefs of Staff were signalling their opinion that the chances of mounting Sledgehammer successfully were remote.[7] On 8 July, Churchill simply stoked the Operation Division's already considerable anger by informing Roosevelt of this conclusion and suggesting that an operation in North Africa could easily take its place: 'This has all along been in harmony with your ideas . . . In fact, it is your commanding idea. Here is the true second front of 1942.'[8] Churchill knew that the President had long favoured Gymnast, even if the operation was vehemently opposed by his military advisers. Here was yet another example of the British Prime Minister subverting their carefully laid plans.

A decision to launch Gymnast would, Marshall believed, not provide any succour to the Russians while at the same time making a cross-Channel assault virtually impossible until 1944. Under these circumstances, the British and Americans would probably have to sit passively while the Germans destroyed the Red Army. This would, in turn, make the German position in Western Europe virtually impregnable to any Allied assault. It was this military logic, combined with a real sense of frustration, that caused Marshall to suggest to the Joint Chiefs of Staff on 10 July 1942 that if the United States engaged 'in any other operation rather than forceful, unswerving adherence to full BOLERO plans . . . we should turn to the Pacific and strike decisively against Japan; in other words, assume a defensive attitude against Germany . . . and use all available means in the Pacific'.[9] Since the British would not seemingly cross the Channel 'except behind a Scotch bagpipe band', it might well be better to abandon all meaningful plans with them and go all out to win the war against Japan.[10]

While this Joint Chiefs paper might well have been a gambit designed to force the President's hand into unconditional support of the army's position, it was equally based on a deadly serious intent to ensure that US strength was not frittered away on what were seen as ineffective British and presidential diversions. However, Roosevelt would have no truck with the proposals. He insisted that Marshall and Hopkins go to London immediately and come to some agreement with the British. If Sledgehammer fell by the wayside, so be it: Marshall would have to agree to Gymnast or some other proposal for the deployment of US troops against Germany during 1942. Roosevelt told Hopkins in no uncertain terms on 15 July that if Sledgehammer could not be mounted, he wanted Gymnast in 1942 and Roundup in 1943.

Marshall arrived in Britain on 20 July 1942 to argue his case directly with the British Chiefs of Staff. Eisenhower, who had been primed to prepare a 'searching analysis' of Sledgehammer for his chief's arrival, noted that 'The decisions to be made are not only highly secret but momentous.'[11] Over the course of the next few days, however, the British chiefs placed themselves on record, time and again, as being definitely against Sledgehammer.[12] It has to be said that their arguments were based on firmer foundations. An Allied attack of a few divisions was highly unlikely to divert German forces from the Eastern Front, and while the British foresaw the distinct possibility of yet another military disaster, the Americans were unable to present a truly convincing case for their concept of an attack on Cherbourg. However, the trump card was held by the British in that the attack would have to be mounted with primarily British troops. British refusal meant that Sledgehammer could not go ahead and that Marshall was forced to bend to British views of the strategic situation. Marshall and his staff officers greeted this determined refusal with dismay. The US Chief of Staff had lost a vital battle with the British that placed his entire strategy for the war in jeopardy. The difficulty was that if Sledgehammer did not go ahead, Marshall believed it would become almost impossible to hold the US Navy to the principle of 'Germany First'.

Marshall and Hopkins were forced to inform Roosevelt of the impasse in London. Roosevelt's reply was unequivocal: they must agree to an operation of some sort in 1942, preferably North Africa, as soon as possible. Gymnast, soon renamed Torch, was on. But it should not be imagined that these strategic disagreements were fought by two competing monolithic groups of opinion: the proposals were complex and there were many factors and considerations to be taken into account. In Washington, both Dill and Dykes had been signalling London, warning them of the consequences of refusing to back Sledgehammer, whereas Bedell Smith admitted to Dykes that he was relieved 'that Sledgehammer has been cleared out of the way, never having felt that it was really on'.[13] In fact, Bedell Smith had always been a consistent advocate of Gymnast, which led some of the American planning staff to consider that he had become more British than the British.

A few days after the dramatic final British refusal, the news had filtered down the chain of command to the American staff officers working in Grosvenor Square. John Dahlquist noted in his diary as late as 25 July that:

It looks as though the plan for Sledgehammer is very dead . . . Personally I feel it was the most impracticable proposition. The critical thing is that we are idle while the enemy is perfecting his defences or completing preparations for his offensive moves. Time is slipping by. I have always felt our theater should start in North Africa and that certainly now steps should be taken to crack Japan before she consolidates.[14]

Marshall, and indeed Eisenhower, might well have rounded upon Dahlquist as an advocate of dispersion if they had been aware of his views. However, Dahlquist was also highly critical of the interventions of some of the American senior officers during the discussions. He considered that General Lee, head of the Services of Supply, had provided inaccurate estimates concerning the capacity for supply, and that General Clark had provided ill-coordinated estimates of available troops. He thought that 'A little less scintillation at the top and more use of the staff would assist a great deal.'[15] Dahlquist's comments show a pragmatic staff officer's view of the Allied arguments.

Roosevelt's clear-cut direction in favour of Gymnast did not immediately settle the matter. Both Marshall and his Operations Division fought a determined rearguard against the plan, and yet the fact was that, taken on their merits, an invasion of French North Africa was a much more viable proposition than a cross-Channel attack in 1942. Even once this had been agreed upon, there remained precious little time to turn an outline plan into the reality of a complex amphibious invasion. In fact, almost all of the details concerning Torch remained to be settled between the two allies. The first decision required was to appoint a commander. The British actually supported the idea of an American commander for Torch, but Marshall was reluctant to commit to a decision in the absence of the President. Admiral King simply remarked that 'Well, you've got him right here. Why not put it under Eisenhower?'[16] In this seemingly casual way, Eisenhower became the US commander in Britain and the commander-in-chief for Torch. Although it had been originally intended that a British officer would be appointed as his deputy commander, it was eventually decided that an American officer should fill the role in order to maintain the fiction towards the Vichy French authorities in North Africa that this was an entirely American enterprise. General Mark Clark, one of Marshall's rising stars, was thus appointed as Eisenhower's deputy. It was not until the beginning of August, and many further meetings of the Combined Chiefs of Staff, that the details were settled. Marshall returned to the United States, while Churchill and Brooke flew out to Egypt to shake up the British Middle East Command.

Churchill was determined to find a British general who could win a victory against Rommel's Panzerarmee Afrika, and was desperate to achieve a clear and resounding victory in the desert to restore Britain's military reputation before Anglo-American operations, in the form of Torch, began. The first change he decided upon was to replace Auchinleck with Lieutenant General Harold Alexander as Commander-in-Chief Middle East. However, Alexander had already been selected as the commander for the British force involved in Torch, and Lieutenant General Bernard Montgomery was hurriedly inserted into his place in the Torch command chain. Ismay had to write an emollient letter to Eisenhower informing him of the change, but events quickly altered even these decisions. William 'Strafer' Gott, who had been chosen by Churchill to command the Eighth Army, was killed when his aircraft was attacked and shot down by German aircraft, and Brooke then intervened to ensure that his protégé, Montgomery, was given command of the Eighth Army. This meant that yet another British commander had to be found for Torch, and Ismay was forced to write another letter to Eisenhower, ensuring him that the third choice for the operation, Lieutenant General Kenneth Anderson, had a fine reputation and would serve him well.[17] This episode smacked of uncertainty in the British commitment towards Torch, and certainly irritated Eisenhower, but it also revealed a deeper, more troubling structural issue: neither Churchill nor Brooke felt there was a large pool of senior general officers in the British Army whom they could trust to fight and win an important battle.

While this high-level shake-up in Britain's desert army was taking place, there were a number of developments at the other end of the military spectrum that revealed the growing cooperation between the British and American armies. On 5 August 1942, Captain J. McLoughlin and 30 tank crew men of the US Army joined the Eighth Army in Egypt, where they were attached to the 3/4th County of London Yeomanry, an armoured regiment in the 22nd Armoured Brigade.[18] They were not quite the first American tank crew to serve in the desert – during June and July 1942, a small group of men had served in the 1st American Tank Detachment under the command of Major Henry Cabot Lodge* – but McLoughlin and his men did represent a visible symbol of growing cooperation at the grass-roots level between these two very different armies.[19] Four days later, the army film unit took a series of photographs of the Americans settling into their new role as members of a British armoured regiment. In fact, the American crews were a welcome reinforcement for the County of London Yeomanry, which had suffered heavy losses during the July fighting at Alamein: the unit was an amalgamation of the remnants of the 3rd and 4th

---

* Cabot Lodge was from a well-known Massachusetts family and had resigned his seat in the Senate so that he could serve in the army.

CLY, and the under-strength unit had only one Grant tank squadron of 15 tanks.

In the event, these American soldiers, along with their new British comrades, were soon to find themselves at the sharp end.[20] On 31 August, Rommel mounted his last, desperate offensive to break through the Eighth Army. The next day, a column of 120 German tanks from the 21st Panzer Division attacked the 22nd Armoured Brigade, which was holding positions on the critical Alam el Halfa ridge. 'Pip' Roberts, the young brigadier of 22nd Armoured Brigade, later related that it seemed 'only a few minutes before nearly all the tanks of the Grant squadron of the CLY were on fire'.[21] Although he wrongly identified them as the 'first American soldiers to fight on African soil', he mentioned that the American crews 'certainly got their battle experience in a somewhat unorthodox battle and I am glad to say without serious casualties, though one or two had to bale out of burning tanks'.[22] McLoughlin and his men had thus achieved the dubious privilege of being amongst the first US tank crew to be fired on by German tanks during the war. They were also witnesses to the first time that the Eighth Army managed to stop a German offensive in its tracks. The British combined use of an anti-tank gun screen, capable Grant tanks, and concentrated artillery fire had dealt very effectively with the German advance. Although Montgomery, the new commander of the Eighth Army, had fought the battle, christened Alam Halfa by the British, in a very cautious and entirely defensive fashion, he had defeated Rommel.

In fact, the tank crews were not the only Americans in the Eighth Army. Five American volunteers had joined the King's Royal Rifle Corps during 1941, conscious of the regiment's eighteenth-century title of 'Royal Americans'. One further volunteer was added to their ranks and all six were wounded in the final battle at El Alamein; two were later killed in Tunisia. Charles Bolte,* who lost a leg in the battle, later observed that 'two got death and three got limps'.[23] However, the link between America and the regiment did not end at Alamein. By the end of 1942, a further 12 Americans had volunteered to fight

* The son of the Charles Bolte who served in the Special Observer Group in 1941–2.

in the corps, and some continued to serve in the regiment through to the war's end in north-west Europe.

While the Americans in the King's Royal Rifle Corps represented an ancient link between the two militaries, August 1942 also saw the creation of a new tradition in the development of the newly raised American Ranger battalions, which grew directly from the inspiration of the British Commando force. The Commandos had been established after the fall of France, when it had seemed that the only realistic means of returning to offensive action was through amphibious raids on the coast of Europe. A Combined Operations Headquarters was created in July 1940 to plan and conduct these raids, along with an all-volunteer force of 440-man battalions.[24] Lieutenant Colonel Dudley Clark, Dill's military assistant, came up with the name, inspired by stories from his South African childhood of the groups of Boer farmers, known as Commandos, who had fought so expertly against the British at the turn of the century, using ponies to mount lightning raids across the veldt.[25] The strenuous training the Commandos underwent soon became a byword for toughness. The gruelling round of specialist infantry instruction, seven-mile route marches with full kit, survival skills, weapons training and the creation of self-reliance produced a strong sense of esprit de corps. The Commandos' hit-and-run raids in Norway and France brought a sense of much-needed glamour and excitement during the gloomy days of 1940–1, even if many members of the British military questioned the real value and cost of the expensively mounted and often risky operations.

The British Commandos first attracted Marshall's attention during his trip to London in April 1942, when he met Lord Louis Mountbatten, the new director of Combined Operations. He was impressed by the suave young naval officer and also saw a chance to develop closer links with this intriguing British organisation. Marshall had met Mountbatten at a propitious moment: Combined Operations were basking in the afterglow of the success of the raid on Saint-Nazaire. The Commandos had used HMS *Campbeltown*, one of the obsolete American destroyers given to Britain the year before, to blow up the lock gates of Saint-Nazaire's dry dock. Even though only 22 of the 200 Commandos who landed were able to escape, the raid was judged a great success and five Victoria Crosses were awarded.

On his return to Washington, Marshall presented Colonel Lucian K. Truscott with the mission of working with Combined Operations to develop an American version of the British Commando force. He hoped that such a force would fulfil a number of different objectives. Firstly, although he was satisfied with the enormous training programmes taking place in the United States, he was well aware that there was no substitute for actual combat experience. If the main invasion of Europe was to take place in 1943, he was determined to ensure that US forces gained such experience, and one of the best means appeared to be to take part in raids on the European coast. American units could be blooded, gain combat experience and reinforce for home consumption the fact that Americans were already fighting. The attachment of American officers and men to British Commando units might well provide them with combat experience; these men could then be spread through larger formations to give them the benefit of their know-ledge and experience. Just as the Commandos had provided valuable, even essential, proof that Britain was still in the fight and hitting back at Germany, so Marshall hoped that the creation of similar units might help to assuage the American public and Roosevelt's demand for military action in Europe during 1942.[26] There must also have been the hope that some of the glamour and mystique that had developed around the British Commandos would rub off on the new American units.

In April 1942, Truscott and a small team of officers, Lieutenant Colonel Haskell Cleaves, Colonel Lauren Hillsinger, Major Guy Embree and Major Theodore Conway, were dispatched to London to study the organisation, training and employment of the British Commandos and to develop recommendations for a similar American unit. The team became working members of the US Combined Operations Group, which was attached to the Combined Operations Headquarters. However, Truscott, who later became one of the US Army's best fighting commanders of the war, very nearly found that his wartime career was over before it had begun. After attending an early planning meeting concerning Operation

Sledgehammer, he wrote a personal memo about the discussion and left it on his desk. This was an innocent example of the lax security that the British suspected was rife within the American services. American officers, used to living and working in peacetime conditions, initially often failed to appreciate the overwhelming importance of security in wartime. When Truscott arrived in his office the next day, his British superior coldly handed him his memo – it had blown off his desk, flown out of the window and landed in the courtyard outside. Had he been a British officer, Truscott would have been sacked immediately; his superior imperiously informed him that it was only due to the 'considerations of Anglo-American relations' that his mistake was to be overlooked.[27] Truscott certainly learnt from the experience.

Conway, in particular, worked closely with Truscott in the foundation of the American Ranger battalions. He visited as many of the Commando units as possible and discovered that 'almost everything they did was unique' and that 'every aspect of their training and administration, discipline and the like was rigorous and purposely so'.[28] Highly impressed with both the Commandos and the tri-service approach of the Combined Operations Headquarters, Conway produced a table of organisation for the new American units that directly copied the Commando structure, with the substitution of American ranks and titles. He had entitled them the 'American Commandos', but when Truscott saw the title he 'picked up his pencil and drew a line through "Commando", and said, "this has got to be an American unit; we have to go back to American tradition"'.[29] In an unconscious echo of the link between the King's Royal Rifle Corps and its American volunteers, Truscott hit upon the name 'Rangers', which connected the unit with the exploits of Roger's Rangers, the irregular raiding force of French and Indian War fame.

The first Ranger battalion was established in June 1942 under the command of Major William O. Darby. Its headquarters were at Carrickfergus in Northern Ireland,[30] and it was trained at the Commando depot at Achnacarry Castle, the seat of the Clan Cameron, in the Highlands of Scotland. These American soldiers, drawn mainly from the infantry divisions stationed in Northern Ireland, were subjected to the same seven-mile speed marches, weapons and fieldcraft instruction, obstacle courses, log races, amphibious training and assault tactics as the Commandos.[31] The development of the US Rangers thus represented the closest cooperation and transference of military knowledge and techniques between the two armies thus far in the war.

As the summer of 1942 wore on, however, Conway became frustrated at the relative dearth of active operations for the new force he had helped to create.[32] The Americans had clearly envisaged a growing programme of raids of increasing intensity that would enable them to rotate hundreds if not thousands of men through the Ranger units. The frequent postponement and then cancellation of numerous Commando raids during the summer of 1942 was evidence of the fact that such raids were in fact highly complex and risky operations, dependent for success upon intangibles such as intelligence, weather and tides. The glamour of the Commando concept had to be balanced against the grim reality of the risks – and potential costs – involved in mounting such operations. Nowhere was that reality demonstrated more graphically than in Operation Jubilee, the raid on Dieppe on 19 August 1942.

The Dieppe raid was the first exposure of the Rangers to actual combat. Fifty Rangers went ashore with the Commandos to capture a German coastal battery above the port of Dieppe. This initial attack was relatively successful and achieved at moderate cost, with seven Rangers killed or listed as missing and seven wounded during the action.[33] However, the main assault, carried out by the 3rd Canadian Infantry Division, which aimed to seize the port and hold it for 24 hours, quickly turned into an unmitigated disaster. When the infantry disembarked, they were met with withering German machine-gun and mortar fire, which cut them down as they attempted to get off the beach. The supporting Churchill tanks arrived late, and then found that they could not mount the high sea wall to support the few infantry who had managed to get into the town. The Canadians suffered 3,367 killed, wounded or prisoner and the Commandos lost 275 casualties. One of Truscott's staff officers, Hillsinger, was killed when the destroyer he was sailing in was sunk by German air attack. The raid had resulted in a true military fiasco and seemed to confirm British fears about mounting a premature cross-Channel attack. However, the American press blew the participation of the Rangers up into a story of real success. Here were American troops, trained in the toughest techniques, now taking part in a daring action in France. Marshall's desire for American troops to see combat as soon as possible had certainly been achieved, and the Rangers who participated in the Torch landings just a few months later had a much clearer, if grimmer, picture of 'the elephant' than had been the case before Dieppe.*

Operation Jubilee was soon the subject of an in-depth examination to attempt to learn from the experience; Mountbatten subsequently claimed that 'the battle of Normandy was won on the beaches of Dieppe. For every man who died in Dieppe at least ten more must have been spared in Normandy in 1944.'[34] While this might well be regarded as hyperbole, there is no doubt that the shocking results of Operation Jubilee intensified British and indeed Allied efforts to overcome the many problems in mounting an amphibious assault. Truscott and his team, who had had no previous experience of amphibious operations before Jubilee, were now regarded as experts, and were drafted in to assist General Patton when he arrived in London in September 1942 to begin planning his task force's part in Operation Torch.

The first weeks of Eisenhower's tenure as the new commander for Operation Torch were fraught ones. The scale of the challenge facing him was enormous. Not only was the time available very short – the invasion was to take place no later than November 1942 – but the resources available continued to fluctuate depending on the available Allied shipping capacity. General Kenneth Anderson later commented that:

> Eisenhower had been pitchforked into a veritable bedlam, and if at times decisions seem to have been by committee and syndicate, yet I know of no man who could have taken all the strings into his own hands at once, simply because the strings were not there to be seized during the first few weeks; they had to be created.[35]

---

* 'Seeing the elephant' was an American Civil War term for having seen combat.

The first thread Eisenhower had to spin himself was the nature and organisation of the Allied Forces Headquarters (AFHQ), which became the model for Anglo-American HQs for the rest of the war. He later argued in his North African dispatch that 'Alliances in the past . . . have often done no more than to name the common foe, and "unity of command" has been a pious aspiration thinly disguising the national jealousies, ambitions and recriminations of high ranking officers, unwilling to subordinate themselves or their forces to a commander of different nationality or different service.'[36] Eisenhower's belief in the necessity of unity of command in Allied operations had clearly been informed by his own experience, his reading of military history and his relationships with Fox Conner and Marshall. He went on to state his determination 'to do all in my power to make this a truly Allied Force, with real unity of command and centralization of administrative responsibility'.[37] A truly allied force required more than just a nominated commander; it also needed a properly integrated and balanced headquarters with staff officers drawn from both nations in order to function in an effective way.

Eisenhower, drawing on his long experience as a staff officer, knew exactly how to develop his headquarters. The key principles underlying the formation of the Allied Force Headquarters were integration and balanced personnel, which meant that, in each of the operational staff sections, the numbers of personnel would be shared as equally as possible between British and American staff officers, and that these officers would be entirely integrated into the same staff system. If one section had an American head, his deputy would be British, and vice versa. However, the principle of the best man for the job was also insisted upon, particularly for section heads. The one exception to this integrated approach lay with the British quartermaster's department and the American services of supply. The supply services, systems and procedures of the two armies were found to be so different that it was deemed impossible to integrate them.[38]

If Eisenhower can be accused of partiality in the establishment of the Allied Force Headquarters, it lay in his decision to organise the headquarters according to the American staff system rather than the British. This was no doubt due to his familiarity with the American system, but it was also due to the fact that American officers found navigating the complexities of the British staff system a real challenge. The lack of previous contact between the two armies during the interwar years meant that their systems, methods, procedures and terminology had all developed organically, with no attempt to make them compatible with or understandable by each other. The British staff system was idiosyncratic and highly confusing for American officers, as it was still based upon divisions of responsibility that would have been recognisable to Wellington's staff officers.[39] Not only was it completely different to the modern American system, but British terminology for staff officers was also confusing, mixing as it did archaic and modern terms in a fashion that could be bewildering to the uninitiated. The very helpful guide to British forces prepared by the American G3 Operations Branch of ETO in August 1943 had a six-page glossary of British military terms, with a further 23 pages of abbreviations and acronyms.[40]

The American staff system had been developed under very different influences to the British. Prior to the deployment of the AEF in 1917, the American Army had lacked a properly organised modern staff system. As part of the preparation for the deployment of the AEF, General Pershing had selected groups of officers to study both the French and British systems as used in 1917. Although there was a trace of British influence, the dominating influence upon the AEF's staff system was French. This was entirely logical, as the AEF had to maintain close coordination and liaison with higher and adjacent French staffs. This meant that the AEF adopted the French 'bureau system' of dividing the staff into five sections, with each section under an Assistant Chief of Staff as well as a special staff group of technical advisers.[41] The AEF also adopted the French system of organising the staff under the control of a Chief of Staff, who was to manage them and support the commander. Indeed, the AEF adopted French methods to the extent that the 'US staff system was fundamentally the same as the French'.[42]

This meant that the Allied Force Headquarters under Eisenhower was organised in a manner that would have been second nature to Foch but completely alien to Haig. There was an Allied Supreme Commander, a Deputy Supreme Commander, and a Chief of Staff. Under the Chief of Staff were the four main staff sections, organised as G-1 Personnel, G-2 Intelligence, G-3 Operations and G-4 Supply. There were also the special staff sections, including Quartermaster, Ordnance, Signals, Transportation, Engineers, Surgeon, Anti-Aircraft, Finance, Headquarters Commandant, Political, and Civil Administration.[43] These structures meant that the two very different staff systems of the British and American armies were fused together in a practical and effective manner. It is difficult to recognise, perhaps, just what a groundbreaking experiment the formation of the AFHQ actually was in 1942. This integrated and balanced headquarters was by no means perfect, nor did it end the problems inherent in the 'national jealousies, ambitions and recriminations of high ranking officers', but it was a major advance on anything that had been attempted before in the coordination and employment of Allied forces. The formation of AFHQ ensured that, at the highest military level, the activities of the British and American armies, navies and air forces were controlled and coordinated by a truly Allied command organisation.

Whatever structure or administrative system Eisenhower had adopted for the Allied Force Headquarters, its growth into a functioning reality also depended on key personalities. The most important person in AFHQ, after Eisenhower, was the Chief of Staff. Even before he had been appointed to command, Eisenhower had already identified the man he wanted: Walter Bedell Smith. Eisenhower made this formal request to Marshall before he left for London, but the Army Chief of Staff was loath to lose such a key figure. The fact was that both men recognised Bedell Smith as a superlative staff officer who not only understood the workings of the American system, in the form of the Joint Chiefs, the US War Department and the White House, but whose work with the Combined Chiefs of Staff and his close relations with the British Joint Staff Mission had given him a real understanding of the British as well.[44] Marshall eventually agreed to Eisenhower's request, but temporised over when Bedell Smith would arrive in London. It was early September when he finally released him to join Eisenhower, and this seems to have been primarily because Marshall feared that Eisenhower required greater support during the tense negotiations over Torch.[45]

As Eisenhower's Chief of Staff, Bedell Smith occupied a very different role to that of a British Chief Staff Officer. He not only served as Eisenhower's main adviser, but also supervised the day-to-day management of the staff. In both roles, his prior experience working for Marshall and the Combined Chiefs of Staff proved invaluable, particularly as there was no real precedent within US Army doctrine or procedure for how a Chief of Staff of an Allied headquarters should function.

Just as importantly, Eisenhower and Bedell Smith possessed very different personalities, which actually dovetailed together almost perfectly. Paul Caraway, who was on the receiving end of Bedell Smith's temper more than once, explained:

> Bedell Smith was the perfect example of the kind of a team you ought to have, if your commander is a softie. You've got to have a son-of-a-bitch as your Chief-of-Staff. Well, if your commander is a SOB like Patton, then you want your Chief of Staff to be a man that can heal the lacerated feelings. Well, Eisenhower could heal the lacerated feelings and get people going together. Bedell Smith could make the thing work. He didn't stand a bit of foolishness out of anybody. Everybody was afraid of him, as far as I could see . . . he was a rattlesnake, but a very efficient and effective man.[46]

Although Eisenhower could have an explosive temper, he had learned early to keep it under control in public. Instead, he used charm, modesty, Midwestern common sense and his famous grin to build trust. Equally, he often hid his impressive intelligence and cold logic behind a cloud of bonhomie. Almost every British senior official and officer warmed to him immediately, even if they considered him lacking in military experience. Bedell Smith's personality was quite different. Suffering from an acute stomach ulcer, he was much more highly strung and could use explosive invective towards

anyone he considered was not meeting his high standards. At the
same time, he also possessed considerable diplomatic skills and
was able to understand and manage the growing staff of AFHQ
in a way that very few people could have achieved.[47] Bedell Smith
was the martinet who kept AFHQ running on rails, while
Eisenhower played the equally important role of keeping the alliance together.

Inevitably, AFHQ had growing pains. When the headquarters
was first formed, it comprised several hundred officers of both
nationalities, all unknown to one another and attempting to learn
how the system would work, alongside planning the coming military operation. After two weeks, Eisenhower addressed his staff
'in a remarkable speech',[48] arguing that:

> the two nations were completely different and only converged at
> one point – a common language. He reminded his mixed audience
> that the Americans regarded the British as 'standoffish conceited
> snobs', whereas the British looked on the Americans as 'loud-
> mouthed braggarts' . . . He pointed out that if we held these views
> and did not realise that they were held it would not be possible for
> a Britisher and American to work in the same office with any degree
> of harmony. He ended by saying that there would be harmony and
> that any officer who produced discord would be thrown out by him
> no matter his nationality or seniority.[49]

Eisenhower later recalled that the British and American officers
'came together like a bulldog meeting a cat' and it took time for
the headquarters to settle down into an efficient pattern.[50] There
were numerous initial problems and frictions based on a lack of
understanding of each other's staff procedures, and a 'fog of mutual
doubts and misgivings' that took time to clear.[51] Even the fact that
the British and American officers spoke the same language appeared
to be a matter in doubt. On his first introduction to a British Chiefs
of Staff meeting in April 1942, Truscott had 'real difficulty in
following the discussions' because of the very different English
pronunciation of his new colleagues:

Their speech was . . . filled with abbreviations or 'short titles' with which we were not familiar; they gave many words a pronunciation not common in America and used familiar words with unfamiliar meanings. They spoke with astonishing rapidity, practically through closed teeth and with little action of the lips. All this made it very difficult for me to understand English 'as she is spoke'.[52]

One American officer put it more bluntly. In his opinion, British officers 'talk so odd that they sound like a bunch of furriners'.[53] British officers, in turn, could struggle to understand a broad Texan accent or the flat vowels of a Midwestern officer, and the very different speech patterns remained a factor, and an obvious point of difference, throughout the war.[54]

Equally, Eisenhower probably overreacted to the first instances of friction in his new headquarters in an attempt to ensure that the officers were under no illusions that they simply *had* to get along with one another. Ismay remembered a heated disagreement between a British and an American officer; Eisenhower looked into the matter, decided that the American officer was at fault and ordered him to be reduced in rank and immediately sent home to the United States. The British officer went to see Eisenhower to plead for his American colleague, saying, 'He only called me the son of a bitch, sir and all of us have now learnt that this is a colloquial expression which is sometimes almost used as a term of endearment.' Eisenhower replied that he had been told that 'he called you a British son of a bitch. That is quite different. My ruling stands.'[55]

Eisenhower was determined that his experiment of a fully integrated headquarters would work, but this was only one of the many difficulties he faced in pulling together the threads necessary to make Torch a reality. All the proposed options had to work within constrained limits, which included the availability of shipping, naval strength, and the preparedness of the troops for the landings. At the same time, the likely Axis response as well as the possible reactions of Vichy France and Spain had to be gauged. Perhaps the greatest difficulty, however, was that the British and American planners in Washington and London could not agree on the best approach to the operation. There was general agreement that the final objective was occupation of the whole of French North Africa, and it was recognised that the capture of Tunis was the key to the control of this theatre, but there was a long-running debate about how this could best be achieved.

While the American planners had been willing to accept almost any risk in the conduct of Sledgehammer, they suddenly took counsel of their fears with regard to Torch. Their fear was that the Axis might react to the landings by attacking Gibraltar through Spain. This could cut the widely dispersed landings in two and cause severe difficulties. Thus the majority American view was that it was better to land at Casablanca on the Atlantic coast than to risk the closure of the Straits of Gibraltar. Meanwhile, having been obstinate in their refusal over Sledgehammer, there were a number of British voices, most notably Admiral Andrew Cunningham, who wished to take the gamble of mounting the landings not only inside the Mediterranean at Algiers and Oran but also at Bone in Tunisia to ensure that at least one landing was as close to Tunis as possible.

These competing views were hard to reconcile, and various alternative plans, memos and signals criss-crossed the Atlantic in what Eisenhower aptly named the 'great transatlantic essay contest'. Marshall sent Major General Thomas Handy, head of the Operations Division, to assist Eisenhower with the planning process while also keeping a watchful eye on progress for the chief. Handy reported to Marshall on 22 August 1942 that he found all the American officers hard at work on the plan but that there was 'a practical unanimity of opinion . . . that the operation is dependent for success upon the favourable outcome of so many uncertain factors as to make our chances considerably less than fifty percent'.[56] This could hardly have been cheering news for Marshall, but Handy's considered conclusion was extraordinary:

> Torch as now set up involves an unjustifiable hazard and should be abandoned entirely or revised and directed toward a less ambitious objective. I believe that the soundest action would be a reversion to the original Sledgehammer–Roundup plan. The next most advantageous action would be for the US to turn to the Pacific.[57]

Not only did this reveal that the head of the Operations Division was far from convinced that Torch would be a success, it also demonstrated that he had not been shifted from the belief that Sledgehammer–Roundup was still the best approach for the European war. The lack of faith in the planning for Torch was in part a reflection of the inexperience of the new AFHQ in planning a major amphibious operation, but it was also due to the almost inevitable tendency to magnify the difficulties involved in an uncertain situation. The planning debate for Torch soon reached a position of deadlock. Just like Sledgehammer, it took the intervention of the President and Prime Minister to break the logjam. It was not until early September that Roosevelt agreed to an assault at Algiers and Churchill agreed to a landing at Casablanca.

Like many political compromises, the resultant agreement was satisfactory to neither side, but it meant that the necessary detailed planning and preparations could finally go ahead in the precious little time left before the operation was launched. The Western Task Force, sailing direct from the United States under the command of Major General George S. Patton, was to capture Casablanca on the Atlantic coast of Morocco;[58] the Centre Task Force, under Major General Lloyd R. Fredendall, was to land at Oran;[59] the Eastern Task Force, commanded by Major General Charles W. Ryder, was to capture Algiers and its nearby airfields.[60] Once Algiers was secured by the American units, Lieutenant General Kenneth Anderson would activate the British First Army, which was then expected to drive towards Tunisia. The lack of shipping and the political compromise necessary to get agreement meant that there were to be no landings at Bone, as Cunningham had wanted. Anderson's men would have to travel over 600 miles to reach Tunis. It was thus almost inevitable that Axis forces would be able to occupy Tunisia before the Allies could reach it, which made the attitude of the Vichy French forces in North Africa more important than ever.

Roosevelt believed that the Vichy French authorities might not resist an American intervention in North Africa. The United States had maintained an ambassador in Vichy, as well as representatives in North Africa. Indeed, Robert Murphy, one of the key American men in North Africa, had managed to convince Roosevelt that, with proper negotiations, the French forces there would not resist American landings. In the event, even the British forces that were to go ashore in the first waves were to wear American flags on their uniforms in the expectation that the French units would not oppose American troops.

As the time for Torch approached, and the final preparations were made, the pressure and anxiety mounted. Churchill became highly impatient waiting for news of the coming attack at Alamein. Finally, on 23 October 1942, the Eighth Army's assault began successfully with a much-publicised 'thousand gun' barrage. Yet after ten days of fierce fighting, Montgomery seemed to be bogged down against the mines, wire and tenacious defence of Rommel's army. When news reached London that he was regrouping for another attack, Churchill was dismayed. He knew that a stalled battle in the desert would be regarded as a British defeat by both allies and enemies alike. He demanded a meeting with Brooke, who was then confronted with:

> a flow of abuse of Monty. What was my Monty doing now, allowing the battle to peter out (Monty was always my Monty when he was out of favour!) . . . Why had he told us he would be through in seven days if all he intended to do was to fight a half-hearted battle? Had we not got a single general who could even win one single battle?[61]

Although Brooke was furious with Churchill and vigorously defended Montgomery, he admitted, if only to himself, that he did suffer a desperate feeling of loneliness because 'there was still just the possibility that I was wrong and that Monty was beat'.[62] Churchill had expressed one of his deepest fears: that the British Army did not have any decent generals and simply was not capable of winning a battle against the Germans. The fact was that Churchill needed a victory; another defeat, whether perceived or actual, would mean that his influence upon Allied decision-making would suffer irretrievable damage.

It was not until 4 November, with the Torch convoys already at sea, that London received the news that the Eighth Army had won a decisive victory and that Rommel's army was in full retreat. The British had indeed finally achieved a success, thanks to intensive training, detailed planning and concentrated use of artillery, all techniques that Montgomery had first learnt as a staff officer in the Great War. Under his tutelage, the Eighth Army had managed to absorb the hard lessons of almost two years of desert fighting. Most importantly, his methodical approach to battle became the model for most British offensives of the war. The successful use of the Sherman tank gave the Americans vital combat proof of the capabilities of the new medium tank, which would equip all of their armoured divisions for the foreseeable future. At Alamein, the Sherman was a battle-winner and the British were effusive in their praise. This was fully justified at the time, but it did have the unfortunate effect that both American and British confidence in the tank persisted until 1944, when it was found to have serious shortcomings against the second generation of German tanks.

It was not surprising that the British, ably supported by Churchill himself, trumpeted this victory. Yet when Churchill wanted to ring the church bells of Britain to acknowledge the triumph, Brooke advised caution. Thinking ahead, he counselled that any celebration could quickly turn to sorrow if Torch proved disastrous. Brooke – and the British public – had become so accustomed to defeat that even a victory seemed too good to be true. Ultimately, the church bells across Britain were rung in joint celebration for Alamein and the success of Torch. The army film unit's film Desert Victory not only made a star of the Eighth Army and its commander, but subsequently won an Academy Award. Montgomery became a household name in Britain, yet his very success sowed seeds of discord amongst the Allies. This awkward, abrasive British general had gained a virtually untouchable reputation as a commander who could win battles.

As Montgomery basked in the glow of victory and sent his army in pursuit of Rommel's men, Eisenhower moved his headquarters to the dank and dripping tunnels of Gibraltar to coordinate the final moves for Torch. Here he found himself almost trapped, with little real communication with the task forces: he could only wait to hear their reports. He later said that it was his loneliest time during the war. However, he still had no real conception of the political quagmire in which he would soon become enmeshed. Like most American officers, he had little or no idea about the complexities, jealousies and bitter divisions of French politics. While General Charles de Gaulle, the leader of the Free French in London, was supported by an exasperated Churchill, Roosevelt hoped to find a more pliable French associate. He and Robert Murphy, his personal representative, had pinned their hopes on General Henri Giraud, who had only recently escaped from a prisoner-of-war camp in Germany. However, when Giraud arrived in Gibraltar, he harangued the hapless Eisenhower on the necessity of his assuming full command of the operation. Eventually Eisenhower persuaded 'Kingpin' (the American code name for Giraud) to go to Algiers to broadcast an appeal to the French forces to cease fighting. Of course, Giraud had no authority amongst the Vichy French forces and his appeal fell on deaf ears.

The Torch landings themselves ultimately succeeded beyond the expectations and fears of the Allied planners. However, the hopes that American troops might be welcomed ashore without a shot being fired proved misplaced. French troops resisted fiercely, particularly at Casablanca and Oran, though the fighting proved mercifully brief. Although Giraud's appeal met with no response, it was soon discovered that, by chance, Admiral Jean Darlan, commander-in-chief of the Vichy armed forces and second only to Marshal Pétain within the regime, happened to be visiting his son in Algiers at the time of the landings. Lieutenant Colonel Dudley Clark, Dill's military assistant, rushed to Algiers to negotiate a deal, and after four days of talks, Darlan agreed to order a ceasefire and take up the post of High Commissioner in North Africa. This armistice, which quickly became known as 'the Darlan deal', was probably the quickest means to end the fighting in French North Africa, but what had appeared to Clark and Eisenhower to be a simple military device soon turned into a full-scale political storm. Churchill was absolutely furious to find that Eisenhower had committed both allies to a deal with a leading member of the Vichy regime.[63] As far as the British administration was concerned, Darlan was a collaborator and a fascist, nor was it the role of a military commander to become involved in matters of high diplomacy. However, neither the armistice nor the resultant political storm did anything to prevent the Germans and Italians rushing troops into Tunis and gaining a firm grip on the Allies' final objective.

Very quickly, Eisenhower and Anderson began to realise that the assumptions made by the Allied planners simply did not hold true on the ground. Eisenhower's forces had made successful landings but were now dispersed between Casablanca, Oran and Algiers, with hundreds of miles between each task force. There had been so much preoccupation with the dangers and risks of the amphibious landings themselves that far less thought had been devoted to the development of subsequent operations. This was to become an unfortunate pattern of Allied operations for the rest of the war. In fact, the campaign quickly became a race for Tunis, with the British troops under Anderson, who had landed at Algiers, in the lead. Anderson later regretted that the press talked of the landing and advance of the British First Army, which gave the impression that powerful forces were moving on Tunis. In fact, the advance guard of his force consisted of only two under-strength brigade groups from the 78th Division and one regiment of tanks. The eventual build-up of forces was slow due to the lack of shipping to bring in regular reinforcements.[64]

With the growth of Axis forces in Tunisia, Eisenhower soon realised that Anderson would not have the strength to reach Tunis, and he began to comb out as many as possible of the American units that had landed at Oran in Morocco, to send them forward to help the British. This decision meant that dribs and drabs of American units were sent up towards Tunisia in a highly piecemeal fashion. Combat Command B of the US 1st Armored Division, which was the first unit sent to support Anderson, became a particular victim of this approach, being attached and detached to various American, British and French units 13 times between November 1942 and February 1943.[65] A mixed bag of field artillery, anti-aircraft units and one battalion of the 26th Infantry Regiment was also dispatched, and all had to cover over 700 miles through Morocco and Algeria before reaching the front line in Tunisia.

Eisenhower readily admitted in a letter to Handy that the campaign was not going according to plan. The rush into Tunisia stretched the limited Allied supply capacity well beyond breaking point, while the great distances, combined with poor weather and lack of airfields, meant that Allied air cover was practically non-existent. 'I think the best way to describe our operations to date is that they have violated every recognised principle of war, are in conflict with all operational and logistic methods laid down in text-books, and will be condemned, in their entirety, by all Leavenworth and War College classes for the next twenty-five years.'[66] The fact was that the Allied plan for Operation Torch had fallen apart the moment it came into contact with the reality of the Axis reaction. This meant that the first weeks and months of Allied operations in French North Africa witnessed a desperate improvisation and scrambling of whatever forces could be scraped together to try and reach Tunis. Nonetheless, Eisenhower firmly believed that 'the hasty pell-mell advance was justified because at the very worst it gave us territory that could, if defended, have been held by a very few troops'.[67]

This scramble towards Tunis meant that much of the cooperation that emerged between the Americans and British was of a highly improvised nature. There was no time or opportunity to ensure that the units knew how to work with one another, and British and American units were often thrown together at very short notice. Not all the improvised cooperation in Tunisia worked well. Indeed, the experience often simply revealed that units of both armies possessed almost no knowledge about their counterpart's organisation, tactics or procedures. Seemingly simple differences in language and vocabulary could and did cause enormous problems, and units were also often employed to meet local crises and problems in a way that differed from their agreed doctrine and the prior training with which they were familiar.

One of the most dispiriting examples of this malcoordination occurred in the final attempt to reach Tunis in 1942. On the night of 22–23 December, the British 2nd Battalion Coldstream Guards was ordered to assault the last major hill on the road to Tunis. Once 'Longstop Hill' had been taken, the defences of the Tunisian capital would be wide open, and it was planned that the positions on the hill would be handed over to the US 18th Regimental Combat Team. The guardsmen made their attack, clambering up the rocky slopes under heavy German machine-gun fire. Eventually the crest of the hill was reached and the Coldstream companies dug in in the hard stony ground. However, unbeknownst to either the British or the Americans, a further crest line, at the Djebel el Rhara, remained in German hands.[68]

Following the assault, the Guards were tired and had suffered heavy casualties, but their relief turned into a disaster. A successful relief requires good communication and a considerable amount of time to ensure that one unit can move into the positions held by the other without a hitch. Unfortunately, none of these preconditions applied when the US 18th Regimental Combat Team attempted to relieve the Coldstream Guards. The different procedures each army used for conducting a relief led to confusion. Heavy German fire held up the relieving American infantry, and chaos ensued when the American commanding officer came forward alone instead of with his headquarters. It took a considerable time to effect the relief in the pitch dark.[69] All the attempts at liaison and coordination (which were conducted very differently in the two armies) ultimately meant that the American soldiers dug in on the lower slopes of the hill, leaving the tactically vital crest undefended. The tired guardsmen stumbled back down and began the long trudge, 12 miles in pouring rain, to a rest camp. However, just a few hours later, one company received orders to return to Longstop Hill as the Americans were in serious difficulty, having lost most of the hill to German counter-attacks. The weary British soldiers had to march all the way back and mount another attack, which subsequently failed.

The episode caused considerable bitterness between the two allies, even though the subsequent Coldstream report on the fighting noted diplomatically that 'although the British and Americans speak the same language, co-operation at the battalion level in battle is very difficult on account of the differences in organization and terminology'.[70] The fighting also proved that the random mixing of Allied units was a recipe for disorganisation and defeat. Finally, the failure to take Longstop Hill, combined with atrocious weather and the breakdown in the supply system, meant that the Allied attempt to rush through to Tunis had failed.

This mixing up of British and American units had a number of other unfortunate consequences. Since the Algerian–Tunisian sector had originally been intended as a British area of responsibility, all Allied troops in Tunisia were supplied through the British supply chain. This meant that the British furnished some 65,000 American and French troops with British rations and clothing, as well as over 400 tons of petrol per day to US units until March 1943. However, with little or no standardisation of arms or equipment, the resupply of ammunition and spare parts became a real problem. American units attached to the British First Army found 'themselves frequently marooned without adequate maintenance, logistical and signal support'.[71] Indeed, one of the American 155 mm artillery regiments that had been rushed up to the First Army had to be almost equally rapidly withdrawn, as it had run out of ammunition and none could be provided through the British supply depots.[72]

For the troops themselves, perhaps the greatest disadvantage to this mingling of units was the fact that American troops had to exist on British rations. In an echo of their fathers' experience in the Great War, American soldiers were unanimous in their complaints about British military food. These criticisms were certainly exacerbated by the logistic difficulties, which also made getting mail through to the troops a constant problem. One American soldier wrote home in early January 1943 complaining that:

> Our living conditions are so poor over here. Haven't had a bath in three weeks and we sleep in our clothes so we can keep warm in our bed rolls. We are on British rations and its hardtack, hot tea, and sausage for breakfast then the other meal at 4 p.m. is hot tea, Irish stew (slop) and hardtack. We're dirty and hungry. No, I didn't expect a picnic but I know none of us can hold out for long.[73]

American soldiers on British rations – and of course all British soldiers – received just two unappetising meals a day. Not surprisingly, many troops complained of constant hunger, which must have affected their morale and their combat effectiveness. Meanwhile, their comrades in Morocco could expect the kind of largesse that only the US Army's Services of Supply could deliver. American rations were described by one soldier as 'good eats . . . We have had turkey on two occasions recently, steak tonight, fresh eggs for breakfast. On the whole we certainly have no complaints coming.'[74]

If the British and American troops holding the front line in Tunisia were tired, hungry and miserable, it might have been small consolation to them to know that their commanders were also despondent. Serious questions were being raised by senior British and American officers about Anderson's ability to command in this new multinational environment. While Eisenhower considered that Anderson 'has worked like a dog and, in my opinion, has done everything that was humanly possible to make the big gamble win', others were less sure.[75] Anderson had a shy, reserved and taciturn manner and could be 'blunt, at times to the point of rudeness'.[76] He found it difficult to establish good working relations with his own British subordinates, and almost impossible with the Americans. This unhappy situation led to Admiral Cunningham, Eisenhower's naval commander, making an unprecedented intervention in army matters. Although he was initially reluctant, he felt it essential to point out to the First Sea Lord (and thereby the other two British Chiefs of Staff) that:

Anderson's relationships with SOs [Senior Officers] both British and American are not as happy as they should be. Anderson is a difficult man to get on with and has not only rubbed Americans wrong way but has also achieved unsatisfactory relationship with our own Air Force even with so equable a man as Tedder [head of the RAF Middle East Command]. The consequence is that there is developing a mutual lack of trust. This lack of trust of Anderson is, I am sure, quite unjustified by his military action and is primarily matter of personalities. It is to my mind, important to check this tendency as soon as practicable to avoid any possibility of undesirable show-down between American and British Armies.[77]

At least some of this criticism was unfair. Anderson was under enormous strain, struggling with a very difficult military situation with insufficient forces and a myriad of intractable problems. While Brooke gave him a faint caution on the importance of good Allied relations, the implications were clear, if not perhaps to Anderson.[78] The days of Braddock, and even of Haig, were over. Military competence was no longer (if it had ever been) enough for a general in command of a British army. Strong personal and diplomatic skills combined with an ability to put others, often from other nationalities, at their ease and to win their confidence were now just as important in the conduct of campaigns.

If Anderson was facing questions over his ability to work as part of an alliance, Eisenhower's military competence and lack of command experience were causing him and his masters real concern. This was probably Eisenhower's most difficult period of the war. Axis air forces, operating from good all-weather airstrips around Tunis, were able to seize and exploit air superiority. Meanwhile, mud, atrocious weather and continual supply problems made conditions at the front very difficult indeed. Facing increasing criticism from both London and Washington over his handling of the campaign, Eisenhower found most of his time absorbed in dealing with the tangled and intractable politics of French North Africa. He complained to a friend that he felt as though 'he was walking a soapy tightrope in the rain, with a blazing furnace on one side, and a pack of ravenous tigers on the other'.[79] Visits to the front became a form of escape from the pressures of Algiers. At least part of the problem was that, throughout November and early December 1942, AFHQ was operating from three separate locations divided by thousands of miles, in London, Gibraltar and Algiers. Bedell Smith was fighting a vital rearguard action in London on behalf of his chief, but it meant that Eisenhower's headquarters in Algiers was not as fully efficient or effective as it might have been. Unsurprisingly, he seemed to be losing his grip of both the military situation and his relations with his military and political masters.

While the Tunisian campaign became bogged down in recriminations and winter mud, there was increasing anxiety on both sides
of the Atlantic about the future strategy of the war. When an
expected full Combined Chiefs of Staff conference failed to mate-
rialise in November 1942, Marshall ordered Bedell Smith to return
to Washington for ten days to contemplate future approaches.[80]
Bedell Smith was grilled by both the Chief of Staff and the President
over the Tunisian campaign and the thinking in London. However,
he also kept Ismay informed on the situation in Washington,
reporting that he found the combined planning there 'to be very
unsatisfactory. Dykes is very low in his mind about the whole thing,
we had one or two long talks while he wept on my shoulder', due
mainly to personality clashes and obstinacy from the US Navy.[81]
He then went on to provide Ismay with a frank summary of
American strategic thinking:

> I found our people rather cold toward the major exploitation from
> this area [the Mediterranean] which so interests the Prime Minister.
> The fact is that China and the Pacific situation have become increas-
> ingly threatening and the US Chiefs of Staff feel most strongly that
> unless some definite action is taken to bolster up the Chinese, there
> is grave danger of a collapse.[82]

The fact was that the fight for Guadacanal in the Pacific was
absorbing the full attention of the US Navy, which, in the person
of Admiral King and his planners, continued to see the war in
Europe as an uninteresting diversion. Bedell Smith's visit to
Washington had convinced him that the Allies were still not working
together and impressed on him:

> the vital necessity for a determination at the earliest possible
> moment of a major strategy for the United Nations. Unless our
> great men sit down and reach a definite decision as to whether
> we exploit the Mediterranean area, push a campaign in the Pacific
> and Burma, or build up in UK for 'Round-Up', we shall continue
> to flounder and will be absolutely unable to pull together. The
> whole thing worries me but I hope that the proposed conference,

which General Marshall thinks might well be held in Egypt, will actually become a fact and will serve to button up this basic difficulty.[83]

The conference was eventually held in Casablanca, rather than Egypt, and while it certainly became one of the most important meetings held by the Allied leaders and their Combined Chiefs of Staff, it could not entirely 'button up' the basic strategic disagreements between the two allies.

7

Growing Pains

For the greater part of military history, collaboration between allied armies has tended to be limited to senior commanders and their staffs. The officers and men in the field have seldom come into close contact with their allies or had much opportunity to meet or understand them as soldiers or individuals. The Allied campaign in North Africa can be seen as a great experiment in which British, French and American soldiers were literally thrown together at short notice and fought shoulder to shoulder. They ate their allies' rations (albeit often unwillingly) and, on occasion, shared each other's equipment. This mixing together of three very different armies brought about some unexpected results. There was, as might be expected, a considerable clash of military cultures. Soldiers from all three armies could be surprised and even shocked at the very different methods, approaches and behaviour of their allies. Even though most of the officers and men were 'civilians in uniform' who had themselves only recently been inculcated into their own national military culture, the six-month process of training had swiftly turned them into soldiers and at the same time cemented national approaches to the business of war. When soldiers of the three nations first met each other, it was invariably the differences, rather than the similarities, that were highlighted. Yet out of the trials and tribulations of this particularly difficult and harsh campaign, soldiers of the British and American armies in particular began to develop mutual understanding and respect even as some senior commanders and their staffs were developing a much more virulent rivalry.[1]

This clash of military cultures could take surprising forms. Major

David Montgomery experienced a bewildering example when he visited British comrades in an anti-aircraft battery who were helping to protect a group of three landing grounds at Negheb in Tunisia. The landing grounds were being used by an American pursuit group, and he had to pass through the American lines to reach the two gun sites manned by the British battery. He noticed that every fifty yards there was an American soldier with a large .50 machine gun as part of the airfield's defences. Once he reached the British battery, his friend Major Bill Emslie explained that there were quite frequent raids by enemy aircraft and that three men had been wounded already that morning during a raid. He added that he didn't mind such shoot-ups, but remarked cryptically that 'It's the American Civil War that gets me down.' Soon afterwards, a dozen Messerschmitts came in on a strafing run, which raked the landing ground with fire. Montgomery recalled that:

As they appeared, anything on the ground that could opened up on them. For just a moment, we could distinguish the heavy crack of the 3.7s and the lighter 'ker-bunk, ker-bunk' of the 40 mms and then their noise was swallowed up in a mighty chorus of machine gun fire, like a hailstorm beating on a tin roof, the sound rising and falling like waves on a beach, deafening and deadening in its intensity. In a second, the air was full of flying bullets, 5 percent German and 95 percent American and we lay prudently flat on the ground, endeavouring to make ourselves as inconspicuous as possible.

When an American fires a machine-gun, he fires a machine-gun; any thought other than keeping the trigger pressed and his sights on the target is excluded from his mind. Not for him are such fussy conventions as 'safety angle' and 'dead zones'. Single-mindedly, he ignores them as ideas devised to prevent him bringing down the enemy. Only when his ammunition belt is exhausted, is his concentration interrupted.

The Me 109s were hedge-hopping and therefore the L[anding] G[round] at ground level was swept with a swathe of half-inch bullets at an almost horizontal trajectory. We could hear them going by just above us like the crack of a thin whip and knocked splinters off the rocks behind us which mewed through the air like plaintive kittens.

This attack took about 45 seconds and then the 109s skated away, brushing the camel thorn with their fuselages, and the firing withered and died away. As far as one could see, little damage was done. Bill Emslie rose to his feet and dusted himself down. 'That', he explained, 'is the American Civil War', as we went back to our lunch.[2]

As a British officer with experience in anti-aircraft gunnery, Montgomery had been trained in the need for safety zones and the conservation of ammunition. He was horrified at the American approach to air defence, which not only wasted ammunition but ensured that the 'defence' of the airfield was probably more dangerous than the German attacks.

American soldiers could find the British Army just as perplexing and infuriating. John Downing was a young infantry lieutenant who was sent to work at a British headquarters as a liaison officer for the US 18th Regimental Combat Team, which was attached to the British 78th Division during December 1942 and January 1943. Downing had to swiftly pick up all the idiosyncrasies of the British Army, and at his very first briefing he realised that there was much to learn. Even when marking up a map, the British symbols 'were designated just the opposite from American custom: friendly units were in red pencil and the enemy in blue'.[3] Differences in how the two armies organised their units could also lead to unfair discrepancies in rank, which were bound to cause a certain resentment between officers in the two armies. British battalions were normally commanded in action by lieutenant colonels, while brigades were generally commanded by a brigadier. However, the British rank of brigadier was not exactly equivalent to that of brigadier general in the US Army, which meant that it was considered something of a hybrid between field and general officer. It also meant that while American regiments were commanded by a colonel, a British brigadier, although also in command of three battalions, outranked his American equivalent.[4]

Downing found his first experience of a British officers' mess

even more disorientating. Each British officer had his own personal
batman, an alien concept to the US Army, and some of the
British batmen had to grudgingly help the new American visitors.
There could be no talk of 'shop' or religion; instead, the officers
enthusiastically discussed the goose for the mess Christmas dinner.
He found the 'whole business . . . extraneous . . . like living in
another world. An attack was coming up and yet the main conversation was about the price of the goose and how it would get
cooked.'⁵ Downing also found the British attitude to shaving
perplexing. British officers and men shaved punctiliously every
morning, even in the front line. He noted that 'Their hands were
red from the cold air, and colder water, but those already shaven
had the pink glowing cheeks of well-scrubbed schoolboys. Luckily
those Spartan regulations were not in force in the American Army.
It would have been another rigor of war to have to shave every
morning in cold water before breakfast.'⁶ Most British officers
saw shaving as an essential mark of soldierly virtue and discipline
that had to be maintained in all circumstances, and took a dim
view of what they regarded as the lax standards of dress and
discipline in many American units.* These differences in military
culture could cause misunderstanding, even resentment and suspicion, and the events of the Tunisian campaign would soon intensify
this yet further.

While the rain and mud of the Tunisian winter stalled operations,
both sides were able to build their resources for renewed offensives
in the spring. This provided time for another meeting between
Churchill, Roosevelt and the Combined Chiefs of Staff, which was
held at Casablanca in January 1943. Although only recently captured
by Patton's Eastern Task Force, Casablanca was far from the battle
front in Tunisia and quite safe for a major meeting. Given that the
Combined Staff planners had failed to agree on the course of future
plans, the conference was of real importance in determining
the direction of the Anglo-American alliance.⁷ Yet once again the

---

* There were, of course, exceptions to this rule. The Long Range Desert Group, the
Special Air Service, and the Chindits, for example, relaxed all strictures concerning
shaving while on operations.

meetings revealed the sharp differences in organisation, strategic thought and military culture of the two allies.

The British view on future strategy was clear: they wished to press the advantage gained in the Mediterranean. The eventual fall of Tunisia would open the shipping route through the inland sea and would also expose Italy as a tempting target. While the continuation of the war in the Mediterranean might be at the expense of a cross-Channel attack in 1943, the build-up of American forces in Britain had been slower than expected anyway. Meanwhile, there were three Allied armies in Tunisia that might be used to knock Italy out of the war. As far as the British were concerned, an offensive in the Mediterranean would distract Hitler and draw troops out of Russia just as effectively as the riskier cross-Channel attack that the Americans were still insisting upon. In contrast with the British, the Americans lacked a fully thought-out strategy for the war beyond the original Bolero–Roundup plan, and worse, there was no agreement between the army and navy so that the British might be met with a united American view of the war.

When the conference began, on 14 January 1943, the Americans soon discovered that they simply did not have sufficient staff to prepare detailed appreciations and calculations for their chiefs as the discussions progressed, and had to hurriedly borrow staff officers from Eisenhower's headquarters. As Ian Jacob noted, 'both they and we were handicapped all the way through by their lack of staff, and nearly every paper produced during the Conference had to be produced by our people with little or no help from the Americans'.[8] The initiative had passed to the British negotiators from the very start. In the initial discussions, Marshall and King wished to decide upon the allocation of resources between the Atlantic and Pacific as a 70/30 percentage split before reviewing courses of action. The British wanted to reach agreement on the objectives first and then allocate resources.

The next day, Brooke gave a detailed exposition of the situation in Europe and the Mediterranean as the British Chiefs of Staff saw it. He argued that there were two broad choices: one was to 'close down in the Mediterranean as soon as the North African coast had been cleared . . . and to devote every effort to building up in the

United Kingdom for an invasion of the North of France at the earliest possible moment'. Under British calculations, it was estimated that only 23 British divisions and 12 US divisions could be ready for such an invasion by 15 September 1943. As far as the British were concerned, this was sufficient to make a landing but insufficient to prevent the Germans from overwhelming the force once ashore. The other choice was 'to maintain activity in the Mediterranean while building up the maximum air offensive against Germany from the UK' and to continue the expansion of US forces in Britain for an eventual cross-Channel attack. Not surprisingly, Brooke expounded on the advantages of the Mediterranean approach. He argued that there were many options, including an attack on Sardinia, Sicily, Crete or the Dodecanese. Threats could be made on all of these points simultaneously, which would force the Germans to disperse their forces. At the same time, a successful assault might force Italy out of the war, thus landing Germany with enlarged commitments throughout the Mediterranean and Balkans.[9]

Opinion quickly swung behind Sicily as the preferred target. Marshall, who remained convinced that a cross-Channel attack at the earliest opportunity remained the best course of action, could only fight a determined rearguard action. Even though 'operations against Sicily appeared to be advantageous' at this point, he wanted to know 'just what part it would play in the over-all strategic plan'.[10] He emphasised that 'he was most anxious not to become committed to interminable operations in the Mediterranean. He wished Northern France to be the scene of the main effort against Germany – that had always been his conception.'[11] Marshall still saw the Mediterranean as a black hole that, if not controlled, would suck all the men and resources away from the vital cross-Channel operation, but he had neither the arguments nor the staff at hand to win the argument. Neither could he gain the support of Admiral King, who was perfectly happy to agree to an operation against Sicily as long as it did not interfere with his plans in the Pacific. Marshall was furious that neither King nor Arnold would support his stance, and being divided, the US Chiefs of Staff were eventually conquered. Once again, it was Dill who acted as interlocutor between the two camps, despite not having a formal role in the discussions.

After four days of intense talks, Marshall finally acquiesced to the British arguments. The main objective for the Anglo-American alliance in 1943 would not be a cross-Channel attack but an invasion of the island of Sicily, which would clear the sea lanes through the Mediterranean for Allied shipping, divert German attention from Russia, and hopefully knock Italy out of the war. However, Marshall was also determined to limit the damage: he refused to sanction any further operations in the Mediterranean. The attack on Sicily, code-named Operation Husky, was thus placed in a strategic vacuum where no real thought could be given to how subsequent operations might develop from a successful occupation of the island.

British strategic thinking had prevailed due to their thorough prep-aration and impressive team of negotiators in the face of divided American counsels. While the British party at Casablanca were certainly gratified that their views had met with acceptance, there was also a sense that this was a temporary victory. The American chiefs had, in a sense, been caught on the cusp of the growth of American military power. The United States had still been strug-gling to expand her armed forces in 1942, but the coming year would see an enormous increase in her military power as the plans laid from 1940 onwards finally bore fruit. By the end of 1942, Britain had recovered from the crisis of 1940 and had reached a position of full mobilisation, but could not expect to experience comparable growth. Soon after Casablanca, Dill remarked to his aide, Major Reginald Winn:

> Reggie, do you realise that from now on the American war effort and war production is going to increase by leaps and bounds? They are going to produce two-thirds of everything to our one-third. Therefore it will become increasingly difficult for us to put forward and sustain our point of view as they will be providing so much more than us.[12]

Dill recognised that Casablanca had perhaps represented the final opportunity for British strategic views to prevail. Wedemeyer was under no illusions about what had happened at the conference. He wrote to Thomas Handy that 'We came, we saw and we were conquered.'[13] But there is no question that Wedemeyer and his team made certain they were not placed in the same position of disadvantage again. Paul Caraway, who joined Wedemeyer's strategy section in the War Department in the autumn of 1942, explained that 'We didn't lose any more conferences we went all the way up. Sometimes we didn't win them without a few knocks and bruises, but we won them. Why? Because we stayed ahead of our British friends the whole time.'[14] The British, having carried their points at Casablanca through ruthless precision and preparation, would be met with a similar US approach in all the subsequent Allied conferences. In many respects, Casablanca represented the high point of British influence upon the alliance, which subsequently waned as the war continued.

Strangely enough, Eisenhower had begun to see the opportunities open to the Allies in the Mediterranean theatre. He wrote to Handy saying that he hoped:

> that history will declare the decisions reached to be wise ones. Frankly, I do not see how the 'big bosses' could have deviated very far from the general course of action they adopted. ROUNDUP, in its original concept, could not possibly be staged before August of 1944, because our original conceptions of the strength required were too low. Inaction in 1943 could not be tolerated and, unfortunately, distances are so great that we could not devote 1943 to one enemy and 1944 to another. One may question, if so minded, the specific objectives chosen, but in all such cases the pros and cons are usually rather evenly balanced and I am happy that a firm decision was reached.[15]

While Eisenhower saw the expansion of the Mediterranean theatre at the expense of a cross-Channel attack in 1943 as logical and possibly inevitable, the issue remains one of the great controversies of the war. Wedemeyer, in particular, never deviated from his view that a cross-Channel attack in 1943 would have been feasible and that, if the British had not been allowed to derail Allied strategy into 'periphery-pecking operations' in the Mediterranean backwater, an Anglo-American occupation of Germany and Eastern Europe would have become a reality.[16] Given the strength of the Wehrmacht and the nature of German defences along the coast of northern France in the summer of 1943, perhaps all that can be reliably said is that if the British and Americans had attempted it, the landings themselves might have been easier than those carried out in 1944, but the battle of the build-up would have been immeasurably more difficult.

One other issue, of the many discussed at the conference, concerned the need for the reorganisation of the command structure in North Africa. Soon Eisenhower would have to coordinate the operations not only of the British First Army, American II Corps and the French forces, but also Montgomery's Eighth Army as it approached Tunisia from Libya. Brooke believed that Eisenhower lacked the 'basic qualities required from such a commander' and he also saw Anderson as incapable of fulfilling the role.[17] While there was some discussion on the desirability of utilising General Patton in this position, Brooke was determined that the post should go to General Alexander. He later explained that by appointing Alexander as deputy to Eisenhower:

> we were carrying out a move which could not help flattering and pleasing the Americans in so far as we were placing our senior and experienced commander to function under their commander who had no war experience . . . We were pushing Eisenhower up into the stratosphere and rarified atmosphere of a Supreme Commander, where he would be free to devote his time to the political and inter-allied problems, whilst we inserted under him one of our commanders to deal with the military situation and to restore the necessary drive and co-ordination which had been so seriously lacking of late![18]

Eisenhower himself soon realised the implications. With Admiral Cunningham as his naval commander and adviser, Air Marshal

Tedder as his new air commander, and now Alexander as his ground force commander, the British had somehow managed to reinsert their system of 'command by committee' under him. Worse still, he knew he would now be advised by three highly experienced British senior officers, and it would be difficult to ignore their advice, even if he disagreed with it. Yet despite his concerns over the implications of the new command arrangements, Eisenhower was to prove himself capable of ensuring that the new system would function efficiently whilst nonetheless refusing to see his personal role relegated to a mere rubber stamp in a British-dominated system.

In fact, while Brooke was dismissive of Eisenhower's skill as a commander, a letter Eisenhower wrote to Thomas Handy revealed just how much he had already learnt from his experience in Tunisia. He asked Handy to help him by 'refusing to deal with our military problems on an American vs. British basis'.[19] Eisenhower argued that 'one of the constant sources of danger to us in this war is the temptation to regard as our first enemy the partner that must work with us in defeating the real enemy', and explained that he used brutal frankness when anyone attempted to represent a purely national as opposed to a United Nations attitude.[20] While he realised that the British and the Americans had divergent national interests, he was not going to allow those to disrupt his conception of unity and cooperation.

> I am not British and I am not ambidextrous in attitude. But I have got a very wholesome regard for the terrific tasks facing the United Nations in this war, and I am not going to let national prejudice or any of its related evils prevent me from getting the best out of the means that you fellows struggle so hard to make available to us.[21]

This one letter, in which Eisenhower outlined his command philosophy so clearly, demonstrates the extent to which Brooke had significantly underestimated the new American Supreme Commander. General Ike, as Eisenhower became known, had never commanded troops in battle, nor heard a shot fired in anger, but he possessed a uniquely broad and powerful vision of how to make the Anglo-American alliance actually work in practice.

While Eisenhower was beginning to demonstrate his unique value to the alliance, the equally indispensable contribution of Vivian Dykes was cut tragically short. Having attended the meetings of the Combined Chiefs of Staff at Casablanca, he was killed when his plane crash-landed in Wales on the return journey. The loss to the alliance was incalculable, and in truth, Dykes, with his experience, efficiency and undoubted ability to work with the American staffs, could never really be replaced. The staff in the British Joint Staff Mission recognised this when they informed London that 'Every member of Missions and his many American friends regard Dykes' death as a cruel personal loss and as a calamity to our combined work here. The Secretariat have lost a great leader and a well loved friend. England never had a finer representative in this country.'[22] Dykes' work and contribution to the Allied cause was further recognised by the posthumous award of the United States Distinguished Service Medal.

With this sad coda to the Casablanca conference, the Allies still had the difficult task of dealing with the war in North Africa, and Eisenhower's insistence on unity of purpose was soon put to one of its greatest tests when the Axis forces in Tunisia moved on to the offensive. Major General Ronald Penney was sent to AFHQ in Algiers on 1 February 1943 to work in what was to become Alexander's new 18th Army Group Headquarters. Penney had served as a Royal Engineer on the Western Front during the Great War, but transferred to the Royal Signals in 1921. During the interwar years, like many of his contemporaries, he had been stationed all across the Empire, in India, China and the North-West Frontier. By 1941 he had become the Signal Officer in Chief, Middle East, and he served in that capacity until appointed to Alexander's new headquarters. Penney was known to be somewhat humourless and had a reputation as 'a man who did everything by the book', but he was highly efficient and effective at providing and maintaining communications.[23] It was in this capacity that he was appointed as Alexander's chief signals officer, which involved visiting all the key headquarters and establishing communications between them.

Penney's first impressions of the situation in the Allied camp were revealing. He found the AFHQ, now established in the Hotel St George in Algiers, to be a 'rabbit warren . . . of incredible proportions' bustling with soldiers, sailors and airmen of every Allied nation.[24] While impressed with both Eisenhower and Bedell Smith, he felt that the entire headquarters was still an experiment in which 'a few British officers were carrying many US officers in key places and exhausting themselves in doing so'.[25] He was also worried that while US Army signals had great potential, they were not being utilised effectively or efficiently.

His sense of unease continued when he visited First Army Headquarters, where he found Anderson 'friendly but difficult as ever'.[26] Having been halted in front of Tunis in December 1942, the Allied forces, deployed in the foothills and passes of the Atlas Mountains in central Tunisia, formed a wide ring around the Axis armies. Anderson's army headquarters was now 200 miles from the front, and although he had one British, one American and one French corps under his command, the units were mixed up together, which increased the problems of command and control.[27]

Penney then went on to visit the headquarters of General Lloyd Fredendall, the commander of the US II Corps. He found the American commander to be 'full of "Jesus" – "Son of a Bitch" – "Goddammed" etc. etc. but without the personality of a George Patton'.[28] Not only were Fredendall's relations with Anderson at breaking point, but with the corps headquarters 60 miles from the front line, he had no clear idea of conditions or circumstances on the battle front. Instead, he had spent an inordinate amount of time preparing an elaborate immobile headquarters, which had been 'literally dug into a hill' and had to be 'approached through a swamp'.[29] While Penney was primarily concerned with the problems this put in the way of efficient communications, the fact that the main Allied headquarters was so far removed from the front line was soon to contribute to a near disaster.

Although Eisenhower had considered concentrating forces for an offensive towards Sfax on the Tunisian coast, the logistic situation had made it impossible. Yet instead of ordering a withdrawal to a more defensible position, he had decided to keep hold of the ground that had been gained during December 1942. This meant that the Allied front of over 300 miles was 'very extended and weakly held', which offered 'many hostages to fortune'.[30] The US II Corps, whose main task was to protect the right flank of the front, was really a corps in name only. Its main strength lay in the US 1st Armored Division, and while this was nearly up to full strength, the positions of its forward troops were badly overstretched, covering a front of almost 70 miles.

This situation presented an opportunity that the German commanders in Tunisia were not slow to exploit. Rommel, who had given up Tripoli, the last Italian colonial capital, on 23 January, pulled his army north. He saw the potential, indeed the necessity, for a spoiling attack that would drive the Allies back and give the Axis forces more room for manoeuvre. While his 15th and 21st Panzer Divisions were a pale shadow of their former selves, these formations still contained hardened desert veterans. Augmented by troops of the 10th Panzer Division, Rommel concentrated 200 Mark IV and Mark III tanks as well as 12 of the new Tiger tanks against the weak American forces at the Faid Pass in the Eastern Dorsale of the Atlas Mountains. This position was held by two battalions of the 168th Infantry Regiment, supported by some reconnaissance elements of 1st Armored Division's Combat Command A. Eisenhower had actually visited the positions the day before, but while he had expressed disquiet at the lack of mines, he had not commented upon the absence of mutual support between the badly dispersed positions.[31] Guided by Allied intelligence, which pointed to a German attack in the north, none of the higher commanders were aware of the German concentration against the Faid Pass.

Early on the morning of 14 February, the German panzers rolled forward under an umbrella of Stuka attacks. The soldiers of the 168th, who came mainly from Iowa, described the dust thrown up by the moving tanks as like 'the swirling yellow haze of drought powdered Oklahoma-Kansas soil' during the dust bowl of the 1930s.[32] The widely dispersed American forces were simply overwhelmed by the onrush of German assault. The panzers made short work of the M3 light tanks and artillery of Combat Command A, and the two battalions of infantry holding the pass were rapidly encircled. That evening, Combat Command C of 1st Armored mounted a prompt counter-attack, only to be encircled and destroyed itself. Soon 165 American tanks and armoured vehicles lay burnt out around Sidi Bou Zid. Elements of the two encircled infantry battalions held out for two days, but ultimately had little choice but to surrender.

The reports received by Anderson's and Fredendall's headquarters were confusing and contradictory, and the Allied commanders made a number of false moves among the chaos. By nightfall on 16 February, 1st Armored Division had been pressed back nearly 25 miles to Sbeitla, and had effectively lost two of its combat commands; only one, Combat Command B, now remained. Almost 4,000 Americans, including Patton's son-in-law, had fallen into German hands.[33] The advancing Germans, including Rommel, marvelled at the vast amounts of equipment that the Americans had abandoned when troops in the shock of their first battle – and an unequal one at that – had panicked and fled their posts, although some had fought bravely against desperate odds. Perhaps worst of all, Fredendall chose this moment to move his headquarters further back, even though it was not directly threatened. At a crucial moment, US II Corps was effectively rudderless. Most reports at the time, and since, attribute the defeat at Faid Pass to the fact that the troops were inexperienced. Yet while this may have been a factor, the main cause was almost certainly the errors of their higher commanders, who had left insufficient forces in poor positions where they were hopelessly vulnerable when the Germans attacked. Rommel's spoiling attack now threatened to unhinge the entire Allied line in Tunisia. This was a real crisis.

Although initially Anderson had delayed the movement of reserves to the threatened sector in the south due to concern over a potential German attack in the north, he managed to seal off the continued German assaults at Sbiba and Thala by rushing whatever troops were available to the threatened sectors. British and American units arrived in the south 'by squadrons, batteries, and even troops, and were armed with every variety of weapon', but were only just enough to stem the German onrush.[34] At Sbiba, the 1st Guards Brigade and the US 18th Regimental Combat Team, supported by two squadrons of Churchill tanks, managed to hold off the advance. However, the badly stretched and deployed American positions in the Kasserine Pass were overwhelmed. The only reserve available was the British 26th Armoured Brigade, which had been re-equipping with Sherman tanks; it had to be rushed forward in its obsolete Valentines and Crusaders to hold a covering position 18 miles south of Thala. Brigadier Charles Dunphie went forward in his scout car to make contact with Colonel Stark, the American officer charged with the defence of the Kasserine Pass. Realising that his brigade formed the last reserve capable of stemming the German onslaught, Dunphie personally organised the defence. At one point this included threatening to shoot an American sergeant who protested that, once he had delivered a half-track tank destroyer to the front line, he must be allowed to return to the rear.[35] The brigade positions were duly stiffened by some American troops and anti-tank guns, along with additional anti-aircraft artillery and infantry in the form of the 2/5 Leicesters, who had only recently disembarked at Algiers.

When the Germans advanced, the Leicesters were quickly overwhelmed, but the rest of the brigade managed to hold on. Amidst scenes of desperate fighting, the beleaguered British were joined by two battalions of American artillery, which provided valuable fire support. After fighting doggedly on 20 and 21 February, the remnants of the brigade, now named 'Nickforce' and powerfully supported by the American artillery, were driven back to a last-stand position just outside Thala. However, this also represented the last gasp of Rommel's offensive: the German attack was halted as much due to a lack of petrol as to the weakening Allied defence, and the next day the Germans withdrew. The Allies, literally fighting shoulder to shoulder, had managed to withstand the onslaught.

A few days later, General von Arnim's 5th Panzer Army mounted an attack against the British 5 Corps in the north but this was rebuffed without difficulty. The crisis was over, but it was clear that much had gone wrong for the Allies. The American defeat at Sidi Bou Zid and Kasserine was serious and caused much soul-searching, yet it had not been on the same scale as the British defeats in Greece, Singapore or at Gazala. While the Battle of Kasserine Pass had cruelly exposed American shortcomings, and certainly inflicted a severe reverse on US II Corps, it had eventually resulted in an Allied defensive success. With the ultimate failure of Rommel's assault, the Axis forces in North Africa could now only expect to delay their inevitable defeat.[36]

There was a certain grim satisfaction amongst many British soldiers that the Americans had been introduced to the reality of war. Major General Richard McCreery, Alexander's Chief of Staff in 18th Army Group, was unsparing in his criticism in a lecture on the subject given to a British audience. He claimed that the US 1st Armored Division was 'over-confident and partially trained' and 'had mistaken three days' growth of beard for toughness . . . In the fighting . . . many bad crimes of defence were committed. The artillery withdrew without informing the infantry. The infantry just withdrew. The Tank-destroyer troops had never worked with infantry and did not begin. There was no attempt at consolidation with wire and mines.'[37] Yet while McCreery was brutally honest in his opinion to a British audience, John Downing, recovering from a wound in hospital, was even more irritated by the way British officers, when commenting on the Kasserine Pass fiasco, 'were so conventionally polite, as if trying to ease the blow and "let us down easy". All of us Americans had been so sure that the war would be over in a hurry once we got into it. So far, spectacular victories had been conspicuously slow in being won.'[38]

With the immediate crisis over, Alexander activated his new head-quarters on 20 February to take charge of the front in Tunisia. In fact, the new command arrangement with Eisenhower as Supreme Commander and Alexander as Ground Force Commander worked well from the start. The two men's personalities were a perfect match and 'their similar temperaments, gracious but firm, smoothed the way to Allied cooperation when it could not be taken for granted'.[39] Eisenhower recognised Alexander's qualities, later commenting to Brooke that 'Alexander seems to have a genius for getting people to work for him just because they want to get a pat on the back from their Commander.'[40] The two men quickly estab-lished a friendship that would outlast the war.

Nonetheless, Alexander soon wrote to Brooke that he was 'frankly shocked at what I have found here – no plans, no policy, no proper direction but complete disorganisation'.[41] Anderson's desperate improvisation had saved the Allies from disaster but had caused considerable confusion and disorganisation, and Alexander now had to reorganise the front into self-contained national sectors. The British First Army, composed of British and French troops, under Anderson, would occupy the northern sector, with the US II Corps in the south and Montgomery's Eighth Army occupying the south-east.[42] He then issued a stream of directives about holding the front, regrouping forces, and the necessity for forming reserves and training. He soon warned Brooke that 'final victory in North Africa is not (repeat not) just around the corner'.[43]

Alexander's changes acknowledged that the Allied armies could not function properly when intermingled in the way that they had been during the desperate fighting in Tunisia. John Downing, who as an American liaison officer had experienced the excitement and frustrations of those early experiments, commented somewhat ruefully:

> We never again during the rest of the war would be as closely under British control as we had been in late 1942 and early 1943. That is not to say we and the British no longer fought and lived side by side, but the units involved were larger and the combat areas too great for the close liaison of the early days.[44]

In fact, this was quite deliberate policy. Attempting to integrate British and American units down to the battalion level in a hurried, piecemeal fashion had not only 'violated every recognised principle of war' but had created confusion, acrimony and dispersion.[45] Both armies had organised their units around the divisional structure, which contained an accepted balance of infantry, engineers, artillery, support weapons, transport and staff functions. The fighting in Tunisia had revealed that when this structure was pulled apart, individual units were simply not able to develop their full combat power. Equally, both armies had found to their dismay that their differing command and control structures, supply and administration chains, doctrine and tactical methods, military terminologies and cultures had frequently clashed and simply did not plug easily together. They could really only develop their full combat power by being organised on national lines.

While Fellers' concept of an entirely separate theatre of operations for the US Army was impracticable, so was the enthusiastic mix-up of Eisenhower and Anderson. In practice, the United States Army and the British Army would henceforth generally fight within separate and clearly defined areas of responsibility: two distinct spheres within one theatre of war. Allied propaganda might suggest that the two armies were comrades-in-arms fighting side by side, but from 1943 onwards they often fought at arm's length from each other.

Reinforcements flowed into Tunisia and quickly repaired the physical damage inflicted at Kasserine. However, Alexander soon decided that the US II Corps was of 'poor fighting value', and warned Brooke that he found the Americans to be 'badly trained – this is the case from top to bottom, and of course entirely inexperienced'.[46] He then used his extensive experience as an infantry officer to set in train a series of measures to rectify the main faults as he saw them. He instituted a mixed 'British American school of tactics', which became known as the 18th Army Group Battle School. This was organised on an Allied basis but taught training in British battle drill to British and American officers and non-commissioned officers in a clear attempt to inculcate British fighting methods into the American units. He also attached a number of British officers 'of proved fighting value' to the US II Corps, while a team amounting to one colonel, four lieutenant colonels and twelve majors was sent to act as staff officers and provide 'advice and encouragement' at every level from the corps headquarters to the combat commands.[47] The officers of the US II Corps would no doubt have been horrified had they realised Alexander's motivation and his honest assessment of their fighting ability, but unaware of this 'with their usual kindness, accepted the members of the British team at once and made them very welcome indeed'.[48] Charles Dunphie, of Thala fame and now acting as head of the team, found himself appointed Assistant Chief of Staff to the corps.

His first meeting with Patton was rather daunting. Patton began by declaring that he 'didn't like the British', but he also mentioned that Dunphie was now an officer of the corps, with the same status and powers as the Chief of Staff, and 'if any American officer is unco-operative you can tell him that he is a Goddam son-of-a-bitch and if he doesn't accept that, tell him that I'll tell him'.[49] After this somewhat inauspicious start, Patton and Dunphie became 'firm friends', and Dunphie worked very effectively with Hap Gay, Patton's Chief of Staff. Indeed, when a serious complaint arrived from AFHQ about a British officer who had threatened to shoot an American sergeant, Patton saved Dunphie's career by tearing up the letter.[50]

Alexander had certainly put his finger on some of the American shortcomings in Tunisia. His comments on poor training and the measures he instigated were certainly a damning indictment of the mass-production methods used by the US Army to rapidly train the vast numbers of recruits. The very speed of this conveyor belt system had allowed many men to pass through training with only the sketchiest knowledge of what was required of an infantry soldier. For example, one replacement soldier who joined the hapless 168th Infantry at Faid Pass was carrying a BAR (Browning Automatic Rifle: the US Army's equivalent of a light machine gun) but had never seen or fired one beforehand. He explained that he had volunteered to be a barman at the replacement depot because he had run a bar in New Jersey.[51] Sending men into action inadequately trained and prepared was not exclusively an American vice but it certainly was a recipe for disaster. Perhaps the final tragedy was that the training techniques of British battle drill were soon recognised by many American officers as superior to American methods, a fact that had first been highlighted by Major Bonesteel, of the American Special Observer Group, over two years previously.

While the campaign saw some senior British officers display an ill-disguised contempt for the combat skill of their American allies, the experience of fighting shoulder to shoulder seems to have engendered a new respect and fellow feeling amongst British and American units. AFHQ was understandably concerned about any hint of tension between the American and British forces. There was worry that the events of the Kasserine Pass might affect morale and relations, and Allied censors were ordered to look especially for any signs of such trouble. However, while there were occasions when British troops did greet GIs to the strains of 'How Green was my Ally', in fact, Kasserine seems to have built more respect than disdain between the ordinary soldiers of the two armies. There were still critical comments: one soldier wrote, 'The poor Yanks have still to depend on us to pull them out of the fire. If their fight was as good as "their Jaw" there would be no need for us here.'[52] Equally, there were American soldiers who found that 'The British are a queer lot – they either act suspicious of us or superior . . . Their kitchens are filthy and the soldiers never look as clean as ours do.'[53] An American officer working within AFHQ even commented on the languid habits of his British colleagues, whom he claimed 'eat from 12 to 1 – sun themselves from 2–3; then have tea at 4: Guess they don't have so much paper work in their army.'[54] But there could be repercussions from expressing openly hostile views concerning allies, and one American officer who had written a letter violently opposing the British and predicting a future Anglo-American conflict was disciplined and sent home.[55]

Over the course of the campaign, many American and British soldiers admitted that their opinion of their allies changed, often radically, when they came into close contact with them on the battlefield. One American officer commented that 'I'll be quite frank with you and say that when I was back in England I didn't have such a good opinion of the English, but when you fight with them, and next to them, they are really all right. They can surely fight, and they can take it, much better sometimes, I think than we.'[56] Another admitted that there had been much talk about the British Army's 'inability to fight. This has all disappeared because the boys at the front lines have been taught in the school of hard knocks.'[57] Instead, there was 'nothing but praise for the English soldiers that are fighting at the front'.[58] One British soldier echoed these comments when he wrote that his first impressions of American soldiers had been gathered from the wrong source: 'We have judged them all by the behaviour of the few that were seen in English pubs, overcome by beverages which were strange to them – they are generous to a degree unseen in the British Army. Honest, impulsive perhaps, but sincere. Their hospitality overawed us until we became accustomed to it. What they have is ours for the asking and we are astonished at the supplies given to us.'[59] One American soldier even wrote that 'If anybody tells you that the British and Americans don't get along – they're crazy. We may not agree on a few things but it's sure been a mutual feeling of respect and being damn glad to see each other over here.'[60]

While fighting for survival against the Germans, there was no time to think badly of another soldier, whatever his uniform or strange habits. Yet this process of breaking down prejudices and coming to see the qualities inherent in the soldiers of another army did not end in Tunisia. In fact, it had to be repeated constantly throughout the war, as fresh soldiers were introduced to combat and to their allies. Some of the most scathing criticisms of the US Army actually came from American soldiers. While one writer suggested that the 'American Army is . . . the most haphazardly trained mass of men in the world', another was even harsher:

> If we could teach these dumb bunnies to fight half as well as they are fed and clothed we'd be getting more done. You may be surprised but the best soldier today is the British soldier . . . Our army is made up of undisciplined, soft, spoiled, untrained thousands of men who are going to get the hell shot out of them until they have learned the hard way.[61]

Such home truths might not have been admitted in front of a British audience, but they revealed that many American officers and men had already learnt from the hard knocks of Kasserine and were determined to rectify whatever mistakes had been made. What neither Alexander nor the many other British critics of the American performance in Tunisia realised was that the Americans were quite capable of recognising their own flaws and putting their house in order.

One of Eisenhower's first steps after Kasserine was to relieve Fredendall and replace him with General George Patton. In giving Patton his new command, Eisenhower stated that his immediate task was 'the rehabilitation of all American forces under your command and . . . preparing with all possible speed' for future offensives.[62] He also stressed the importance of 'a spirit of partnership between ourselves and the British forces', but Patton felt that Eisenhower had 'sold his soul to the devil on "Cooperation", which I think means we are pulling the chestnuts for our noble allies . . . It is clear that I too must "cooperate or get out".'[63] Patton's mistrust and suspicion of the British had been learnt not only from his history books but also through his experience as Pershing's aide in the First World War, and the events of the Second would only confirm and intensify them. Eisenhower had also sent Omar Bradley to act as his personal representative, but Patton insisted that he would have no spies in his headquarters and appointed Bradley as his deputy commander.[64] Patton and Bradley would have a tense and awkward yet ultimately creative relationship as commanders throughout the war. While Patton always respected Bradley's professionalism, Bradley came to despise Patton's over-the-top command persona along with his profanity, drinking and egotism.[65] Both men brought important attributes to help rebuild the fighting power of II US Corps. Patton insisted upon smartness (including wearing the correct uniform and shaving) and discipline, and through his constant haranguing began to inspire the men under his command. Bradley, with his long experience as the commandant of the Infantry Training School at Fort Benning, was a solid commander who began to methodically solve the problems of tactics, training and equipment that had emerged during the course of the campaign. Between them, Patton and Bradley worked with a will to achieve 'the rehabilitation' of the troops under their command.

Rommel was comprehensively rebuffed when he attacked the Eighth Army at Medenine, in southern Tunisia, on 6 March 1943 and the initiative passed to the Allies. Patton took his rebuilt corps and launched it in an attack which by 23 March had not only recovered Gafsa, El Guettar and Maknassy from the Italian Centauro Division but had also begun to restore the confidence and fighting spirit of his men. This relatively minor victory had an important effect: the Americans in Tunisia began to put the humiliation of Kasserine behind them.

Alexander was keen to maintain the pressure on the Axis forces, and on 20 March the Eighth Army drove from Medenine towards the Mareth Line, which included French defences built in the thirties. The initial frontal attack on the line stalled against a fierce Italian defence, but a daring outflanking manoeuvre by the 2nd New Zealand Division finally unhinged the Axis positions. The Eighth Army continued to push northwards pursuing the retreating Axis forces. After a further stiff fight at the Wadi Akarit, north of Gabes, over 6–7 April, patrols of the Eighth Army and the US II Corps were able to meet one another for the first time. However, when US signals officers went to link their communications with the Eighth Army, they were 'tactlessly rebuffed'.[66] The Eighth Army signals officers later explained to Penney that 'We were trying to get the Americans into our Eighth Army signal system, i.e. absorb them.' Penney commented that the Eighth Army 'didn't then admit the existence of anyone else – bless them!'[67] Having fought an isolated war in the deserts of Egypt and Libya for so long, the Eighth Army could not yet conceive of having to work as part of an Allied team. Indeed, their entry into the group of Allied armies in Tunisia brought a fresh clash of military cultures, as severe between the British First and Eighth Armies as it was between the British and Americans. The Eighth Army appeared 'overbearingly confident' and dismissed both the First Army and the Americans as inexperienced.[68]

One of the most powerful ways of building morale and fighting spirit amongst groups of soldiers is to convince them that they are members of the best section, platoon, company, battalion, brigade, division, corps or indeed army in the world. This can be a very powerful motivating force but it can also have significant side effects in creating rivalry between units and certainly between allies. The Eighth Army, with their scruffy caravans of yellow-painted vehicles, their distinctly non-regulation dress sense and their unique vocabulary developed over two years of desert fighting, now had an unrivalled record of success and had been told by their egotistical commander that they were the best soldiers in the world: they

believed him. The British First Army, which had fought through
the Tunisian campaign, remained much closer in spirit to the 'home'
British Army of spit and polish, regulation dress, orthodox doctrine
and olive-green-painted vehicles. The First Army and the American
troops had also just come through a very difficult period of disap-
pointments and adversity. Unfortunately, the British Eighth Army
made no secret of the fact that it considered itself to be superior
in every respect to the poor benighted members of the First Army
and the clearly incompetent Americans. The Eighth Army's sense
of a unique separate identity would last for the rest of the war.

This uneasy sense of rivalry was heightened by an unfortunate
episode during the next Allied push. Alexander now prepared an
offensive to be mounted by the newly created British 9 Corps of
the First Army, under the command of Lieutenant General John
T. Crocker. Alexander hoped to break through the enemy defences
at Fondouk in the Eastern Dorsale mountains, drive forward to
capture Kairouan and thus strike in the flank of the retreating Axis
forces. However, Crocker's main forces were the British
6th Armoured Division and the 34th US Infantry Division, which
had lost two of its battalions at Faid Pass. Understandably, Patton
was very unhappy about an American division being placed under
British command. Matters became much worse when Crocker
ordered the 34th Division to renew its assault against the hills
overlooking the Fondouk Pass while at the same time removing
much of their promised support.

The division had already made one attack against these positions
but had found the 2,000 yards of open poppy fields in front of the
pass too difficult to cross under heavy German fire.[69] Patton did
not make himself popular when he ordered Lieutenant Colonel
Robert Moore, still smarting from the loss of two of his battalions
at Faid Pass, to 'Take those hills or bring me back a truckload of
dog tags.'[70] Rather than display such 'a death or glory' attitude,
General Ryder, the commander of the 34th Division, remonstrated
with Crocker and asked for a postponement of the attack until
nightfall, when his men would have a better chance of approaching
the German positions. Crocker insisted on his timetable, and
predictably, the attack failed again, with heavy loss of men. It took

a further assault by the leading elements of 6th Armoured Division to knock out some of the German positions. The leading regiment, the 17th/21st Lancers, then advanced directly against the gap, in what can only be described as another Charge of the Light Brigade. The Lancers found themselves in a dense minefield and came under heavy fire from German anti-tank guns, suffering heavier casualties than they had done at Balaclava, but they did manage to unlock the German defences.[71] That night, the soldiers of the 34th Division were able to assault and capture the German hilltop positions.

The delay in forcing the Fondouk Gap meant that any chance of catching Rommel's retreating forces evaporated. Crocker blamed this result upon the 34th Division's performance in action. He recommended to Alexander that the division be withdrawn for further training under British tutelage, but worse, he vented his frustration to war correspondents, complaining that their performance had been disappointing and had allowed Rommel's forces to slip through the intended trap.[72] Crocker's disdain found its way into both the British and American press and caused real recrimination between the British and Americans. Eisenhower, ever vigilant for tension between the allies, commented, 'It was disturbing, the more so because it was so unnecessary . . . Nothing creates trouble between allies so often or so easily as unnecessary talk – particularly when it belittles one of them.'[73] Eisenhower was right to label Crocker's words unnecessary. While the attack had not achieved its primary purpose, the combined British and American forces had succeeded in driving the Germans back and taking many prisoners. Patton seethed with anger over the open criticism. He believed the 34th Division had been sent on an 'impossible mission with both flanks open', but he also considered that Eisenhower was now 'more British than the British and is putty in their hands'.[74] While Eisenhower had issued a strict edict that there was to be no overt American criticism of the British, Crocker had seemingly demonstrated that the British held to no such strictures. In fact, Patton was right to be suspicious and resentful of the British commanders' attitudes towards the US II Corps. Crocker's had not been an isolated statement: it is clear that Alexander shared his views and had not sought to control his staff or his commanders over disparaging comments in the way that Eisenhower, as the senior American officer in the theatre, had.

Indeed, Alexander had just admitted his full assessment of American combat performance in a remarkable memorandum to Brooke. He believed that 'the men simply do not know their job as soldiers, and this is the case from the highest to the lowest, from the general to the private soldiers . . . In fact they are soft, green and quite untrained.'[75] He was concerned that unless something was done, 'the American Army in the European theatre of operations will be quite useless and play no useful part whatsoever'.[76] Despite his harsh criticism, Alexander also understood the need for tact and a careful approach on such matters. Most importantly, he believed that the 'Americans themselves must do something to raise the morale of their own troops and try to develop the spirit of battle and the will to fight and die for their country. No army is worth a damn without it and it is sadly lacking with them at the moment.'[77] Alexander's comments on the American Army were just as damning as Fellers' had been about the British Army the previous year, yet Eisenhower and Patton were already working to correct many of the deficiencies that Alexander had identified. Ironically, Alexander was the one British commander most American officers found they could work with constructively, but it took a long time for his pessimistic view of the American Army to become more realistic.

Meanwhile, the campaign in Tunisia continued to wrest mountain after mountain from the Axis defenders through very heavy and difficult fighting. By mid-April, the Axis forces had withdrawn into a tight bridgehead covering the Cap Bon peninsula, Tunis and Bizerte. On 25 April, Longstop Hill, which had marked the limit of the Allied advance in December 1942, was finally taken by the 38th (Irish) Brigade, with close support from Churchill tanks of the North Irish Horse.

Yet as the Tunisian campaign began to reach its end, a fresh controversy arose between the Allies stemming from Alexander's poor view of American troops and his misreading of American sensibilities. With the Axis being driven back towards Tunis, and the front lines shrinking as a consequence, Alexander saw this an ideal opportunity to place the US II Corps into reserve, where it could conduct training for the forthcoming invasion of Sicily. Only one US division would then participate in the final destruction of the Axis forces. Alexander's usual tact and diplomacy had failed him, and he was blissfully unaware of the reaction this would cause within US II Corps. He was guilty of treating an American force in the same way he would any British or Canadian unit rather than as the single formation in Tunisia that represented the forces of the United States.[78]

Both Patton and Bradley were furious when they realised that American forces would only have a small part to play in the final act. Eisenhower had to insist on the employment of the 'entire II Corps as a unit'. He argued, quite rightly, that 'Success would make the unit, and it would give a sense of accomplishment to the American people that they richly deserved in view of the strenuous efforts they had made thus far in the war.' Not surprisingly, on realising his faux pas 'Alexander instantly concurred'.[79] The change in plan required the move of the entire II Corps to the northern sector, across the supply lines of the First Army, and giving them the capture of Bizerte as their main objective.

The final operation to take Tunis went entirely according to plan. US II Corps troops entered Bizerte on 7 May at almost the same time as soldiers of the First Army took Tunis. Von Arnim surrendered with his staff five days later, 'very dazed and on the edge of a breakdown'.[80] Once the Cap Bon peninsula had been cleared on 13 May, all Axis resistance in Africa had come to an end and an entire army had been destroyed: over 250,000 troops, along with all their equipment and materiel, were captured. The power of the Allied air and naval forces had ensured that there could be no Axis Dunkirk, and the British considered that their humiliation of three years before had been amply avenged.

Nonetheless, many American officers at the time, and many historians since, saw the lengthy Tunisian campaign as merely postponing the final victory over Germany. If Tunis had been taken in December 1942 as planned, Marshall might have won the argument at Casablanca, and all the reinforcements that went to Africa could have been available for a cross-Channel attack. In the event, 'Tunisgrad' followed only a few short months after the surrender of the German Sixth Army at Stalingrad, and these two events marked the true passing of the initiative from the Germans to the Allies.

Perhaps just as importantly, during six months of continuous engagement, British and American soldiers had learnt to fight in harsh and testing conditions. The British Eighth Army was no longer the only battle-hardened and confident Allied army, but had been joined by the British First Army and the US II Corps. Tunisia had been not only a great experiment in Allied cooperation, but also a challenging experience for thousands of Allied troops. Eisenhower had learned the bitter lesson of his near failure as a field commander in Tunisia, and his AFHQ had developed into a fully forged Allied headquarters. However, the campaign had sealed the fate of General Anderson: he was returned to the UK, where he commanded the British Second Army until the spring of 1944, but he was never given an active operational command again.

On 30 May 1943, the Allies staged a massed victory parade in Tunis to mark the end of the campaign in Africa. This should have been a supreme moment of Allied unity and celebration, and it was certainly an impressive display. Twenty thousand French, American and British soldiers marched past Eisenhower and Giraud on the saluting dais, where they were joined by all the other senior Allied generals. For at least some of the onlookers, the parade fixed an image of Allied success and solidarity in their minds. Anderson later claimed that:

> Never have I seen the equal of those men marching twelve deep in solid phalanx for more than two hours; magnificent in physique, bronzed and clear-eyed, conquerors they were and conquerors they looked as they swung by to the music of massed pipes and drums, British and American regimental bands and the 'musique' of the Foreign Legion playing its famous slow march 'Le Boudin'.[81]

Yet most observers agreed that the British looked the 'most striking'.[82] The GIs were somewhat sombre and drab in their standard fighting kit and steel helmets while the British soldiers marched in their colourful berets, bonnets and caps. The massed pipes and drums of the Highland Division formed a notable highlight in the parade.[83] Patton, crammed behind a group of French generals on the platform, felt that the American contribution to victory had been marginalised in the parade just as it had in its execution.[84] As far as he was concerned, Tunisia had been one of the most difficult periods of the war, when American forces had been placed under British command, disparaged by patronising British officers and hindered from showing their true mettle. While the Allied unity Eisenhower insisted upon had indeed become a reality, much of it remained only a surface sheen. Underneath, misunderstanding continued to breed rivalry, resentment and suspicion.

8

Sicilian Feud

Sicily is a large three-cornered island that sits just off the south-western tip of mainland Italy, between the eastern and western basins of the Mediterranean Sea. This strategically important location has meant that it has attracted the attention of almost every group of peoples who have used the Mediterranean as their highway. As Major General John Lucas* commented, 'Sicily has been invaded at times by the Greeks, Carthaginians, Romans, Phoenicians, Saracens, Goths, Vandals, Normans, Germans, French, Spanish and maybe some others. Now by the British and Americans. What a life.'[1] The Anglo-American allies of 1943 were simply the latest in a long line of armies to have set foot there.

The island had loomed large in British thoughts ever since June 1940, when the Italian air force had begun using it as a giant airbase to attack the British island of Malta and the convoys sent to its aid. Malta became the most heavily bombed place on earth in April 1942, and the vast majority of those bombs had been loaded on to Axis planes on Sicilian airfields. The capture of Sicily would deny the Axis those airfields and ensure a clear sea passage through the Mediterranean, thus saving nearly one million tons of Allied shipping space. This was why the British had pressed so hard at Casablanca for what became known as Operation Husky: the conquest of Sicily.

Any Allied landing on Sicily had to expect to encounter a determined Axis defence. This demanded a 'triphibious' approach to the problem, in which naval, air and ground forces were all utilised to

---

* An old friend of both Patton and Eisenhower, and the man who acted as Eisenhower's deputy during Operation Husky.

best effect to ensure a successful landing on a hostile shore and the subsequent capture of the island.[2] It was the need to reconcile the competing demands of all three services that led to the majority of the troubles in planning Operation Husky. The arguments and controversy that surrounded the process eventually moved in an entirely unexpected and unintended direction, and the consequent feud not only engulfed all three services but did untold and long-lasting damage to the relationship between the British and American armies in Europe.

The original strategy for Operation Husky was prepared in London by the British Joint Planning Staff. As with any plan involving the combined action of the three military services, it had to be a compromise between the needs and demands of the naval, air and ground elements, with each conferring particular but different advantages and limitations on the conduct of the operation. Reconciling those differences while developing a workable plan was never going to be easy; indeed, the various requirements for Husky simply brought the differences into sharp focus.

Sicily had first been chosen as an appropriate objective for an Allied attack because it lay within the (short) range of Allied fighters flying from Tunisia and Malta. Nonetheless, air support of the naval task forces at sea and the armies ashore would be limited until the Axis airfields on the island were captured. As far as the air planners were concerned, the capture of the groups of airfields around Syracuse, Comiso, Ponte Olivo and Palermo was of the first importance. But for the British naval planners, the prevention of heavy Axis air attack on the naval task forces was also critical. The Royal Navy had suffered grievous losses from air attack while defending the passage of convoys to Malta over the past two years, and was understandably anxious to avoid this, particularly while the naval task forces were at their most vulnerable during the landing phase of the operation, when they would be stationary off the Sicilian beaches. This meant that the naval planners wanted widely dispersed landings that would limit the impact of air attacks while also maximising the ability of amphibious forces to stretch any defence by attacking multiple points simultaneously. The early capture of the main ports on the island – Syracuse, Augusta and

Palermo – was also seen as vital to the operation, as this would enable rapid build-up and maintenance of the ground forces once ashore, while also reducing the naval commitment to bring those forces on to the island across open beaches. The nature and capacity of available shipping was critical, as this would determine the number of troops that could be not only landed on the island but also sustained during the subsequent fighting.

Reconciling these competing demands was a complex problem in itself, but the entire enterprise was further complicated by the number of different military headquarters that all had to play a part in the development of the plan. In January 1943, Alexander's 18th Army Group headquarters was given the task of fusing all these elements together and developing the outline plan received from London into a detailed and workable assault. However, neither Alexander nor his Chief of Staff, Richard McCreery, felt able to devote sufficient attention to Husky while the difficult fight for Tunisia continued. Alexander delegated the task to Force 141, a small headquarters staff based in Algiers. Major General Charles Gairdner was appointed as the Chief of Staff of Force 141. The team of planners for the Eastern Task Force, known as Force 545, were based in Cairo, while the headquarters for the US Western Task Force, known as Force 343, resided at Rabat in Morocco. Admiral Cunningham, as the naval commander-in-chief, had his headquarters in Alexandria, and Air Marshal Tedder, the air commander-in-chief, had established his headquarters firstly in Algiers but moved subsequently to Tunis. Thus the headquarters of the relevant forces and services were dispersed across 2,000 miles of the Mediterranean coast. This was hardly an auspicious start for Husky.

Nonetheless, Gairdner set to work establishing his team and preparing the plan. In this he was ably supported by Brigadier General Arthur S. Nevins, an experienced American planning officer who had worked in London on the British Joint Planning Staff since April 1942. However, the fact that Alexander, his nominal commander, was actually at the front in Tunisia and 'naturally uninterested', while Eisenhower 'made it abundantly clear that at the moment he did not want to be worried with Husky' did not bode well, and

Gairdner quickly realised that he would not be able to ask either man for any decisions regarding the plan.[3] Eisenhower did in fact have his own preferred concept, which was for a concentrated attack on the south-eastern corner of the island, but remembering his bruising experience during the planning process for Torch in North Africa, the Commander-in-Chief had clearly decided to leave Husky well alone. This lack of interest from the responsible commanders was to be the root cause of many of the subsequent difficulties. As early as late February 1943, Gairdner had started to feel that 'The problems are beginning to multiply at an alarming rate. Washington, London, AFHQ and ME all have a big finger in the pie – and yet we are the people who are to be ultimately responsible. I feel that I am hardly up to the job – but I certainly didn't ask for it and no man can do more than his best.'[4] As it turned out, the entire episode of Husky planning revealed a real weakness in the Anglo-American alliance. While there were mechanisms, however flawed, for thrashing out Allied strategy, there remained a gap in translating that strategy into realistic operations.

By mid-March, after a month of concentrated effort by Gairdner and his staff, the overall plan was accepted by a 'high powered conference', which was attended by Eisenhower, Cunningham, Alexander, Tedder and General Carl Spaatz, the commander of the Allied Northwest African Air Force. This amended plan involved two main naval task forces. The Eastern Task Force would land British troops on the southern coast of Sicily around Gela to capture the airfields at Ponte Olivo, as well as further forces on the south-eastern shore of the island around Avola and the Pachino peninsula. These forces would then move north-east to capture Syracuse and Augusta. The Western Task Force would land US troops around Palermo to secure the capture of that port and its surrounding airfields. While the plan certainly met the requirements of the navies, air forces and supply, the Allied ground forces would land at either end of Sicily, which would make any concentration of force or mutual support once ashore impossible. Unfortunately, the total shipping requirements also meant that the landings had to be staggered over three days, with the Western Task Force making its assault two days after the Eastern Task Force. Nonetheless, 'the plan was approved in every particular'.[5]

Gairdner also met with Lieutenant General Miles Dempsey, Montgomery's deputy for Husky, who had discussed the plan with Montgomery for four hours; he now felt confident that 'we will get a measure of agreement' from Montgomery.[6] The very next day, however, a telegram arrived from Montgomery addressed to Alexander. His message was blunt:

> Dempsey and Ramsay visited me today on way to Algiers and before they came I studied Husky. In my opinion the operation as planned in London breaks every commonsense rule of practical battle fighting and is completely theoretical. It has no repeat no hope of success and should be completely recast. Have given Dempsey letter for you stating my views as to lines on which planning should proceed.[7]

Gairdner was, not surprisingly, upset by Montgomery's intervention, particularly given that Montgomery had had the original outline plan for four weeks but had left it until now to signal his disapproval. He speculated that perhaps Montgomery wanted 'his Army etc. to think that it was he & he alone that got it changed or what? Anyhow it is a nice baby for me to hold.'[8]

Montgomery's main objection was based on the fundamental principle of war that an army had to be able to concentrate its forces to achieve success and ensure against defeat. Widely dispersed landings staggered over three days seemed to offer the Axis forces on the island the opportunity to focus on each of the Allied forces and overwhelm them in turn. Montgomery was a convinced advocate of the concentration of force and demanded the provision of at least one more division for the assault against Gela in the south-east. While Gairdner understood that the south-eastern assaults were an essential part of the operation, he was also aware of the shipping and logistic implications, which made Montgomery's demand very difficult to fulfil. As the question was examined, it became clear that the extra division could not come from British sources, but it might be possible to use an American division. This, of course, would weaken the Western Task Force and place an American division under British command. When this modification was accepted by Eisenhower and Bedell Smith, Gairdner found that 'a horrible feeling of hostility at once arose' in his headquarters.[9] Arthur Nevins felt so strongly about this fresh subordination of US troops to British command that he wrote a memo to Eisenhower pointing out the dangers of the new plan. With his staff officers now thoroughly unhappy about the changes, there remained uncertainty over whether Montgomery would actually agree to the operation. Gairdner felt convinced that there would be a showdown, and on 1 April confided to his diary that:

> I can see that Monty is going to be a prima donna who will act as a hair-shirt to me. I can get no decision re the outline Plan. Alex won't come to a definite decision because of Monty & he doesn't realise how short time is. The best I could do was to say I would come up again in 3 days and we would then go and see Monty. It is the devil.[10]

While Gairdner could see the gathering storm, there was little he could do to avert it. Alexander was not willing to come to a definite decision while Montgomery remained unhappy about the plan. Even when Gairdner attempted to arrange a final conference by flying with Alexander to see Montgomery, Eighth Army Headquarters replied that the army commander was far too busy preparing for another battle. Eventually, on 5 April, Gairdner was able to meet with Montgomery's Chief of Staff, Freddie de Guingand, who agreed with all the main points in the plan. Unfortunately, Gairdner seems to have taken de Guingand's agreement as also signifying Montgomery's assent, which was to prove a costly miscalculation. With the seeming agreement of all the main commanders, he flew to London to explain the plan to the Prime Minister and the Chiefs of Staff.

Meanwhile, Eisenhower also miscalculated over a report he sent to the Combined Chiefs of Staff on 7 April warning that if there were more than two German divisions on Sicily, the operation offered 'scant promise of success'.[11] This misplaced comment drew

Churchill's ire, as he was astonished to learn that an additional two German divisions could wreck all the Allied plans. He thundered that it was 'perfectly clear that the operations must either be entrusted to someone who believes in them, or abandoned. I trust the Chiefs of Staff will not accept these pusillanimous and defeatist doctrines from whoever they come.'[12] This was one of the few times during the war that Churchill criticised Eisenhower more or less openly, and Gairdner was severely heckled by the Prime Minister when he presented the plan to the Chiefs of Staff.

Gairdner returned to Algiers believing that the outline for Operation Husky was now accepted and that the detailed planning for the naval task forces, air forces and ground elements could begin in earnest. It was at this point, on 24 April 1943, that a further cable was received from Montgomery's headquarters. Montgomery claimed that this was the first occasion he had been able to thoroughly examine the problems confronting the Eastern Task Force with his corps commanders. He argued that the existing plan had been 'based on the assumption that opposition will be slight and that Sicily will be captured relatively easily. Never was there a greater error.'[13] He believed that since the Germans and Italians were fighting hard in Tunisia, it must be assumed that they would do the same in Sicily, and that this, combined with the 'dispersion of effort' in the plan, would lead to 'a first-class military disaster'.[14] Instead, he argued, 'We must plan the operation on assumption that resistance will be fierce and that a prolonged dogfight battle will follow the initial assault.'[15] So far Montgomery was simply expounding a difference of military opinion that he should have expressed perhaps two months previously. However, he went on:

> I am prepared to carry the war into Sicily with the 8th Army but must do so in my own way. The fight will be hard and bitter.
>
> In view of above considerations my army must operate concentrated with corps and divisions in supporting distance of each other. CENT and DIME [between Licata and Scoglitti] landings must be given up and the whole initial effort be made in the area of ACID and BARK [between Avola and Syracuse]. Subsequent operations will be developed so as to secure airfields and ports and so on. The

first thing to do is to secure a lodgement in a suitable area and then operate from that firm base.

Time is pressing and if we delay while above is argued in LONDON and WASHINGTON the operation will never be launched in July. Whole planning and work in CAIRO is suffering because everyone is trying to make something of a plan which he knows can never succeed.

I have given orders that as far as the army is concerned all planning and work as regards ETF [Eastern Task Force] is now to go ahead on lines indicated.

Admiral RAMSAY is in complete agreement with me and together we are prepared to launch the operation and see it through and win. It is essential that the air plan should provide close and intimate support for 8th Army battle.[16]

Montgomery was essentially stating that whatever had been agreed, he was now going to plan on a different basis without reference to Force 141, Alexander or the naval and air chain of command. Gairdner believed that the telegram would 'lead to a first class crisis . . . It is impossible to treat admirals of the Fleet and air chief marshals as if they were ignoramuses in the art of war. Furthermore the Americans are beginning to feel that the British Empire is being run by Monty.'[17] Admiral Ramsay had rather unwillingly allowed his name to be mentioned in the telegram, and Admiral Cunningham, furious that his subordinate was now working on a plan without any reference to his headquarters, ordered that Ramsay was not to do anything without his permission. Montgomery sent a further telegram stating that he would stake his military reputation on his plan and suggested a meeting to explain his ideas; he seems not to have understood that he was not the only commander involved in Husky. His intervention and declaration that he would now only follow his own plan gave the Americans 'the impression that Force 141 was unable to issue orders to its subordinate British formations which would be obeyed by them'.[18]

A further conference had to be convened at which Montgomery could expound his plan to all of the main commanders. However, Montgomery came down with an attack of tonsillitis and was confined to bed. He sent Freddie de Guingand in his place, but Guingand's plane crashed in the desert and so one of Montgomery's corps commanders, Oliver Leese, was sent in his stead. At the meeting, which took place on 29 April, Patton and Nevins were the only Americans present amongst the large number of British senior officers, who included Alexander, Leese, Cunningham, Tedder, Ramsay, Air Marshal Arthur Coningham, Air Marshal Philip Wigglesworth, Commodore Dick, Major General Frederick Browning, Gairdner and Brigadier Charles Richardson. It was not surprising given this situation that Patton felt that the British were unfairly dominating Allied strategy. Yet far from this being a matter of the British presenting a united front and sewing up the Husky plan between them, Patton was instead about to witness the full range of jealousy, resentment and suspicion that pervaded many of the relations between high-ranking British commanders.

Oliver Leese read out a paper from Montgomery that reiterated his arguments for a concentrated assault on the beaches south of Syracuse. However, Tedder and Cunningham were already furious with Montgomery, and they were not about to listen to one of his corps commanders or agree to his plan. They reiterated their argument that they refused to adopt a plan that left significant airfields in Axis hands within 30 miles of the landing beaches and massed so many ships in one location. The conversation came to a deadlock. Alexander simply refused to take sides, saying that he 'accepted [the] Eighth Army Plan from a purely military point of view, but, of course, did not reject the RN and RAF views'.[19] Not surprisingly, Patton considered that Alexander was a 'fence walker'.[20] Patton had supported Tedder and Cunningham during the meeting by pointing out that his landings were widely separated, but had also stated that he himself was prepared to take the risk. He considered this stalemated meeting as 'one hell of a performance. War by committee.'[21] It was precisely the kind of event Marshall had sought to avoid by pressing the concept of the Supreme Commander on the Combined Chiefs of Staff. Eisenhower had also feared the re-establishment of the British committee system, and those fears had now apparently been realised. A large group of senior British commanders were arguing amongst themselves without reference to their own commander, and consequently failing to agree upon a viable plan.

Yet since there was a complete impasse, Eisenhower became involved in the controversy whether he liked it or not. He had experienced similar situations over the Torch planning but it would appear that he did not entirely understand the relationship between Alexander and Montgomery. While Montgomery was theoretically Alexander's subordinate, the reality was that Alexander would not gainsay the commander of the Eighth Army. By 1 May, with Montgomery now demanding an extra two divisions for his task force, Gairdner believed that:

> General Ike is evidently going to be put on the spot. As far as I can see it, he will have to adopt one of three courses:
> (a) Adopt Monty's plan
> (b) Adopt our plan and sack Monty
> (c) Say the operation isn't on.
> As neither (b) or (c) are 'on', the result would appear to be fairly obvious![22]

Gairdner had correctly divined Montgomery's method of winning an argument. Montgomery had quite deliberately created a crisis over Husky in 'a technique whereby he would paint a picture of deadlock or failure, only to produce, *deus ex machina*, a practicable solution – if all was left up to him'.[23] He may have sincerely believed that only his plan was practical and that the original plan would lead to disaster, and he clearly believed that neither Eisenhower, Alexander nor Gairdner had a clue about what he called the practical realities of battle, but the bombastic and egotistical tone he adopted in his telegrams and statements ensured that he alienated almost every one of the other commanders involved in Husky.

Montgomery finally arrived in Algiers on 2 May. After a brief meeting in the hotel bathroom, he convinced Bedell Smith to take his latest amendment to Eisenhower. In the new plan, Montgomery's Eighth Army would land on the Pachino peninsula and at the beaches around Avola, while the US forces would land not around Palermo but instead on the beaches at Gela and Scoglitti, which had originally been earmarked for the Eastern Task Force. This would meet the objections of the air force but completely alter the role of the US forces, who would have to come ashore over the open beaches, for there was no port of any size on the south coast of the island. While each task force would land en masse, the British and American forces were still separate and would not be mutually supporting in the initial phases of the operation.

Eisenhower, who had originally favoured a concentrated assault on the south-eastern corner of the island, gave the new plan his approval. It had been Eisenhower's apparent disinterest in the planning for Husky and lack of clear direction, combined with Alexander's refusal to confront his subordinate, that had allowed Montgomery to undermine and then entirely dominate the planning for the operation. Bedell Smith apparently admitted to Patton that 'the reason everyone yields to Monty is because Monty is the national hero and writes direct to the Prime Minister; and that if Ike crossed him, Ike might get canned'.[24]

Winning the argument over Husky certainly seemed to strengthen Montgomery's already unshakeable position. He had, in effect, been able to dictate terms to the Anglo-American alliance over how the campaign should be conducted. Beloved by the British public, and with the clear support of both the Prime Minister and CIGS, Montgomery was at the zenith of his strength and prestige. However, having indulged in such brinkmanship successfully, he would continue to use these methods in the future. Meanwhile, the suspicion of American officers that 'the British Empire is being run by Monty' now only intensified their dislike and distrust of him.[25] Yet although attitudes to Montgomery have often been seen in terms of an Anglo-American divide, the Sicilian episode demonstrated that antagonism was not confined to American officers. Montgomery's behaviour had made enemies of Cunningham and Tedder as well as their staffs. The much-vaunted rivalry between Patton and Montgomery was minor compared to the depths of hostility that developed within the Royal Air Force; at one point Tedder gossiped to Patton that Montgomery was 'a little fellow of average ability who has had such a build-up that he thinks of himself as Napoleon – he is not'.[26] These Anglo-American and interservice rivalries and resentments would fester with unfortunate repercussions in the years to come.

Montgomery's triumph seemed complete when he pushed his argument one step further. Given that it was his headquarters that had developed the accepted plan, and given that all the forces would now come ashore at the south-eastern end of the island, he believed that he should command the entire operation and that the forces of the US II Corps should be subordinated to Eighth Army headquarters. Gairdner, who felt that his own position was untenable, discussed with Patton whether '8th Army should now de jure as well as de facto take over the whole operation. That is the logical answer but it may be that the Americans are not prepared to face up to such a complete elimination.' Not surprisingly, Bedell Smith baulked at this latest gambit and made it clear that 'no Americans are to be put under Monty'.[27] Montgomery could see nothing other than military logic in his suggestion and seems to have been entirely ignorant of the damage caused by such an argument. As far as he was concerned, there was only one island to be attacked and it thus made perfect sense to have one headquarters in control of the whole operation. He may have understood the command of an army intimately, but he remained ignorant as to how to manage the more complicated relationships required of a multinational and interservice operation, and seems to have been blissfully unaware that his brinkmanship had entirely wrecked any real chance of smooth cooperation between the air, naval and ground forces involved.

Marshall would not tolerate such behaviour, but his response from Washington also revealed his acute political awareness. He signalled to Eisenhower that if Montgomery was to command a British Army in Sicily, then there was no reason why there should not also be an American Army commanded by Patton. It was decided that once Patton was ashore, the I US Armored Corps headquarters would transform into the Seventh US Army. This simple mechanism ensured that the American forces could not suffer complete 'elimination' at the hands of the British. Patton had begun to resent the seeming domination of British decision-making in the Mediterranean theatre. He now saw Eisenhower as a 'straw man' in thrall to the British and objected to the occupation of so many senior command positions by British officers. For Patton, and many other American officers, the coming operation in Sicily would be as much a fight for national prestige and a demonstration of what the US Army could achieve as it was a military campaign to defeat the Axis.

Nonetheless, Patton's sense of destiny and the personal rivalry that developed between him and Montgomery should not be misunderstood. Patton could be very generous to British officers who had gained his respect. In June 1943, with the preparations for Husky reaching their climax, he met Charles Dunphie again in Marrakesh. Patton asked Dunphie sharply, 'Why aren't you wearing the Silver Star ribbon?' Patton had recommended the award of the medal for Dunphie's service in US II Corps, but the British officer had to reply that he had not heard anything about it. Patton duly took the ribbon off his own uniform for Dunphie to wear on his. That small piece of ribbon became one of Dunphie's most treasured possessions.[28]

With Eisenhower's assent to Montgomery's plan, the preparations for Husky could begin in earnest. Each of the task forces began training and exercising for amphibious landings, but this was complicated by the continuance of the Tunisian campaign, and the overall effect of muddled and amateurish rehearsals did not inspire much confidence that the amphibious assault would go smoothly. Part of the problem was that while the Eighth Army (with the exception of the 2nd Canadian Division) would go ashore with veteran divisions, the majority of US formations allocated to the operation were filled with fresh troops.[29] Although the 1st Infantry Division had seen combat in Tunisia, neither the 3rd nor the 45th, which were tasked with making the assault landings, had been in action before. However, while the troops may have been inexperienced, their commanders most certainly were not. Troy Middleton, the commander of the 45th Division, had already gained a fine reputation as the best regimental commander in the AEF in 1918, while Lucian Truscott, now in command of the 3rd Division, was acknowledged as having 'trained the 3rd Division . . . to the most effective degree of any US Division in the Mediterranean'.[30] The rapid marching pace he insisted upon during both training and action soon became famous as the 'Truscott trot'.

Nonetheless, many senior British officers continued to take a dim view of American military efficiency. Clarence Huebner had the unenviable task of acting as the US liaison officer at Alexander's 18th Army Group Headquarters, and there is no doubt that he found it a difficult role. He complained to Penney over a particularly tactless exchange overheard between two British officers, one of whom remarked: 'Hope you've seen that no American commander is in a position of responsibility.' To which the other replied, 'Of course I have, in accordance with your own particular orders.'[31] As Huebner pointed out, this was deeply unfair, and he resented British interference in American preparations. It seemed the US Army would have to prove itself all over again to its rather disdainful and dismissive ally. Not surprisingly, the preparations for Husky were a febrile time of frantic activity mixed with reserve and suspicion between the allies.

Although Operation Husky has faded from popular consciousness today, in 1943 it represented the greatest Anglo-American effort of the war so far. As the forces embarked on to the ships that would transport them across the Mediterranean, the scale of the invasion fleet was breathtaking: more than 2,500 warships, troopships, merchant ships and landing craft were assembled in five task forces. This armada also represented the second stage of development for one of the trump cards of the Anglo-American alliance that is often taken for granted: their ability to project air, land and maritime power across considerable distances. These convoys converged on Malta before sailing on to the landing beaches on the southern and eastern coast of Sicily.

While the high seas and bad weather on the morning of 10 July 1943 produced many awkward moments for the naval commanders, these conditions were disastrous for the airborne assaults that preceded the landings. The high winds over the parachute drop zones meant that the men of the US 82nd Airborne were scattered all over southern Sicily. Despite this, a much-denuded party of determined men were able to seize their objectives around the

Ponte Dirillo and hold them against numerous Italian counter-attacks. The British glider assault, however, met with tragedy: more than 260 paratroopers drowned when their gliders ditched in the sea. The small numbers of troops that landed near their target, the Ponte Grande, fought a fierce battle against the Italian defenders of Syracuse. The amphibious landings themselves met with only light and patchy resistance. By the end of the first day, both the British and American forces were strongly established ashore. Charles Gairdner, who had returned to England under a cloud and dropped from his wartime rank of major general back to his substantive rank of colonel, heard about the successful invasion on the radio. He commented bitterly: 'What a pathetic way for me to have to listen to this news!'[32]

The initial Italian reaction to the landings had been weak, giving the lie to Montgomery's dire predictions of immediate and fierce Axis resistance. The majority of the men in the Italian coastal divisions simply melted back into their nearby homes when confronted with one of the largest invasion forces in history. Alexander later commented in his dispatch that these divisions, 'whose value had never been rated very high, disintegrated almost without firing a shot and the field divisions, when they were met, were also driven like chaff before the wind'.[33] However, on 11 July, the mechanised battle groups of the Hermann Göring Division, one of only two German divisions on the island, moved forward with the intention of driving the invading forces back into the sea. It was the American units holding positions around Gela, not the Eighth Army, that took the full brunt of the German and Italian counter-attacks. The desperate fighting lasted all day, and at one point German tanks were just a thousand yards from the beach. Although one German commander had sent an enthusiastic signal claiming that his attack had forced the Americans to re-embark, there was no repeat of Kasserine on Sicily. A combination of staunch defensive tactics and heavy naval gun fire finally drove off the depleted German forces.

Meanwhile, the Eighth Army had consolidated its hold over the southern tip of the island and was pushing north towards the vital Catanian plain. However, in the expectation of immediate combat, it had landed its numerous infantry divisions without all their transport, which meant that the foot-bound infantry could only march slowly across the rugged terrain. The British were thus simply not able to move fast enough in the first few days to take full advantage of the Axis disarray and bounce the relatively weak German rearguards out of their blocking positions towards Catania. Montgomery launched a bold airborne operation to capture the Primasole Bridge, the last major obstacle before the plain, but this failed by the narrowest of margins. In a textbook operation, the lead elements of the German 1st Parachute Division landed on the very same drop zones the British 1st Parachute Brigade used one night later. A messy, confused and desperate fight developed, and even when troops from the main force arrived, they were unable to drive the German paratroops away. Eventually the British were able to take the bridge, but the delay had given the Germans time to prepare defences further back, which meant there would be no easy or swift march into Catania. Montgomery's dogfight had finally developed, but it would not bring an early end to the campaign. With his main advance stymied, Montgomery looked to shift one of his corps further west to try and outflank the German defences. It was Montgomery's change of plan and his attempted imposition of a secondary role on the US Seventh Army that caused the greatest controversy of the campaign.

On 13 July, a directive from Alexander arrived at Seventh Army Headquarters. This stated bluntly that after the development of the initial operations, 'Eighth Army will . . . drive the enemy into the Messina peninsula advancing by three main axes'.[34] These routes would take the Eighth Army north of Catania, across the centre of the island from Leonforte to Regalbuto and on to Adrana at the base of Mount Etna, and on the eastern side of the island from Nicosia to Troina and on to Randazzo in the north. The directive instructed: 'Seventh Army will protect the rear of Eighth Army in two phases. (1) Establish a secure base with one division . . . (2) Thrust north to hold the road junctions at Pethalia and . . . south of Resuttano.'[35] The Seventh Army's only projected offensive operation was to capture Agrigento and Porto Empedocle, but only if it could be achieved without 'getting committed seriously'.[36]

This directive made the roles of the two Allied armies on Sicily quite clear: the Eighth Army would drive north towards Messina while the Seventh Army protected the flank and rear of the British.[37] What was not made clear to the Seventh Army was that this directive had originated in a suggestion from Montgomery. He had signalled Alexander's headquarters on 12 July, arguing that 'the maintenance and transport and road situation will not allow of two Armies both carrying out extensive offensive operations. Suggest my Army operates offensively Northwards to cut the island in two and that American Army holds defensively.'[38] Montgomery was attempting to provide 'grip' on the campaign, which he felt was lacking, and in effect to exercise overall command (which had been denied him) through Alexander's 15 Army Group headquarters. His suggestion chimed not only with Alexander's low opinion of American capabilities but also with the supply situation. Without access to a major port, the American forces had to rely upon supply across the open beaches, which was very much an untested experiment at the time. They were also receiving 1,000 tons of supplies per day from Syracuse, but this was an awkward arrangement given the port's location on the south-eastern corner of the island. It thus seemed to make sense to give the Seventh Army a defensive task that would not unduly test its green troops and would limit its supply needs, while the veteran Eighth Army would drive north sustained by the ports it had already captured.

However, what might have appeared like plain military logic to Alexander or Montgomery caused a storm of protest in Seventh Army headquarters: here was yet another attempt by the British to hinder the progress of the American Army. The implications of Alexander's directive were that the Seventh Army, starved of supplies, would perform only a secondary role to the British Eighth Army. Albert Wedemeyer, who was serving as a War Department observer during Husky, told Patton:

> I felt that the operations visualized were incompatible with American participation in the HUSKY effort, and were not justified by the developing situation; that we had the enemy back on his heels and continued aggressive action was indicated and, in my opinion, imperative; further, that such aggressive action on the part of the

Seventh Army would provide incidental but effective security for the rear of the British Eighth Army.[39]

Wedemeyer's forcefully expressed opinion gave Patton indirect War Department permission for his next move. The following day, the two men flew to see Alexander and protest against the directive. They 'courteously and tactfully' put their point of view with the help of three maps that had been made up depicting Patton's vision of future operations for the Seventh Army.[40] Patton wanted to advance northwards towards Palermo. The capture of this major port would then enable the Seventh Army to sustain itself on a push into the northern corner of the island. Alexander approved his request.

General Lucas gratefully noted in his diary on 21 July that 'Seventh Army had been given the mission of advancing on Messina north of Mount Etna. Three rousing cheers. By the Grace of God, we are still a Republic!'[41] Alexander had certainly abdicated his responsibility to properly coordinate the operations of the two armies on Sicily, but at least Patton now had a chance to prove what the Seventh Army could do. Indeed, Robert Henriques, the British liaison officer at Seventh Army Headquarters, remarked to General Lucas that 'the British High Command has no clear conception of the power and mobility of the American Seventh Army. The British vehicles are so inferior that neither commander nor staffs understand what can be accomplished by good equipment.'[42]

Unshackled from Alexander's directive, the Seventh Army was now able to demonstrate the speed and mobility of the American infantry division. US Army doctrine emphasised the importance of rapid movement, and US formations were liberally equipped with highly effective vehicles. Lucas commented in his report on Husky that 'the 2½ ton truck is the outstanding cargo vehicle in the Army and without it this rapid campaign would have bogged down long before its completion because of lack of supplies. I have seen nothing belonging to our enemies or our Allies that can compare with it.'[43] The US Army had another equipment success in Husky that made their rapid movement possible. The DUKW was essentially an amphibious truck that made possible the rapid unloading of stores from ships across open beaches. These two types of vehicles kept the Seventh Army supplied on its rapid march. As the Axis forces withdrew from the south-western part of the island, so Patton's men drove rapidly north to Palermo, which was entered on 23 July 1943 to much rejoicing by the local inhabitants.

Meanwhile, the Eighth Army had been encountering fierce resistance and numerous delays as it fought across the grain of the island. Lucas in fact commented that:

> The British are rather surprisingly slow. Two reasons, I think: (1) Strong opposition and (2) Montgomery is notorious for the meticulous care with which he prepares for his operations. This virtue, like any other, can become an obsession that finally defeats its object. He will not move until everything, every last ration and round of ammunition is ashore and in its proper place.[44]

Lucas was expounding a perspective that would come to form the received American perception of Montgomery's generalship, and indeed the entire performance of the British Army in the Second World War. The accusation that Montgomery was cautious and that the British were slow would grow as the war developed. However, the accusation was unfair with regard to Sicily. Montgomery's original plan for a rapid seizure of the island had been bold but had been checked at the Primasole Bridge by the Germans. The Eighth Army was held back not by Montgomery's caution but by the fierce resistance of a determined enemy who made full use of the very difficult country. The German general Hans Hube had shouldered the nominal Italian commander, General Guzzoni, aside and taken control of the Axis defence of the island. Hube, a hard-bitten veteran of the Eastern Front, was under no illusions about the contest on Sicily; he developed a series of strong defensive lines, anchored on hilltop villages, to hold the Allies for as long as possible so that his forces could slowly withdraw and eventually evacuate the island. In the absence of any better approach, the Allies were forced to fight for every hilltop to slowly press the Germans and Italians back.

While the fighting in Sicily continued, Lucas, who travelled back and forth between the island and Eisenhower's headquarters in

Algiers, had detected dangerous undercurrents. He wrote in his diary that:

> The feeling about the British domination seems to run high among the junior members of the staff. I think the situation, which may be dangerous if not watched, is more the fault of senior members of the staff than of Ike. Ike has to lean in that direction from matters of policy. I think he is getting blazed for many things that he knows nothing about. If I get the chance I will tell him so but it is like talking to a man about his wife.[45]

Matters became worse before they got better because these Allied tensions exhibited themselves most clearly in Alexander's own head-quarters. While Alexander saw Montgomery's suggestions concerning the development of the campaign as a purely military matter, American officers regarded the subordination of the Seventh Army as a devious, politically motivated manoeuvre. American officers might have been overly wont to read Machiavellian scheming into every British action, but British commanders and their staff were equally at fault in apparently remaining blithely ignorant of the impact of their actions and behaviour on American sensibilities. Relations between Clarence Huebner, the American liaison officer at Alexander's headquarter, and the rest of Alexander's staff became increasingly frosty, and Penney remarked in his diary that 'Rightly or wrongly it is getting near murder with most of us!'[46] A few days later, Penney recorded that the rest of the staff had simply decided to ignore Huebner.[47] This breakdown in rela-tions simply reflected the wider and growing tension between the two armies on Sicily, culminating in Alexander sacking Huebner on 28 July.

Although this incident might well have been dangerous, it actu-ally marked the start of a certain degree of rapprochement. Huebner was replaced by Lyman Lemnitzer, who Penney described as 'a much more cheerful soul'.[48] Lemnitzer found it easy to work with Alexander and his staff and became an accomplished and highly effective liaison officer who helped to smooth over similar difficulties throughout the Italian campaign. Huebner was not returned to the States under a cloud, but instead took over command of the 1st Infantry Division from Terry Allen. Commanding one of the best American divisions proved much more suitable to his undoubted talents as an infantry officer than the very awkward role of liaison.

Meanwhile Lucas felt that the growing resentment among the 'rank and file of American officers against British arrogance and calm assumption of authority was a dangerous thing' but the fact that 'no harm was done was due, not to any effort on our Allies part, but entirely to the firm hand of Eisenhower. The British owe him a debt of gratitude because any serious cleavage would have done more immediate damage to the Empire than to America.'[49] While Eisenhower's solution to these tensions remained careful and patient negotiations between the allies, Patton's approach was more direct. He informed Troy Middleton, commander of the 45th Division, that the campaign was now 'a horse race, in which the prestige of the US Army is at stake. We must take Messina before the British. Please use your best efforts to facilitate the success of our race.'[50] Patton wanted to win this race not only to enhance his own prestige but also to prove that the American Seventh Army could match and indeed beat Montgomery's Eighth Army.

It was the BBC that caused the last breach between the Allies on Sicily. The BBC's broadcasts were the only Allied programmes that could be picked up by wireless sets in either army. The BBC had infuriated commanders and soldiers in both armies during Tunisia – Montgomery had been particularly incensed when a careless broadcast had revealed his intentions during the Mareth battle – and American soldiers already considered its reporting openly biased against them. However, an off-hand remark at the end of one news report claiming that the Eighth Army had engaged in heavy fighting while their American allies were sunning themselves and eating grapes in the olive groves of western Sicily caused a storm of protest amongst the Seventh Army. Eisenhower was furious and immediately wrote to Churchill demanding a retraction. Lucas commented that with 'the Boss, being mad at our Allies, all the little people are running for cover. At great expense to ourselves we are saving the British Empire and they aren't even grateful.'[51] This incident forced the BBC to attempt to balance its coverage, but thoughtless reporting would continue to cause problems between the allies during the war.

Ultimately, Patton's men won the race for Messina by a few hours. When the leading troops of the Eighth Army reached the town, they were greeted by American calls of 'Hey! Where've you tourists been?' Patton had achieved the victory and recognition for his army that he sought – but at a heavy price. Lucas described the outstanding characteristic of the campaign as 'a continuous and unrelenting attack. From the time American troops landed on the beach until they entered Messina the pressure on the enemy was never relinquished . . . The men of the Seventh Army marched tremendous distances over the roughest terrain I have ever seen. They, in many cases, reached the limit of physical exhaustion.'[52] But despite these hardships, Lucas stressed the importance of what the Seventh Army had achieved: 'the speed with which the Sicilian show was brought to its culmination filled many people with astonishment, especially our allies, the British, who regarded us with the oblique eye a professional always turns on one he considers an amateur'.[53] The performance of the Seventh Army had restored the prestige of the US Army and proven its British critics wrong. This ensured that British senior commanders, however grudgingly, now had to recognise US troops as equals rather than as inexperienced allies who needed to be subordinated to British command.

As Lucas had noted, Patton's relentless offensive had cost many casualties and had been mounted at an exhausting pace. When Patton made two visits to field hospitals on the island, he was confronted with the human price of the Sicilian campaign. He treated soldiers suffering from physical wounds pleasantly, but when he saw men with psychological wounds caused by exhaustion and the stress of combat, he behaved disgracefully. On two separate occasions he 'slapped' soldiers suffering from combat fatigue and verbally abused them as cowards.[54] The reaction from Eisenhower was immediate, and he sent a letter to demand that Patton apologise to everyone involved. At the same time, however, he attempted to prevent the incidents from reaching the American press. Nonetheless, Patton's entire career was placed in jeopardy and he

spent many months in limbo. It was only Eisenhower's protection
of his old friend that saved him from military oblivion.

Sicily has often been viewed in retrospect as a 'bitter victory' and
indeed almost a failure for the Allies because the Germans were
able to evacuate virtually their entire force from the island.[55]
Montgomery railed in his diary at the lack of 'grip' by senior
commanders without once acknowledging that his heavy-handed
interventions had wrecked any real chance of the interservice cooperation essential to preventing the Germans' escape.[56] But
Operation Husky had achieved the goals that the Chiefs of Staff
had set at Casablanca. The Mediterranean sea route could now be
opened, Mussolini had been removed from power, and the Allies
had successfully carried the war into Europe. The Germans may
have accomplished a highly professional evacuation of the island,
but it remained a retreat. And while the British and Americans had
been fighting in Sicily, the Red Army had comprehensively blunted
the Wehrmacht's summer offensive at Kursk. These two widely
separated battles marked the passing of the initiative to the Allies.
After Sicily and Kursk, there would never be another 'Blitzkrieg'
that reshaped the map of Europe; retreat would become all too
familiar to the Wehrmacht.

Operation Husky also marked another important watershed. Its
completion represented the limit of British domination of Allied
policy. Casablanca had seen the imposition of a British Mediterranean
strategy on the Anglo-American alliance. Montgomery's intervention in the planning process for Husky had signified virtually
complete British domination over the execution of that strategy.
Neither would be tolerated again by the United States, whose army
had categorically demonstrated its prowess during the campaign.
Unfortunately, the battle for Sicily, marked by its harsh terrain and
bitter fighting against a determined opponent, was also simply a
taste of what was to come in the rest of the Italian campaign.

9

Stomach Ache

Eisenhower broadcast the news of the Italian surrender on 8 September 1943, across the BBC and US radio stations. Mussolini had been removed from power on 25 July, and the Italian king, Emmanuel III, and his newly chosen prime minister, Marshal Pietro Badoglio, had spent the next two months in agonies of indecision. Both reaffirmed their determination to continue the fight as an Axis power while secretly opening negotiations with the Allies, as they faced the dilemma that remaining with the Axis would lead to an Allied invasion while siding with the Allies would bring German occupation. Faced with Allied demands for unconditional surrender, Badoglio had temporised until the last possible moment. Eisenhower's broadcast even reached the troopships of the Allied task forces already en route for the Bay of Salerno. These ships were part of an operation code-named Avalanche, a hurriedly arranged invasion of mainland Italy. The news of the Italian surrender was greeted with surprise and relief by the troops on board the ships and hopes flared that their landings might become an unopposed stroll ashore.

In fact, the key decisions concerning Italy had been made before the invasion of Sicily, at the Trident conference held in Washington in May 1943. While the chiefs had authorised the capture of Sicily at the Casablanca conference in January 1943, there had been no agreement at that time concerning further moves in the Mediterranean. With the projected cross-Channel attack scheduled for the spring of 1944, there appeared to be a gap of nine or ten months in Allied activity. At the Trident conference, the British chiefs argued that it was 'unthinkable' for the Allies to remain inactive during this period and suggested that the main task in the interim should be the 'elimination of Italy', which would go 'a very long way towards defeating Germany'.[1] Brooke rehearsed these arguments during the conference itself, warning that the Germans were still too powerful for any forces the Allies might land in France but that operations to occupy Italy would stretch German defences yet further. The British Chiefs of Staff were advancing the same arguments in favour of a 'peripheral' strategy that had dominated Allied conferences over the past two years.

However, Marshall had managed to gain agreement amongst the US Chiefs of Staff for his approach to the problem. In a previously prepared paper, the US chiefs argued that the overall strategy for the defeat of Germany must not be compromised for local successes in the Mediterranean, which had to be seen as a 'secondary theater' that could not deliver 'decisive and final operations'.[2] During the conference, Marshall reiterated his arguments in favour of concentration on a cross-Channel attack, which remained unchanged in their inspiration since his memorandum of spring 1942. He expressed his fear that landing forces in Italy 'would establish a vacuum' that would suck yet more troops into the Mediterranean and might eventually prejudice the success of the cross-Channel attack. He simply would not accept an open-ended commitment to operations in the Mediterranean.

These decisions were confirmed at the Quadrant conference, held in Quebec in August 1943. Thus, Overlord, the new name given to the cross-Channel attack, was to have overriding priority over Italy in Allied resources. Nonetheless, it was hoped that Italy could be eliminated as a belligerent, and airbases established as far north as Rome. After the capture of Sardinia and Corsica, the Allies would place 'unremitting pressure' on German forces in northern Italy, and create favourable conditions for an assault into southern France.[3] These decisions meant that all the subsequent operations in Italy took place within strict limits, whilst the build-up of forces in the United Kingdom for Overlord had first call on any resources. The difference in the outcome at Trident and Quadrant lay in the level of preparation and unity the US Chiefs of Staff brought to the table. Wedemeyer, back in harness at the War

Department after his Sicilian travels, informed Eisenhower of the results of the Quebec conference and observed that:

> It was gratifying to note the teamwork that has at last been attained on the US Joint Chiefs of Staff level. In earlier conferences the British Chiefs of Staff . . . represented a united front. They presented and defended their views pertaining to strategy and related problems very effectively. On the other hand, Admiral King would differ with Marshall or with Arnold, and Admiral Leahy evidenced only perfunctory interest in anything but the processing of papers with the minimum of effort. At Quebec the attitude was different, with Marshall carrying the ball and Leahy, King, and even old Hap Arnold swinging in to provide timely and effective interference.[4]

Yet Marshall's views about how the war should be conducted had not changed: what had changed was his ability to weld the US Joint Chiefs of Staff together and agree on a common view of American and Allied strategy.

These Allied decisions, taken at the highest level, had profound consequences for the conduct of the Italian campaign. Even before the first Allied soldier landed in Italy, it was clear that this was a secondary theatre that would have to be conducted with definite limits to the resources expended. The Allied chiefs had taken these decisions for sound strategic reasons but also in an atmosphere of optimism. Brooke had expressed the commonly held view at Trident that he did not believe that 'Germany would try to control an Italy which was not fighting'.[5] There was an expectation that, in the event of an Italian surrender, the Germans would rapidly withdraw to the eminently defensible Alps, leaving the Allies to simply occupy Italy and utilise its airbases to mount strategic bombing raids against the Third Reich.

These decisions meant that while the invasion of Sicily had been mounted with the full panoply of Allied power, the invasion of mainland Italy had to be planned and executed with far fewer resources. The profusion of Allied plans for the invasion of Italy produced by Eisenhower's AFHQ – Giant, Gangway, Avalanche,

Buttress, Baytown, Goblet, Musket and Slapstick* – simply reflected
the uncertainty concerning the likely response to Allied intervention on mainland Italy and ever-changing calculations of the available
shipping and landing craft capacity. None took account of Napoleon's
advice that Italy was like a boot and thus best entered from the
top. This was due to the need to coordinate the activities of all
three services. It was theoretically possible for the Allies to have
made a landing in northern Italy but practically impossible due to
the need to provide air cover over the assault beaches.

Eventually Eisenhower settled on three operations. In Giant, the
82nd Airborne Division would be dropped on to the airfields around
Rome and, in cooperation with Italian units, deny the city and its
vital transport hub to the Germans. Avalanche would see the Fifth
Army, with one British and one American corps, land on beaches
in the Gulf of Salerno. And before either of these operations took
place, the Eighth Army was to cross the Messina Straits from Sicily
on to the mainland in Operation Baytown. As the negotiations with
the Italians proceeded at a frustratingly slow pace, Eisenhower
attempted to persuade Montgomery to cross the Messina Straits
at the earliest opportunity. But Montgomery believed the Germans
would resist any landing on the toe of Italy. Eisenhower disagreed,
and at one point even told Alexander that he thought 'we could
do it in a row boat', but Montgomery would not be moved: he
wanted to wait until he could cross in strength.

While Baytown appeared a relatively straightforward operation,
Eisenhower always recognised that not only was Avalanche a more
risky venture but that the US Fifth Army was something of an
unknown quantity. It had been established in January 1943 under the
command of Lieutenant General Mark Clark, a relatively young
American officer who had received meteoric promotion, leapfrogging

---

* Giant was an airborne operation designed to drop the 82nd Airborne Division on
to the airfields around Rome; Gangway was the projected landing of the Fifth Army
north of Naples; Avalanche was the landing of the Fifth Army at Salerno; Buttress
was a potential landing of the Eighth Army on the northern coast of Calabria; Baytown
was the crossing of the Messina straits by the Eighth Army, while Goblet was an
operation by 5 Corps against Crotone; Musket and Slapstick concerned two landings
at Taranto.

ahead of many older, more experienced officers. He had served briefly as an infantry company commander in the Argonne in 1918, but had really come to prominence in 1940 when he became General MacNair's right-hand man at GHQ Army Ground Forces, developing the 'mass production' methods for training the new US Army.[6] Eisenhower considered Clark to have 'no superior' in the fields of 'organization and training', a view shared by Marshall, who consistently supported him in his rapid promotion.[7] Clark had been given command of the US II Corps in England while also serving as Eisenhower's deputy commander in London during 1942, where he had impressed Churchill as just the kind of pugnacious and dynamic commander favoured by the British Prime Minister. Churchill insisted thereafter on referring to Clark as 'the Eagle', in reference to his aquiline features and hawkish attitude. Clark had then been involved in the cloak-and-dagger attempt to secure French support in North Africa before the Torch landings, for which he was awarded the Congressional Medal of Honor. There was no question that his star was in the ascendant, and when Eisenhower offered him the command of the Fifth Army, even though it was initially a replacement and training organisation, Clark jumped at the chance.

While Clark had many of the essential attributes for an army commander in his ambition, his organisational ability and his relentless and ruthless pursuit of objectives, these were combined with less attractive characteristics. He was a vain man, anxious and almost aggressive in his desire for publicity, yet highly sensitive to any criticism, whether real or perceived. He had to fret on the sidelines in relative inactivity during the Tunisian and Sicilian campaigns as the Fifth Army were not directly involved, but he was well aware of the rumours of British dominance and the biased publicity that surrounded them. From the first, he was determined to prove the superiority of American troops and to ensure that they received adequate recognition for their achievements. Even before his army went into combat, he had begun to see the British as rivals and competitors rather than allies.

Clark assembled a strong staff in the Fifth Army. Most people who came to know him considered Al Gruenther to be one of the finest chiefs of staff of the war. Brigadier Charles Richardson, who had served with distinction on Montgomery's staff, joined with a small team to help coordinate the British forces within the army. He considered that Gruenther 'had a brilliant mind and was completely devoid of intellectual arrogance' while also being totally unbiased towards either the British or American forces in the army.[8] Clark also possessed a talented head of G3 (Operations) in the form of Brigadier General Don Brann, a contemporary of Eisenhower. Richardson noted, in the final briefing before the Salerno landings, that it was Brann who set the scene, stated the objectives and explained the tactics to be used. Richardson, schooled in Monty's 'master plan' approach, considered Clark to be 'too much in the hands of his staff'.[9]

This was, in part, a common British misunderstanding of the functioning of the American staff system, which did expect more calculation and product from the staff before the commander made decisions. However, it was also true that in August 1943, neither Clark nor his staff had had any real practice in the planning or conduct of army operations. Clark had briefly commanded a battalion in 1918 but had little or no further experience in the command of formations. Although he realised from the first that Clark possessed the 'courage and personality of a leader', Richardson doubted whether he really understood 'operations at Army level'.[10] The essential qualification within the British Army for high command was prior experience of commanding a division in battle, something Clark simply did not have. This was precisely the kind of situation that had prompted Alexander to state that the American generals of the war were 'not professional soldiers, not as we understand that term'.[11] In fact, over the course of the Italian campaign, Clark proved himself to be an able commander, but the planning for Avalanche betrayed the inexperience of the Fifth Army's commander and staff. Although Clark had wanted to make the landings at Gaeta, just north of Naples, Tedder had insisted that the Bay of Salerno was as far north as the Allied air forces could guarantee coverage. While the beaches at Salerno appeared attractive, there were many inherent problems with their hinterland. The plain of Salerno was large and flat but broken up with numerous ditches, settlements and agriculture, which severely limited visibility; it was also dominated by a range of hills, which encircled the wide plain.

With many troops earmarked for a return to the United Kingdom, there were now insufficient Americans left for the Fifth Army to be an all-American force. Instead, it comprised the British X Corps, under the command of Major General Richard McCreery, and the American VI Corps under Major General Ernest J. Dawley. McCreery was an austere and rather severe man who did not warm to Clark, and the feeling was mutual. In planning the landings, the British X Corps were to land to the north of the Sele river around Salerno, while the US VI Corps were to land at Paestum. This meant that, after the landings, the two corps would be divided by a six-mile gap and a river. Each corps would essentially fight its own unsupported battle. The Fifth Army planners had made the same basic errors of dispersion and lack of mutual support that Montgomery had railed against during the Husky planning.

Meanwhile, the German High Command, uncertain as to the status of their erstwhile Italian allies, had been readying their own plans. There had been a serious debate about the best way of dealing with Italy in the event of an Italian surrender. Hitler had already prepared Operation Axis for a German takeover of northern Italy, and German divisions had been quietly filtering through the Brenner Pass for such an eventuality. However, Field Marshal Rommel, who had been placed in charge of an army group in northern Italy, favoured a withdrawal to the Alps in the event of an Allied invasion. Kesselring, on the other hand, still in charge of the German forces in southern Italy, believed the best approach had been proven during the fighting on Sicily. He wanted to make full use of the excellent defensive terrain by forcing the Allies to wear themselves out against a series of well-prepared defensive lines. Just as importantly, Kesselring had correctly divined that the Bay of Salerno marked the limit of Allied air cover, which made it the most likely location for an Allied landing. Kesselring saw to it that there were three German divisions deployed around Salerno, which were able to shoulder aside the original Italian garrison when the Italian armistice was announced.

When the Eighth Army crossed the Messina Straits under the

cover of a tremendous artillery bombardment, it met almost no resistance.[12] Perhaps Montgomery can be forgiven for using a sledge-hammer to crack a nut, but his continued insistence that the Germans would resist any landings fiercely now appeared faintly ridiculous: the only casualty after the landings was an unfortunate Canadian soldier who was savaged by a lion that had been released from its cage in a local zoo by the artillery bombardment. Montgomery's forebodings of doom did come to pass, albeit at Salerno rather than in Calabria. The Allied plan for a swift descent on Italy began to unravel when Eisenhower was forced to cancel Giant II, the proposed air drop on the Rome airfields. At the very last minute Badoglio had retracted his commitment that the Italian army would support the operation. Indeed, when news of the armistice broke, the Italian army were left without any firm orders, and in the confusion, most of its units were easily disarmed by the Germans.

Meanwhile, Kesselring's far-sighted arrangements ensured that when the Allied assault troops landed on the beaches at Salerno and Paestum, they were greeted not as liberators by the Italians, as they had expected, but by a storm of fire from determined German defenders. For most of the Allied soldiers, this was their first introduction to combat, and it proved a real shock. The American infantry found German tanks prowling around just off the beach at Paestum, while a British battalion was overrun by panzers as it marched inland: a sense of crisis gripped the Fifth Army almost immediately after the landings. Salerno was a tough battle, and one that Clark struggled to control. He established his command post in the VI Corps sector, visiting McCreery in the northern half of the beachhead only infrequently. While British and American soldiers both fought hard to establish, maintain and deepen the beachhead, they did not fight as a unified army. Divided by the River Sele and nearly six miles of difficult terrain, the two corps, British and American, fought essentially separate battles.

The worst moment at Salerno arrived on 14 September when the Germans gathered together sufficient troops to mount a deter-mined counter-attack. The German tanks and their supporting panzer grenadiers overran a number of American positions and drove within a few miles of the beach. The advance caused consternation and panic at Fifth Army headquarters, whose positions were in danger of being overrun. That evening Clark even contemplated the re-embarkation of VI Corps, a move that would almost certainly have led to disaster. Montgomery was kept informed of these events by one of his ADCs, who reported to him that 'The Army, Corps and Div staffs were completely untrained, and there were chaotic scenes, with lack of news, little control over the air, less control over formations and units, and so on.'[13] This was somewhat exaggerated, as in fact the German attack had already run out of steam and the Allied measures to regain control, such as the air drop of an American parachute regiment on to the beaches, had already taken effect.

Anxiety over the course of the battle at Salerno spread to the very top of the Allied command chain. At the height of the crisis, Churchill, worried that none of the commanders had fought a large-scale battle before, encouraged Alexander to be 'on the spot' so that he could exert direct influence on the fighting. The Prime Minister reminded Alexander that General Sir Ian Hamilton had lost the Battle of Suvla Bay by remaining remote during the critical phases.[14] Alexander was able to soothe Churchill's nerves by informing him that he had already anticipated his wise advice by visiting the Fifth Army. In fact, Alexander visited the embattled beachhead three times, and while he was impressed by Clark's calmness under fire, and was convinced that McCreery had his corps under control, he became concerned over Dawley's ability to command the American VI Corps. Clark and Dawley had already fallen out over Clark's interference in the deployment of VI Corps; Dawley clearly felt that Clark was treading on his toes as corps commander. After one meeting, Dawley called Clark a 'Boy Scout' and Clark then drove off, leaving Dawley without transport back to his command post.

The next day, after expressing doubts about Dawley, Clark took Alexander and Lemnitzer to visit VI Corps. Lemnitzer recalled that, when asked about the situation on the corps front, Dawley, 'obviously under great strain' and 'with his hands shaking like a leaf', 'made a pitiful effort to explain the dispositions of his troops and what he

planned to do'.[15] Alexander concluded that he would have to be
relieved. This was a difficult moment. Not only was the relief of a
corps commander a very serious step, but Clark had, until very recently,
been considerably more junior than Dawley. Clark may have hesitated
for another, more personal reason. Dawley was a close friend of
General MacNair, who had been Clark's main patron in his rise to
the top. Although Alexander was convinced that Dawley should go,
he clearly did not feel that he could interfere directly in what was a
matter for the US Army, and relied on Lemnitzer to inform Eisenhower
about the matter. When Lemnitzer explained the situation to him,
Eisenhower reputedly exploded: 'Well G—— D——, why in the hell
doesn't he relieve Dawley?'[16] Eisenhower's outburst was somewhat
ironic given his own initial failure to grasp the nettle of Fredendall's
relief during the Tunisian campaign, but he had clearly learnt the
importance of replacing a failing subordinate, regardless of qualms
over seniority or sentiment. Nonetheless, it was only after Eisenhower
visited Salerno for himself, on Alexander and Lemnitzer's recommendation, that Dawley was relieved. He was rapidly replaced by
John Lucas, who had recently taken over command of II US Corps.
Bradley, its previous commander, had gone to take charge of US
preparations in Britain. While Dawley was, in some respects, the
scapegoat for Clark's inexperience at Salerno, his relief was a clear
example of Alexander's growing experience in handling Anglo-
American issues, and also of Lemnitzer's unsung worth as a senior
liaison officer. Without his skill and tact, the episode might have led
to a further deterioration in Allied relations.

The crisis at Salerno was surmounted and Dawley had actually
played a full part in ensuring that the American defence held
against the German assaults. The German forces had put everything they had into driving the Allies back into the sea, and failed.
On 17 September, Kesselring issued orders for General Heinrich
von Vietinghoff's Tenth Army to withdraw. The next day, German
units began to pull out and the pressure on the Allied units in the
Salerno beachhead began to slacken. Eisenhower later commented:

I . . . went into this operation in the firm belief that naval gunfire
and overwhelming air support could sustain us on the beaches while

we were waiting for the build-up. Therefore the situation we faced on the 13th was not unexpected and there was no reason to get too glum about the matter. It is a rather odd thing, though, that no matter how much one foresees and prepares for an adverse situation, wishful thinking always intervenes following on early success and there results in a staff a too hopeful spirit of optimism, which is badly shattered when the enemy reacts exactly as you figured he would.[17]

While Eisenhower was almost certainly displaying a sangfroid he did not feel at the time of the crisis at Salerno, it was certainly true that naval gunfire and air cover in support of amphibious landings had become the Allies' trump card. In Sicily, and now at Salerno, German forces, even under favourable conditions, had been unable to throw the Allies back into the sea. Even though Salerno proved that the Germans had no answer to the threat of Allied amphibious landings, Kesselring won the debate over how to defend Italy. He had shown that the Germans could delay and possibly forestall the Allied advance. Hitler decided to support him and agreed to the forward defence of Italy.

Here lay the ultimate paradox of the entire Italian campaign. Had the Allies mounted a more powerful invasion, unrestricted by the needs of the build-up for Overlord in the UK, it is possible that they might have overwhelmed the German defence at Salerno. This might well have discredited Kesselring's arguments and precipitated a German withdrawal to the Alps. By using more strength in Italy, the Allies might have achieved the objective they sought: a relatively easy occupation of the Italian peninsula. By allocating strictly limited resources to this 'secondary theatre', they ultimately ensured that the Germans would mount a determined defence in Italy. While the Allied planners had expected the Germans to withdraw in the face of an Allied occupation force, this proved to be wishful thinking. The Allied troops in Italy were thus condemned to fight a hard campaign against a determined opponent even when, had more resources been available, complete and resounding success often appeared tantalisingly close. Due to the strategic decision to give Overlord overriding priority, there were never enough troops, ships or landing craft for the Allies to exploit their maritime superiority along the Italian coast by mounting major amphibious operations that could have unlocked whatever linear defence Kesselring mounted. Yet the campaign in Italy did have another paradoxical effect in drawing German troops and resources away from France, the intended target for Overlord. The Allied campaign in Italy became far harder as a result of Salerno, but the eventual landings in France became that much easier.

Unfortunately, differing Allied arguments as to just why the Germans had withdrawn began to inflict serious damage on Allied relations. Montgomery considered the advance of the Eighth Army from the toe of Italy towards Salerno – a distance of almost 300 miles in 17 days in the face of a skilled German retreat that mined and demolished the roads behind them – 'an amazing achievement' that ranked as 'as one of its finest efforts'.[18] He also believed that the Eighth Army advance had relieved the pressure on the Fifth Army and saved the beachhead at Salerno. Although Clark sent a generous signal to Montgomery on 16 September thanking him for his assistance and expressing a desire for partnership between the two armies, he was soon appalled to find that stories were circulating that the Eighth Army had saved his troops at Salerno. This interpretation seemed to be confirmed by the photographs of the historic meeting between Clark and Montgomery on 24 September, which portrayed a 'victorious' Eighth Army commander reaching down from his armoured car to shake the hand of the 'rescued' Fifth Army commander. Clark became convinced that the British intended to steal the honours from the American Army in a repeat of Tunisia, and he became equally determined to prevent this. The myth that the Eighth Army had saved the Fifth was soon in competition with the countering legend that the Eighth Army had dawdled on the road towards Salerno. Neither view of events was likely to foster a sense of partnership and common effort in the coming campaign, and the recriminations between the British and Americans that began at Salerno became a long-running theme in Anglo-American relations in Italy, lasting virtually until the war's end.

On 17 September, Montgomery informed Alexander of his vision for future operations, arguing that as the armies advanced up the Italian peninsula, the west should be taken by the American Fifth Army, and the east by the British under Montgomery's command.[19] In fact, the terms 'American' and 'British' concealed the multinational nature of the Allied armies in Italy. Clark would have dearly loved for his Fifth Army to have been an exclusively American formation, but there were never enough American troops in Italy to make this a reality, and the Fifth Army consistently had British and French troops attached to it. Later in the campaign, a Brazilian Expeditionary Force (FEB) joined Fifth Army. While this entered the line as a regiment, by the end of the war it had reached divisional strength.[20] 'British', meanwhile, was a catch-all term encompassing soldiers drawn not only from the United Kingdom but from all over the British Empire – and beyond. Indian, South African, New Zealand, Polish and Greek formations served in the nominally British Eighth Army.

Nationalities aside, the predominant reason for the two armies to operate on either side of Italy was supply. Having separate ports designated for each army's use considerably simplified this already complex problem. However, the solution inevitably led to a situation in which the two armies, Fifth and Eighth, advanced with only a minimum of coordination and contact. Montgomery soon became worried by this, and confided to his diary that:

> As this campaign goes on the more clear it becomes that 15 Army Group is very ineffective. There is no grip of the battle. In the end I decide what I want to do, and what is best. I then get Clark (5 Army) to agree, and between us we fix up a plot, boundary and so on. As it happens this is probably the best way to do it; but it is not the proper way to make war.[21]

Montgomery certainly did not rate Alexander as a battlefield commander. He believed Alexander relied on 'ideas being produced which will give him a plan; he does not come . . . with his own plan, and then give out clear orders'.[22] On the other hand, Montgomery himself had consistently demonstrated that he was perfectly capable, if given orders that he disliked, of ignoring them, subverting the Allied command chain and conducting business on his own terms.

In fact, Alexander had already submitted his outline plan to Eisenhower and to the CIGS. He explained that his phase one would see the south of Italy secured, while phase two envisaged the capture of Naples and the cluster of airfields at Foggia. These airfields were considered of prime importance as they would enable the strategic bombing forces to begin operations against the Ploesti oilfields in Romania, and other targets in the Third Reich. Phase three was aimed at the capture of the glittering prize of Rome, the Italian capital and 'eternal city', which also possessed vital road and rail communications. Alexander admitted that his phase four, the capture of Ravenna, was only a forecast, since he did not have 'accurate information of the main body of the German formations, and where they intend to stand'.[23] Unfortunately, the timetable he was working to was wildly optimistic: he envisaged the capture of Naples by 7 October 1943, the capture of Rome one month later, and the fall of Ravenna on the far side of the Apennine mountains by the end of November. The simple truth was that, even after Salerno, the Allies still did not expect the Germans to fight in Italy.[24] At this point, no one seems to have identified the importance of Monte Cassino or imagined that Kesselring would make his stand south of Rome. Alexander was already thinking beyond a gradual progression up the leg of Italy in suggesting that the Allies should 'take full advantage of our command of the sea and skies to put ashore small but hard-hitting mobile forces behind the enemy so as to cut him off . . . Later, when we are in a position to break into the valley of the Po, it may be possible to stage a seaborne operation in some strength based on Corsica and aiming at securing a bridgehead in the Genoa area.'[25] In expressing his desire to utilise amphibious forces, Alexander seems to have believed that he could draw upon the full resources of the Allies to achieve his aims. He would soon find that his visions of a fast-moving campaign that rapidly occupied Italy shrivelled in the reality of German resistance and straitened circumstances.

In the autumn of 1943, the two armies slowly pushed forward

up the leg of Italy. John Lucas, now in command of US VI Corps, experienced the full frustration of the conditions. He wrote that after Salerno, 'The mountains were serious military obstacles which became ever more difficult as the advance continued and the ranges progressively increased in height . . . The enemy, therefore, always held commanding ground and was able to observe our movements and direct his fire on us with disconcerting freedom.'[26] Italy was a beautiful land of rivers, mountains and valleys studded with ancient hilltop villages, but it was those very features that made it a terrible place to fight. It was comparatively simple in such terrain for the German rearguards to cause seemingly endless delays. This was no war of movement but a 'war of engineers. The retreating enemy placed every possible obstacle in the way of our advance. All bridges were destroyed, railroad as well as highway, roads blown from the faces of cliffs, towns demolished so that streets were filled with rubble.'[27] Even if Allied soldiers had never visited Italy before, its reputation as 'Sunny Italy' preceded it,* but the reality was quite different: torrential rain and mud imposed almost as much drag on Allied operations as the Germans did.

By the middle of October 1943, Alexander wrote to Brooke of his growing concerns:

> I am not happy about the situation and our prospects of getting to Rome early. The Germans have heavily reinforced the front and they are now fighting for every foot with extreme tenacity. Our troops can only progress very slowly at heavy cost and they are getting tired. The Germans have in front of me 9 Divisions which I am opposing with 11 Divisions. As I see it we shall have to carry out another amphibious operation of probably a division plus in order to turn his flank. And as far as I know we have not got the required craft for this.[28]

He had begun to realise that the campaign in Italy was not going to be easy. He understood only too well that an unimaginative drive up the Italian peninsula placed heavy demands on the Allied

---

* The Great Western Railway, for example, had compared Cornwall with Italy for sunshine and beauty in a famous interwar poster campaign.

troops and offered no prospect of decisive success. His answer to
the dilemma was an amphibious landing to outflank the German
line. This was the genesis of what became Operation Shingle, the
landings at Anzio. But the Allies still had to stand by their earlier
agreement that the commitment to Italy had to be constrained
whilst Overlord continued to be prioritised. Brooke, in his reply to
Alexander, stated that he was under no illusions concerning the
difficulties, and that he had had trouble persuading the Americans
that 'our commitment in Italy would be a heavy one'.[29] Alexander
had suggested that a visit to Italy by the Director of Military
Operations might help to secure his theatre greater resources, but
Brooke warned against this by arguing that any opinion that came
from a British source 'would be suspect by the Americans who
seem to have an ineradicable impression that our hearts are not in
OVERLORD and that we take every opportunity of diverting to
the Mediterranean resources which they consider should be concentrated in Great Britain'.[30] He suggested that Alexander should
provide Eisenhower with his plan in the hope that the Combined
Chiefs of Staff would agree to allot greater resources to the Italian
campaign.

By airing his thoughts directly with Brooke, Alexander had sought
help from his British superior, the CIGS, without reference to the
Allied chain of command, and this was just the sort of 'conspiracy'
to siphon resources away from Overlord that the American chiefs
continually suspected the British chiefs of condoning. In fact,
Alexander had already alerted Eisenhower to his difficulties,
pointing out that the removal of landing craft from Italy for
Overlord would 'seriously prejudice our operations to gain Rome'.[31]
When these craft had gone, there would be none available on the
east coast and only nine at Naples. Alexander argued that at least
twenty landing craft were necessary for working the port at Naples,
and perhaps another twenty for mounting 'cutting out assaults'
along the coast. He warned Eisenhower that the shortage of landing
craft would 'force us into frontal attacks which will undoubtedly
be strongly contested and prove costly. At the same time if the
frontal attacks make rapid progress, then maintenance will not
keep pace.'[32] It was thus only in October 1943 that Alexander truly

realised the horns of the dilemma of operating on a secondary front with insufficient resources.

This gulf between ambitious objectives and insufficient resources meant that more was demanded of the ordinary soldier. On 1 November 1943, Lucas wrote in his diary: 'There is no discharge in the war. This is a heart breaking business. An advance of a few miles a day, fighting a terrible terrain and a determined enemy, building bridges, removing mines, climbing mountains. The men get punch drunk, but we must keep on going. Continuous pressure is the answer.'[33] His view that 'continuous pressure' on the Germans was the only solution was shared by Fifth Army headquarters, and by Clark in particular. Indeed, the concept of an unrelenting advance that would break any enemy was an ingrained feature of American military thought in the Second World War. The vision of a 'power drive' to Berlin was simply one feature of a belief, almost unchanged since Pershing's day, that the enemy must be given no respite no matter what demands that placed on formations and individual soldiers. While American divisions could draw soldiers from a large replacement pool to make up losses due to combat, illness or exposure, the same divisions had to be committed to action day after day, month after month. Combat historian Sidney T. Matthews remembered that troops frequently 'stayed in the line for 30, 60, in some cases even 70 or 80 days without relief. The result was that frequently one battle and one day merged into the next in the mind of the soldier.'[34] Seeing service in this 'secondary' theatre actually increased the demands placed upon the ordinary soldiers. By November 1943, Lucas's three divisions had been in action continually for over three months since landing at Salerno, and most of the men were absolutely exhausted.[35]

By this time, both Alexander and Eisenhower were convinced that an amphibious operation to draw German troops away from the main front was essential if the Allies were to have any hope of reaching Rome. Eisenhower's warnings to the Combined Chiefs of Staff had the desired effect of postponing the withdrawal of landing craft from the Italian theatre. Alexander got Lemnitzer and Fifth Army headquarters to work on plans for the 'end run' to

Rome. This was originally envisaged as a five-division assault, which would include divisions earmarked for Overlord that were still in the Mediterranean theatre.[36] Although a landing on the coast near Rome was considered, the beaches were found to be unsuitable and the target became Anzio, south of Rome and over 75 miles north of the main Fifth Army front. This would be an ambitious assault that would seize the high ground of the Alban hills around Colli Laziali. With a powerful Allied force thus threatening the German lines of communication to the main battle front, Alexander expected the Germans to withdraw, uncovering Rome in the process, rather than fighting it out.[37] Such a large amphibious assault might well have achieved Alexander's objectives, but the resources it demanded were simply not available: the divisions earmarked for Overlord could not be used, and uncertainty over the number of landing craft led to delay and cancellations.

Meanwhile, Montgomery pushed north on the Adriatic coast towards the vital Foggia airfields. He mounted a successful operation at Termoli, using what remained of the available landing craft, but the Eighth Army's drive ended at the River Sangro, where fierce German counter-attacks stalled British attempts to expand their bridgehead. Beset by foul weather and a sea of mud, Montgomery realised that any attempt to continue the advance on the Adriatic coast was impossible.

At a command conference held on 3 November at Carthage in North Africa, it was decided that the Fifth Army would continue the drive up the west coast of Italy, past Monte Cassino and up the Liri valley towards Rome. Meanwhile, a two-division amphibious assault would take place at Anzio Nettuno, where there were suitable beaches and a small port. However, such a small force could only survive if the Fifth Army could advance rapidly and secure a link-up within ten days of the landings. Meanwhile, the Eighth Army would mount attacks north of the Sangro to provide Kesselring with the dilemma of responding on three simultaneous fronts. In order to accomplish this complicated plan, Eisenhower asked the Combined Chiefs for permission to retain, until 15 December, 68 landing craft that were currently earmarked for dispatch to Britain.[38] But when mid-December came, the Eighth Army remained bogged down in the mud, and the Fifth Army's long and weary fight amongst the mountains had left them far short of the Liri valley. The dearth of landing craft, the lack of progress and a general shortage of enthusiasm for the project forced Clark to cancel the operation on 18 December.

Operation Shingle might well have been stillborn but for Churchill's intervention, which resurrected the project. Lieutenant General Kenneth Strong, Eisenhower's intelligence chief, certainly believed that Anzio 'was executed because the PM wanted it'.[39] While the vast majority of Allied operations were planned as part of an agreed overall strategy that flowed from Roosevelt and Churchill through the Combined Chiefs of Staff and on to the appropriate Allied Supreme Commander, Operation Shingle formed an exception to this rule. It just so happened that Churchill was in North Africa recovering from a minor heart attack after the strenuous debates of the Cairo conference. Alexander and Eisenhower visited him at Carthage on 23 December 1943 in an attempt to gain his support for the project that the Combined Chiefs of Staff had refused. Shingle seemed to offer a chance to break the deadlock in Italy and enable the Allies to reach Rome. Over the next few days, Churchill held a series of meetings concerning the operation in an attempt to revive it.[40] As with so many military impasses during the war, he went over the heads of the military and persuaded Roosevelt to agree that the landing craft vital for the operation should be retained in the Mediterranean until mid-February.[41]

The reason that Churchill was able to dominate the military process over Shingle also lay in the fact that December 1943 witnessed a hiatus and rapid personnel change in the Allied chain of command. Omar Bradley, Patton's deputy commander, had left for London soon after the conclusion of the Sicilian campaign, and Eisenhower left Allied Forces Headquarters in Algiers soon after seeing Churchill on 23 December. Nor did he go alone: he stripped the vast majority of key staff officers from Algiers and took them with him to form the new Supreme Headquarters Allied Expeditionary Force in London in preparation for Operation Overlord. When the British general Henry Maitland 'Jumbo' Wilson took over Eisenhower's post as Supreme Commander Mediterranean, he had to reassemble his headquarters almost from scratch. Not surprisingly, this greatly altered the dynamics of command in the Mediterranean. While Alexander had deferred to Eisenhower on a number of issues, he was never willing to surrender any real decision-making to Wilson. This temporary fracture in the Allied command chain enabled Churchill to exert an unusual amount of influence and pressure on the planning for Operation Shingle.

In effect, Operation Shingle – having been a starved problem child of Alexander and Clark – became a personal project of the Prime Minister. With Churchill's whirlwind of energy behind the project, new forces could be allotted to it. But although Churchill, by dint of a flurry of communications to Roosevelt and the Combined Chiefs, managed to gain sufficient landing craft for the operation to proceed, there was insufficient strength for its success to be assured.

It was decided to use Major General John Lucas as the commander, and he turned over command of the US VI Corps on 31 December 1943 in order to devote himself to the planning for Shingle. Almost immediately, he encountered difficulties in lack of shipping and lack of time to prepare for the operation. He was also informed that, along with the US 3rd Infantry Division, his force would consist of the 1st British Infantry Division. Both Lucas and Truscott, the commander of the 3rd Infantry, recommended that the assault should be mounted by two American divisions. This would simplify the supply and administrative arrangements, which were complicated and strained as it was. Of course, from Churchill's perspective it was essential that a British division be included in the assault to drive home the fact that this was an Allied undertaking. He wrote to Roosevelt that 'it is fitting that we should share equally in suffering, risk and honour'.[42]

The multinational nature of the force may have suited Churchill's political purposes, but it complicated an already difficult military problem. In some respects, it simply revived many of the awkward features of the Tunisian campaign without any compensating benefits. When, on 8 January 1944, Lucas visited the British 1st Division, he was greatly impressed, and declared it 'the British Army at its best'.[43] However, the truth was that Lucas neither understood nor had real confidence in British formations. He shared Clark's view that the 'British never went all out to take an objective'.[44] He certainly expressed a sceptical, not to say suspicious, view of the British when he later wrote:

> The officer of the British Army is only secondarily a military man. He is primarily 'Empire Conscious' and, with the sea and its lanes kept open by a justly famed and powerful Navy, the British Army has built the Empire. This has required force at times and diplomacy always. These men are, from their extreme youth, trained to think in terms of Empire safety and advancement and every action they take is coloured by a long-term policy which is, in many cases, only dimly understood by their Allies.[45]

There is little doubt that these views would have shocked his British counterparts, who would not have recognised themselves in such a description. If there was a long-term policy held by the British government concerning the Empire, it was only dimly understood by most British officers, who believed that they approached the military problems of the Italian campaign with pragmatic military professionalism.

To complicate matters, Lucas did not hit it off with Ronald Penney, the new commander of the British 1st Division. Penney had so impressed Alexander as his Chief Signals Officer that Alexander had recommended him for field command. It was rare for a signals officer to be given command of a division in the British Army of the Second World War, and virtually unheard of in the American. Clark unfairly quipped that Penney was 'not too formidable a general but a good telephone operator', which said as much about the prejudice amongst American officers towards signals as it did about Penney's competence.*[46] Penney, in his turn, quickly labelled the white-haired Lucas 'Buffalo Bill', and although he considered him 'a nice man' did not rate him as a corps commander.[47]

From the outset, Lucas was concerned by the small size of his

---

* In the American Army of the Second World War, infantry and cavalry officers were far more likely to rise to field command than an officer from one of the specialist branches. It should also be pointed out that Heinz Guderian, the German 'father' of the Panzerwaffe, began his career as a signals officer.

forces and the distance between his beachhead and the main lines
of the Fifth Army. Two days into his new command, he was
informed that, due to the lack of landing craft, his force would be
put ashore with seven days' supplies and then 'abandoned to its
fate'.[48] The plan was that the rest of the Fifth Army would have
reached the beachhead before the supplies ran out, which he considered an 'example of blind optimism that showed such a lack of
appreciation of the fighting qualities of the German soldier that I
could not believe it to have been seriously considered'.[49] He later
reflected that the 'whole affair had a strong odor of Gallipoli' about
it, an impression that can only have been heightened by Churchill's
enthusiastic sponsorship of the operation.[50]

After one of the last high-level conferences regarding the Anzio
landings, Alexander mentioned that Churchill had said that the
operation '"will astonish the world" and added, "It will certainly
frighten Kesselring"'.[51] However, Lucas did not share such unguarded
optimism:

> [I] felt like a lamb being led to the slaughter but thought I was
> entitled to one bleat, so I registered a protest against the target date
> as it gave me too little time for rehearsal . . . I have the bare
> minimum of ships and craft. The ones that are sunk cannot be
> replaced. The force that can be gotten ashore in a hurry is weak
> and I haven't sufficient artillery to hold me over but on the other
> hand I will have more air support than any similar operation ever
> had before.[52]

These were hardly the words of a confident corps commander who
expected his assault landings to 'astonish the world'. Churchill was,
as usual, quite innocent of the military realities surrounding the
rather desperate gamble of landing two divisions at Anzio, and
Alexander seems to have been guilty of ignoring inconvenient facts
in the blind hope that all would go well. That left Lucas as the sole
bearer of responsibility for making sure that the operation actually
worked, and that was clearly a burden that was already too much
for him.

After two rushed and almost farcical amphibious rehearsals for the men of the 3rd US and 1st British Infantry divisions, the final preparations for Operation Shingle went ahead at breakneck speed. Alexander said farewell to Lucas with the heartening endorsement, 'We have every confidence in you. That is why you were picked', but Clark's last words contained a warning: 'Don't stick your neck out, Johnny. I did at Salerno and got into trouble.'[53] The stage was set for one of the most awkward episodes in Anglo-American relations amidst one of the most desperate battles of the war.

10

Hauling on the Rope

As the troop convoys set off for Anzio, the Fifth Army's main offensive against the German defences at Monte Cassino began.[1] These defences, known as the Gustav line, were some of the most elaborate and formidable of the entire war. Clark's intention was to divert attention away from the Anzio landings taking place 60 miles to the north. However, he seemed to expect that his troops could take the Gustav line at a run, pushing the Germans back as they had had to do since landing at Salerno. No one in the Fifth Army appeared to realise just how formidable an obstacle the combination of terrain and prepared positions around Monte Cassino would prove to be. Equally importantly, there were no real reserves available to exploit any success: the same tired troops of the British X Corps and the US II Corps were expected to advance on a broad front and penetrate the German line at the same time.

Unfortunately, this situation was complicated by the fact that Clark had developed a real dislike for Lieutenant General Richard McCreery and the British troops under his command. He had even called McCreery a 'feather duster' to his face.[2] Clark had little trust in British capabilities and so planned to use McCreery's X Corps in a diversionary assault on the southern sector of the Garigliano river. The main assault would be made by the US 36th Division, which was chosen to mount the critical crossing of the Rapido river. Once across, the American infantry was then to hold a firm bridgehead for the US 1st Armored Division, which could then drive up the Liri valley and reach the gates of Rome.*

---

* Confusingly, the Rapido river, so named while it flowed through Monte Cassino and the Liri valley, became known as the Garigliano when it joined the Liri river.

Quite contrary to Clark's expectations, when the British X Corps attacked under a heavy bombardment on 17 January 1944, they achieved complete surprise and managed to seize a secure bridgehead over a 10-mile front. Kesselring, duly alarmed by this development, sent two of his reserve divisions to help plug the gap. Clark, however, did not take advantage of this breakthrough by diverting American troops to support the British. Instead, his refusal to re-inforce the British success led him to commit a series of piecemeal attacks that were doomed to failure.

General Alphonse Juin's French Expeditionary Corps, which was composed mainly of tough French colonial troops and Moroccan soldiers well used to the demands of mountain warfare, attacked towards Monte Cairo at the same time as the US attack across the Rapido, but it was at too great a distance to offer any real mutual support. The Rapido river, as it flows within sight of the ominous massif of Monte Cassino, seems a relatively minor obstacle, but, swollen by winter rains, it lived up to its name: its waters were fast-flowing and dangerous to cross. With the Germans in complete possession of the heights that dominated the valley, the US 36th Division was committed to the appalling prospect of an assault river crossing with no subsidiary attacks to draw the attention and fire of the defenders. In an 'alarming scene', Dick McCreery, having learned of the plan, told Charles Richardson in a voice 'choked with emotion . . . "It's not on! Tell your Army Commander he will have a disaster".'[3]

The results were only too predictable: the assault on 20 January, although pressed twice with a fatalistic courage by the Texan soldiers, became a terrible, bloody fiasco. The German defenders were not even aware that they had broken up what was considered to be the main attack of the offensive. The pressing of the attack by Clark and Fifth Army headquarters later led to a 1946 Congressional inquiry. Faced with a lack of manpower and no viable reserves, the Fifth Army had simply not had the strength to force the Gustav line. Clark's first attack at Monte Cassino had been a dismal failure. Far from opening the gates to the Liri valley, he had found the way resolutely shut. This was the worst possible outcome, as the main body of the Fifth Army was stalled at the very moment the assault landings were taking place at Anzio. General Lucas could not now expect any help to arrive swiftly from the south.

As it turned out, far from meeting heavy German resistance, as had been feared, the assault troops landed at Anzio and Nettuno on 22 January 1944 almost without incident. Kesselring had in fact withdrawn troops from the area only a few days before the landing to help shore up the weakened position on the main Gustav line. The road to the Alban hills, and indeed to Rome itself, seemed wide open. By the end of the day, the vast bulk of the Allied inva-sion force, over 36,000 men, had been landed. Lucas recognised that his landings had 'achieved what is certainly one of the most complete surprises in history', but the question remained whether he could exploit that fleeting advantage.[4] In the event, he held to his plan. He did not send a light force to race for the Alban hills or for Rome as Alexander and Churchill had expected, but instead consolidated his position on the flat featureless plain that stretched beyond Anzio. The Grenadier Guards and the Irish Guards, which landed as reserve battalions for the British 1st Division, had pleaded with their brigade commander to be landed as mobile striking columns, which could then drive up the road to Albano to form roadblocks on the main highway to Rome. Permission for this bold move was refused, even though this was precisely the kind of manoeuvre Alexander had expected.[5] When the Irish Guards landed safely, there was 'an atmosphere of jubilation, mixed with a sense of "this is too good to be true"'. By the end of the day, however, 'there was a sickening feeling of anti-climax' as the precious time when the Germans were clearly unprepared and in some disarray was frittered away in inactivity.[6]

The troops themselves were thus only too conscious that an opportunity had been missed, but there were reasons for this. On 12 January, just days before the invasion force sailed, Lucas had been issued with a new Fifth Army order. This included the signif-icant alteration that the VI Corps was now to advance towards the Alban hills rather than the previously more categorical instruction to reach them. Phase one of the operation was now to establish a beachhead, while phase two was for VI Corps to attack in the direction of Colli Laziali, at Lucas's discretion. In giving Lucas the new set of orders, General Donald Brann, Clark's head of operations, had made it clear that his 'primary mission was to seize and secure a beachhead. He stated that much thought had been put on the wording of this order so as not to force me to push on at the risk of sacrificing my Corps.'[7] These fresh orders not only revealed that Clark had misgivings about the operation but placed the decision for moving out of any bridgehead firmly in Lucas's hands. There were reasons for such caution. As Marshall later observed, every further mile of advance meant that there would be another seven miles of front for the men of VI Corps to defend as the lines stretched further back towards Anzio.[8] With only two assault divisions, Lucas was well aware that his corps simply did not have the forces to gain a solid beachhead and drive for Rome. He later confided to his diary that:

more has been accomplished than anyone had a right to expect. This venture was always a desperate one and I could never see much chance for it to succeed, if success means driving the German north of Rome . . . Had I been able to rush to the high ground . . . immediately upon landing, nothing would have been accomplished except to weaken my force by that amount because the troops sent, being completely beyond supporting distance, would have been immediately destroyed. The only thing to do was what I did. Get a proper beachhead and prepare to hold it.[9]

There is little doubt that Lucas had become tired and depressed by the grinding attritional advance through Italy. While Lucas knew the paucity of his strength, the Germans did not initially have that advantage. It is just possible that a rapid advance by forward elements of VI Corps on to the lines of communication of the German 10th Army might – just might – have shocked the German High Command into a precipitate retreat from the Cassino position. Such bold and risky strokes in military history have sometimes succeeded, but Lucas, cautious and only too well aware of the German army's ability to recover from reverses, decided to wait until he was strong enough to advance from his limited, shallow beachhead. Unfortunately, his caution meant that he surrendered the initiative, and his fears of an overwhelming German response became a self-fulfilling prophecy.

Once he realised the danger, Kesselring grabbed reserves from wherever he could find them, including France, northern Italy and the Balkans, to seal off the Anzio beachhead. Lucas's methodical approach had denied his men the opportunity to seize key pieces of terrain when the Germans were weak. As German reserves flowed into the area, the men of VI Corps soon found themselves outnumbered and forced to fight a desperate defensive battle on some very unpromising terrain. The Allied defensive positions in the beachhead had to be dug on a flat plain with no obvious features to anchor them. Meanwhile, the Germans occupied all the high ground around the plain, which gave them perfect observation to direct artillery fire and coordinate their attacks. It was later said that the 'German observers in the Alban Hills . . . could sit in comfort . . . and direct their guns as if they were playing on a sand-model'.[10]

Clark and Alexander had initially expressed satisfaction with the landings at Anzio, which had been accomplished with such little loss. When Alexander visited Lucas on 25 January, he commented that the landings had been 'a splendid piece of work', but Lucas, rather gloomily, reminded him that 'it wasn't over yet'.[11] By this time, the Allied troops had pressed forward and the beachhead was now 10 miles deep, yet Alexander concealed his disappointment that Lucas had not even attempted to send light forces forward to the Alban hills.[12] However, on the same day, Ronald Penney, the commander of the British 1st Division, was becoming increasingly anxious at the lack of any forward planning by the corps headquarters. He was worried that instead of close coordination between the two divisions, there was only 'a lot of waffle', and that separate plans were made by the two divisions for everything.[13] Penney communicated his fears to Alexander. Clark, too, began to be dismayed by the fact that the Anzio landings had not caused any redeployment from the Gustav line around Monte Cassino. The grand gesture of the Allied landing appeared to have become a damp squib. Churchill fumed in a memo to the British Chiefs of

Staff on 29 January at the lack of progress in what he saw as his project: 'We hoped to land a wild cat that would tear the bowels out of the Boche. Instead we have stranded a vast whale with its tail flopping about in the water.'[14]

Churchill, with incredible unfairness, placed the blame squarely on his allies: he stated that Anzio had become 'an American operation, with no punch in it'.[15] Yet it was his insistence that VI Corps should include both British and American troops that had complicated the command, supply and coordination difficulties without providing any extra forces. At the same time, the forces in the beachhead found that communication between the British and American divisions was awkward, and that VI Corps headquarters was entirely unable to cope with the additional demands placed upon it. Lucas and his staff had experience of operating an undivided American corps but were unequal to the challenge of coordinating an Allied force. One regimental historian emphasised that:

> Most British and American soldiers admired each other and were anxious to help each other, but they rarely knew what the other was doing. Time and again the British units made attacks with the assurance of Corps HQ that American troops would support and conform, only to find that the Americans concerned had heard nothing, and so did nothing, about it. The same must have happened equally frequently the other way round. When the British and American battalion commanders could talk to each other personally there were no difficulties, administrative or tactical. That amorphous body, Corps HQ, on the other hand, always put a complete block in the normal channels of communication.[16]

Thus, the same kind of administrative friction that had bedevilled Allied operations in Tunisia soon came to afflict the troops at Anzio. But such problems were to assume greater importance at Anzio given the constrained nature of the beachhead and the desperate nature of the fighting.

By the end of January, Lucas, perhaps needled by a growing sense of disappointment from Alexander and Clark, and with further transfusions of strength in the form of the US 1st Armored

Division and 45th Infantry Division, felt able to move on to the offensive. Unfortunately, Kesselring had by now found enough troops to block all approaches off the Anzio plain, and the Allied forces ran into a solid German defence. The outcome was predictable. In the northern sector, the British 1st Division pushed towards Campoleone but failed to take the town. Unfortunately, these attacks simply pressed the division forward into a dangerous salient that made it highly vulnerable to German counter-attacks. The US 3rd Division pushed forward on a broader front towards Cisterna. In the initial attack, two Ranger battalions that had slipped behind German lines were cut off and forced to surrender. Although the American infantry fought hard and did gain some ground, they too were unable to reach their objective. Both towns might have fallen almost without effort on the first day after the landings, but now the Germans were ready to begin a series of powerful counter-attacks with the much more ambitious objective of wiping out the Allied beachhead altogether. The German attacks, which were mounted with growing intensity, placed the British 1st Division in real peril.

While Penney was struggling with an increasingly difficult situation, Lucas admitted to himself that he had lost confidence 'in the British Division and its commander'. Lucas understood the American Army, its strengths, weaknesses and limits of endurance, but he frankly admitted that he didn't 'understand the British very well':

> They seemed unable to make even a simple reconnaissance without getting into trouble. They would advance with the greatest possible bravery but always with heavy losses, which could not be replaced, and always on a narrow front which gave the enemy an opportunity for his favourite 'pinching off' tactics.[17]

The breakdown in trust and confidence was mutual. With his division under heavy attack, Penney felt isolated and devoid of support from a corps commander who did not seem in touch with his difficulties.

By the time Alexander visited the VI Corps again, on

1 February 1944, it was clear that German pressure on the beach-head was increasing. Far from it being a question now of when the Allies would break out towards Rome, the question seemed to be whether the beachhead could survive. Lucas found Alexander difficult to talk to, 'as he really knows very little of tactics as Americans understand it'.[18] Given Alexander's considerable experi-ence of infantry tactics, this seemed a strange comment. It certainly showed that there was no meeting of minds between the two men. Lucas could only comment that Alexander 'was kind enough but I am afraid he is not pleased. My head will probably fall in the basket but I have done my best.'[19] When Lucas suggested that VI Corps should be heavily reinforced, 'Alexander just smiled'.[20] Alexander's polite silence concealed the fact that he was now disappointed in the VI Corps commander.

As the German attacks increased in intensity, Penney found himself under enormous pressure. By 4 February, Lucas considered the 'news very bad. The British are in serious trouble and I am greatly disturbed about them. They have occupied an advanced position for days and are now in danger. I ordered General Penney this morning to withdraw . . . General Penney objected strenuously to any retrograde movement and I had the greatest sympathy for his point of view. I could, however, see no alternative and, therefore, gave him a direct order to pull out.'[21] Yet even once the 1st Division had pulled back – with great difficulty – from its exposed positions, it still found it hard to hold its more entrenched positions against the increasingly determined German counter-attacks. Penney repeatedly asked Lucas for more support, but although Lucas real-ised that the British division was 'badly disorganized and knocked to pieces', he had little to offer.[22] The dangerous position of the entire VI Corps, combined with the frustrations of an intense defensive battle, brought the relations between the two men to breaking point.

Alexander was by this time deeply concerned by the events in the Anzio beachhead and well aware of the breakdown between Penney and Lucas. Lucas expressed his concerns about Penney to Clark, who passed them on to Alexander. Yet when Clark mentioned that Lucas 'did not think much of Penney's ability', Alexander simply replied, 'Well, I do.'[23] Meanwhile, Penney made sure that his old chief knew of his concerns about his corps commander, pointing out that Lucas never visited the front and also informing Alexander of the move of the corps headquarters into wine cellars under the town of Nettuno. This certainly protected the staff from the heavy German bombardment, but it also isolated the head-quarters from the fighting troops while creating an unhelpful bunker mentality. Relations between Alexander and Lucas cannot have been helped by the fact that the Irish Guards had suffered severely in the heavy fighting, and Alexander was bound to feel a sense of proprietorial interest in the battalion he had commanded during the Great War.

The fighting had become increasingly desperate. The commanding officer of the Irish Guards, Colonel Scott, wrote to the War Office informing them of the scale of losses: 'There came with me into this place 794 men, and 286 followed from the infantry reinforce-ment training depot and the central reinforcement unit, making a total of 1,080. Against this we have had 560 casualties, which leaves the battalion at a nominal strength of 520. There are no more replacements available.'[24] Heavy losses like these had been experi-enced throughout the British 1st Division, which was now so weak-ened from continuous battle that it was incapable of offensive action, and there were virtually no replacements available in the Mediterranean theatre to make up the losses. When Alexander visited Anzio on 14 February, his first port of call was to the Irish Guards, and although there were 'no heroic speeches . . . you could almost feel the confidence and pride radiating from the Battalion as the General walked briskly round the area . . . He congratulated the Battalion on "a fine performance in a very tough slogging match", and that was enough.'[25] It could be said that Alexander was at his best when, through his visits to the front, he slipped back into the role of battalion commander. For all his faults as an army group commander, he never lost his touch for inspiring confidence in ordinary soldiers.

Yet although Alexander made the Irish Guards his first stop when visiting Anzio, his most important appointment was with Lucas. Alexander understood the requirements of battlefield command,

and as far as he was concerned, sitting in a wine cellar was simply not good enough. After this visit, he decided that Lucas needed to be replaced. However, when he broached the subject with Clark, the American commander simply told him that he was wrong and that 'Lucas was a good man'. Alexander had to raise the issue three times before Clark relented. Alexander understood that 'ambition was a key' to Clark's actions and, on the third occasion, pointedly implied that if a disaster occurred at Anzio, both Lucas and Clark would be sacked. It was only then that Clark agreed to relieve Lucas.[26]

The next day, Alexander informed Brooke in a personal telegram that he was disappointed in Lucas and his headquarters: 'They are negative and lack the necessary drive and enthusiasm to get things done. They appear to have become depressed by events.'[27] He explained that he needed 'a thruster like George Patton' in command and even suggested that VI Corps headquarters might be replaced by a British commander and staff. He did, however, realise that this would be a rather too drastic move, and that instead he would seek Eisenhower's advice on the best available American commander. He also repeated his belief that the 'trouble is the lack of battle experience', which seems hardly fair considering Lucas had been in continuous action since October 1943, and reveals that Alexander's prejudice concerning American commanders and their lack of experience was still alive and well.[28]

Alexander's telegram was designed to keep the CIGS informed of events, but it very nearly caused a full-scale rift in Anglo-American relations when Eisenhower received a copy. It was of course part of a commanding general's role to ensure that his subordinates were capable and to replace them if they were found wanting. Throughout the war, British commanders at every level seldom hesitated to sack or transfer officers who were believed to be unequal to the task, and American commanders were, if anything, even more ruthless in returning subordinates stateside if they were found wanting. However, it was a very different matter if a British commander suggested that an American officer should be removed – or vice versa. Not only had Alexander declared that an American general was inadequate and needed to be replaced, but by stating that he did not know of any American commander in Italy who was up to the job of commanding a corps, it appeared that he was casting doubt on the professionalism and quality of the entire US Army officer corps. An individual issue thus quickly became an alliance problem.

In the event, President Roosevelt and General Marshall were the final arbiters of who should, and should not, command a US corps in battle. The politically astute Eisenhower worked quickly to minimise the damage. He replied to Alexander that any decisions on American officers lay with Generals Devers and Clark, and that it was simply impossible to shift the command of a unit between nationalities during 'a period of crisis', since this would be interpreted 'as an attempt to "pass the buck" and would create repercussions that would be felt throughout the allied forces everywhere'.[29] He even went so far as to agree to send George Patton to Italy, but warned that he could only spare him for one month. In addition, he named Truscott as his top choice of American divisional commanders already in Italy and suitable for corps command. Eisenhower also immediately informed Marshall of the exchange of telegrams, explaining to him that he had kept the matter strictly secret and advising him to do the same, as he believed that, although he was convinced that Alexander was 'acting according to his honest convictions . . . many people would misinterpret and misconstrue the purposes of General Alexander'.[30]

When Alexander met with Generals Wilson, Devers and Clark, the issue was rapidly resolved, and the very next day Eisenhower was able to signal Marshall with the news that Clark and Devers agreed that Truscott, currently the commander of the 3rd US Division, should take over command of VI Corps. The takeover was not immediate, as it was an inopportune time to change commanders, and it was decided to appoint Truscott as Lucas's deputy, while General Eveleigh was sent to act as a British deputy. Lucas was not deceived. He realised that these changes almost certainly presaged his relief, but he was pleased with the presence of Eveleigh, whom he described as a 'fine fellow' who could help him with the British troops. Penney also felt reassured by the presence of Eveleigh, who put 'great heart and experience' into the corps headquarters.[31] These initial changes were a belated recognition that an Allied corps required a greater degree of coordination and liaison than any other; the presence of a British deputy from the start of the operation might well have smoothed over many of the problems that had developed between Lucas and Penney.

The Germans had mounted an all-out attempt to destroy the beachhead, but the Allies held firm and inflicted enormous casualties on the German troops with concentrated artillery fire and intense air support. Yet although VI Corps had fought and won a desperate defensive battle, it was at this point that Lucas was relieved. Clark returned to the beachhead on 22 February, and that evening, at his command post in the Villa Borghese, he broke the news, telling Lucas that:

> he could no longer resist the pressure which came from both Alexander and Devers. That Alexander said I was defeated and Devers said I was tired. I was not surprised at General Alexander's attitude. He had been badly frightened, but what I heard about Devers was a great shock. All of us were tired. And I thought I was winning something of a victory.[32]

Even when Operation Shingle was in its planning stages, Lucas had been placed between the Scylla of unrealistically optimistic objectives and the Charybdis of severely limited means. At no point did Churchill, Alexander or Clark ever admit their responsibility in placing VI Corps in an almost impossible situation. At the same time, although Lucas was a professional and experienced soldier, he was simply not up to the task of commanding a multinational corps in battle. Yet in an ironic echo of Dawley's experience at Salerno, Lucas and VI Corps had weathered the German storm before he was replaced. Given the way in which Alexander had levered Lucas out of command, Clark's suspicion and distrust of British motives in general and Alexander in particular only increased. He had just witnessed the demise of an old friend through Penney's whispering campaign and the approval of both Alexander and Alan Brooke, the CIGS. Alexander had even used the threat of Clark's relief in order to gain his assent. Given this situation, it is not surprising that Clark became increasingly paranoid about his British 'allies'.

After Lucas's unhappy experience, it has to be said that Lucian Truscott was the right man to command the beleaguered VI Corps. Alexander had initially asked for Patton, but Truscott, with his low husky voice and his insistence on strict discipline, had also already proved himself a very capable battlefield commander. When he took command, he soon inspired both British and American soldiers with a belief in victory. Penney remarked that 'a new spirit came with the new Corps Commander and a new atmosphere of confidence and improved staff work'.[33] Even though the doctrine, tactics and techniques of the British and Americans remained different, these issues became of lesser importance when the force was commanded by Truscott, who had, by now, considerable experience and understanding of both British and American methods. While Lucas had become increasingly isolated from the troops under his command, Truscott made sure that he visited those in the front line regularly, and his presence became 'an inspiration to all'.[34]

Yet if relations between the commanders and staff of the British and American forces in the Anzio beachhead had been strained beyond breaking point, the same was not true of the soldiers. Anzio was one of the few places where British and American troops literally fought shoulder to shoulder in some of the most intense defensive battles of the war. While significant differences in tactics and outlook remained, a shared sense of hardship led to a cementing of respect and understanding between the fighting soldiers. British morale reports stressed the fact that relations between US and British troops were 'nowhere better than at Anzio, where they had fought side by side'.[35]

While the crisis at Anzio had passed by the end of February 1944, the main front of the Fifth Army remained fixed at Cassino. Instead of the amphibious assault unlocking the advance, Clark now had to order attacks at Cassino in an attempt to take pressure off the troops at Anzio. Most of these were conceived and launched hurriedly without sufficient time to properly prepare them. In early

February, Clark sent what was left of the US II Corps into an attack across the flooded Rapido north of Cassino. The aim was to penetrate the German defences and then turn south, moving across the massif towards the abbey, which was increasingly seen as the key to the whole German position. Struggling against seas of mud and a determined defence, it took eight days of heavy fighting for the soldiers of the 34th Division to claw out a bridgehead and push forward into the belt of mountains north of Monte Cassino. They then attacked south across a jumble of rocky broken ridges towards the monastery. By 7 February, the leading troops were within 400 yards of its walls, but they were also exhausted. Worn out and suffering from exposure, the American infantry could go no further, and, as was so often the case in Italy, there were no fresh troops available to exploit the hard-won gains.[36] Clark later maintained that 'if he had had one extra combat team he could have taken the Monastery. But he did not have it.'[37] It is certainly true that the American soldiers came within just a few hundred yards of severing the German supply route to the monastery, which might have unlocked the defence. Yet a final effort to seize the position was simply impossible: the Americans had been pushed beyond their limits by exposure, exhaustion and casualties. Indeed, Alexander became so concerned about morale that he sent Lemnitzer to inspect the condition of the troops. Lemnitzer reported back that they had become so disheartened by the nature of the fighting that they were 'almost mutinous'.[38] Alexander then insisted that if Monte Cassino had not been taken by 12 February, the Americans would be relieved by the troops of the newly formed New Zealand Corps, commanded by General Bernard Freyberg.

Major General Howard Kippenberger, a highly experienced officer of the 2nd New Zealand Division, who had fought on the Somme in the Great War and throughout the desert war, personally went up to the American positions on the bare slopes of Snakeshead Ridge to make a reconnaissance of the situation. On his return he informed General Freyberg that he had found the American soldiers in 'bad condition' and he believed that the division was now 'simply not capable of making a new attack'.[39] Kippenberger was also shocked to learn that neither the American divisional commander nor his deputy had gone up to the front lines, and thus 'had no first hand knowledge of their ability to continue the attack'.[40] Clark was forced to accept Freyberg's judgement that the 34th Division needed immediate relief.

Kippenberger watched the troops as they trudged off the mountainside at Cassino, where they were served hot food from New Zealand field kitchens. He later stated that he would 'never forget the condition of the 34th Div men as they came out of the line. Many of the men had frozen feet, they were weather beaten – many were hungry.'[41] Fifty of the American soldiers were so exhausted that they had to be carried off the mountain on stretchers.

This episode placed in stark relief the contrast between British and American officers in their attitudes to the men under their command. Clark and Major General Geoffrey Keyes, commander of the US II Corps, had been willing to push their troops to the very last extremity in order to take the monastery, but British and Commonwealth officers like Kippenberger had been schooled through their service in the Great War that their first duty lay with their men's welfare. British officers of the Second World War were only too conscious of the criticisms levelled at the Great War generals and their staff officers – the 'bloody red tabs'. The received memory was that they had led a privileged existence, utterly ignorant of and remote from the conditions experienced by the troops at the front. Whether apocryphal or not, the story of Lieutenant General Sir Lancelot Kiggell, Haig's Chief of Staff, breaking down in tears *before* he reached the front line at Passchendaele in 1917 and exclaiming, 'Good God, did we really send men to fight in this?' had entered the collective consciousness of British officers of the Second World War. Men as disparate as Brooke, Montgomery, Alexander, Freyberg and Auchinleck shared a common generational reflex: that they would not make those mistakes while in command. This was at least one of the reasons why Kippenberger had gone to see the positions of the 34th Division for himself.

British generals in Italy were also only too conscious of the fact that if their units sustained heavy losses, these simply could not be replaced. The British attitude towards casualties thus emphasised the need to conserve strength and made commanders 'careful about making hard, slogging attacks that would be costly unless such operations were really necessary'.[42] American commanders, on the other hand, had a seemingly inexhaustible supply of manpower and were more willing to suffer losses to achieve their objectives; Oliver Leese, the commander of the Eighth Army, described how 'they treat their man-power as a mass production commodity in the same way as they do their vehicles and guns'.[43] These differences in tactical approach can be seen as the genesis of the broad front/narrow front controversy that would come to dominate the north-west Europe campaign. The British emphasis on concentration of force along narrow axes of advance was simply incompatible with the American espousal of constant pressure all along a front in a search for weak spots. Clark believed that throughout the Italian campaign, the American troops in the Fifth Army 'carried the ball', having to push forward while the British, overly concerned about casualties, hung back. Worst of all, he believed that the British then tried 'to steal the credit for the hard fighting the Americans had done during the war in Italy'.[44] In his turn, Richard McCreery had terrific arguments with Clark because he believed Clark's methods would cause unnecessary loss of life.[45]

This gulf of understanding was doubly unfortunate: very few British or American commanders fully recognised the merits of the other's approach. The respective attitudes and methods reflected different national approaches to battle and, in its widest sense, a contrasting political, economic and demographic context to operations. Unfortunately, it often seemed beyond the Allied commanders to play to the strengths of these different approaches, and instead the unequally yoked armies more often pulled against each other.

The terrible irony was that the fighting around Monte Cassino from January to May 1944 most closely resembled the nightmarish attritional battles of the Great War in its ferocity and seeming futility. With the US II Corps driven beyond the point of exhaustion, Clark and Keyes were finally forced to acknowledge that they simply did not have the remaining strength to take the abbey and unlock the Gustav line. The New Zealand corps of the 4th Indian

Division and 2nd New Zealand Division were taken from the Eighth Army and brought from the Adriatic front to reinforce the Fifth Army for another attempt to break the deadlock.

With the front at Anzio under increasingly heavy German counter-attacks, and the entire Fifth Army pinned under the seemingly malevolent gaze of the abbey of Monte Cassino, General Freyberg requested that the abbey be bombed before his troops made their attack. This request was highly controversial, since the Germans had declared that they would not use the abbey for defence, and Clark refused to sanction the bombing. Ultimately, it was Alexander who had to order the attack. On 15 February, the Allies used heavy and medium bombers to target the ancient building, turning it into an eminently defensible wreck of rubble and debris. Whatever military advantage might have been gained from the bombing was thrown away, however, since the 4th Indian Division was not ready to launch its main attack from Snakeshead Ridge until two days later. The outcome was predictable. The three leading battalions advanced into a storm of fire from the German defenders, whose virtually invisible dugouts within the ruins had been prepared long before the Allies reached Cassino. After enormous exertion, the attack petered out with heavy losses.

It is fair to say that the Allied commanders became fixated upon the capture of the abbey, believing that it would unlock the German defences and enable the drive on Rome to continue. Yet this fixation and the frustration it generated simply played into the hands of the tenacious German defenders. By bombing the abbey, the Allies were using high explosive as a substitute for clear military thinking, which might have told them that the keys to Rome actually lay in outflanking the Germans in the surrounding mountains. Freyberg made another attempt to break through on 15 March, this time by assaulting the town of Cassino, below the ruins of the monastery. In another demonstration of Allied firepower, a massive bombing raid, which dropped 1,000 tons of bombs, was followed by a concentrated artillery bombardment by the 'best part of 800 guns', completely destroying the town. This battering shook but did not break the German defence, and the chaos of rubble, mud and craters created by the bombardment proved an impossible barrier for the advancing New Zealand and Indian troops.[46] Nonetheless, with almost incredible exertion, men of the 1/9th Gurkhas managed to reach Hangman's Hill, halfway up Monastery Hill, and the 1/4th Essex took Castle Hill, while the New Zealanders fought room by room in the ruins.[47] The Welsh Guards arrived in Cassino after this attack, which had 'captured about half the town, only after tons of bombs and uncountable shells had shattered every building, obliterated every road, let loose the waters of the Rapido and sown the ruins with undiscovered death'.[48] Alexander later admitted to Brooke that 'towns can be completely obliterated by the air, but it doesn't necessarily follow that the garrison won't hold out – and it's a certainty that the roads will be so blocked that tanks or other vehicles will not be able to pass through'.[49]

When General Wilson suggested continuing the battle, Freyberg just said one word: 'Passchendaele': there could be no other response to this than closing down the attack.[50] These awesome displays of firepower simply revealed the frustration of commanders who seemingly had no answer to the tenacious German defence. The vision and concentration of the Allied leaders was inexorably sucked into a narrow-minded obsession with taking the abbey, or what was left of it. The deadlock Alexander had feared as early as October 1943 had become an all too concrete reality. The amphibious landing that he and Clark had hoped would unlock the front had bogged down at Anzio, and the German main line of defence, anchored on Monte Cassino, remained stubbornly firm. This was the antithesis of the imagined war of movement the Allied strategists and planners had hoped for once they reached Europe. It also marked a failure of imagination amongst Allied commanders, and a low point in Allied relations. Alexander's 15th Army Group did not appear to be a cohesive unit but rather an awkward assembly of national forces whose whole seemed worth less than the sum of the individual parts.

Much of the problem seemed to lie with Alexander and his group headquarters. There was no question that he was a talented soldier with a real feel for the battlefield, but he seemed unable to provide a vision or plan to energise his subordinates. Instead he relied upon discussion with his army commanders for ideas that might be developed into a plan. This approach was unequal to the challenge posed by the grim deadlock at Monte Cassino. Yet while Alexander seemed unable to extricate the Allies from this trap, John Harding, his new Chief of Staff, would prove more successful. Harding had served in the desert from its early days as a theatre of war, and had gained a reputation as a soldier with the rare ability to handle both staff and command appointments with equal success. This had culminated in his command of 7th Armoured Division during the Battle of Alamein, where he had been badly wounded in the drive towards Tripoli. Sent home to recover, he had just taken over command of VIII Corps when, much to his chagrin, he was summoned to Italy to act as Chief of Staff to Alexander.[51]

Harding had arrived in Italy in January 1944, but it was only after the second Battle of Cassino in February that he was able to fully assess the situation. While the fighting at Cassino continued, he developed his ideas in a staff appreciation that became the basis for the renewed attack on the Gustav line. This new approach formed the basis for Operation Diadem, the Allies' final attempt to break through to Rome. As his biographer noted: 'All of Harding's clarity of mind, downright, straightforward, realistic commonsense, practical military experience, determination and courage . . . shone through this example of what a military appreciation . . . was designed to achieve.'[52] Like most successful military plans, Harding's vision was clear and simple. Italy might be a secondary front, but it was necessary to force the Germans to commit the maximum number of forces against Alexander's armies in order to support Overlord. Harding realised that the only means of achieving this was to break through the Gustav line and destroy as many enemy divisions as possible so that German forces would be drawn from other fronts to repair the damage. He argued that the Allies needed a much greater concentration of forces, good weather, and time to repair and refit their armies before making the attempt.[53] He understood that the root cause of the Allies' travails at Cassino lay in a basic military problem: it was an accepted fact in both the American and British armies that for an attack to succeed, the attacker should outnumber the defender by three to one, but given the formidable nature of the terrain at Cassino, Harding realised that this ratio might need to be even higher, and although lavish weight of firepower might assist an attack, it could not entirely replace the required number of troops. By this point in the war, planners in the Red Army had learned through hard experience that for an attack to succeed and achieve a rapid breakthrough, force ratios of up to ten to one, and even forty to one, were necessary.[54] Such figures were never achieved by the Western Allies. Given the paucity of troops in Italy, the Allied commanders had become accustomed to attacking – and often succeeding – with far less than this accepted ratio, but the policy had met with disaster at Cassino.

For Harding's plan to work, additional divisions would need to be found, and the armies in Italy reorganised. Clark's Fifth Army would concentrate along the lower Garigliano, and he would also command the reinforced VI Corps at Anzio. Meanwhile, the Eighth Army would cross Italy to join the Fifth Army on the Cassino front, taking over responsibility for the main sector in the Liri valley. This would enable the Allied armies to regroup. British-equipped divisions would come under the Eighth Army on the right flank, and American-equipped divisions, including the French Expeditionary Corps, would be placed under the Fifth Army on the left.[55] All these changes and preparations would take time, and the armies would not be ready to launch the attack until May.

Having amassed much greater forces on the Cassino front, the Eighth and Fifth Armies would launch a simultaneous assault on the Gustav line. The Eighth Army, now on the main axis, was to 'lay on, stage, mount and run the break into . . . the Liri Valley'.[56] The British XIII Corps would initially capture a bridgehead over the Rapido. Even greater concentrations of fire were planned for this assault, but this time, there would be sufficient troops available to exploit the bombardment. Alexander placed his trust in Leese and his Eighth Army, commenting to Alan Brooke that 'between ourselves, Clark and his Army HQ are not up to it, it's too big for them'.[57] Meanwhile, Clark was to command the Fifth Army from the Anzio beachhead. These forces were to prepare to launch 'the main offensive aimed at getting astride the German L of C [line of communication] by a breakout'.[58] Significantly, the timing of the breakout from Anzio would be determined by Alexander. The advance from Anzio was designed to cut off the retreat of the German Tenth Army. Diadem was to be an encirclement battle in which the forces from the Anzio bridgehead would trap the retreating German forces from the Cassino front. Harding's plan, enthusiastically endorsed by Alexander, was a real attempt to end the tug of war and bend the formidable strength of the two Allied armies towards a single goal. The defeat and destruction of the German Tenth Army was the main objective: Rome would merely fall to the Allies as a result of the battle. Yet Alexander's lack of faith and trust in Clark was certainly reciprocated, and would eventually hamstring Diadem.

The vast movement of the Eighth Army and the reshuffling of the Allied line all took place under the strictest secrecy, and utilised careful deception measures to ensure that the Germans gained no inkling of the massing Allied forces. It was not until 11 May that Alexander finally put his armies into the attack. Even with a clear advantage in numbers, the Eighth Army still struggled to achieve its objectives. The Polish Corps were given the dubious honour of attacking Monastery Hill, as Leese was convinced that there were no viable alternatives to yet another frontal assault.[59] For the first three days, the pattern of failure at Cassino appeared to repeat itself as the Poles were beaten back to their start line with grievous casualties. Although 13 Corps did manage to cross the Rapido, its gains were limited in the face of determined resistance. However, the French Expeditionary Corps, operating in the trackless Aurunci mountains south of Cassino, managed to achieve unlooked-for success. Juin's Moroccan Goums were expert mountain fighters, and they managed to confuse and surprise the relatively sparse German defenders by searching for weak points and attacking enemy posts in the flank and rear. It was thus the French attack that unlocked the German defence, enabling the American troops near the coast to press forward. These outflanking attacks weakened the German resistance against the Eighth Army, which, by dint of heavy fighting, now managed to gain ground. Kesselring was forced to order a final withdrawal from the Gustav line, which had been held against so many Allied attacks, back to the Hitler line six miles further up the Liri valley. Finally, at 09.50 hours on 18 May, a Polish patrol entered the abbey, and raised a hurriedly made Polish flag above the devastated ruins of Monte Cassino.[60]

Although the Eighth Army's advance was soon stalled by German resistance further up the Liri valley, the moment was soon approaching for Alexander to unleash Truscott's VI Corps. Unfortunately, Mark Clark was by no means an enthusiastic supporter of Harding's plan. Clark knew that any attempt to block the German escape route would place VI Corps at the centre of the storm. He later maintained that VI Corps was not strong enough to take Highway Six and the numerous parallel roads, which would be necessary to cut off the Germans. It would also seem that he was concerned that not only might VI Corps be mauled by German forces desperate to escape, but that this might hand the British an 'easy victory' at his expense. Yet if Clark did harbour reservations about Diadem, he certainly did not raise them with Alexander. There seems little doubt, however, that Clark's real motivation was his heartfelt desire to reach Rome. Indeed, he explained his decision-making in these terms in his memoirs:

> My own feeling was that nothing was going to stop us on our push towards the Italian capital. Not only did we intend to become the first army in fifteen centuries to seize Rome from the south, but we intended to see that the people at home knew that it was the Fifth Army that did the job and knew the price that had been paid to do it.[61]

There is no question that Clark put a particular emphasis on favourable publicity: any journalist who filed a report had it returned unless it contained the phrase 'with General Mark Clark's Fifth Army in Italy'. His pursuit of publicity did not meet with Marshall's approval, but the US Chief of Staff was prepared to overlook this particular flaw in view of Clark's undoubted talents as a commander.[62] Clark was also aware that Patton had put himself and his Seventh Army on the map with his high-profile captures of Palermo and Messina; why should he not do the same with

Rome? Ensuring good publicity for his army would not only build Clark's personal profile but would also be one way of reminding the American people living thousands of miles from the battle fronts of the sacrifices made by American soldiers on their behalf. Clark's hunger for publicity was not simply an individual personality flaw, but an integral part of the Allied way of making war. The fact is that a certain degree of rivalry and competition is not only encouraged but inherent in military training. Soldiers have to believe that the unit they have joined is the best, and the bonds of comradeship, which can bind a fighting unit of men tightly together, can also create an atmosphere of 'them and us'. Thus there were deeper underlying reasons for Clark's desire to seize Rome, but they had particularly unappealing consequences during Operation Diadem.

While Alexander had made it clear through a series of staff conferences that VI Corps was to concentrate upon a rapid drive to Valmontone, Clark had ordered Truscott's staff to plan for three differing possibilities. The main prospect was Plan Buffalo – an attack towards the town of Artena, 'with the final objective of cutting Highway 6 near Valmontone'[63] – but Clark stressed the need for flexibility to respond to changing circumstances. The attacking forces were to be solely American, and the remaining, battered British divisions in the beachhead were assigned to a holding role only.[64] Here was an ironic reversal of Alexander's intended division of labour between the Allies on Sicily.

When the US VI Corps began its breakout from the Anzio beachhead, it achieved rapid success. German reserves had been drawn into the battle for the Gustav line, leaving only a weakened Fourteenth army to watch the beachhead. Finally the Allies had achieved the combination of pressure from both fronts, which was too much for the German defence. By the evening of 25 May, all the first objectives were in VI Corps hands, and the attack had been 'quicker, less expensive, and more devastating to the enemy than had been hoped'.[65] Plan Buffalo was already on the verge of success, and the capture of Valmontone, with the consequent cutting of the German line of communications, seemed to be in VI Corps' grasp. This was certainly the fitting climax to the operation as Harding and Alexander had envisioned it. However, on that day

Clark issued orders to Truscott that shifted the axis of the VI Corps towards the north-west and Rome, leaving the thrust towards Valmontone to be continued by much weaker forces. On the morning of 25 May, he had visited Truscott at his command post, and while he had discussed the possibility of changing the main thrust, he had not ordered it. It was only that afternoon that Brigadier Don Brann informed Truscott that Clark was ordering him to change the direction of the attack. Truscott was surprised and protested, saying that he would only accept the order once he had spoken to Clark. Brann simply told him that Clark was now out of the beachhead and could not be contacted. Faced with little alternative, Truscott carried out the order.[66]

Whether Truscott's attack would have been successful in cutting off and destroying von Vietinghoff's army remains a matter of debate, but the stark fact is that Clark's change of orders ensured that this outcome could never take place. Truscott himself was convinced at the time, and ever after, that a golden opportunity had been missed. The change of direction caused delay amongst the advancing units, and when they resumed their attack in the new direction towards the Alban hills, they met stronger resistance from German units holding the Caesar line – the last line of defence before Rome – than they might have by driving on Valmontone. What made Clark's behaviour even more culpable was that he sent Al Gruenther, his Chief of Staff, to inform Alexander of the changes only after twenty-four hours had elapsed. It was now too late to alter the decision. Harold Macmillan, the British political representative in Italy, saw Alexander soon after this meeting and noticed that, under a calm exterior, Alexander's eye was twitching. When Macmillan asked him why he had not put his foot down, Alexander snapped, 'Why do you talk nonsense? How can I give orders?'[67] Alexander may not have shown it to anyone else at the time, but Richard McCreery later confessed that Clark's behaviour during the breakout from Anzio had 'made Alexander livid' and 'had rankled with him ever since'.[68]

Clark focused on the prestige value of Rome, and his position in history as its conqueror, for many reasons: because he craved the publicity and political impact that would follow his capturing 'the Eternal City'; because he did not trust his British allies; and because neither he nor his British counterparts really understood how to conduct an encirclement battle in the first place. However, it is not surprising that, given his flagrant disregard for Harding's operational design, and his threats to order his men to fire on any troops of the Eighth Army who attempted to reach Rome first, neither Alexander nor Harding ever forgave him for his behaviour.

Alexander could only watch as Diadem came apart in his hands. The remnants of the German Tenth Army were able to make their escape as the Eighth Army, snarled up in enormous traffic jams, jostled its way up the Liri valley, while VI Corps had to battle heavy German resistance in its drive toward Rome. Mark Clark did achieve his aim: American patrols entered Rome at daybreak on 4 June, and he drove into an empty and silent city early on the morning of the 5th, holding an immediate press conference on the Capitoline Hill as the modern 'conqueror of Rome'. Yet the exploits of 'Mark Clark's Fifth Army' held the front pages of the American newspapers for only one day: from 6 June onwards, the campaign in Italy would only ever be a secondary front, of minor interest to American newspaper editors.

The failure to complete Diadem has to be seen as one of the most serious consequences of the tension that had developed between the British and American commanders in Italy. In this respect, the episode cannot simply be explained by reference to Mark Clark's personality but must also be seen in the light of the series of misunderstandings, arguments and slights – real or imagined – that had clouded the minds of British and American commanders from Tunisia onwards. Yet it also revealed a wider flaw in the Anglo-American approach to the conduct of war. The fact was that neither the British nor the Americans had a level of understanding concerning the encirclement battle comparable to that of the Germans or the Soviets. Unlike the Anglo-American armies, both the Germans and the Soviets had, by 1944, considerable experience of conducting such battles. They knew that the encirclement and destruction of enemy forces was the first and most important task of any military force exploiting a breakthrough, and that once enemy forces had been encircled, their destruction was only a matter of time, at which point the glittering prizes of captured towns, cities and territory would be within easy reach. By contrast, the Western Allies had invariably fought their battles using linear methods, which were able to push the Germans back but not destroy them. Neither the British nor the Americans had real experience of encirclement operations, and neither did they have a common lexicon of terms or methods with which to express themselves. Thus, in one sense, Clark was only able to change Truscott's orders because the Allies lacked any agreed vision of exploitation.

Yet the understandable focus on the flawed climax of Diadem tends to detract from the fact that the fourth Battle of Cassino had resulted in a major military success for the Allies. As Alexander reported to Brooke, his armies had given the Germans a 'fair cop': some 20,000 German troops had been taken prisoner, and Kesselring's armies had suffered nearly 10,000 battle casualties.[69] Harding's original conception had achieved its primary aim: not only had the Allied offensive tied up considerable enemy resources, but the German forces had been comprehensively defeated, if not destroyed. They had had to seek safety in flight, and badly needed reinforcements if they were to make a further stand in Italy. This meant that the Italian theatre drew in further German strength at precisely the moment when Germany could no longer afford it. The next major defensive line on which Kesselring proposed to hold the Allies was the Gothic line, which lay along the crest of the Apennine mountains beyond Florence.[70] Yet the Allies had also suffered 43,746 casualties in the fierce fighting. The American replacement system soon refilled the ranks of the Fifth Army but with every fight, the Eighth Army continued to lose strength.

If Clark's actions had marred the crowning moments of Diadem, fundamental disagreements between the British and Americans over strategy were soon to alter the whole dynamic in the Mediterranean theatre. Alexander hoped that his victorious armies would now be able to keep the Germans on the move, and thus drive them out of Italy altogether. However, the resolution of the competing priorities between the British and American chiefs was soon to deprive his troops of the strength they needed to continue their successful drive.

Operation Anvil, the invasion of southern France, had first been mooted at the Quadrant conference, and, like many Allied plans during the war, had a long gestation period and went through many vicissitudes before actually being implemented. At the Sextant conference held in Cairo in November 1943, it was agreed that Anvil would amount to a two-division assault, which would take place simultaneously with the Overlord landings. However, it had also been assumed that by this date, the forces in Italy would have reached the Pisa–Rimini line. It was during the summer of 1944 that the disagreement over Anvil developed into a bitter controversy that revealed the very different approaches towards strategy held by the British and Americans. Anvil had been an integral part of US planning since the occupation of French North Africa, and offered numerous logistic and indeed political benefits. The United States had spent much time and treasure re-equipping the French army in North Africa, and the opening up of the great ports of Marseilles and Toulon was seen as an essential means not only of ensuring the return of the army to its home country but also of enabling the delivery of vast quantities of supplies into the European theatre by an alternative route. The British, meanwhile, preferred to see Anvil as a possible option that might prove obsolete if conditions changed. Churchill had already voiced such concerns in the autumn of 1943, when it appeared that the Italian front was losing out to Overlord. At one point he bemoaned the lack of troops in Italy, claiming that 'this is what happens when hostilities are governed by lawyers' agreements made in all good faith months before and persisted in without regard to the ever changing fortunes of war'.[71] Yet the American response might well have been that such lawyers' agreements were absolutely essential in ensuring that the British, led by their prime minister, did not back out of their agreements altogether. The American strategic dilemma by 1944 lay in coordinating the resources required not just for Overlord and the Mediterranean but for the Pacific war as well, which by 1944 had progressed far beyond a mere poor relation of the European conflict. Unfortunately, by the summer of 1944, Anvil remained an essential operation for the US Chiefs of Staff, yet for their British counterparts it now seemed an unwelcome diversion that would simply starve the successful armies in Italy of the means to achieve a sweeping victory.[72]

Alexander himself weighed in to the controversy with a brief to the Chiefs of Staff outlining the possibility of advancing through Italy and then swinging through the 'Lubljana gap' in Yugoslavia, with Vienna as the ultimate objective. Brooke realised that such arguments were doomed to failure. He commented on 30 June that 'It is very unfortunate that Alex and Winston ever started this wild scheme about going to Vienna. This has made our task with the Americans an impossible one.'[73] If the US Chiefs of Staff had been unwilling to give extra resources to the Italian campaign when stalemate threatened, they proved even less enthusiastic about providing greater resources when Alexander wished to exploit his victory. His vision of charging into Austria and the Balkans simply alerted the Americans to their old fears of Italy acting as a 'suction pump' by drawing strength away from the cross-Channel attack.

While Brooke realised that this was a fight that was not going to be won, Churchill refused to be reconciled to Anvil, and continued to argue vociferously against the operation, culminating in a six-hour conference with Eisenhower on 7 August 1944 in which he attempted to wear down the Supreme Commander with his impassioned arguments. Eisenhower remained immovable. But when the Prime Minister returned to the charge two days later, accusing the Americans of dominating their ally and remaining deaf to British strategic ideas, Eisenhower had had enough. He subsequently wrote to Churchill:

> I do not, for one moment, believe that there is any desire on the part of any responsible person in the American war machine to disregard British views, or cold-bloodedly to leave Britain holding an empty bag in any of our joint undertakings. I look upon these questions as strictly military in character – and I am sorry that you seem to feel we use our great actual or potential strength as a bludgeon in conference. The fact is that the British view has prevailed

in the discussions of the Combined Chiefs of Staff in many of our undertakings in which I have been engaged, and I do not see why we should be considered intemperate in our long and persistent support of ANVIL.[74]

Of course, none of these wider strategic decisions were purely military in character, but Eisenhower, astute as ever, had put his finger on Churchill's frustrations. The British, and Churchill in particular, had become accustomed to prevailing in conference, and now found it difficult to adapt to the changed strategic situation where the United States was undoubtedly the stronger partner, with new confidence in its views.

However hotly argued at the time, the controversy over Anvil, and the inherent choice between southern France and Italy, was always going to be an option of difficulties. Anvil was indeed essential to reinsert the bulk of the French army into France and provide an important alternative logistic route to feed Overlord, but at the same time, the loss of large numbers of troops from Italy robbed those armies of momentum at precisely the moment when it might have been decisive. Since the Italian campaign had never been favoured by the US Chiefs of Staff, it was not surprising that Eisenhower eventually chose to support Anvil. However, if the United States had held to the letter and spirit of their 'lawyers' agreement' that the defeat of Germany should come first, he might not have had to make such a difficult choice. The troops, resources and landing craft required for Overlord, Anvil *and* Italy existed, but some were deployed in the Pacific.

Anvil, which was renamed Dragoon at Churchill's insistence, since he had been dragooned into acceptance, duly took place on 15 August 1944 against limited German opposition. Toulouse and Marseilles were quickly secured, and the forces of General Alexander Patch's US Seventh Army and General Jean-Marie de Lattre de Tassigny's French army quickly drove up the Rhône valley. As early as 12 September, Patch's men linked up with Patton's Third Army near Dijon. Yet the gain of Anvil/Dragoon had to be set against the loss of troops in Italy. The US Fifth Army lost not only Juin's French Expeditionary Corps but also Truscott and his veteran VI Corps.

Dragoon was thus a real success, but it did mean that Alexander had to cope with a drastic reduction in strength for his next moves in Italy.

During the early summer of 1944, the Germans fought a series of actions through the Italian countryside north of Rome. This was intended to delay the Allied approach to the Gothic line north of Florence, but the Allies continued to press the Germans back. By late August, the Allied armies were beginning to close up on the Gothic line itself. Alexander once again relied on Harding's military judgement to find a means of breaking these formidable defences. His original conception had been to concentrate both the Fifth and Eighth Armies in the Florence area and break through the Appenine mountains on a broad front towards Bologna. This time, it was Oliver Leese, the commander of the Eighth Army, who disliked the plan. His initial experience in command of the Eighth Army was not a happy one, not least because he had to hand over more and more British divisions to the Fifth Army for service in the Anzio beachhead or at Cassino. He did so 'with much reluctance and great apprehension'; he always wanted his whole strength concentrated under his own hand.[75] Although he admired Mark Clark as a 'gallant fighting soldier', he also saw him as a 'complete egoist', and relations between the two men were never entirely cordial.[76]

When the fighting reached the outskirts of Florence, Leese visited a forward observation post with General Sidney Kirkman, the commander of British XIII Corps. They looked at the dominating wall of the Apennines beyond the city, and agreed that with the now sadly attenuated forces at their disposal, the original plan was now not suitable. Leese later commented that it came as 'a bitter disappointment . . . as we had planned to cross the mountains on a broad front and I feel confident that we could have done this, if the 5th Army had been left intact'.[77]

He decided instead that shifting his entire army to the Adriatic coast would enable a 'major battle' to be fought 'in country where we could best exploit our great advantage in tanks, guns and aircraft'. After a hurried meeting with Alexander and Harding beneath the wing of an aircraft at Orvieto airfield, Leese gained his chief's agreement. However, while Leese had hoped to concentrate the whole striking power of the Eighth Army under his hand, when the plan was broached with Clark, the American general insisted that the British XIII Corps should be placed under Fifth Army command to act as a link between the two armies and to provide the weakened Fifth Army with sufficient strength. Leese later related that 'it was a bitter decision to make, but I just had no alternative except to agree – somewhat grudgingly I must confess'.[8] Thus his desire to fight a battle with the concentrated force of his whole army ended in a fatal compromise. Instead of uniting their strength, the two armies would once again fight separate battles, with neither strong enough individually to make a complete breach through the German defences. The tug of war had resumed.

Eighth Army's offensive, Operation Olive, began auspiciously. The movement of the Eighth Army across Italy was an enormous endeavour but was skilfully accomplished by its experienced staff and without alerting the Germans to the move. On the night of 25 August, the leading elements crossed the Metauro river without incident, and over the next few days, the Canadian Corps was able to overrun the first lines of German defences rapidly. As Leese gleefully narrated to Montgomery: 'We caught the enemy completely by surprise and swept him back to the Gothic Line. I expected to have to check on the Gothic Line and organise a main attack. But once again . . . we gate-crashed our way into the line before the enemy was ready.'[79]

But the fighting became increasingly fierce as German reserves rushed to the area. The battle for the little hilltop town of Gemmano was so bitter that it was christened 'the Cassino of the North' by the troops who had to assault it eleven times before it fell into their hands. By 12 September, everything seemed poised for a major armoured breakout into the Romagna plain, but unfortunately, Eighth Army's great gatecrash came to a bitter end on the Coriano ridge, where a charge by the 9th Armoured Brigade was brought to a grinding halt. The Germans had managed in the nick of time to stop the Eighth Army pushing out on to the Bologna plain. Fighting continued for days before the autumn rains turned the battlefield into a quagmire. The rest of the autumn became a bitter disappointment when instead of the inviting open ground for manoeuvre they had imagined, the men of Eighth Army found that the Romagna plain contained a mesh of interconnected watercourses, swollen by the rains into an almost impassable swamp. The Eighth Army ground slowly forward over the autumn and winter of 1944, but it was by no means the dramatic end to the campaign that had been fondly imagined in the good summer weather.

Meanwhile, the Fifth Army tackled the defences of the Gothic line perched on the Apennine mountains north of Florence. Fortunately, intercepted communications alerted them to the fact that the German engineers had concentrated their main defences on the lower heights of the Futa pass, which enabled the US II Corps to mount a diversionary assault at Futa and put its main attack into the comparatively lightly defended Giogo pass. The American assault began on 12 September 1944, and the thrust towards the Giogo pass achieved considerable surprise. Nonetheless, the men of the 91st and 85th Divisions had to attack in extremely difficult terrain, which included 'numerous mountain peaks, streams, deep valleys, broken ridges, and rugged spurs', which all offered excellent defensive positions to the German defenders.[80] The 91st Division's capture of Monte Altuzzo and the Monticelli ridge remains one of the finest feats of arms of the war, and the American infantry entirely proved – if any further proof were needed – its prowess in battle. Over the course of just two days, the infantry had not only climbed the virtually sheer mountainside in the face of a determined German defence but held out against desperate German counter-attacks.

The fighting had witnessed numerous acts of valour by American soldiers, yet the sad fact remained that by now, the rest of the world was not watching the fight in Italy, regardless of the valour or skill displayed by the troops in combat. After six days of fierce fighting, II Corps had suffered 2,731 casualties but had seized the Giogo pass, outflanking the main German positions at Futa, and enabled the American drive through the narrow gorges and passes of the Apennines to continue.[81] Not surprisingly, it

became increasingly difficult to push troops through the mountains, and the American advance became channelled into one
thrust by the US 88th Division, which advanced towards Monte
Battaglia, a narrow ridge 2,345 feet high, which ran from south
to north and culminated at its northern point in a ruined castle.
It was here that the men of the 350th Infantry Regiment faced
repeated counter-attacks in perilously exposed positions.[82] After
three days of intense fighting, the men of the Blue Devil's Division
had held on, but were exhausted and needed relief. It took three
nights in early October for the Welsh Guards, the Coldstream
Guards and the Grenadier Guards to complete the relief of the
American troops on the exposed slopes of Monte Battaglia.[83]
Holding these positions turned out to be one of the most
unpleasant experiences of the war for the guardsmen. The regimental historian Michael Howard later related that:

> the Germans overlooked the Battaglia positions from three sides,
> and from the incessant pounding of his guns and mortars the
> guardsmen could find refuge only in their slit trenches. But for the rain
> this might have been tolerable; but the ceaseless downpour had
> filled the slits with water to a depth of several feet, and no covering
> could keep it out. The men and their blankets were quickly
> drenched, and for the three weeks that the Brigade remained on
> Battaglia they could never get really dry. The platoon areas were
> filthy with old ration-tins and excrement, and all around there spread
> a waste of mud and rock and shell-scarred tree stumps, scattered
> with shell-holes and with unburied corpses of German and
> American dead.[84]

Had the weather been better, the men might have been able to
see the city of Bologna, their final objective, in the distance. As it
was, the American drive through the Apennines, which had started
so well, had been stalled at Monte Battaglia. The operations to
breach the Gothic line, which had achieved great initial success,
had ended in frustration, and the men of both the Fifth and Eighth
Armies had to reconcile themselves to spending yet another winter
among the mountains of Italy. The fact was that neither army had

the strength individually to defeat the Germans in Italy. It is more than likely that if, utilising Harding's original conception, the two had attacked the Gothic line together, even in their weakened state they may well have achieved the victory they sought. Once again, the unwillingness or inability of the two allies to work together had cost them dearly.

It was not until the spring of 1945 that the Allied armies in Italy finally demonstrated what they could achieve as a united force. Over the winter of 1944–5 there were many changes in the Allied command structure, which served to smooth over some of the previous rifts. General 'Jumbo' Wilson was sent to Washington to replace Dill, and Alexander was elevated to Supreme Allied Commander in the Mediterranean. There was never any question, however, that his primary focus remained on the armies in Italy. Mark Clark was now placed in command of 15th Army Group, while Truscott was rewarded with the command of the Fifth Army. Richard McCreery, Clark's 'feather duster', took over command of the Eighth Army when Leese was sent out to the Far East. Truscott and McCreery had worked closely together before, and much of the tension and friction that had bedevilled the relationship between the two armies evaporated with the new commanders.

Both armies spent the winter of 1944 and early spring of 1945 in intensive training and preparation, and while their strength was now attenuated, they both received significant quantities of new equipment. Meanwhile, the German forces in Italy were a shadow of their former strength, lacking numbers and equipment while still having to hold extensive defensive positions. While the Fifth Army concentrated its forces in a drive north towards Bologna, the Eighth Army prepared to cross the River Senio and drive for the Argenta gap – a narrow spit of land between the river and Lake Comacchio. When the offensive began, on 1 April 1945, the Allied armies achieved complete surprise and made rapid gains. The use of amphibious forces on Lake Comacchio outflanked the German positions, and although the fighting for the Argenta gap was fierce, by 21 April, the British 6th Armoured Division had broken out into open country behind the German defences, and American soldiers had entered Bologna. Two days later, the leading spearheads of the two armies met, appropriately enough, at the town of Finale.[85] The Allies in Italy had finally achieved the encirclement battle that had been sought the year before. The German forces were overwhelmed and began to disintegrate, while the Allied spearheads crossed the River Po and drove on towards the Alps and Trieste.

British and American cooperation certainly went much further than ever before in these final battles. Due to a crippling shortage of American artillery ammunition, the British 7th Army Group Royal Artillery (AGRA), consisting of two field regiments, one medium regiment, two anti-aircraft regiments and one survey regiment, provided all the artillery support for the US IV Corps in the offensive. Close artillery support requires good communication but also real trust between the infantry units and the artillery. British artillery observers were attached to every US and Brazilian unit to handle the requests for fire. In supporting the 10th US Mountain Division, the 1st Armoured Division, the 92nd Infantry Division and the Brazilian Expeditionary Force, the artillery units of the AGRA covered 250 miles and fired a total of 23,000 rounds. The 7th AGRA report stated that 'The close integration of US infantry and British Artillery during these battles bodes well for the continued friendship of American and British Forces.' This unremarked-upon example of cooperation showed how far the two armies had travelled from the mistrust and suspicion of late 1943, but it also revealed how long it had taken to develop a close bond of trust.[86]

Amidst dramatic scenes, the SS General Wolff negotiated the first major surrender, with the capitulation of all German and Italian forces in Italy taking place on 2 May 1945.[87] Alexander had finally achieved the decisive battle he had so ardently desired, but it came too late to have any meaningful effect on the course of the war. The world's eyes were now focused on the dramatic events in Germany that eventually brought the Second World War to a close. Indeed, it must even be questioned whether this final offensive in Italy was really an essential operation of war.

Churchill, however, was understandably delighted. He exulted in a cable to Alexander:

I rejoice in the magnificently planned and executed operations of the 15th Group of Armies which are resulting in the complete destruction or capture of all the enemy forces south of the Alps. That you and General Mark Clark should have been able to achieve these tremendous results . . . after you have made great sacrifices of whole Armies for the Western Front, is indeed another proof of your genius for war and of the intimate brotherhood-in-arms between the British Commonwealth and Imperial Forces and those of the United States. Never I suppose have so many nations advanced and manoeuvred in one line victoriously. The British, Americans, New Zealanders, South Africans, British-Indians, Poles, Jews, Brazilians and strong forces of liberated Italians have all marched together in that high comradeship and unity of men fighting for freedom and for the deliverance of mankind. This great final battle in Italy will long stand out in history as one of the most famous episodes in this Second World War.[88]

Churchill had allowed his enthusiasm to paint an unrealistic picture of the Italian campaign. The Allied forces in Italy were certainly the most diverse, with contributions from a wide range of nations, but the campaign had not always resulted in an 'intimate brotherhood-in-arms'. It often seemed to be dominated by intense rivalry and suspicion between its British and American commanders. But Alexander, despite his many flaws as an army group commander, counted among his essential talents the ability to keep such a wide variety of polyglot forces together. And perhaps most importantly, the Allied campaign in Italy, for all its faults and imperfections, did actually achieve its main aim, forcing the Germans into defence and thus drawing some of their strength away from the decisive theatres of war.

The course of the Italian campaign reveals the hard truth that multinational operations are rarely sleek, efficient or glamorous, due to the suspicions and resentments that can build up between allied forces, leading to friction and inefficiencies. This does not mean, however, that multinational forces cannot achieve their aims. The tug of war between the American Fifth Army and the British Eighth Army was not an isolated historical event, but rather an example of behaviour that is all too common in multinational operations. Yet it was when the tug of war was suspended that the Allied armies in Italy achieved their greatest successes. Ensuring that coalition forces do not indulge in competition and rivalry but actually work together to achieve a common goal remains the key challenge of alliance warfare.

II

Over There, Over Here

The first sight of Britain for the 'average' GI was of a rain-washed green island, more often than not under a leaden grey sky. The majority of GIs travelled across the Atlantic on troopships convoyed by naval escorts, yet fully 30 per cent made the journey on the British ocean liners the *Queen Mary* and the *Queen Elizabeth*. The two ships had been converted into vast troop carriers, each able to take 15,000 soldiers in one crossing, and their high speed meant that they could travel unescorted;[1] indeed, the men often mistook the ships for American vessels because they were so modern and fast. The soldiers disembarked at the great western ports of Britain: Glasgow, Liverpool and Bristol.* Once on dry land again, most GIs were welcomed with a speech by a British dignitary or retired general and music from a military band.[2] Many of their immediate impressions concerned the bomb damage around the ports, and the rather dowdy and threadbare clothes people wore. Britain often seemed both familiar and yet foreign at the same time: there could be no mistaking that it was a country at war. After refreshments provided by British voluntary organisations, most soldiers boarded a train, which looked small and dirty in comparison to American rail stock, before being whisked away on a disorientating journey to 'somewhere in England'.

The genesis for this influx of American troops was to be found in Marshall's memorandum to the British Chiefs of Staff in April 1942. Marshall proposed to send one million American soldiers and airmen to Britain so that 30 American divisions would be available

---

* The first convoys in 1942 had landed at Belfast in Northern Ireland.

for an invasion of Europe by 1 April 1943. The code name for
the transport of vast numbers of Americans across the Atlantic, the
construction of housing and bases to accommodate them while in
Britain and the stockpiling of stores and equipment was Bolero.
The dry details of the outline plan, even with the staggering statistics involved, could prepare no one – whether GI or British subject
– for the reality of what, by the spring of 1944, amounted to a
virtual invasion and occupation of large parts of the British Isles,
and Operation Bolero, rather like the strategic intention behind
Marshall's memorandum, followed a chequered and by no means
straightforward path before its eventual completion.

Bolero committees were quickly established in both Washington
and London to deal with the vast amount of detailed planning and
preparation required to make the plan a reality. However, it very
quickly became apparent that the original plan was optimistic to
say the least: the one million men envisaged would amount to a
force of only 16 to 18 divisions rather than 30. Nonetheless, Bolero
remained an enormous operation that would stretch Allied logistics
and ingenuity to the limit if it was to be achieved. Under the
original estimates, 849,300 US troops would have to arrive in Britain
by 9 April 1943, with 120,000 men arriving every month until June
1943.[3] It made sense for the American soldiers, as well as the bulk
of their supplies, to disembark at ports on the west coast of Britain;
it followed that the best locations to accommodate them would be
South Wales and south-west England, as this would rationalise the
transport and delivery of both men and supplies, and many existing
British Army bases in Wales and the west were cleared to make
room for the incoming Americans. The task of accommodating so
many soldiers and their kit was staggering. The area of covered
storage eventually requisitioned or built to house the vast quantities
of American equipment amounted to 17,944,186 square feet, while
the area of open storage amounted to 34,636,905 square feet.[4]

All of this machinery was beginning to accelerate when, in July
1942, the strategic decision in favour of Operation Torch changed
the whole basis for Bolero. Initially, the actual numbers of troops
reaching Britain was not far behind the planning estimates, but by
the end of September, when Torch planning reached its climax,

only 183,110 men had arrived against an estimate of 264,000.[5] In fact, the cargo programme for Bolero had fallen far behind the optimistic estimates even by midsummer. The simple fact was that, since the Royal Navy was still struggling against the U-boat threat in the Atlantic, there was almost bound to be a serious shortage of shipping for such a large programme. Had Bolero continued unchanged by Torch, the supply of shipping and the capacity of British ports to handle ships at the frequency required would have created a serious bottleneck that might well have upset much of the plan.

Although Churchill seems to have pressed Torch upon Roosevelt with the blithe assumption that it would not necessarily prejudice a cross-Channel attack in 1943, there is no question that Bolero was 'thrown out of gear by Torch'.[6] Since there no longer seemed any urgent need to transfer large quantities of American assets or men to Britain, far fewer troop convoys sailed across the Atlantic, while troops and stores originally earmarked for the European assault were diverted to North Africa. The US Army had built up one armoured and three infantry divisions in Britain by November 1942, and all but one of these were sent to North Africa. Army Air Corps forces were even more drastically reduced, with some going to North Africa but many being diverted to the Pacific. This period of indecision concerning the fate of Bolero was not fully ended until the Casablanca conference in January 1943, by which time the transport of men and supplies to Britain had come to a virtual standstill. By 15 December 1942, there were only 96,537 Americans in Britain: Bolero almost seemed to have gone into reverse.[7] At this point, the American troops seemed to be simply another small contingent amongst the many Allied nations – including the Canadians, Poles, Czechs and French – that had forces resident in Britain.

Marshall may have lost the strategic argument for a cross-Channel attack, but Bolero was again placed on the Allied priority list for shipping. However, with so many competing demands, including the needs of British defence, imports, Torch, Husky, assistance to Turkey and a projected attack in Burma, all of which took precedence, little was achieved in the first few months of 1943. Indeed, the Allies experienced an acute crisis over shipping due to renewed U-boat attacks. Not only were Allied shipping losses serious, but it meant there were simply insufficient escort ships to provide protection for the projected convoys. All these factors meant that by the end of March 1943 there were still only 114,489 American soldiers and airmen in Great Britain, and the stores programme for Bolero was badly behind schedule. This renewed delay in the Bolero programme was caused partly by the Allied strategic decision to make 1943 'the Mediterranean Year', but also by the exigencies of the war. It meant that Bolero, as originally conceived, was unlikely ever to have worked. Eisenhower, who had had input into Marshall's memorandum, later admitted that the original estimates would have proved too optimistic: a cross-Channel attack in the summer of 1943 might well have proved impossible even if Marshall had won the strategic argument in July 1942.

It was entirely fortuitous that just as the Allies began to devote serious attention to the problems of the cross-Channel attack, the U-boat threat in the Atlantic was finally mastered. With the closing of the North Atlantic air gap, renewed Enigma intelligence and improved anti-submarine techniques amongst convoy escorts, the U-boats suffered a 'Black May' of losses from which they never entirely recovered. By the summer of 1943, Allied shipping losses had fallen dramatically and most convoys were now experiencing little difficulty in crossing the Atlantic. Meanwhile, the two liners that had been used to transfer Australian troops from the Middle East were returned to the North Atlantic route. The conditions were now set for a major acceleration in Bolero, and what had been a trickle suddenly turned into a veritable flood of American soldiers and supplies arriving in Britain from the summer of 1943 onwards. It was thus not just the numbers of Americans but the speed of the build-up that undoubtedly heightened the social impact of the arrival of the US Army in Britain.

It was certainly unfortunate that the first American troops started to arrive in the United Kingdom in the spring of 1942, when the overall morale of the British Army at home was at its lowest ebb, following the fall of Malaya and Singapore in February. The following month, General Ronald Adam, the Adjutant General, decided to establish a committee to investigate the morale of the British Army, believing as he did that 'This war is going to be won or lost on morale. We are too apt to leave the problem alone. Morale is a psychological problem like sex, and therefore the Britisher is almost ashamed to talk about it.'[8] There certainly was a widespread belief that low morale was a contributory factor to the defeats suffered in the Far East, and there was a growing sense amongst the army's commanders that it was a serious problem.

The fact was that the British Army had suffered defeat after defeat with seemingly no victories to counterbalance them. Yet the problem of poor morale seemed to weigh most heavily on the forces garrisoned at home, perhaps because there appeared to be a lack of real purpose for the soldiers there. By the spring of 1942, the army had grown to over two and a quarter million men, and the vast majority of these were stationed in Britain. The British Army had prepared to meet the expected German invasion with frantic energy well into 1941, but as the immediacy of the threat subsided, it had been left almost in a state of limbo. Army units trained hard in numerous exercises, but it was difficult to engender a real sense of purpose and urgency into this interminable activity when there seemed no prospect of immediate action.[9] Thus the negative consequence of the British strategic decision to win the war through air power and blockade without a decisive role for the army was felt in declining army morale.

The British Army also had a poor public image. Memories of the Great War remained fresh, and perceptions of the appalling losses of that war had shifted from a grievous but necessary sacrifice to a futile waste of young life. While soldiers gained some sympathy from the press, the leadership of the army was lampooned through the popular stereotype of David Low's cartoon figure of 'Colonel Blimp', an old-fashioned, pompous and incompetent officer out of touch with modern realities. Army leaders certainly felt that 'the persistent criticism and scorn directed by the Press against Army leadership and institutions is beginning to affect the confidence of the troops both in their leaders and in their weapons'.[10]

There was thus precious little, if any, glamour associated with

serving in the British Army during the early years of the Second
World War. The RAF had achieved considerable fame in defending
the country during the Battle of Britain, while its bombing raids
were seen as actually hitting back directly against Germany.
Meanwhile, the navy had also caught the public imagination with
the raid on Taranto, the Battle of Matapan and the hunt for the
Bismarck.[11] Soldiers' conditions in cold, crumbling Victorian
barracks appeared poor next to service in the RAF or the navy, and
even their uniform was the least attractive of the three services.
The khaki battledress, made of rough woollen serge, had been
adopted by the army in 1939 and was an eminently modern and
practical form of clothing for active service, but it could certainly
never be described as smart.[12] Only Polish soldiers, by dint of great
persistence and effort, were able to put creases into their trousers.
Soldiers wearing their sack-like battledress and heavy hobnailed
boots came to be nicknamed 'brown jobs' by the other services,
which seemed to be a comment not just on their uniforms but on
the experience of being a British soldier.[13] One army report lamented
this sense of inferiority:

> The ordinary soldier suffers from a lack of respect for himself as a
> member of the Army. Reasons for this are not far to seek. First,
> the feeling . . . that the Army is not justifying its existence by any
> noteworthy action. Second, the better publicity accorded to the
> other Services and to Dominion . . . troops. Dominion troops have
> enjoyed a disproportionate share of the credit for what fighting has
> taken place in Europe and in the Middle East, and both the wireless
> and the newspapers 'boost' the RAF, the Canadians, and everyone
> except the British soldier, who does not fail to comment bitterly
> on the fact.[14]

Perhaps most importantly, the British soldier knew that he was
the 'worst paid of the Services, worse paid than other soldiers, and
worse paid than the average civilian worker – facts which are
brought home to him every time he enters a public house and
almost every time he seeks female society'. Not surprisingly, this
fact was considered 'most damaging to his self-respect'.[15] As one

regimental sergeant major put it: 'The soldier really begins to grouse when he goes into a pub and finds that he can only afford a single glass of beer, whilst the munition worker slaps down a £1 note and asks for whisky or gin.'[16] British soldiers had invariably been poorly paid: in the Great War they received a shilling a day; by contrast, Australian troops had received five shillings a day. This had created resentment and protest during and after the Great War, but little had been done to remedy the situation.

All these factors, combined with 'defeat, inactivity and bullshit', meant that morale in the British Army at home reached its lowest point just as American troops first started arriving in Britain.[17] It was thus not surprising that the first GIs were greeted with a mixture of curiosity and resentment by many British soldiers. Relations between American soldiers and British civilians on the street, in shops and in the pub could range from the frosty to the cordial but it was a well-known fact that British and American soldiers tended not to mix in Britain, and when they did, the results were often hostile.[18] If the British soldier generally felt undervalued and unappreciated in comparison to the other British services, it was natural that he would feel a mixture of envy, resentment and jealousy when confronted with his American counterpart. American soldiers were paid more, wore smarter uniforms, enjoyed a quantity and quality of food unknown in British messes, and possessed seemingly inexhaustible supplies of lavish equipment. The common taunt of British soldiers said it all (or at least most of it): the GIs were 'overpaid, oversexed and over here'.

John Keegan, the military historian, has winningly described the difference between the two armies when in late 1943 the area around his home 'overflowed almost overnight with GIs'. Keegan, with the eyes of a ten-year-old, noted:

> How different they looked from our own jumble-sale champions, beautifully clothed in smooth khaki, as fine in cut and quality as a British officer's . . . and armed with glistening, modern, automatic weapons . . . More striking still were the number, size and elegance of the vehicles in which they paraded about the countryside in stately convoy. The British Army's transport was a sad collection

of underpowered makeshifts, whose dun paint flaked from their tinpot bodywork. The Americans travelled in magnificent, gleaming olive green, pressed steel, four-wheel-drive juggernauts.[19]

The British soldier's apparent disadvantage began with the clothes he wore. The American Army had started the war wearing an olive drab (a greener hued version of khaki) single-breasted service dress tunic, with matching trousers and shoes or boots. In fact, the first American troops to arrive in Britain in 1942 looked distinctly old-fashioned, since they were still wearing the British pattern steel helmets that their fathers had worn in the Great War. However, the army had recently introduced a series of modern field jackets and trousers for wear while on duty, which meant that the smart service dress tunic, shirt and tie, trousers and shoes could be worn when off duty.[20] British soldiers, meanwhile, were expected to wear their unflattering battledress and hobnail boots both on and off duty. The fact that all American soldiers wore shirts and ties when out on the town could prove a source of severe embarrassment to some British soldiers, who found themselves saluting American privates 'on account of their uniforms'.[21]

The lavish scale of American equipment was another obvious difference, where British units often had to struggle with shortages or inappropriate kit. One American officer, after visiting a British unit, commented that:

> I have seen very little here that can compare in quality or quantity with what we have; it takes a visit to the other fellow to appreciate how well we are fixed. Little things like overshoes, warm gloves, woollen underwear, knit caps to wear under our helmets etc., that we have taken for granted assume a different aspect at 04.00 a.m. in an 80 mile gale, they make all the difference between comparative comfort and misery.[22]

'Uncle Sam' certainly seemed to provide his soldiers with everything they needed, and that included mountains of food. Although British soldiers ate greater quantities of food than British civilians, food in wartime Britain was strictly rationed. The same was not true, however, for the American Army in Britain, which imported its own rations for its men. It had originally been intended that American units in Britain would eat the same rations as the British troops, but this was abandoned after it was rapidly discovered that American soldiers complained vociferously when placed on the meagre British Army rations.[23]

The Ministry of Information kept a close eye on British morale at home during the war, and one of the prominent topics of its weekly surveys was the relations between American and British troops. As early as July 1942, reports warned of 'trouble brewing' between soldiers of the two armies due to 'the lavish way in which the Americans fling their money about'.[24] Part of the problem lay in the fact that the men did not tend to mix while on duty, being kept busy with training, drill and other duties in their separate camps and barracks. This meant that it was only when they were off duty and looking for entertainment, drink and the company of women that the British and Americans tended to meet. As one British Army correspondent noted, it was the 'street corner and public-house contact between the two Forces that leads to trouble . . . relations improve remarkably on closer acquaintance'.[25]

It was also in the pub that the far greater spending power of the American soldier was only too obvious to the British Tommy; although direct comparisons of pay between an American and British soldier of equivalent rank are complex, it is fair to say that the British soldier did not come out well. American soldiers also received their pay monthly, and often saved it up for a night on the town, whereas British soldiers were paid weekly and had correspondingly less to spend on a night out. American soldiers, unfamiliar with the strange British currency, but delighted with their spending power, would often pull out 'wads enough to choke a cow' and wave them about.[26] Perhaps not surprisingly, there were numerous stories of American soldiers being overcharged or cheated of change by unscrupulous shopkeepers and publicans.[27] Even when American troops were being generous towards British soldiers in an attempt to break the ice, the gesture could backfire. In one incident, an American soldier walked into a Blackpool pub and, with commendable generosity, shouted, 'Well, boys, the lot's on me – what'll you have?' Rather than welcoming their new-found American comrade, the British soldiers in the pub felt embarrassed because they certainly could not 'afford treating on this scale, and angry because they were in an awkward position'.[28] American troops in pubs would often insist on buying whisky for British soldiers, which they would struggle to buy in return, making the British soldiers appear 'diffident and stand-offish'. The official suggestion that GIs should treat British soldiers only to beer was hardly calcu- lated to improve the situation. Yet American soldiers quite rightly resented any suggestion that they were overpaid – most knew that munition workers back in the States were earning far more than they were. Although British soldiers' anger and envy focused on lavish American spending, the comparison simply demonstrated how badly paid they were by their own government.

Other encounters were even less calculated to win friends. Stories soon circulated of American soldiers going into pubs and calling out, 'Get me a drink as fast as you got out of Tobruk', or mentioning that there were four colours in the Union Jack: red, white, blue and yellow.[29] GIs certainly gained a reputation for being brash and overconfident, and British soldiers were reported to be irritated by American 'big talk, their swagger' and their boasts that 'they have come here to teach us how to do the job'.[30] British soldiers also complained about what they saw as the sloppy manner and behav- iour of the Americans. One British civilian remembered that most of the Americans at the nearby base were 'just young lads and very few of them shaved regularly – dead scruffy really. There were an awful lot of them that just worked and slept, not going out much, except to the pub . . . they could all dance really well, but couldn't march to save their lives.'[31] Such evidence confirmed British suspi- cions that the GIs might talk 'big' and have money and lavish food, but they didn't 'look like a soldier', and probably wouldn't fight like one either.[32] American soldiers in their turn complained about the snobbery and stand-offishness they experienced at the hands of British troops.

Perhaps not surprisingly, much of the envy and jealousy concerning American soldiers revolved around their perceived success with British women. The fact that every American soldier looked like an officer to the untutored eye gave them a certain advantage with the opposite sex. It was not difficult to see the attraction of smartly dressed young American men who could spend lavishly and had access to all kinds of unknown luxuries, such as nylon stockings and good-quality American cigarettes. Reports were soon mentioning that the generosity of American soldiers was causing real resentment amongst British soldiers because 'all the girls are going mad about them and giving their own fellows up'.[33] It was often claimed that American soldiers had no respect for British girls. 'They think they can buy them body and soul, if they take them into a pub and buy them a drink.'[34] As one British soldier rather plaintively put it, 'What chance has a poor Tommy with a couple of bob jingling in his pocket?'[35]

The presence of American troops in Britain did not just cause friction with British soldiers at home. Indeed, British troops serving in the Mediterranean and Middle East may well have developed greater anxiety and suspicion concerning the American presence for the very reason that they were serving overseas. One army report claimed that 'Press and other accounts of infidelity foster a feeling of hostility towards those now in the UK, particularly members of overseas forces, which is reaching dangerous proportions.'[36] Another declared that anxiety about the possible infidelity of wives and girlfriends back in Britain was 'wrecking the peace of mind of a very large proportion of the MEF'.[37] Certainly, by October 1942, there were nearly 2,000 divorce cases pending in the Middle East Forces, with new cases received every day.[38] One padre even claimed that 'The most efficient fifth column work done out here is carried out by the women in England.'[39] The 'Dear John' letter, in which a girlfriend, fiancée or wife informed her man that she had found love elsewhere, became not only legendary but genuinely feared in the British Eighth Army. Long and continuous absence from home made such break-ups inevitable, but they also caused real bitterness amongst British troops seemingly marooned in the desert wastes of North Africa or fighting in the mountains of Italy. When such letters involved an American soldier or airman, the feelings of helplessness and resentment were only intensified; here was a British soldier, fighting for his country many miles from home, whose wife or girlfriend had been 'stolen' by an American. At the same time, British soldiers serving in the Middle East had no sense of the wider context in which these letters were sent, and couldn't appreciate that wartime conditions had changed Britain markedly during the time they had been away.

All these factors meant that relations between British and American soldiers in Britain were far removed from the official picture of comrades marching arm in arm to victory. In fact, it could be argued that the root cause of the poor relations came down to bad first impressions that were not subsequently corrected by closer contact. Hearsay, rumours, press reports and unfortunate incidents on street corners and in pubs meant that soldiers of both armies tended to pre-judge one another and thus, if at all possible, keep out of each other's way when off duty. This tendency was reinforced by local agreements between American and British commanders to give their men leave on different nights or to set aside certain towns for troops of one nationality. One British cadet wrote, 'Thank heavens the Yanks are barred from the Nuffield. They swarm everywhere else and are disliked by all. In fact a Yank was asked how he liked England, and he said "Sir, we like you and you like us and that's our orders, sir."'[40] A British sapper wrote home that he liked his posting in Southampton but that 'the only snag is the town is infested with Yanks, and they are popular as sin with us. These blokes blow too much. They keep telling us they are winning the war for us (I don't think) so you can guess how popular they are.'[41] It has to be said, however, that while soldiers' complaints about American troops tended to be vociferous and gain notice, good relations, where they developed, could often go unnoticed. Most Ministry of Information reports stressed the fact that the bulk of accounts recorded favourable impressions of American soldiers while continuing to worry about the minority of adverse opinions. As might be expected, there was always a range of opinions on both sides.

It is impossible to sum up all the myriad experiences, both good and bad, that American soldiers encountered while in Britain. For George MacIntyre, a soldier in a combat engineer battalion, 'Landing in England was to be, for me, the most exhilarating, pleasant and heartwarming experience I had ever undergone . . . I was to enjoy my stay in this hospitable country more than any place I had been up to that time.' Indeed, MacIntyre found Britain to be a home from home. He disembarked at Liverpool but was soon sent south to Totnes in Devon, where many units of the American First Army were billeted. He was quartered in the small hamlet of Berry Pomeroy, just outside Totnes. On his first evening off, he made the trip into Totnes rather timidly since 'it was our first trip to a foreign land, and we didn't quite know how to act. We weren't timid very long for we found the average English citizen a very friendly person. Despite their reputation, we found they had a reserved but acute sense of humor . . . We were brash with our kidding but they were subtle and very thorough.' MacIntyre enjoyed nights in the pub and he met some families who adopted him during his stay in England. Soon he was spending most of his time off with the Prince family, including visits for Sunday dinner. He was embarrassed about eating their food when he knew they were severely rationed, but soon found ways of repaying them with surplus rations from his company kitchen. For the Princes, the extra sugar, butter, flour and fruit must have seemed like amazing largesse. MacIntyre felt he had found 'more genuine hospitality in England than I did in many parts of my own country. I mean they went without themselves in order to show the "Yanks", as they called us, that we were welcome.'[42]

Yet while there were many American soldiers who were delighted to be adopted by British families while stationed in England, there were others who were frustrated by British customs and practice. One soldier wrote home that he thanked God he was 'an American and that you are there. I sure don't like England, and I don't like the people. They are very old fashioned, they do things the way their fathers did and don't have the least ambition to improve their ways. I don't understand them. They are very friendly, but I don't like the slow way they do things. The towns are awful.'[43] Another American soldier, writing just before the war ended, believed that many English people would 'dance with joy when they see us go. I've seen a lot of bastards, but these take the cake. If ever we had a war with England I'd volunteer right away.'[44]

Just as had already occurred in Tunisia, Sicily and Italy, whenever British and American soldiers actually worked closely together, the results were generally more positive and led to much-improved relations. As one report mentioned, 'Wherever men of the two Forces are compelled by circumstances actually to live or work together, relations almost invariably improve. Several Commanders report that relations are good where the contact is really close.'[45]

It was in an attempt to solve the problems of ignorance and frosty relations between the two armies – who would soon have to fight together – that the Army Council established an Anglo-American relations committee in August 1943. American representatives joined the committee a month later. Not every idea for improving relations proved suitable. One American suggestion was to explain to British soldiers that GIs actually saved a large proportion of their pay in life assurances and other securities. It was eventually decided that this would simply highlight the disparity in pay even further and the matter was shelved.[46] The most promising idea lay in developing an inter-attachment scheme in which small groups of soldiers of all ranks would be exchanged for two weeks' service in the other army. This was designed to bring about the close contact and knowledge that, it was hoped, would improve relations, as well as being 'essential for the efficient co-operation of the two forces in the field'.[47]

When the inter-attachment scheme started on a very small scale in the autumn of 1943, it met with a favourable reception. One factor that almost certainly helped was that the British Army was no longer quite the Cinderella service it had been in the spring of 1942. Soldiers' pay and allowances had been improved, if only marginally, and the army now had successes in North Africa, Tunisia and Sicily to its credit. With the British Army 'back on the map', soldiers' grievances were no longer quite as sharp as they had been a year before. In this changed atmosphere, the inter-attachment gathered momentum during the winter and into the spring of 1944. The scheme was soon felt to be a great success for the comparatively small number of men who took part in it, both in fostering good Anglo-American relations and also in stimulating thought and discussion in the units concerned, although some minor issues inevitably remained. Overall, it was felt that the 'British soldier's opinion of the American was, in many cases, radically changed for the better as the result of the visit'. Most British soldiers on the scheme realised that American soldiers, while on duty, worked as hard as if not harder than themselves. American soldiers who had visited British units were said to be full of admiration for the professionalism of the British non-commissioned officers.

Of course, it was not just British soldiers who changed their opinions on closer acquaintance. American Corporal Del Sahlberg found service in England interesting, although he did not care for English food, with the exception of fish and chips. On 5 May 1944, he was driving a truck when he stopped to help an elderly man whose car had broken down. Sahlberg was able to quickly fix the engine with some wire and refused payment even though the old man insisted. He had climbed back into the cab of his truck when he heard the man call out, 'Yank.' 'I got down and asked what he wanted. After a few moments staring at [me] intently, he said "Do you know, you have completely destroyed my opinion of your kind?" I said "Thank you" and drove off.'[48] Letters from British soldiers on the scheme told the same story. One private wrote: 'We have had about six Yanks staying with us for the last fortnight to start mixing with the British Army to see how we live and to mix with us, so that when we do go into action together we shall be more sociable than they have been before. All I can say about them is this, that if all the others are the same as these fellows then they are a nice set of fellows indeed.'[49] However, one infantry private felt sympathy towards the dozen American soldiers who had joined his battalion and felt they would be glad when they could go back to their own unit because 'they look proper miserable, they can't make out when they go on parade. I saw one standing in parade today with his hands in his pockets.' He explained that his NCO had orders not to put the Americans on charge for such heinous breaches of military discipline because 'their discipline is different to ours'.

One American engineer commented that he got along fine with his British 'buddies', and that it was much easier to understand them having worked with them. Perhaps revealingly, he believed that 'there is not so much difference in British and Americans than North and South'.[50]

Just as had been intended, the inter-attachment scheme was useful in breaking down prejudices between the soldiers involved, but these were still comparatively few. By 10 May 1944, a total of 338 British officers and 3,080 men had visited American units, while 915 American officers and 4,726 men had worked with British formations, with the average length of stay being 12 days.[51] By this time, unit commanders were beginning to complain that the scheme was interfering with essential training for Overlord and the visits began to tail off.[52] The inter-attachment scheme was certainly a genuine attempt to foster better relations between the soldiers of the two armies, but it could only really influence a small fraction of the mass armies encamped in Britain. The Anglo-American relations committee had held regular monthly meetings during 1943 and 1944, with its members giving reports on the progress of the inter-attachment scheme and various publicity initiatives, but the meetings stopped abruptly. The date of the next meeting had been agreed as 7 June 1944, but it was never held. By that time the British and American armies that had been held in Britain for so many months were flowing out of the country in a continuous stream: Operation Overlord had begun.

While the American 'invasion' of Britain resulted in a profound impact upon British society that continues to this day, on the other side of the Atlantic, the infiltration of North America by the British Army Staff was both unheralded and almost unnoticed even at the time. Nonetheless, the work undertaken by this organisation resulted in a degree of liaison, collaboration and even integration between the British and American armies that had never 'been attempted previously in history . . . between Allies'.[53] The volume of work for the British Army Staff, combined with a large increase in the variety of its functions, resulted in a steady growth in its numbers from its tiny beginnings in Michael Dewar's tank mission. By its peak in mid-1944, the British Army Staff had become a substantial organisation of some 400 officers, 500 other ranks and

1,000 (mainly Canadian and American) civilians in 45 different stations all over North America.[54] Even a simple list of its branches reveals the range and complexity of work as well as the level of collaboration achieved by the two armies; these included Operations, Plans and Intelligence; Staff Work, Training and Service Arms (infantry, armour, artillery, engineers and signals); Assignments and Requirements, which dealt with the business and management of Lend-Lease; Civil Affairs in liberated and captured territories; Public Relations; Quartermaster and Services; Supplies and Transportation; and Ordnance.[55]

From the British perspective, perhaps the most important branch was Assignments and Requirements, which had to argue for British needs in the allocation of resources from American industry. Since the requirement for munitions and equipment consistently exceeded the amount actually produced during 1943, the competition between the various Allied theatres for the limited output became intense. The problem was compounded by the fact that the US had tended to underestimate their requirements, which meant that their bids, when it came to the assignment stage, were higher than their agreed allocation. Since these bids could only be met at the expense of other Lend-Lease nations, the British officers often had to argue long and hard to gain acceptance of British needs. Although higher US demands did dislocate British plans and assumptions concerning equipment, the supply department of the British Army Staff certainly had its hands full by the middle of 1944, dealing with a programme that included the dispatch of more than half a million tons of stores a month from 80 ordnance depots and 30 ports, which were then shipped to 20 different destinations overseas. Britain may have become a supplicant at the American table, but through the mechanism of Lend-Lease, she certainly did not lack for resources while the war lasted.

Some branches of the British Army Staff were more successful than others in promoting liaison and collaboration between the two armies. In the vital field of intelligence, a critical decision to pool all information on enemy countries was taken as soon as the United States entered the war. Since the military intelligence given to American planning staffs on fundamental issues such as the size, deployment and reserves of enemy forces varied greatly from British estimates, it would have been virtually impossible for the British and Americans to work successfully together without reconciling such differences. This work required 'tact, patience and firmness in presenting British views', as well as a cooperative attitude from the American intelligence community, and it took time as well as 'mutual confidence and respect on both sides before the doors to complete collaboration were fully opened'.[56] Thus, it was not until October 1942 that there was no material difference between British and American intelligence estimates of German strength.[57] Over time, the Allies moved to a system where, although each intelligence service still carried out their own computations, the responsibility for the analysis of the German order of battle took place in London, while similar work on Japanese forces occurred in Washington. The British and Americans had thus moved towards 'complete integration' of their intelligence work in a manner unprecedented in military history.

The same was also true in the realm of airborne forces, where virtually complete integration was achieved. The interchange of ideas on this new form of warfare led to an agreed method of paratroop training for both armies, and ultimately to the creation of the First Allied Airborne Army, which was staffed jointly by British and American personnel. A similar result was achieved in the field of engineering, where both armies agreed to establish a combined stockpile for the vast array of equipment and stores that was required. This led to the 'complete integration of all aspects of supply of engineer stores from procurement to despatch', which resulted in the most efficient use of resources for both armies.[58]

The story was somewhat different when it came to the exchange of tactical and technical information in other branches and services. Although the volume of this work grew enormously after Pearl Harbor, the dissemination of British advice on tactics and training was not always welcomed. British officers found that 'The US Army was not prepared to accept pure theory from the British Army whom they regarded as singularly unsuccessful up to 1943', and that any influence had to be exerted on a 'very personal basis', as 'Personal experience and particularly first hand combat experience impressed them more deeply than encyclopaedic knowledge . . . They were a little proud about accepting new British ideas, and if they did accept them they quite rightly and usually successfully improved upon them.'[59] It was only by selecting officers for their 'personality, character and ability to mix well' that British ideas could gain any traction in American circles. Given the 'remarkable ignorance about each other' at the beginning of the war, it took a great deal of time and effort to create the machinery and 'the psychological atmosphere' in which effective exchanges of information could take place.[60]

Thus, it was not until 1943 that full liaison was established in many fields of work, but once achieved, 'there was a noticeably greater freedom in the exchange of training ideas'.[61] The sheer volume of the exchange of tactical and technical information that took place between the armies was extraordinary. British officers were attached to all of the important US army schools, with exchanges of students at the schools, the army and navy staff colleges, and the US Army Command and General Staff School at Leavenworth. The acceptance of British officers as 'directing staff' at Leavenworth was seen as a great step forward in promoting understanding between the two armies, although unfortunately, this important American gesture was not immediately reciprocated by the British staff college. But while the British Army in the UK had 'ample opportunity of getting to know its American ally . . . it was only through the medium of the few BAS officers at US schools and Boards that many Americans learnt anything about the British Army alongside which they were shortly destined to fight'.[62] Indeed, it might be argued that by the time the full programmes of liaison and exchange had been arranged in 1943, it was almost too late: many of the officers and combat troops of both armies who would fight in Europe had already been trained and sent to the United Kingdom.

Unfortunately, the level of collaboration and integration varied greatly in different areas. British methods of anti-aircraft defence met with a receptive audience in America, since the success of the British air defence during the Battle of Britain had 'made a deep impression' on their American counterparts,[63] and when

British Army Staff officers advised major changes to the layout
of American anti-aircraft defences in the continental United States,
their suggestions were readily accepted. However, similar attempts
to standardise methods and procedures in field artillery were not
so successful. The British did make an early attempt to persuade
the American Army to adopt the British 25-pounder field gun and
the 3.7 inch anti-aircraft gun (both of which proved to be excellent weapons), but the US Army had already made the decision
to equip its field artillery batteries with 105 mm guns, and 'neither
side ever convinced the other of the superior merits of their own
weapons'.[64] This was a major setback for true integration, since
had both armies been equipped with the same field and anti-aircraft
guns, it would have resulted in highly significant economies of
scale and much greater flexibility in the field. Even in tank and
anti-tank guns there was no common solution: the only guns that
were standardised between the two armies were the six-pounder
(57 mm) anti-tank gun and the 40 mm Bofors light anti-aircraft
gun.

Similarly, although both armies shared their experience in
armoured warfare freely, collaboration in the design of tanks did
not develop in the way that might have been imagined after the
signal success of the Lee/Grant and Sherman tanks. The fact was
that the American authorities now tended to see the British as
customers for rather than designers of armoured vehicles, since
the virtual failure of the British tank programme to provide the
army with decent armoured vehicles meant that the British Army
became increasingly reliant on American equipment. Nearly 28,000
US tanks and armoured vehicles were delivered to the British Army
and imperial forces by the end of the war, and the value of these
tanks and all their components and spare parts exceeded 200 million
dollars.[65] This enormous scale dwarfed the original orders of the
British Tank Mission back in the heady days of 1940. Such depend-
ency caused understandable anxiety at the War Office that the
British Army would become wholly reliant on the United States
for any future tank programme. Ultimately, both nations still went
their own way in tank and gun design, despite sharing a great deal
of technical and tactical knowledge. Opportunities for greater

collaboration were thus sometimes missed, with unfortunate consequences for the soldiers in the field.

The record of collaboration, cooperation and integration
achieved by the British Army Staff was thus mixed and varied
greatly between the many branches, arms and services that went
to make up the immensely complex machinery of the two armies.
Much depended on the personal connections between like-minded
British and American officers, and not surprisingly, if these were
not present, the two armies tended to go their own way. Yet
although its efforts were often lost in the noise of war, the achievements of the British Army Staff and those of the American
departments and staff that worked with it were nonetheless
profound. For the first time in military history, two armies had
attempted to collaborate as closely as possible during a conflict.
The astonishing fact remains that it was attempted at all.

One of the pre-eminent examples of the integration that could
take place between the two armies was the creation and development of COSSAC in 1943. This strangely named organisation grew
out of the need to develop detailed planning for the cross-Channel
attack. It had been agreed at the Casablanca conference to appoint
a Chief of Staff to push forward with this planning before the
eventual appointment of an Allied Supreme Commander who
would lead the operation. The Chief of Staff was to establish a
combined American and British staff to work on the vast amount
of detail required to mount a successful invasion. Since it was
assumed in early 1943 that the Supreme Commander, when
appointed, would be a British general, the British Lieutenant
General Frederick E. Morgan was appointed as interim Chief of
Staff, with Brigadier General R. W. Barker of the US Army as his
deputy. General Ismay presented Morgan with a file of papers
'some inches thick' (the result of the Combined Operations and
Combined Planners' work on the subject) and required him to
come up with an outline plan within 24 hours. The resulting memo
formed a basis for discussion with the Chiefs of Staff on 24 March
1943. When Morgan was later briefed by Brooke, the CIGS bluntly
stated, 'Well, there it is; it won't work, but you must bloody well

make it.'[66] Such has been the lot of many a staff officer throughout history, but Morgan was placed in the particularly invidious position of having to grow a headquarters and staff and formulate plans without the authority of an appointed commander. From the start, he was only too well aware of the difficulties this created. He was faced with the same challenge as the unfortunate Charles Gairdner, who had to coordinate the planning for Operation Husky. However, while Gairdner had struggled to cope with such problems, Morgan set about his task with real energy and vision. He christened his new organisation COSSAC (Chief of Staff Supreme Allied Commander), giving it the sense of permanence and authority that initially had been lacking.

Morgan had wanted to keep his staff as compact as possible, and planned to use the small but effective headquarters of Marshal Foch in 1918 as a model. He believed the Supreme Commander's headquarters should ideally be 'a really small body of selected officers who dealt with the major decisions on broad lines, the day-to-day work of the war being delegated completely to commanders of army groups'.[67] However, as the COSSAC planning continued, and the range of potential operations increased, so the numbers of staff involved grew far beyond those of Foch's tiny group. Morgan also drew inspiration from Eisenhower's integrated Allied Headquarters in the Mediterranean, and followed Eisenhower's lead in creating a properly combined staff of British and American officers. Initially, the work of COSSAC was grouped into three main branches: Operations (with navy, army and air sections, each of which had American and British components), Administrative (with American and British sections) and Intelligence (which was unified under a single British principal staff officer). In October 1943, the divisions along national lines were abolished and the headquarters was reorganised on purely functional lines, each branch becoming fused, with a single officer, whether British or American, at its head. The one area that was impossible to properly integrate remained supply, which, as Eisenhower had found in the Mediterranean, was simply too complex and difficult to achieve.[68]

This process of reorganisation and integration was the natural outcome of the increasing weight of American representation on the COSSAC staff, in respect of both numbers and ranks, by the autumn of 1943. At first, when the forces of the United States in Britain had been comparatively small, COSSAC had been predominantly British in character; but as the flow of troops across the Atlantic continued, so the balance between the allies adjusted. The reorganisation of COSSAC produced closer integration of effort between the American and British component staffs, and the 'elimination of national divisions' meant that COSSAC achieved a 'very real unity of aims and methods' in its work. Indeed, the sense of working on a common endeavour meant that close bonds of trust and loyalty grew up amongst members of COSSAC staff.

Morgan noticed some amusing differences between the national habits of his American and British officers. He found that there was a 'sharp divergence in eating habits', since the American officers had 'breakfast in the middle of the night, lunch half way through the morning and dinner at teatime', which meant that mealtimes could be staggered conveniently. However, this could also cause problems for the American officers 'when they found themselves . . . getting up American and going to bed British, which did not leave much interval for sleep'.[69] Morgan also noticed differences in the way that American and British officers responded to difficult problems. An American officer, once convinced that the course of action was correct, would respond enthusiastically:

> 'We will deliver what you demand up to not less than 110%. You bet. And as far your schedule, it's a cinch. The boys will be there a week ahead of time. This is right up our street' . . . Sure enough the dirt would begin to fly in prodigious quantities all over the place. The inevitable snags would be encountered. There would be a series of rousing reports, a certain number of individuals would cross the Atlantic at high priority and sure enough the goods would be delivered right on time at 100% of requirement.[70]

A British officer, by contrast, when confronted with the same problem, would first give 'a look of incredulous horror' and then ask:

'My dear old boy, is all this really necessary. Well if it really is, couldn't we do it just as well with half the bother. At any rate we can't get anywhere near the numbers you want, 90% of your figure would be the absolute limit. And as for time, I don't see how it can possibly be done in less than at least a week longer than you seem prepared to give us. If you insist we'll have a crack at it only don't expect much of a show. But we will do our best.' In the event of course it would happen exactly as required.[71]

Morgan's rather wry description of these differing reactions can almost be seen as a microcosm of the Allied strategic disagreements in the lead-up to the invasion of Normandy in 1944. While the Americans had enthusiastically promoted the idea of a cross-Channel attack, the British had cavilled and emphasised all of the difficulties involved, and yet by late 1943 both nations were working flat out to ensure that all the preparations for the operation were in place.

While COSSAC worked on a multitude of plans, covering many different eventualities, the planning for Overlord, the full-scale invasion of Europe, constituted its most vital and important work. Morgan and his staff prepared an initial appreciation for Operation Overlord with surprising swiftness, and a report was delivered to the Chiefs of Staff on 15 July 1943.[72] This was an outstanding piece of staff work, a model of clarity and vision that provided a blueprint for one of the greatest endeavours of military history. That it was produced by a properly integrated headquarters of soldiers, sailors and airmen drawn from the armed forces of both Britain and America was an apt demonstration of just how far the Anglo-American alliance had come in two short years.

The beaches north of Caen in Normandy were selected as the target for the invasion, with the intention of securing a beachhead that would enable further operations deep into France to be developed. The target date for the invasion was set as 1 May 1944. However, the number of divisions taking part in the assault landing was restricted to just three due to the limited number of landing craft available. Indeed, one of the most difficult problems for the COSSAC staff lay in the number of landing craft – not just for the initial landings but for the subsequent landing of follow-up formations and the maintenance of the entire force as it expanded in the beachhead. Once ashore and established, the Allied armies would thrust south- and south-westward with a view to destroying enemy forces, acquiring sites for airfields, and gaining depth for a turning movement into the Cotentin peninsula directed on Cherbourg. The capture of this important port would provide the supply necessary to deepen the bridgehead in order to establish additional airfields in the area south-east of Caen. It was estimated that within 14 days of the initial assault, Cherbourg should be taken and the bridgehead extended, by which time some 18 divisions would be ashore and 14 airfields would be operational to command the skies above Normandy.[73]

The entire plan was based on 'concentration of force and tactical surprise' and rested on a number of key assumptions. These included adequate training in amphibious assault for the naval forces, control of the air over the beaches, and a distinct limit on the number and quality of German reserves in France. Morgan also realised the importance of sustaining the forces once ashore, and emphasised that 'Unless adequate measures are taken to provide sheltered waters by artificial means, the operation will be at the mercy of the weather.' If these preconditions were met, he believed there was 'a reasonable prospect of success'.[74]

This bold plan was the fruit of many years of thought, combined with lessons from the experience of the Torch and Husky landings, but in some of its basic planning assumptions there lay the seeds of much controversy during the hard-fought campaign of 1944. In the summer of 1943, it was still reasonable to expect that the Germans were unlikely to stage a last-ditch defence of Normandy but would instead mount a fighting withdrawal in the face of the Allied invasion. Morgan's underlying assumption was that the Germans would then gather their strength and fight the decisive battle for France using all their skill in manoeuvre and armoured formations. Such optimism was still possible in the summer of 1943, and also guided Allied thinking in Italy, but by the time Overlord became a reality, it was only too clear that the Germans were unlikely to withdraw from any battle. This meant that the COSSAC planning assumptions about how far the Allies would progress over time were unrealistic, yet much of the plan, and in particular the capture of airfields, depended upon them.

Other assumptions of the COSSAC plan also fundamentally shaped the subsequent nature of the Allied campaign in Europe without any seemingly conscious decision by Allied leaders or commanders. The plan stated that it would 'simplify the development of the operation if formations of both nationalities take part in the initial assault. United States on the right, British on the left; any other arrangement is likely to lead to very great confusion'. The suggested command and control arrangements were also designed to ensure simplicity and clarity: command of the initial assault and operations up to the capture of Brittany or the establishment of a United States Army Group HQ would rest with the commander of the British–Canadian group.[75] Yet this was also a legacy of the British desire to command the operation in its entirety, which would have been appropriate in 1942 but was not in 1944. It was also stressed that 'except in an emergency' a British or American formation lower than a corps would not be placed under command of a different nationality. This was to ensure that the confusion of Torch was avoided. Given where the American and British forces were encamped in Britain, such a principle made perfect sense, yet it also had serious implications for the subsequent development of the campaign in Europe.

As Morgan later explained, 'the bland statement that the American Army would obviously leave England for Europe on the right of the British Army' was actually a big strategic decision, one that determined where each of the two armies would fight in the drive across Europe.[76] The original Bolero planning, which had quartered the American Army in the west of England, by inexorable logic determined the location of the armies in the Overlord assault and the subsequent campaign in Europe. The British, who would land on the left, would naturally take the northern approach, through the Low Countries and into Germany, which meant that the American armies had to be on the southern flank of the Allied drive. Yet the northern approach into Germany offered the potentially most decisive axis of advance, as well as access to all of the ports of northern Europe. In a meeting with his chiefs in November 1943, Roosevelt discussed the possible occupation of Germany and argued that:

> The United States should take northwest Germany. We can get our ships into such ports as Bremen and Hamburg, also Norway and Denmark, and we should go as far as Berlin. The Soviets could then take the territory to the east thereof. The United States should have Berlin. The British plan for the United States to have southern Germany, and he did not like it.[77]

As Marshall reminded him, the British proposals were based on the military considerations of Overlord. Von Moltke once pointed out that errors in deployment can rarely, if ever, be corrected, and the decision in 1942 to quarter the American Army in western Britain thus shaped the whole of the Allied campaign in Europe.

Yet the military balance between these two partners as they embarked on Overlord had changed irrevocably. In November 1943, at a meeting with his military chiefs, Roosevelt asked what the total forces were now available to the United States and Britain. The figures were astounding, particularly given the fact that the British had calculated just three years before that the United States would struggle to put six divisions in field.[78] The total of British and American forces expected to be available by January 1944 was:

Total forces
US 10,529,400
UK 3,822,000 plus 1,070,000 Dominion.

Overseas
US Army 2,550,000
US Navy 1,229,600[79]

One crucial aspect of these statistics was that the main strength of the United States was still at home and had not yet been deployed to the battle fronts. As Morgan realised, the US Army in Britain was only ever a vanguard of America's total strength. The real power of the US Army would only develop once the beachhead in France was established and the reserve divisions from the continental United States could take their place in the line. As Marshall later observed, the US had fought the campaigns in Tunisia and Italy with few troops 'in the shop window', which had left the British as very much the senior partner for most of these campaigns, with all the attendant frustrations involved for commanders like Patton and Clark.[80] These facts meant that in 1944, the British public, and even elements of the British Army, could still believe that the two armies were roughly equal in strength given the respective forces deployed in Britain. The fact that the British and American forces that went ashore on D-Day were comparable in strength continued this fiction, but while Britain had by this point reached the limit of her resources, the United States could claim she had 'not yet begun to fight'.*

This change in the balance of power between the two partners also meant that the Supreme Allied Commander for Overlord would now be an American, not a British officer as had been originally expected. Brooke, who had hoped to be nominated and indeed had been virtually promised the post by Churchill, now found, to his bitter disappointment, that he would have to continue in the vital yet exhausting and exasperating job of CIGS. Yet although the baton had passed to the United States, Roosevelt seemed unable or unwilling to nominate his choice for this vital position. Throughout the summer and autumn of 1943, Morgan pressed as hard as he could for the immediate appointment of a commander for Overlord. He knew that many vital decisions could only be taken by the Supreme Commander with the full authority of the Combined Chiefs of Staff behind him. He complained in one letter to General Jacob Devers, then the US Commanding General, European Theater of Operations, that it seemed he had to 'function without a Commander . . . indefinitely. While I hate the sight of the whole of this business, I am completely at a loss to suggest anything better, short of course

---

* This was John Paul Jones's famous retort when called upon to surrender by the captain of HMS *Serapis* during a naval engagement in the American War of Independence.

of appointing the great man himself, which appears to be utterly impossible.'[81]

By September 1943, it appeared that the matter was more or less settled. It was expected that Eisenhower would return to the United States to take over the role of US Army Chief of Staff from Marshall, who would in turn take command of Overlord, with General Bernard Montgomery as his British deputy. Eisenhower's place as Allied Commander in the Mediterranean would be taken by General Alexander.[82] Churchill was now alive to the difficulties that this hiatus in command was creating, but even though he barraged Roosevelt with pleas for an immediate decision and subsequent announcement, the President stayed his hand. When whispers about Marshall's impending appointment reached the American press, they had a field day with the information, but the rumours were not confirmed.[83] Throughout October 1943, Churchill continued to press Roosevelt to announce the decision, but by the end of the month, the President admitted that he would not be able to make Marshall available immediately. As ever, it was Dill who was able to provide the inside story and help the rather confused British understand what was going on in Washington. After a talk with Marshall, Dill explained that the President, as well as 'many highly placed Americans', feared

> that if Marshall were to disappear to England and Eisenhower were replaced by Alexander and nothing under American leadership happened in Europe for some six months the effect on American public opinion would be serious. Marshall's disappearance from the American public eye would tend to confirm fear that he was being kicked upstairs, this with removal of Eisenhower would create strong public urge to ease off in Europe and turn 'full bore' to the Pacific[84]

The episode provided an interesting contrast to the received wisdom that it was the British who were 'sticky' about Operation Overlord. While the British had presented every difficulty and delayed the operation for as long as possible, they now pressed for the necessary steps to ensure that it was a success. For Britain,

there could be nothing more important than the liberation of
Europe, but for the American public there had always been two
wars: one in Europe and one in the Pacific. Commanding Overlord
was considered a demotion for Marshall in the eyes of the American
public, and even in late 1943, Roosevelt and Marshall still had to
contend with the large body of public opinion that favoured
the Pacific war. It also appeared that Roosevelt, the true author of the
'Germany First' strategy, was baulking at the final political decision
necessary to make the plan a reality.

The fact was that Marshall, with his deep understanding of both
the American Army and the political shoals of Washington, had
made himself indispensable to Roosevelt. And so the days dragged
on and Roosevelt did not make a clear-cut decision. It was only at
the last minute, on 13 December 1943, that he decided he simply
could not spare Marshall and nominated Eisenhower for the
Overlord command instead. Thus, Brooke and Marshall both shared
the bitter disappointment of having the command they ardently
desired snatched away from them for political reasons. Even the
timing of the announcements caused numerous difficulties, given
the need for both Churchill and Roosevelt to be seen to appoint
their commanders. It was not until 24 December that Eisenhower's
appointment was announced by Roosevelt in a radio broadcast.

Eisenhower, who had never expected to take on the role, thus
became the Supreme Allied Commander for Overlord almost by
accident rather than design. Yet through his hard apprenticeship as
the Allied commander for Torch in Sicily and Italy, he had learned
exactly what the job entailed. In September 1943, Lord Louis
Mountbatten had asked Eisenhower for advice before he took up
his post as Allied Supreme Commander in South East Asia. In a
detailed memorandum, Eisenhower gave his friend sound and clear
advice on the role and responsibilities of an Allied Supreme
Commander. He explained that the real basis for Allied unity of
command was to be found:

> in the earnest cooperation of the senior officers assigned to an allied
> theater. Since cooperation, in turn, implies such things as selfless-
> ness, devotion to a common cause, generosity in attitude and mutual

Crisis at Salerno.

Alexander, Clark and McCreery walk along the beach at Salerno on 15 September 1943. The outcome of the Allied landings still seemed in doubt when this picture was taken.

Supreme Command or war by committee?

enhower, Tedder, Alexander id Cunningham in Algiers, pril 1943. Behind them are old Macmillan, Walter Bedell iith and two British officers.

'Buffalo Bill' and Clark's 'good telephone operator'.

Rear-Admiral Troubridge, General Lucas and General Penney discuss matters on HMS *Bulolo* during the Anzio landings, 22 January 1944. Relations between Lucas and Penney were never good and deteriorated under pressure.

Training.

Guards NCOs being instructed in the use of the 'bazooka', the US anti-tank rocket launcher, in Italy. The Italian campaign more closely resembled a 'tug of war' between the Allies than effective co-operation.

Anzio.

Relations between British and American troops were never better than in the desperate crises of the Anzio fighting.

xander and Truscott
cuss the next move,
March 1944. Truscott
k over command of
Corps during the
io battle and proved
self one of the most
pable and effective
erican commanders
of the war.

Firepower.

he bombardment of Cassino, 15 March 1943. The town's destruction proved counter-productive.
remaining German defenders managed to frustrate the advance of the 2nd New Zealand Division
the tangle of rubble and wreckage. The ruins of the town and the monastery of Monte Cassino
would not be finally 'liberated' until 18 May 1944.

Another valley, another mountain.

US soldiers of the 370th Infantry Regiment march through Prato, 9 April 1945. When this image was ta
the campaign in Italy was almost over, yet it seems to sum up the experience of the Italian campai

The Great Crusade.

Eisenhower speaks with the soldiers of Company E, 502nd Parachute Infantry Regiment, at Greenham Common on the evening of 5 June 1944. Eisenhower later saluted each plane as it took off.

Grim faced GIs board the landing craft which will take them to France. The American 'invasion' of Britain was about to end and the invasion of France was about to begin.

Command.

Patton, Eisenhower and Bradley are shown here in Bastogne, Belgium, after the Battle of the Bulge. The complex mix of friendship and rivalry between these three American commanders was a major influence on the campaign in Europe.

Liberation.

A British Sherman tank is mobbed under a jubilant crowd during the liberation of Brussels, 3 September 1944. The Allies had just advanced far further and faster than expected but had effectively reached the limit of their ability to supply their forces.

The War in Germany.

A British sergeant during the battle for Geilenkirchen, one of the first German towns to fall to a combined American and British assault, 5 December 1944.

An American landing craft under fire at St Goar during the Rhine crossing, 22 March 1945.

American tanks and infantry move into a smoke-filled street in Wernberg, 22 April 1945. British and American troops met pockets of stubborn German resistance until the very end of the war.

The Final Act.

Montgomery accepts the surrender of all German forces in Northern Germany, May 1945. Montgomery understood the vital importance of the act of surrender. This image set British perceptions of the victory in 1945. The final surrender instrument was signed by Bedell Smith on behalf of Eisenhower in Rheims.

confidence, it is easy to see that actual unity in an allied command depends directly upon the individuals in the field . . . It will therefore never be possible to say the problem of establishing unity in any allied command is ever completely solved. This problem involves the human equation and must be met day by day. Patience, tolerance, frankness, absolute honesty in all dealings, particularly with all persons of the opposite nationality, and firmness, are absolutely essential.[85]

Eisenhower now understood that the role and effectiveness of a Supreme Commander rested almost entirely on trust and personal relationships, and warned Mountbatten that the senior commanders of the army, navy and air forces in the theatre would 'each have a great degree of independence in his own field' and would almost certainly communicate directly to their own heads of service and their own heads of government'. He recognised that the job of the Supreme Commander was to strive for *mutual respect and confidence among the group of seniors making up the allied command*. All of us are human and we like to be favourably noticed by those above us and even by the public.'[86] He also realised that while a Supreme Commander was 'not really a commander' in the sense of commanding an army or fleet, he was also not just a 'figurehead or a nonentity. He is in a very definite sense the Chairman of a Board . . . he must execute those duties firmly, wisely and without any question as to his own authority and his own responsibility.'[87] In listing the attributes required of a Supreme Commander, Eisenhower had unconsciously described the virtues most people actually saw in him, and his personal memo to Mountbatten was clear proof that no one else understood the role as intimately – or as well – as he did. He was indeed the right man, perhaps the only man, for the job.

Eisenhower also explained that the senior commanders who operated under the Supreme Commander were not chosen by him but were named by the Combined Chiefs of Staff. The authority of the Supreme Commander, which had 'no legal basis', could 'be wrecked at any moment not only by dissatisfaction on the part of either Government, but by internal bickering'.[88] Although he was an American, almost all of his immediate subordinates were British. Air Chief Marshal Arthur Tedder was appointed as his deputy commander, 'on account of the great part the Air will play in this operation', a successful appointment that maintained the close relationship the two men had forged during the North African and Italian campaigns. Admiral Bertram Ramsay was placed in charge of the naval effort due to his 'unique experience': he had not only worked on most of the Allied amphibious operations in the Mediterranean but had also masterminded the evacuation of the BEF from Dunkirk in 1940. Air Chief Marshal Sir Trafford Leigh-Mallory, who unlike the other two had not been part of Eisenhower's Mediterranean team, would command the air forces for Overlord.[89]

While General Omar Bradley had returned to England in the summer of 1943 to prepare the US First Army for the invasion and thus had long been the preferred candidate to become the commander of the US 12th Army Group once it was activated on the continent, the nomination of his British counterpart was a matter for some debate. Churchill had not made up his mind between Bernard Montgomery and Harold Alexander, but Brooke most certainly had. He was convinced that only Montgomery had the military judgement, determination and skill to command the British liberation army successfully. Eisenhower was equally convinced that he wanted Alexander, with whom he had worked successfully in both Africa and Italy. With Churchill recovering from illness in Marrakesh, Brooke was able to influence the British War Cabinet in Montgomery's favour, and it was eventually decided that Montgomery would be a better choice than Alexander based on 'their military merits for this job'. Churchill admitted that 'Eisenhower would have chosen Alexander' but explained to Roosevelt that 'Montgomery is a public hero and will give confidence among our people'.[90] If the weight of American public opinion had helped to keep Marshall in Washington, British public opinion had played its part in giving Montgomery command of the 21st Army Group of 2nd British and 1st Canadian Armies.

The one place where Eisenhower was able to choose his man lay in the matter of his Chief of Staff. He was determined to have Bedell Smith, his indispensable right-hand man, which meant that

Morgan had to be shunted from the post he had done so much to create and define. Eisenhower finally took command of Overlord on 17 January 1944, but COSSAC was not exactly disbanded: its 320 officers and 600 other ranks formed the nucleus of Eisenhower's new Supreme Headquarters, Allied Expeditionary Force. Yet although COSSAC had developed a plan for the invasion of Europe and formed a core headquarters staff, much remained to be done. Eisenhower and Montgomery both came to the same conclusions about the outline plan: the number of beaches was too small and the weight of troops to be put ashore on the first day too weak. More beaches and troops would have to be added to the initial assault, which therefore required yet more landing craft. Morgan had foreseen these problems, but only Eisenhower, with his full authority as Allied Supreme Commander, could request – and receive – the additional resources from the Combined Chiefs of Staff. These changes not only meant that Overlord had to be postponed until June 1944, but also that landing craft had to be removed from the Pacific theatre and extra production developed in the United States.

Preparations gathered even greater speed and momentum during the early months of 1944, which saw Britain transformed into 'a huge storehouse, workshop, arsenal, armed camp and aircraft carrier'.[91] Tens of thousands of aircraft and millions of soldiers had flowed into Britain, while thousands of ships of every type and size were anchored in every port and estuary. Rationing, the blackout, the most extensive conscription of men and women of any of the combatant nations, along with wartime shortages, all combined with the massive influx of British, American and many other Allied nations' soldiers, sailors and airmen to give the impression that Britain had become an 'india-rubber island' that had been stretched to its maximum capacity.[92]

Although Montgomery's appointment had been announced as commander of the 'British and Canadian Expeditionary Group' of armies, Eisenhower kept to the original COSSAC conception: Montgomery would act as the overall land commander for the amphibious assault and the subsequent campaign until such time as he decided to activate the Supreme Headquarters Allied

Expeditionary Force (SHAEF) on the continent.[93] Montgomery was thus in overall charge of the development of the plan for the establishment and development of the beachhead. Characteristically, he disparaged the original COSSAC plans, calling them 'hardly a sound operation of war', and instead formed his own strategy for the invasion and beachhead.[94] In fact, he developed his 'master plan' with surprising speed, delegating all of the staff work to his Chief of Staff de Guingand and his subordinates. Once it had been approved by Eisenhower, on 21 January 1944, Montgomery saw his primary role during the build-up to the invasion as visiting as many of his commanders and troops as possible, both British and American, to energise and inspire them, just as he had done with the Eighth Army before the Battle of Alamein two years before.[95] De Guingand's development of an efficient and effective staff system within the Eighth Army now paid dividends, as he thrashed out the details of a much larger and more complex plan. In view of the fact that the US 12th Army Group would be activated at some point during the campaign, de Guingand did not create an integrated Anglo-American headquarters, but rather developed two parallel staffs so that the US army group could begin its functions as rapidly as possible when the time came.[96] Although de Guingand was in effect fulfilling the role of both deputy commander and chief of staff, Montgomery characteristically refused any suggestion that he should be promoted to lieutenant general.

As the Allied armies engaged in their vast preparations, relations between the senior land commanders, Montgomery, Eisenhower and Bradley, had never been better. Montgomery visited many American units, giving them the same pep talk he used with British units. He, along with all the other Allied commanders, helped to paint a picture of an unstoppable Allied effort. He also took the time to visit British factories and docks to encourage everyone to do their bit for the invasion. He confided to his diary on 20 February:

> In my journeying around the country I am seen by the civil popu-
> lation; their re-action is immediate, and great enthusiasm results
> from my visits. I have been asked to address the railwaymen, the
> dockers and the stevedores, the workers in the big factories, and so

on . . . The result of all this is that the nation is beginning *to look to me* to lead them to victory.[97]

While he understood some of the pitfalls of such public popularity, and knew that he was 'bound to make enemies whatever I do', Montgomery was now both a representative and a national symbol of the British war effort.[98]

Nonetheless, he had produced a clear and workable plan for the coming campaign, while de Guingand and the staff of 21st Army Group had laboured hard to refine and check its details. Montgomery held a series of conferences at his headquarters – St Paul's School in London, where he had once been a pupil – to ensure that every senior officer involved understood his master plan. The first of these included a two-day exercise, Thunderclap, with all the general officers of the four field armies, which began on 7 April 1944. Montgomery's clear exposition outlined the Overlord plan and the role of each of the armies. He explained that the First US Army was:

(a) to assault astride the Carentan estuary.
(b) to capture Cherbourg as quickly as possible.
(c) east of Carentan, to develop operations southwards towards
    St Lo in conformity with the advance of Second British Army.
After the area Cherbourg-Gaumont-Vire-Avranches has been
captured, the Army will be directed southwards with the object of
capturing Rennes and then the ports of Nantes and St Nazaire.[99]

The Second British Army would meanwhile drive south from Caen to capture airfield sites and work 'to protect the eastern flank of First US Army while the latter is capturing Cherbourg. In its subsequent operations the Army will pivot on its left and offer a strong front against enemy movement towards the lodgement area from the east.'[100]

Montgomery emphasised the need both to drive inland rapidly and to secure space for administrative development and airfields. Much of his plan for the development of the lodgement area was predicated on the need to secure Caen on the first day through bold and vigorous action. With Caen in British hands, the wide-open plain to the south of the city not only provided good 'tank country' to mount a major armoured threat but also made a perfect site for numerous airfields to develop the Allied air effort to its maximum.

With the two assault armies ashore and established, the First Canadian Army would reinforce the area of the Second British Army, while in the American sector, the US Third Army would land with the task of clearing the Brittany peninsula and opening its ports. Montgomery then explained how he envisaged that operations would be developed over time, and used a modified version of the COSSAC phase lines to show how the armies would press forward over the first 90 days of the campaign. He projected his usual confidence in explaining that 'Given close cooperation between the air forces and the land armies, I do not see how the enemy can stop us from developing the operations as we plan – if only we can get a good lodgement in the first four days and capture Cherbourg quickly.'[101] Unfortunately, his confident predictions of the rapid expansion of the lodgement area would cause much trouble and controversy during the campaign itself.

By early June 1944, the enormous military machine of Overlord, comprising millions of men and women, was ready: everyone and everything now waited for the order to go. Eisenhower had moved down to a concealed trailer in the grounds of Southwick Park, near Portsmouth, the site of Ramsay's headquarters. After a month of perfect weather, however, Group Captain Stagg, SHAEF's chief meteorologist, had to report that conditions were changing for the worse. With the date of the invasion looming, Eisenhower confided to his diary that 'no one who does not have to bear the specific and direct responsibility of making the final decision as to what to do can understand the intensity of these burdens'.[102] That the decision to launch the invasion was left in his hands now seems even more remarkable than it was at the time. Neither Hitler nor Stalin would have allowed a mere military man to make such a momentous judgement replete with such enormous consequences. It is also hard to imagine any contemporary politician surrendering this sort of responsibility into another's hands. Yet both Roosevelt and

Churchill, along with their military chiefs, understood that it had to be a military decision untrammelled by extraneous political considerations. The fact that Eisenhower was left to give the green light to launch the invasion was perhaps the measure of the Anglo-American alliance. Eisenhower's position, and his decision, depended not on personal rivalries, jealousies or competition between the Allies, but on trust.

On Saturday 3 June, in the face of continued reports of bad weather that would last until at least the 5th, Eisenhower was faced with no choice but to provisionally postpone the invasion for 24 hours. At 04.15 hours on 4 June, he held another meeting of his senior commanders and asked their advice. While the airmen were against it because air support would be impossible in bad weather, and Ramsay counselled caution given the poor sea state, Montgomery wanted to go ahead. Eisenhower simply remarked, 'The question is just how long can you hang this operation on the end of a limb and just let it hang there? . . . I am quite positive we must give the order. I don't like it but there it is . . . I don't see how we can do anything else.'[103] It was decided to go ahead on 6 June, subject to confirmation the following morning. Thus it was not until 04.15 hours on the 5th that Eisenhower was confronted with the final necessity of making the decision: either the invasion went ahead or the entire operation would have to be postponed for at least a month. Stagg was able to suggest that there might be a narrow window of better weather on 6 June, but conditions would still not be ideal. As Eisenhower sat and pondered the matter for what seemed to him to be thirty seconds but which Bedell Smith later recorded as five minutes, he held the fate of the alliance in his hands. When he made his final decision with the words 'Okay – let's go', and the room emptied in a blink of an eye, the Anglo-American alliance had never been closer or stronger.[104]

12

The Great Crusade

As the thousands of ships in the greatest invasion force ever assembled began their journey across the English Channel, the outcome of the endeavour remained very much in doubt. No one could know for certain whether the five Allied assaulting divisions would succeed in getting ashore and establishing a beachhead, or be thrown back into the sea.

At one of the last full briefings of the plan, Churchill exclaimed: 'Gentlemen, I am hardening toward this enterprise', a comment that struck Eisenhower 'with peculiar force' as he realised that it was only now, with just weeks before Overlord took place, that the Prime Minister believed the operation might work.[1] Just hours before the invasion, Brooke confided to his diary :

> It is very hard to believe that in a few hours the cross Channel invasion starts! I am very uneasy about the whole operation. At best it will fall so very far short of the expectation of the bulk of the people, namely all those who know nothing of its difficulties. At the worst it may well be the most ghastly disaster of the whole war. I wish to God it were safely over.[2]

The wellsprings of Churchill and Brooke's anxiety were obvious. Their personal experience of the power of the German army to inflict grievous losses dated back to the Great War. Even in this war, the examples of British disasters at the hands of the German army were legion. At Salerno, the ferocious German counter-attack had created crisis; just a few months earlier, the long stalemate at Anzio had cost thousands of casualties for little result. Perhaps the memory that loomed largest in their minds was the Somme. If D-Day became a 'ghastly disaster' like the first day of the Somme, the result would snuff out Allied hopes of successfully ending the war.

D-Day did not become a 'Somme by sea' as Brooke feared, and only on Omaha Beach did the events of 6 June 1944 come close to approximating the carnage of 1 July 1916. Almost everything that could go wrong did go wrong at Omaha. The impressive aerial and naval bombardments that preceded the landings did not suppress the German defenders, who remained safe in their bunkers. The heavy sea state not only made many of the troops seasick but also meant that most of the supporting DD tanks foundered offshore.* Coming ashore into an inferno of German fire, the leading waves of the US 1st and 29th Divisions suffered 90 per cent casualties. As one early report claimed, 'to one like myself who saw the terrain only a few days later . . . I could come to but one conclusion. Those bluffs were captured and those exits opened solely through the plain undaunted heroism of those infantry teams of the 1st and 29th Divisions and their attached engineer units.'[3] At the cost of 3,000 casualties, through inspired leadership and bravery, as well as the full support of the US Navy, the soldiers on Omaha managed to claw out a narrow beachhead. German resistance on the other beaches was patchier but could still be fierce: on Sword Beach, the 2nd South Lancashires landed directly opposite a German strongpoint and suffered 250 casualties within a few minutes.[4]

By the end of the day, success had been achieved on all five beaches – Utah, Omaha, Gold, Juno and Sword – and some troops had advanced up to eight miles inland. At the cost of some 10,000 casualties, over 130,000 troops had been successfully landed in a masterpiece of naval staff planning and preparation, while a further 23,000 men had dropped from the skies.[5] Even with the terrible losses of Omaha, the success of D-Day had exceeded almost all expectations, with perhaps one exception. The British 3rd Division had been expected to drive forward and seize the key city of Caen,

---

* DD stood for 'duplex drive'. These were Sherman tanks fitted with a large canvas buoyancy screen and propellers to drive them through the water.

but its leading troops had been blocked just a few miles short of the outskirts. The early capture of Caen had been fundamental to the development of Montgomery's plan, and the failure to take the city was to have serious repercussions as the Normandy campaign developed.

One of the key reasons for the Allied success was the lacklustre German response. The Luftwaffe had withdrawn the vast majority of its remaining planes from France while the Kriegsmarine was unable to make any effective response in the face of the Allied naval might. This left only the German army to defend the coast of France, but it suffered from a fractured command system that split responsibility between Rommel and Field Marshal Gerd von Rundstedt as commander of the Armies in the West. The two men had indulged in a long argument over how to best defend France, which eventually resulted in Hitler taking direct personal control of the reserve panzer divisions. Confusion, the intervention of the Allied air forces, and the attendant hold-up in gaining Hitler's approval meant that none of these vital armoured divisions saw action on D-Day itself. The only panzer formation in the area, 21st Panzer Division, spent much of the day in delay and disorder. Late in the day, its battle groups mounted an attack that suffered heavy casualties, and although some troops reached the coast, they were eventually ordered back to Caen. The Germans had responded to the invasion with all the frailties of a divided coalition, whilst the Allies came ashore with the unified strength of their many nationalities. The sixth of June 1944 was the longest day not for the Allies but for the Germans.

The results of D-Day may have exceeded expectations, but what ensued did not follow anyone's script. As the Allies continued to pour men, equipment and supplies ashore in the 'battle of the build-up', the Germans pushed troops forward to contain the Allied toehold in Europe. The stage was set for one of the most intense and attritional battles of the war.

Although both Allied armies were animated by a single plan, they fought effectively separate battles in Normandy. The city of Caen was the first major objective for the British Second Army, while

Bradley's First US Army was to capture the Cherbourg peninsula. The two armies thus fought side by side but the focus of their activity was on either flank. There was no mixing up, no confusion of US and British units under Montgomery's gaze. The greatest level of contact between the two armies was through liaison officers and headquarters staff at the army level: the combat units did not mix. This fact helps to explain the misunderstandings that developed between the armies during the campaign, as it was easy for each to feel that it was carrying the burden of the fighting alone, when the reality was that all the Allied armies were intensively engaged throughout the campaign.

Yet although the two armies fought separately, their efforts were combined through the exercise of Montgomery's overall role as land forces commander. He, at least, saw the evolving battle as a whole and planned operations to utilise the strength of both armies. In essence, he envisaged that the British Second Army would operate to suck in the majority of German reserves opposite its front, which would draw German resources and attention away from the American front and allow Bradley's army to seize the Cherbourg peninsula quickly. Montgomery's broad plan was simple but ensured that there would be none of the drift and dissipation of effort that had afflicted operations in Italy. Yet the greatest controversy surrounding the Normandy battles still swirls around Montgomery's consistent claims that the entire campaign worked out exactly according to his master plan.

One of Montgomery's considerable strengths as a commander was his 'projection of personality', in which he portrayed himself to his troops as a confident, expert commander whose plans always succeeded. As commander of the Eighth Army and 21st Army Group, he had repeatedly told his soldiers that he would not commit them to battle without a foolproof plan that ensured their lives would not be wasted. Given the long run of defeats and reverses the British Army suffered during the early years of the war, Montgomery's projection of personality – a subject he had first lectured on at staff college in the twenties – had considerable psychological benefits for the men under his command. He continued to project this air of confidence and determination throughout the Normandy battles, but this time there was another audience he had to win over. Montgomery had previously fought all his battles under the command of General Alexander, who had given him virtually free rein in his conduct of operations. In effect, Alexander's role as coalition commander had insulated Montgomery from many of the demands and potential frustrations of operating in a broader arena where the actions of land, sea and air forces had to be coordinated within an alliance. But Montgomery's behaviour during the planning for Sicily was an unfortunate harbinger of the difficulties that arose during Normandy and beyond. He had many strengths as a commander, but his abrasive egocentric personality was a real limitation in this new environment, where he was no longer acting as a single army commander who could devote all his time to the troops under his command, but was instead fulfilling a much wider role as land forces commander under Eisenhower. This time, there was a much broader constituency, including Eisenhower and SHAEF, who needed to know what was happening.

Montgomery did not change his command style or the focus of his efforts. He moved across to France as quickly as possible and established his famous 'Tac HQ'. This was a small mobile headquarters, while the main headquarters of 21st Army Group remained in Britain for much of the campaign. This meant that even some of Montgomery's key staff officers were badly informed about the course of the battle. While Montgomery did visit Bradley and his army commanders during the campaign, he refused to visit Eisenhower, nor did he attend the major SHAEF conferences to which he was invited. In his stead, he sent the affable and well-liked de Guingand, who became an essential link between SHAEF and Montgomery. While such behaviour undoubtedly helped Montgomery maintain his legendary grip over operations, it was counterproductive in his new role as 21st Army Group commander. He also kept in much closer touch with Brooke than with Eisenhower. While he admitted to some of his worries in his letters to the CIGS, he did not do the same in his less frequent and less informative letters to Eisenhower. Equally, when Eisenhower visited Normandy, he stayed with his old friend Bradley rather than with

Montgomery. Ike thoroughly enjoyed living like a soldier and watching Bradley's battle unfold. He did meet with Montgomery, but the visits were relatively brief. Montgomery remained in his sparse Tac Headquarters, from which he had banned all unnecessary visitors, and his effective isolation from SHAEF contributed to the breakdown in understanding that developed between himself and Eisenhower during the campaign.

However, the first major spat of the Normandy campaign, known as the 'airfields controversy', did not begin as an Anglo-American quarrel but developed from the mistrust and rivalry between Britain's air commanders and Montgomery. The delay in capturing Caen and the land to the south-east that had been earmarked for airfields caused real disquiet amongst the air commanders, who saw the development of airfields in France as fundamental to the maintenance of air supremacy over the battlefield.

While Montgomery had had a number of arguments with Air Chief Marshal Sir Trafford Leigh-Mallory, Commander-in-Chief of the Allied Expeditionary Air Forces, before D-Day, both men recognised the need to work closely together. Indeed, Leigh-Mallory became a consistent advocate of the need to provide as much support as possible to the ground forces in Normandy. Unfortunately, personal relations between Arthur 'Mary' Coningham, the commander of the British 2nd Tactical Air Force, and Montgomery had broken down long before D-Day. Coningham believed that Montgomery had stolen the credit for the successes in the Western Desert, which had put the achievements and efforts of his Desert Air Force in the shade. He had consequently developed a bitter personal hatred for Montgomery, while at the same time he had little if any respect for Leigh-Mallory as his commander. Arthur Tedder, now acting as Eisenhower's Deputy Commander, was also dismissive of Leigh-Mallory but had formed a close relationship with Coningham during the desert war. Tedder had also developed a strong dislike of Montgomery after the interservice feuding over Sicily, and no longer trusted the commander of 21st Army Group. A tendency developed in which Tedder and Coningham froze Leigh-Mallory out of decision-making, yet Leigh-Mallory was the only commander Montgomery would communicate with on a regular basis.[6] This situation meant that the chain of command for air operations was troubled from the start and riven with personal agendas, which spilled over into the arguments concerning the development of airfields in Normandy.

Montgomery was certainly in no doubt that dominance of the air was vital to the overall success of the campaign, and he pressed this point to his army commanders and encouraged them to work closely with their air counterparts. Before the invasion, he had emphasised the importance of developing airfields in France as soon as possible: 'As we secure airfields, and good areas for making airfields, so we get increased air support, and so everything becomes easier. It is very important that the area to the SE of Caen should be secured as early as Second Army can manage.'[7] The flat plain south-east of Caen offered the perfect location for numerous airfields, but with a tenacious German defence making the capture of the city impossible, let alone the ground to the south, the plans for the establishment of airfields were bound to go awry. As von Moltke had usefully pointed out: 'No plan of operations extends with certainty beyond the first encounter with the enemy's main strength.'[8] While Montgomery and Eisenhower undoubtedly understood this, it transpired that the air chiefs regarded the forecasts and phase lines given before D-Day more as 'solemn promises' than the estimates they really were, and were no longer prepared to trust Montgomery.[9]

Montgomery's insistence, both at the time and post-war, that the entire battle had progressed according to his plan was not only infuriating to his critics, but also drew the focus away from his genuine skill as an operational commander. He was at the height of his powers as a battlefield commander during the Normandy campaign. He exerted his legendary grip over his formations – British, Canadian and American – while adjusting and modifying his plans with the constant aim of maintaining balance (never allowing the Germans to cause a major setback) and always wrestling to maintain the initiative and set the tempo of events so that the battle would eventually swing the Allies' way. Few, if any, other contemporary Allied generals would have been able to cope with the intense pressures of the Normandy campaign as expertly and successfully as he did. In this sense, whether Montgomery altered his plans (which he most certainly did) or whether the campaign shaped up in exactly the way he planned (which it did not) was virtually irrelevant: it was his constant adaptation of his master plan that actually ensured that the German commanders were left with no real opportunity to turn the battle in their favour. Unfortunately, Montgomery's overly optimistic reports to Eisenhower infuriated the air commanders and eventually disturbed the Supreme Commander himself. Meanwhile, the air commanders misread the reality of the fighting in Normandy and became voluble in their recriminations about Montgomery's failure to capture the ground they saw as vital but which could only be a tactical objective for the troops on the ground. In this way the rather theoretical, and in the event unrealistic, phase lines that had been developed before the invasion became the sticking point and focus of controversy that caused real damage to the Anglo-American alliance.

While the COSSAC planners and Montgomery had both envisaged that once the Allies landed, the Germans would mount an orderly withdrawal to the line of the River Seine to fight the decisive battle for France on ground of their own choosing, the Germans simply did not match these expectations. Once they recovered from the initial surprise and shock of the invasion, they fought for every yard of ground just as they had in Italy. Over the first few days, the Allied armies were able to link up all five beaches into a firm lodgement area, and as far as both Montgomery and Bradley were concerned, progress had been satisfactory. On 9 June, Montgomery identified a gap in the rapidly solidifying German front and, in one of his boldest moves, attempted to slip the 7th Armoured Division behind the German front lines to cut off the Panzer Lehr Division. Unfortunately, this rapid advance came to grief in the town of Villers Bocage on 13 June, when the lead elements of the British division were shot up by Michael Wittman's small unit of heavy Tiger tanks. As further German reinforcements from the 2nd Panzer Division arrived, General George Erskine decided to withdraw his 7th Armoured Division from their exposed position with the approval of his corps commander, General Gerard Bucknall.[10] This setback was disappointing when the prospects of success had appeared so favourable, and the result was that the Germans were able to contain the British in their narrow beachhead for the present.

As the battle for Normandy intensified, the air commanders became increasingly concerned about the schedule of airfield construction. By 14 June, only two landing strips had been prepared out of the target of five airfields in the British sector. Although a further eight strips were in the process of construction, the air commanders became alarmed that the battle was not progressing in the manner they had hoped. On 14 June, at a meeting of the air commanders, Coningham claimed that 'there was an element of crisis in the central sector', while Tedder warned that the situation might develop into 'a dangerous crisis'. The army liaison officers at the meeting certainly did not share this interpretation, but nor were they able to convince the air chiefs that their fears were misplaced. Although the territorial gains around Caen had been disappointing, and the promising 'hook' around Villers Bocage had come to grief, both Allied armies were still making progress. There is no question that Montgomery had hoped to extend the lodgement area on his eastern flank more deeply, but his seeming inability to capture Caen did not necessarily mean that his general plan had failed or that the Allied beachhead was in crisis. However, two days later, Coningham thundered that 'He would like the Army to keep in mind what they had planned and where they had planned to be by D+10, and to admit that the plan had failed. He thought that nothing was to be gained by the Army saying that all was well, and that a greater sense of urgency was needed.'[11] Coningham was clearly angered by Montgomery's confident reports, yet ironically, the air commanders' focus on phase lines was almost a throwback to the Great War obsession with ground. Montgomery could not afford to throw men into attacks simply to capture territory. His wider operational concern had to be that Allied activity maintained sufficient tempo to ensure that Rommel could not build up his forces to mount a full-scale counter-stroke against the Allied lodgement area.

There was no question that the eastern flank of the lodgement was cramped and congested and grew more so daily as more and more troops, supplies and munitions arrived. However, at the moment that Montgomery had planned to mount a major assault – Operation Epsom – to push around Caen to the west, the 'great storm' of 19–21 June hit the Normandy coast. This was the worst summer Channel storm for 60 years and it might have wrecked the Allied campaign in Normandy entirely. As it was, the storm destroyed the American Mulberry harbour at Omaha Beach and severely damaged the British one at Arromanches. While some American observers were highly critical of the British concept of artificial harbours, believing them to be a waste of resources and manpower, in fact they were vital during the storm. Thousands of small craft that otherwise would have been wrecked sheltered in the lee of the Mulberry harbour at Arromanches. Just as Morgan had predicted, without the harbours the Allies would have been entirely at the mercy of the weather and might well have lost the majority of the small craft vital for unloading supplies across the open beaches. Had the Allies invaded Normandy without the artificial harbours, the ravages of the great storm might have finished the invasion altogether. As it was, the unloading of supplies was drastically reduced, which put a major brake on Allied plans and progress.[12] However, the pressure for results and the impatience with the seeming deadlock in Normandy during July grew to such an extent that almost everyone seemed to have forgotten that the great storm caused at least a week of disruption and delay while also giving the Germans their best chance for turning the situation to their advantage.

Eisenhower sent a letter to Montgomery on 25 June, just as Operation Epsom began:

All the luck in the world to you and Dempsey. Please do not hesitate to make the maximum demands for any air assistance that can possibly be useful to you. Whenever there is any legitimate opportunity we must blast the enemy with everything we have.[13]

In some ways, encouragement was all Eisenhower could offer at this stage, since with his headquarters still in Britain, he could do little himself to bring about the success of the campaign.

Unfortunately, the soldiers of the 15th Lowland Scottish Division and 43rd Wessex Division went forward that morning in a heavy drenching mist, and air support was notably lacking. Although Montgomery had referred to the coming offensive as a 'Blitz attack', the fierce battle that followed did not live up to such hopes.[14] The congested lodgement area made it difficult to deploy properly the full weight of the two British corps, XXX and VIII, in a major attack. Narrow country roads with numerous choke points in the form of Norman farmhouses and small stone bridges over streams in deep ravines, combined with a ferocious German defence, conspired to limit the British gains. Nonetheless, the British did grind slowly forward in what became known as the battle of the 'Scottish corridor'.

The fighting around Hill 112, the furthest point of the British advance, was perhaps the bitterest of the entire campaign. Caen lay just five miles to the north-east, but on 29 June, General Dempsey, the commander of the British Second Army, decided to withdraw from Hill 112 and go over to the defensive. This was in response to Enigma intelligence of a looming German counter-attack, but when the German attack came, it was stopped dead in its tracks by a solid British defence. Any hope of outflanking Caen had passed. While Epsom's gains looked disappointing, it had pre-empted and disrupted the last serious German effort to counter-attack the Allied front with formed panzer reserves.[15] The German panzer commanders were despondent. One described how the panzer 'units were senselessly pounded to pieces before they could employ their infantry forces effectively. It was a one-sided battle of materiel on a scale never before experienced.'[16] The British air chiefs were unimpressed by such results, since the airfield construction programme was now badly behind schedule, and those airfields that had been built had to be crammed together into the already congested lodgement area.[17] They believed that Montgomery had wasted another opportunity and that Epsom simply represented a further example of his inability to match his optimistic assess-ments to actual results.

Yet if British progress on their flank had been disappointing, the same could not be said of the American sector. Bradley had mounted an offensive to the south, which had to be called off after limited progress and heavy casualties, but VII Corps, under the command of General J. Lawton 'Lightning Joe' Collins, managed to drive across the Cherbourg peninsula by 18 June and isolate the German defenders of Cherbourg. As the Germans withdrew into their defences, the Americans rapidly followed up and laid siege to the considerable fortifications of the port. After heavy fighting, the German defenders surrendered on 30 June, but only after they had comprehensively wrecked the port facilities.[18] Nonetheless, the capture of Cherbourg was the first major Allied success of the campaign. Although it took some considerable time to bring the port back into operation, its capture reduced the reliance on the single surviving Mulberry harbour and ensured that yet more men and supplies could flow into France.

It was during this period that Basil Liddell Hart, one of Britain's foremost military historians and commentators, met with General George Patton. Patton was still kicking his heels in England and fretting that the fighting would be over before he was allowed to activate his Third Army in France. In fact, he was playing a vital role as the fictitious commander of the First US Army Group, a major Allied deception effort that convinced the German High Command that the Allies still intended to land major forces at the Pas de Calais. Throughout the Normandy fighting, the German Fifteenth army sat in its positions around Calais waiting for an attack that never came.[19] During his conversation with Liddell Hart on 19 June, Patton claimed that the American forces had penetrated much deeper than the British at every stage, and while the British had failed to gain any of their objectives around Caen, the Americans were now overrunning the Cherbourg peninsula. Liddell Hart, who certainly could not be described as either a friend or supporter of Montgomery, challenged this by pointing out 'that the British forces had, surely, absorbed the enemy's strength at the critical time, and thus provided the shield under cover of which the American advance across the Cherbourg peninsula had become possible'.[20] In fact, without any inside knowledge of Montgomery's plan, Liddell Hart had divined its essence. Whether every operation reached its objectives or not, the activity of the British Second

Army around Caen was bound to draw the attention of the German High Command – and the bulk of the German reserves. This inevitably made it harder for the British Second Army to reach its objectives, but every German division drawn into the fight around Caen meant that there was one fewer available to contest the American progress. Patton's Anglophobia and dislike of Montgomery had not cooled over his months of enforced inactivity – if anything, they had grown stronger – which meant he simply could not acknowledge the validity of Montgomery's plan. He was not alone.

As July 1944 opened, the Allies were certainly not as far advanced as they had expected and the German grip around Normandy appeared as tight as ever. Montgomery claimed in a directive to his two army commanders, Dempsey and Bradley, that his policy of drawing the main enemy forces on to the eastern flank to enable territorial gains on the western flank had been successful. However, Montgomery expected the British Second Army to push towards Caen while guarding against the likely possibility of a 'full-blooded enemy counter-attack'.[21] This meant that the US First Army would have to carry the main burden by developing an offensive to the south from 3 July. Although Montgomery had predicted rightly that 'Once we can capture Caen and Cherbourg, and all face in the same direction, the enemy problem becomes enormous', the first weeks of July were the tensest of the campaign for the Allied commanders and the most difficult for the Allied soldiers.[22]

The American drive south towards the key town of Saint-Lô encountered enormous difficulties. Montgomery explained to Brooke on 7 July 1944:

> The American offensive on my western flank is gathering momentum slowly. When it began on 3 July the weather was too awful; driving rain, mist, low cloud, no visibility; and since then we have had fine periods only, and no continued spell of good weather. The country over that side is most difficult; it is very thick and approximates to jungle fighting.[23]

Instead of mounting the expected 'power drive' into France, the

US First Army had found itself enmeshed in the heart of the Normandy bocage, a vast patchwork of tiny fields each surrounded by high, thick hedgerows that had grown up over centuries of cultivation. As one American report ruefully admitted, 'Each hedgerow is an ideal defensive position "made to order" for delaying action.'[24] The nature of the terrain, combined with an expert German defence, divided the all-arms combination of infantry, armour and artillery into their separate, vulnerable constituents. The poor weather grounded the American air support, while the closeness of the country made accurate artillery fire impossible when the opposing sides were so close together. Tanks that climbed the high banks of the hedgerows were easy targets for German anti-tank guns and panzerfaust teams.* The American infantry, who then had to advance across hedgerows without support, found themselves pinned down in the open by intense German machine-gun and mortar fire. Snipers hidden in the dense tree growth could take a frightening toll of soldiers who tried to find cover.

The American drive towards Saint-Lô became an infantryman's war, with men fighting literally from one hedgerow to the next. Casualties began to mount alarmingly, and a grim joke went around the men that General Charles Gerhardt, the commander of the US 29th Division, was actually a corps commander, because he had one division in the field, one division in the hospital and one division in the cemetery.[25] The relentlessly high casualties amongst the dense hedgerows gave the bocage fighting the same character and atmosphere as that of an earlier war: General Ulysses S. Grant's men had suffered the same bloody attrition and seeming lack of progress amongst the tangled undergrowth of the Wilderness battles in 1864.[26]

Bradley, faced with tactical deadlock, exerted his control by sacking a number of divisional commanders who failed to make sufficient progress. Not surprisingly, disquiet amongst American commanders grew. Captain Chester B. Hansen, Bradley's aide, noted in his diary that:

Talk is beginning to mount on the situation as it now exists . . .

---

* The Panzerfaust was a simple hand-held anti-tank weapon which could be fired and then thrown away.

While Monty prepares for buildup – he now has 3500 tanks – he must weather this storm of public condemnation which is growing up round about him. People blame Monty for things the way they stand now. Must not forget situation at Anzio before the break-through came.[27]

American casualties were rising alarmingly and American criticism of their 'slow' British allies became more pointed. They did not know that the British were facing the same problems, and often suffering just as grievous casualties. This led to the accusation that the British were not doing their fair share of the fighting. American commanders began to see Montgomery – and the British Second Army – as overly cautious, too slow and unwilling to press home attacks to their fullest extent, just as Mark Clark had criticised the British in Italy. In contrast, Colonel Charles Bonesteel, now a US planning officer with 21st Army Group Headquarters, argued that Bradley used 'doughboy tactics of maintaining constant pressure all along the line, punching continuously with battalions to stretch the Germans to a point where a breakthrough could succeed',[28] the same tactics Pershing had espoused in the First World War: constant attacks that relied on the infantry to make ground. Just as in Italy, such tactics could succeed, but they placed a great burden on the American infantryman. In the bocage, the American commanders' faith in constant pressure caused murderous casualties amongst their infantry units.

Montgomery's experience in both the Great War and the Second World War had led him to eschew such tactics. Instead, he placed his faith in preparing and organising a major attack on a narrow front in which every infantry advance was properly supported with massive weights of artillery fire, tank and air support. This was what he called taking a 'colossal crack' at the Germans.[29] Yet such attacks took time to organise, and in the meantime, British troops often found themselves involved in actions much closer to the American experience. Even when major offensives, such as Epsom, were launched, their results were often disappointing for the amount of effort – and ammunition – expended.

The blunt truth was that neither Allied army had really found a simple answer to the tenacious German defence. All Allied attacks depended on advance of the infantry, and it was correspondingly in the infantry that 70 per cent of the casualties were suffered.[30] British infantry battalions in Normandy suffered the same percentage rate of casualties – 30 per cent – as those suffered in the First World War; the only difference lay in the length of the fighting.[31] American infantry casualties were comparatively much higher, but this meant that American criticism of British caution and slowness had a grim counterpoint. While Montgomery and his British subordinates had to be careful with their soldiers' lives to ensure that the British Second Army did not wither away entirely, American commanders had no such compunction. Here was the devil's bargain for the better pay, equipment, uniforms and food that had caused such resentment amongst British soldiers: American soldiers came to realise that their lives were a commodity their commanders were willing to spend in order to reach their objectives.

Yet the growing losses in Normandy concealed the combined impact of the Allied efforts on the Germans. Although each army believed they were fighting their own battle that had little or anything to do with the other, in fact Montgomery viewed and coordinated their separate battles as an indivisible whole. Although controversial at the time, and the source of argument ever since, this was a tremendous advance over the disorganisation of Tunisia or the divided pull of the two armies in Italy.

Both Allied armies attacked using air and artillery support in prodigious quantities, which inflicted severe losses upon the defending German infantry. Indeed, the differing approaches of the two armies were actually complementary. The constant pressure of attacks in the American sector meant that the German defenders, no matter how successful they were, also suffered a drain of casualties that could not be replaced. Meanwhile, each set-piece offensive in the British sector was followed by the looming build-up to another. These twin approaches confronted the German commanders with an impossible dilemma. As July wore on, they had to abandon any thought of a major counter-stroke for the bankrupt substitute of simply holding on against the increasing weight of the Allied armies.

By the end of June, Montgomery had become fully aware of

the criticism levelled against him by Coningham (whom Montgomery described as 'a bad man, not genuine and terribly jealous') and he decided to launch what can only be described as a counter-attack.[32] Eisenhower had asked Tedder to keep in close touch with Montgomery, and when the two men met on 29 June, Montgomery tackled Tedder on the subject of Coningham, arguing that 'the Army', which was of course synonymous with Montgomery himself, was losing confidence in Coningham, and beginning to wonder if he was a 'loyal member of the team'. This was a thinly veiled threat to take the matter to Brooke, which, given his firm support of Montgomery, could only result in Coningham's removal. Not surprisingly, this conversation had the desired effect: once Tedder had spoken to Coningham, Montgomery found that 'his attitude has been very different, and his advances almost an embarrassment'.[33] Montgomery had certainly won this round in his battle with the 'air barons'.

As the US First Army ground slowly towards Saint-Lô, Montgomery decided to launch a frontal assault to finally capture Caen. Leigh-Mallory asked for the support of heavy bombers, and with Eisenhower's insistence the request was somewhat grudgingly acceded to by RAF Bomber Command.[34] The Germans had developed a chain of villages north of Caen into a formidable belt of defences that would have to be tackled by the attacking infantry, so the heavy bombers were ordered to bomb the rear of the enemy's defences on the outskirts of the city.[35] Caen had been a target for Allied air attack and naval gunfire since D-Day, but this time it suffered the impact of a full-scale bombing raid. Tragically, the heavy bombers overshot the intended targets and unloaded their bombs on to the centre of the city. In just one hour, Caen was hit by as many bombs in an hour as Bomber Command had dropped on Hamburg over the course of one night the year before.[36] The medieval heart of the city was destroyed, and civilian casualties were heavy. Although the bombing shocked the Germans, it left their formidable chain of defended villages untouched, which meant that the Canadian and British infantry still had to fight hard to pierce the German defensive belt.

By the evening of 9 July, the 3rd British Division had finally reached the centre of Caen, but could go no further through the rubble-choked remains of the city. It proved impossible to seize the bridgeheads over the Orne that Montgomery had hoped would finally open the way to the south.[37] Air Marshal Sir Arthur Harris, head of Bomber Command, fumed that his bomber crews had suffered more casualties than the British Army since D-Day. Although he was mistaken in this, Harris fervently believed that his bombers could win the war independently and felt that using them to support the army was a waste of a strategic asset. Caen had finally fallen, but the Allied armies still seemed to be locked in a futile battle of attrition.

The pressure on Montgomery – and equally on Eisenhower – to achieve a breakthrough was now intense. The Allied armies in Normandy were badly behind the schedule that had been so confidently predicted before the invasion. All the effort, all the firepower of the Allied armies, navies and air forces did not seem to be able to break the firm grip of the German army around their positions. This generated intense pressure on both Eisenhower and Montgomery, but while Montgomery could isolate himself in his headquarters and focus on the battle, Eisenhower felt increasingly powerless to influence events in a positive way. He was also becoming worried about Montgomery's conduct of the campaign.

The first real hint of Eisenhower's concerns came in a letter to Montgomery on 7 July 1944. He observed that the Allies were approaching the limit of their capacity to bring new troops into the theatre, while the Germans could still reinforce and increase their relative strength. He urged Montgomery to 'examine every single possibility with a view to expanding our beachhead and getting more room for manoeuvring so as to use our forces before the enemy can obtain substantial equality'. He re-emphasised the need to 'use all possible energy in a determined effort to prevent a stalemate or of facing the necessity of fighting a major defensive battle with the slight depth we now have in the bridgehead', and advised Montgomery to attempt a 'major full-dress attack on the left flank supported by everything we could bring to bear'. He concluded: 'What I want you to know is that I will back you up to the limit in any effort you may decide upon to prevent a deadlock.'[38]

While this was a far gentler missive than Tedder wished Eisenhower to send, the Supreme Commander had suggested that not only was a stalemate possible but the continuation of Montgomery's approach might well condemn the Allies to deadlock. In his reply, Montgomery simply professed to be 'quite happy about the situation. I have been working throughout on a very definite plan, and I now begin to see daylight.' He summed up by stating: 'I think the battle is going very well. The enemy is being heavily attacked all along the line; and we are killing a lot of Germans. Of one thing you can be quite sure – there will be no stalemate.'[39] Eisenhower's subsequent reply demonstrated that he was reassured by Montgomery's arguments, but his point had nonetheless been made, however subtly: Montgomery needed to make greater gains and show greater results.

Under intense pressure to achieve, Montgomery now planned his next attempt to lever the Germans out of their positions. He had admitted to Brooke (but not to Eisenhower) on 7 July that 'we cannot be 100% happy on the eastern flank until we have got Caen. We have pulled such a weight of enemy on to our eastern flank that I want to get 100% happy there!'[40] Even the subsequent capture of Caen did not immediately improve the British position, nor did it enable the construction of any further airfields.

Yet even as the tension within the Allied High Command reached crisis point, their German counterparts had come to the conclusion that the battle was lost. On 15 July, Rommel felt forced to inform Hitler of the reality of the situation:

> The position on the Normandy front is becoming more difficult by the day and is approaching a grave crisis. Our losses are so high that the fighting power of the divisions is rapidly sinking . . . The fighting has shown that even the bravest unit is gradually worn out by the enemy's material . . . Everywhere, the troops fight heroically, but the unequal battle is nearing its end. In my opinion it is necessary to draw the appropriate conclusions from the situation. It is my duty as the Commander-in-Chief of the Army Group to express my views unequivocally.[41]

Rommel had, of course, equivocated. He could not quite bring himself to state baldly the fact that he now believed that the battle, and thus the war, was lost. The 'appropriate conclusions' were that Germany would somehow have to negotiate surrender terms with the powers bent on her destruction. But just two days later, Rommel was seriously injured when his car was attacked by one of the ever-present Allied fighter-bombers. It would take him many months to recover from his injuries, and in the meantime, Field Marshal Gunther von Kluge took his place as commander of Army Group B and the Normandy front.

The fighting in Normandy had been so intense, its burden placed primarily on the infantry, that the British Second Army was running short of infantry replacements. Montgomery's solution was to use his three fresh armoured divisions in VIII Corps, which had suffered relatively little loss, to carry out a blitz attack southwards, supported by the full weight of Allied airpower. Utilising heavy bombers to blast the German front lines, the British armour would be unleashed 'from the bridgehead over the Orne to the NE of Caen' on the far eastern flank of the British sector.[42] In so doing, Montgomery was actually following Eisenhower's suggestion for a major full-dress attack on the left flank, while also attempting to economise on what was becoming his scarcest resource: British infantry.

Montgomery announced Operation Goodwood in glowing terms. He asked Eisenhower on 12 July for the 'whole weight of air power' for each army on the day of their assault, and explained that 'We must have the air to ensure success . . . My whole Eastern flank will burst into flames . . . The Operation . . . may have far-reaching results.'[43] This was not only exactly what Eisenhower wanted to hear, but it hinted that this attack might result in the long-awaited breakthrough. The next day, Montgomery elaborated further with the news that there would in fact be *two* 'very big attacks next week'. While the British attacked on 18 July, the US First Army would launch 'a heavy attack with six divisions about five miles west of St Lo on Wednesday 19th July'. The Supreme Commander immediately responded to Montgomery's request for air support with characteristic enthusiasm: 'All senior airmen are in full accord because this operation will be a brilliant stroke which will knock loose our present shackles . . . we are so pepped up concerning the promise of this plan.'[44] Montgomery had, however, inserted a certain ambiguity as to which attack he now saw as the decisive one. Was it the British attack, or would it be the impact of the two attacks when taken together?

Montgomery moderated his enthusiasm regarding the British attack in a letter to Brooke when he said that the operation:

> may have far reaching results. Anything may happen. We may 'muck up', and write off, a great many of the enemy troops east of the Orne . . .
>
>   . . . I shall watch over the battle very carefully myself; we must be certain that we neglect no chance of inflicting a real heavy defeat on the enemy; we must also be certain that we do nothing foolish, and so lay ourselves open to a German come back which might catch us off balance – and lead to a set-back.[45]

A note of caution, and perhaps of realism, had entered his thinking, but he had not communicated this to Eisenhower. The Supreme Commander was now convinced that the plan would:

> reap a harvest from all the sowing you have been doing during the past weeks. With our whole front line acting aggressively against the enemy so that he is pinned to the ground, O'Connor's* plunge into his vitals will be decisive. I am not discounting the difficulties, nor the initial losses, but in this case I am viewing the prospects with the most tremendous optimism and enthusiasm . . . I hope you will forgive me if I grow a bit exuberant.[46]

Yet while Eisenhower was under the impression that this was the crucial attack, Montgomery had changed his mind. While SHAEF and the air headquarters were still following his earlier, more optimistic instructions of 13 July, Montgomery issued a personal directive to Dempsey two days later revising and limiting

---

* General Richard O'Connor, commander of VIII Corps

the objectives for the operation. The directive made it clear that Goodwood was not to be a breakthrough battle after all. Instead, the main purpose of the attack was:

> To engage the German armour in battle and 'write it down' to such an extent that it is of no further value to the Germans as a basis of the battle.
>
> To gain a good bridgehead over the Orne through Caen, and thus to improve our positions on the eastern flank.
>
> Generally to destroy German equipment and personnel, as a preliminary to a possible wide exploitation of success.[47]

Montgomery's emphasis that the eastern flank was a bastion that must remain firm was hardly calculated to inspire his commanders into an all-out attempt to break through the German positions. He had changed the purpose of the attack, but at no point did he inform either SHAEF or the air chiefs of this important alteration. Dempsey later admitted that Montgomery had painted 'his canvas in rather glowing colours' in order to win the support of Spaatz and Harris, the 'bomber barons'. To mislead the air commanders as to the nature of the assault was one thing, but Dempsey also admitted that Montgomery would often say, 'there's no need to tell Ike'.[48] Montgomery had actually made a fatal mistake. He had allowed the internecine conflict between himself and the air barons to spill over into his relations with Eisenhower and SHAEF. Montgomery's disdain for Eisenhower as a soldier and commander meant that he had kept vital information from his superior officer, and his behaviour over Goodwood was bound to fracture the trust that had previously developed between the two men. Needless to say, he himself would not have tolerated such sleight of hand from any of his own subordinates.

Operation Goodwood did not have an auspicious start. Squeezing three armoured divisions from a congested beachhead through the narrow Orne bridgehead across just six bridges meant that each division came into action sequentially rather than as a united powerful force. Just as unfortunately, the relatively small numbers of infantry attached to each armoured division became snarled up in fierce village fighting soon after the start line was crossed, leaving the armour to drive deep into the German rear unsupported. Perhaps worst of all, the artillery of each division had to be left on the far side of the bridges, which limited the range and weight of fire support that the advancing spearheads could rely on. Nonetheless, the 7,000 tons of bombs laid in 'carpets' by the heavy bombers of Bomber Command literally blasted apart the German front lines, and soon the British armour was motoring deep into the German rear lines. Unfortunately, the British planners had miscalculated the full depth of the German defences, and the final German lines on the Bourguébus ridge had been left intact. As the 11th Armoured Division drove up to the base of the ridge, tank after tank was knocked out by concealed German anti-tank guns, which brought the British advance to a shuddering halt. By midday on 18 July, just a few dramatic hours after the start of the operation, Goodwood was effectively over.

The ferocity of the British attack shocked von Kluge, since the German front line had been completely ruptured and the best part of two infantry divisions had disappeared in the firestorm. Goodwood had proved that with the support of heavy bombers, the Allies could now grind to dust the forward German defences. Yet more German reserves had to be hurried to the sector to close the door on the British Second Army, which had actually come close to achieving a breakthrough. However, although Montgomery professed himself satisfied with the results, and issued a press communiqué on the evening of 18 July that suggested a breakthrough was likely, Goodwood did not even approach the glowing colours he had sketched out.

Not surprisingly, when the reality became known, Eisenhower was monumentally angry. He bemoaned the fact that 7,000 tons of bombs dropped had only resulted in an advance of seven miles, and he was now only too aware that Montgomery had been economical with the truth. Tedder was, if anything, even more furious. He later wrote to Air Chief Marshal Trenchard:

on this last affair I feel we all (that includes 'Ike' and myself) have been had for suckers. I do not believe there was the slightest intention to make a clear break-through. Moreover, as has happened before, deliberate and cold-blooded endeavours are being made in high quarters in Normandy to hide the facts.[49]

As far as Tedder was concerned, Montgomery had lied about the entire operation in order to gain the use of the heavy bombers. This was the final straw, and he 'positively demanded Montgomery's head'.[50] It was a delicate moment for the British commander: Churchill was equally angry to learn that he had been 'banned' from visiting 21st Army Group Headquarters, and it took Brooke to soothe him while also alerting Montgomery to the necessity of allowing the Prime Minister to visit him in France. Eisenhower was far-sighted enough to realise that this was not the time to remove Montgomery from his command, and instead went to visit him at his headquarters,[51] subsequently putting his thoughts on paper to ensure 'that we see eye to eye on the big problems'.

> A few days ago, when Armored Divisions of Second Army, assisted by tremendous air attack, broke through the enemy's forward lines, I was extremely hopeful and optimistic. I thought that at last we had him and were going to roll him up. That did not come about.
>
> Now we are pinning our immediate hopes on Bradley's attack, which should get off either tomorrow or on the first good day. But the country is bad, and the enemy strong at the point of main assault, and more than ever I think it is important that we are aggressive throughout the front.[52]

This was certainly a highly restrained letter from the Supreme Commander, but the sharp barb of criticism was obvious. Indeed, the controversy over Goodwood had caused real damage to the relationship between Eisenhower and Montgomery. The two men were now communicating with each other through formal letters rather than frequent face-to-face meetings, and the gulf of misunderstanding between them could only grow.

Eisenhower was right: all immediate hopes were now pinned on Bradley's attack. Bradley had been developing his ideas for a breakthrough since D-Day, but they bore little resemblance to the usual broad-front approach of US Army attacks. Operation Cobra, at least on paper, seemed more similar to the British method of selecting a narrow front and using all available firepower to make a breach. Indeed, a key feature of the plan was the intense aerial bombardment of a 'box' approximately 2,500 yards deep and 6,000 yards wide by fighter-bombers and medium and heavy bombers.[53] It was hoped that this would rupture the front, in the same manner as Goodwood, and enable the US First Army to finally break out of its hedgerow prison. Although US Army Intelligence estimated that there were 8,000 German defenders in the vicinity of the chosen breakthrough area, in fact there were closer to 5,000, with the now understrength and battle-weary Panzer Lehr Division the only armoured division.[54] Goodwood, if it achieved nothing else, had at least focused German attention on the British sector. With everything ready for the attack, Bradley had to wait for the one element he could not control: the weather. On the afternoon of 20 July, torrential rain fell in France.[55] Eisenhower, over on a visit to Bradley, only half jokingly remarked, 'When I die they can hold my body for a rainy day and bury me during a thunderstorm for this weather will be the death of me yet.'[56] Mist, low clouds and heavy rain blanketed Normandy for the next few days, causing seemingly endless postponements.

Yet while Bradley fretted at his inability to launch his long-prepared attack, dramatic events were taking place in Germany. On the morning of 20 July, Count von Stauffenberg had planted a bomb intended to kill the Führer in his bunker in East Prussia. The assassination attempt failed and Hitler exacted a terrible revenge on the members of the German resistance who had sought to end his life and the war with one stroke. As the Nazi regime exerted an even tighter grip over the German army in the aftermath of the failed putsch, there could be no debate or discussion about following Hitler's orders to stand fast in the Normandy theatre.

On 24 July, Leigh-Mallory took the chance of improving weather to order the heavy bombers into the air, but did not inform the army of his decision. While most of the bombers did not reach their target due to the persistent rain, one group did drop their bombs, but tragically, many of them fell short on to the American lines. The US 30th Division lost 24 killed and 131 wounded to American bombs. The friendly fire combined with the false start to his offensive infuriated Bradley, who feared that this abortive attempt might alert the Germans to the danger. Yet as the US troops withdrew to the agreed safety line, the panzergrenadiers of Panzer Lehr followed them up and dug in directly in the target area. The next day, the heavy bombers tried again, and this time more than 1,500 of them dropped their destructive cargoes over the target. Although the fighter-bombers and the first groups of bombers dropped their bombs on target, the smoke and dust raised by the bombing obscured the area, and there was a tragic repeat of the previous day. Bradley's aide, Captain Hansen, recounted the experience in the American trenches: 'The ground belched, shook and spewed dirt to the sky. Scores of our troops were hit, their bodies flung from the slit trenches . . . Huebner who is an old front line campaigner said it was the most terrifying thing he had ever seen.'[57] Around 61 American soldiers were killed and 600 wounded by bombs, including General Leslie MacNair, the Commander of Army Ground Forces. As one of the primary architects of the vast expansion of the US Army, he had come to France to witness his army in action, but it tragically cost him his life. His mangled corpse was only identified by the stars on his collar. The tragic repetition of short bombing was 'morale-shattering' for the men who were then expected to carry on and mount an attack.

However, if the effect of the bombing on the American troops was grievous, it was devastating to the German defence. Fritz Bayerlein, the commander of Panzer Lehr, remembered that the planes kept coming over 'like a conveyor belt' and the bomb carpets rolled back and forth relentlessly over the German positions. He estimated that out of perhaps 3,200 soldiers in his division, the bombing had caused some 700 casualties. The immediate shock of such a terrible experience made many of the German defenders helpless for hours afterwards, and they were captured by the Americans wandering around in a daze.[58] But there were other men still able to fight back, and frustratingly, American progress on 25 July seemed just as slow and deadly as on any other occasion. However, over the course of the next few days of hard fighting, the American commanders realised that they had torn a five-mile hole in the German defences and there were simply no more German reserves to stop them.

As the US VII Corps pushed forwards into the German rear, Bradley finally placed Patton in command of the US armoured divisions who were now pouring through the gap, although his new Third Army would not be officially activated until 1 August.[59] Patton told Bradley, 'I must get in and do something spectacularly successful . . . if I am to make good.'[60] He proved as good as his word: within days, he had achieved the incredible feat of pushing his leading divisions through the narrowest of choke points at Avranches, reassembling them on the far side and driving on into Brittany.

On 28 July, Montgomery was able to write to Brooke: 'It begins to look as if the policy we have been working on for so many weeks is now going to pay a dividend . . . The Americans are going well.' Whether Montgomery had indeed followed the same policy throughout the Normandy campaign would become one of the great post-war controversies. Yet in the same letter he admitted that he was no longer aiming the British Second Army towards Falaise, because 'the enemy is very strong in that (quarter)', and instead was shifting the weight of the British attack from Caumont towards Vire in Operation Bluecoat,[61] which, although it proved to be one of the most successful British attacks of the campaign, could not be as decisive as a thrust towards Falaise might have proved. Just as Montgomery ordered Dempsey to 'step on [the] gas for Vire', Churchill reminded him that British prestige was at stake: 'very glad that the Americans had a good success today. It would be fine if this were matched by a similar British victory. I realise that you have the main weight of the enemy against you and I am sure you will overcome them. This is the moment to strike hard.'[62]

Patton's superb drive into Brittany seemed glamorous and dramatic next to the grindingly slow progress of the British Second Army. Yet while the controversies of the Normandy campaign and the subsequent Battle of Falaise have so often been portrayed as an Anglo-American divide, little of that was apparent at the time.

On 28 July, Montgomery and Dempsey visited Bradley's headquarters to congratulate him on his great success. Hansen related that 'Brad's welcome to them was warm and refreshing, came out of his truck, wrung their hands and said he was glad to see them. Brad gets along remarkably well with anyone, beautiful with these two.'[63] Any sense of tension between the key Allied commanders seemed to have evaporated in the glow of the American success. Much of the bitterness that developed subsequently between Montgomery and Bradley was not apparent in the days after Cobra.

Even at this stage, when Patton's men were driving into open country, there was little expectation amongst the Allied commanders that they might win a conclusive victory. As late as 27 July, Montgomery reminded his army commanders that it was essential to secure the Brittany ports before the winter,[64] and Patton's forces were consequently directed westwards, not eastwards. It had been a long-agreed part of the Allied plan that the Brittany ports, most notably Brest, were vital to the long-term sustainment of the Allied armies in France. Patton's forces thus dashed off towards an objective that had real long-term value but that would do nothing to destroy the German armies in France. On 3 August, Major General John Wood of the 4th Armoured Division remonstrated with his corps commander, Troy Middleton, that 'we're winning this war the wrong way, we ought to be going toward Paris'.[65] Although Middleton had to order Wood to follow orders and push towards L'Orient on the southern coast of Brittany, Bradley had in fact decided on that day to occupy Brittany with one corps and to use the rest of the available forces to turn east and drive towards the Seine. That same day, General Wade Haislip's XV Corps turned east.

While the Allied commanders had expected that the German army would withdraw back to the Seine, Hitler refused to follow such conventional military logic. Instead, he ordered von Kluge to prepare a counter-attack that he hoped would cut off the American troops now pouring into Brittany. Over the first week of August, the German panzer formations thus moved west away from safety and towards encirclement. With the weight of the British Second Army now around Caumont, Montgomery ordered the newly activated First Canadian Army, under General Harry Crerar, to drive on to Falaise. Operation Totalise was a full-scale attempt to advance on the open ground south of Caen, and although it made progress, the Canadians were held far short of their goal.

When von Kluge launched Operation Luttich towards Mortain on 7 August, the result was predictable. The US 30th Division earned fresh laurels mounting a desperate defence at Mortain, but the Allied fighter-bombers soon put paid to any rapid advance by the panzers. Bradley, who was now in command of 12th Army Group, having handed over command of the US First Army to General Courtney Hodges, now recognised the opportunity the German counter-attack presented. When he gathered his staff on 6 August, he ebulliently announced, 'Let's talk big turkey . . . I'm ready to eat meat all the way.' With XV Corps now driving eastwards against little opposition, Bradley saw the opportunity to thrust his forces east to Le Mans before turning north at Alençon and pushing on to Argentan. He explained that he wanted the 'Armor to strike quickly especially on lower line where Ger resistance does not exist, strike through, pour on infantry, burst up to coast, cut off and destroy the German Army in France'.[66] With the Canadians pushing south towards Falaise, the Germans would be trapped between the advancing jaws of the two armies.

On 8 August, in Eisenhower's presence, Bradley telephoned Montgomery for approval of his change of plan. Montgomery acceded, and also agreed that the existing army boundaries could be ignored. While he now urged the Canadians to press their offensive, he did not reinforce them with units of the Second Army. This meant that the subsequent Canadian advance was slow and hesitant, opposed as it was by German units who were now alive to the danger they faced. However, perhaps the most controversial decision of the Falaise battle was taken by Bradley on 12 August. During the morning, Haislip informed Patton that since his forces would soon capture Argentan, he now had no further assigned mission. Patton ordered him to 'push on slowly in the direction of Falaise'. However, later in the day, Patton telephoned Bradley and, 'in a moment of lightheartedness', asked, 'We now have elements in Argentan. Shall we continue and drive the British into the sea for another Dunkirk?'[67] Bradley, who had been so confident and ebullient just days before, replied: 'Nothing doing. You're not to go beyond Argentan. Just stop where you are and build up on that shoulder.'[68] There is no doubt that the forward positions of XV Corps were exposed, and Bradley feared that a German counter-attack might place his highly extended forces in danger. He later admitted full responsibility for this decision: 'In halting Patton at Argentan, however, I did not consult with Montgomery. The decision to stop Patton was mine alone; it never went beyond my CP . . . I much preferred a solid shoulder at Argentan to the possibility of a broken neck at Falaise.'[69] There were sound reasons for halting the American drive at Argentan and ensuring that his forces were not exposed to a significant reverse; however, given the slow Canadian progress, Bradley's decision ensured that the gap would remain open and that large numbers of German troops would escape the trap.

What is less understandable is the rumour that spread around American headquarters that it was Montgomery who had halted the American troops due to considerations of national prestige. Patton certainly believed – quite wrongly – that the order originated from Montgomery and that it was 'either due to jealousy of the Americans or to utter ignorance of the situation or to a combination of the two'.[70] Similarly, G-3 (Operations) staff in Bradley's own headquarters suggested that 'we were ordered to hold at Argentan rather than to continue the drive to Falaise since our capture of that objective would infringe on the prestige of forces driving south and prevent them from securing prestige value in closing the trap'.[71] Major Hansen was certainly under the impression that Montgomery had 'subscribed to the vice of extreme over-caution and has made the error of many commanders in denying sound tactics for the prestige value of objective'.[72] Such rumours made the American staffs all the more anxious for 12th Army Group to be removed from 21st Army Group control. Yet it does seem remarkable that Bradley would allow his own staff to subscribe to such unsubstantiated rumours when he had taken the decision himself.

Ultimately, the Falaise gap was closed further east at Trun and Chambois, and the troops who had to place themselves in the greatest danger to do so were neither British nor American but Canadian and Polish. Major David Currie's small battle group had to fight a desperate battle at Saint-Lambert-sur-Dives to deny the last crossing points over the Dives river to the Germans. However, it was the troops of the 1st Polish Armoured Division who truly became the 'cork in the bottle'. Deployed in positions around the high point of Mont Ormel above the plain of Falaise, the Poles resisted the full fury of the German army as it attempted to escape, fighting a desperate battle in isolated positions for three days. By midday on 21 August, they were finally relieved by Canadian forces and the battle for Falaise was effectively over.[73]

Yet almost immediately a sense developed amongst the Allies, prompted by news reports, that the Falaise battle somehow represented a lost opportunity, and this has lingered ever since. In one report, British censors commented that the public were concerned with the tone of over-optimism and exaggeration about the possibilities of the Falaise battle, in which 'the first impression was that the whole German Seventh Army had been trapped, then it was daily softened down till only remnants were left'.[74] The Battle of Falaise did not end in a conclusive general surrender of the German army, and this lack of finality left the British and American public with a vague sense of dissatisfaction. Historians have searched the personalities of the generals and the fragmentary record of their decisions in vain to explain the errors that led up to the closing of the pocket. Accusations were made at the time, and ever since, that somehow Montgomery's personal vanity or his vainglorious desire for prestige had robbed the Allies of greater success. These were baseless rumours: neither Montgomery nor Bradley's decisions during the Battle of Falaise can be remotely compared to Mark Clark's behaviour during the battle for Rome.

The failure, if failure it was, to close the Falaise pocket earlier than was actually achieved originated not in Anglo-American rivalry but in the same fundamental flaw of Anglo-American war-making that had resulted in the inability to trap Kesselring's forces south of Rome. Neither Montgomery nor Bradley had recourse to a common understanding and doctrine of how to successfully execute an encirclement battle. This meant that the fighting that developed into the Battle of Falaise was by its nature entirely improvised, hasty and messy, and with little clarity of direction. It was not surprising that during such a fast-moving engagement, some questionable decisions were made by both commanders.

This unsatisfied hunger for a conclusive victory also obscured, both at the time and ever since, the real magnitude of the Allied success. Even though the Allies might not have executed a perfect encirclement – like Napoleon at Ulm or von Moltke at Sedan – the overall effect on the German forces in Normandy was devastating. If the Allies did not close the pocket on the ground as efficiently as might have been hoped, their air forces executed a vertical envelopment that exacted a terrible price from the German army. Retreating German forces had to run the gauntlet of devastating Allied artillery and air power. Ten thousand German soldiers died in the inferno of the Falaise pocket, and a further 50,000 were taken prisoner. Perhaps 40,000 German troops managed to escape from the encirclement, but the vast majority fled with nothing more than their personal weapons: virtually all the German army's equipment had to be left behind. The real measure of the Allied victory is perhaps reflected in the fact that when the remnants of seven panzer divisions were reassembled on the far bank of the Seine, the total force amounted to 1,300 men, 24 tanks and 60 artillery pieces.[75]

In one climactic and entirely unexpected engagement, the Allies had won the battle for France as decisively as the Germans had in 1940. As the British, American and Canadian armies drove across France at full speed, it was not surprising that a sense of euphoria and an anticipation of an early victory infused the troops and their commanders. The war seemed to have been won. It was in this atmosphere of impending triumph that Eisenhower announced that he would take full control of the armies in his capacity as Supreme Commander on 1 September 1944.

13

SHAEF at War

On 2 August 1944, Alan Brooke wrote to General Sir Henry Wilson, the Supreme Allied Commander in the Mediterranean, revealing his fears regarding the dominance of the United States in the direction of the war:

> The Americans now feel that they possess the major forces at sea, on land and in the air, in addition to all the vast financial and industrial advantages which they had from the start. In addition they now look upon themselves no longer as the apprentices at war, but on the contrary as full blown professionals. As a result of all this they are determined to have an ever increasing share in the running of the war in all its aspects. I can assure you that we are watching these unpleasant new developments very carefully.[1]

The American moment had most certainly arrived. One of the frustrations for American commanders in North Africa and Italy had been that the US Army had only a few troops 'in the shop window'.[2] They knew that there was a Grand Army of the Republic training and equipping at home, but there were relatively few men on active service. With the successful Normandy invasion, the United States could finally put forth its strength on the continent of Europe and there could no longer be any doubt that they were the predominant ally. Of course, the US had actually become the senior partner in 1941 with the passing of the Lend-Lease Act, but most British decision-makers had managed to ignore such inconvenient truths.

While American commanders could now take pride in the full

strength of the US Army on campaign, their British counterparts
had to cope with the nagging doubts and jealousies of having run
a race only to be 'pipped at the post'. The British Liberation Army
of 1944 was, after all, the second largest British Army ever sent to
the European continent, yet this great outpouring of strength at the
end of an exhausting war now seemed doomed to a poor second
place. The British had to watch uncomfortably as the political and
military leverage they had enjoyed for much of the war evaporated
in front of them. It was in this changing context that Montgomery,
willingly supported by Brooke, fought a long and ultimately unsuccessful rearguard action to win back the command authority over
the Allied armies that he had relinquished at the conclusion of the
Normandy campaign.

This issue, which became one of the longest-running and most
corrosive sources of tension between the British and American
armies in the last campaign of the war, had actually begun before
the end of the Normandy battles. As early as 7 July 1944, Montgomery
had informed Brooke that there was 'great pressure' from SHAEF
to establish a US army group, but that he was 'keeping right clear'
of all such discussions. In his inimitable way, however, Montgomery
had pointed out that if Eisenhower wished to take control of the
campaign, 'he . . . must come over here and devote his whole and
undivided attention to the battle. Any idea that he could run the
land battle from England, or could do it in his spare time, would
be playing with fire. Eisenhower himself has, I fancy, no delusions
on this subject.'[3] Montgomery's basic argument was that running
the land battle was a 'whole-time job for one man', and that man
was him. Bedell Smith later suggested that Monty 'always had it
in the back of his mind' that he would continue as the land force
commander, and Freddie de Guingand mentioned that Montgomery
refused to discuss the movement of US staff officers from 21st Army
Group Headquarters during the Normandy battle, perhaps in the
hope 'that somehow it would never take place'.[4]

However, it had always been part of the COSSAC, and latterly
the SHAEF, plan that as the American Army in France grew in
strength, a US Army group would be formed. It had also long been
part of the plan that once the Allies were fully established ashore,

the Supreme Allied Commander would then take direct charge of the land battle. Eisenhower decided to form the US army group under Bradley but placed it under Montgomery's command while the battle in Normandy continued, and reserved judgement on when he might take direct command of the army groups in France. Many of the Americans in Bradley's headquarters began to chafe under the continued command of 21st Army Group, believing that now was the time to show what the American Army could do.

With the destruction of the German Seventh Army at Falaise, the Allied armies were able to drive eastwards, virtually unhindered by the Germans, whose only option was to retreat to escape destruction. It was in this period of euphoria, when anything seemed possible and the war seemed to have been won, that the Allied commanders had to consider their next moves as the front now pushed forward faster than anyone had expected. Under the COSSAC and SHAEF plans, it had been assumed that, after a gradual build-up, the Allied armies would move to confront the Germans along the line of the River Seine, where a climactic battle for France would be fought. The advance would then continue, stage by stage, until the border with Germany was reached. Instead, the Allies had fought an intense campaign in Normandy with seemingly little progress until the German Seventh Army was destroyed, and there now seemed to be nothing to stop an immediate drive into Germany. The fact was that the Allied armies and their commanders had run out of any pre-prepared script – the next moves would have to be improvised.

Montgomery characteristically informed Brooke of his future thinking before he revealed it to Eisenhower:

After crossing Seine 12 and 21 Army Groups should keep together as a solid mass of some 40 divisions which would be so strong that it need fear nothing. The force should move northwards. 21st Army Group should be on western flank and should clear the channel coast and the Pas de Calais and west Flanders and secure Antwerp. The American armies should move with right flank on Ardennes directed on Brussels Aachen and Cologne. The movement of American armies would cut the communications of enemy forces on channel coast and thus facilitate the task of British Army Group. The initial objects of movement would be to destroy German forces on coast and to establish a powerful air force in Belgium. A further object would be to get enemy out of VI or V2 range of England. Bradley agrees entirely with above conception.[5]

Here was the genesis of what became known as Montgomery's 'narrow front' concept. Both Allied army groups would advance together through the Low Countries and thence into Germany itself. As with most of Montgomery's plans, this had the benefit of concentration of force but does not seem to have been based on secure knowledge of whether 40 divisions could be supplied in one sector of the front. However, even as the balance of strength swung decisively in favour of the Americans, Montgomery could not envisage his 21st Army Group as fulfilling anything other than the dominant, decisive role in the advance into Germany. Just as had been the case in Tunisia, Sicily and Italy, he saw the American forces as helping to 'facilitate the task of British Army Group'. It would also appear that he still hoped that he would remain the land force commander, guiding both army groups in their advance. Montgomery's thinking certainly took account of the damage being caused by Hitler's *Vergeltungswaffen* or 'vengeance weapons'. The Germans had begun bombarding London and the south of England with V-1 flying bombs on 13 June 1944, and these were soon joined by the V-2 rocket, which was first fired against England on 8 September 1944.* These attacks caused considerable destruction and loss of life, and made an advance through northern France and Belgium an important priority, as it would drive the Germans away from the launch sites.

Yet Montgomery's plan also bore an ominous resemblance to the Dyle Plan of 1940, in which the most powerful French and British armies had advanced into Belgium to confront the Germans. While Montgomery intended this mass of 40 divisions to drive on into Germany, the Allies in 1944 did not possess even the advantages of the French army in 1940: there could be no equivalent to the

---

* Montgomery had been briefed on the imminent operational use of the V-2.

French forces that had covered the Ardennes and the line of Maginot defences four years before. And whereas Montgomery considered that an advance of 40 divisions would be powerful enough to 'fear nothing', in the context of the Second World War such a force was small. Although the Western Allies had never deployed any force as large since 1940, 40 divisions on the Eastern Front would have represented little more than a pinprick. At the same time, Montgomery does not seem to have ever fully explored whether they could be properly positioned, supplied and usefully employed on the relatively narrow front he suggested. Most SHAEF estimates concluded that it was not feasible, but on the one occasion when the senior SHAEF supply officer visited Montgomery's headquarters, he was thrown out and never went back.[6]

While Montgomery believed that Bradley agreed 'entirely' with his ideas, this could not have been further from the truth. Far from being satisfied with a secondary task in facilitating the advance of the British, Bradley had developed his own ideas for the future campaign. On the same day that Montgomery wrote to Brooke, Bradley met with Eisenhower to suggest an altogether different plan. He proposed driving directly east towards Metz and the German border, 'rather than diverting too much strength up over the northern route to the Lowlands'.[7] At a SHAEF conference on 19 August, both commanders aired their ideas to Eisenhower. The Supreme Allied Commander was now faced with two very different plans from his two army group commanders, neither of which was compatible with the other. Unfortunately, both Montgomery and Bradley somehow got the impression that Eisenhower favoured their plan at the expense of the other.

In fact, Eisenhower had his own conception for the advance into Germany, and on 24 August he gave notice to Montgomery and Bradley that he would soon take direct command of the theatre. He explained that he would soon issue a brief directive to both army groups. The Army Group of the North, which was effectively Montgomery's 21st Army Group, would be given the task of 'operating northeast', driving through the Pas de Calais region and pushing on into Belgium with the intention of gaining 'a secure base at Antwerp' and the ultimate goal of advancing 'eastward on the Ruhr'. He also envisaged the use of the Allied airborne army to accelerate the advance of Montgomery's army group. This was the genesis of what became Operation Market Garden.

Meanwhile, Bradley's army group was to 'thrust forward on its left', in order to support Montgomery. Bradley was ordered to 'clean up' the Brittany peninsula, where the Germans were still holding out in Brest, but then develop sufficient forces to 'advance eastward from Paris toward Metz'. Eisenhower stressed the importance of speed in execution, since German resistance had collapsed, but he also added an important rider: 'All of the supply people have assured us they can support the move, beginning this minute – let us assume that they know exactly what they are talking about and get about it vigorously and without delay.'[8]

As his directive revealed, Eisenhower had already conceived a broad campaign plan for the Allied armies in Western Europe. In fact, the planners at SHAEF had completed a study on the long term strategy for the campaign even before D-Day. While it was acknowledged that Berlin was the ultimate objective, the planners considered that an attack on the Ruhr, the industrial heartland of Germany, was considered 'likely to give us every chance of bringing to battle and destroying the main German Armed Forces'.[9] Thus, Eisenhower had long seen an attack on the Ruhr as the necessary precursor for the final, decisive battle. There were four main routes to the Ruhr, of which only two were considered suitable: the first was through the Metz gap, south of the Ardennes, while the most direct route was north of the Ardennes on the line of Maubeuge–Liège in Belgium. The SHAEF planners considered that 'our main chance of success would appear to be in advancing astride the Ardennes with two mutually supporting forces, extending the enemy forces, and, by surprise and deception, achieving superiority of force in one or other of the gaps and defeating the enemy in detail'.[10] Montgomery's army group would drive forward through the Low Countries and into Germany from the north, while Bradley would advance across central France to pierce the Reich beyond Metz. Eisenhower's thinking on the campaign envisaged an advance on a broad front, with one major thrust in the north, another in the centre, while the south would be covered by the 6th Army Group supplied from Marseilles. This plan, as Montgomery never ceased to point out, had the flaw of dispersion but had the advantage that supply could be drawn from the north and south coasts of France while also ensuring that the Germans could not focus their attention on one sector of the new, vast front, which ran from the sea to Switzerland, just as it had done during the Great War. It was also an integral part of this plan that the great ports of Antwerp and Marseilles would have to be opened as Allied supply bases to sustain the drive into Germany. The eventual intention was for the two thrusts to eventually meet in a great encirclement behind the Ruhr.

While Montgomery saw the argument over strategy as an entirely binary problem in which he was right and Eisenhower was wrong, the reality was never that simple. Both approaches contained advantages and problems in almost equal measure. Montgomery's choice had the virtue of concentration and a single aim – crossing the Rhine and aiming for the Ruhr. Yet such a *Schwerpunkt*, or 'point of main effort', would be easily identified by the Germans, enabling them to direct all their reserves to the threatened northern sector while the other Allied armies waited immobilised in France by lack of supply. Eisenhower's plan ensured that the Germans could not concentrate on one sector of the front but risked stretching Allied resources to the point where they would not be strong enough to break through the German defences. Eisenhower was clear, however, on some important fundamentals that seem to have eluded Montgomery. The Supreme Commander understood that the Allies needed to maintain a continuous front to prevent German recovery, ensure the safety of the flanks of each Allied army and gain ground cheaply wherever possible. Perhaps most importantly of all, he was absolutely clear on the paramount need to capture the port of Antwerp and open it as a major entry point for Allied supply. Without Antwerp and Marseilles working at full capacity, there could be no sustained advance to carry the Allies to the Rhine and beyond.

Montgomery's contemptuous disdain for Eisenhower's abilities seems to have blinded him to the fact that Eisenhower did in fact have a secure grasp of the fundamentals required for success in

Europe. Eisenhower took a broad view of the theatre as a whole and he was thinking big: about multiple lines of advance, about airpower and, most critically, about supply. Montgomery's plan, by contrast, seemed trammelled by considerations that limited his chosen field of operations to the area of northern Europe – Belgium, Holland and Germany – that Britain's armies had traditionally and invariably fought over since the late seventeenth century. Brooke also had serious reservations about Eisenhower's plan, which he considered might add 'another 3 to 6 months on to the war!' The British CIGS disapproved of Eisenhower's aim to 'split his forces' but also mused that 'If the Germans were not as beat as they are, this would be a fatal move, as it is it may not do too much harm.'[11]

The arguments concerning the best strategy for the rest of the campaign soon became intertwined with the question of who should command the Allied armies. Eisenhower had already made it clear that he would assume overall command when the River Seine was reached: that time was now fast approaching and the date was set for 1 September 1944. However, in late August 1944, Wes Gallagher, an American journalist for Associated Press, found out about the coming changes to the command set-up and managed to slip a story through the censors that Bradley now commanded an army group and was thus no longer under Montgomery's command. This story was reported in Britain as a demotion for Montgomery. Gallagher's scoop had stolen Eisenhower's thunder: the Supreme Commander's announcement a few days later that he was taking overall command of the Allied armies on 1 September now lacked impact and caused disquiet amongst the British public. It also led to Eisenhower's assumption of command becoming a divisive issue within the Anglo-American alliance. The public in both countries was now highly sensitive to any slight, real or perceived, that might be dealt to one of 'their' generals, and judging the British mood, Churchill told Brooke that he had decided to promote Montgomery to the rank of field marshal, as a gesture to 'mark the approval of the British people for the British effort that had led to the defeat of the Germans in France through the medium of Montgomery's leadership'.[12]

Eisenhower did not learn of Montgomery's promotion until the morning of 1 September, which caused anger amongst many American officers, who considered it 'poor taste' to make the announcement at the same time as Eisenhower's assumption of command.[13] Churchill's gesture, however, does not seem to have had the desired effect even with its target audience. It was noted by Home Intelligence reports that the majority of people were 'very pleased at [Montgomery's] promotion' but there were lingering doubts that it was 'a sop for his recent demotion', or 'an Irishman's rise'.[14]

However, although the political fallout of Eisenhower's decision was deeply worrying for the cohesion of the Anglo-American alliance in its final campaign, the military consequences were much more serious. SHAEF had remained in England throughout the course of the Normandy battles, but in late August 1944, this vast organisation moved across the Channel. Eisenhower decided to open his headquarters at Grainville, a small resort town in western Normandy. This proved to be the very worst location for the Supreme Allied Headquarters at a time when the spearheads of the Allied armies were driving forward at a dramatic pace. Grainville was soon left far behind, and what was worse, communications between SHAEF and its army groups became very difficult. Although Eisenhower wished to avoid the ostentation of SHAEF occupying Versailles or Paris, by September 1944 these were the only logical choices. By choosing Grainville, Eisenhower had made himself land commander in name only during a crucial period of the campaign when events moved very swiftly indeed.[15]

As these command changes were being implemented and argued over, the Allied armies were advancing at a blistering pace. Brian Horrocks, the commander of the British 30 Corps, later related:

> On 29th August we burst out of the bridgehead on the Seine and set off on our chase northwards. This was the type of warfare I thoroughly enjoyed. Who wouldn't? I had upwards of 600 tanks under my command and we were advancing on a frontage of fifty miles . . . scything passages through the enemy rear areas, like a combine harvester going through a field of corn.[16]

With the German army in France routed, there seemed nothing to stop the Allied advance. On 1 September, with his armoured spearheads driving across France at speed, Patton begged Bradley, 'Give me 400,000 gallons of gasoline and I'll put you in Germany in two days.' Bradley himself reckoned that by turning 'everything toward Germany', his army group could get at least six divisions to the Rhine very quickly.[17] It was perhaps inevitable that, after the bitter campaign of Normandy, the Allied commanders would become infused with optimism: the end of the war seemed to be in sight.

Within days, Patton's Third Army had reached the Moselle river, close to the border with Germany; it now seemed likely that he would be able to breach the defences along the German frontier, known as the Siegfried Line, and enter Germany immediately. In the north, Montgomery's 21st Army Group 'scythed' forward with Horrocks' 30 Corps in the lead. Brussels was liberated, to much rejoicing, on 3 September, by which time 30 Corps had covered 250 miles in just six days.[18] Horrocks ordered his lead division, the 11th Armoured Division under Major General Pip Roberts, to go even further the next day and reach the docks at Antwerp. This was by far the largest port available to the Allied armies on the coast of France and Belgium, and its possession would enable a massive transfusion of supplies for the assault on Germany. Horrocks gave a rather sceptical Roberts the objective of securing the docks before the Germans had time to destroy them. The following day, Roberts' men duly reached Antwerp and the elaborate port facilities fell into British hands entirely undamaged. The port of Antwerp was truly a mighty prize, with its 30 miles of wharves, 632 cranes, 186 acres of warehousing, and storage facilities for 100 million gallons of oil.[19] This was a major achievement, but its capture marked the temporary end of the northern British drive. Horrocks was ordered to halt, and he later identified 4 September 1944 as the critical day when the Allied momentum was lost:

Had we been able to advance that day we could have smashed through this screen and advanced northwards with little or nothing to stop us. We might even have succeeded in bouncing a crossing over the Rhine. But we halted, and even by that same evening the situation was worsening.[20]

While Horrocks believed that his corps was on the verge of complete success in early September, so too did Patton in his southern drive towards Germany. Both men had tantalising objectives seemingly within their grasp, but the reality was disappointingly different. The simple fact was that after an astonishingly rapid advance, the Allies had outrun their ability to supply their armies. With so few ports available, the vast majority of supplies still had to arrive in France over the open beaches in Normandy – which were now at least 300 miles away from the front line. Neither rail transport nor pipelines could be relied upon because Allied bombing and German demolitions had wrecked them.[21] The advance had been so rapid that there had been no opportunity to build up supply dumps, which meant that the available motor transport had to work even harder. Expedients like the Red Ball Express – a loop of one-way roads on which trucks drove hell-for-leather up to the front and back to the beaches – made a difference but could not alter the basic problem.[22] By early September, three newly arrived US divisions had to be immobilised in Normandy in order to reserve the transport capacity for the front, and it still was not enough. The tantalising vision of a complete and rapid victory in the autumn of 1944 withered in the glare of harsh logistic reality. Unfortunately, the pause that was forced upon the Allies gave the battered German forces what they most needed – a breathing space in which to organise their defence of the Reich.

A heated argument soon developed between the proponents of the two competing thrusts, with Bradley and Patton arguing that their advance into Germany should be given top priority for the lion's share of the dwindling total of resources, while Montgomery contended that his plan to 'bounce' the Rhine offered the best opportunity to maintain the momentum of the Allied advance. Just at the point when Eisenhower needed to give clear direction, the patchy communications between the Supreme Commander in Grainville and his generals' forward headquarters failed, adding to

the rising tempers on all sides. On 4 September, Montgomery wrote
to Eisenhower with his revised version of how to win the war:

1. I consider we have now reached a stage where one really
    powerful and full-blooded thrust toward Berlin is likely to get
    there and thus end the German war.

2. We have not enough maintenance resources for two full-
    blooded thrusts.

3. The selected thrust must have all the maintenance resources it
    needs without any qualifications and any other operations must
    do the best it can with what is left over.

4. There are only two possible thrusts one via the Ruhr and the
    other via Metz and the Saar.

5. In my opinion the thrust likely to give the best and quickest
    results is the northern one via the Ruhr.

6. Time is vital and the decision regarding the selected thrust
    must be made at once.

7. If we attempt a compromise solution and split our maintenance
    resources so that neither thrust is full-blooded we will prolong
    the war.

8. I consider the problem viewed as above as very simple and
    clear-cut.[23]

One of Montgomery's real talents as a commander was his ability
to simplify complex issues into clear statements of intent. However,
while this skill had served him well while an army commander, he
was now dealing with much wider issues, where such simplicity
was not always so helpful. Inherent in his statement was also the
same challenge and threat he had used to engineer acceptance to
his plans throughout the war. Ultimately, Montgomery was challenging Eisenhower to either adopt his plan or face accusations
that he had prolonged the war, while also implicitly arguing that
only he could serve as the overall commander for such a thrust.
    Nonetheless, there was merit in Montgomery's 'Schlieffen Plan
in reverse'. If the available transport and supplies had been ruth-
lessly stripped from all other forces, and concentrated behind
21st Army Group and Hodges' First US Army, it is just conceivable

that a drive by 18 fully supplied divisions might have been able to reach the Ruhr. However, 12 out of the 43 available Allied divisions would have been immobilised, and any 'full-blooded' thrust on the Ruhr would have been reliant on supply dumps and communications stretching back for hundreds of miles to the Normandy beaches. There were also dangers: the difficult question was not, perhaps, whether the force could reach the Ruhr, but what would happen when it did. Operating at the very limit of the supply chain, and without the possibility of support from the rest of the Allied force, such a thrust would almost certainly have opened itself to a dangerous German counter-attack.

Not surprisingly, Eisenhower refused to take such a gamble. Not only did he consider Montgomery's plan too risky, but it did not accord with his overall conception of the campaign. Montgomery's attempt to regain command of the ground forces – or at least of those in combat – was also politically impossible for Eisenhower. He had already tried to explain this situation to Montgomery when, during a conversation on 23 August, he had argued that American public opinion would object to a situation where Bradley's 12 Army Group had only one army in it while 21st Army Group also commanded Hodges' First US Army. Montgomery queried why 'public opinion should make him want to take military decisions which are definitely unsound'. Eisenhower's response was that Montgomery 'must understand that it was an election year in America; he could take no action which was calculated to sway public opinion against the President and possibly lose him the election'. He also emphasised that, given the preponderance of American strength in theatre, 'there could be no question of the American Army Group being under the operational direction of a British general'.[24] Montgomery could not accept that such political matters might influence the command organisation of the Allied armies, but in fact Eisenhower had softened the blow somewhat: the reality was that Montgomery as overall commander was simply no longer acceptable to Bradley or Patton – or to American public opinion. Eisenhower had attempted to let Montgomery down gently but the British field marshal had been unable to read between the lines.

★   ★   ★

Faced with insistent demands from both Bradley and Montgomery, Eisenhower compromised. He decided to support Montgomery's plan to 'bounce' the Rhine, while still providing 12th US Army Group with sufficient supplies to mount a limited offensive towards Metz. Bradley and Patton were livid that Eisenhower refused to support their thrust fully, while Montgomery complained that the Americans were absorbing resources that his army group needed. The fact that Eisenhower compromised is often seen as evidence of his failure to command, but actually demonstrated that he was executing his function as Supreme Commander under very difficult circumstances. He knew that he needed to ensure that the Allied armies kept up momentum, maintained the cohesion of the alliance and defeated the German army all at the same time. Both Montgomery and Bradley's plans, whatever their possible risks or merits, were almost calculated to destroy Allied cohesion, which was the one factor Eisenhower saw as essential to victory.

By 10 September, Eisenhower had approved Montgomery's Operation Market Garden, a bold and risky venture that nonetheless offered real opportunities. Montgomery later explained:

> The basic idea for the drive northwards towards Arnhem was to use one airborne division as a sort of carpet which was unrolled like a stair-carpet along a narrow axis. The para troops were dropped mainly at the canal and dyke crossings.
>
> Up the stair-carpet went the 30 Corps thrust, two lines abreast on one road – just barging through by sheer weight and impetus.
>
> At the top of the stair-carpet two large drawing room carpets were put down, each of one airborne division – one at Nijmegen and Grave, and one at Arnhem.[25]

While the airborne forces laid down these 'carpets', the British 30 Corps would drive 80 miles into Holland, crossing the Maas and Waal rivers at the points secured by the airborne forces before reaching the last crossing at Arnhem over the Lower Rhine. The hope was that an early crossing of the Rhine would outflank this major river barrier and enable a rapid drive into the Ruhr.[26]

Certainly the plan seemed to re-orientate the Allied drive in

Montgomery's favour, but it also appeared to Eisenhower to be the 'boldest and best move the Allies could make at the moment'.[27] The First Allied Airborne Army, commanded by Lieutenant General Lewis Brereton, represented Eisenhower's strategic reserve. There had been numerous plans for its use during the pursuit from Normandy, but all the operations had been stillborn due to the speed of the advance. Operation Market Garden appeared to offer an opportunity to employ it to maintain Allied momentum under favourable conditions. The First Allied Airborne Army also represented a truly integrated Allied force, comprising of two British and three American airborne divisions, an attached Polish parachute brigade, along with an American troop carrier command and two British troop carrier groups. This was a powerful reserve, which 'had in effect become coins burning holes in SHAEF's pocket'; not only did the airborne forces desperately want to demonstrate what they could do, but Eisenhower wanted to use them to achieve a strategic success. This accorded not only with his own thinking but with that of Generals Marshall and Arnold, who had consistently encouraged him to use airborne forces deep in the German rear.[28]

Operation Market Garden soon became a reality. It was launched on 17 September 1944 amidst growing hopes that this might be the battle to knock Germany out of the war. Initially the airborne drops went according to plan, and 30 Corps was able to drive up the narrow corridor, linking up with the 101st Airborne Division at Eindhoven and pushing on for Nijmegen. In that Dutch city, one of the most remarkable examples of tactical cooperation between British and American troops led to a signal success. The 82nd Airborne Division had managed to secure the high ground south of the River Waal but had been unable to capture the town of Nijmegen itself, which included the major bridge over the wide Waal river. Major General James Gavin, the commander of the 82nd Airborne Division, 'decided that the best and quickest method would be to rush the bridge with tanks' once 30 Corps arrived. Unfortunately, the advance into Nijmegen by a mixed group of British tanks, a company of British infantry and a battalion of American paratroops to seize the road and railway bridges met with heavy resistance. On the evening of 19 September, Gavin came up with an original, if risky plan: while the advance through Nijmegen continued, one parachute regiment would cross the Waal in British assault boats to outflank the defence. The crossing would be given maximum support, including Typhoon fighter-bombers, an artillery bombardment and smokescreen and an armoured regiment, the 2nd Armoured Irish Guards, to fire across the river.[29]

This dangerous task was given to the 504th Regimental Combat Team, under the command of Lieutenant Colonel Reuben Tucker. None of the men had seen – let alone practised in – the British assault boats, and yet the crossing depended on them. The trucks carrying the flimsy boats struggled through the enormous traffic jams up the single route, christened 'Hell's Highway', that led to the front. This led to postponement after postponement for Tucker's assault. Eventually the boats arrived, but they still had to be manhandled nearly a thousand yards to the riverbank. With 14 men in each plywood boat, they were 'rather overloaded'.[30] The crossing began at 1500 hours, but 'soon after the journey had started it was seen that the smoke screen had passed its best and gaps were forming'. Tucker asked Lieutenant Colonel Vandeleur of the Irish Guards, who was standing with him watching the attack from the top of a factory, to get his tanks to thicken the smokescreen. Even so, when the boats were halfway across the 400-yard-wide river, they 'came under murderous fire, 20 mm, machine gun and rifle fire from the opposite bank'.[31] Only half the boats made it across, but once the Americans reached the bank, they charged forward to deal with the German posts, taking very few prisoners. By the end of the action, the two supporting squadrons of the Irish Guards had fired off all their ammunition; without their support, the para-troops would have suffered even higher casualties.

As more troops were ferried across, Tucker's men advanced towards the railway bridge and then the road bridge. After hard house-to-house fighting, the Grenadier Guards and 505th Parachute Infantry managed to deal with the last German resistance on the approaches to the road bridge. As dusk fell, four Sherman tanks of the Grenadier Guards were able to motor across the bridge and link up with the American paratroops. Remarkably, all the German attempts to blow the bridge with planted 500 lb charges had failed.[32] The Allies were now only 11 miles from Arnhem, where the British 1st Parachute Division was struggling to hold its positions against determined German counter-attacks.

The crossing of the Waal at Nijmegen was remarkable in that a rapidly organised and improvised cooperation between British and American units had resulted in a 'great feat of arms which will surely rank very high in the annals of our history'. The British report considered that 'there has never been a finer example of unison and good team work' than 'the perfect liaison, co-ordination and understanding between ourselves and the Americans which was the keynote to the capture of the Nijmegen bridge'.[33] The fact that British and American soldiers could cooperate so seamlessly demonstrated just how far the two armies had come since the early days of Tunisia.

Yet the day did not end with such a warm glow of self-satisfaction. Tucker had expected that once the bridge was captured, the British would immediately continue on their way towards Arnhem, where 1st British Parachute Division desperately needed their help. Instead, the tanks stopped. Tucker was incredulous that, after the sacrifice made by his men, the British had been ordered to wait for infantry support rather than continue the pursuit,[34] and even considered continuing the advance with his own depleted, exhausted regiment. When he saw Gavin 12 hours later, he was still incandescent, shouting, 'What in the Hell are they doing? We have been in this position for over twelve hours, and all they seem to be doing is brewing tea. Why in Hell don't they get on to Arnhem?'[35] This famous outburst seems to sum up the differences between the two armies, yet Tucker's fury was the result of both a cultural and a military misunderstanding.

The drinking of tea by British soldiers in the Second World War was legendary, but it was also essential. British tank crews had first perfected a rapid means of brewing up in the desert campaign. The radio operator and hull machine-gunner had an additional role in a British tank: it was also his job to leap out and make the tea whenever there was an opportunity. Some petrol was poured into a tin filled with sand. The sand was then stirred and lit, and the resulting fire would boil a dixie can of water in under three minutes.[36] Mugs of hot, sweet army tea would then be gratefully drained by the crew. The sign 'WHEN IN DOUBT BREW-UP' was a common one in the British Army's sector. It was also an example of the British Tommy's mordant humour – when a tank was hit and caught fire, it had also 'brewed up'. The British soldier's love of a mug of tea was not a sign of rigidity or tradition but a vital means of giving often tired men a boost and ensuring tank crews were hydrated during long days of fighting. The crewmen that Tucker saw brewing up had, after all, been in action for an entire day.

Yet there was also a serious military aspect to the misunderstanding. In the plan for Operation Market Garden, 30 Corps had been expected to drive down one road for over 100 miles, on 'almost a one tank front', while crossing seven major water obstacles. This task was described as 'threading a piece of cotton through the eyes of seven needles in a row'.[37] Far from having a fresh reserve ready to exploit the success that had been achieved, the troops of the Guards Armoured Division that crossed the Waal represented the fingertip of 30 Corps, which had stretched as far as was possible. The three armoured groups of the Guards Armoured Division were either engaged in fighting to clear Nijmegen or support the 82nd Airborne on the Groesbeek heights, or were in real need of rest, reorganisation and resupply. Behind them, the rest of 30 Corps stretched in a 23,000-vehicle tailback covering 60 miles. Although tantalisingly close, they could go no further that night.[38]

Ultimately, the delays imposed on 30 Corps as they struggled up one route towards Arnhem doomed Operation Market Garden. After a legendary five-day battle, Lieutenant Colonel John Frost's 2nd Parachute Battalion, the one unit of the British 1st Airborne Division that had managed to reach Arnhem Bridge, was forced to surrender. On the night of 25 September, the remnants of the British 1st Airborne Division crossed the Rhine. Out of 10,600 men who had gone into action, 1,485 had been killed and 6,414 captured. Market Garden had, by a narrow margin, failed, leaving Montgomery's 21st Army Group holding an awkward 60-mile salient that led nowhere. The ferocious fighting along Hell's

Highway and at Nijmegen and Arnhem also demonstrated the unwelcome fact that the German army was far from beaten and had staged a remarkable recovery: the end of the war no longer seemed so close. Market Garden had been a risky venture but perhaps one that needed to be taken. However, with its failure, the Allies could no longer ignore their logistic predicament. Having attempted to subordinate logistic reality to the tempting strategic and operational opportunities available, there was now no alternative but to plan future operations around the necessity of securing lines of communication, opening up port capacity and building supply dumps close to the front.[39]

The operation also marked the last chance for a British-inspired victory that might have ended the war. In fact, the British had missed a much more important, even vital, opportunity over their capture of Antwerp. Although the port had been taken intact, its facilities were useless until the 40 miles of the Scheldt estuary were cleared of mines and its banks of German defenders. Unfortunately, by halting after the capture of Antwerp, the British had allowed the Germans to stiffen their defences. Horrocks later wrote:

> It never entered my head that the Scheldt would be mined, and that we should not be able to use Antwerp port until the channel had been swept and the Germans cleared from the coastline on either side . . . If I had ordered Roberts, not to liberate Antwerp, but to by-pass the town on the east, cross the Albert canal and advance only fifteen miles towards Woensdrecht, we should have blocked the Beveland isthmus and cut the main German escape route.[40]

Perhaps Horrocks might be forgiven the error, but the importance of such an issue should certainly have occurred to Montgomery. The fact was that in early September 1944, the British supply situation was under control. The British had access to more roads and their supply columns had a shorter distance to travel, which meant that they did not need Antwerp opened immediately. However, the American forces operating further south, with longer lines of communication, most certainly did.[41]

After the failure of Market Garden, Eisenhower held a conference on 5 October 1944 that not only provided a post-mortem on the operation but in which he reiterated his strategy for the campaign. Brooke, who was present as an observer, noted that Ike's strategy continued to focus on the clearance of the Scheldt estuary, followed by an advance to the Rhine, the capture of the Ruhr and a subsequent advance on Berlin. After a full and frank discussion in which Admiral Ramsay criticised Monty freely, Brooke was moved to write, 'I feel that Monty's strategy for once is at fault, instead of carrying out the advance on Arnhem he ought to have made certain of Antwerp in the first place . . . Ike nobly took all blame on himself as he had approved Monty's suggestion to operate on Arnhem.'[42] The Allied leaders had realised that there was no alternative to a long, methodical and bitter fight during the winter of 1944: the war would not now end in a rapid blaze of glory.

If the Allies had not immediately recognised the importance of the Scheldt estuary, or of Antwerp, the Germans most certainly had. London had been the first target for the German *Vergeltungswaffen*, but in October 1944, Antwerp became the priority. Montgomery gave the unglamorous yet essential task of clearing the Scheldt estuary to the Canadian First Army. They had to fight a fiercely contested and waterlogged battle to clear the Breskens pocket and take the island of Walcheren, before the Scheldt was properly free of German resistance. Antwerp was finally opened for Allied shipping on 8 November.[43] The Germans realised that if they could render the port unusable through heavy bombardment, or mining the Scheldt channel, they could place a heavy brake on Allied progress. The protection of Antwerp, being firmly in the 21st Army Group sector, was a British responsibility, but it was soon realised by Brigadier P. G. Calvert-Jones, the commander of GHQ AA Troops in 21st Army Group, that American assistance would be required. Not only was the Royal Navy concerned about the threat from magnetic mines in the Scheldt channel, but V-1s and V-2s might also be used against the city. Given the vital importance of protecting both Antwerp and the Scheldt, an elaborate defence involving three anti-aircraft brigades, two British and one American,

was undertaken. On 19 October, Calvert-Jones was alerted by
Brigadier Belchem, the Brigadier General Staff (Ops) of 21st Army
Group, that flying bomb attacks could be expected within the next
24 hours. Belchem ended the interview by saying drily, 'Your job,
old boy, I am busy.'[44]

The first flying bombs fell on Brussels on 21 October, and four
days later on Antwerp. Initially the scale of attack was relatively
low, which gave time to organise and prepare the Allied defence,
but this proved a much greater challenge than the defence of
London, since the German missiles could approach from a very
wide arc and there was no possibility of early warning. Furthermore,
due to the dense civilian population, there were significant restrictions on the areas in which shooting could take place. This meant
there was no possibility of deploying an effective defence around
the whole of the threatened perimeter. In these circumstances, it
was clear that more anti-aircraft guns were needed, as well as
American equipment in the form of SCR-584 radar sets and No. 10
predictors, which had proved so successful against flying bombs in
England. Given the importance of Antwerp, SHAEF agreed to
dispatch three US anti-aircraft battalions to thicken up the defence.
When a second US brigade arrived, control of the defences was
turned over to the American Brigadier General G. Armstrong, who
took command on 11 November 1944.

These defences proved their worth. Although the Luftwaffe
attempted to drop aerial mines into the Scheldt channel almost every
night, all their attempts met with failure. The vengeance weapons
were another matter, and Antwerp became the most heavily bombed
city in Europe during the winter of 1944. There was no practical
defence against the supersonic V-2, and Antwerp soon gained the
moniker of 'the City of Sudden Death'. However, the combined
efforts of the British and American anti-aircraft batteries achieved
great success against the V-1. Of the 4,900 V-1s launched at Antwerp,
2,400 might have hit the docks but 2,356 were destroyed by the
defences, and only 200 reached their intended target. In mid-
December 1944, the Combined Chiefs of Staff agreed to the use of
the top-secret VT proximity fuse by the artillery batteries defending
Antwerp. The VT fuse was essentially a miniaturised radar that could

be fitted into the nose cap of an artillery shell, enabling it to explode in close proximity to a fast-moving aerial target. It was invented in Britain, but the United States placed vast scientific and engineering resources behind the project to bring it to fruition. With its introduction at Antwerp, 90 per cent of V-1s were brought down.

While the civilian casualties in Antwerp and its surroundings were grievous, with 3,700 civilian deaths and 6,000 injured over the 154 days of attack, the German bombardment did not prevent the Allies from using the port. Allied military casualties were 32 killed and 298 wounded, while 30 million tons of supplies were unloaded during the period.[45] The successful defence of Antwerp owed much to the seamless cooperation between the British and American anti-aircraft units, but also to the unseen yet vital scientific and technical collaboration between the two allies.

After the high hopes of the summer, the autumn of 1944 proved to be one long disappointment as Allied soldiers were pushed into unrewarding assaults against determined German resistance in foul weather. Patton's Third Army, which had raced across France, was baulked by the German defence around the great fortress city of Metz. Advancing on a broad front, and suffering from supply shortages and the awful weather, Patton's units were held by a thin German defence. The siege of Metz lasted for over three months and cost 50,000 American casualties. By December 1944, Patton's army had advanced just 46 miles.[46] The campaign was later described as 'dogged, grim and dirty, lacking glamour', which was representative of the fighting all across the long Western Front in the autumn of 1944.[47]

Meanwhile, the First US Army fought their way into Germany. The battle for the ancient city of Aachen, once the seat of Charlemagne's empire, lasted for nearly the whole of October and ended with the virtual destruction of the city. In November, another offensive was launched towards Cologne by the newly activated Ninth US Army under the command of General William Simpson. The Ninth US Army never gained the high public profile of the other American armies; it often worked in close touch with the British Second Army due to its deployment on the northern end of the

American line. As one member of SHAEF observed, 'Simpson worked well with them [the British], but he had to do the giving.'[48] Simpson's generosity towards the British began early: while training his force in the United States, his army had been known as the Eighth US Army, but in deference to the British Eighth Army, this was changed when the formation reached Europe.[49] However, such minor issues did not concern Bill Simpson. An austere Texan who was not made in the same flamboyant mould as Patton, he was judged to be a 'crack commander' and his staff 'the most professional . . . on the continent' by members of SHAEF.[50]

Simpson's 'giving' continued during his offensive, when he asked General Horrocks, the commander of the British 30 Corps, if he would support his left flank by capturing the German town of Geilenkirchen. This placed Horrocks in a difficult position, since 21st Army Group was neither willing nor able to spare any additional troops for the attack. At a meeting with Simpson and Eisenhower, the Supreme Commander asked Horrocks whether he could take the town: 'I replied that the spirit was willing, but the flesh, in the shape of one extra division, was weak. Eisenhower then turned to Simpson and said "Give him one of ours."' Thus the 84th US Division was placed under 30 Corps command for the attack. The division was also assisted by British mine-clearing tanks and Crocodile flamethrower tanks, which made their tasks considerably easier.[51] After the capture of the town on 16 November, the fighting became static in the waterlogged country between the Meuse and the Roer and the division returned to Simpson's command. If American troops had been placed under British command in 1917 or 1942, it would have been seen as a highly important political matter, but in late 1944, the incident passed off almost without comment.

Further south, the First US Army was engaged in one of the most costly and futile battles of the war. Fighting in what became known to the American soldiers as 'Huertgen Forest', a mass of trees 20 miles long and 10 miles wide, lasted from 14 September for 'three miserable, interminable months'.[52] Five American infantry divisions and one armoured combat command were sucked into the battle, which cost 33,000 American casualties. Ernest Hemingway called it 'Passchendaele with tree bursts', and tragically, it was just as futile as that grim Great War battle. The problem was that, without control of the Roer dams, neither the Ninth nor the First US Armies could cross the River Roer, since any attempt would result in the Germans opening the dams. This would flood the river and cut off any assaulting force. Ultimately, the dams were not finally seized until the end of February 1945. Once again, the American units advanced on a broad front, which meant there was not sufficient strength to punch through and reach their objective quickly.[53] Instead, unit after unit was sucked into 'a misconceived and basically fruitless battle that could have, and should have, been avoided'.[54] The continued American attacks in the rain, mud and later snow of a European autumn and winter followed Pershing's dictum of exerting continuous pressure regardless of the circumstances. Yet these offensives opened up the American generals of the Second World War to the bitter criticisms of the First: of mounting futile attacks that had little if any chance of success, leading to the waste of their soldiers' young lives for no purpose.

There is no question that by the end of October 1944, Eisenhower's broad front strategy had run into the sand. There were many reasons for this, including poor weather and lack of supplies, but there were also deeper, structural factors at work. When Wedemeyer had drafted the 1941 Victory Program, he had envisaged a US army of 200 divisions – a veritable steamroller that would crush the Germans by virtue of its very weight. By 1944, such grandiose ambitions had been reduced to a total force of some 90 divisions. With units still training in the States, and others committed to the war in the Pacific, Eisenhower and his generals realised that the '90-division gamble' that had been played by Washington left him with fewer than 60 divisions in Europe. This was simply not enough to pursue Eisenhower's broad front strategy and provide a sufficient reserve. At the same time, the US Army began to suffer shortages, not simply because of the demands of the Pacific theatre, or the fact that Antwerp took time to be opened, but also because American industry, in the expectation of an early European victory, was already turning over to civilian production. Artillery ammunition in particular became a scarce commodity in the winter of 1944, and some American units had to be supported by more plentifully supplied British artillery batteries. In fighting the culminating campaign against Germany, the United States army seemed to have reached the end of its reserves of manpower and supplies prematurely.

It was in this depressing atmosphere of a campaign gone awry that bad news arrived from Washington. After a long struggle with aplastic anaemia, Sir John Dill died on 5 November 1944. Brooke was truly grieved by Dill's passing; he commented in his diary that 'His loss is quite irreparable and he is irreplaceable in Washington. Without him I do not know how we should have got through the last 3 years.' He later added a more fulsome tribute to his predecessor: 'In my mind we owe more to Dill than to any other general for our final victory in the war. If it had not been for the vital part he played in Washington we should never have been able to achieve the degree of agreement in our inter-Allied strategy. The war might have taken a very different course.'[55] In Washington, Marshall too was genuinely grief-stricken at the loss of his close personal friend. He insisted that Dill be accorded the honour of burial in Arlington National Military Cemetery, and acted as one of the pallbearers at his funeral. Churchill never publicly – or privately – acknowledged Dill's critical importance and contribution to the development and success of the Anglo-American alliance. It was Marshall who ensured that after the war a fine equestrian statue was raised at Arlington to remember a prophet of the Anglo-American partnership who had not been accorded due honour in his own country.[56]

Yet while Brooke felt Dill's loss deeply, he could not quite emulate his predecessor's even-handedness and generosity of spirit, and in November 1944 came to side with Montgomery in mounting a serious challenge to Eisenhower's authority. Montgomery had continued to criticise Allied strategy and question Eisenhower's competency after the failure of Market Garden. In early November, he had returned to Britain for a short break and had briefed Brooke on the situation as he saw it. Brooke commented that Montgomery had become fixated on the command arrangements:

He has got this on the brain as it affects his own personal position, and he cannot put up with not being the sole controller of land operations. I agree that the set up is bad but it is not one which can be easily altered, as the Americans have now the preponderating force in France, and naturally consider they should have a major say in the running of the war. Perhaps after they see the results of dispersing their strength all along the front it may become easier to convince them that some drastic change is desirable.[57]

At this point Brooke seemed able to take a reasonably detached view of proceedings in Europe. However, over the course of the month, continued missives from Montgomery persuaded him to become actively involved in these issues. Montgomery argued that Eisenhower should either take full control or appoint a land force commander. He felt that 'If we go drifting along as at present we are merely playing into the enemy hands, and the war will go on indefinitely.' Yet when he asked Brooke whether he should take the initiative again in the matter, Brooke's response was immediate and adamant: he advised Montgomery to remain silent.[58] This advice was not because Brooke intended to remain passive and simply watch the campaign unfold. He explained to Montgomery that 'the Command organisation and strategy had to prove themselves defective by operational results before they could be satisfactorily attacked'[59]. He believed that there would soon be 'ample proof of the inefficiency of the present set up', which would enable him to go on the attack by forcing the Combined Chiefs of Staff to 'reconsider the present Command Organization and present strategy on the Western Front'.[60]

Brooke then discussed the subject with Churchill, arguing that 'American strategy' and 'American organization' were both faulty. He considered that the American approach of 'always attacking all along the front, irrespective of strength available, was sheer madness', and that the only solution to the command conundrum was to make Bradley commander of land forces, with one group of armies north of the Ardennes under Montgomery, and another group of armies to the south under Patton. Brooke's gambit was now clear: he hoped to insert a deputy beneath Eisenhower, thus taking real control out of his hands.[61] This time, given American strength, the deputy would have to be American, but the effect was the same: he intended that Eisenhower should be deprived of any real operational command. Brooke was now involved in what might well be termed a conspiracy to reassert British control and direction of the war against a commander in whom the American Chiefs of Staff had expressed their full confidence.

Although Montgomery had agreed not to broach the subject with Eisenhower again, when the Supreme Commander came to visit him on 29 November, he could not resist labouring the same points. Eisenhower was angered by Montgomery's accusation of strategic failure, and when the two of them met with Bradley and Tedder at Maastricht on 7 December, Montgomery found that he was 'alone against the other three' and that Eisenhower had 'reversed all his views which he previously agreed upon'. Montgomery believed that Eisenhower had been '"got at" by the American generals'.[62] What he never seemed to understand was that his own forceful articulation of opinions did not mean that Eisenhower necessarily agreed with him. Montgomery's unwilling-ness to participate in collective discussions at SHAEF with the principal commanders and their staffs meant that his perspective on Eisenhower's views was narrow and skewed. He had lost the ability to see the wider picture – which included understanding the opinions of his fellow commanders in Europe.

But Brooke had by now gone to the British Chiefs of Staff and called Eisenhower to account for the failures in the Allied campaign. Eisenhower was invited to London to brief the cabinet on 12 December 1944, and the meeting did not go well. Brooke provided savage criticism of Eisenhower's plans, arguing that they involved a 'dangerous dispersal of forces' and that neither of the two main thrusts towards Ruhr and Frankfurt would be powerful enough to succeed, and renewed his attempt to insert a land force deputy beneath the Supreme Commander. On 18 December, the British Chiefs of Staff agreed a paper proposing that the issue of command on the Western Front be discussed by the Combined Chiefs of Staff. Brooke had by now become fixated on the same issues as his lieutenant, Montgomery.

These disagreements over command and strategy appeared to be final proof that the Allied campaign had reached its nadir. The winter of 1944 seemed to offer no prospect other than a slow, grinding advance by the Allied armies into Germany at the cost of far too many lives. Hitler, however, had quite different ideas. Since September, he had been building up reserve forces in strict secrecy opposite the Ardennes region of Belgium. This was to be Germany's last throw of the dice: an all-out offensive over the same ground that had witnessed the Wehrmacht's extraordinary victory in 1940, with a similar aim – the shattering of the Anglo-American alliance. The spearheads of the German Fifth and Sixth Panzer Armies and the Seventh Army were to drive for the Meuse, cross the river and head for Antwerp, the key Allied supply base. Most of the German generals had severe reservations about the offensive, and von Rundstedt commented that if the German spearheads even reached the Meuse, it would be a miracle. But Hitler had heard such talk in 1940 as well, and he was adamant that the offensive, taking advantage of poor weather to negate the Allies' crushing air superiority, and with its preparations undertaken in strict secrecy, would not only catch the Allies by surprise but would shake the Anglo-American alliance to its very foundations. As the soldiers of three German armies prepared for battle in the early hours of 16 December 1944, it seemed that Hitler's prediction might be proved right: that the blow would 'bring down this artificial coalition with a mighty thunderclap'.[63]

Supreme Commander

At 0530 hours on 16 December 1944, the whole horizon erupted as thousands of German guns pounded the thinly stretched American lines in the Ardennes.[1] The opening bombardment was one of the most ferocious ever experienced by American soldiers during the war. Major General Troy Middleton's VII Corps took the brunt of the German assault, and Middleton, who had been noted as the finest infantry regimental commander in the AEF in 1918, knew that his defences were paper-thin.[2] That morning, American troops fought desperate defensive battles only to find themselves overwhelmed and overrun by superior numbers.

It took time for the gravity of the situation to get through to Middleton's headquarters and for the information to flow up the command chain to Hodges' First US Army and thence on to SHAEF. It was not until a 2 p.m. briefing that Major General Kenneth Strong, the chief intelligence officer at SHAEF, received news that 'the situation had become serious'.[3] When Eisenhower heard the news, Bradley was fortuitously with him. Bradley initially dismissed it as a minor attempt by the Germans to distract attention from the American attack against the Roer dams, and suggested that it could be dealt with easily. However, Eisenhower understood the position immediately. He realised that there were no minor objectives along the Ardennes front; this had to be an unexpected major offensive by the Germans. He took rapid steps to counter the threat and ordered Bradley to send the 7th and 10th Armored Divisions from the Ninth and Third Armies as immediate reserves. He then ordered his only available reserve, the 82nd and 101st Airborne Divisions, which had been resting and refitting after Operation

Market Garden, to the Ardennes sector.[4] There is no question that the weakness of the American forces there was a direct result of Eisenhower's broad front strategy. The Ardennes, as a 'quiet' sector of the front, had been stripped of reserves in order to reinforce other, more active areas, which left it highly vulnerable to the German blow. However, Eisenhower's immediate response to the news of the German assault at least began to repair the weakness caused by his own strategy. At this moment of crisis, his responses were calm, unhurried and correct – precisely what the British and American governments required of a Supreme Commander. Eisenhower had just received the news that he was to be promoted to the rank of five-star general, and that evening he celebrated with Bradley and a bottle of champagne. Chester Hansen, Bradley's ADC, joined the celebrations briefly, but then went on to the Lido, 'where we saw bare breasted girls do the hootchy kootchie until it was late and we hurried on home'.[5] The contrast with the desperate battle for survival being fought by the GIs in the frozen forests of the Ardennes could hardly have been greater.

The situation at the Ardennes front rapidly grew worse. The inexperienced 106th Infantry Division had been holding an impossibly wide frontage of 22 miles when the Germans attacked. Although the men had fought back with real courage, their commander, Major General Alan Jones, had mistakenly kept his forces in position instead of pulling them back as quickly as possible. This doomed two of his three infantry regiments to encirclement and capture in what became the largest surrender of American troops in the European theatre.[6] However, even as disaster engulfed some of the American units, Middleton recognised that the towns of St Vith and Bastogne, with their important roads, could act as choke points. If these places could be held, the German advance might be channelled, disrupted and eventually prevented from becoming an irresistible flood westwards. He used the only reserves available in the form of engineer battalions to form piecemeal blocking forces to delay the German advance while the defences of these towns could be organised and time bought for reinforcements to reach the area.

On 18 December, Eisenhower held an important conference in the gloomy surroundings of Verdun. This was a highly significant meeting in which all the key commanders, including Bradley, Devers, Tedder and Patton, were present bar one. Montgomery was represented by Freddie de Guingand, his Chief of Staff, since he had decided (once again) that he was unable to leave his own command.[7] Kenneth Strong later remarked that:

> The meeting was crowded and the atmosphere tense. The British were worried by events. As so often before, their confidence in the ability of the Americans to deal with the situation was not great. Reports had been reaching them of disorganization behind the American lines, of American headquarters abandoned without notice . . . Stories of great bravery on the part of individual American units and soldiers did not change their opinion.[8]

Yet Eisenhower opened the conference by emphasising that 'The present situation is to be regarded as one of opportunity for us and not of disaster. There will be only cheerful faces at this conference table.'[9] He went on to state firmly that 'the enemy must never be allowed to cross the Meuse'.[10] He explained that since the Allies were holding firm on both 'shoulders of the penetration', steps must be taken to slow and hold the German attack while preparing counter-attacks from both the northern and southern shoulders. He recognised that Patton's Third Army could be disengaged from its operations in the Saar relatively quickly and could hold the south, while the northern counter-attack would take longer. The policy there would have to be 'to plug the holes and get things straightened out'.[11] However, when he asked Patton how long it would be before he could wheel his army north and begin his counter-attack, the Third Army commander responded with 'forty-eight hours'. This caused an outbreak of laughter, particularly from the British officers in the meeting, yet Patton had meant what he said. In fact, his headquarters had already begun planning such a move, and in just over two days, the bulk of the Third US Army had disengaged, swung through 90 degrees and begun its drive north. This was one of the most exceptional feats of command

and staff work of the war. Yet while Patton's exemplary generalship during the Battle of the Bulge, as it came to be known, was rightly lionised, it was Eisenhower who had revealed his real talent as a commander at the Verdun conference.

Eisenhower sent a report to the Combined Chiefs of Staff explaining his new policy:

The whole front south of Moselle passes to strict defence immediately giving up all penetrations across the Saar River. Devers takes over most of present Third Army front. Patton moves north with six divisions and taking over VIII Corps temporarily will organize major counter blow with target date of 23 or 24th. Our weakest spot is in direction of Namur. Enemy is expected to attack with armour near Monschau to broaden his penetration and may attack with lesser strength from Triers region. He also may try to attack on north of Ninth Army but Montgomery has reserves capable of dealing with him there. The general plan is to plug the holes in the north and launch coordinated attack from the south.[12]

Here was the proof of his capability as a commander. Within 48 hours of the German attack, he had not only taken the correct steps to hold the assault but had developed a clear plan for a counter-attack to finish off any chance the Germans had of success. While it might not be an example of 'grip' in the sense that Montgomery understood, this was a clear, coherent plan to deal with the crisis. If Eisenhower had been an over-promoted figurehead with no real knowledge of war and no understanding of how to command troops – as Montgomery constantly suggested – his response to the crisis would most likely have been indecision, command paralysis and, ultimately, disaster.

That same day, Brooke confided to his diary that he doubted whether the Americans had the skill required to deal with the German offensive. He continued: 'It is a worrying situation, if I felt that the American Divisional, Corps, Army Commanders and Staff were more efficient than they are, there is no doubt that this might turn out to be a heaven sent opportunity. However, if mishandled it may well put the defeat of Germany back for another

6 months.'¹³ Brooke had yet again unfairly underestimated Eisenhower and his American commanders. Meanwhile, Montgomery continued to hold his critical view of Eisenhower because, unlike every other senior Allied general and airman, he had not been present at this vital meeting.

Yet not all American commanders had necessarily measured up to the crisis. Omar Bradley, although the most trusted of Eisenhower's American subordinates, proved lacklustre in the first, critical days of the attack. He had not identified the seriousness of the German threat and had even cavilled when Eisenhower ordered him to move reserves. Worse, he did not visit the headquarters of the First and Ninth Armies during the early days of the battle but attempted to control them through telephone and radio contact. This was unusual behaviour for Bradley, who normally emphasised the importance of personal contact during periods of crisis. The fact was that he had been ill for a number of days and had not fully recovered before the German attack began. Bradley had relieved numerous subordinate commanders for lesser crimes than exhaustion, but when his doctor warned Eisenhower of Bradley's tiredness, Eisenhower simply replied 'Well, aren't we all.'¹⁴

Meanwhile, Lieutenant General Courtney Hodges, commander of the US First Army, was rapidly overwhelmed by the scale of the crisis caused by the German attack against his badly strung-out forces. Although Montgomery had not attended the SHAEF conference, he had not been idle. He had given warning orders to 30 Corps, now in reserve, to be ready to move south, and had sent a liaison officer to make contact with US First Army. This officer, acting as Montgomery's eyes and ears, found that the First Army headquarters at Spa had been abandoned very hurriedly, with 'stores and office equipment lying about'.¹⁵ The rapid drive of Kampfgruppe Peiper, the leading unit of 1st SS Liebstandarte SS Adolf Hitler Division, had caused real concern. On 18 December, when it was realised that 'only a small road block and half-tracks stood between them and our headquarters', the majority of the personnel were sent to man the road leading into town.¹⁶ Eventually, the reports claiming that the German tanks were just a mile away proved false, but by then the decision had been taken to evacuate the headquarters back to its rear position at Chaudfontaine. Unfortunately, in the confusion, not to say panic, of the move, no one at First Army informed subordinate units of the move, which left them without any guidance or control at a critical moment. This was the situation Montgomery's liaison officer had stumbled into. The worried Montgomery reported to Brooke that there was a 'definite lack of grip' and warned that the:

> general situation is ugly as the American Forces have been cut clean in half and the Germans can reach the Meuse at Namur without any opposition. The command set up has always been very faulty and now is quite futile with Bradley at Luxembourg and the front cut into two. I have told Whiteley that Ike ought to place me in operational command of all troops on the northern half of the front. I consider he should be given a direct order by someone to do so.[17]

While Montgomery's assessment was overly pessimistic, since the American forces had not been cut in two and there remained determined opposition between the Germans and the River Meuse, there was nonetheless a serious problem. The Germans had advanced deep into the American position, which made Bradley's headquarters at Luxembourg badly placed to control the forces on the northern half of the German penetration. Further, Bradley's refusal to relocate his headquarters due to issues of prestige meant that the difficulties of command and control would only get worse as the Germans advanced. Given the despondency at First Army headquarters, and Bradley's refusal or inability to visit Hodges, Montgomery was right to suggest that the command arrangements needed to be changed.

Kenneth Strong's memoirs give the impression that he arrived at the same conclusion, but there seems little doubt that the inspiration for what happened next came from the field marshal. Strong and Major General John 'Jock' Whiteley, deputy to the Assistant Chief of Staff, Operations, no doubt alarmed by the receipt of Montgomery's message in the early hours of 20 December, went straight to Bedell Smith's bedroom and woke him up. They explained the danger that if the Germans reached the Meuse, Bradley's command would be split in two, making effective control of his three armies impossible. They suggested that there should be a 'temporary change in command arrangements; all troops taking part in the eventual attack north of the penetration must be under the command of one man, and Montgomery seemed the obvious choice'.[18] Whiteley added that, 'to his sure knowledge', Bradley and First Army had been out of contact for two days. In fact, this was untrue: Bradley had been in telephone contact but had not visited personally. Whiteley then added the devastating information gleaned from the British liaison officer that he had 'found considerable confusion and disorganization' behind the American lines.[19]

Bedell Smith immediately phoned Bradley, who, not surprisingly, argued against this change of command but admitted that, had Montgomery been an American commander, the proposal would possess sound military logic. Bedell Smith's own reaction to Whiteley and Strong's deputation revealed the tensions that still existed in the Anglo-American alliance. He argued that 'whenever there was any real trouble the British did not appear to trust the Americans to handle it efficiently. Our proposal, he said, would be completely unacceptable to the Americans.' Given Brooke and Montgomery's ill-disguised – and ill-informed – disdain for the capabilities of the senior American commanders, Bedell Smith had placed his finger on the heart of the matter. Bedell Smith was understandably angry and declared that, given their view of the situation, Whiteley and Strong would no 'longer be acceptable as staff officers to General Eisenhower'.[20]

However, the next morning, instead of being relieved, Whiteley and Strong were told by Bedell Smith that he now intended to put their proposals to Eisenhower as his own, 'since such a proposal would come much better from an American'.[21] The pair were present when Bedell Smith approached Eisenhower. After a brief word with Bedell Smith, and without speaking any further, the Supreme Commander phoned Bradley to inform him of his decision that the US First and Ninth Armies would now come under Montgomery's command. Bedell Smith later apologised to Whiteley and Strong and explained that 'What made me really mad was that I knew you were right. But my American feelings got the better of me because I also knew of the outcry there would be in the United States about your proposal, if it was put into effect.'[22] The proposal would almost certainly have foundered if Bedell Smith had known that Montgomery had been its originator.

This move was tantamount to a vote of no confidence in Bradley's leadership and was almost bound to revive the tedious and corrosive debate with Montgomery concerning overall land command. Yet Eisenhower acted immediately because he understood that Bradley could not effectively command three armies when two of them were physically separated from his headquarters. His decision was testament to his guiding vision of the vital importance of unity, and in making this difficult decision he once again placed the needs of the alliance before any other consideration.

That same morning, Eisenhower telephoned Montgomery to give him command of the northern shoulder. Montgomery later related to General Sir Frank 'Simbo' Simpson that Eisenhower:

> was very excited and it was difficult to understand what he was talking about; he roared into the telephone, speaking very fast. The only point I really grasped was that 'it seems to me we now have two fronts' and that I was to assume command of the northern front. This was all I wanted to know. He then went on talking wildly about other things; I could not hear, and said so; at last the line cut out before he had finished.[23]

Montgomery had got what he wanted, but he also believed that this represented complete vindication of his views on Allied strategy and his proposed command structure. His letter to Simpson continued:

> There is no point now in examining the past. If I produced all the correspondence and telegrams that have passed between me and Eisenhower since 1st September last, it could be proved in any court of law that Eisenhower persisted in pursuing the course he took in direct defiance of all British advice; it was pointed out to him on

paper that if he neglected to concentrate his main strength on his
left and instead attempted to develop two thrusts, and if he refused
to have a sound and simple set up for command, he would get no
good results and would prolong the war. He refused to listen to my
advice; he was quite unable to make up his mind himself as to what
he *did* want to do; and now the blow has fallen and the war has
been put back *for months*.[24]

It is understandable that Montgomery would see no irony in his
own ideas and arguments, but the events of the Battle of the Bulge
actually proved the soundness of Eisenhower's strategy and
command. Montgomery and Brooke had always claimed that
Eisenhower was a hopeless commander with no conception of how
to command in war. If this had been true, the Allies might well
have been faced with a real military disaster in December 1944. But
the truth is that much of their irritation and contempt for
Eisenhower stemmed from the fact that he had simply refused to
agree to their views and advice. Eisenhower had defied British
advice on at least another two significant occasions. Firstly, he had
refused to cancel Operation Anvil/Dragoon: the landings in the
south of France. If he had caved in to Brooke's arguments and
Churchill's considerable pressure over this issue, then there would
have been no 6th US Army Group in the line. There would thus have
been many fewer Allied troops holding the broad Western Front
and, without the port of Marseilles, far fewer resources. In the
wake of the German offensive, and in the face of severe protests
from Charles de Gaulle, Eisenhower ordered a limited withdrawal
around Strasbourg. This enabled the US Third Army to mount its
powerful counter-attack. Ultimately, Patton's remarkable drive to
Bastogne in the Battle of the Bulge was only possible because
Eisenhower had not bent to British will over the landings in the
south. These considerations alone proved that his insistence upon
Operation Dragoon had been correct.

Eisenhower had also been forced to engage in a long-running
and tiresome paper 'battle' with Montgomery solely because he
refused to accept the British field marshal's arguments over the
conduct of the campaign and the appropriate command structure.

If he had accepted Montgomery's counsels, the combined forces of 21st and 12th Army Group would have mounted a drive into Germany north of the Ardennes. These forces might have progressed further into Holland and Germany during the autumn of 1944. With the bulk of the Allied armies in northern Belgium, Holland and perhaps Germany, only weak and ill-supplied forces would have been available to hold the front further south. In this situation, the powerful German forces that had been gathered secretly in the Ardennes might well have ruptured the thinly held Allied front entirely, crossed the Meuse before the Allied armies could redeploy, and then been able to encircle the northern Allied armies in an almost exact replay of 1940. Eisenhower's plan for the campaign in France and Germany had resulted in compromise; there were some flaws in the command structure, and his broad front approach had indeed led directly to the weakness of the American position in the Ardennes. Yet without his determined defence of the Anvil/ Dragoon landings earlier in the war, and his insistence on two major axes of advance into Germany, the German Ardennes counter-offensive might have resulted in a major Allied reverse. Eisenhower had made mistakes and the Allied campaign in the autumn of 1944 was far from perfect but he had been correct about the major issues of strategy on the Western Front. If he had been the weak-minded and poor commander of Montgomery's accusations, he might well have listened to the repeated and strongly worded British advice and the results could have been catastrophic.

Montgomery certainly did not indulge in such introspective analysis: he believed that events had entirely vindicated his opinions. Nonetheless, when Eisenhower gave command of the First and Ninth Armies to Montgomery, the British field marshal visited their commanders as soon as he could. He arrived at the headquarters of First Army to meet with both Hodges and Simpson at 1.30 p.m. on 20 December. One of his staff later commented that Montgomery's cavalcade, with a prominent Union Jack on his staff car, was 'like Christ come to cleanse the Temple'.[25] However, his visit certainly began to restore that grip to operations for which he was justly famous. He later reported to Brooke that 'Neither

Army Commander had seen Bradley or any of his staff since this battle began. Ninth Army had three divisions and First Army 15 divisions and there were no reserves anywhere behind front. Morale was very low. They seemed delighted to have someone to give them some firm orders.'[26]

Yet while Montgomery always claimed that both armies were in 'a complete muddle' before he arrived, this was particularly unfair to the commander of the Ninth Army.[27] Simpson was in full control of his troops and had begun shifting units south to the threatened sector on the very first day of the German attack. Indeed, his calm and his unstinting generosity, which saw his own army denuded of troops while his divisions began to transfuse the battered First Army with strength, were the measure of the man. Simpson garnered little or no fame for his actions during the Battle of the Bulge, yet his action in sending assistance was as vital as Patton's in stemming the German advance. While Bradley understandably reacted to Montgomery's control of two of his armies with horror and a serious case of wounded pride, Simpson wrote to Eisenhower that 'I and my Army are operating smoothly and cheerfully under the command of the Field Marshal. The most cordial relations and a very high spirit of cooperation have been established between him and myself personally and between our respective staffs.'[28]

The situation in First Army Headquarters was rather different. After four days of battle and crisis, Hodges was physically and mentally exhausted and Montgomery actually recommended his immediate relief. However, Montgomery's assumption of command, the movement of British forces to cover the Meuse bridges and the continued tenacious defence by determined American units had already begun to make the difference in the northern sector. By the next day, when Montgomery again visited Hodges' headquarters, the American Army commander, when asked 'if things looked better', could reply in the affirmative.[29] By Christmas Day, the immediate crisis seemed to have passed in the northern sector, particularly as the Allied air forces had been able to operate for three days providing much-needed support to the hard-pressed ground troops.

There was no question that the US First Army had been badly battered by the German attack. One indication of this was the loan of 200 Sherman tanks from 21st Army Group to help replace the 250 Shermans that had been lost since the German attack began. These were to be returned to the British 'only when convenient to do so'.[30] Here was a clear example of the benefits of industrial cooperation, which had begun with the British Tank Mission in the very different conditions of 1940.

With the immediate crisis surmounted, attention at SHAEF turned to organising the counter-attack. While Patton reached Bastogne on 27 December, relieving the 101st Airborne Division after a legendary week-long siege, both Eisenhower and Bradley became highly frustrated at Montgomery's slowness in organising the northern counter-attack. Montgomery was methodical in the movement of his reserves, and the difficulties of coordinating the movement and deployment of a British corps in the rear of an American army were not to be underestimated, but the fact was that the US First Army had taken the brunt of the German offensive. Many of its units required considerable reorganisation, resupply and re-equipment before any offensive could be launched. It was not until 3 January that Montgomery finally launched his counter-attack.

Ultimately, the results of the Allied counter-attacks were disappointing. They were not launched from the shoulders of the 'bulge' as Eisenhower had originally envisaged, and instead had the effect of slowly squeezing the bulge out. Instead of catching large numbers of German troops in a repeat of the Falaise pocket, the Germans were able to retreat in a well-organised phased withdrawal. However, in the final analysis, the German attack had been defeated at a heavy cost in men, equipment and fuel. Hitler's last gamble had failed.

The closing stages of the Battle of the Bulge came to be remembered not for the deadly battles fought in the snow of a bitter winter but for the fierce Anglo-American controversy that swirled around Eisenhower and Montgomery. The two men met at Hasselt in Belgium on Eisenhower's train on 28 December. The Supreme Commander wanted to discuss the details for dealing with the now

vulnerable German salient and to urge Montgomery to mount a
rapid counter-attack, but the British field marshal wanted to settle
the master plan for the future conduct of the war.[31] Eisenhower
explained that he would place Simpson's Ninth Army under
Montgomery's command for the northern thrust into Germany.
This was to be the primary, but not sole, attack towards the Ruhr
that Eisenhower hoped would precede the final campaign in
Germany itself. Montgomery, however, reopened old wounds,
arguing that all available power must be given to the northern
thrust, and that this must be commanded by one man. After much
badgering, Montgomery believed that Eisenhower:

> finally agreed to comply with both conditions and to give me powers
> of operational control and coordination over Army Groups
> employed for northern thrust. We have reached agreement on these
> matters before and then he has run out. But I have a feeling that
> this time he will stick to the agreement. He was very pleasant and
> the meeting was most friendly but he was definitely in a somewhat
> humble frame of mind and clearly realised that present trouble
> would not have occurred if he had accepted British advice and not
> that of American generals.[32]

Nothing could have been further from the truth. Once again
Montgomery had mistaken Eisenhower's tact for agreement. It was
at this point that Montgomery overplayed his hand. Clearly
believing that he, and his views on command and strategy, had
been entirely vindicated by the events of the Battle of Bulge, he
now wrote an extraordinary letter to his Supreme Commander.
Even though he had promised in both October and November 1944
that the command issue was closed and he would not raise it again,
he now did just that. He argued that the time for coordination had
passed and that it was essential that the 'operational control of all
forces engaged in the northern thrust' – which meant both his own
21st Army Group and Bradley's 12th Army Group – must now be
placed under his command. He even went so far as to suggest the
text that Eisenhower should use in a directive on the subject.[33] This
really was too much for Eisenhower. Montgomery's tactless

reopening of an old issue was made worse by the fact that a campaign to have him reinstated as land forces commander had begun in the British press, no doubt stimulated by correspondents at 21st Army Group. He had been as patient as humanly possible with his key British subordinate, but Eisenhower rightly felt that he had reached the end of the road.

While Montgomery seemed oblivious to the storm that he had created, Freddie de Guingand, his Chief of Staff, who always had his ear close to the ground, had become deeply worried. He realised that 'an extremely dangerous situation had developed, and that unless something was done, and done quickly, a crisis would occur in the sphere of inter-allied relationships'.[34] After a worrying telephone conversation with Bedell Smith, he decided to fly to SHAEF immediately. On his arrival, he met with Bedell Smith and found that SHAEF 'was very much disturbed at the virulent anti-British campaign in the American press. Apparently the American press had got heated over certain articles in the British press which tended to criticise General Eisenhower's handling of his forces and the American papers were in return opening an attack on FM Montgomery.'[35] Bedell Smith then showed de Guingand in strict confidence a telegram from Marshall to Eisenhower referring to the press campaigns and telling Eisenhower that 'it would be quite unacceptable to give a British general command of any substantial American forces. He informed General Eisenhower that the latter had the full confidence of the President himself and the whole of America in his handling of the land campaign.'[36] De Guingand then saw Eisenhower, who mentioned the damage being done to Bradley's position and indeed the alliance by the British press campaign and Montgomery's indiscreet remarks. Eisenhower explained that he was tired of the whole business and that it was 'now a matter for the Combined Chiefs of Staff to make a decision'.[37] The threat was clear: either he or Montgomery would have to be removed, and given Marshall's forthright support for the Supreme Commander, it was obvious that it was Montgomery who would have to go.

In a draft letter to Montgomery, Eisenhower explained that he 'would deplore the development of such an unbridgeable gulf of

convictions between us that we would have to present our differences to the CC/S. The confusion and debate that would follow
would certainly damage the good will and devotion to a common
cause that have made this Allied Force unique in history.'[38] Despite
this, Eisenhower had finally reached the point of no return with
Montgomery. Many commentators and historians have expressed
surprise that he had been so patient, and that it was not until late
December 1944 that the crisis really came to a head. Paul Fussell
considered it 'amazing that the egotism and arrogance of one mere
man could occasion so much trouble'.[39] Although Montgomery's
removal would have been a personal disaster for him, and would
have been regarded as an insult to the British people by the British
press, it is almost certain that he would have been replaced by
General Sir Harold Alexander, whom Eisenhower had wanted in
the first place. On the other hand, Montgomery's removal, and the
subsequent heated exchanges across the Atlantic, would also have
been a personal disaster for Eisenhower. Montgomery had, after
all, just demonstrated his qualities as a commander in helping to
reorganise the northern shoulder of the Bulge, but much more
importantly, Eisenhower had built his entire philosophy of command
on the central importance of Allied unity. As he had once explained
to his driver, Kay Summersby, 'If I can keep the team together,
anything is worth it.'[40]

De Guingand considered the possible outcomes of Montgomery's
deposition 'too frightful even to contemplate' and asked Eisenhower
for a stay of execution of 24 hours so that he could speak to
Montgomery. When de Guingand returned to Montgomery's headquarters and bluntly told his commander that he might have to go,
he believed that Montgomery was 'genuinely and completely taken
by surprise and found it difficult to grasp what I was saying'.[41]
Montgomery's bluff, after all his arguments and threats, had finally
been called. 'What shall I do, Freddie?' he asked his Chief of Staff,
and de Guingand drafted a placatory message, which Montgomery
duly signed.[42]

Despite this conciliatory gesture, both SHAEF and 12th Army
Group were now entirely exasperated by Montgomery's behaviour,
and any meaningful cooperation in the future was going to be

difficult. Ultimately, as on so many occasions during the war, it was Eisenhower who made the relationship work. Air Marshal James Robb, the British Chief of the Air Staff at SHAEF, later related his astonishment at the fact that, throughout the final campaign, Montgomery '*never* visited Supreme Headquarters, not even to pay a courtesy call on his Supreme Commander'.[43] Robb knew that Eisenhower's response would have been explosive 'if either of the two American generals commanding Army Groups failed to visit him occasionally, or if they communicated direct to the US Chiefs of Staff in Washington on questions of Command, strategy or policy without informing him'.[44] Throughout the campaign, Montgomery was communicating directly with Brooke and even Churchill, yet it was Eisenhower who, 'without a word to anyone of what must be on his mind, himself pays the visit to his Army Group Commander'. Robb believed that history would 'reveal in due course, I hope, how much we owed to the tolerance and wisdom of a leader to whom personal considerations, even discourtesy of subordinates, meant nothing if they interfered in any way with the conduct of the war or the happy relations between staffs or forces of different nationalities'.[45]

Montgomery later related to Brooke that the command discussion was finished and that it would 'be quite useless to open it again', which was precisely the advice Brooke had given him back in November. However, his blithe assurance that 'everything is very friendly' could hardly have been further from the truth.[46] The news that Montgomery had been placed in command of all Allied troops on the northern shoulder of the salient was not made public until 6 January 1945. While the crisis of the Battle of the Bulge had since passed, the SHAEF announcement provoked a renewal of the battle between the British and American press. Chester Hansen recorded the disgust in Bradley's headquarters when the announcement reached the British press, and commented that 'the real unfortunate part of this affair is the fact that it will have permanent effect on the relationships of our countries after the war'.[47] Whether the front-line troops were actually concerned by the controversies of higher command and the press is difficult to determine. There is, however, no doubt that Bradley was deeply wounded by the command changes precipitated by the Battle of the Bulge, and further infuriated by the portrayal of events in the newspapers.

It was clear that something needed to be done to help calm these troubled waters and begin to rebuild some of the trust and understanding between the higher-level headquarters in Europe. Montgomery decided to hold a press conference, and informed Churchill that he intended to tell the story of the battle as he saw it but also relate how 'the whole Allied team rallied to the call and how national considerations were thrown overboard'. He stressed that he would make a 'strong plea for Allied solidarity' and emphasise the 'great friendship' that existed between himself and Ike. Taking Montgomery's intentions at face value, it was understandable that Churchill replied that what was proposed 'would be invaluable'.[48] In the event, it would have been far better if Montgomery had remained silent.

Montgomery held his press conference on 7 January 1945, and did indeed cover the ground mentioned to Churchill. His prepared speech was certainly not designed to cause offence, but even though it praised Allied unity, it still managed to hit the wrong note. He explained that when:

> the situation began to deteriorate . . . the whole allied team rallied to meet the danger; national considerations were thrown overboard. General Eisenhower placed me in command of the whole northern front. I employed the whole available power of the British group of armies: this power was brought into play very gradually and in such a way that it would not interfere with the American lines of communication. Finally it was put into battle with a bang, and today British divisions are fighting hard on the right flank of the United States First Army.
>
> The battle has been most interesting – I think possibly one of the most interesting and tricky battles I have ever handled, with great issues at stake.[49]

It was Montgomery's use of the personal pronoun 'I' that made all the difference to an otherwise unobjectionable statement. His comments thus implied that he, and he alone, had managed the battle, and that his actions, and his British forces, had saved the situation. He paid a handsome tribute to the American forces and saluted the 'brave fighting men of America' in general, but there was no mention of their commanders, suggesting they did not share the fine fighting qualities of the American soldier. He made a plea for teamwork and even stated that uncomplimentary articles about Eisenhower in the British press grieved him. Unfortunately, he continued beyond his prepared text, and his unscripted comments made it appear that everything was 'untidy' before he had sorted it out, that he had been placed in charge of the entire battle (which he had not), and that he had won the battle for the Allies.

Nonetheless, initial reaction from the press on both sides of the Atlantic was broadly favourable, concentrating on Montgomery's tribute to the American soldier and his plea for support for Eisenhower. However, on the morning of 8 January, a German propaganda radio station commandeered a wavelength used by the BBC for broadcasts to the Allied forces in Europe, transmitting what purported to be an official BBC comment but which was designed to give maximum offence to any Americans who might be listening.

> Field Marshal Montgomery came into the fight at a strategic moment . . . The American First Army had been completely out of contact with General Bradley. He quickly studied maps and started to 'tidy up' the front. He took over scattered American forces, planned his action and stopped the German drive. His staff, which has been with him since Alamein, deserves high praise and credit. The Battle of the Ardennes can now be written off, thanks to Field Marshal Montgomery.[50]

As was intended, large numbers of American soldiers, who relied on the BBC for much of their news, believed this was a genuine broadcast and were horrified at its implications. The *New York Daily Mirror* summed up the mood with the headline 'Monty Gets Glory: Yanks Get Brush-off!'[51] More seriously, American officers at both SHAEF and 12th Army Group believed the broadcast was genuine, which only increased their anger over the original text of the press conference. Brendan Bracken, the British Minister for Information, was able to repudiate the German broadcast on 10 January, but by then the damage had been done. Bradley, already furious with Montgomery after the initial press conference, felt compelled to issue his own account of the battle, which was carried by many papers. His moderate and factual report was pilloried in the British press, particularly by the *Daily Mail*, which claimed that it was a 'slur on Monty'.[52] Such an aggressive tone in a British newspaper was bound to create a reaction in the United States, particularly after the ire raised by the fake broadcast. Eisenhower later claimed that the ensuing press battle 'caused me more distress and worry than did any similar one of the war'.[53]

Churchill understood the damage that had been done when he wrote to Ismay:

> I fear great offence has been given to the American Generals . . . not so much by Montgomery's speech as by the manner in which some of our papers seem to appropriate the whole credit for saving the battle to him. Personally I thought his speech most unfortunate. It had a patronizing tone and completely overlooked the fact that the United States have lost perhaps 80,000 men and we but 2,000 or 3,000. Through no fault of ours we have been very little engaged in this battle, which has been a great American struggle with glory as well as disaster. Eisenhower told me that the anger of his Generals was such that he would hardly dare to order any of them to serve under Montgomery. This of course may cool down, but also it may seriously complicate his being given the leadership of the northern thrust.[54]

Churchill subsequently made a statement to the House of Commons that helped to calm the situation. He made it clear that 'the United States troops have done almost all the fighting and have suffered almost all the losses', comparing those losses to those suffered by both sides at the Battle of Gettysburg in the American Civil War. He reminded his audience that 'in telling our proud tale not to claim for the British Army an undue share of what is undoubtedly the greatest American battle of the war and will, I believe, be regarded as an ever famous American victory'.[55]

Churchill's generous and clear statement helped to calm matters, but real damage had been done to relations between Montgomery and the American commanders in north-west Europe. The incident marked the end of any real rapport between Montgomery and Bradley, and fatally weakened Monty's relationships with Eisenhower and SHAEF. The final tragedy of the entire incident was that what had been Eisenhower's finest moment – in which the commanders and forces under his command, both American and British, had indeed worked together as an unshakeable Allied team – became remembered for the shadow boxing of a press battle. Even emphasising that the Ardennes battle was 'an ever famous American victory' took away some of the potency of the fact that it had been the greatest battlefield test of the Anglo-American alliance.

At no time during the battle had there been any hint of real crisis on the scale of 1914 or 1940. There had been no evidence of the Anglo-American alliance pulling apart under pressure as had occurred in the Anglo-French alliance in 1914, 1918 and 1940. One of the defining characteristics of the Anglo-American response to the crisis of the Battle of the Bulge had been sheer calm military professionalism. It would have been very easy under such pressure to make a fatal mistake, but none was made, and with Eisenhower continuing to hold his nerve, the German offensive was doomed to failure. It was for these reasons that the Battle of the Bulge was the greatest test and also the greatest triumph not only of Eisenhower's command but of the Anglo-American alliance. Unfortunately, the misguided energies of the press resulted in anger, mistrust and suspicion between the main architects of success. The reservoir of trust and confidence that had existed between the senior commanders at the outset of the invasion of Europe in June 1944 had been entirely drained.

Yet many British troops serving in north-west Europe and beyond recognised the canard that Montgomery's press conference represented. One soldier, serving in Italy, wrote home that:

If you hear anyone running the Yanks down over that withdrawal in France, even if our own troops had been in that position Jerry would have come through just the same, it was just a weak spot and Jerry found it. These Yanks are great in battle and that is first hand information for I have fought with and beside them . . . ever since we landed at Anzio.[56]

Another soldier, on another front, provided similar sentiments:

Do not be narrow minded and think the American soldier is no good, that is the nonsense that people who never fought with them say and think . . . They are as good a soldier as any. Because they had a push-back in France some people say they are no good, but how many push-backs did the British Army have and no one said anything about it. People who criticize are only causing bad blood and prolonging the war.[57]

While the greatest defensive success of the alliance caused a breakdown in relations between the higher commanders, it is clear that the same was not true of the fighting troops at the front. As had been observed from the battles in Tunisia onwards, British and American soldiers who worked, lived and fought together could develop a real bond of comradeship and trust that was stronger than the influence of newspaper headlines.

Clearly not everyone who read the British press over the incident believed what they were seeing. Nor was Montgomery universally despised amongst American senior commanders. General Hasbrouck, commander of the US 7th Armored Division, which had fought a fierce delaying action at St Vith, believed it was Montgomery's controversial decision to pull his unit back that saved them from destruction.[58] On 16 January 1945, Hodges' First US Army returned to Bradley's command. Montgomery visited them the same day, and Hodges told him 'what a great honor it had been to serve under the Marshal's command and what great assistance had been given by the cooperation of the British – in the way of tanks, in the way of movement of troops, and tactical decisions'.[59] His words were later backed up by a 5 lb tin of coffee, which was deposited at Montgomery's headquarters.

However, Montgomery's visit to Bradley's headquarters on 4 February 1945, which de Guingand had insisted upon, did not go so well. Chester Hansen admitted that 'no one looked forward with much eagerness to Montgomery's visit here today' and that he had a 'great numbers of enemies among the American commanders'.[60] De Guingand later related that 'the visit was not a roaring success. The atmosphere throughout was distinctly cool. We stayed to lunch but few words were spoken other than were necessary for the transaction of business.'[61] There is no doubt that the events of the Battle of the Bulge marked the final nail in the coffin of Montgomery and Bradley's relationship, and there was very little in the way of real cooperation between the 21st and the 12th Army Groups in the last months of the war.

While Hodges' First Army returned to Bradley's command, Simpson's Ninth Army remained under the command of 21st Army Group for the next major push. In accordance with Eisenhower's directive, 21st Army Group were to form the main thrust to the Rhine. In fact, Simpson himself proposed that the Ninth Army should put in a strong attack to the Rhine in cooperation with the First Canadian and Second British Armies.[62] Simpson's inspiration eventually led to a directive from 21st Army Group that envisaged a converging attack, with First Canadian Army attacking south-eastwards in Operation Veritable, while the Ninth Army would attack north-eastwards in Operation Grenade. This time the Ninth Army would make the main assault and the First Army would protect its flank.[63]

The First Canadian Army's attack opened on 8 February 1945 with one of the greatest artillery bombardments of the war. However, the close forest of the Reichswald presented a real challenge to the advancing troops. The Germans, who realised the importance of holding this ground, had constructed very powerful defences. Three belts of mines, wire and pillboxes covered the front, and much of the open ground surrounding the forest had been inundated. German resistance was fierce, and progress through the

gloomy Reichswald was slow. The history of the 11th Armoured
Division summed up the fighting as a 'slow, miserable and costly
operation . . . confronted by impenetrable forests, impassable bogs,
numerous craters, roadblocks, mines and every form of demoli-
tion'.[64] As the fighting progressed, almost the whole of the First
Canadian and Second British Armies were sucked into the fray.
Indeed, the Germans were so determined to hold this ground that
many of their few remaining reserve divisions were pulled into the
fighting. This slowed the Canadians and British but ultimately made
the Ninth Army's subsequent advance easier. It took a month of
some of the heaviest and bitterest fighting experienced by the British
Army during the war to drive through to the Rhine, at the cost of
15,500 casualties.[65]

While the Canadians and British slugged it out, Operation
Grenade had something of a false start. The Ninth Army began
its assault on 10 February, but the main dilemma confronting its
advance remained the Roer river dams. If these were blown by
the Germans, there would be rapid and widespread flooding,
which would cut any attacking forces off from their support.
Although the US First Army attempted to secure the reservoirs
that controlled the headwaters of the Roer, the Germans destroyed
the control mechanisms of the dams to create a sustained flood
on 9 February. The entire Roer river valley flooded and made any
advance impossible, which forced a frustrating two-week delay
on Ninth Army's plans. However, when Simpson launched
Operation Grenade at 3.30 a.m. on 23 February, the flood waters
were beginning to recede and the attack could begin secure in
the knowledge that bridges could be built to support the leading
troops. The Ninth Army mounted a successful assault crossing
over the Roer under a very heavy artillery and air bombardment,
and with the securing of a bridgehead, the main defensive line
that had held them up in this sector since late November 1944
had finally been breached.[66] The advance towards the Rhine
quickly gathered pace as German commanders scrambled to
evacuate their units to the far bank. By 5 March, the Ninth Army
had closed up to the river between Mors and Dusseldorf, and a
few days later, its troops linked up with the Canadian drive from

the north. Montgomery's converging attack involving three Allied armies, British, Canadian and American, had been a great success and, indeed, a model of alliance cooperation. Only the Rhine now remained as the last major physical barrier between the Allies and the heart of Germany.

The 21st Army Group had been designated as the main thrust for the Rhine crossing by SHAEF, but both the First and Third US Armies had also made rapid advances to the river during February and March. It had been anticipated that the Germans would blow all of the bridges over the Rhine – and they did, sometimes literally as the leading American tanks arrived – but on 7 March, the troops of Hodges' First Army were able, by a stroke of luck and decisive action, to capture a railway bridge over the river at Remagen. This was certainly not on the planned axis of advance, and SHAEF initially cavilled at the idea of exploiting the bridgehead. A frustrated Bradley could only ask: 'What in hell do you want us to do, pull back and blow it up?' Bradley met with a more supportive response from Eisenhower, who ordered him to secure the bridgehead.[67] In fact, the rapid advance to the Rhine all along the front, as well as the large number of prisoners taken, proved the soundness of Eisenhower's strategy of multiple thrusts. With the exception of 21st Army Group's operations, the Germans had been unable to concentrate their forces, and once Allied forces had reached the Rhine, the river acted as a barrier to the withdrawal of the large German forces on the western bank.

It was now obvious that the crossing of the Rhine would be the first scene in the final act of the war against Germany. While the river was a formidable obstacle for much of its length, it was a particularly difficult challenge in the 21st Army Group sector, where it was 500 yards wide and in flood, with the German forces concentrated to oppose any crossing in the area.[68] But the Allies had been engaged in extensive planning and vast preparations for over six months.[69] These included detailed studies of likely crossing points, the construction of the necessary equipment and the training and preparation of the engineers to undertake the vital task of bridging the river.[70] For the first time in its history, parties of the US Navy and their specialised vessels were used inland to support an army river crossing.[71]

It was as these comprehensive plans were close to fruition that the hitherto cordial relations between Montgomery and Simpson began to fray. It had been long understood that, while the Royal Engineers of the British Second Army would be able to construct bridges at a number of crossing sites, the operation would have to rely on the far greater resources of the US Army's corps of engineers. Yet Montgomery's original directive for the operation envisaged the Second Army, reinforced by an American corps of two divisions, mounting the crossing. There was no mention of the Ninth Army whatsoever, which 'flabbergasted' Simpson and his staff, since this 'left General Simpson's command with no part to play in the assault across the Rhine'.[72] After heated protests, Montgomery's final directive, issued on 21 February, took a different shape and ordered a coordinated assault by First Canadian army in the north, British Second Army in the centre, and a one-corps assault by Ninth Army at Reinberg.[73] Yet this included an awkward compromise in which the most important and numerous crossings at Wesel would be built by American engineers but used by the British for a number of days after the assault.[74]

Even once the armies closed up to the Rhine, disagreements remained. Simpson and his staff were convinced that a surprise crossing north of Dusseldorf was possible, but Montgomery vetoed the plan. Given the race to reach the Rhine that occurred in the other American armies, and the dramatic and successful capture of the Remagen bridge, it is understandable that Simpson would chafe under such orders, but Montgomery wanted to make a coordinated crossing on a broad front that could be held and, more importantly, sustained. Given the width of the river and the relative strength of the German defence, his caution may well have been correct, but the Ninth Army remained convinced that 'it could have been done, and done successfully'.[75]

The final preparations took some time, and it was not until the night of 23 March that the assault was launched under the supporting fire of 3,500 guns.[76] After such a lengthy planning and preparation process, the assault itself was 'accomplished so spectacularly as to appear simple', although of course this was only as a result of the painstaking prior effort.[77] The assault succeeded, although German forces fought back determinedly. The 51st Highland Division encountered some of the fiercest resistance and suffered heavy casualties, including the death of its divisional commander.[78] The second phase of the operation, code-named Varsity, saw the British 6th Airborne and the US 17th Airborne dropped on landing zones to link up with the assaulting troops in order to disrupt German artillery positions and rear defences. However, intense anti-aircraft fire caused heavy casualties amongst the transport aircraft and their paratroops.[79] Overall, the operation exceeded expectations: the Allies had crossed the last major German barrier seemingly effortlessly. With this success, it appeared that the German defence of their homeland could not long endure.

Winston Churchill, who, much to his annoyance, had been prevented from witnessing D-Day first-hand at Eisenhower's insistence, had been adamant that he be present at the crossing of the Rhine. On 24 March, Brooke and Montgomery accompanied him to the river to watch the aircraft of the airborne divisions as they flew over on their missions. After lunch, they met with Eisenhower, Bradley and Simpson, and discussed Eisenhower's plans for the immediate future.[80] During the course of these discussions, as Eisenhower later related in his memoirs, Brooke, elated with the success of the Rhine crossing, said to him, 'Thank God, Ike, you stuck by your plan. You were completely right and I am sorry if my fear of dispersed effort added to your burdens. The German is now licked. It is merely a question of when he chooses to quit. Thank God you stuck by your guns.'[81] Perhaps predictably, Brooke took exception to this version of events and later responded that he had been misquoted. He accepted the broader statement that Eisenhower's policy 'was now the correct one, that with the German in his defeated condition no dangers now existed in a dispersal of effort', but he was convinced that he never said 'You were completely right'.[82] It could be said that the differing memories of the conversation on the banks of the Rhine simply marked the start of the long-running post-war controversies concerning the entire north-west Europe campaign.

★   ★   ★

From 25 March, the expansion of the bridgehead quickened pace as German resistance weakened, and the key question for the Allies became how quickly they could pass their forces over the newly bridged Rhine to intensify their pursuit. It was in this situation of impending success that the bridges over the Rhine at Wesel, constructed by Ninth Army engineers, became a major bone of contention and finally soured the otherwise good relations between the Ninth and Second Armies. Boundaries between military formations, although seemingly just lines on a map, were of vital importance in managing the movements of the Allies' immense mechanised military forces. They were often drawn to include particular roads and to make quite clear which formation could utilise which routes. The Allied armies absolutely depended on having sufficient roads along which their combat units could drive, and these were just as important for maintaining the constant flow of supplies necessary to sustain the fighting at the front. Any dispute over a road or a boundary could lead to enormous traffic jams, and frayed tempers at headquarters.

The nature of the engineering problem in bridging the Rhine meant that the British Second Army and the US Ninth Army were forced into a very awkward compromise: they had to share the use of the bridge at Wesel. The original agreement had been that Ninth Army would have it for the first five hours after its completion, in order to supply the 17th Airborne Division, but that it would then be turned over to the British for the next 10 days.[83] However, without use of the bridge, the Ninth Army was effectively penned on the wrong side of the Rhine and unable to exploit the situation that was rapidly developing. On 27 March, Simpson met Montgomery and Dempsey to discuss the army boundaries for the final advance on Berlin, and use of the vital bridge. When Dempsey explained that he 'didn't see how he was going to let the Ninth Army have the bridge for an indefinite time', Simpson lost his patience.[84] Montgomery sided with Simpson and ordered that the bridge should return to Ninth Army control at 0700 hours on 31 March. This frustrating situation led to the Ninth Army staff giving full vent to their prejudices about the British Army. Simpson's personal calendar, updated by his staff, noted that 'Dempsey with his "time out for tea" army . . . stopping at night to sleep, for tea and moving slowly at best, were just wasting invaluable time with their ten-year war'.[85] Even with the revised agreement in place, Ninth Army still had to watch and wait while the British used the precious bridge.

General James E. Moore, Chief of Staff of Ninth Army, felt that he had been taken in by Major General Harold 'Pete' Pyman, the Chief of Staff of Second Army, over the negotiations for the bridge. He believed he had agreed to the Second Army sending one armoured regiment across to support the paratroops and was furious when he realised that the bridge was being used by the entire Guards Armoured Division. When the time came for the bridge to be turned over to Ninth Army, Moore phoned Pyman and warned:

> 'One thing more, Pete, I just want you to know that tomorrow morning I'm sending my provost Marshal with three tanks up there, and if they find one damn British vehicle anywhere near that bridge it's getting knocked off in to the ditch.' He said, 'You wouldn't do that!' I said, 'The hell I wouldn't!'[86]

At 0700 hours on 31 March, the bridge was finally turned over to Ninth Army use. With orders to throw any British vehicle off the road, the 5th Armored Division and the 84th Infantry Division crossed over the Rhine as quickly as possible. This final argument had come about because British needs had been prioritised over the equally legitimate demands of the Ninth Army. In this instance Montgomery, acting as adjudicator, had actually sided with Simpson and his American Army, yet there is also no doubt that Simpson had increasingly chafed under British command. It was doubly unfortunate that this final breakdown of trust occurred in the moment of victory.

Yet while the arguments over bridges, routes and crossings had undoubtedly soured the otherwise friendly and efficient relations between Simpson and the British Second Army, one of the armoured battalions the British had managed to squeeze over the Wesel bridge became involved in one of the last examples of tactical cooperation between American and British forces in north-west Europe. Even as the 3rd Tank Battalion, Scots Guards, was crossing the Rhine at Wesel, it found that the 'whole plan was changed'. It became part of a brigade group, including American paratroops, hastily formed to mount a bold advance that it was hoped would lead to a big breakthrough in the German line.[87]

After crossing the Rhine on 24 March, the battalion picked up the American paratroops of the 2nd Battalion of 513th Parachute Regiment, commanded by Lieutenant Colonel Allen C. Miller. By 3 p.m. 'the Americans were on board and the great enterprise had begun'.[88] With American paratroops on every tank as protection against German panzerfaust and panzerschreck teams, the British tanks drove through a succession of small German towns, including Dorsten, Haltern and Potthol, often against fierce but patchy opposition. By 3 April, after an advance of 50 miles, Munster had been reached. This German town, the largest to have fallen to the British at this point was 'in an indescribable state from bombing'. The next day, the Scots Guards 'said goodbye with real regret to Lt Col Miller and his splendid American battalion'.[89] Even if their senior commanders were now hardly on speaking terms, this rapid drive into Germany with American infantry and British tanks was perhaps the final proof that British and American soldiers could indeed work and fight successfully together.

As the Allied advance into Germany gathered pace, Simpson's army drove south-east while the First Army pushed north-east. These moves rapidly encircled the considerable German forces defending the Ruhr industrial area. On 1 April, the two thrusts of the American armies met at Lippstadt, trapping 430,000 German soldiers in a vast encirclement. Although pockets held out until late April, the main German resistance quickly crumbled. Field Marshal Walter Model, commander of army Group B of the German army, committed suicide rather than surrender.[90] Eisenhower's vision of a vast encirclement battle around the Ruhr had finally come to fruition. On 4 April, Simpson's Ninth Army was finally returned to Bradley's 12th Army Group, and this marked 'the beginning of the breathless race all the way to the Elbe'.[91] As one American sergeant put it when he wrote home in April, 'Ever since wading the Rhine and coming out un-perforated of hide my morale has been climbing. Now all I've got to do is shake hands with a Russian. We've almost got Germany crammed down Hitler's throat and I don't imagine he likes the taste too much.'[92]

With the war in its final stages, the American people, and indeed much of the world, were stunned by the news of President Roosevelt's death on 12 April. Roosevelt's health had been deteriorating for a number of months, but this was not public knowledge. The great architect of America's war effort, and the personal linchpin of the Anglo-American alliance, was no more. President Harry S. Truman would lead America into the post-war world.

While the final act of the war had long been envisaged as a triumphant assault by the united American and British armies on the German capital, Eisenhower had already decided that Berlin, while of great political value, was no longer important as a military objective. At the Quebec conference in September 1944, the Allied powers had raised the issue of the occupation of Germany. In decisions that were later ratified at the Yalta conference in February 1945, it had been agreed that the country would be divided into four occupation zones. Berlin was also to be divided between the four occupying powers of the United States, the Soviet Union, Britain and France, but it would lie deep within the Soviet sector. Given this political settlement, and the fact that massive Soviet armies were poised in April 1945 to lay siege to the city, there seemed little purpose to Eisenhower in driving American and British forces to Berlin, and on 15 April, Simpson was ordered to halt his army 65 miles away, on the line of the River Elbe. It has to be said that many people disagreed with the decision. Bradley, Patton and Simpson were truly dismayed by the orders to halt on the Elbe, and at that point, Simpson believed that the leading elements of his army could have reached the outskirts of the city in just 48 hours.[93]

Eisenhower's decision also caused one of the most bitter strategic arguments with the British. He had already overstepped his authority by communicating directly with Stalin on 28 March about future Soviet intentions. This in itself infuriated Churchill and Brooke, but their main point of contention was that Berlin remained a vital strategic target. Eisenhower stuck to his position even as

Churchill, Brooke and Montgomery railed against it. Added to their arguments was the fact that Montgomery's army, shorn of Simpson's support, was now accorded the secondary role of supporting Bradley's advance. Ultimately, Eisenhower saw no reason to suffer thousands of Allied casualties for an objective that could no longer affect the outcome of the war or alter the agreed occupation zones. Notwithstanding the long and bitter controversy over the issue that rumbled on throughout the Cold War, he may well have been correct. Even Simpson, who had been highly disappointed and frustrated at the time, later wrote:

> I believe that General Eisenhower acted correctly in stopping us when he did. Since the occupation zones of Germany already had been agreed upon by the governments of the United States, Great Britain and Russia, his action had no impact on future events in Germany – and it did prevent further American casualties and enabled us to have an orderly meeting up with the Russians.
>
> While I am convinced we could have taken BERLIN, I do not see that we lost anything in not doing so.[94]

However, for Churchill and Brooke, the loss of the argument and their lack of traction with Eisenhower, who had the full support of the US Chiefs of Staff, also brought into sharp relief the loss of British power and influence over Allied decision-making. By this point, American strength was no longer latent or hidden. The 61 American divisions formed the bulk of the Allied armies, supported by 13 British, 11 French, 5 Canadian and 1 Polish.[95] While Britain was now a significant ally amongst many, the United States' emergence as a superpower was all but complete.

One of the immediate consequences of Eisenhower's decision not to regard Berlin as a military objective was that direct co-operation between the British and American armies in Europe was virtually at an end. With the First Canadian army concentrated to break into Holland, it was left to the British Second Army to race into northern Germany while Patton's Third Army drove south into Austria. German resistance had clearly been broken, as the soldiers of the Scots Guards realised on their 'swan' to Lubeck.

They noted that 'all the way there and back the eye could see practically nothing but streams of grey-clad German soldiers flooding back in countless thousands to the [prison] Cages'.[96] While the British move was isolated, it was also rapid, and it ensured that Hamburg, Kiel and Denmark were swiftly liberated by the Western Allies. The British reached the Baltic Sea at Lubeck just hours before the advancing Soviet troops.

When Hitler committed suicide in his bunker on 30 April, the war was clearly drawing to an end, and yet the fighting dragged on into May. Chester Hansen noted in his diary: 'Everyone now feels that the end is here but the feeling is a lifeless one. The war is petering out, not running out. We wish it would end sharply and decisively. The boredom of waiting for the German army to make up its mind is tiring.'[97] The rump of the German authorities, now led by Admiral Karl Dönitz, were in fact playing for time. They wanted to make separate capitulations with each of the Allies, in order to delay their final surrender to the Russians and thus enable the escape of as many soldiers and civilians as possible from the advancing Red army.[98]

It was for this reason that on 3 May 1945, German envoys arrived at Montgomery's headquarters on Lüneburg Heath offering to surrender the three German armies in north Germany. When the German representatives were presented to him, Montgomery played the part of victorious commander perfectly, returning the German salute casually and shouting at the last representative, who had the misfortune to be a mere major. One of Montgomery's aides whispered to his colleague that 'the Chief was putting on a pretty good act'. His colleague replied 'Shut up, you SOB, he has been rehearsing this act all his life.'[99] After negotiation, the surrender included all German forces in Holland, north-west Germany and Denmark. The following day, the German envoys returned to sign the surrender document. Montgomery understood the essential theatre of the moment. It was vital that the defeated German commanders sign the instrument of surrender in his presence so that there could be no doubt in anyone's mind about the scale and nature of the defeat. This also ensured that the famous photographs and newsreel footage of Field Marshal Montgomery signing the document on a trestle table covered in an army blanket became the image fixed in the minds of the British people.[100]

Yet this separate, regional surrender did not mean the end of the war. Dönitz sent Admiral Hans von Friedeburg to the SHAEF forward headquarters, housed in a French school in Rheims, in an attempt to negotiate the surrender of the German forces in the west. Eisenhower refused to accept any partial surrender and insisted that a general surrender take place on both Eastern and Western Fronts simultaneously.[101] It took a number of exchanges and threats before Dönitz and Field Marshal Alfred Jodl accepted that there would be no separate surrender. It was thus not until the early hours of the morning of 7 May that Jodl, along with von Friedeburg and a military aide, eventually signed the full and unconditional surrender of all German forces.[102] Eisenhower, however, based on his deep antipathy towards the Germans, had decided not to take part in the ceremony. Instead, he paced back and forth in his office while Bedell Smith orchestrated the signing of the documents. While Jodl was brought in briefly to speak to him, Eisenhower's personal conviction meant that the world was denied the image of the German armed forces making that final, unconditional surrender to the Supreme Commander himself. Eisenhower did, however, personally draft the message to the Combined Chiefs of Staff, which read simply: 'The mission of this Allied force was fulfilled at 0241 local time, May 7, 1945.'[103] This modest, unadorned signal was the measure of the man who had done most to ensure that the Anglo-American armies worked together and finally achieved their objective.

15

Born on the Battlefield

An American soldier who found himself in London on 8 May 1945 wrote home that he was 'glad to be here to help the English people to celebrate the Victory that all of us have fought so hard for. The English people, in themselves, sacrificed as much as any people in the world. The people back home will never realize how much this Victory has meant to the English.'[1] While American life had also been transformed by the war, for the British people victory in Europe meant a final end to the danger and fear of the front line. Yet as they were soon to discover, victory against Nazi Germany had been bought at a heavy price. One American officer mused that it would see the end of British strength:

> One gets the feeling these people [the British] are done when Germany is defeated. The forces they commit to the Pacific will not much exceed what they had in Singapore, etc. in peacetime. Certainly their factories are re-converting already, resorts are crowded and little attention is paid to the Government's half-hearted reminders of Japan . . . if our peace depends on a strong Britain, and I sincerely believe it does, then we must get her industry going again and give her first shot at the tremendous markets a ravaged continent will offer. There is little doubt that she's a bankrupt nation too.[2]

In fact, his predictions of a minimal British effort towards the defeat of Japan were inaccurate. The British Fourteenth Army fought a spectacular campaign against the Japanese in Burma, while a powerful Pacific Fleet was dispatched to work with the US Navy in the final assault on Japan. However, although this force was one of the biggest ever assembled by the Royal Navy, it was dwarfed by the might of the US Navy in the Pacific.[3] It was all too obvious that Britain had ceded its position as the world's greatest naval power to its ally. The dispatch of the Pacific Fleet was a clear sign by the British government that it wanted to make an important contribution in the Pacific, but Admiral King had no desire to share his war with any incomer. Concern grew within the British government that the American people had no knowledge or interest in the final British effort during the war.

While the Allies were preparing for a final assault on the Japanese home islands in the spring of 1946, the war came to an unexpected end. On 6 August 1945, General Wilson in Washington wrote urgently to Brooke in London that 'we have just got news that the first TA bomb was dropped on Japan this morning'.[4] TA, or Tube Alloys, was the Allied code name for the atomic bomb. Wilson then provided a report of the effect of the bomb on the Japanese city of Hiroshima. The explosion of a second atomic device over Nagasaki convinced the Japanese emperor that the war must be ended. Japan surrendered on 14 August 1945.

In common with the experience of every previous coalition and alliance throughout history, once the danger and emergency of war had passed, the ties that bound the Anglo-American alliance began to fray. The end of the war against Japan saw the rapid dismantling of almost all of the organisational structures that had made the alliance function so effectively. Surprising as it may seem, there had never been a formal treaty signed between Britain and the United States to regularise the vast and unprecedented cooperation that had developed during the war. Anglo-American collaboration ultimately depended upon informal agreements made between the Prime Minister and the President. However, Roosevelt had died before the war in Europe ended, and Churchill's Conservative Party lost the July 1945 general election to Clement Attlee's Labour Party. Since so much had depended upon the personal relationship between these two men, there was no legal barrier to prevent the new American president, Harry C. Truman, and his administration from taking a very different view of many of the most vital wartime agreements.

These ranged from the secrets of the atomic project to Lend-Lease, which by 1945 was largely keeping Britain's economy afloat. British industry had been turned over to war production for the past six years and exports had fallen to one third of their pre-war scale: Britain faced an enormous post-war trade deficit. The reconversion of British industry would take great effort and capital investment, but while Roosevelt had given commitments of American help towards this process at the Quebec conference in 1944, these offers of aid had not been forthcoming.[5] With the end of hostilities, the United States ended Lend-Lease abruptly in September 1945, which caught Britain completely unprepared. Millions of dollars' worth of military equipment and supplies were suddenly halted in transit, but most seriously of all, without shipments of food, the British government could not, in the short term, feed its people.

The British had hoped that the agreements reached at Quebec would be honoured, which would have seen American aid continued while Britain reconverted her industry. Ultimately, the new Labour government had to send a delegation to Washington in the autumn of 1945 to negotiate a loan from the United States in order to stave off the bankruptcy that had been threatening since at least 1941. The terms of the loan, and the pressure exerted upon Britain to accept American proposals for free trade, dismayed the British. The United States was now treating Britain as an economic competitor and forcing her to accept proposals she had resisted during the war.[6]

In this very different atmosphere, the nature of British and American military cooperation was also bound to alter. Even before the end of the war, the British Chiefs of Staff had made a plea to their American counterparts that the machinery of the Combined Chiefs of Staff should be retained. In a memorandum submitted during the Terminal Conference held in Berlin from 17 July to 2 August 1945, the British chiefs argued that it would be a 'retrograde step to allow this machinery to fall into disuse merely because Germany and Japan have been defeated and there are no supreme allied commanders to receive the instructions of the Combined Chiefs of Staff', considering that 'the world, all too unfortunately, is likely

to remain in a troubled state for many years to come. Major problems will constantly arise affecting both American and British interests.'[7] They argued that a method of mutually exchanging
information and developing uniformity in weapon design and
training would also be beneficial. The reply from the US Chiefs of
Staff was short and to the point: 'The political relationship of the
United States with other nations in the period following this war
is not yet sufficiently defined to permit the United States Chiefs of
Staff to discuss at this date the post-war relationships between the
respective military staffs.'[8]

The Combined Chiefs of Staff had always been much more than
a useful device to share information or develop common weapons
procurement. It had been the key mechanism by which the United
States and Britain fused their strategy in order to win the war. The
heated arguments over Allied strategy that developed within the
Combined Chiefs of Staff had not been a weakness but a strength,
since it ensured that, ultimately, both governments abided by the
decisions reached in open conference. However, its operation had
depended upon an unprecedented level of openness between the
two governments and their armed forces, which had been enabled
by the clear and overriding common interest of defeating Germany
and Japan. The establishment of the Combined Chiefs of Staff had
also represented a tacit agreement by both sides of rough equality.
Yet while in the crisis of 1941 and 1942 both sides were willing to
accept this fiction, it no longer reflected the relative power of the two
governments in 1943, let alone 1945. Just as importantly, the operation of the Combined Chiefs of Staff had represented an exclusive
relationship between Britain and the United States. Even during
the war, important allies such as Canada and China had clamoured
for representation on its committees and in its decision-making.
American post-war interests were likely to be more expansive than
an exclusive relationship with the fading British Empire would
allow. It was not surprising, then, that the US Chiefs of Staff
refused to be unequally yoked with an impoverished and weakened
Britain in peacetime when the United States was now unquestion-
ably the most powerful nation on earth. The American Century
had well and truly begun, and measures adopted in the emergency

period of the war in a very different political and military context were not going to be allowed to determine American policy in the future.

The demobilisation of the American Army in Europe proceeded apace in 1945 and 1946, and inevitably, much of the lower-level cooperation between the two armies withered away almost as quickly as it had been established. In one striking example, in April 1945, a somewhat bored American liaison officer at the British School of Infantry recommended that his post be discontinued.[9] Similarly, in Washington, the British Army Staff had rapidly shrunk to three peacetime branches with a very limited staff by the end of 1946.[10]

Yet there remained a recognition amongst many of the officers and men that the unique relationship that had developed during the war should be remembered and maintained in some form. General Miles 'Bimbo' Dempsey, the commander of the British Second Army, which had fought alongside the US Ninth Army for many months in 1944–5, wrote to General Bill Simpson at the end of the war that he counted himself 'as very fortunate to have met you in this war. Now that it is over, we must not let our friendship die. It was born on the battlefield. I hope you realise how much we of Second Army admire your splendid Ninth – and your great achievements.'[11]

The impulse to maintain the relationship that had developed between the two armies was widely felt. Yet the majority of the schemes to continue these bonds, which included a scholarship programme and a fellowship organisation, were relatively short-lived.[12] The one permanent and tangible connection was formed by the establishment of the Kermit Roosevelt lectures, which enabled the exchange of military addresses by British and American officers.[13] General Albert C. Wedemeyer, the man who had crafted the 1941 Victory Program and sat in on some of the Combined Chiefs of Staff's most heated meetings, was selected as the first American Kermit Roosevelt lecturer in 1947. In his lecture, Wedemeyer emphasised the importance of the relationship between the United States and Britain:

We have fought side by side against aggressor nations in two world wars, and have been victorious. But the relationship between our countries is more than a war-time alliance of convenience or necessity. We have mutual interests inherent in our common origins and strongly reinforced by marked similarities in our political and economic structures.[14]

There was more than a little irony in the fact that Wedemeyer, one of the arch-Anglophobes of the War Department in 1941, was now a confirmed advocate of Anglo-American cooperation. While his experience during the war may have modified his views, the real reason for his change of heart was the emergence of a new threat. As he explained:

In the world today there are two divergent groups which appear to be creating situations incapable of peaceful resolution. Soviet Russia and her satellites comprise one group, Anglo-American peoples and their adherents represent the other. A state of moral belligerency exists. In a political, economic and psychological sense, we are virtually at war with the Soviet Russian group.[15]

By 1947, the outlines of the Cold War, which would dominate international relations for a further 40 years, were already apparent. It was this new and unwelcome situation which ensured that Anglo-American military cooperation, which had come to an abrupt end in 1945–6, would continue and deepen in the conditions of new global confrontation between East and West.

Wedemeyer's final thoughts on the Second World War were sobering. He explained that, ultimately:

Our strategy was defective in that it was incomplete. We failed to relate or to integrate the military factor in strategy with political and economic considerations. Military victory was achieved, but today we find that the national aims for which we fought are jeopardized by the very conditions of victory. We liberated most of Europe from one totalitarian system only to let it fall under the aegis of another.[16]

In fact, this perceived inability to transform military victory into a lasting political settlement was neither new nor unique to the Second World War. To this day it remains one of the great questions surrounding the use of force. Wedemeyer's views of the threat from the Soviet Union in 1947 also shaped his opinion on many of the strategic decisions taken during the Second World War under very different circumstances. One of the most controversial subjects throughout the Cold War remained Eisenhower's decision not to drive on Berlin. In 1945, his decision had been arrived at through clear military logic, yet even two years later it appeared short-sighted due to the new conditions of the confrontation with the Soviet Union.

Yet while the relationship between the two armies continued in new directions during the Cold War and beyond, the memory of the cooperation during the Second World War was soon shaped by the burgeoning public interest in memoirs and histories of that conflict. Unfortunately, in the conditions of the Cold War, the importance and contribution of the Red Army to the defeat of Hitler's Germany came to be overlooked or ignored. This was as much due to the fact that it had been very difficult to gain accurate information about the Red Army's campaigns during the war as it was impossible afterwards. It was not until the 1970s and 1980s that any real information began to be available in the West about the vast scale of the war in the East. This meant that the focus of the books about the war was almost exclusively Anglo-American, and they generally focussed upon personalities rather than broader issues. This trend was set early with the publication in 1946 of Ralph Ingersoll's *Top Secret*, and Harry Butcher's *My Three Years with Eisenhower*.[17] Ingersoll's book was inaccurate, sensational and highly critical of both Eisenhower and the British, and thus sold very well. Butcher, however, possessed a distinct sales advantage in that he had worked directly for Eisenhower and had kept Eisenhower's headquarters diary for much of the war. His book gave a glimpse into the higher counsels – and the disagreements – of the war, which was not what Eisenhower had intended. While Eisenhower later argued that he had had nothing to do with the production of the book, it is clear that he did read the manuscript, and even insisted that a passage concerning Churchill was rewritten before publication. He cautioned Butcher to reconsider any mention of foreign officials, including General de Gaulle and Field Marshal Montgomery, 'where the promotion of bad feeling would be to defeat the very purposes that I strove so hard to advance during the war'.[18]

While Ingersoll's book could be dismissed as a piece of sensational journalism, Eisenhower was much exercised by the publication of Butcher's, which became an instant best-seller. He went so far as to write to Brooke to tell him that he had been upset by these 'so-called "war histories"', which were as concerned with selling their stories as with accuracy. A recent headline had claimed that 'Eisenhower nearly sacked Montgomery', and Eisenhower stressed that he had not collaborated with Butcher and that he did not want 'either to lose personal friends through no fault of my own, or to appear in the light belittling the war effort of the British Fighting Forces or of the individuals composing them'.[19] In his reply, which was probably the warmest letter he sent to Eisenhower, Brooke reassured him:

> You need have no fear, no number of Captain Butchers, or of so called 'war histories' could ever begin to affect the opinions we all formed of you during the war. We know only too well that your main objective has always been to promote a practical basis of co-operation between all Commands, regardless of nationalities. We also know that the successes you achieved could never have been realised without the wonderful qualities you showed in this respect.
>
> You can therefore rest fully assured that your old friends on the Chiefs of Staff Committee completely understand the facts, and will do all in their power to remove any misunderstandings with reference to this matter that they may come across.[20]

Yet in many respects, the damage had been done. Montgomery had been greatly annoyed by Butcher's account and the attention-grabbing headlines in the press. In a letter to Eisenhower, he declared that this exposure of Allied disagreements was all 'a terrible pity. And the repercussion is bound to be that some British author will retaliate by getting at you.'[21] What he did not inform Eisenhower of was that he had given Alan Moorehead, an Australian journalist, access to his papers. Moorehead's biography of Montgomery was published later that year.[22]

These early war books, for all their inaccuracies, were popular, sold well and were a gift for newspaper editors looking for lurid headlines. Millions of men and women had served in the Allied armies and there was a ready market for books about the recent conflict. With their focus on personalities, controversies and disagreements, these publications, which were often serialised in newspapers, exposed to an eager reading public glimpses of the war that had been unknown at the time. Eisenhower bemoaned this fact in a letter to Montgomery in 1946 when he wrote that:

> It seems too much to hope that so-called military writers will ever come to understand that the great story of the Allied operation in Europe lies in the essential unity that was achieved; committed to the theory that only in clashes and quarrels is there any interest for the public, they magnify every difference of opinion into a world-shaking battle.[23]

Controversy did indeed sell, and these early books set a pattern that continued for many decades. The first few books of 1946 soon turned into a flood, as many people began to write memoirs and histories of the war. These included Freddie de Guingand whose reasonably balanced *Operation Victory* was one of the first memoirs written by a wartime chief of staff; and Kay Summersby, whose *Eisenhower Was My Boss* angered Eisenhower. Summersby had been Eisenhower's driver and secretary, and, it was rumoured, his lover.

It was partly in response to the flood of books, and partly due to the fact that any book he wrote would earn a substantial sum of money, that Eisenhower penned his own memoir, *Crusade in Europe*, which was published in 1948. While Basil Liddell Hart, the British military writer, considered it the 'most fair-minded book that any great soldier of any country has written about either of the last two wars',[24] it reopened the arguments concerning command

and strategy in 1944 and clearly angered Montgomery. When a hostile review was published in the *Sunday Times*, Ismay moved to ensure that favourable reviews were printed in other newspapers.[25]

Further books, most notably Bradley's memoir, *A Soldier's Story*, published in 1951, brought another storm of headlines and wounded feelings on both sides of the Atlantic. Bradley justified his decisions during the war and did not refrain from making observations about Montgomery and the British.

It was in response to the new Soviet threat that the United States and Britain began to synchronise their military efforts once again. A series of diplomatic initiatives coalesced in 1949 with the formation of the North Atlantic Treaty Organization, or NATO, which was established as a collective defensive security body to prevent Soviet encroachment in Europe. It has been argued that the United States' ratification of this treaty marked a revolution in US foreign affairs – for the first time, America entered into a permanent 'entangling' alliance.[26] In 1950, Eisenhower was appointed as the first Supreme Allied Commander Europe of NATO. His deputy was none other than Field Marshal Bernard Montgomery, who had been working as the military chairman of the Western Union Defence for the previous three years.[27] Eisenhower's prestige and experience, combined with Montgomery's influence, undoubtedly set NATO's military alliance on a firm path in a period when the Soviet challenge seemed very real indeed.

Eisenhower went on to become President of the United States, while Montgomery went into retirement to write his memoirs, the publication of which, in 1958, set in train a number of controversies with former British as well as American generals. Montgomery's memoirs certainly painted Eisenhower in a poor light while justifying his own actions and decisions. Unfortunately, with the publication of his memoirs, and his continued criticisms that a soldier should never dabble in politics, the rift between Montgomery and Eisenhower became permanent. The claims and counter-claims that had characterised the publication of each man's memoirs built up a confusing and overlapping series of arguments about what had actually happened during the campaigns of 1944–5. These controversies also had the effect of placing in the spotlight the personalities and relationship of Eisenhower and Montgomery almost to the exclusion of every other issue. Ultimately, the debates surrounding the two men as commanders during the Second World War came to represent a multitude of opinions and views about Britain and America in the very changed conditions of the 1950s and 1960s.

Of course, the controversy over command and strategy in 1944 was only one of many debates between the Allies during the war. While it was of great personal importance to the protagonists – and indeed to their many supporters – the inordinate focus upon this issue came to dominate but also obscure the reality of what had happened during the war. Through their service in the founding years of NATO, but more particularly through the battle of the memoirs, the persons and, later, the memories of, Eisenhower and Montgomery became archetypes for the relationship between the United States and Britain in a strikingly similar fashion to the way that Braddock and Washington were remembered in the eighteenth century. Over the ensuing decades, the memory of the Anglo-American alliance of the Second World War was distorted by an increasing wave of nostalgia, particularly in a Britain that had lost its power, but also by an increasing focus on the personal rivalries of the commanders.

The Anglo-American alliance had always been more than the sum of its parts and far greater than the relations between a few men. It had been born in the great emergency of 1940–2, and the spectre of seemingly imminent defeat had been a spur to co-operation in a bewildering range of fields. Its strength had rested on both the breadth and depth of that cooperation, ranging from an unprecedented sharing of scientific and technical information to British and American soldiers eating the same rations and firing the same ammunition. Much of the success of the alliance had actually been based on innovation far from the battle fronts. In this wider context, the actions and collaboration of the two armies was only one part of a much wider whole, which encompassed navies, air forces, industries, transport, governments and people of both countries.

Equally, the relationship between the two armies in the Second

World War was actually deeply rooted in a distant past. Neither army was a stranger to the other in 1941, but the long absence of meaningful contact during the interwar years certainly made the resumption of contact more awkward than might have been the case. Neither understood the other nor saw clearly how the war should be prosecuted together. Once the United States joined the war, the cooperation between the armies developed at breakneck speed and soon took unforeseen forms. The early reports and debates from military attachés in London and Egypt, as well as the US Observer Mission, helped to establish contact and develop meaningful avenues of collaboration. The British Tank Mission ultimately not only primed the pump of American tank production but also helped to ensure that both armies had a viable combat tank in 1942–3. Thus the American observer missions and the British Army Staff in the United States had acted as enablers for an unprecedented level of cooperation, just as the Combined Chiefs of Staff had enabled the Allies to thrash out in heated argument the agreed strategy for a global war.

Even on the battle fronts, the personal rivalries and disagreements between generals were only ever part of a wider and more detailed picture. The relationship between the two armies was never perfect. Prejudices, rivalries and political and military differences remained between the two forces to the end of the conflict, but this should not obscure the very real cooperation that was achieved. The campaigns in North Africa, Tunisia and Italy were hard fought – and sometimes desperate – battles in their own right but also served as vital testing grounds to enable the final amphibious assault on the shores of France. Ultimately, while the campaigns in Normandy and north-west Europe saw the culmination of the Anglo-American alliance under very different circumstances to those of 1941, and sparked controversies that continue to this day, they were highly successful military operations that resulted in the achievement of the alliance's ultimate political objectives. Eisenhower's Victory Order of the Day on 8 May 1945 counselled against 'the profitless quarrels in which other men will inevitably engage as to what country, what service, won the European war'.[28] While the majority of the fighting in Europe undoubtedly took place on the Eastern Front, it is not too much to say that without the industrial, economic and military contribution of the Anglo-American alliance, Nazi Germany could not have been defeated.

The secret of the Anglo-American success was not the fact that the two allies often held competing national interests, or approached strategic questions from different directions. In these circumstances, and given the enormous stakes, it was not surprising that there were heated arguments and disagreements and that these played out at every level of the respective governments and armies. Equally, the record of the war proved that there was no monopoly of effective strategy-making or thought on either side of the Atlantic. Indeed, what have often been considered to be British or American strategic perspectives were in fact multi-faceted, with politicians, officials and officers from both sides taking different positions on what were complicated, intractable and dynamic problems. It was the collective nature of Allied planning and the unified execution fusing the power of the two armies together that made Anglo-American strategy effective.

Perhaps it is, after all, human nature to focus on argument and disagreement rather than cooperation. Yet it seems regrettable that in remembering the relationship between the British and American armies in the Second World War, Eisenhower's firm vision of honesty, frankness and wholehearted cooperation between the two nations and armies in spite of their differences tends to be overshadowed by arguments about personalities. Just as importantly, as the events of the Second World War receded into the past, the success of the Anglo-American alliance came to be taken for granted, as if the campaigns that had begun in North Africa were simply part of the inevitable triumphant march of the democracies towards victory. Eisenhower summed up his views in a letter to his confidante, Pug Ismay:

> While it is true that during the war we had the compelling motive
> of a common fear to stick together, the fact is that we had present
> in early 1942 and during most of that year, all of the ingredients
> for a profound pessimism and for mutual recrimination. In spite of
> the black outlook we buckled down and did the job. Extremists on

both sides of the water can indulge in all the backbiting and
name-calling that they please – they can never get away from the
historical truth that the United States and the British Empire,
working together, did a job that looked almost impossible at the
time it was undertaken.[29]

For too many years, this pre-eminent fact has been obscured by
the emphasis placed upon the command controversies. Collaboration,
not conflict, was the touchstone of this alliance. Even in the face
of rivalry and suspicion, the American and British armies combined
their efforts and won the hard-fought battles of the Second World
War together.

Notes

Introduction

1   See Danchev, *Very Special Relationship*.
2   Dimbleby and Reynolds, p.115.
3   Duncan Hall, p.353.
4   Historical Record, British Army Staff Part II, p.7, WO202/917, TNA.
5   See Reynolds, *Rich Relations*.
6   See Stoler.
7   One of the best is Kimball.
8   See Burk.

I
Family Legacy

1   Goodhart, *Colonel George Washington*, p.8
2   Lewis, p.156.
3   Kopperman, p.17.
4   Ferling, p.6.
5   Parkman, p.151.
6   Kopperman, p.18.
7   Lewis, p.181.
8   Parkman, p.165.
9   A. G. Bradley, pp.100–1.
10 Cope, p.2.
11 Kopperman, p.93.
12 Ibid.
13 Ibid.
14 Goodhart, *Colonel George Washington*, p.32.

15 Benjamin Franklin, *Autobiography*, quoted in Parkman, pp.140–1.

16 Cooper, pp.13–14.

17 Ibid., p.14.

18 Lewis Butler, p.2.

19 Ibid., pp.16–17.

20 Ibid., p.3.

21 Goodhart, *The Royal Americans*, p.33.

22 Ferling, pp.5–6.

23 Burk, pp.108–9.

24 Jeremy Black, 'Could the British Have Won the American War of Independence?', *Journal of army Historical Research*, 74, 2006, p.150.

25 Quoted in Esmond Wright, *The Fire of Liberty: The American War of Independence seen through the eyes of the men and women, the statesmen and soldiers who fought it*, p.33.

26 Weigley, *History of the United States army*, p.73.

27 Vetock, p.18.

28 Palmer, p.157.

29 Waldo, p.30.

30 Vetock, p.11.

31 Ford, IX, p.366.

32 Weigley, *History of the United States army*, pp.116–17.

33 Vetock, p.20.

34 Weigley, *History of the United States army*, pp.131, 144.

35 Graves, pp.186–7.

36 Henry Adams, *History of the United States During the Administration of Jefferson and Madison*, p.45, quoted in Weigley, *History of the United States army*, p.117.

37 Quoted in Longford, p.379.

38 See Gleig, *Narrative*, pp.156–8. Gleig also wrote one of the best British memoirs of the Peninsular War: *The Subaltern*.

39 Gleig, *Narrative*, p.162.

40 Ibid., pp.156–8.

41 Ibid.

42 Ibid.

43 Ibid., p.380.

44 Ibid.

45 Keegan, *The Face of Battle*, p.116.

46 'Poor 27th! in a few days they had not two hundred men in the ranks.' Smith, p.26.

47 Luvaas, p.185.

48 Shaw, p.2.

49 Strachan, pp.vii–ix.

50 Vetock, p.19.

51 Ibid., p.15.

52 Henderson, p.238.

53 Ward with Burns and Burns, p.xvi.

54 See Griffith.

55 Ibid., pp.23–5.

56 See Luvaas.

57 See the four volumes of Johnson and Buel.

58 army Historical Series, *American Military History*, p.300.

59 General Ulysses S. Grant became the commander-in-chief of the Northern Armies in 1864. General William T. Sherman was one of his key subordinates. His march through Georgia in 1864–5 was a deliberate attempt to destroy the South's ability to wage war. It remains controversial to this day. Henderson, *The Science of War*, p.57.

60 Quoted in Weigley, *History of the United States army*, p.347.

61 Holmes, *The Little Field Marshal*, pp.64–6.

62 Ibid.

2
The Great War

1 Keegan, *The Face of Battle*, p.209.

2 Turner, p.72.

3 Ibid.

4 Ibid., p.85.

5 Taylor, p.105.

6 See Gregory.

7 Holmes, *The Little Field Marshal*, p.201.

8 Terraine, p.37.

9 Holmes, *The Little Field Marshal*, p.201.

10 Fox Conner, 'The Allied High Command and Allied Unity of Direction', 19 March 1934, army War College, USAMHI.

11 Greenhalgh, p.10.

12 William Philpott, 'Haig and Britain's European Allies', in Bond and Cave, p.133.

13 Sheffield and Bourne, pp.165–6.

14 Charteris, p.235.

15 Ibid., p.236.

16 Ibid., pp.306–7.

17 Joffre, Vol. 2, p.568.

18 Fox Conner, 'The Allied High Command and Allied Unity of Direction', 19 March 1934, army War College, USAMHI.

19 'A Study of Anglo-American and Franco-American Relations during World War I. Part II: Franco-American Relations', USAMHI.

20 Pershing, Vol. I, pp.150–1.

21 Grotelueschen, pp.31–2.

22 'A Study of Anglo-American and Franco-American Relations during World War I. Part II: Franco-American Relations', USAMHI.

23 'A Study of Anglo-American and Franco-American Relations during World War I. Part I: Relations between American Expeditionary Forces and British Expeditionary Forces 1917–1920', USAMHI.

24 Ibid.

25 Ibid.

26 Ibid.

27 Ibid.

28 Ibid.

29 Ibid.

30 'A Study of Anglo-American and Franco-American Relations during World War I. Part II: Franco-American Relations', USAMHI.

31 Ibid.

32 Fox Conner, 'The Allied High Command and Allied Unity of Direction', 19 March 1934, army War College, USAMHI.

33 Greenhalgh, pp.178–85.

34 Trask, pp.62–4.

35 Mead, p.146.

36 Charteris, p.292.

37 Ibid.

38 Ibid.

39 Ibid., pp.294–5.

40 Trask, p.55.

41 Ibid., p.51.

42 Fox Conner, 'The Allied High Command and Allied Unity of Direction', 19 March 1934, army War College, USAMHI.

43 Trask, p.53.

44 Ibid.

45 Ibid., p.64.

46 Bean, pp.276–9.

47 De Groot, p.388.
48 Smythe, p.47.
49 Pogue, *Education of a General*, p.154.
50 Ibid., p.183.
51 Ibid., p.190.
52 Smythe, pp.49–50.
53 D'Este, *A Genius for War*, pp.170–7.
54 Sheffield and Bourne, p.304.
55 Smythe, p.54.
56 Harris with Barr, p.207.
57 General Sir Henry Rawlinson diary, 29/9/18, NAM.
58 Mead, p.336–9.
59 Maurice, p.251.
60 Charteris, p.298.

3

Tanks in Washington

1 Pogue, *Ordeal and Hope*, p.2.
2 Gabel, p.8.
3 Pogue, *Ordeal and Hope*, p.22.
4 Ibid., p.18.
5 Duncan Hall, p.41.
6 Ibid., pp.39–54.
7 See Bond.
8 Duncan Hall, pp.39–54.
9 Ibid.
10 Fraser, p.139.
11 18 September 1945, Ironside, CAB106/223, TNA.
12 Horrocks, *A Full Life*, p.80.
13 Fraser, p.139.
14 Hamilton, *The Making of a General*, pp.326–7.
15 Nicolson, p.100.
16 Jackson, p.108.
17 12 June 1940, RG319/57/304, USNA.
18 Leutze, pp.xiii–xvi.
19 Dean Acheson, in Leutze, p.ix.
20 Ismay, *Memoirs*, p.212.
21 Leutze, pp.3–4.

22   Ibid., p.5.

23   Strachan, p.102.

24   Lee to Washington, 25 June 1940, RG319/57/304, USNA.

25   Wingate, p.50.

26   Strachan, pp.233–5.

27   Ibid.

28   'Losses of British equipment in 1940', CAB106/209, TNA.

29   Fletcher, *The Great Tank Scandal*, p.34.

30   Loewenheim, Langley and Jonas, p.5.

31   Ibid., p.89.

32   Ibid., p.94.

33   Ibid., pp.94–5.

34   Corey Ford, pp.11–94.

35   Ibid., p.95.

36   Reynolds, *From Munich to Pearl Harbor*, p.79.

37   J. R. M. Butler, pp.345–6.

38   Matloff and Snell, p.17.

39   Ibid., pp.13–14.

40   C. T. Ballantyne, Secretary General, Anglo-French Purchasing Board, to Col. E. E. MacMorland, War Department, 22 June 1940, RG156/506/J663, USNA.

41   Calder, p.125.

42   J. R. M. Butler, pp.223–4; Playfair, pp.133–7.

43   Leutze, p.10.

44   Ibid., p.11.

45   Ibid., p.13.

46   Lee to W. D., 25 July 1940, RG319/57/304, USNA.

47   Lee to W. D., 31 July 1940, ibid.

48   Lee to W. D., 31 July 1940, ibid.

48   Duncan Hall, p.183.

49   'Historical Record of the British Army Staff', Part I: Historical Outline, WO202/916, TNA.

50   Anglo-French Co-ordinating Committee, Allied Purchase of War Material in the United States of America, 14 June 1940, WO185/40, TNA.

51   Dewar, Michael Bruce Urquhart, Who Was Who, A & C Black, 2008, online edition.

52   Pratt, Major General Douglas Henry, Who Was Who, A & C Black, 2008, online edition.

53   AVIA38/42, TNA.

54   Fletcher, *The Great Tank Scandal*, p.89.

55   Koistinen, pp.17–18.

56   Fletcher, *The Great Tank Scandal*, p.90.

57   Bonesteel interview, Bonesteel MSS, USAMHI.

58   Pogue, *Ordeal and Hope*, p.67.

59   Stout, pp.12–13.

60   Fletcher, *The Great Tank Scandal*, p.90; AVIA38/42, TNA.

61   VCIGS to Pakenham-Walsh, 21/08/1940, AVIA38/42, TNA.

62   Ibid.

63   The main contracts were: Pullman Standard Car Manufacturing Company 500; Baldwin Locomotive Works 685; Pressed Steel Car Company 501; Lima Locomotive Works 400; see 'The Launching of the Tank Programme', AVIA38/42, TNA.

64   Ibid.

65   Exchange Requirements Committee 31 revised, 16 November 1939, AVIA38/42, TNA.

66   'Recommended Immediate Changes to the Medium Tank Programme', AVIA38/137, TNA.

67   Dewar to Burton, 31 August 1940, WO185/40, TNA.

68   Dewar to Burton, 1 September 1940, WO185/40, TNA.

69   Liddell Hart, Vol. 2, pp.490–1.

70   Dewar to Burton, 5 March 1941, WO185/45, TNA.

71   'Buffalo Bill', WO193/311, TNA.

72   See Greg Kennedy.

73   'Buffalo Bill', WO193/311, TNA.

74   Brief on CCS (40) 538 (J. P.), 'Buffalo Bill', WO193/311, TNA.

75   Matloff and Snell, p.22.

76   Leutze, p.32.

77   'Security Measures with Regard to Documents', 8 August 1940, 'Buffalo Bill', WO193/311, TNA.

78   Leutze, pp.32–3.

79   'Buffalo Bill', WO193/311, TNA.

80   Note signed by Newall, Pound and Dill, 28 July 1940, 'Buffalo Bill', WO193/311, TNA.

81   Leutze, p.36.

82   'Staff Conversations with the USA', 'Buffalo Bill', WO193/311, TNA.

83   Note by L. C. Hollis, 1 August 1940, 'Buffalo Bill', WO193/311, TNA.

84   Matloff and Snell, p.341.

85   16 August 1940, Anglo-American Standardisation of Arms Committee, p.6, WO193/311, TNA.

86   Leutze, p.36.

87 Ibid.

88 Ibid., pp.36–7.

89 'Buffalo Bill', WO193/311, TNA.

90 J. R. M. Butler, p.343.

91 'Buffalo Bill', WO193/311, TNA.

92 Ibid.

93 Ibid.

94 Leutze, p.57.

95 Matloff and Snell, p.24.

96 Ibid., pp.24–5.

97 Ibid.

98 *The Times*, 23 September 1940, p.4.

99 J. P. 735 (s) Annex VI, Staff Conversations, 27 June 1940–12 Dec 1941, WO193/305, TNA.

100 Ibid.

101 No. 425, 15 September 1940, RG319, USNA.

102 Leutze, p.58.

103 Ibid., p.341.

104 Leutze, p.xviii.

105 Mark Bernstein and Alex Lubertozzi, *World War II on the Air: Edward R. Murrow and the Broadcasts that Riveted a Nation*, pp.3–7; 89–119.

106 Kendrick, pp.172–228.

107 Black, *Roosevelt*, p.577.

4
Special Observers

1   Cole, *Imperial Military Geography*, pp.14–59.

2   Duncan Hall, pp.1–2.

3   Dobson, *US Wartime Aid*, p.5.

4   Ibid., p.28.

5   Gilbert, p.686.

6   Ibid., p.687.

7   Dobson, *US Wartime Aid*, pp.25–8.

8   Blaine, *The Arsenal of Democracy*, p.96.

9   Stettinius, p.73.

10 Sherwood, p.233.

11 Ibid., p.232.

12 Kimball, p.78.

13   Sherwood, p.237.

14   Ibid., p.233.

15   Ibid., p.245.

16   Gilbert, p.688.

17   Sherwood, pp.246–7.

18   The United States representatives were: Maj. Gen. S. D. Embick, Brig. Gen. S. Miles, Brig. Gen. L. T. Gerow, Col. J. T. McNarney, Rear Admiral R. L. Ghormley, Rear Admiral R. K. Turner, Capt. A. G. Kirk, Capt. D. C. Ramsey and Lt Col. O. T. Pfeiffer. The British representatives were: Rear Admiral R. M. Bellairs, Rear Admiral V. H. Danckwerts, Maj. Gen. E. L. Morris, Air Vice Marshal J. C. Slessor and Capt. A. W. Clarke. See the official report, 'ABC Staff Conversations', PREM3/489/1, TNA.

19   'History of First Days in England', Bolte MSS, USAMHI.

20   Matloff and Snell, p.33.

21   'Staff Conversations', 27 June 1940–12 December 1941, WO193/305, TNA.

22   'ABC Staff Conversations', PREM3/489/1, TNA.

23   Ibid.

24   Early Days in England, USAMHI.

25   'ABC Staff Conversations', PREM3/489/1, TNA.

26   The Earl of Avon, *The Eden Memoirs: The Reckoning*, p.169.

27   Ibid.

28   Ibid., p.178.

29   John Kennedy, p.63.

30   Ford, pp.98–9.

31   Ibid.

32   Danchev, *Establishing the Anglo-American Alliance*, p.19.

33   Ford, p.99.

34   Danchev, *Establishing the Anglo-American Alliance*, p.51.

35   Marshall-Cornwall, p.185.

36   John Kennedy, p.75.

37   Ibid.

38   Stettinius, p.89.

39   Ibid., p.90.

40   Fellers to W. D., 22 April 1941, RG319/57/218, USNA.

41   Fellers to W. D., 30 April 1941, RG319/57/218, USNA.

42   Fellers to W. D., 16 June 1941, RG319/57/218, USNA.

43   Fellers to W. D., 17 April 1941, RG319/57/218, USNA.

44   Wavell to Dill, 'Tanks for Middle East', 31 May 1941, WO193/565, TNA.

45   Dill to Churchill, 'Tanks for Middle East', 5 June 1941, WO193/565, TNA.

46   See WO193/565, TNA.

47 Charles L. Bolte, 'History of First Days in England', Bolte MSS, USAMHI.

48 Five of the 17 officers, including General Chaney, were army Air Force officers, with just one representative officer drawn from the G1, G2, G3, G4, plans, ordnance, quartermaster, signal, medical, and adjutant general branches of the general staff. Bolte interview, Bolte MSS, USAMHI.

49 Bolte interview, Bolte MSS, USAMHI.

50 'History of First Days in England', Bolte MSS, USAMHI.

51 Bolte interview, Bolte MSS, USAMHI.

52 'ABC Staff Conversations', PREM3/489/1, TNA.

53 Dahlquist diary, Dahlquist MSS, USAMHI.

54 Ibid.

55 Bolte interview, Bolte MSS, USAMHI.

56 'History of First Days in England', Bolte MSS, USAMHI.

57 'Historical Record of the British Army Staff', Part I: Historical Outline, WO202/916, TNA.

58 A. T. Cornwall-Jones to 'C-J' (sic), 24 April 1941, CAB122/1, TNA.

59 Ibid.

60 'History of First Days in England', Bolte MSS, USAMHI.

61 Clifford, p.3.

62 'History of First Days in England', Bolte MSS, USAMHI.

63 Clifford, p.5.

64 Ibid., pp.5–6.

65 Ibid.

66 Ibid., p.7.

67 Ibid., p.9.

68 'History of First Days in England', Bolte MSS, USAMHI.

69 Mark Skinner Watson, p.353.

70 Pogue, *Ordeal and Hope*, p.140.

71 Ibid., p.58.

72 Mark Skinner Watson, pp.353–4.

73 Matloff and Snell, p.61.

74 Mark Skinner Watson, p.355.

75 Matloff and Snell, p.59.

76 J. P. (41) 444, 14 June 1941, War Cabinet Joint Planning Staff, Future Strategy Review, CAB122/30, TNA.

77 Ibid.

78 Matloff and Snell, p.61

79 J. P. (41) 444, 14 June 1941, War Cabinet Joint Planning Staff, Future Strategy Review, CAB122/30, TNA.

80   Ibid.

81   Ibid.

82   Kimball, p.99.

83   'Overture to Overlord', p.48, CAB106/1038, TNA.

84   1 July 1941, Wemyss to VCIGS, WO32/9464, TNA.

85   Oral interview, Bonesteel MSS, USAMHI.

86   Ibid.

87   Ibid.

88   Cerami, p.37.

89   Gabel, p.193.

90   Ibid.

91   Pogue, *Ordeal and Hope*, p.89.

92   Gabel, pp.192–4.

93   'Recommended Immediate Changes to the Medium Tank Programme', AVIA38/137, TNA.

94   Floyd E. Coleman, http://www.warriorsaga.com/, accessed on 20 November 2009.

95   Fellers, Middle East Reports, September 1941, RG319/57/218, USNA.

96   Ibid.

97   Ibid.

98   Ibid.

99   Ibid.

100 Ibid.

101 Fellers to W. D., 27 November 1941, RG319/57/222, USNA.

102 Floyd E. Coleman, http://www.warriorsaga.com/, accessed on 20 November 2009.

103 Fellers to W. D., 1 December 1941, RG319/57/222, USNA.

104 See Baily, pp.32–51.

105 Fellers to W. D., 31 December 1941, RG319/57/222, USNA.

106 Dahlquist diary, Dahlquist MSS, USAMHI.

107 Ibid.

108 Ibid.

109 'History of First Days in England', Bolte MSS, USAMHI.

5

Combining the Chiefs

1   Danchev, *Very Special Relationship*, p.10.

2   John Kennedy, pp.179–80.

3   Danchev and Todman, p.209.

4   Arcadia Box No. 1/3, Arcadia Conference, Combined Chiefs of Staff: Conference Proceedings, 1941–5, Bedell Smith MSS, EL.

5   Danchev, *Establishing the Anglo-American Alliance*, p.70.

6   Ian Jacob diary, Alanbrooke MSS, 6/7/2, LHCMA.

7   Ibid.

8   Ibid.

9   Ferrell, p.40.

10   Arcadia Box No. 1/3, Arcadia Conference, Combined Chiefs of Staff: Conference Proceedings, 1941–5, Bedell Smith MSS, EL.

11   25 December 1941, Ian Jacob diary, Alanbrooke MSS 6/7/2, LHMCA.

12   Eisenhower, 'Command in War', EPPF, EL.

13   Danchev, *Establishing the Anglo-American Alliance*, p.70.

14   Ibid., p.71.

15   Bourne MSS, IWM.

16   Danchev, *Establishing the Anglo-American Alliance*, p.81.

17   Crosswell, pp.76–80.

18   Ibid., p.92.

19   Danchev and Todman, 9 February 1942, p.228.

20   Ferrell, p.48.

21   Newell, p.8.

22   George B. Jarrett MSS, Box 2, USAMHI.

23   Ibid.

24   Ibid.

25   Ibid.

26   Matloff and Snell, pp.175–6.

27   Ibid., p.181.

28   Ferrell, p.44.

29   Matloff and Snell, p.177; Ambrose, pp.30–1.

30   Stoler, pp.28–30.

31   Ibid., p.35.

32   Matloff and Snell, p.183.

33   Enclosure by the sub-committee of the Combined Staff Planners, 3 April 1942, CAB122/301, TNA.

34   Ibid.

35   Matloff and Snell, p.185.

36   John Kennedy, p.224.

37   Matloff and Snell, p.186.

38   Danchev and Todman, p.246.

39   Wedemeyer, p.105.

40 Ibid.

41 Bourne's visit to London, 12–20 April, 26 April 1942, Bourne MSS, IWM.

42 Ibid.

43 Ibid.

44 Matloff and Snell, pp.189–90.

45 Dill to Brooke, 5 May 1942, Bourne MSS, IWM.

46 Ibid.

47 Ibid.

48 Kennedy, *Business of War*, p.233.

49 Matloff and Snell, p.196.

50 Ambrose, p.44.

51 Ferrell, p.59.

52 Ibid., p.60.

53 Dill to Chiefs of Staff, 15 June 1942, CAB122/30, TNA.

54 Fellers to W. D. 14 March 1942, RG319/57/204, USNA.

55 Fellers to W. D. 14 March, 11 April, ibid.

56 CAB122/153.

57 Ibid.

58 Fellers to W. D., 15 May, RG319/57/223, USNA.

59 Dill to CIGS, 5 June 1942–10 June 1942, CAB121/284, TNA.

60 The Contribution of the Information Service to the May–June 1942 Offensive in North Africa, RG457/1035, USNA.

61 Ibid.

62 Behrendt, pp.145–6.

63 Churchill, p.344.

64 Gilbert, p.723.

65 American Expeditionary Force Middle East, WO193/333, TNA.

66 The Contribution of the Information Service to the May–June 1942 Offensive in North Africa, RG457/1035, USNA.

67 Ibid.

68 CAB121/284, TNA.

6
Cats and Bulldogs

1 Butcher, pp.29–30.

2 Barr, pp.151–74.

3 Glantz and House, pp.119–20.

4 Ferrell, p.64.

5   Dahlquist diary, 25 June 1942, Dahlquist MSS, USAMHI.

6   Stoler, p.76.

7   Ibid., p.54.

8   Ibid.

9   Ibid., pp.54–6.

10   Ibid.

11   Ferrell, p.72.

12   Ibid.

13   Danchev, *Establishing the Anglo-American Alliance*, p.179.

14   Dahlquist diary, Dahlquist MSS, USAMHI.

15   Ibid.

16   Ambrose, p.78.

17   Ismay to Eisenhower, 1 September 1942, EPPF, EL.

18   5 August 1942, 3rd County of London Yeomanry War diary, http://www.sharpshooters.org.uk/news/item.aspx.

19   Lodge to Auchinleck, 24 June 1942, AUC/955, JRL.

20   G. P. B. Roberts, p.93.

21   Ibid., p.100. Three American soldiers were wounded; four British soldiers were killed and one officer and three troopers wounded in the regiment. 1 September 1942, 3rd County of London Yeomanry War diary, http://www.sharpshooters.org.uk/news/item.aspx.

22   G. P. B. Roberts, p.93.

23   Goodhart, *The Royal Americans*, p.1.

24   Combined Operations History, CAB106/3, TNA.

25   Messenger, pp.26–7.

26   David W. Hogan, Jr, *Raiders or Elite Infantry? The Changing Role of the US Army Rangers from Dieppe to Grenada*, p.13.

27   Truscott, p.34.

28   Theodore J. Conway interview, Conway MSS, Box 1, USAMHI.

29   Ibid.

30   David W. Hogan, Jr, *Raiders or Elite Infantry? The Changing Role of the US Army Rangers from Dieppe to Grenada*, p.18.

31   Ibid., p.19.

32   Theodore J. Conway interview, Conway MSS, Box 1, USAMHI.

33   Ibid.

34   Combined Operations History, CAB106/3, TNA.

35   'The Allied Campaign in North Africa', CAB106/708, TNA.

36   C-in-C Dispatch, North Africa, p.1, EPPF, EL.

37   Ibid.

38 'History of Allied Forces HQ and HQ NATOUSA 1942–1944', Vol. 1, pp.13–14, RG498, USNA.

39 See S. G. P. Ward.

40 G3 Operations, ETOUSA, 'Notes on British Forces', August 1943, United States army, European Theatre of Operations, USAMHI.

41 Hittle, p.211.

42 Ibid., p.212.

43 'History of Allied Forces HQ and HQ NATOUSA 1942–1944', Vol. 1, p.21, RG498, USNA.

44 Crosswell, *The Chief of Staff*, p.100.

45 Ibid., pp.104–5.

46 Paul Caraway Oral Interview, Paul Caraway Papers, USAMHI.

47 Croswell, *The Chief of Staff*, p.110.

48 'The Allied Campaign in North Africa', CAB106/708, TNA.

49 Ibid.

50 Ambrose, p.80.

51 'History of Allied Forces HQ and HQ NATOUSA 1942–1944', Vol. 1, p.14, RG498, USNA.

52 Truscott, p.32.

53 Field Base Censor No. 1, 12–18 March 1943, WO204/3900, TNA.

54 'History of Allied Forces HQ and HQ NATOUSA 1942–1944', Vol. 1, p.16, RG498, USNA.

55 Ambrose, p.81.

56 Handy to Marshall, 22 August 1942, Handy Files, EPPF, EL.

57 Ibid.

58 The Western Task Force was composed of five regimental combat teams and one armoured combat team, comprising a total of 36,000 officers and men. 'The Allied Campaign in North Africa', CAB106/708, TNA.

59 The Centre Task Force was built around the 1st US Infantry Division, one combat command of 1st Armored Division and one Ranger battalion with a total of 40,000 officers and men. Ibid.

60 The Eastern Task Force consisted of two US regimental combat teams, two British infantry brigade groups and two Commandos with mixed US and British personnel in a total of 23,000 British and 10,000 American troops. Ibid.

61 Danchev and Todman, p.335.

62 Ibid., p.336.

63 Churchill, pp.653–4.

64 'The Allied Campaign in North Africa', CAB106/708, TNA.
65 Paul A. Reuben interview, Reuben MSS, USAMHI.
66 Eisenhower to Handy, 7 December 1942, Handy Files, EPPF, EL.
67 Ibid.
68 Howard and Sparrow, p.112.
69 Ibid., p.114.
70 Hill, p.175.
71 Jenkins MSS, USAMHI.
72 'Notes from Theatres of War, No. 16: North Africa, November 1942–May 1943' (War Office), Allied Inter-Operability Study, USAMHI.
73 AFHQ Morale Report, 1–7 January 1943, WO204/3900, TNA.
74 Ibid.
75 Eisenhower to Handy, 7 December 1942, Handy Files, EPPF, EL.
76 Dwight D. Eisenhower, p.83.
77 Cunningham to First Sea Lord, 19 December 1942, Alanbrooke MSS 6/2/53, LHCMA.
78 Brooke to Anderson, December 1942, Alanbrooke MSS 6/2/53, LHCMA.
79 Ambrose, p.144.
80 Croswell, p.135.
81 Bedell Smith to Pug, 15 December 1942. Ismay MSS 4/29/1a, LHCMA.
82 Ibid.
83 Ibid.

7
Growing Pains

1   'The Allied Campaign in North Africa', CAB106/708, TNA.
2   David Montgomery, 'An Innocent Goes to War', unpublished manuscript, pp.413–15, D. Montgomery Papers, IWM.
3   Downing, p.138.
4   Ibid., pp.143–4.
5   Ibid., p.141.
6   Ibid., p.135.
7   'Mediterranean Strategy', CAB122/32, TNA.
8   Ian Jacob diary, Alanbrooke MSS 6/7/4, LHCMA.
9   Ibid.
10 Ibid.
11 Ibid.
12 'Washington 1942–4', Winn MSS, IWM.

13   Wedemeyer, p.192.

14   Caraway MSS, USMHI.

15   Eisenhower to Handy, 26 January 1943, Handy Files, EPPF, EL.

16   Wedemeyer to Liddell Hart, 30 December 1961, LH1/735/3, LHCMA.

17   Danchev and Todman, p.365.

18   Ibid.

19   Eisenhower to Handy, 26 January 1943, Handy Files, EPPF, EL.

20   Ibid.

21   Ibid.

22   Joint Staff Mission to War Cabinet Offices, 29 January 1943, CAB122/274, TNA.

23   Greacen, p.268.

24   1 February, Penney diary 1943/1944, Penney MSS 3/2, LHCMA.

25   Ibid.

26   Ibid.

27   8 February, ibid.

28   Ibid.

29   Ibid.

30   'The Allied Campaign in North Africa', CAB106/708, TNA.

31   Ankrum, p.180.

32   Ibid., p.185.

33   Bruce Allen Watson, p.95.

34   'Notes from Theatres of War, No. 16: North Africa, November 1942–May 1943' (War Office), Allied Inter-Operability Study, USAMHI.

35   Memoirs of Major General Sir Charles Dunphie, p.55, Charles Dunphie MSS.

36   Bruce Allen Watson, p.98.

37   Lecture Notes, 'Lessons of Tunisian Campaign', by Major General R. L. McCreery, CGS 18th Army Group, 18 June 1943, CAB106/895, TNA.

38   Downing, p.173.

39   Nicolson, p.175.

40   Eisenhower to Brooke, 3 July 1943, Alanbrooke MSS 6/2/27, LHCMA.

41   Alexander to Brooke, 27 February 1943, ibid.

42   Nicolson, pp.178–9.

43   Alexander to Brooke, 27 February 1943, Alanbrooke MSS 6/2/17, LHCMA.

44   Downing, p.204.

45   Eisenhower to Handy, 26 January 1943, Handy Files, EPPF, EL.

46   Alexander to Brooke, 27 February 1943, Alanbrooke MSS 6/2/17, LHCMA.

47   Alexander to Brooke, 3 April 1943, ibid.

48   Memoirs of Major General Sir Charles Dunphie, pp.57–9, Charles Dunphie MSS.

49   Ibid.

50   Ibid., p.61.

51   Ankrum, p.180.

52   AFHQ, Field Base Censor No.1, week ending 13 March 1943, WO204/3903, TNA.

53   Ibid.

54   Ibid.

55   Ibid., 12–18 March 1943.

56   135th Infantry, ibid.

57   Ibid.

58   Ibid.

59   AFHQ Morale Report 1–7 January, 8–14 January 1943, WO204/3900, TNA.

60   11–17 April 1943, Base Censorship Detachment No. 2, AFHQ Mail Reports, WO204/3903, TNA.

61   752nd Tank Battalion, ibid.

62   Blumenson, *The Patton Papers*, p.181.

63   Ibid.

64   6 March 1943, Memorandum for General Patton, Patton Files, EPPF, EL.

65   D'Este, *A Genius For War*, pp.464–8.

66   8 April 1943, Penney diary, Penney MSS 3/2, LHCMA.

67   Ibid.

68   Jackson, p.195.

69   Ankrum, p.244.

70   Ibid., p.233.

71   Ffrench Blake, pp. 132–6.

72   Ibid., p.256.

73   Dwight D. Eisenhower, p.151.

74   Blumenson, *The Patton Papers*, p. 218.

75   Alexander to Brooke, 3 April 1943, Alanbrooke MSS, LHCMA. Titled Most Secret Private and Confidential, yet four copies were made on 12 April 1943, Alanbrooke MSS 6/2/17, LHCMA.

76   Alexander to Brooke, 3 April 1943, Alanbrooke MSS, LHCMA.

77   Ibid.

78   Jackson, p.194.

79   Dwight D. Eisenhower, p.152.

80   'The Allied Campaign in North Africa', CAB106/708, TNA.

81   Ibid.
82   Ibid.
83   30 May 1943, Penney diary, Penney MSS 3/2, LHMCA.
84   D'Este, *A Genius for War*, p.497.

8
Sicilian Feud

1   Lucas MSS, USAMHI.
2   Churchill would appear to have coined the phrase 'triphibious' in 1941
      to denote the use of air, land and sea forces in an amphibious landing
      on a hostile shore, and Eisenhower also used the phrase in his *Crusade
      in Europe*, but, perhaps fortunately, the phrase never became popular
      and is little used today. See Wilmot R. Jones, Wilmot Files, EPPF, EL.
3   22 February 1943, Gairdner diary, Gairdner MSS, IWM.
4   26 February 1943, ibid.
5   'Planning for Operation Husky between February and May 1943',
      WO106/5823, TNA.
6   15 March 1943, Gairdner diary, Gairdner MSS, IWM.
7   'Planning for Operation Husky between February and May 1943',
      WO106/5823, TNA.
8   15 March 1943, ibid.
9   20 March 1943, ibid.
10   1 April 1943, Gairdner diary, Gairdner MSS, IWM.
11   Eisenhower to Combined Chiefs of Staff, 7 April, 1943, Marshall Files,
      EPPF, EL.
12   Tedder, p.433.
13   'Planning for Operation Husky between February and May 1943',
      WO106/5823 TNA.
14   Ibid.
15   Ibid.
16   Ibid.
17   24 April 1943, Gairdner diary, Gairdner MSS, IWM.
18   'Planning for Operation Husky between February and May 1943',
      WO106/5823 TNA.
19   Ibid.
20   Blumenson, *The Patton Papers*, p.254.
21   Ibid.
22   1 May 1942, Gairdner diary, Gairdner MSS, IWM.

23   Hamilton, *Master of the Battlefield*, p.261.

24   Blumenson, *The Patton Papers*, p.254.

25   Lucas diary, Lucas MSS, USAMHI.

26   Blumenson, *The Patton Papers*, p.254.

27   6 May 1943, Gairdner diary, Gairdner MSS, IWM.

28   Memoirs of Major General Sir Charles Dunphie, p.65, Charles Dunphie MSS.

29   'Planning for Operation Husky between February and May 1943', WO106/5823, TNA.

30   Wedemeyer Observer Report, Wedemeyer Files, EPPF, EL.

31   5 June 1943, Penney diary, Penney MSS, LHCMA.

32   10 July 1943, Gairdner Diary, Gairdner MSS, IWM.

33   Alexander Dispatch, Alexander Files, EPPF, EL.

34   Wedemeyer Observer Report, Wedemeyer Files, EPPF, EL.

35   Ibid.

36   Ibid.

37   Ibid.

38   12 July 1943, Montgomery's diary, Montgomery MSS LMD 42/1, IWM.

39   Wedemeyer Observer Report, Wedemeyer Files, EPPF, EL.

40   Ibid.

41   21 July 1943, Lucas diary, Lucas MSS, USAMHI.

42   14 July 1943, ibid.

43   Lucas Observer Report, Lucas Files, EPPF, EL.

44   14 July 1943, Lucas diary, Lucas MSS, USAMHI.

45   Ibid.

46   20–28 July 1943, Penney diary, Penney MSS 3/2, LHCMA.

47   Ibid.

48   Ibid.

49   Lucas diary, Lucas MSS, USAMHI.

50   Blumenson, *The Patton Papers*, p.306.

51   Ibid.

52   Lucas Observer Report, Lucas Files, EPPF, EL.

53   Lucas diary, Lucas MSS, USAMHI.

54   See the testimony of Col. F. Y. Leaver, commanding officer of 15th Evacuation Hospital, to Col. Richard T. Arnest, surgeon, II Corps, 4 August 1943; and Col. Donald E. Currier, Medical Corps, commanding officer of 93rd Evacuation Hospital, to Col. Richard Arnest, surgeon, II Corps, 12 August 1943. Patton Files, EPPF, EL.

55   See D'Este, *Bitter Victory*.

56   7 August 1943, Montgomery's diary, Montgomery MSS LMD36/1, IWM.

9
Stomach Ache

1   Box No.2, Trident Conference Minutes, Bedell Smith MSS, EL.

2   Box No.2, Quadrant Conference Minutes, Bedell Smith MSS, EL.

3   Ibid.

4   Wedemeyer to Eisenhower, 2 September 1943, Wedemeyer Files, EPPF, EL.

5   Box No.2, Quadrant Conference Minutes, Bedell Smith MSS, EL.

6   Interview with Brig. Gen. Charles E. Salzman, Matthews MSS, USAMHI.

7   Blumenson, *Mark Clark*, p.112.

8   Richardson, *Flashback*, p.159.

9   Ibid., p.160.

10 Ibid., p.157.

11 Alexander to Brooke, 3 April 1943, Alanbrooke MSS 6/2/17, LHCMA.

12 The bombardment was carried out by more than 300 field guns, 80 British medium guns and 48 medium guns. Oliver Leese considered the bombardment 'even more impressive and devastating than the opening of the barrage at Alamein'. 'Battle for Sicily', Leese MSS, IWM.

13 17 September 1943, Montgomery diary, Montgomery MSS LMD 41/1, IWM.

14 Churchill to Alexander, 14 September 1943, Alanbrooke MSS 6/2/18, IWM.

15 Lemnitzer interview, Matthews MSS, USAMHI.

16 Ibid.

17 Eisenhower to Thomas Handy, 26 September 1943, Handy Files, EPPF, EL.

18 9 September 1943, Montgomery's diary, Montgomery MSS LMD 41/1, IWM.

19 17–18 September 1943, Montgomery's Diary, Montgomery MSS, LMD 42/1, Montgomery Papers, IWM.

20 See Mascarenhas.

21 27 September 1943, ibid.

22 Ibid.

23 Alexander to Brooke, 21 September 1943, Alanbrooke MSS 6/2/18, LHCMA.

24 Molony, pp.332–3.

25 Alexander to Brooke, 21 September 1943, Alanbrooke MSS 6/2/18, LHCMA.

26 10 November 1943, Lucas diary, Lucas MSS, USAMHI.

27 Ibid.
28 Alexander to Brooke, 17 October 1943, Alanbrooke MSS 6/2/18, LHCMA.
29 Brooke to Alexander, 18 October 1943, Alanbrooke MSS 6/2/18, LHCMA.
30 Ibid.
31 Alexander to Eisenhower, 12 October 1943, Alexander Files, EPPF, EL.
32 Ibid.
33 1 November 1943, Lucas diary, Lucas MSS, USAMHI.
34 Matthews MSS, USAMHI.
35 6 November 1943, Lucas diary, Lucas MSS, USAMHI.
36 Lemnitzer interview, Matthews MSS, USAMHI.
37 D'Este, *Fatal Decision*, p.72.
38 Ibid., p.71.
39 Kenneth Strong interview, Matthews MSS, USAMHI.
40 Gilbert, pp.763–4.
41 D'Este, *Fatal Decision*, p.77.
42 Gilbert, p.765.
43 8 January 1944, Lucas diary, Lucas MSS, USAMHI.
44 John Lucas interview, Matthews MSS, USAMHI.
45 'From Algiers to Anzio', pp.6–7, Box 1, Lucas MSS, USAMHI.
46 Greacen, p.268.
47 3 January 1944, Penney diary, Penney MSS, LHCMA.
48 2–10 January 1944, Lucas diary, Lucas MSS, USAMHI.
49 Ibid.
50 Ibid.
51 24 January 1944, Lucas diary, Lucas MSS, USAMHI.
52 Ibid.
53 Ibid.

10
Hauling on the Rope

1 Alexander to Brooke, 26 January 1944, Alanbrooke MSS 6/2/19, LHCMA.
2 Weintraub, p.179.
3 Richardson, *Flashback*, p.160.
4 7 January 1944, Lucas diary, Lucas MSS, USAMHI.
5 Alexander interview, Matthews MSS, USAMHI.
6 Fitzgerald, pp.215–19.
7 12 January 1944, Lucas diary, Lucas MSS, USAMHI.
8 George C. Marshall interview, Matthews MSS, USAMHI.

9   29 January 1944, Lucas diary, Lucas MSS, USAMHI.

10 Fitzgerald, p.239.

11 25 January 1944, Lucas diary, Lucas MSS, USAMHI.

12 Alexander interview, Matthews MSS, USAMHI.

13 25 January 1944, Penney diary, Penney MSS 3/2, LHCMA.

14 Gilbert, p.767.

15 Ibid.

16 Fitzgerald, p.210.

17 1 February 1944, Lucas diary, Lucas MSS, USAMHI.

18 Ibid.

19 Ibid.

20 Ibid.

21 4 February 1944, ibid.

22 Ibid.

23 John Lucas interview, Matthews MSS, USAMHI.

24 Fitzgerald, p.321.

25 Ibid., p.325.

26 Harold Alexander interview, Matthews MSS, USAMHI.

27 Alexander to Brooke, 20 February 1944, Alanbrooke MSS 6/2/19, LHCMA.

28 Ibid.

29 Eisenhower to Marshall, 16 February 1944, Alexander Files, EPPF, EL.

30 Ibid.

31 20 February 1944, Penney diary, Penney MSS 3/2, LHCMA.

32 22 February 1944, Lucas diary, Lucas MSS, USAMHI.

33 20 April 1944, Penney diary, Penney MSS 3/2, USAMHI.

34 Grace, p.141.

35 MEF May–July 1944, Notes on British Army Morale, WO32/15772, TNA.

36 Magdalany, p.87.

37 Mark Clark interview, Matthews MSS, USAMHI.

38 Harold Alexander interview, Matthews MSS, USAMHI

39 Howard Kippenberger interview, Matthews MSS, USAMHI.

40 Ibid.

41 Ibid.

42 Alexander interview, Matthews MSS, OCMH, USAMHI.

43 Leese to Montgomery, 10 July 1944, Leese MSS, IWM.

44 Mark Clark interview, Matthews MSS, USAMHI.

45 Harpur, p.121.

46 Alexander to Brooke, 22 March 1944, Alanbrooke MSS 6/2/19, LHCMA.

47 John Ellis, *Cassino*, pp.221–63.

48   L. F. Ellis, *Welsh Guards at War*, p.140.

49   Alexander to Brooke, 22 March 1944, Alanbrooke MSS 6/2/19, LHCMA.

50   Magdalany, p.193.

51   Carver, p.121.

52   Ibid., pp.129–30.

53   Ibid., p.126.

54   Charles Dick, 'The Operational Employment of Soviet Armour in the Great Patriotic War', in Harris and Toase, *Armoured Warfare*, p.108.

55   Oliver Leese, 'I take over the 8th Army in Italy from Gen. Montgomery', Leese MSS, IWM.

56   Alexander to Brooke, 22 March 1944, Alanbrooke MSS 6/2/19, LHCMA.

57   Ibid.

58   Ibid.

59   Oliver Leese, 'I take over the 8th Army in Italy from Gen. Montgomery', Leese MSS, IWM.

60   John Ellis, *Cassino*, p.336.

61   Mark Clark, p.321.

62   Mark Clark interview, Matthews MSS, USAMHI.

63   'Fifth Army History', p.106, RG407/427/1620, USNA.

64   Ibid., p.107.

65   Ibid., p.116.

66   D'Este, *Fatal Decision*, pp.366–7.

67   Trevelyan, p.292.

68   Harpur, p.74.

69   Alexander to Brooke, 4 June 1944, Alanbrooke MSS 6/2/20, LHCMA.

70   Holland, p.183.

71   'The Anvil Debate', CAB106/1117, TNA.

72   Ibid.

73   Danchev and Todman, p.564.

74   Eisenhower to Churchill, 11 August 1944, Churchill Files, EPPF, EL.

75   Oliver Leese, 'I take over the 8th Army in Italy from Gen. Montgomery', Leese MSS, IWM.

76   Ibid.

77   Ibid.

78   Ibid.

79   Leese to Montgomery, 10 September 1944, Leese MSS, IWM.

80   Oland, *North Apennines 1944–45*, p.10.

81   Fisher, p.336.

82   Captain Robert E. Roeder, the commander of G Company, 2nd

Battalion, 350th Infantry Regiment, was posthumously awarded the Congressional Medal of Honor for his valour during the fighting. When his company was overrun, Roeder led the fighting to recover the positions. When he was seriously wounded, he stayed by the entrance to the ruined castle, fighting and encouraging his men until he was killed by a mortar shell. See ibid., p.351.

83   L. F. Ellis, *Welsh Guards at War*.

84   Howard and Sparrow, p.238.

85   Shepperd, pp.353–71.

86   History of 7 AGRA, WO204/7212, TNA.

87   Richard Lamb, *War in Italy 1943–1945: A Brutal Story*, pp.272–95.

88   Churchill to Alexander, 29 April 1945, Alanbrooke MSS 6/2/20, LHCMA.

11
Over There, Over Here

1   L. F. Ellis, *The Battle of Normandy*, p.29.

2   A British survey in 1943 found that on average, 45% of the troops heard the speech, 65% heard the band, 83% enjoyed the refreshments, but only 9% received the welcome leaflet that had been printed. 25% of those who heard the speech believed it to have been delivered by an American officer. While 95% of those who did hear the speech and the music were enthusiastic in their satisfaction at the welcome, those who did not hear the speech or the music were not! 'army Morale', WO32/1557, TNA.

3   'Bolero', CAB106/1097, TNA.

4   Ibid.

5   Ibid.

6   Ibid.

7   Ibid.

8   'Morale in the Army', 3 March 1942, WO32/15772, TNA.

9   Executive Committee of the Army Council, 31 October 1941, WO259/62, TNA.

10   'Morale in the Army', 3 March 1942, WO32/15772, TNA.

11   Executive Committee of the Army Council, 31 October 1941, WO259/62, TNA.

12   Andrew Mollo, *World Army Uniforms since 1939*, Poole: Blandford Press, 1981, p.30.

13 Calder, pp.248–9.

14 WO32/15772, TNA.

15 WO32/15772, TNA.

16 Ibid.

17 Calder, p.250.

18 This book cannot hope to provide a full survey of the social impact of American soldiers in Britain. However, an excellent picture of the US Army's influence on British life is provided by Norman Longmate, *The GIs in Britain*, and David Reynolds, *Rich Relations*.

19 Keegan, *Six Armies in Normandy*, pp.11–12.

20 Andrew Mollo, *World army Uniforms since 1939*, Poole: Blandford Press, 1981, p.58.

21 3 September 1942, INF1/292/Pts 3–4, TNA.

22 Extracts from censorship reports concerning the 'inter-attachment' scheme (January–February 1944), WO32/15772, TNA.

23 'Logistical Build-Up in the British Isles', Report of the General Board United States Forces, European Theater, USAMHI.

24 2 July 1942, Intelligence Weekly Reports, INF1/292/Pts3–4, TNA.

25 'Army Morale', WO32/15772, TNA.

26 27 August 1942, Intelligence Weekly Reports, INF1/292/Pts3–4, TNA.

27 Ibid.

28 10 September 1942, ibid.

29 30 July 1942, ibid.

30 2 July 1942, ibid.

31 Summers, p.39.

32 31 December 1942, Intelligence Weekly Reports, INF1/292/Pts3–4, TNA.

33 6 August 1942, ibid.

34 Ibid.

35 30 July 1942, ibid.

36 May–July 1943, Morale Report, WO32/204/3900, TNA.

37 Ibid.

38 August–October 1942, ibid.

39 May–July 1942, ibid.

40 1–31 December 1944, censorship report on United States Army Mail No. 29, FO371/44601, TNA.

41 Ibid.

42 Macintyre MSS, USAMHI.

43 16–31 January 1945, censorship report on United States Army Mail No. 29, FO371/44601, TNA.

44 1–30 April 1945, ibid.

45   May–July 1943, Morale Report, WO32/204/3900, TNA.

46   19 November 1943, Anglo-American relations committee, WO193/ 455, TNA.

47   14 September 1943, ibid.

48   Summers, p.32.

49   Anglo-American relations committee, WO193/455, TNA.

50   Ibid.

51   Ibid.

52   Ibid.

53   Historical Record, British Army Staff, Part II, WO202/917 TNA.

54   Historical Record, British Army Staff, Part I, WO202/916 TNA.

55   See Historical Record, British Army Staff, Parts I–X, WO202/ 916–925.

56   Ibid.

57   Ibid.

58   Ibid.

59   Ibid.

60   Ibid.

61   Ibid.

62   Ibid.

63   Ibid.

64   Ibid.

65   Historical Record, British Army Staff, Part II, WO202/917 TNA.

66   Frederick Morgan, 'Overture to Overlord', TNA; also published as Frederick Morgan, *Overture to Overlord*.

67   Ibid.

68   Ibid.

69   Ibid., p.64.

70   Ibid., p.100.

71   Ibid., p.101.

72   'History of COSSAC', CAB106/969, TNA.

73   Ibid.

74   Ibid.

75   Ibid.

76   Frederick Morgan, 'Overture to Overlord', p.162, TNA.

77   19 November 1943, Minutes of Meeting, Matthews MSS, USAMHI.

78   J. P. 735 (s) Annex VI, Staff Conversations, 27 June 1940– 12 December 1941, WO193/305, TNA.

79   19 November 1943, Minutes of Meeting, Matthews MSS, USAMHI.

80   Marshall interview, Matthews MSS, USAMHI.

81　'History of COSSAC', CAB106/969, TNA.

82　Churchill to Attlee, 1 September 1943, PREM3/336/1, TNA.

83　Roosevelt to Churchill, 5 October 1943, PREM3/336/1, TNA.

84　Dill to Chiefs of Staff, 8 November 1943, CAB106/329, TNA.

85　14 September 1943, Memorandum Prepared for Lord Louis Mountbatten, Mountbatten Files, EPPF, EL.

86　Ibid.

87　Ibid.

88　Ibid.

89　Churchill to Attlee, 14 December 1943, PREM3/336/1, TNA.

90　War Cabinet to CIGS, 15 December 1943; Churchill to Roosevelt, 18 December 1943, ibid.

91　L. F. Ellis, *The Battle of Normandy*, p.29.

92　A common joke of the time was that only the barrage balloons prevented the island from sinking into the sea under all the weight. Calder, p.306.

93　Churchill to Roosevelt, 24 December 1943, PREM3/336/1, TNA.

94　Notes for the Commander-in-Chief for Supreme Commander's Meeting, 21 January 1944, Montgomery MSS LMD 54/4, IWM.

95　Richardson, *Send for Freddie*, pp.145–6.

96　De Guingand, *Generals at War*, p.100.

97　20 February 1944, personal diary, Montgomery MSS LMD 54/1, IWM.

98　Ibid.

99　Brief Summary of Operation 'Overlord' as affecting the Army. Given as an address to all General officers of the four field armies in London on 7 April, 1944, Montgomery MSS LMD 55/4, IWM.

100　Ibid.

101　Ibid.

102　D'Este, *Eisenhower, A Soldier's Life*, p.519.

103　Ibid.

104　Ibid., p.526. See also Ambrose, fn.417.

12

The Great Crusade

1　Dwight D. Eisenhower, p.245.

2　Danchev and Todman, p.554.

3　Colonel E. G. Paules, Report No. 23, Observations of Invasion of France and Fall of Cherbourg, June 3–July 6, 1944, RG407/427/24635, USNA.

4　Scarfe, pp.72–3.

5   The British and Canadian forces had suffered over 4,000, while American casualties amounted to 6,000. See L. F. Ellis, *The Battle of Normandy*, pp.222–3.

6   Orange, pp.256–66.

7   Notes by C-in-C 21 Army Group, 20 March 1944, Montgomery MSS LMD 54/25, IWM.

8   Hughes, pp.45–7.

9   'The Airfields Controversy', CAB106/1120, TNA.

10 L. F. Ellis, *The Battle of Normandy*, pp.254–5.

11 'The Airfields Controversy', CAB106/1120, TNA.

12 'The Story of the Mulberries', CAB106/1039, TNA.

13 Eisenhower to Montgomery, 25 June 1944, Montgomery Files, EPPF, EL.

14 Montgomery to Eisenhower, 25 June 1944, Montgomery Files, EPPF, EL.

15 L. F. Ellis, *The Battle of Normandy*, pp.275–86.

16 Hargreaves, p.112.

17 'The Airfields Controversy', CAB106/1120, TNA.

18 Harrison, pp.386–442.

19 F. H. Hinsley, *British Intelligence in the Second World War: Its Influence on Strategy and Operations*, Vol. 3, Part II, pp.44–9, 177–82.

20 Talk with Lieutenant General G. S. Patton, 19.6.44, Liddell Hart MSS LH11/1944/39, LHCMA.

21 Montgomery to Bradley and Dempsey, 30 June 1944, Montgomery Files, EPPF, EL.

22 Montgomery to Bradley and Dempsey, 18 June 1944, Alanbrooke MSS 6/2/25, LHCMA.

23 Montgomery to Brooke, 7 July 1944, Alanbrooke MSS 6/2/26, LHCMA.

24 'Hedgerow Fighting', HQ Twelfth army Group, OCMH, USAMHI.

25 Balkoski, pp.253–4.

26 James M. McPherson, *Battle Cry of Freedom: The Civil War Era*, pp.75–731.

27 12 July 1944, Chester B. Hansen diary, Hansen MSS, USAMHI.

28 Charles Bonesteel interview, Matthews MSS, USAMHI.

29 See Stephen A. Hart.

30 John Ellis, *The Sharp End of War*, p.158.

31 Ibid.

32 Montgomery to Brooke, 27 June 1944, Alanbrooke MSS 6/2/25, LHCMA.

33 Montgomery to Brooke, 7 July 1944, Alanbrooke MSS 6/2/26, LHCMA.

34 Orange, p.269.

35 L. F. Ellis, *The Battle of Normandy*, p.311.

36   Keegan, *Six Armies in Normandy*, p.188.

37   L. F. Ellis, *The Battle of Normandy*, p.316.

38   Eisenhower to Montgomery, 7 July 1944, Montgomery Files, EPPF, EL.

39   Montgomery to Eisenhower, 8 July 1944, ibid.

40   Montgomery to Brooke, 7 July 1944, Alanbrooke MSS, LHCMA

41   Hargreaves, p.135.

42   Montgomery to Brooke, 14 July 1944, Alanbrooke MSS 6/2/27, LHCMA.

43   Montgomery to Eisenhower, 12 July 1944, Montgomery Files, EPPF, EL.

44   Ibid.

45   Montgomery to Brooke, 14 July 1944, Alanbrooke MSS 6/2/27, LHCMA.

46   Eisenhower to Montgomery, 14 July 1944, Montgomery Files, EPPF, EL.

47   Notes on Second Army Operations 16 July–18 July, Alanbrooke MSS 6/2/27, LHCMA.

48   'The Airfields Controversy', CAB106/1120, TNA.

49   Orange, p.271. Trenchard, the 'father of the Royal Air Force', had been the first commander-in-chief of the Royal Air Force.

50   Ibid.

51   D'Este, *Decision in Normandy*, p.394.

52   Eisenhower to Montgomery, 21 July 1944, Montgomery Files, EPPF, EL.

53   'VII Corps in Operation Cobra', Collins MSS, EL.

54   Ibid.

55   Ibid.

56   20 July 1944, Hansen diary, Hansen MSS, USAMHI.

57   25 July 1944, ibid.

58   Ibid.

59   Weigley, *Eisenhower's Lieutenants*, p.171.

60   27 July 1944, Hansen diary, Hansen MSS, USAMHI.

61   Montgomery to Brooke, 28 July 1944, Alanbrooke MSS 6/2/28, LHCMA.

62   Churchill to Montgomery, 27 July 1944, Alanbrooke MSS 6/2/28, LHCMA.

63   28 July 1944, Hansen diary, Hansen MSS, USAMHI.

64   Montgomery's directive to Bradley, Dempsey, Patton and Crerar, 27 July 1944, Alanbrooke MSS, LHCMA.

65   Weigley, *Eisenhower's Lieutenants*, p.179.

66   6 August 1944, Hansen diary, Hansen MSS, USAMHI.

67   12 August 1944, ibid.

68   Omar Bradley, p.376.

69   Ibid.

70   Blumenson, *The Patton Papers*, pp.508–9.

71   13 August 1944, Hansen diary, Hansen MSS, USAMHI.

72   Ibid.

73   Keegan, *Six Armies in Normandy*, pp.249–82.

74   24 August 1944, Home Intelligence Weekly Reports, INF1/292/Pts3–4, TNA.

75   L. F. Ellis, *The Battle of Normandy*, p.214.

13
SHAEF at War

1   Brooke to Wilson, 2 August 1944, Alanbrooke MSS 6/3/6, LHCMA.

2   George C. Marshall interview, OMHI interviews, USAMHI.

3   Montgomery to Brooke, 7 July 1944, Alanbrooke MSS 6/2/26, LHCMA.

4   Bedell Smith interview, OMHI interviews, USAMHI.

5   Montgomery to Brooke, 18 August 1944, Alanbrooke MSS 6/2/26, LHCMA.

6   Major General Robert W. Crawford interview, OCMH interviews, USAMHI.

7   18–19 August, Hansen diary, Hansen MSS, USAMHI.

8   Eisenhower to Montgomery, 24 August 1944, Montgomery File, EPPF, EL.

9   The 'Broad Front' versus the 'Narrow Front' Controversy, CAB106/1106, TNA.

10   Ibid.

11   Danchev and Todman, p.585.

12   Ibid., p.586.

13   22 September 1944, Hansen diary, Hansen papers, USAMHI.

14   7 September 1944, Home Intelligence Weekly Reports, INF1/292/Pts3–4, TNA.

15   D'Este, *Eisenhower*, p.593.

16   Horrocks, *A Full Life*, p.195.

17   1 September 1944, Hansen diary, Hansen MSS, USAMHI.

18   Horrocks, *A Full Life*, p.195.

19   Baldwin, p.273.

20   Horrocks, *A Full Life*, p.206.

21   Greenfield, p.322.

22   Van Creveld, p.220.

23   Montgomery to Eisenhower, 4 September 1944, Montgomery Files, EPPF, EL.

24   Montgomery to Archibald Nye, 26 August 1944, Alanbrooke MSS 6/2/31, LHCMA.

25   Montgomery to Simpson, 20 September 1944, Alanbrooke MSS 6/2/32, LHCMA.

26   Greenfield, p.329.

27   Pogue, *Supreme Command*, pp.281–2.

28   Greenfield, p.335.

29   Buckingham, p.135.

30   'The Capture of Nijmegen Bridge, 20 September 1944', WO205/1125, TNA.

31   Ibid.

32   Buckingham, pp.138–40.

33   'The Capture of Nijmegen Bridge, 20 September 1944', WO205/1125, TNA.

34   Buckingham, p.141.

35   Powell, p.163.

36   Forty, p.140.

37   'The Capture of Nijmegen Bridge, 20 September 1944', WO205/1125, TNA.

38   Lloyd Clark, p.168.

39   Greenfield, p.328.

40   Horrocks, *A Full Life*, p.204.

41   Van Creveld, p.229.

42   Danchev and Todman, p.600.

43   See Zuehlke.

44   'The Diver Defences of Brussels and Antwerp', CAB106/1057, TNA.

45   Baldwin, p.274.

46   Rickard, pp.228–35.

47   Blumenson, *Patton*, p.241.

48   Ben Lear interview, OMHI interviews, USAMHI.

49   Eisenhower to Marshall, 15 May 1944: 'In order to avoid confusion with the British Eighth Army when the two Theaters are combined, I recommend that the designation of our new army Headquarters be not the Eighth US Army as specified . . . Further reason is a natural British feeling for their famous Eighth Army, which feeling I share.' WO219/546, TNA.

50   Major General Ewart, G Plan, CG ADSEC ETO, OMHI interviews, USAMHI.

51   L. F. Ellis, *The Defeat of Germany*, p.161.

52   MacDonald, p.1.

53   Ibid., pp.199–202.

54   Ibid., p.205.

55 Danchev and Todman, p.617.

56 Danchev, *Very Special Relationship*, p.1.

57 Danchev and Todman, p.620.

58 Montgomery to Brooke, 17 November 1944, Alanbrooke MSS 6/3/1, LHCMA; Brooke to Montgomery, 20 November 1944, ibid.

59 Danchev and Todman, p.628.

60 Ibid.

61 Ibid., pp.629–30.

62 Montgomery to Brooke, 7 December 1944, Alanbrooke MSS 6/3/1, LHCMA.

63 Danny S. Parker, p.14.

14
Supreme Commander

1   Morelock, p.293.

2   Price, p.135.

3   Strong, p.157.

4   Morelock, p.60.

5   16 December 1944, Hansen diary, Hansen MSS, USAMHI.

6   Morelock, p.295.

7   Strong, p.162.

8   Ibid.

9   Ambrose, p.558.

10 David Eisenhower, p.567.

11 Strong, p.163.

12 SHAEF to Combined Chiefs of Staff, 19 December 1944, Alanbrooke MSS 6/3/1, LHCMA.

13 Danchev and Todman, p.636.

14 3–11 December 1944, Hansen diary, Hansen MSS, USAMHI.

15 Montgomery to Brooke, 20 December 1944 (sent on 19 December, received 0255 20 December), Alanbrooke MSS 6/3/1, LHCMA.

16 18 December 1944, First US Army, war diary, 2 June 1944–7 May 1945, Box 25, Hodges MSS, EL.

17 Ibid.

18 Strong, p.165.

19 Ibid.

20 Ibid., p.166.

21 Ibid.

22 Ibid.

23 Montgomery to Simpson, 25 December 1944, Alanbrooke MSS 6/2/36, LHCMA.

24 Ibid.

25 Hamilton, *The Field Marshal*, p.213.

26 Montgomery to Brooke, 20 December 1944, Alanbrooke MSS 6/2/36, LHCMA.

27 Montgomery to Simpson, 25 December 1944, ibid.

28 Weigley, *Eisenhower's Lieutenants*, p.615.

29 20 December 1944, First US Army, war diary, 2 June 1944–7 May 1945, Box 25, Hodges Papers, EL.

30 28 December 1944, ibid.

31 Montgomery to Brooke, 28 December 1944, Alanbrooke MSS 6/2/36, LHCMA.

32 Ibid.

33 Montgomery to Eisenhower, 29 December 1944, Box No. 74, Montgomery Files, EPPF, EL.

34 De Guingand, *Generals at War*, p.106.

35 Ibid.

36 Simpson to Brooke, 31 December 1944, Alanbrooke MSS 6/2/36, LHCMA.

37 De Guingand, *Generals at War*, p.108.

38 Eisenhower to Montgomery, 31 December 1944, Montgomery Files, EPPF, EL.

39 Fussell, p.20.

40 Summersby, p.205.

41 De Guingand, *Generals at War*, p.111.

42 Ibid.

43 'Higher Direction of War', Box No. 1, Robb MSS, EL.

44 Ibid.

45 Ibid.

46 Montgomery to Brooke, 2 January 1945, Alanbrooke MSS 6/2/36, LHCMA.

47 6 January 1945, Hansen diary, Hansen MSS, USAMHI.

48 Montgomery to Simpson, 13 January 1945, Alanbrooke MSS 6/3/1, LHCMA.

49 'Field Marshal Montgomery's Press Conference, January the 7th, 1945', CAB106/1107, TNA.

50 Ibid.

51 Ibid.

52 Ibid.

53 Eisenhower, *Crusade*, p.356.

54 Ibid.

55 Ibid.

56 Censorship report on United States Army Mail No. 29, FO371/44601, TNA.

57 Ibid.

58 Morelock, p.150.

59 16 January 1945, First US Army, war diary, 2 June 1944–7 May 1945, Box 25, Hodges MSS, EL.

60 4 February 1945, Hansen diary, Hansen MSS, USAMHI.

61 De Guingand, *Generals at War*, p.112.

62 Theodore W. Parker, pp.138–9.

63 Ibid., p.141.

64 Palamountain, *Taurus Pursuant*, p.85.

65 L. F. Ellis, *The Defeat of Germany*, pp.253–71.

66 Ibid., pp.170–90.

67 Weigley, *Eisenhower's Lieutenants*, p.628.

68 L. F. Ellis, *The Defeat of Germany*, p.285.

69 Timothy, p.13.

70 Ibid.

71 Ibid., p.1.

72 Theodore W. Parker, p.290.

73 Ibid., p.211.

74 Ibid., p.208.

75 Ibid., p.190.

76 Ellis, *The Defeat of Germany*, p.288.

77 Timothy, p.29.

78 Lieutenant General Tom Rennie was killed by a mortar shell while driving up to the front. Rennie had seen continuous service since the Battle of El Alamein in 1942. Fergusson, pp.308–9.

79 Ellis, *The Defeat of Germany*, p.290.

80 Danchev and Todman, pp.673–6.

81 Dwight D. Eisenhower, p.372.

82 Danchev and Todman, p.677.

83 27 March 1945, Personal Calendar, Box 12, Simpson MSS, USAMHI.

84 Ibid.

85 Ibid.

86 Oral History Program, Moore MSS, USAMHI.

87 On this operation, 6th Guards Armoured Brigade comprised 3rd Tank

Battalion, Scots Guards; 4th Tank Battalion, Coldstream Guards; 513th Parachute Regiment of the 17th US Airborne Division; 3rd British Division Reconaissance Regiment; 6th Field Regiment, Royal Artillery and 61st Medium Regiment, Royal Artillery. 3rd Tank Battalion, Scots Guards, 20 July 1944–8 May 1945, CAB106/1029, TNA. One of the officers of the Scots Guards was Lieutenant Robert Runcie, who was awarded the Military Cross during this operation. He later became the Archbishop of Canterbury.

88   Ibid. See also 17th Airborne Division, Rhine Crossing, WWII Operations Reports 1940–48, Folders 67 to 69, RG407/427/24030, USNA.

89   3rd Tank Battalion, Scots Guards, 20 July 1944–8 May 1945, CAB106/1029, TNA.

90   Friedrich von Mellenthin, *Panzer Battles*, p.260.

91   Box 16, Simpson MSS, USAMHI.

92   Censorship report on United States Army Mail No. 29, FO371/44601, TNA.

93   'Situation of Ninth US Army on Elbe River on April 15, 1945, William H. Simpson, 29 March 1966, Simpson MSS, USAMHI.

94   Ibid.

95   'NW Europe 1944–5, Comparison of Strengths', CAB106/1001, TNA.

96   3rd Tank Battalion, Scots Guards, 20 July 1944–8 May 1945, CAB106/1029, TNA.

97   30 April, Hansen diary, Hansen MSS, USAMHI.

98   Dönitz, p.458.

99   Hamilton, *The Field Marshal*, p.502.

100   Ibid., p.513.

101   Ambrose, p.662.

102   Ibid., p.663. The proceedings at SHAEF marked the final unconditional surrender of Nazi Germany. However, the Soviets insisted that the terms of the surrender document were not those that had been agreed by the European Advisory Commission. There was thus a second act of military surrender in Berlin on 8 May 1945.

103   Ibid., p.668.

15
Born on the Battlefield

1   1–30 May 1945, censorship report on United States Army Mail No. 29, FO371/44601, TNA.

2   Ibid.

3   See Robb-Webb.

4   General Maitland Wilson to General Alan Brooke, 6 August 1945, CAB127/47, TNA.

5   See Dobson, *US Wartime Aid*, pp.185–227.

6   Dobson, *Anglo-American Relations*, pp.89–90.

7   Terminal Conference, Bedell Smith MSS, EL.

8   Ibid.

9   11 April 1945, WWII Operations Reports, 1940–48 Special File, RG94, Box No. 24636 [407/427/24636], USNA.

10   Historical Record, British Army Staff, Part I, WO202/916, TNA.

11   General Miles Dempsey to General William Simpson, 11 May 1945, Simpson MSS, USAMHI.

12   See Eisenhower–Alexander Foundation WO204/427, TNA; CAB122/1036, TNA; and Morgan Files, EPPF, EL.

13   The lecture programme was funded by a donation by Mrs Kermit Roosevelt in memory of her husband. See Mrs Kermit Roosevelt to George Marshall, 17 June 1944, Winn MSS, IWM.

14   Ibid.

15   Ibid.

16   Ibid.

17   See Ralph Ingersoll, *Top Secret*, New York: Harcourt, Brace, 1946; Butcher, *My Three Years with Eisenhower*.

18   Butcher Files, EPPF, EL.

19   Eisenhower to Brooke, 4 March 1946, Brooke Files, EPPF, EL.

20   Alan Brooke to Eisenhower, 19 March 1946, Brooke Files, EPPF, EL.

21   Montgomery to Eisenhower, 28 January 1946, Montgomery Files, EPPF, EL.

22   G. E. Patrick Murray, *Eisenhower Versus Montgomery: the Continuing Debate*, Westport CT: Praeger, 1996, p.16.

23   Eisenhower to Montgomery, 5 November 1946, Montgomery Files, EPPF, EL.

24   Liddell Hart to Eisenhower, 3 January 1949, Liddell Hart File, EPPF, EL.

25   See Ismay Files, EPPF, EL.

26   Kaplan, pp.1–5.

27   Ismay, *NATO*, pp.35–8.

28   Chandler and Galambos, Vol. 6, p.17.

29   Eisenhower to Ismay, 13 July 1946, Ismay Files, EPPF, EL.

Bibliography

Unpublished primary sources

The National Archives, Kew (TNA)

AVIA12, 38
CAB106, 121, 122,
FO371
INF1
PREM3
WO32, 106, 185, 193, 202, 204, 205, 259

Imperial War Museum,
Department of Documents, London (IWM)

Bourne MSS
Gairdner MSS
Leese MSS
Macready MSS
Montgomery MSS
D. Montgomery MSS
Morgan MSS
Winn MSS

Liddell Hart Centre for Military Archives, King's
College London (LHCMA)

Alanbrooke MSS
Ismay MSS
Penney MSS

Joint Services Command and Staff College Library (JSCSC)

Kermit Roosevelt Lecture Programmes

United States Army Military History Institute (USAMHI)

Bolte MSS
Bonesteel MSS
Caraway MSS
Conway MSS
Dahlquist MSS
Hansen MSS
Jarret MSS
Jenkins MSS
Lucas MSS
Macintyre MSS
Matthews MSS
Moore MSS
OCMH interviews
OMHI interviews
Reuben MSS
Simpson MSS

United States of America National Archives, Washington, DC (USNA)

RG94
RG156
RG319
RG407
RG457
RG498

Eisenhower Library, Abilene, Kansas (EL)

Bedell Smith MSS
Collins MSS
Eisenhower Pre-Presidential Files (EPPF)

Hodges MSS
Robb MSS

John Rylands Library, Manchester University, Manchester (JRL)

Auchinleck MSS

Major General Sir Charles Dunphie MSS, Private Collection

Memoirs of Major General Sir Charles Dunphie

National Army Museum, Chelsea (NAM)

General Sir Henry Rawlinson MSS

Published primary sources

Blumenson, Martin, *The Patton Papers*, 2 vols, Da Capo Press, 1992

Brooks, Stephen, *Montgomery and the Eighth Army: a selection from the diaries, correspondence and other papers of Field Marshal the Viscount Montgomery of Alamein, August 1942 to December 1943*, Bodley Head for the Army Records Society, 1991

Brooks, Stephen, *Montgomery and the Battle of Normandy: a selection from the diaries, correspondence and other papers of Field Marshal the Viscount Montgomery of Alamein, January to August 1944*, The History Press for the Army Records Society, 2008

Chandler, Alfred D., and Louis Galambos, *The Papers of Dwight David Eisenhower*, 9 vols, Johns Hopkins University Press, 1978

Danchev, Alex, and Daniel Todman, *War Diaries 1939–1945: Field Marshal Lord Alanbrooke*, Weidenfeld & Nicholson, 2001

Ferrell, Robert H., *The Eisenhower Diaries*, W. W. Norton & Company, 1981

Published secondary sources

Ambrose, Stephen E., *The Supreme Commander: the War Years of General Dwight D. Eisenhower*, Cassell, 1971

Ankrum, Homer R., *Dogfaces Who Smiled Through Tears: The 34th Red Bull Infantry Division in World War II*, University Press of Mississippi, 1999

Atkinson, Rick, *An Army at Dawn: The War in North Africa 1942–1943*, Abacus, 2004

Atkinson, Rick, *The Day of Battle: The War in Sicily and Italy 1943–1944*, Little Brown, 2007

Atkinson, Rick, *The Guns at Last Light: The War in Western Europe, 1944–1945*, Little Brown, 2013

Baily, Charles M., *Faint Praise: American Tanks and Tank Destroyers during World War II*, Archon Books, 1983

Bairne, A. J., *The Arsenal of Democracy: FDR, Detroit, and an Epic Quest to Arm an America at War*, Houghton Mifflin Harcourt, 2014

Baldwin, Ralph B., *The Deadly Fuze: Secret Weapon of World War II*, Presidio Press, 1980

Balkoski, Joseph, *Beyond the Beachhead, the 29th Infantry Division in Normandy*, Stackpole Books, 2005

Barr, Niall, *Pendulum of War: The Three Battles of El Alamein*, Jonathan Cape, 2004

Bean, C. W., *The Official History of Australia in the War of 1914–1918 Vol. VI: The Australian Imperial Force in France during the Allied Offensive, 1918*, Angus & Robertson, 1929

Behrendt, Hans Otto, *Rommel's Intelligence in the Desert Campaign*, Kimber, 1985

Bernstein, Mark, and Alex Lubertozzi, *World War II on the Air: Edward R. Murrow and the Broadcasts that Riveted a Nation*, Sourcebooks, 2003

Bidwell, Shelford, and Dominic Graham, *Tug of War: The Battle for Italy, 1943–1945*, Hodder & Stoughton, 1986

Black, Conrad, *Franklin Delano Roosevelt: Champion of Freedom*, Weidenfeld & Nicholson, 2003

Blumenson, Martin, *Mark Clark*, Jonathan Cape, 1985

Blumenson, Martin, *Patton: the Man Behind the Legend, 1885–1945*, Jonathan Cape, 1986

Bond, Brian, *British Military Policy Between the Wars*, Clarendon, 1980

Bond, Brian and Nigel Cave, *Haig: A Reappraisal 70 Years On*, Leo Cooper, 1999

Bradley, A. G., *The Fight with France for North America*, Constable & Co., 1902

Bradley, Omar, *A Soldier's Story*, Henry Holt & Co., 1951

Buckingham, William F., *Arnhem 1944: A Reappraisal*, Tempus, 2004

Buckton, Henry, *Friendly Invasion, Memories of Operation Bolero: The American Occupation of Britain 1942–1945*, Phillimore, 2006

Burk, Kathleen, *Old World New World: The Story of Britain and America*, Little Brown, 2007

Butcher, Harry C., *My Three Years with Eisenhower: The Personal Diary of Captain Harry C. Butcher, USNR, Naval Aide to General Eisenhower, 1942 to 1945*, Simon and Schuster, 1946

Butler, J. R. M., *Grand Strategy, September 1939–June 1941*, HMSO, 1957

Butler, Lewis, *The Annals of the King's Royal Rifle Corps Vol. I: 'The Royal Americans'*, John Murray, 1913

Calder, Angus, *The People's War*, Jonathan Cape, 1986

Carver, Michael, *Harding of Petherton*, Weidenfeld & Nicholson, 1978

Cerami, Joseph R., 'The 1941 Louisiana Maneuvers', *Military Review*, October 1987

Charteris, John, *At GHQ*, Cassel, 1931

Churchill, Winston S., *The Hinge of Fate*, Cassell, 1966

Clark, Lloyd, *Arnhem: Operation Market Garden, September 1944*, Headline Review, 2009

Clark, Mark, *Calculated Risk*, Harrap, 1951

Clifford, Kenneth J., *The United States Marines in Iceland 1941–1942*, US Marine Corps, 1970

Cole, D. H., *Imperial Military Geography*, Sifton Praed, 1936

Cooper, James Fenimore, *The Last of the Mohicans: A Narrative of 1757*, Empire Books, 2011

Cope, William H., *The History of the Rifle Brigade (The Prince Consort's Own): formerly the 95th*, Chatto & Windus, 1877

Crang, Jeremy, *The British Army and the People's War 1939–1945*, Manchester University Press, 2000

Crosswell, D. K. R., *The Chief of Staff: The Military Career of General Walter Bedell Smith*, Greenwood, 1991

Danchev, Alex, *Establishing the Anglo-American Alliance: The Second World War Diaries of Brigadier Vivian Dykes*, Brassey's, 1990

Danchev, Alex, *Very Special Relationship: Field Marshal Sir John Dill and the Anglo-American Alliance 1941–44*, Brassey's, 1986

De Groot, Gerard, *Douglas Haig, 1861–1928*, Unwin Hyman, 1988

D'Este, Carlo, *Decision in Normandy: The Unwritten Story of Montgomery and the Allied Campaign*, Collins, 1983

D'Este, Carlo, *Bitter Victory: The Battle for Sicily July–August 1943*, Collins, 1988

D'Este, Carlo, *Fatal Decision: Anzio and the Battle for Rome*, Harper Collins, 1991

D'Este, Carlo, *A Genius for War: A Life of General George S. Patton*, Harper Collins, 1995

D'Este, Carlo, *Eisenhower, A Soldier's Life*, Cassell, 2003

Dimbleby, David, and David Reynolds, *An Ocean Apart: The Relationship between Britain and America in the Twentieth Century*, Guild Publishing, 1988

Dobson, Alan P., *US Wartime Aid to Britain 1940–1946*, Croom Helm, 1986

Dobson, Alan P., *Anglo-American Relations in the Twentieth Century*, Routledge, 1995

Dönitz, Karl, *Ten Years and Twenty Days: Memoirs*, Greenhill, 1990

Downing, John P., *At War with the British*, JP Downing, 1980

Duncan Hall, H., *North American Supply*, HMSO, 1955

Eisenhower, David, *Eisenhower at War*, Collins, 1986

Eisenhower, Dwight D., *Crusade in Europe*, William Heinemann, 1948

Ellis, John, *The Sharp End of War: The Fighting Man in World War II*, David & Charles, 1980

Ellis, John, *Cassino: the Hollow Victory, The Battle for Rome January–June 1944*, Deutsch, 1984

Ellis, L. F., *Welsh Guards at War*, Gale & Polden, 1946

Ellis, L. F., *Victory in the West Vol. I: The Battle of Normandy*, HMSO, 1962

Ellis, L. F., *Victory in the West Vol. II: The Defeat of Germany*, HMSO, 1968

Fergusson, Bernard, *The Black Watch and the King's Enemies*, Collins, 1950

Ferling, John, *The World Turned Upside Down: The American Victory in the War of Independence*, Greenwood, 1988

Ffrench Blake, R. L. V., *A History of the 17th/21st Lancers 1922–1959*, Hamilton, 1968

Fisher, Ernest F., *Cassino to the Alps*, US Army, 1977

Fitzgerald, I. D. J. L., *History of the Irish Guards in the Second World War*, Gale & Polden, 1949

Fletcher, David, *The Great Tank Scandal: British Armour in the Second World War*, Part 1, HMSO, 1989

Fletcher, David, *The Universal Tank: British Armour in the Second World War*, Part 2, HMSO, 1993

Foley, Robert, *Alfred Von Schlieffen's Military Writings*, Frank Cass, 2003

Ford, Corey, *Donovan of OSS.*, Hale, 1971

Ford, Paul L., *The Works of Thomas Jefferson*, Putnam & Sons, 1893

Forty, George, *Desert Rats at War: North Africa*, Ian Allen, 1977

Fraser, David, *Alanbrooke*, Collins, 1982

French, David, *Raising Churchill's Army: The British Army and the War against Germany, 1919–1945*, Oxford University Press, 2000

Fuller, J. F. C., *Sir John Moore's System of Training*, Hutchinson, 1925

Fussell, Paul, *The Boys' Crusade: American GIs in Europe: Chaos and Fear in World War Two*, Weidenfeld & Nicholson, 2004

Gabel, Christopher R., *The US Army GHQ Maneuvers of 1941*, US Army, 1991

Gilbert, Martin, *Churchill: A Life*, Heinemann, 1991

Glantz, David M., and Jonathan House, *When Titans Clashed*, University Press of Kansas, 1995

Gleig, George Robert, *A Narrative of the Campaigns of the British Army at Washington, Baltimore, and New Orleans under Generals Ross, Pakenham, & Lambert, in the Years 1814 and 1815*, John Murray, 1826

Gleig, George Robert, *The Subaltern*, Blackwood & Son, 1845

Gooderson, Ian, *A Hard Way to Make a War: The Allied Campaign in Italy in the Second World War*, Conway, 2008

Goodhart, Philip, *Colonel George Washington: Soldier of the King*, Philip Goodhart, 1993

Goodhart, Philip, *The Royal Americans*, Wilton, 2005

Grace, Edward, *The Perilous Road to Rome via Tunis*, Parapress, 1993

Granatstein, J. L., *Canada's Army: Waging War and Keeping Peace*, University of Toronto Press, 2002

Graves, Derek E., *Red Coats and Grey Jackets: The Battle of Chippawa, 5th July 1814*, Dundurn, 1994

Greacen, Lavinia, *Chink: A Biography*, Macmillan, 1989

Greenfield, Kent Roberts, *Command Decisions*, US Army, 1960

Greenhalgh, Elizabeth, *Victory Through Coalition*, Cambridge University Press, 2005

Gregory, Adrian, *The Silence of Memory*, Berg, 1994

Griffith, Paddy, *Rally Once Again: Battle Tactics of the American Civil War*, Crowood, 1987

Grotelueschen, Mark, *The AEF Way of War: The American Army and Combat in World War I*, Cambridge University Press, 2007

Guingand, Francis de, *Generals at War*, Hodder & Stoughton, 1987

Guingand, Francis de, *Operation Victory*, Hodder & Stoughton, 1947

Hamilton, Nigel, *Master of the Battlefield: Monty's War Years 1942–1944*, Hamish Hamilton, 1983

Hamilton, Nigel, *Monty: The Field Marshal 1944–1976*, Hamish Hamilton, 1986

Hamilton, Nigel, *Monty: The Making of a General 1887–1942*, Hamish Hamilton, 1981

Hargreaves, Richard, *The Germans in Normandy*, Pen & Sword, 2006

Harpur, Brian, *The Impossible Victory: A Personal Account of the Battle for the River Po*, William Kimber, 1980

Harris, J. P., with Niall Barr, *Amiens to the Armistice: The BEF in the Hundred Days Campaign, 8 August–11 November 1918*, Brassey's, 1998

Harris, J. P., and F. H. Toase, *Armoured Warfare*, Batsford, 1990

Harrison, Gordon A., *Cross-Channel Attack*, Konecky & Konecky, 1951

Hart, Russell, *Clash of Arms: How the Allies Won in Normandy*, Lynne Reiner, 2000

Hart, Stephen A., *Colossal Cracks: Montgomery's 21st Army Group in Northwest Europe 1944–1945*, Praeger, 2000

Hastings, Max, *Overlord: D-Day and the Battle for Normandy*, Michael Joseph, 1984

Hastings, Max, *Armageddon: the Battle for Germany, 1944–45*, Macmillan, 2004

Hinsley, F. H., *British Intelligence in the Second World War: Its Influence on Strategy and Operations*, Vol. 3, Part II, HMSO, 1988

Henderson, G. F. R., *The Science of War: A Collection of Essays and Lectures, 1892–1903*, Longmans, 1905

Hill, E. R., 'The Coldstream at Longstop Hill', *army Quarterly and Defence Journal*, July 1944

Hittle, J. D., *The Military Staff: Its History and Development*, Military Service Publishing, 1944

Hogan, Jr, David W., *Raiders or Elite Infantry? The Changing Role of the US Army Rangers from Dieppe to Grenada*, Greenwood Press, 1992

Holland, James, *Italy's Sorrow: A Year of War 1944–1945*, St Martin's Press, 2008

Holmes, Richard, *The Little Field Marshal: Sir John French*, Jonathan Cape, 1981

Holmes, Richard, *Firing Line*, Jonathan Cape, 1985

Horrocks, Brian, *A Full Life*, Collins, 1960

Horrocks, Brian, *Corps Commander*, Sidgwick & Jackson, 1977

Howard, Michael, *The Mediterranean Strategy in the Second World War: The Lees-Knowles Lectures at Trinity College, Cambridge, 1966*, Weidenfeld & Nicolson, 1968

Howard, Michael, and Peter Paret, *Carl von Clausewitz: On War*, Oxford University Press, 2007

Howard, Michael, and John Sparrow, *The Coldstream Guards 1920–1946*, Oxford University Press, 1951

Hughes, Daniel, *Moltke on the Art of War: Selected Writings*, Presidio Press, 1993

Hunnicutt, R. P., *Firepower: A History of the American Heavy Tank*, Presidio Press, 1988

Irving, David, *The War Between the Generals*, Penguin, 1981

Ismay, Hastings, *NATO: The First Five Years 1949–1954*, NATO, 1955

Ismay, Hastings, *The Memoirs of General the Lord Ismay*, Heinemann, 1960

Jackson, W. G. F., *Alexander of Tunis as Military Commander*, Batsford, 1971

Joffre, Joseph J. C., *The Memoirs of Marshal Joffre*, trans. T. Bentley Mott, Geoffrey Bles, 1932

Johnson, Robert Underwood, and Clarence Clough Buel, *Battles and Leaders of the Civil War*, The Century Co., 1887

Kaplan, Laurence S., *The Long Entanglement: NATO's First Fifty Years*, Praeger, 1999

Keegan, John, *The Face of Battle*, Jonathan Cape, 1976

Keegan, John, *Six Armies in Normandy, From D-Day to the Liberation of Paris*, Jonathan Cape, 1982

Keegan, John, *Churchill's Generals*, Weidenfeld & Nicolson, 1991

Kendrick, Alexander, *Prime Time: The Life of Edward R. Murrow*, Dent, 1970

Kennedy, Greg, *Imperial Crossroads: Anglo-American Strategic Relations and the Far East, 1933–1939*, Frank Cass, 2002

Kennedy, John, *The Business of War*, Hutchinson, 1957

Kimball, Warren, *Forged in War: Churchill, Roosevelt and the Second World War*, W. Morrow, 1997

Koistinen, Paul A. C., *Arsenal of World War II: The Political Economy of American Warfare, 1940–1945*, Eurospan, 2007

Kopperman, Paul E., *Braddock at the Monongahela*, Feffer & Simons, 1977

Korda, Michael, *Ike: An American Hero*, HarperCollins, 2007

Lamb, Richard, *War in Italy 1943–1945: A Brutal Story*, John Murray, 1993

Leutze, James (ed.), *The London Observer, The Journal of General Raymond E. Lee, 1940–1941*, Hutchinson, 1971

Lewis, Thomas A., *For King and Country: George Washington, the Early Years*, Wiley, 1993

Liddell Hart, B. H., *The Tanks*, 2 vols, Cassell, 1959

Loewenheim, Francis L., Langley, Harold D., and Manfred Jonas, *Roosevelt and Churchill: Their Secret Wartime Correspondence*, Barrie & Jenkins, 1975

Longford, Elizabeth, *Wellington: The Years of the Sword*, Weidenfeld & Nicholson, 1969

Longmate, Norman, *The GIs in Britain,* Hutchinson, 1975

Luvaas, Jay, *The Military Legacy of the Civil War: The European Inheritance*, University Press of Kansas, 1988

MacDonald, Charles B., and Sidney T. Matthews, *Three Battles: Arnaville, Altuzzo and Schmidt*, Office of the Chief of Military History Department of the Army, 1952

MacDonald, Charles B., *The Battle of the Huertgen Forest*, Lippincott, 1963

Macready, Gordon, *In the Wake of the Great*, William Clowes and Sons Ltd, 1965

Magdalany, Fred, *Cassino: Portrait of a Battle*, Longmans, 1957

Marshall-Cornwall, James, *Wars and Rumours of Wars: A Memoir*, Cooper, 1984

Mascarenhas, J. B., *The Brazilian Expeditionary Force by its Commander*, US Govt Printing Office, 1966

Matloff, Maurice, *American Military History, Office of the Chief of Military History*, 1969

Matloff, Maurice, and Edwin M. Snell, *Strategic Planning for Coalition Warfare*, 2 vols, Office of the Chief of Military History, Dept. of the army, 1952

Maurice, Frederick, *The Last Four Months: The End of the War in the West*, Cassell & Co., 1919

Mead, Gary, *The Doughboys: America and the First World War*, Allen Lane, 2000

Messenger, Charles, *The Commandos: 1940–1946*, Kimber, 1985

McPherson, James M., *Battle Cry of Freedom: The Civil War Era*, Oxford University Press, 1988

Molony, C. J. C., *The Mediterranean and Middle East, Vol. V, Part I: The Campaign in Sicily, 1943, and the Campaign in Italy, 3rd September 1943 to 31st March 1944*, HMSO, 1973

Morelock, J. D., *Generals of the Ardennes: American Leadership in the Battle of the Bulge*, National Defence University Press, 1994

Morgan, Frederick, *Overture to Overlord*, Hodder & Stoughton, 1950

Newell, Clayton R., *Egypt–Libya: 11 June 1942–12 February 1943*, US Army Center of Military History, 1993

Nicolson, Nigel, *Alex: The Life of Field Marshal Earl Alexander of Tunis*, Weidenfeld & Nicolson, 1973

Oland, Dwight D., *North Appenines 1944–1945*, United States Army Center of Military History, 1996

Oman, Carola, *Sir John Moore*, Hodder & Stoughton, 1953

Orange, Vincent, *Tedder: Quietly in Command*, Frank Cass, 2004

Palamountain, Edgar W. I., *Taurus Pursuant: History of 11th Armoured Division*, British Army of the Rhine, 1946

Palmer, John McAuley, *General von Steuben*, Yale University Press, 1937

Parker, Danny S., *Battle of the Bulge, Hitler's Ardennes Offensive, 1944–1945*, Greenhill, 1991

Parker, Theodore W., *Conquer, the Story of the Ninth Army, 1943–45*, Infantry Journal Press, 1947

Parkman, Francis, *Montcalm and Wolfe: France and England in North America*, Macmillan, 1884

Patrick Murray, G. E., *Eisenhower Versus Montgomery: the Continuing Debate*, Praeger, 1996

Pershing, John J., *My Experiences in the World War*, Frederick A. Stokes, 1931

Playfair, I. S. O., *The Mediterranean and Middle East, Vol. I: The Early Successes Against Italy*, HMSO, 1974

Pogue, Forrest C., *Supreme Command*, Office of the Chief of Military History, 1954

Pogue, Forrest C., *George C. Marshall: Education of a General, 1880–1939*, McGibbon & Kee, 1964

Pogue, Forrest C., *George C. Marshall: Ordeal and Hope, 1939–1942*, Viking Press, 1966

Pogue, Forrest C., *George C Marshall: Organizer of Victory, 1943–1945*, The Viking Press, 1973

Poston, M. M., *Design and Development of Weapons: Studies in Government and Industrial Organisation*, HMSO, 1964

Powell, Geoffrey, *The Devil's Birthday: The Bridges to Arnhem 1944*, Leo Cooper, 1992

Price, Frank James, *Troy H. Middleton: A Biography*, Lousiana State University Press, 1974

Reynolds, David, *Rich Relations: The American Occupation of Britain 1942–1945*, HarperCollins, 1996

Reynolds, David, *From Munich to Pearl Harbor, Roosevelt's America and the Origins of the Second World War*, Ivan R Dee, 2001

Reynolds, David, *In Command of History: Churchill Fighting and Writing the Second World War*, Allen Lane, 2004

Richardson, Charles, *Flashback: A Soldier's Story*, Kimber, 1985

Richardson, Charles, *Send for Freddie*, Kimber, 1987

Rickard, John Nelson, *Patton at Bay: The Lorraine Campaign, September to December 1944*, Praeger, 1999

Robb-Webb, Jon, *The British Pacific Fleet Experience and Legacy, 1944–50*, Ashgate, 2013

Roberts, Andrew, *Masters and Commanders: The Military Geniuses Who Led the West to Victory in World War II*, Allen Lane, 2008

Roberts, G. P. B., *From the Desert to the Baltic*, Kimber, 1987

Ryder, Rowland, *Oliver Leese*, Hamish Hamilton Ltd, 1987

Scarfe, Norman, *Assault Division: A History of the 3rd Division from the Invasion of Normandy to the Surrender of Germany*, Collins, 1947

Shaw, A. G. L., *Great Britain and the Colonies 1815–1865*, Methuen, 1970

Sheffield, Gary, and John Bourne, *Douglas Haig: War Diaries and Letters, 1914–1918*, Weidenfeld & Nicholson, 2005

Shepperd, G. A., *The Italian Campaign 1943–45: A Political and Military Re-Assessment*, Barker, 1968

Sherwood, Robert E., *The White House Papers of Harry L. Hopkins: An Intimate History: Vol. I: September 1939–January 1942*, Eyre & Spottiswoode, 1948

Smith, Harry, *The Autobiography of Lieutenant General Sir Harry Smith*, John Murray, 1902

Smythe, Donald, 'St Mihiel: The Birth of an American Army', in *Parameters*, Vol. XIII, No. 2

Stettinius, Edward R., *Lend-Lease: Weapon for Victory*, Penguin, 1944

Stoler, Mark, *The Politics of the Second Front: American Military Planning and Diplomacy in Coalition Warfare, 1941–1943*, Greenwood Press, 1977

Stout, Wesley W., *Tanks are Mighty Fine Things!*, Chrysler, 1946

Strachan, Hew, *Military Lives*, Oxford University Press, 2002

Strong, Kenneth, *Intelligence at the Top: The Recollections of an Intelligence Officer*, Cassell, 1968

Summers, Don, *A Short History of Grove Airfield*, Ridgeway Military and Aviation Research Group, 1997

Summersby, Kay, *Eisenhower Was My Boss*, Werner Laurie, 1949

Taylor, A. J. P., *The First World War: An Illustrated History*, Penguin, 1966

Tedder, Arthur, *With Prejudice: The War Memoirs of Marshal of the Royal Air Force, Lord Tedder*, Cassell, 1966

Terraine, John, *Mons: The Retreat to Victory*, Pen & Sword, 2010

The Earl of Avon, *The Reckoning: The Memoirs of Anthony Eden, Earl of Avon*, Houghton Mifflin Co., 1965

Timothy, P. H., *The Rhine Crossing, Twelfth Army Group Engineer Operations*, US Army Engineer School, 1946

Trask, David F., *The AEF and Coalition Warmaking, 1917–1918*, University Press of Kansas, 1993

Trevelyan, Raleigh, *Rome '44: The Battle for the Eternal City*, Secker & Warburg, 1981

Truscott, Lucian, *Command Missions: A Personal Story*, Arno Press, 1979

Turner, William, *Pals: The 11th (Service) Battalion (Accrington), East Lancashire Regiment*, Leo Cooper, 1991

van Creveld, Martin, *Supplying War: Logistics from Wallenstein to Patton*, Cambridge University Press, 2004

Vetock, Dennis J., *Lessons Learned: A History of US Army Lesson Learning*, US Army Military History Institute, 1988

von Mellenthin, Friedrich, *Panzer battles, 1939–1945: a study of the employment of armour in the Second World War*, Cassell, 1956

Wakefield, Ken, *Operation Bolero: The Americans in Bristol and the West Country 1942–45*, Crecy Books, 1994

Waldo, S. Putnam, *Memoirs of Andrew Jackson, Major General in the Army of the United States and Commander in Chief of the Division of the South*, 1818

Ward, Geoffrey C., with Ric Burns and Ken Burns, *The Civil War: An Illustrated History*, Bodley Head, 1991

Ward, S. G. P., *Wellington's Headquarters: A Study of the Administrative Problems*, Oxford University Press, 1957

Watson, Bruce Allen, *Exit Rommel: The Tunisian Campaign 1942–1943*, Praeger, 1999

Watson, Mark Skinner, *Chief of Staff: Prewar Plans and Preparations*, Historical Division, Department of the Army, 1950

Wedemeyer, Albert, *Wedemeyer Reports!*, Devin-Adair, 1958

Weigley, Russell, *Eisenhower's Lieutenants: The Campaigns of France and Germany 1944–1945*, Indiana University Press, 1984

Weigley, Russell, *History of the United States Army*, Indiana University Press, 1984

Weintraub, Stanley, *15 Stars: Eisenhower, MacArthur, Marshall, Three Generals Who Saved the American Century*, Free Press, 2007

Wingate, Sir Ronald, *Lord Ismay: A Biography*, Hutchinson, 1970

Wright, Esmond, *The Fire of Liberty: The American War of Independence seen through the eyes of the men and women, the statesmen and soldiers who fought it*, Hamish Hamilton, 1984

Zuehlke, Mark, *Terrible Victory: First Canadian Army and the Scheldt Estuary Campaign: September 13–November 6, 1944*, Greystone Books, 2001

Acknowledgements

This book has had a far longer gestation period than I ever expected. There is, thus, a particular satisfaction, and feeling of trepidation, in being able to thank the many people who have helped me along the way. I would like to thank Will Sulkin, at Jonathan Cape, for first believing in the project and Dan Franklin for seeing it through to completion. It has been a real pleasure to work with Katherine Ailes who has shaped and refined the final text greatly. I also need to offer a very particular thanks to Veronique Baxter at David Higham who has shown levels of patience, understanding and support far beyond the ordinary. I can only hope that her levels of trust and belief have some small reward in the finished product. Laura West has also been very helpful and a model of efficiency.

I have been assisted greatly by many librarians and archivists without whom such a work would be impossible. The librarians of the Joint Services Command and Staff College have been unfailingly helpful and I would also like to thank Patricia Methven at the Liddell Hart Centre, Dwight Strandberg at the Eisenhower Library, and David Keogh at the US Military History Institute, and the archivists at the National Archives, Kew, the US National Archives and the Imperial War Museum. I would particularly like to thank Christopher Dunphie for granting me access to his father's papers. Rebecca Maryan assisted me with some of the research for which I am very grateful.

I have also benefited greatly from research funding which enabled me to visit many of these archives. I would like to thank the Defence Studies Department, King's College London, which supported much of the initial work, the British Academy, which awarded me a Small Research Grant at a critical stage in the research, and The US Army Heritage and Education Center for awarding me a General and Mrs Matthew B. Ridgway Military History Research Grant.

I have a particular debt of gratitude to pay to the commanders, General Richard Shirreff, General James Bucknall and General Tim Evans, and staff of Headquarters Allied Rapid Reaction Corps. General Richard Shirreff first invited me to support an ARRC staff ride to France in 2008, and, over the years, HQ ARRC Staff Rides have given me a priceless opportunity to visit many of the battlefields mentioned in this text, and to learn greatly from many highly experienced military officers.

I am also very grateful to Professor David French, Professor Keith Neilson, Professor Jeffrey Grey, Professor Andy Wiest and Professor Geoffrey Jensen for their help and advice. Their sustained interest has been of real encouragement and support over the years.

I consider myself fortunate to have had the pleasure of working with my colleagues in the Defence Studies Department at the Joint Services Command and Staff College. I would also like to thank all of my students for their interest and insight into a myriad of issues. The remarkable body which comprises the students and staff of the Higher Command and Staff Course have had a powerful influence on the nature of this work. Although it is invidious to single out individuals from such a group, I feel I must do so. Major General Andrew Sharpe, who also read the manuscript, Commodore Keith Winstanley, Commodore Toby Williamson, Brigadier Mitch Mitchell and Brigadier Charlie Herbert all deserve a particular vote of thanks for their interest, support and friendship. Colonel Tom Torrance offered me gracious and generous hospitality on my trips to Carlisle.

I would particularly like to thank Tim Benbow, Greg Kennedy, Christina Goulter, Patrick Porter and Chris Tripodi who all read and commented on all or parts of the manuscript. Their suggestions have improved the finished work considerably while all errors or omissions are, of course, my own.

I must also thank my friends for their unwavering support over what have turned out to be some difficult years. Keith Blackmore, Warren Chin, Huw Davies, Nicola Rodgers, Debs Sanders, Gary Sheffield, Victoria Syme-Taylor, Chris Tuck and Kate Utting have all helped me more than they realise and more than I can ever repay them. I must particularly thank Guy Finch, that remarkable font of technical and military knowledge, for offering me a safe haven in the middle of a storm and for remaining a firm and constant friend. There is always a concern when writing acknowledgements such as these that there may be some important omissions. I can only say that any omissions are not intended and that my gratitude for all of the many people, named and unnamed, that have helped with this project is very real indeed.

It is a matter of deep regret that I must dedicate this book to another mentor, colleague and friend who passed away when they still had so much left to give to the field of military history and beyond. I first met Richard when I was a young and callow lecturer at Sandhurst but I really got to know him on the many HCSC Staff Rides that he conjured into vivid life in his role as the senior historian and mentor of the course. To share a car with Richard on a nine-day staff ride across northern France was to enter a living and rich world of history, personal reminiscences, humour and fellow-ship unlike any other I have experienced. Richard was a truly remarkable gentleman whose enthusiasm and knowledge of military history was only matched by the warmth and generosity of his spirit. He gave unstintingly of his time and provided me with powerful support and guidance. I know that I was by far from the only member of the military history community to have benefited from his selfless enthusiasm and knowledge and I will always consider myself truly privileged to have witnessed a master at work. In however small a fashion, this book represents my tribute to him and it is with the warmest sense of gratitude that I dedicate this work to the memory of Richard Holmes.

Image Credits

The death of British Commander General Braddock near Fort Duquesne (engraving), French School, (18th century) / Private Collection / Peter Newark Military Pictures / Bridgeman Images

Eisenhower's Wedding Day, courtesy of the *Eisenhower Presidential Library & Museum*

The Tyneside Irish Brigade, Battle of the Somme, 1 July 1916, during the attack on La Boisselle © Imperial War Museums, Q53

American and British soldiers (members of the regimental band of the 1/7th Battalion, Lancashire Fusiliers; Royal West Kent and Manchester Regiments) near Pas, 18 May 1918 © Imperial War Museums, Q8847

Training of the 77th American Division with the 39th British Division, near Moulle, 22 May 1918 © Imperial War Museums, Q9079

General Marshall and General Sir John Dill on board HMS *Prince Of Wales* © Imperial War Museums, A4986

Churchill and Roosevelt on the Quarterdeck of HMS *Prince Of Wales* during the Atlantic Conference, 10 August 1941 © Imperial War Museums, A4811

An American sergeant instructor lecturing troops about the Grant tank, 17 February 1942 © Imperial War Museums, E8493

A very early production M4A1, Sherman Tank, named 'Michael', reproduced courtesy of The Tank Museum, Bovington

An American M3 Stuart tank being hoisted from a ship onto the quayside at Alexandria, 19 July 1941 © Imperial War Museums, E4310

Private Milburn Henke, who was presented to the press as the 'first' United States soldier to step ashore, lands at Dufferin Quay, Belfast, Northern Ireland © Imperial War Museums, H16847

Five GIs being served pints of beer in the NAAFI in Britain © Imperial War Museums, EA9010

Lance Sergeant Brown and Sergeant A Randall during the link-up between the Eighth and First Armies on the Gabes–Gafsa Road, 7 April 1943 © Imperial War Museums, NA1821

Stretcher bearers of the East Surrey Regiment during the attack on Longstop Hill, 23 April 1943 © Imperial War Museums, NA2237

Winston Churchill leaves the old Roman amphitheatre at Carthage, Tunisia, with Lieutenant General Kenneth Anderson after addressing British troops on 1 June 1943 © Imperial War Museums, NA3253

Winston Churchill, General Dwight D Eisenhower and General Harold Alexander in Tunis on 25 December 1943 © Imperial War Museums, NA10074

Chiefs of Staff in conference in the Anfa Hotel, Casablanca © Imperial War Museums, A14041

Harold Alexander, Mark Clark and Richard McCreery on the Salerno beaches on 15 September 1943 © Imperial War Museums, NA6822

Eisenhower, Tedder, Alexander and Cunningham, courtesy of the Eisenhower Presidential Library & Museum

Rear-Admiral Troutridge, General Lucas and Major General Penney on HMS Bulolo © Imperial War Museums, NA11048

An American soldier instructs Guards NCOs in the use of the bazooka, 3 November 1943 © Imperial War Museums, NA8376

A soldier with the 2/7th Middlesex Regiment shares a cup of tea with an American infantryman in the Anzio bridgehead, 10 February 1944 © Imperial War Museums, NA11770

General Sir Harold Alexander, with American General Truscott at Anzio, 4 March 1944 © Imperial War Museums, NA12364

The bombing of Cassino during the Allied barrage on 15 March 1944 © Imperial War Museums, EA17892

Moving up through Prato, Italy, Bull, April 9, 1945, reproduced courtesy of the US National Archives, 111-SC-205289

Eisenhower gives the order of the day, Moore, June 6, 1944, reproduced courtesy of the US National Archives, 111-SC-194399

US troops file aboard a Landing Craft Assault at a British port prior to embarkation on D-Day 6 June 1944 © Imperial War Museums, EA25357

Patton, Eisenhower and Bradley in Bastogne, Belgium © Imperial War Museums, EA52043

The liberation of Brussels, 4 September 1944 © Imperial War Museums, BU508

An infantry sergeant during the advance into Germany near Geilenkirchen, 5 December 1944 © Imperial War Museums, BU1434

Crossing the Rhine under enemy fire at St. Goar. March 1945, reproduced courtesy of the U.S. National Archives, 208-YE-132

Wernberg, Germany, Pvt. Joseph Scrippens, April 22, 1945, reproduced courtesy of the U.S. National Archives, 111-SC-205298

Field Marshal Bernard Montgomery signing the Instrument of Surrender of German forces in North-West Europe at Luneberg Heath © Imperial War Museums, BU5207

Index